Victorian Architecture

G. A. Bremner is Professor of Architectural History at the University of Edinburgh. He received his PhD from the University of Cambridge in 2004, where he was a Gates Scholar at Gonville and Caius College. His books include *Imperial Gothic: Religious Architecture and High Anglican Culture in the British Empire*, c. *1840–1870* (2013) and *Building Greater Britain: Architecture, Imperialism, and the Edwardian Baroque Revival*, c. *1885–1920* (2022).

Oxford History of Art

Titles in the *Oxford History of Art* series are up-to-date, fully illustrated introductions to a wide variety of subjects written by leading experts in their field. They will appear regularly, building into an interlocking and comprehensive series. In the list below, published titles appear in bold.

WESTERN ART

Archaic and Classical Greek Art
Robin Osborne

Classical Art From Greece to Rome
Mary Beard & John Henderson

The Art of the Roman Empire AD 100–450
Jaś Elsner

Early Medieval Art
Lawrence Nees

Medieval Art
Veronica Sekules

Art in Renaissance Italy
Evelyn Welch

Northern European Art
Susie Nash

Modern Art 1851–1929
Richard Brettell

After Modern Art 1945–2017
David Hopkins

WESTERN ARCHITECTURE

Roman Architecture
Janet DeLaine

Early Medieval Architecture
Roger Stalley

Medieval Architecture
Nicola Coldstream

Renaissance Architecture
Christy Anderson

European Architecture 1750–1890
Barry Bergdoll

Modern Architecture
Alan Colquhoun

Architecture in the United States
Dell Upton

WORLD ART

Aegean Art and Architecture
Donald Preziosi & Louise Hitchcock

Early Art and Architecture of Africa
Peter Garlake

African-American Art
Sharon F. Patton

Twentieth-Century American Art
Erika Doss

Byzantine Art
Robin Cormack

Art in China
Craig Clunas

Indian Art
Partha Mitter

Mesoamerican Art
Cecelia Klein

Native North American Art
Janet C. Berlo & Ruth B. Phillips

Polynesian and Micronesian Art
Adrienne L. Kaeppler

WESTERN DESIGN

Twentieth-Century Design
Jonathan M. Woodham

Design in the USA
Jeffrey L. Meikle

Fashion
Christopher Breward

PHOTOGRAPHY

The Photograph
Graham Clarke

WESTERN SCULPTURE

Sculpture Since 1945
Andrew Causey

THEMES AND GENRES

Landscape and Western Art
Malcolm Andrews

Portraiture
Shearer West

Beauty and Art
Elizabeth Prettejohn

REFERENCE BOOKS

The Art of Art History: A Critical Anthology
Donald Preziosi (ed.)

Oxford History of Art

Victorian Architecture

G. A. Bremner

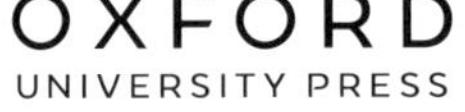

OXFORD
UNIVERSITY PRESS

Great Clarendon Street, Oxford, OX2 6DP,
United Kingdom

Oxford University Press is a department of the University of Oxford. It furthers the University's objective of excellence in research, scholarship, and education by publishing worldwide. Oxford is a registered trade mark of Oxford University Press in the UK and in certain other countries.

Published in the United States of America by Oxford University Press
198 Madison Avenue, New York, NY 10016, United States of America

British Library Cataloguing in Publication Data
Data available

Library of Congress Control Number: 2025944758

ISBN 9780198835394

DOI: 10.1093/oso/9780198835394.001.0001

Printed in the UK by
Bell & Bain Ltd., Glasgow

The manufacturer's authorised representative in the EU for product safety is Oxford University Press España S.A. of Parque Empresarial San Fernando de Henares, Avenida de Castilla, 2 – 28830 Madrid (www.oup.es/en or product.safety@oup.com). OUP España S.A. also acts as importer into Spain of products made by the manufacturer.

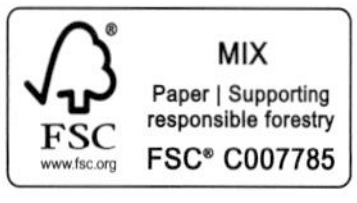

Acknowledgements

As this book represents the cumulation of 30 years' study of the Victorian built environment, there are many people to thank. Without trying to name them individually, I will only say that I owe an enormous debt of gratitude to all those who have encouraged me to study Victorian architecture, who have challenged my assumptions about it, who have discussed it with me at length, and who have generously read and commented on my work relating to it. If nothing else, these friends and interlocutors have inspired my love for Victorian architecture. They know who they are. Without them, I would not have attempted such a book.

Having taught a senior-level course on the history of Victorian architecture at university for over 20 years now, I also owe considerable thanks to my students who have exhorted me to present the Victorian built environment in ways that are meaningful and relevant to them. As the future study of Victorian architecture is in their hands, these students see and interpret the built environment in ways that are different from, but no less important to, those of previous generations. I have learnt from them, just as they have learnt from me. If we are to keep the study of the Victorian built environment alive and well, then we must remain alert to the concerns of current and future generations. In many respects, this book is for them.

I also wish to acknowledge the generous support of the Paul Mellon Centre for Studies in British Art, London, for awarding me a Senior Fellowship to complete this book. Many thanks also to Oxford University Press, the patience and professionalism of whose staff has been tremendous, including Cathryn Steele and Imogene Haslam, and to Matthew Cotton, especially, who commissioned the book. Without them, I would not have been able to bring this book to the level of finish it has acquired. And last, but by no means least, I must thank my wife Marla, and my two children, Victor and Alexandra, who have been by my side and a constant support throughout the process. This book is also for them.

Contents

DOMINION
OF CANADA
Vancouver
Winnipeg
Montreal
Toronto
Halifax
St John's
Edinburgh
Manchester
Dublin
London
UNITED STATES
OF AMERICA
Atlantic
Ocean
Honolulu
Hawaiian Islands
BRITISH
HONDURAS
Jamaica
GAMBIA
SIERRA
LEONE
GOLD
COAST
Georgetown
BRITISH
GUIANA
Pacific Ocean
St Helena
Tristan da Cunha
Falklands
The British Empire
c.1900
British territory

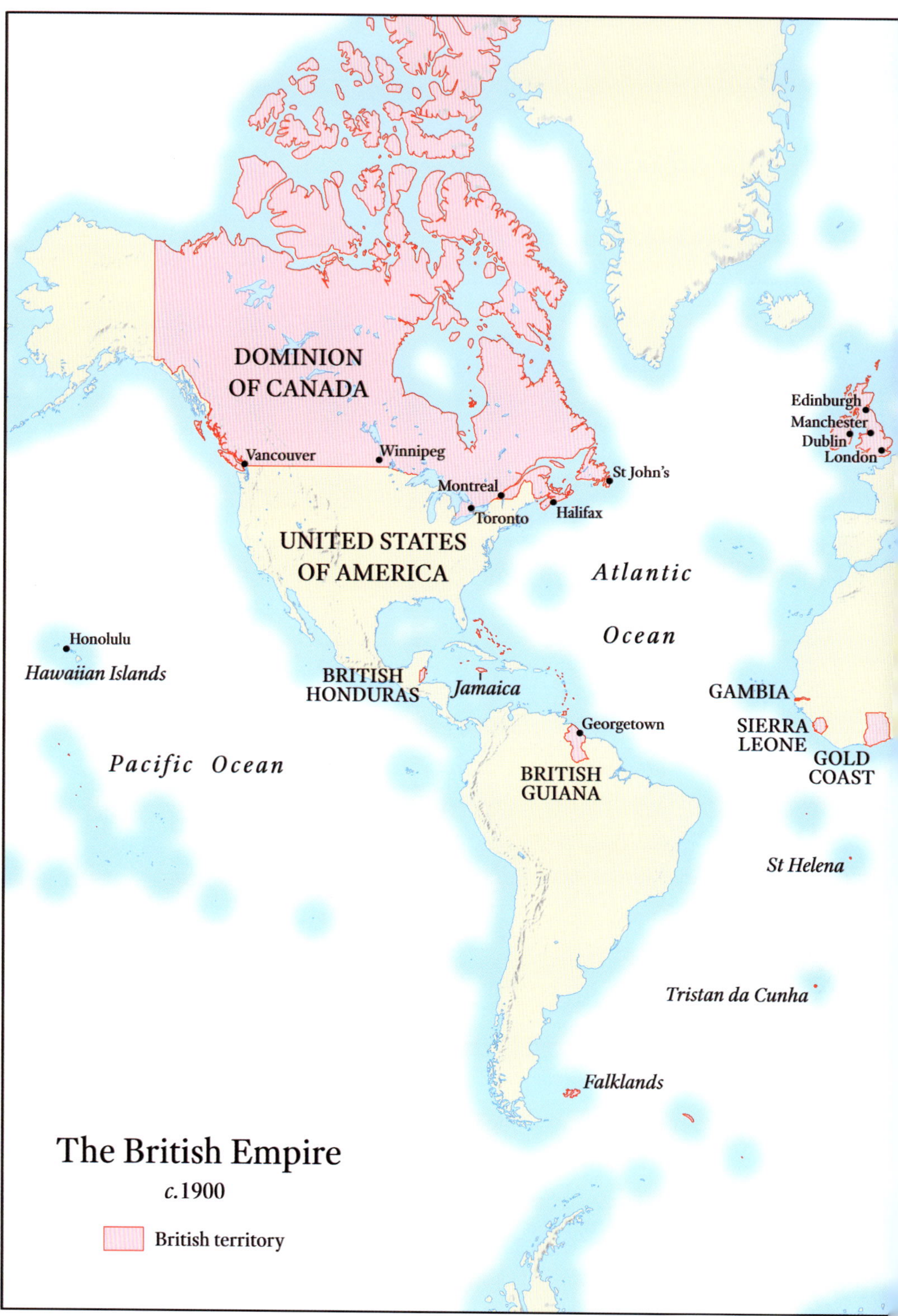

Map 1

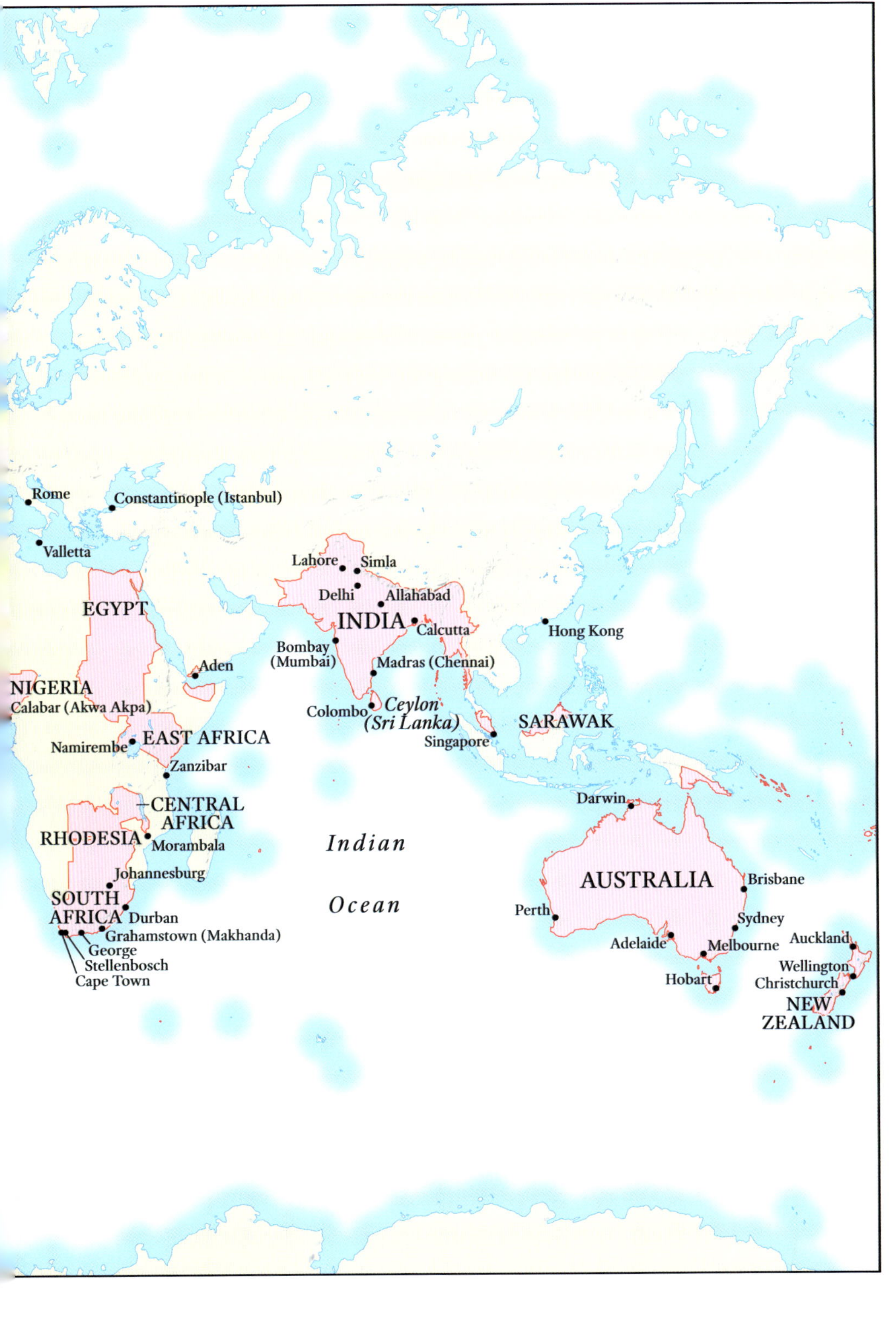
Rome
Constantinople (Istanbul)
Valletta
EGYPT
Aden
NIGERIA
Calabar (Akwa Akpa)
EAST AFRICA
Namirembe
Zanzibar
CENTRAL AFRICA
RHODESIA
Morambala
Johannesburg
SOUTH AFRICA
Durban
Grahamstown (Makhanda)
George
Stellenbosch
Cape Town
Lahore
Simla
Delhi
Allahabad
INDIA
Calcutta
Bombay (Mumbai)
Madras (Chennai)
Colombo
Ceylon (Sri Lanka)
Singapore
Hong Kong
SARAWAK
Indian Ocean
Darwin
AUSTRALIA
Brisbane
Perth
Sydney
Adelaide
Melbourne
Hobart
Auckland
Wellington
Christchurch
NEW ZEALAND

The British Isles
British territory
Coal field
1. Saltaire
2. Todmorden
3. Copley
4. Hyde
North
Sea
Peterhead
Inverness
Aberdeen
Helensburgh
Glasgow
Edinburgh
Paisley
Cathcart
Rothbury
Newcastle
Wreay
Belfast
Appleton-le-Moors
Studley Royal
Skelton-on-Ure
Sledmere
Bradford
York
Howsham
Preston
Hull
Leeds
Rochdale
Halifax
Manchester
Sheffield
Liverpool
Cheadle
Lincoln
Denbigh
Crewe
Galway
Maynooth
Dublin
Pontcysyllte
Derby
Nottingham
Hoar Cross
Loughborough
Jackfield
Leicester
Foxton
Aberystwyth
Warley
Bournville
Rugby
Birmingham
Cambridge
Northampton
Cork
Abergavenny
Selsley
Leafield
Colchester
Maidenhead (Boyne Hill)
Cardiff
Swindon
Oxford
London
Cowbridge
Bristol
Reading
Stone
Ramsgate
Burrington
Canterbury
Bridgwater
Winchester
Horsham
East Grinstead
Treverbyn
Saltash
Truro

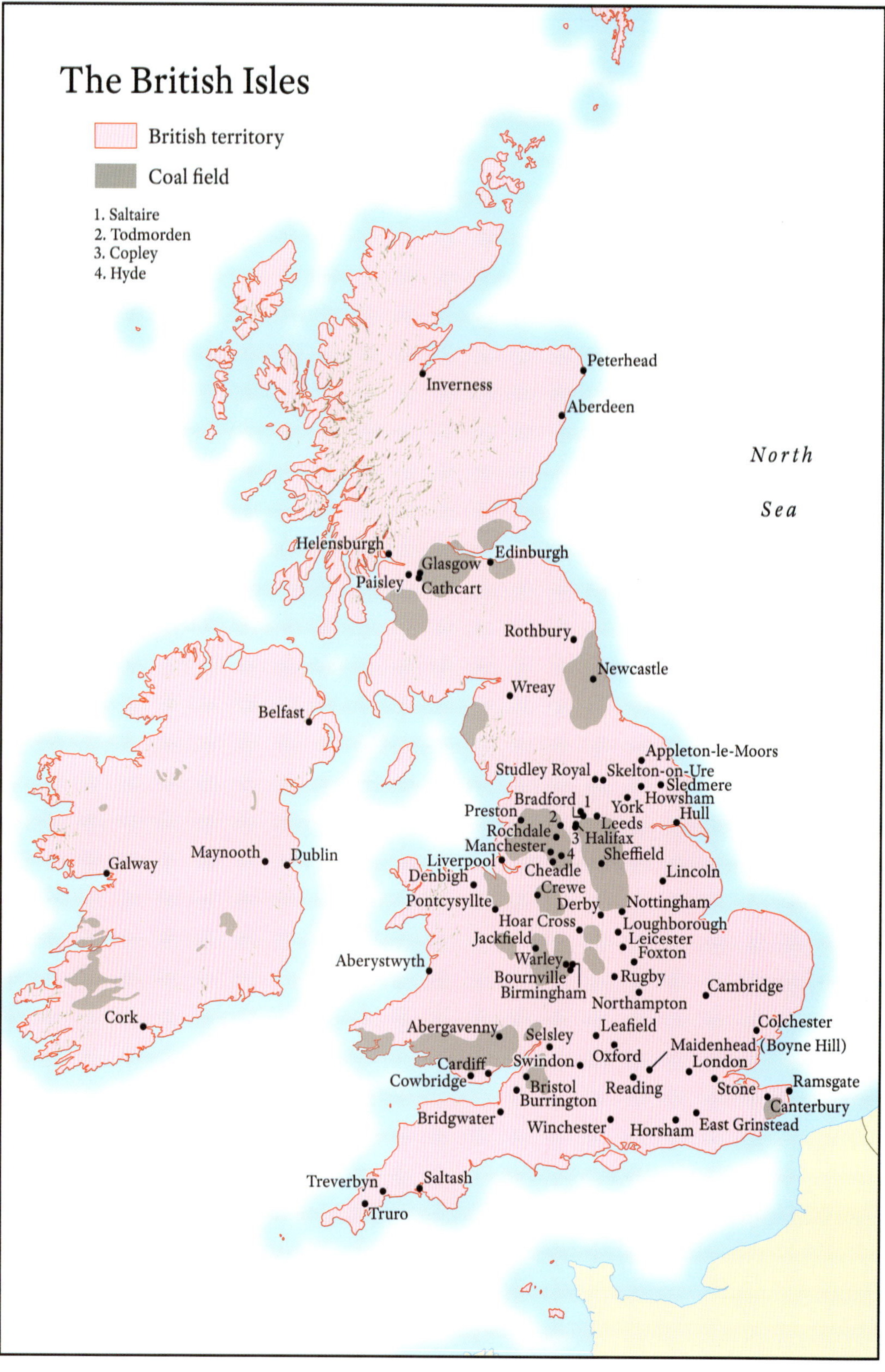

Map 2

North-West Territories
British Columbia
Alberta
Saskatchewan
DOMINION OF
Manitoba
Regina
Winnipeg
Barons
Vancouver
Victoria
Fort William, Port Arthur (Thunder Bay)
Wisconsin
Delafield
UNITED STATES
OF AMERICA
Illinois
St Louis
Missouri
San Francisco
California
Pacific
Ocean
MEXICO
Gulf of
Mexico
BRITISH
HONDURAS
British Territories
in North America and the Caribbean
British territory
Bison range
Original
1870
1889

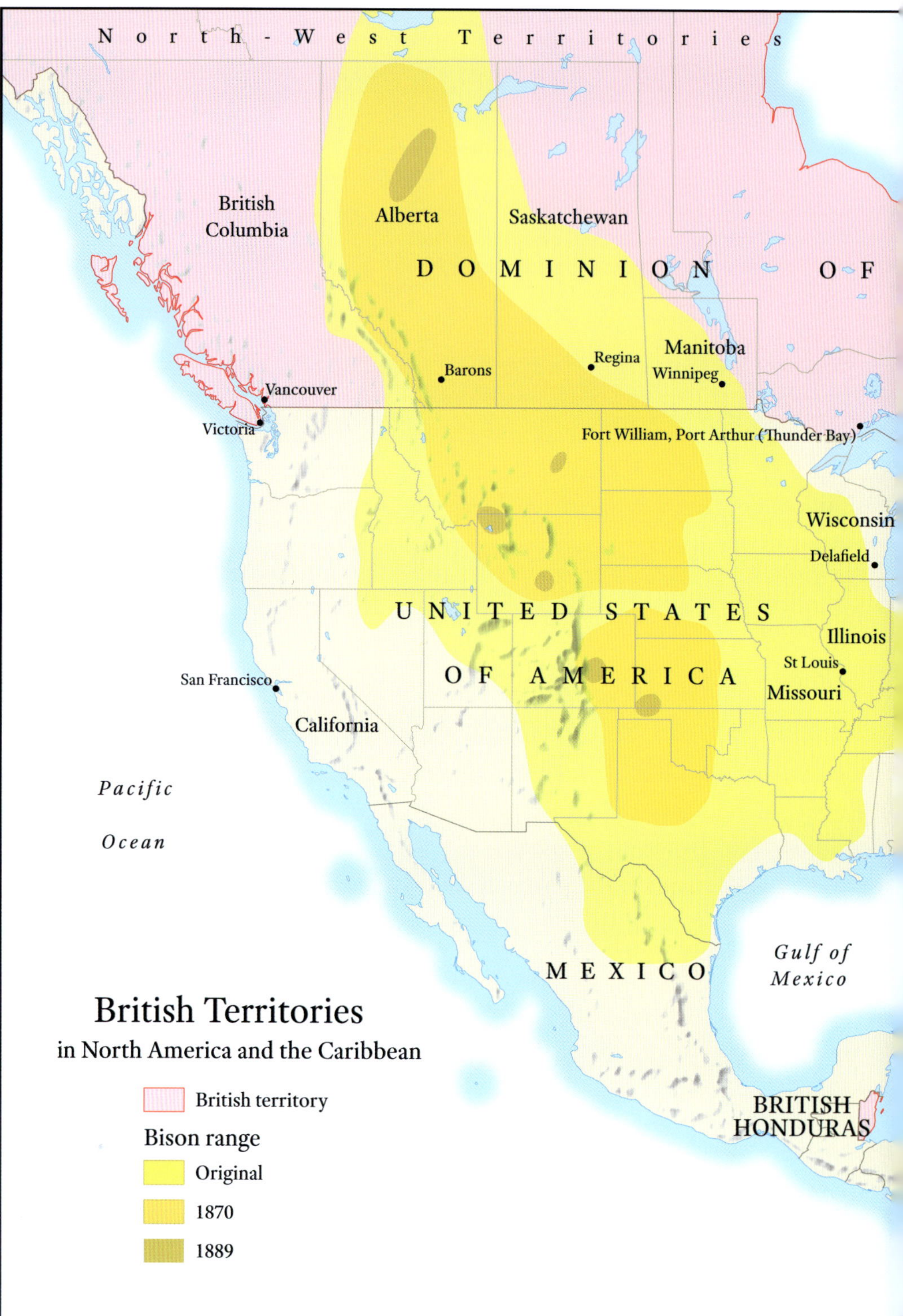

Map 3

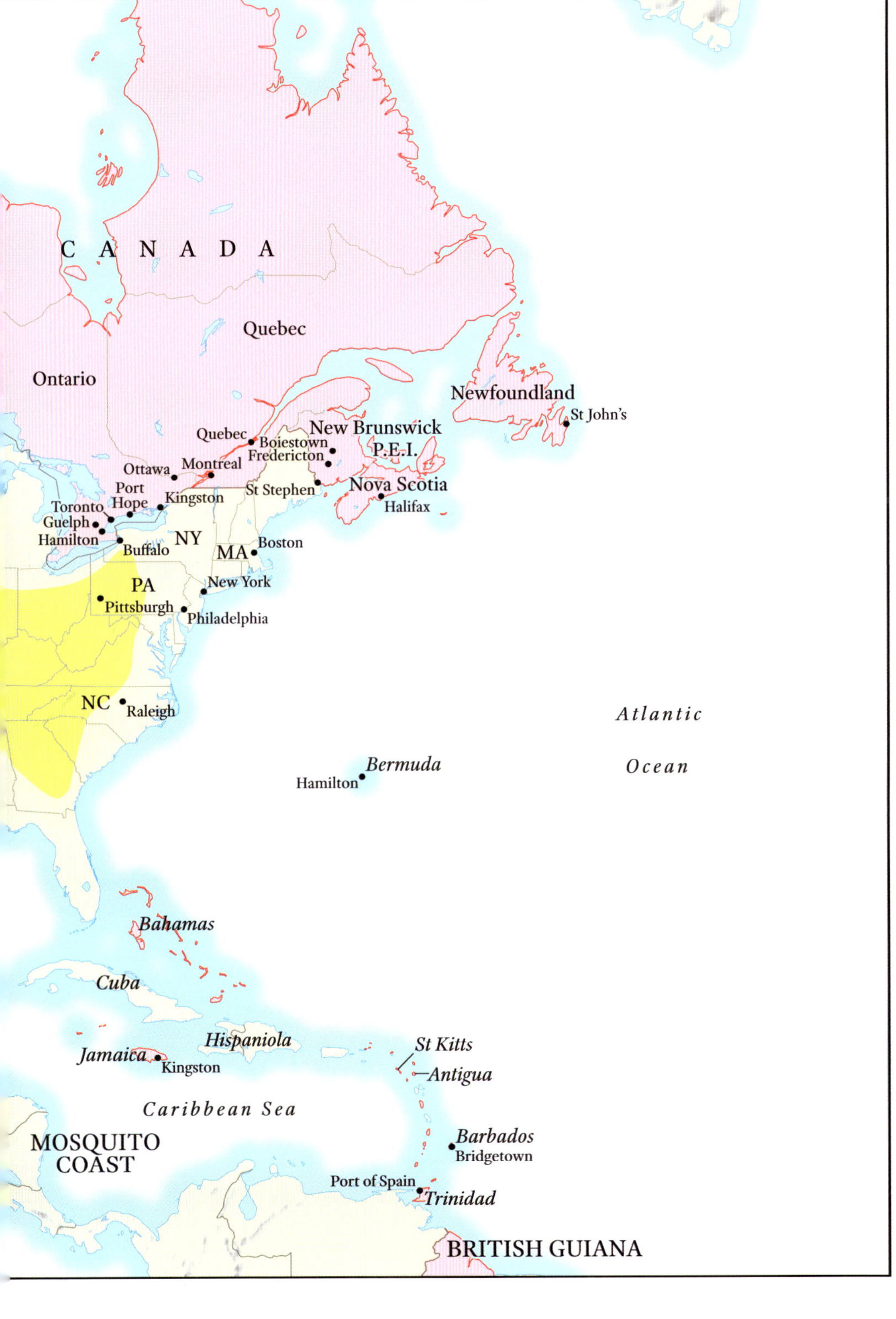
C A N A D A
Quebec
Ontario
Newfoundland
St John's
Quebec
New Brunswick
Boiestown
Fredericton
P.E.I.
Ottawa
Montreal
Nova Scotia
St Stephen
Halifax
Port Hope
Kingston
Toronto
Guelph
Hamilton
Buffalo
NY
MA
Boston
PA
New York
Pittsburgh
Philadelphia
NC
Raleigh
Atlantic
Ocean
Bermuda
Hamilton
Bahamas
Cuba
Hispaniola
St Kitts
Antigua
Jamaica
Kingston
Caribbean Sea
Barbados
Bridgetown
MOSQUITO COAST
Port of Spain
Trinidad
BRITISH GUIANA

C H I N A
Ajmer
Jaipur
Allahabad
I N D I A
Dhaka
Calcutta
BURMA
Bhavnagar
ARAKAN
Bombay (Mumbai)
ANNAM
Hainan
Formosa
Hong Kong
Arabian
Sea
Madras
(Chennai)
SIAM
South
China
Sea
Philippine
Islands
TENASSERIM
CAMBODIA
Ceylon
(Sri Lanka)
Colombo
Galle
MALAY
STATES
BRUNEI
Kuala Lumpur
SARAWAK
Singapore
Kuching
Sumatra
Borneo
Celebes
DUTCH EAST
INDIES
Java
Tarnagulla
Bendigo
Castlemaine
Victoria
Ballarat
Sunbury
Werribee
Melbourne
Geelong
Camperdown
Bass Strait
Launceston
Van Diemen's
Land
(Tasmania)
Ross
Oatlands
Buckland
Hobart
Port Arthur
0 50 100 km
0 25 50 mi
Western
Australia
Perth
Fremantle

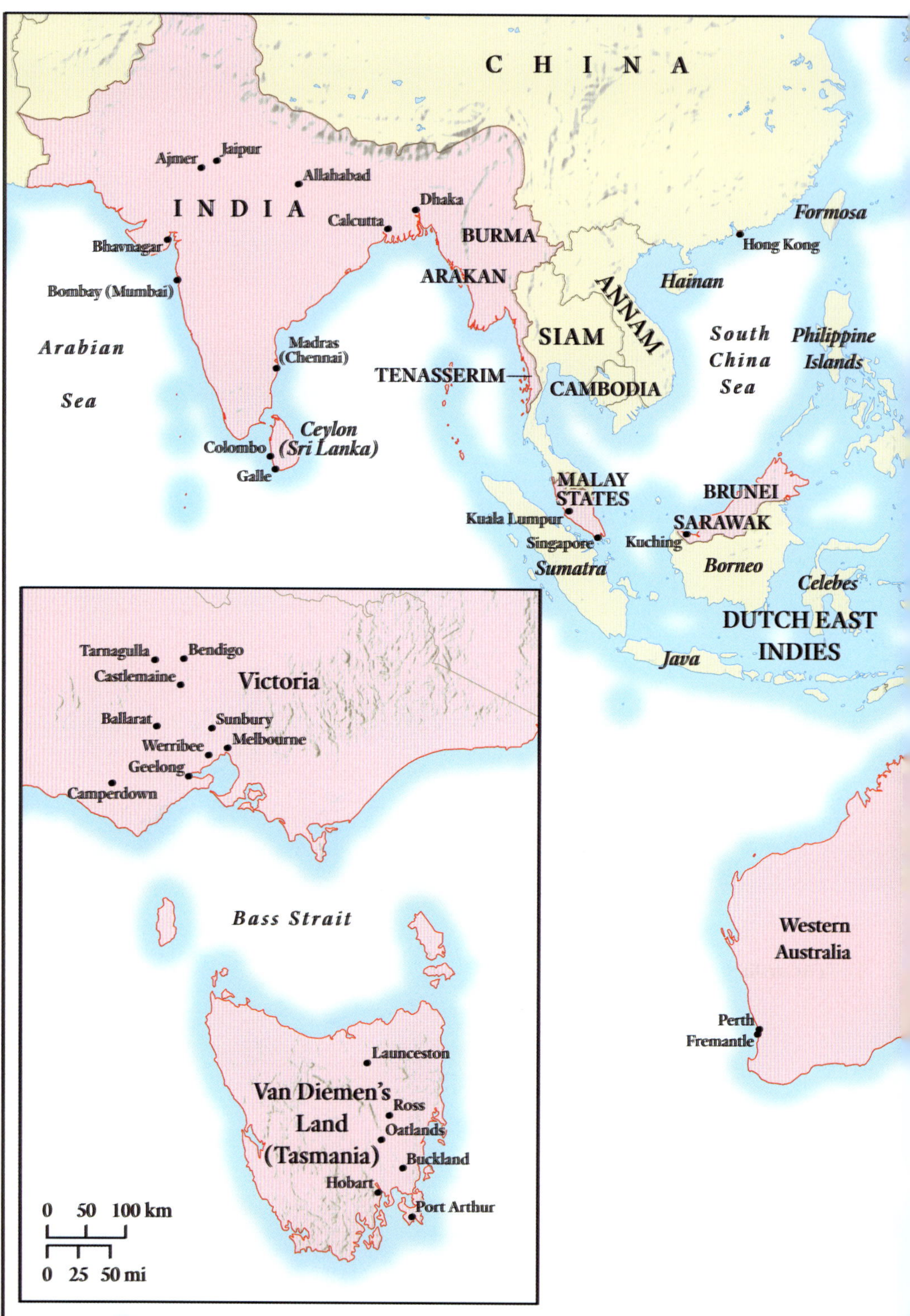

Map 4

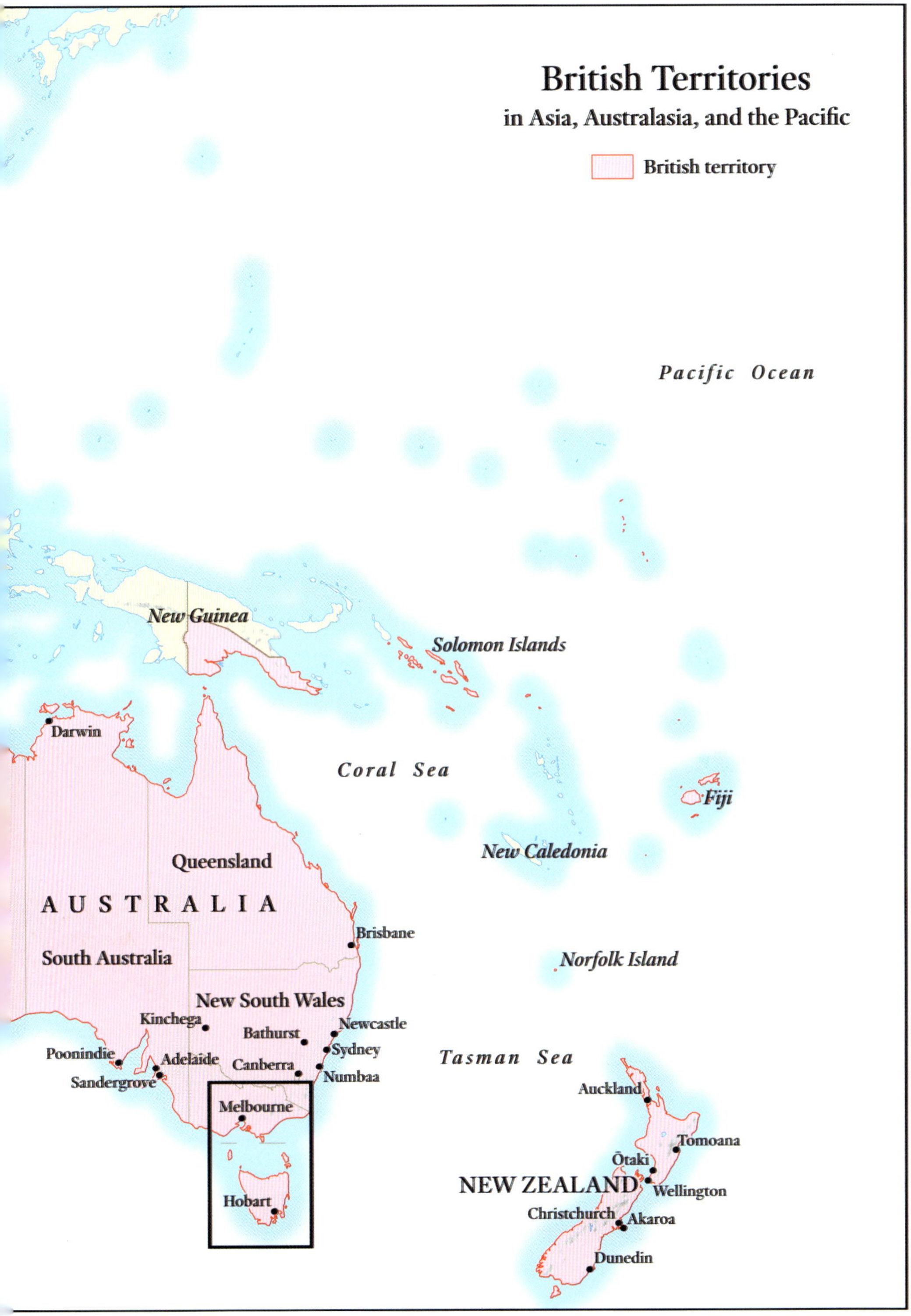

British Territories
in Asia, Australasia, and the Pacific

British territory

Pacific Ocean

New Guinea

Solomon Islands

Darwin

Coral Sea

Fiji

New Caledonia

Queensland

AUSTRALIA

Brisbane

South Australia

Norfolk Island

New South Wales

Kinchega

Newcastle

Bathurst

Sydney

Poonindie

Adelaide

Canberra

Numbaa

Sandergrove

Tasman Sea

Auckland

Melbourne

Tomoana

Ōtaki

NEW ZEALAND

Wellington

Hobart

Christchurch

Akaroa

Dunedin

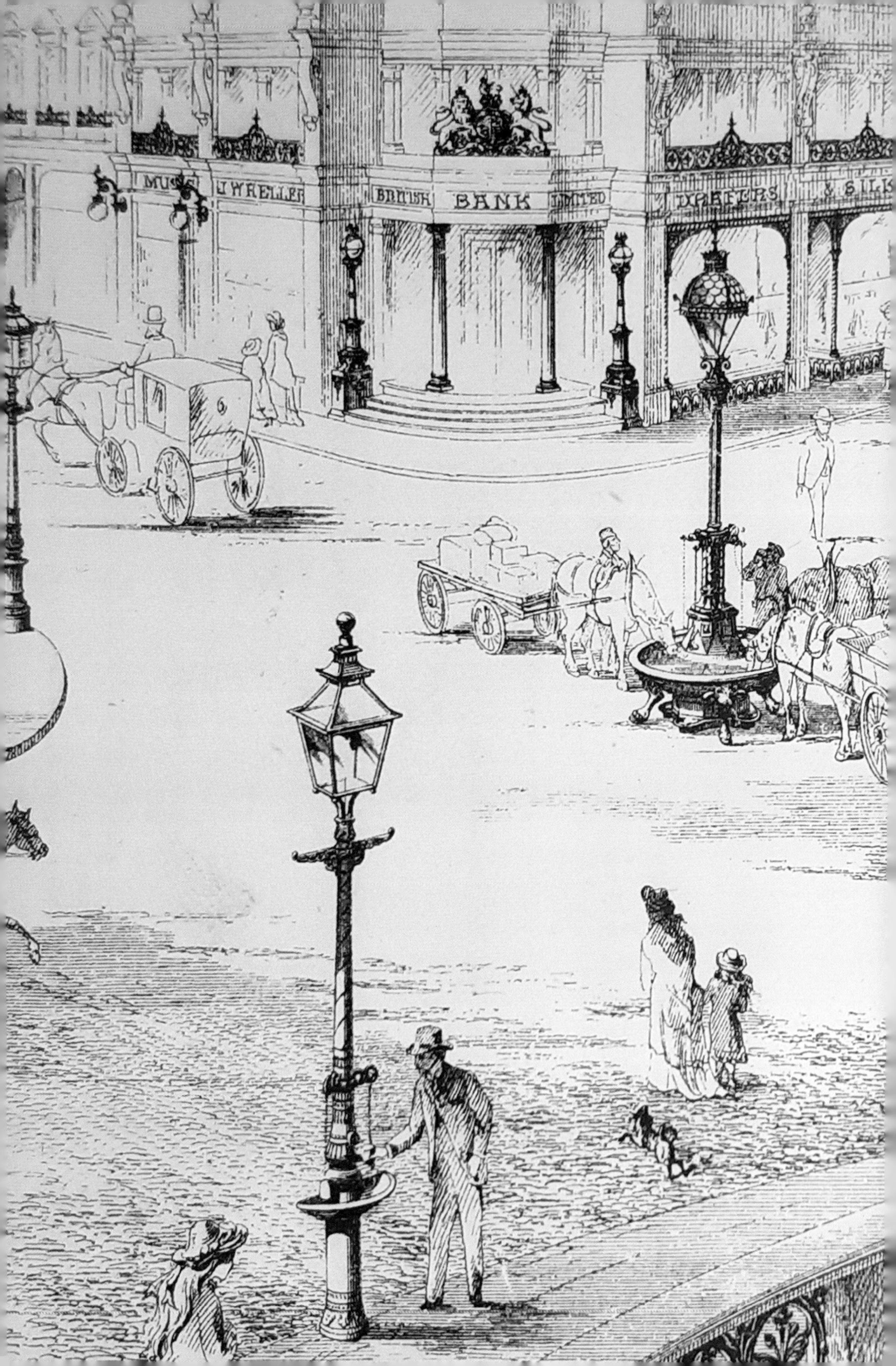
BRITISH
BANK
LIMITED
DRAPERS

Introduction: The World of Victorian Architecture

This book is both an account of Victorian architecture and a primer for understanding something about the period—its culture, politics, and social mores—through its buildings. In this respect, it is neither a handbook, guide, nor gazetteer. It differs from previous accounts of its kind in that it proceeds from the premise that what we call Victorian architecture was more than merely an insular phenomenon. Indeed, the *world* of the Victorians was global. Never before, it might be argued, had the horizons of Britons been so distant, or their allotment so wide, than during the Victorian period. To be sure, Queen Victoria was the hereditary monarch of a small group of islands situated off the western edge of continental Europe, 'The United Kingdom of Great Britain and Ireland', incorporating what is ordinarily termed the British Isles. But she was also, and concurrently, sovereign of extensive overseas territories, habitually referred to as 'the colonies'. By 1876 she had even acquired the grandiose if controversial title 'Empress of India'. Her successive governments held sway over considerable portions of the world (both formally and informally), exercising degrees of power and authority that the history of humanity had scarcely known. Having seen off major rivals throughout the course of the eighteenth and early nineteenth centuries, in particular Spain and France, and despite having lost most of its North American colonies, the United Kingdom had emerged by 1850 as the world's undisputed superpower. Turning eastward, it came to command an empire that encompassed nearly a quarter of the earth's surface, and a fifth of its population. By 1868 it was no longer a case of Great Britain, opined the Liberal politician Charles Dilke, but 'Greater Britain' **[1]**.

A Wide Prospectus

This Greater British world comprised territories that had accrued to the Crown either through inheritance, war, trade, or by occupation. The period strictly covered by Victoria's reign (1837–1901) was, as we shall see, undoubtedly one of rapid industrialisation and social 'improvement', of large-scale political and institutional reform, but it was also an imperial one. Thus, the modern history of the British Isles is very much the story of this outward expansion: politically, economically, and culturally, not to mention ideologically. No account of Victorian Britain, let alone its architecture, is complete without recognising this essential fact. The modern British state was the metropolitan centre of a world system, one that achieved hegemony not

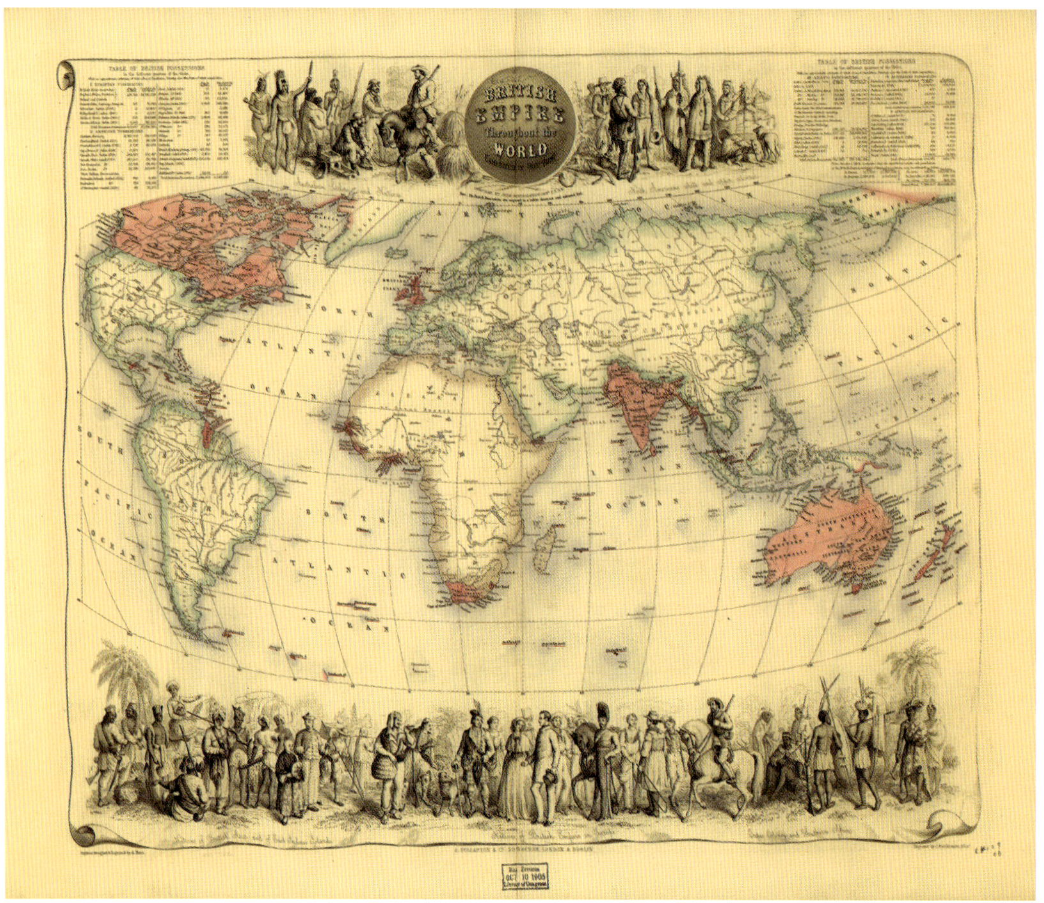

Fig. 1

Map showing the extent of the Victorian world by the 1850s (in pink). *British Empire Throughout the World Exhibited in One View*, c.1855 (Archibald Fullarton & Co.).

only through the developmental forces of science and technology, but also (and equally) through political coercion and military violence, including the systematic manipulation of space.

This history of Victorian architecture therefore starts from the premise that in order to give a fuller and more up-to-date account of the built environment during this period, we must include this wider British world. The presumption here is that Victorian architecture, by definition, is a global phenomenon. People and ideas were increasingly mobile, with the nature and distribution of British architectural forms providing ample evidence of this. British architects were designing buildings not just in the British Isles, but ever farther afield, in lands as far apart as Barbados and Bombay, Newfoundland and New South Wales. Indeed, the Victorian period witnessed the beginnings of what today would be described as the global architectural practice, including those of George Gilbert Scott, William Butterfield, and Aston Webb. 'Starchitects', such as Scott, designed buildings for places as geographically diffuse as South Africa, Australia, India, New Zealand, Canada, and China. This fact points to an ecology of design traditionally overlooked by historians of Victorian architecture: that people inhabiting the wider Victorian world, or designing for it, were creating new and hybrid forms of Victorian architecture, continuously, in multiple locations. This includes architects not born in Britain, and those who never in fact set foot in it, such as the distinguished Bombay Parsi engineer Khan Bahadur Muncherji Cowasji Murzban.[1]

Through the leading journals of the day, such as *The Builder* and *The Building News*, the profession in Britain was kept abreast of developments overseas, and vice versa. Architectural 'progress' in the colonies was reported as if it were an extension of that in Britain, with many of the émigrée architects involved, particularly in the latter part of the century, being fellows or associates of the RIBA (Royal Institute of British Architects). This suggests that Victorian architects were themselves cognisant of their place and influence within a wider field of opportunity and action, including within the formal political structures of colonialism. Such opportunity, it should be noted, also encompassed places outside British territory, including the United States, Continental Europe, and Latin America. It is important to recognise that architecture in Britain was therefore part of this wider activity, and was in turn affected by it, as knowledge and experience of architecture moved between different parts of the British world, and beyond.

Markets for British-made building materials also multiplied during this period, with companies producing and exporting products as diverse as cast iron, encaustic tiles, and stained glass in huge quantities. Even whole buildings were packed and shipped abroad. Scottish foundries, such as Sun, Lion, and Saracen, were particularly entrepreneurial in this regard. Indeed, so successful were they that their products are still readily identifiable in places like Argentina, India, Australia, and South Africa. Encaustic tile manufacturers, too, such as Mintons and Maw & Co., along with stained glass producers, including Clayton & Bell, Hardman & Co., and Ballantine & Allan, established important export markets in the colonies. Their products can be found in many hundreds of buildings across the British world to this day, including many major cathedrals.

In addition to manufactured products, there was also a burgeoning and globally networked market in raw materials. Although forms of liberal commerce assisted in opening markets for the procurement of such materials from around the world, including a brisk trade in marble, Britain's possession of a substantial territorial empire provided levels of access and privilege that accrued advantage. In a period of ongoing international rivalry, such advantage amounted to what these days would be called 'resource security'. We find it, for instance, in the transatlantic and trans-Tasman timber trades between Canada and Britain, and the Australian colonies and New Zealand respectively, not to mention the circulation of exotic timbers from the Caribbean and Southeast Asia around the British empire.[2] Naturally, these products and materials were made to conform to British modes and standards of design, adapted where appropriate, leaving a vast and conspicuous architectural legacy, both in Britain and across its former empire.

This trade, and the wider commerce that accompanied it, was facilitated by Britain's preferential access to mineral resources. This included not only precious metals, which enriched Britain enormously, but also sources of energy. Securing reserves of coal to power Britain's locomotive and steamer fleets was obviously paramount in transporting people and goods around the British world. Coaling stations dotted at strategic locations along primary shipping routes relied upon ready supplies of coal not just from Britain, but from India, parts of Southeast Asia, China, Australia, and Japan.[3] This points to an important factor in the development of architecture during the 'long' Victorian period: the rise of a new and intrinsic energy regime based around the frenzied extraction and consumption of fossil fuels. The dominance of this regime has long been taken for granted in the history of Victorian architecture, especially in discussions on the impact of industrialisation, but rarely inflected as a primary determinant in the shape, scale, and appearance of buildings. To what extent, we might ask, would the Victorian building world have been possible without the economic and technical forces that structured this energy revolution? As we today confront the toxic environmental legacies of the industrial-scale combustion of fossil fuels, it is worth reflecting upon how the possibilities of 'modern', High Victorian architecture were shaped by their relationship to thermodynamic processes pegged to this new energy economy. One of the aims of this book is to take this aspect of the history of Victorian architecture seriously.

This is therefore a different history of Victorian architecture. It is not a rehash of old ways of seeing, of architecture categorised by either typology, chronology, style, form, materiality, patronage, or personality. Naturally, categories of this kind will be invoked, as they are useful to any history of architecture, but they are not used as a primary structuring device. We already have a rich and impressive tradition of such writing on Victorian architecture, which, on its own terms, is difficult to surpass. Instead, this history will be structured around themes that I consider, in one form or another, fundamental to how Victorians perceived and experienced their world, themes that were in themselves constitutional of the Victorian frame of mind, such as urbanism, industry, government, faith, empire, modernity, social order, family, collecting, and consumerism. These themes will offer an alternative perspective on Victorian architecture, making for a more wide-ranging interpretation of architecture and its various uses and meanings.

Understanding Victorian Architecture

The first question a book such as this must ask is what *is* Victorian architecture? This is not an easy question to answer, and is really the task of the book at length. Nevertheless, it is worth offering some preliminary thoughts on the fundamental complexities that attend the subject. With this in mind, it is necessary to ask not only what constitutes 'Victorian architecture' historically, but also how we define it as a category of study.

History, Chronology, and Architecture

What may be considered Victorian has long been assumed to be obvious. But closer inspection reveals otherwise. Indeed, all-encompassing categories such as 'Victorian' can be as elusive as they are illuminating. Over the years, those writing on the history of art and architecture have tended to corral discussion of objects and buildings into chronological frames of reference, referring to 'periods', movements, and genres of creativity and production.

The discipline as it evolved has naturally coalesced around patterns or taxonomies of apparent order, helping make sense of art and architecture as socially constructed (and thus limited) phenomena. One of these ordering devices has been the loose labelling of artistic output within the timeframe of dynastic rule (what Hugh Casson called 'royal parcels'), whether it be the art of ancient Egypt, medieval Europe, or indeed modern Britain. In the case of Britain, it is possible to speak of Tudor, Elizabethan, or Jacobean art and architecture, just as it is of Georgian, Victorian, and even Edwardian. These terms have become conventional. Although they do not necessarily explain very much in themselves, we are now accustomed to their use in distinguishing and analysing broad periods of artistic production. Sub and overlapping genres are of course permitted. In the case of Victorian art and architecture, there is 'Pre-Raphaelite', 'Arts and Crafts', 'High Victorian', and 'Gothic Revival', but these are still seen as part of a broader period or mentality of creative intent that we associate with the Victorian age.

There is no inherent logic to this periodisation other than it being a way of bringing historiographic containment to what might otherwise be seen as disparate activity. What it contains, to be sure, is often fragmentary, paradoxical, if not incoherent, especially when viewed from end to end. After all, there is not a great deal in common between what architects were doing (or how they did it) in 1838 and 1898. Some historians, such as the urban geographer David Ward, for instance, refer to not one but *three* distinct if overlapping phases of Victorian urban morphology: a regional one (prior to the full impact of the railway age); a national one (once transport systems integration had been achieved); and an international or global one (when telecommunications were developed, and people and investment had become fully mobile), each of which affected the city in different ways.[4] Whether we accept this or not, it demonstrates the nebulous and somewhat slippery nature of the problem. Despite these limitations, I contend that the term Victorian is still useful.[5] It helps us form an immediate mental picture of what is being referred to, a kind if perceptual shorthand, once we understand the period's basic formal and theoretical parameters. This 'picture', as it were, is akin to what John Summerson once described as that which is 'most profoundly, most typically and, very often, most ludicrously Victorian'.[6] Thus, when we talk of Victorian art or architecture, an essential if not particularly nuanced image comes to mind. In short, we know it when we see it.

However, there are serious chronological and geographical implications to consider that both challenge and disrupt such periodisation. Appreciating this is necessary in establishing the scope of this book. To begin with, the long-accepted practice of bracketing periods of history by century for the sake of convenience—i.e., sixteenth-century weapons, or eighteenth-century literature, etc.—has been unsettled somewhat by the insistence that historical phenomena are neither contained by nor exclusively shaped within arbitrary dates; that, in fact, such phenomena nearly always transgress such rigid boundaries. Hence, for the past few decades in historical scholarship we have become used to categories such as the 'long eighteenth century' (1688–1815) or the 'long nineteenth century' (1789–1914). This might equally apply to regal periodisations, as Casson observed of the Victorian era.[7] We could speak of a 'long' Victorian period, for instance, in which certain social and technical transformations—the evolution of new moral sensibilities, the idea of 'improvement', the effective harnessing of steam power, or the full effects of reform culture—were observable in the decades leading up to Victoria's accession to the throne, before becoming associated with what Walter E. Houghton and Asa Briggs, among others, called Victorianism.

Such transformations and their antecedents must be seen to affect our understanding of Victorian architecture, too. The moral and spiritual revolutions that underpinned the mature phase of the Gothic Revival, for instance, certainly predate Victoria's reign, as do the technological developments that led to the possibilities of polychromy in High Victorian architecture of the 1850s and 1860s. At the other end of Victoria's reign we have the 'New Imperialism', which, as a sentiment, carried well over into the Edwardian period, and beyond. This also affected architecture either side of 1901, as evidenced, for example, in the rise of so-called Edwardian Baroque architecture from the late 1880s. It is also worth remembering that there were architects' careers that firmly bridged either the late Georgian and early Victorian periods, or the late Victorian and Edwardian, such as Charles Barry and C. R. Cockerell, at one end, and John Belcher and Aston Webb, at the other. Hence, nothing is quite as it seems. This book is aware of the shortcomings of such periodisation, and will take a longer rather than shorter perspective on its traditional limits.

Substance and Meaning in Victorian Architecture

But chronology is only one factor. Matters of substance and meaning are others. The term 'Victorian architecture' can also refer to buildings seen to embody characteristics peculiar to the Victorian age, or to discrete movements that fell within its broad chronology, such as the Arts and Crafts. On this point it may be said that 'High Victorian' architecture—represented, say, by a structure such as All Saints' church, Margaret Street, in London—is indicative of a certain attitude towards design that was informed by a confluence of concerns relating to history, morality, religious reform, scientific thought, and innovations in building technology. This is not something that has been revealed in hindsight by art-historical scholarship, but something that those living through it fully appreciated. It is worth recalling that in 1861 A. J. B. Beresford Hope, one of Britain's leading architectural theorists, observed that the architecture of his age was, for lack of a better term, 'Victorian'. Looking back over the first 25 years of Victoria's reign, he could see the vast changes that had swept across the architectural scene in Britain, especially in the availability of and attitude towards new materials.[8] The 'development' of architecture in this regard, as he and his colleagues were wont to describe it, seemed clear.

Victorian architects were also acutely aware that they were revivalists, but not inane copyists. There is (and has been) much confusion surrounding so-called historicism and the clash of styles during this period, exacerbated by the Modernist myth of Victorian architectural discombobulation. Architects were inspired by the past, and understood, as George Gilbert Scott did, the limitations of creating something 'new' or 'modern' from a given set of stylistic constraints. Indeed, talk of creating a new, indicative, and entirely original style of architecture for modern Britain exercised the Victorian architectural imagination, and remained something of a monkey on the back of British architecture until the 1930s. Pressure in this regard was particularly keen given the arrival of novel building materials into mainstream practice during the first half of the nineteenth century, such as cast iron, plate glass, and mass-produced terracotta. The effects of these changes on the visual and spatial experiences of not just architects but the Victorian public in general fashioned what some scholars see as a peculiar condition of 'nineteenth-century modernism', and one that must be taken seriously on its own terms rather than positioned as a prelude to that of the twentieth century.[9] If there is one *leitmotif*, as it were, that tracks through the history of Victorian architecture, it is this conscientious quest for 'modernity' and the 'modern', in one form or another.

This anxiety was embodied in publications such as Thomas Harris's *Victorian Architecture* (1860), where the pursuit of a new and distinctly 'national' architecture bordered on a frantic plea. For most, however, achieving absolute novelty seemed beyond their grasp, even if it was desirable. In fact, John Ruskin decried that architects ought to 'get rid of' any such idea. What the leading lights of the profession (and their critics) wanted most of all, it seemed, was to produce something representative of its time, an architecture that was true to itself. In his influential *Remarks on Secular & Domestic Architecture* of 1857, Scott was honest enough to advise his fellow professionals that, 'if we can devise . . . a [new] style for ourselves, by all means let us do so; but if not, let us endeavour to develop it out of that of some former period'. Given this, he cautioned: 'our business' ought simply to be 'to cull from works of any date [in his case Gothic], or from our own conceptions, such ideas as are practically suited to meet our requirements, and to express them consistently . . .; and if the result should differ from anything before done, so much the better, if only it be good'.[10] In making these remarks, Scott was also invoking that sense of responsibility so characteristic of and consistent with Victorian notions of moral probity. It also suggests to us how the idea of history, and modern architecture's place within it, was something that the Victorians grappled with perpetually.[11]

The 'Problem' of Style

Even in their own time Victorian architects and critics bemoaned the enervating consequences of eclecticism. For instance, Banister Fletcher could still observe as late as 1896 that his ardent hope was for 'a style or manner in architecture' that would 'become the free expression of our own civilization, and the outward symbol of our nineteenth century progression'.[12] Long before this hard-line Gothic Revivalists, such as Scott and George Edmund Street, had warned against eclecticism (for its own sake) as a form of cognitive dissonance, if not dishonesty. In some respects this is not surprising. With the profession in its infancy, and architectural education largely reliant on the pupillage system, even at century's end there was little consensus as to what modern architecture should be.[13] Not even the rise of the professional print media in the 1840s could bring much unanimity, but instead

Fig. 2

Alexander Thomson, St Vincent Street United Presbyterian Church, Glasgow (1859).

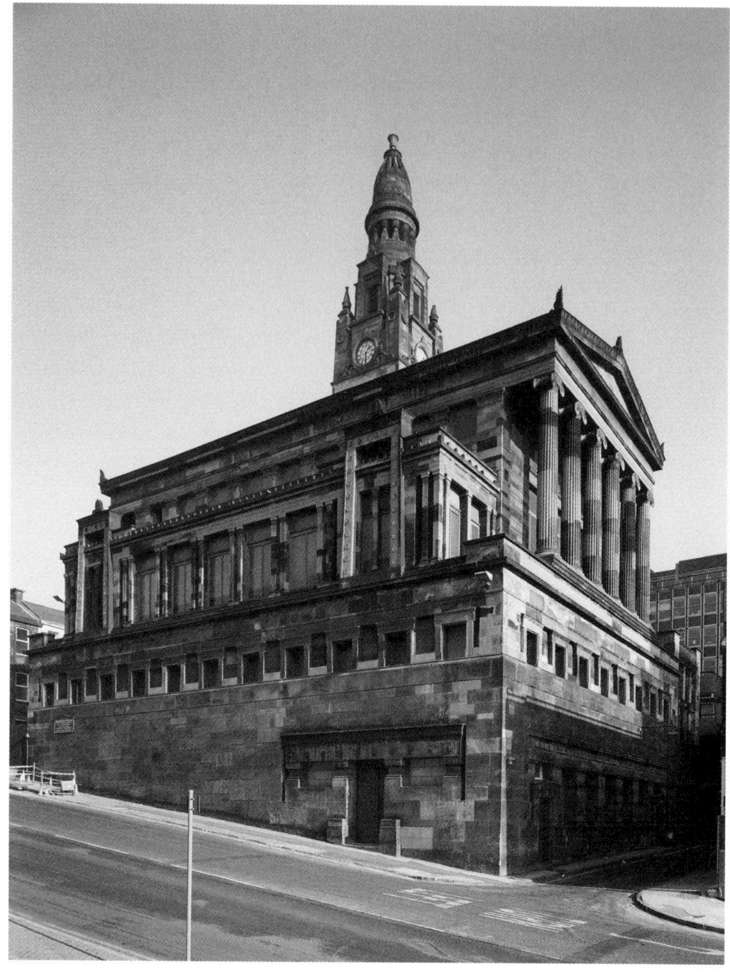

tended to exacerbate divisions as competing ideas became more widespread, backed by ever more sophisticated moral and theoretical argument.

The 'battle' over style, as it became known, was inflamed by the highly influential and impassioned pleas of those such as A. W. N. Pugin and John Ruskin, which blew revolutionary winds of change through the creaking shibboleths of British architecture in favour of a revived Gothic.[14] At the other end of this ideological divide was the powerful, evangelically inspired intellect of Alexander 'Greek' Thomson, who, from the ultra-Protestant viewpoint of his Presbyterian faith, saw Gothic architecture as nothing less than a 'popish' conspiracy. As will be discussed further in Chapter 3, for Thomson, the inherent beauty of the best classical architecture (such as the Parthenon) was far from deceptive, but instead evidence of God's sublime truth on earth **[2]**.[15] Even by century's end, when new, nationally inspired forms of 'grand manner' Classicism such as the Edwardian Baroque came to dominate architecture in Britain, architects, critics, and commentators alike were still grumbling about seeking eternal truths in architecture, only this time on different premises.

While many architects were content to follow 'taste', for the likes of Pugin, Ruskin, and Thomson, along with their growing bands of followers, the 'principle of truth' was paramount, being one of the guiding 'lamps' of Victorian respectability.[16] In its communicative capacity, architecture was therefore understood by many leading practitioners as a form of virtue signalling. The material signs of morality were designed for display. Moreover, in considering the seeming muddle of Victorian architecture, we need to remember that Victoria's reign of 63 years is a long time in the history of architecture, being quite a bit more than the life expectancy of an average person of the period. We also need to remember that new building types and functions were emerging in real time: train stations, exhibition buildings, large hotels, grand museums, town halls, workhouses, and state schools, among others. Thus, the creative output of the Victorian period represents more than a lifetime's worth of transformation.

For the Victorians, truth was both religious and scientific. But these competing truths were not necessarily contradictory, and great efforts were made at reconciling them. We see this in ecclesiastical architecture, for example, where associational ideas relating to science, such as evolutionary theory, affected aesthetic outcomes in relating God to nature. The application of scientific thought to building solutions, as in engineering, also became a lively sub-branch of architectural design. Unsurprisingly, architects were keen to exploit the potential of new technology, whether in terms of construction, comfort, or aesthetics. This concern for technical modernity led not only to landmark structures such as the Crystal Palace, but also to buildings such as the Reform Club (1841), the Houses of Parliament (1837–67) **[3]**, and

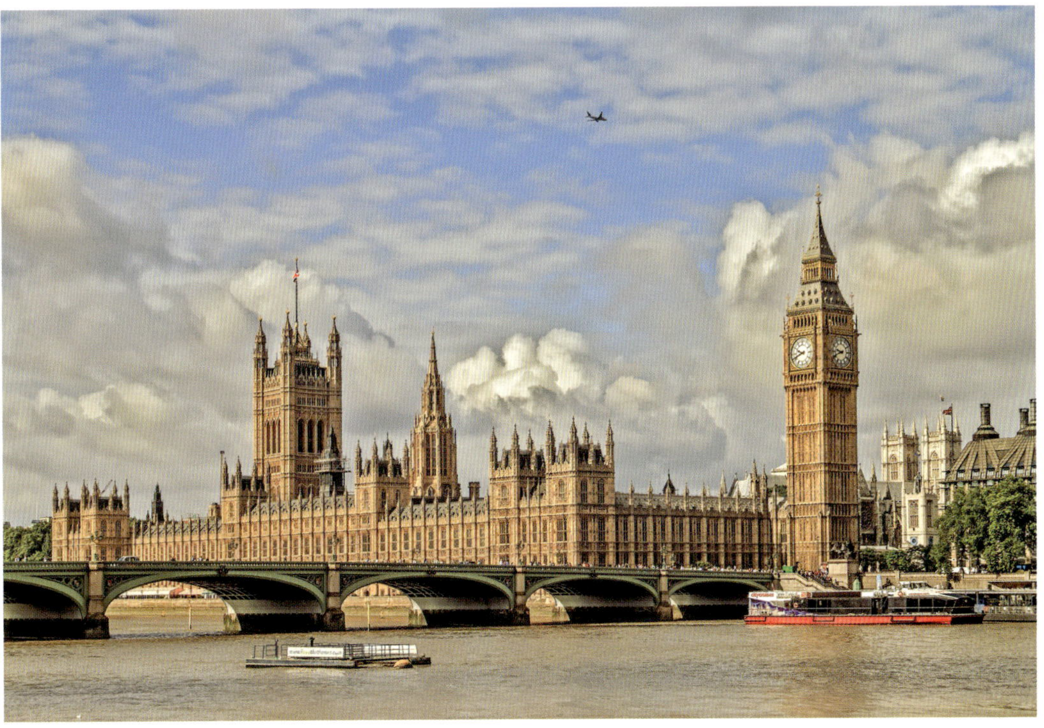

Fig. 3

Charles Barry, A. W. N. Pugin, and E. M. Barry, Houses of Parliament, Westminster (1837–67), London.

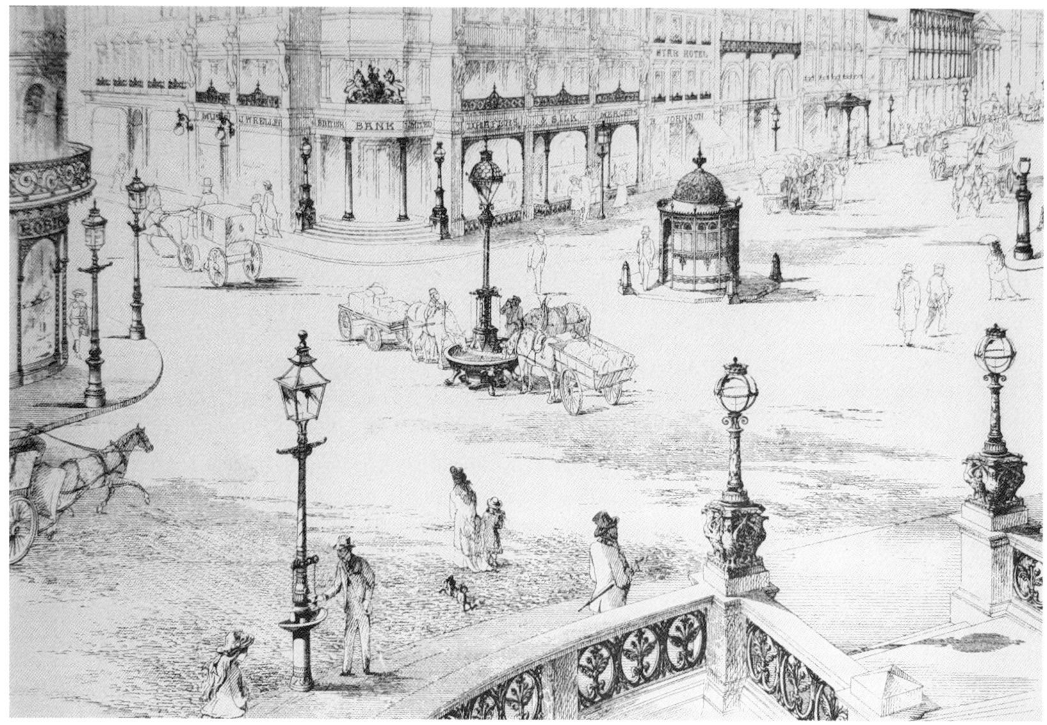

Fig. 4

Cast iron and the Victorian urban environment. 'Central Thoroughfare with Examples of Architectural and Sanitary Castings', *Macfarlane's Castings*, 6th edition, 2 vols (Glasgow, 1882), facing title page to volume 2.

Pentonville Prison (1840–2), all of which were among the most advanced buildings then erected. Indeed, the effort that went into making the new Palace of Westminster the most efficient and comfortable public building that modern ingenuity could devise was quite extraordinary. In this sense, the co-productive association between science, architecture, and social reform in Britain, at scale, is one of Victorian architecture's defining characteristics.

To be sure, in searching for a new and unique style, and failing by their own standards, architects during the Victorian period did in fact create many novel building forms. This is what makes Victorian architecture such a rich field of inquiry. 'Buildings', or indeed infrastructure, such as sewerage pumping stations, train sheds, viaducts, warehouses, factories, even street furniture, were part of a design-orientated matrix that created degrees of thematic continuity across the Victorian built environment **[4]**. Therefore, any revised history of Victorian architecture must be alert to the different and diverse registers of design that are evident in the wider built environment, where these overlapped with science and engineering, and how they contributed to what may be described, in retrospect, as a 'Victorian-ised' landscape.

Looking Forward

The complexities and contradictions inherent in the term Victorian architecture are therefore apparent. While a certain essence (ethos, even) is identifiable in much architectural design during the period, the edges of what we call Victorian architecture are necessarily blurry if not indistinct.

We must appreciate it as an architecture of geographical diffusion and ideological incoherence; of material diversity and social prescription; and of great formal variety in the service of programmatic constraint. All this makes the study of architecture during the Victorian period challenging, often surprising, and even inspiring. Therefore, in asking what Victorian architecture is, we can safely say that it is many things. The aim of this book it to embrace this diversity, and to showcase Victorian architecture in all its wondrous, sublime, and at times disturbing glory.

This book thus engages with the history of Victorian architecture and urbanism in both familiar and unfamiliar ways. The aim is to renovate the presentation of Victorian architecture for a twenty-first-century audience. In doing this I take the widest possible view of what 'architecture' is understood to encompass. The intention is to avoid perpetuating abstract or arbitrary divisions between architecture (with a capital 'A') and vernacular/industrial building forms. Instead, I embrace the whole of the Victorian built environment, including critical infrastructure and its impact on architecture and the city. I believe this is important in gaining a fuller understanding of what Victorian architecture includes and can mean. However, in a book that aims to incorporate so much more than has traditionally been attributed to the subject, certain things must necessarily be excluded. With this in mind, I have privileged discussion of the principles of Victorian architecture and design over complete typological coverage. Also, treatment of the United States of America, the late nineteenth-century architecture of which is often referred to as 'Victorian', has also been largely omitted. Despite the numerous overlaps and correspondences American architecture had with that in Britain, especially between about 1840 and 1870, the limitations of this format do not allow analysis of it here. This would require a much larger book, or indeed a separate volume altogether. Therefore, architectural developments in the United States are only mentioned in passing, or where they are seen to have had an appreciable impact on architecture in the British world.

As with other volumes in the *Oxford History of Art* series, the overall ambition is to fashion an authoritative, concise, and visually attractive book aimed at both students and general readers, as well as serving as a useful reference point for professional scholars. The buildings discussed are placed in their proper social and cultural contexts in order that they may be seen as products, formations, and assemblages expressive of deep and intersecting cultural concerns. In this respect, the volume's approach takes advantage of the key methodological and historiographic changes that have transformed the historical study of architecture in recent decades. In short, this is a *new* general history of Victorian architecture.

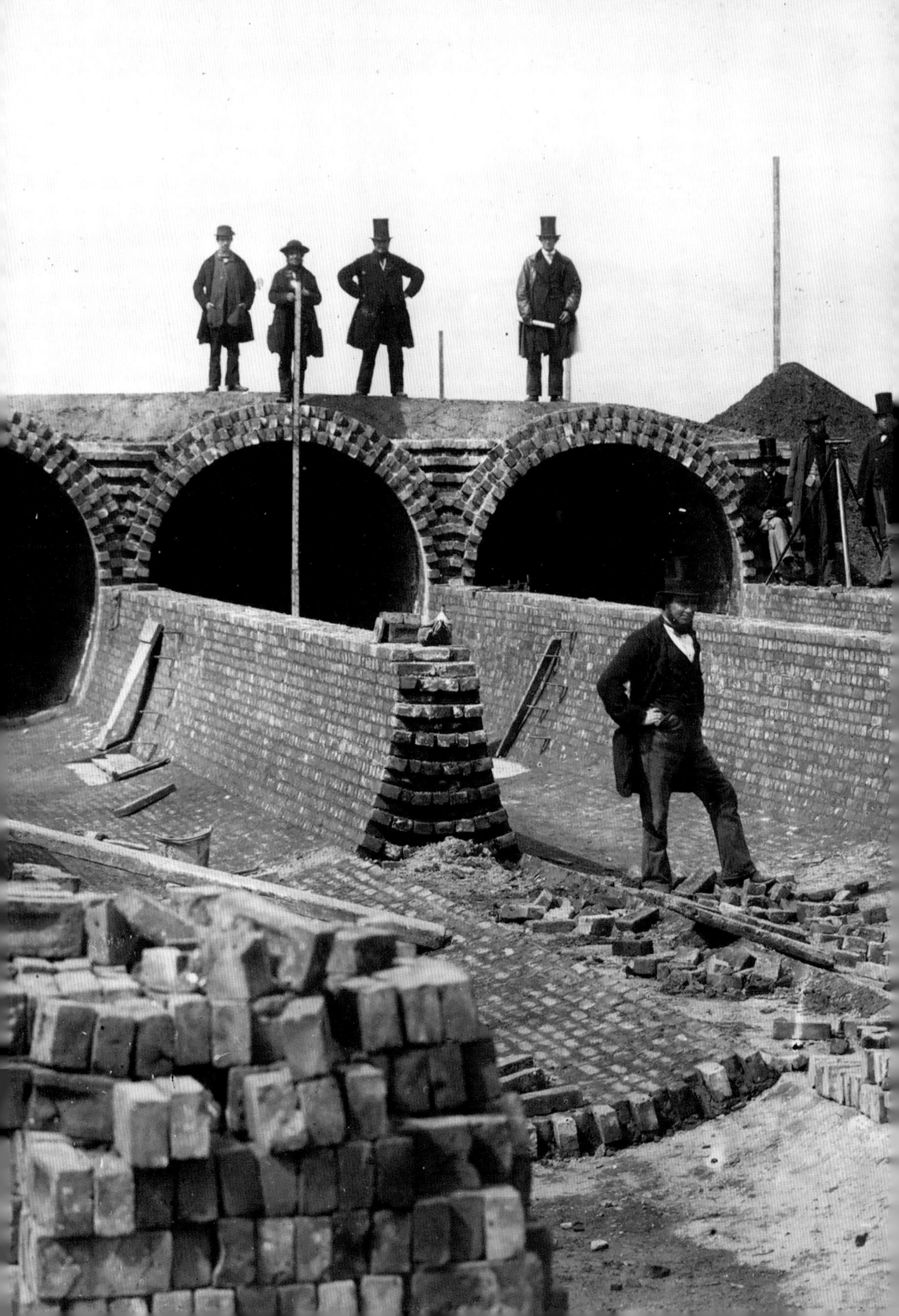

1

Steam and Speed: Industry, Infrastructure, and the City

It is difficult to understand the rapid and spectacular transformation that took place within Victorian building culture without first appreciating its relationship to the infrastructures that drove and sustained it. In many ways, these infrastructures were indicative of an altered architectural imagination, and responsible for making most of the features we identify with Victorian architecture possible to begin with. These include not only those structures commonly associated with modern industry, such as warehouses and factories, but also canals, railroads, aqueducts, viaducts, suspension bridges, modern gas and sewerage works, telegraph equipment, and docking facilities. These should not be dismissed merely as products of civil engineering. They signified something peculiarly *modern* in their systematic and disruptive (near violent) reordering of a settled mode of existence. Indeed, with the continued expansion of the British empire throughout the late nineteenth century, such infrastructures were instrumental in shaping patterns of settlement, industry, and social control right across the world. Thus, lying at the foundation of global Britain's economic power and success, they constitute an extended assemblage germane to any study of Victorian architecture.

The explosive growth of cities and their attendant conurbations was also a notable feature of the age. Even for those who know little about the history of the Victorian built environment, there is a general awareness that from around the second quarter of the nineteenth century Britain's population grew rapidly, and that it was the period during which the modern city, warts and all, was born. This comes down to us not only through the art and literature of the period, but also via the vast remnants of the Victorian built environment, despite much of it having already been swept away, either through war or modern urban regeneration. Nevertheless, the context of the Victorian city provides an important social, spatial, and technological register through which to understand the aim and function of specific architectural interventions during the period.

In this sense infrastructure and the city were connected, both physically and imaginatively. Those types of infrastructure mentioned above often converged on cities, serving their daily needs as well as their demands for growth. They stretched their tentacles further afield, too, across the countryside, linking Britain's new and rapidly expanding centres of industry, constituting a larger 'technosphere'.[1] Indeed, the problem of urban growth as an index to industrialisation became central to the political economy of Victorian Britain, as the 'condition of England' question became urgent. It was not only large, existing cities such as London that grew rapidly during this period; other, much smaller ones, in becoming centres of industrial production, expanded exponentially to become the 'shock cities' of the age. This included cities in the industrial Midlands and North, such as Birmingham, Sheffield, Manchester, Leeds, Newcastle, and Glasgow. In this chapter I will trace some of these developments with a view to setting the scene out of which the architecture of the Victorian period emerged.

The Built Landscapes of Industrialisation

Infrastructure and the processes of industrialisation were synonymous in nineteenth-century Britain. One of the primary motivations behind infrastructural development was the high cost of inland transportation. These costs were a major constraint on the British economy. Investment in new and sophisticated transport technologies was therefore understood as a means of not only reducing these costs but also increasing economic output. The subsequent transport revolution led to more reliable, secure, and greater-capacity modes of delivery, not to mention faster and cheaper ones, too. Taking the railways as indicative of this change, by 1865–70 freight charges per ton mile cost one-twentieth (in real terms) of what they did by horse-drawn wagons in 1700. Over the same period average transportation speeds increased more than ten times (from 1.96 to 23.2 mph). Even taking into consideration the vast improvements in roads and coach technology that had occurred by the early nineteenth century, travel by rail was still nearly three times faster. Similar rates of efficiency were achieved in the wider British world. In British India, for instance, the coming of the railways in the late nineteenth century reduced average overland freight charges by more than 90 per cent, with tens of millions of tons of cargo being transported by rail annually.[2]

A key factor in this transformation was coal. With coal increasingly recognised as a ready and powerful source of energy in the United Kingdom, it became a crucial input in the growth of the British economy and its full-scale industrialisation. Britain's accessible abundance of coal was coincident with a high-wage economy in comparison to other parts of Europe and Asia during the eighteenth and early nineteenth centuries. This incentivised British business to invent technology that effectively substituted energy for human labour.[3] But coal was a dense, heavy material that was expensive to transport. The development of the British canal system, particularly around burgeoning industrial centres such as Birmingham, was beneficial not only to the efficient movement of goods, but also (and especially) for the transportation of coal. However, although reliable, canal transport was slow. For improved passenger transport, and the movement of both high-value and perishable goods, only the railways could offer the speed and comfort required.

High-pressure steam locomotives required large amounts of coal to operate. This created an industrial ecology in Britain increasingly based upon a technological multiplier effect centred around the thermodynamic properties inherent to the combustion of fossil fuels. Once James Watt's improved steam engine had proven its utility in the efficient rotary propulsion of machinery, the benefits of steam power were hard to resist. This ushered in regimes of time and scale against which all economy was measured (positively or negatively), including in architecture. As the architect G. E. Street observed at the time: '[s]urely all our facilities of locomotion, of friendly intercourse and acquaintance with foreign lands, and the like, are so many points in which we have a great advantage'.[4] With the heavy investment in railway lines in the 1830s and 1840s, by the time of the Great Exhibition of 1851 an embryonic national rail network of over 6,000 miles had been constructed.[5] The temporal and thus economic efficiency of railways increased demand for certain industrially produced materials, such as iron and steel, thus fostering the development of these industries. To this one might add certain other building materials typical of the Victorian age, such as manufactured bricks, terracotta, tiles, and polished granite (see Chapter 2).

The Canal Network and Its Equipment

One of the earliest and most extensive infrastructural developments in this transport revolution was the building of the British canal network. Although the vast majority of Britain's canals were laid before the Victorian period, they were continually added to and modernised throughout the nineteenth century. This is mainly because canals were still useful for haulage that was either close in proximity, bulky, or not particularly time sensitive. The canals themselves were major and often conspicuous engineering works, especially when emerging as aqueducts, such as the daring examples at Chirk and Pontcysyllte in Wales **[5a]**. At intervals along their length canals were also dotted with structural accretions referred to as 'canal machinery', including cranes, sluice-operating gear, paddles, bridges (lifting, swinging, and draw), and locks, either single, double, or multiple **[5b]**. To this can be added other, more traditional structures that surrounded key nodal points, such as wharves, warehouses, stables, and lock houses and navigation offices, many of which were extended and upgraded during the Victorian period.

Some of the more impressive Victorian-era improvements to the British canal system included the installation of so-called inclines, designed to connect adjacent canals at different levels. The Blackhill Incline, some 1,000 feet in length, was opened near Glasgow in 1850. There boats were moved in floating tanks (caissons) up the 1/10 slope between canals using two 25hp steam engines. Between March and August 1851 alone this incline shifted 5,227 boats. A similar, yet more substantial piece of infrastructure was installed in 1900 at Foxton, on the Grand Union Canal, in Leicestershire **[6a]**. This was capable of moving 70-ton barges between canals in under 13 minutes. To these huge structures may be added the incredible Anderton hydraulic boat lift, near Manchester. First erected in 1875, this structure was able to elevate barges over a height of 50 feet, from the River Weaver up to the Trent and Mersey Canal **[6b]**. But perhaps the greatest such construction of the Victorian age was the Ganges Canal network in British India, the 'upper' section of which was completed in 1854, the 'lower' in 1880.

Fig. 5a

Thomas Telford, Pontcysyllte Aqueduct, Wales (1795–1805).

Fig. 5b

'Neptune's Staircase', staircase lock on the Caledonian Canal (1803–22), near Fort William, Scotland, designed by Thomas Telford. At the base of the lock a train can be seen crossing the Banavie cast-iron swing bridge (1901).

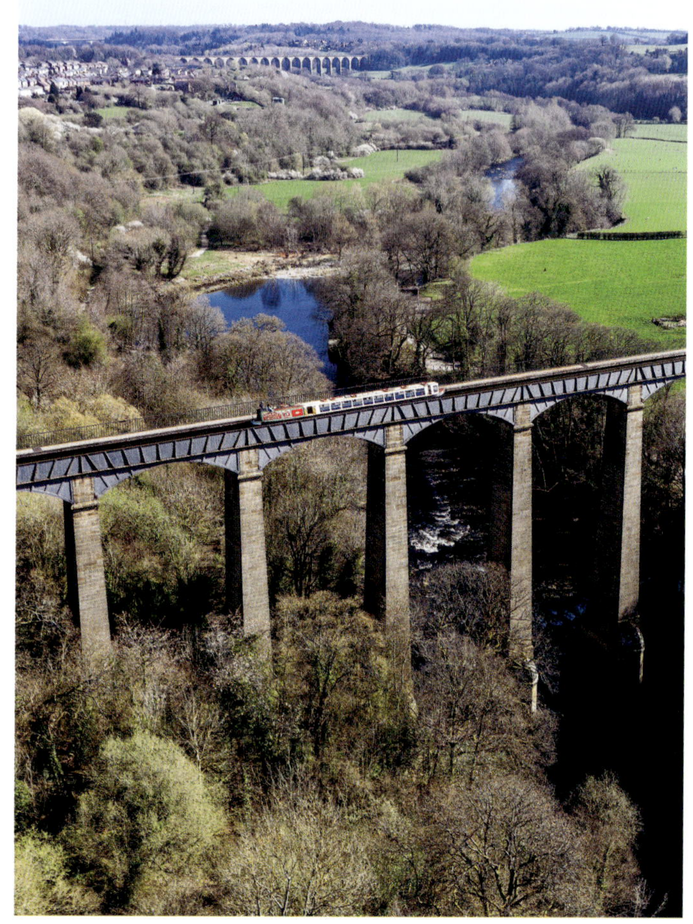

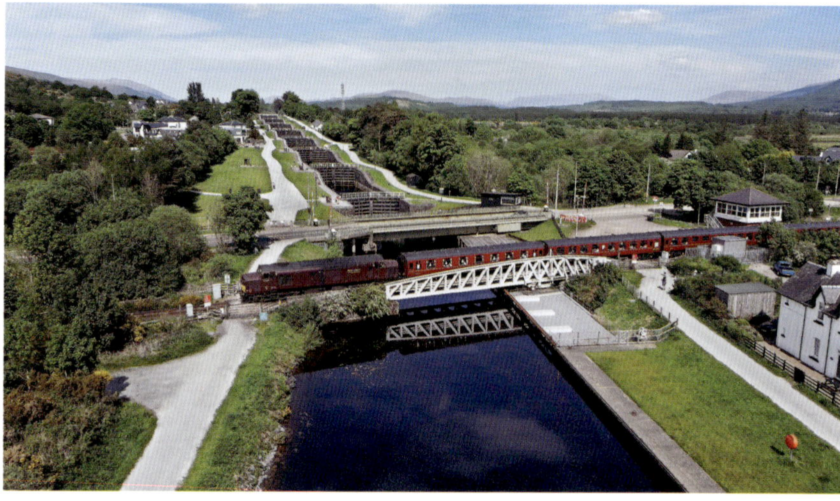

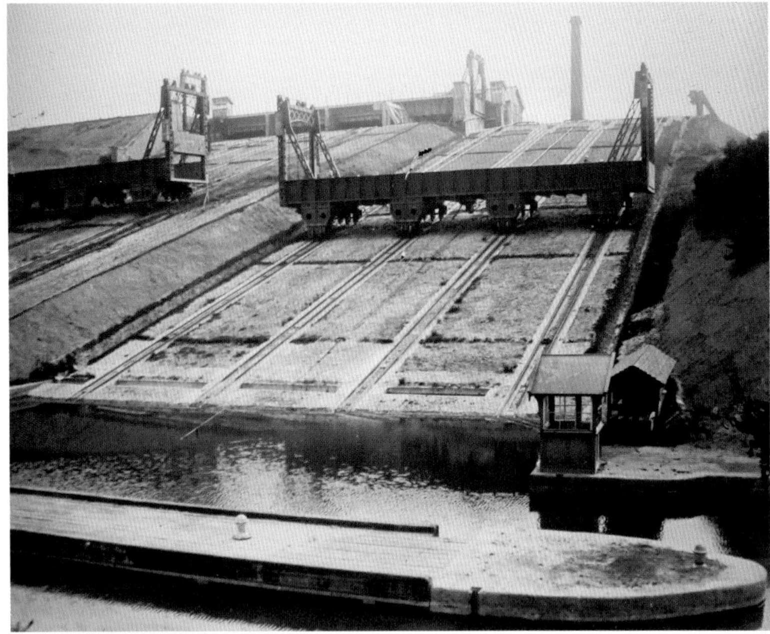

Fig. 6a

Victorian industrial sublime. Inclined plane boat lift, Grand Union Canal at Foxton Locks, Leicestershire (1900), by Gordon Cale Thomas.

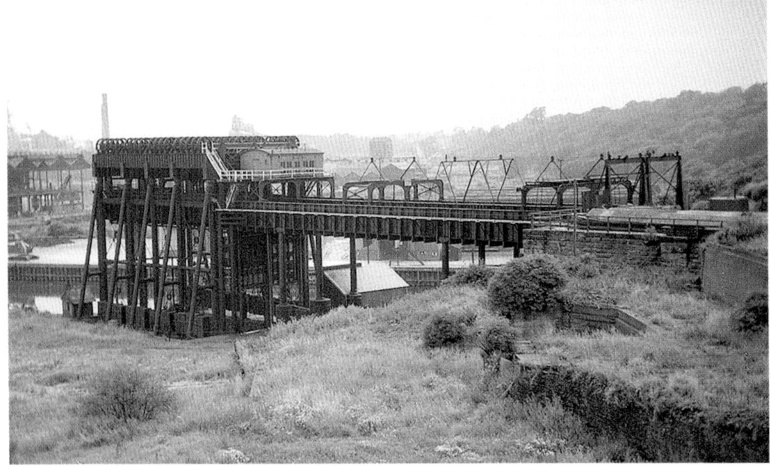

Fig. 6b

Anderton hydraulic boat lift, near Manchester (1875), connecting the River Weaver and Trent and Mersey Canal.

Stretching for some 800 miles—from Haridwar, at the foot of the Shivalik ranges, to Cawnpore (Kanpur) in central Uttar Pradesh, including several thousand miles of feeder canals—the network was initially built for the East India Company by the engineer Proby Cautley in response to the Agra famine of 1837–8. Intended mainly for irrigation purposes, it was also used extensively for transportation **[7]**.

The heroic scale, novelty, and affective impact of structures such as these began to evoke what has since been called the Victorian industrial sublime. Indeed, in some ways it is useful to think of canal systems and their equipment as continuous megastructures—like the roots of a tree, or the vascular system of a living creature—representing *in toto* a new type of industrialised landscape from which there was no return. In this sense they were hyper-

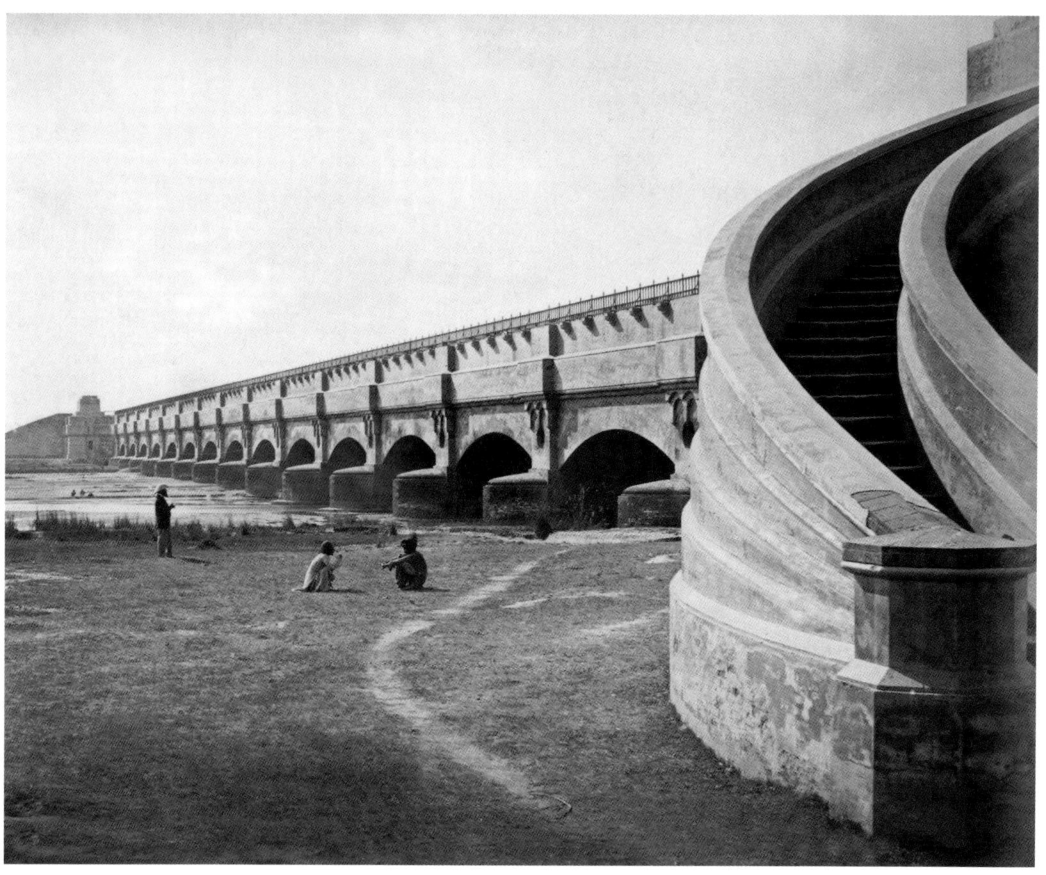

Fig. 7
Solani Aqueduct (1846), Ganges Canal, Roorkee, India.

objects: manifest locally and deployable, but difficult to comprehend fully. As such they symbolised the full-scale transformation of the British world economy. In the colonies, this translated into the rise of public works departments, which were responsible for authorising infrastructural development as part of land enclosure and governance.

The Railways and Associated Infrastructure

The infrastructure that best represents this new economy was the railways. It may be a cliché to point to J. M. W. Turner's famous painting, *Rain, Steam, and Speed—The Great Western Railway* (1844) as indicative of this, but it is difficult to surpass the emotional power this picture conveys regarding the rather sudden and dramatic appearance of locomotive technology **[8]**. The initial reaction to steam-powered locomotion in Britain was of course mixed. Some lauded it, others feared it; others yet still rejected it. Despite its promise of markedly shorter travel intervals, it took time to garner trust, especially where passenger transportation was concerned. Turner's painting captures this promise and foreboding in equal measure, at the dawn of the technology's lasting impact. It also depicts the infrastructure that accompanied this technology, not only the track but, in this instance, the Maidenhead Railway Bridge, designed by one of the greatest engineers of the age, Isambard

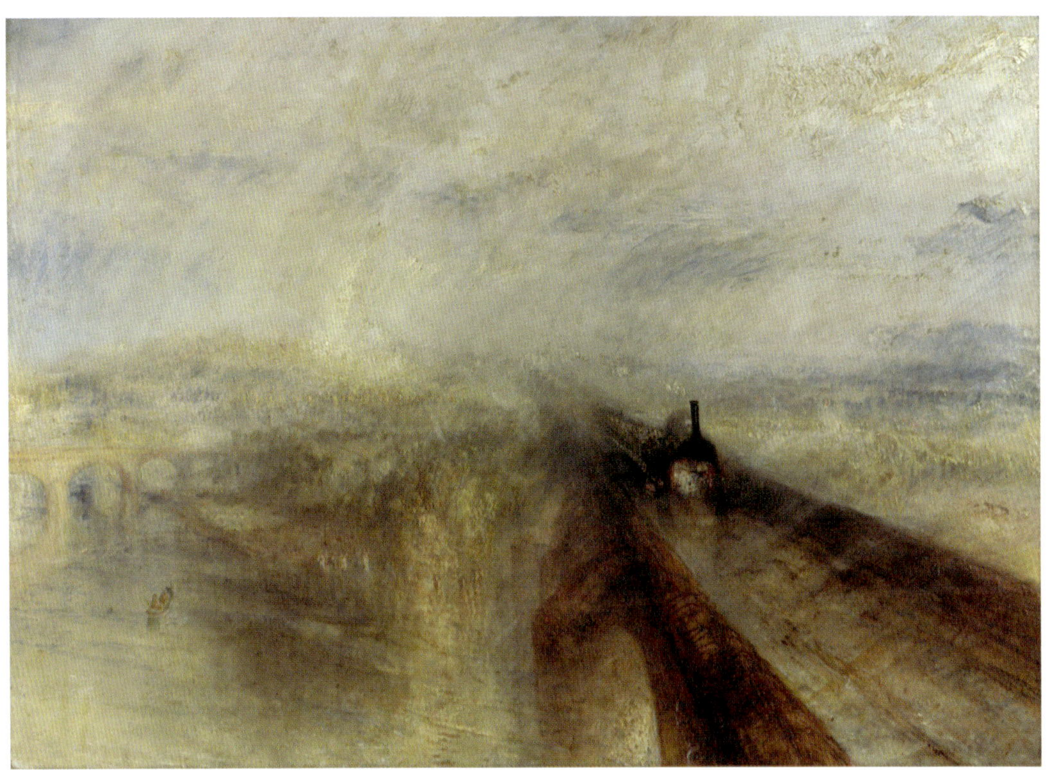

Fig. 8

J. M. W. Turner, *Rain, Steam, and Speed—The Great Western Railway* (1844).

Kingdom Brunel. In an almost visceral sense, Turner's image evokes the sounds and smells that would become so much a part of Britain's steam age, as the locomotive punches its way through the vagaries of the natural world.

With the snaking to and fro of tracks, tunnels, cuttings, embankments, viaducts, and bridges, not to mention the great stations that pushed their way into so many Victorian towns and cities, in both Britain and the wider British world, the railways were a true Victorian phenomenon. Given the type of vehicle involved, the infrastructure for railways was necessarily much heavier and bulkier than that for canals. In an effort to traverse low-lying country, the passage of railways was almost always more obtrusive. Railway embankments and cuttings were conspicuous interventions in a landscape that had remained largely untrammelled for hundreds of years. But it was viaducts and bridges that had the most dramatic effect. These remarkable feats of engineering were among the most striking built structures of the Victorian era, many of which remain in service to this day. Constructed of all kinds of materials, including brick, stone, timber, and eventually concrete, it was those made of iron, and later steel, that were the most novel and spectacular. The Britannia wrought iron 'tube' bridge by Robert Stephenson over the Menai Strait (1849–50), in Wales, set an early standard. But it was those based on the suspension principle that offered the greatest opportunity for experimentation. Two of the more interesting renditions of this approach can be found in Brunel's iron bridge at Saltash (1859), Cornwall, and the incredible Forth Bridge (1883–90), in Scotland, by John Fowler and Benjamin Baker **[9a&b]**.

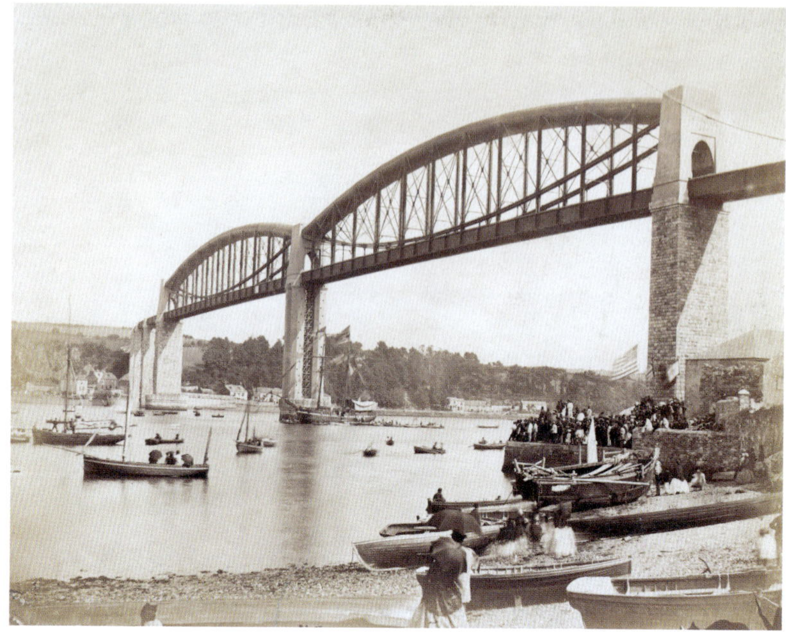

Fig. 9a

Royal Albert Bridge (1854–9), over River Tamar at Saltash, Cornwall, by Isambard Kingdom Brunel.

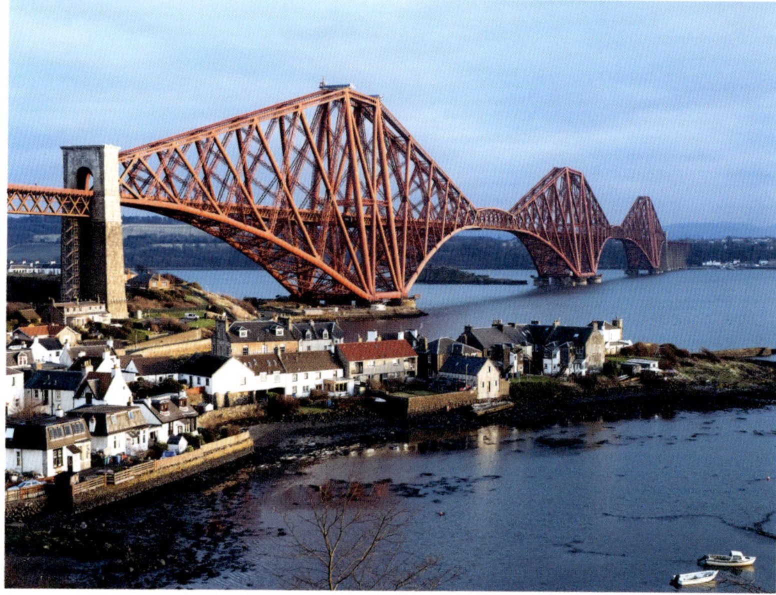

Fig. 9b

Forth Bridge (1883–90), cantilever railway bridge over Firth of Forth, near Edinburgh, Scotland, by John Fowler and Benjamin Baker. The first major structure in Britain made using steel rather than iron, being at the time the world's largest all-steel bridge.

In Britain alone, the growth of the railways was extremely rapid, at over 13 per cent per annum between 1840 and 1870. Beyond passenger traffic, they were responsible for a continual fall in freight rates, becoming the cheapest and fastest mode of inland transport by the third quarter of the nineteenth century. Their construction not surprisingly employed many thousands of humans and animals, but by the last quarter of the nineteenth century the use of steam-powered technology, including excavators and cranes, was increasingly common. The railways also became huge consumers of bricks, especially extra strong

Staffordshire blues, which often had to be sourced at distance. All this added considerably to the embodied energy of these great structures, the combined extent of which had reached 13,500 miles by 1870, and some 20,000 by 1914.

Being a service-based industry, the railways were accompanied by all manner of buildings, large and small. This led to a spate of building activity along and around railroads and stations throughout the Victorian period. Industry wished to be as close to the railway network as feasible, and oftentimes the railway was brought to it, as in the case of coal mines, ports, and important centres of manufacturing. Such locations required not only their own sidings (connecting tracks) but also large and elaborate storage facilities. These took the form of warehouses and goods stations, either along routes, linking inland (usually agricultural) production with the network, or at major termini, particularly in towns and cities. Smaller, local goods sheds were usually quadrangular utilitarian structures in brick, timber, or stone. Occasionally the architects and engineers who designed them introduced a level of architectural pretence, as seen in those at Acklington (1847), Axbridge (1869), and Langwathby (1876), for instance, with their rudimentary Gothic appearance. Those in densely populated urban areas were often large and conspicuous structures the likes of which had hardly been seen before, such as the Great Northern Railway's goods depot at King's Cross, London (1852), or the Midland Railway's goods station and warehouse at Crosshall Street, Liverpool (1874) **[10a]**. Indeed, the Midland's goods yard at Somers Town in London (1883–6), adjacent St Pancras station, had considerable architectural merit, with its perimeter wall designed in harmony with the station itself. This wall—three-quarters of a mile long, 30 feet high, some three feet thick, and comprising over 8 million bricks—was a sight to behold, and would have been among the first images of the metropolis to have pressed itself upon the minds of visitors leaving the station **[10b]**.

Other railway related structures that would have been difficult to ignore, and which contributed substantially to the fabric and spatial organisation of the Victorian city, were the companies' own service facilities. These facilities, congregated in 'yards', took up dozens, and sometimes hundreds of acres of land in central locations in many of Britain's major cities. Apart from goods stations, these structures included coal depots, workshops, and engine sheds, set near or alongside stations. Engine or 'running' sheds often occupied large tracts of land, partly owing to the challenge of parking, servicing, and turning locomotives on a regular basis. They were usually rectangular, but innovative designs for polygonal and round sheds centring on an engine turntable were also employed. Among the earliest of this latter type were those built at Derby (1839–40), for the North Midland Railway company, and at Manchester (1848), for the Manchester, Sheffield & Lincolnshire company. The first housed thirty engines, servicing sixteen tracks; the second was marked by its single-column, wrought-iron roof with double track turntable **[11]**. Then there were the workshops for the construction of locomotives. Such works could take up three-quarters of the land in railway towns, as seen, for instance, at Swindon and Crewe. The Cowlairs (1840s) and St Rollox (1854, enlarged 1886) locomotive works in Springburn, on the north-eastern edge of the city of Glasgow, occupied huge amounts of land,

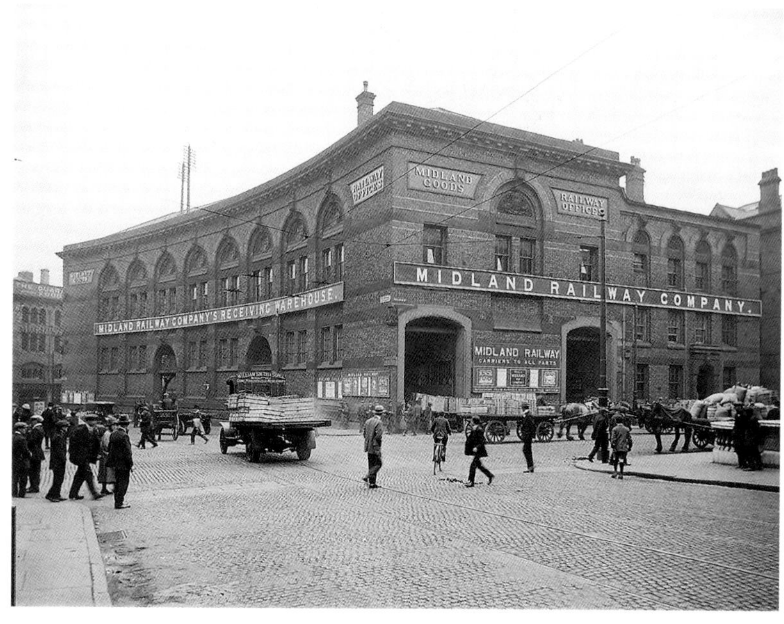

Fig. 10a

Midland Railway Goods Warehouse and Offices (1874), Crosshall Street, Liverpool, by Henry Sumners.

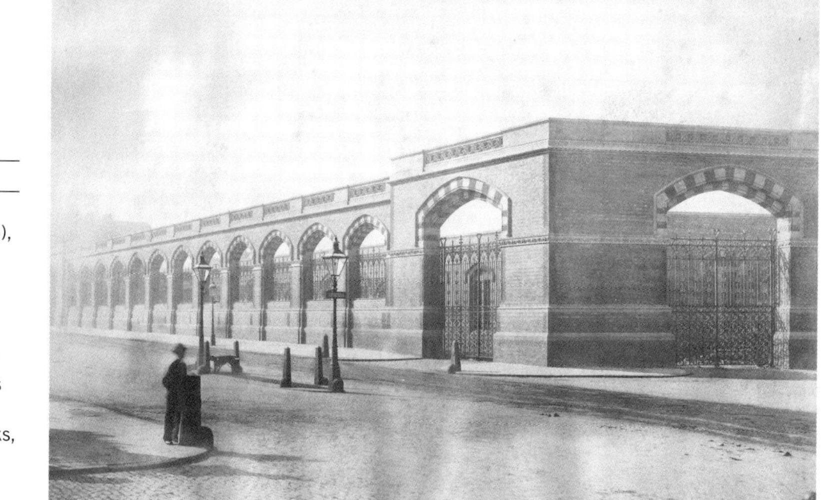

Fig. 10b

Exterior wall of Somers Town Goods Yard (1883–6), Midland Railway Co., St Pancras, London, by John Underwood and Joseph Firbank. The area was heavily industrialised, over many acres with numerous structures, such as coal storage depots, canal docks, and the gasometers of the Imperial Gas Works.

with Cowlairs comprising 167 acres by 1920. The workshop buildings alone at St Rollox were 15 acres in extent. Added to these structures one could point to signal boxes and gantries, which were located along the length and breadth of the network. By 1922 these boxes totalled some 11,000 in number.

Railway Stations and Related Buildings

Railway stations were among the more conspicuous, frequented, and therefore familiar manifestations of the corporate superstructure that comprised the British rail network. They included everything from major urban termini to smaller wayside platforms. Many, especially in major towns and cities, were accompanied by hotels for the convenience of travellers. So characteristic were

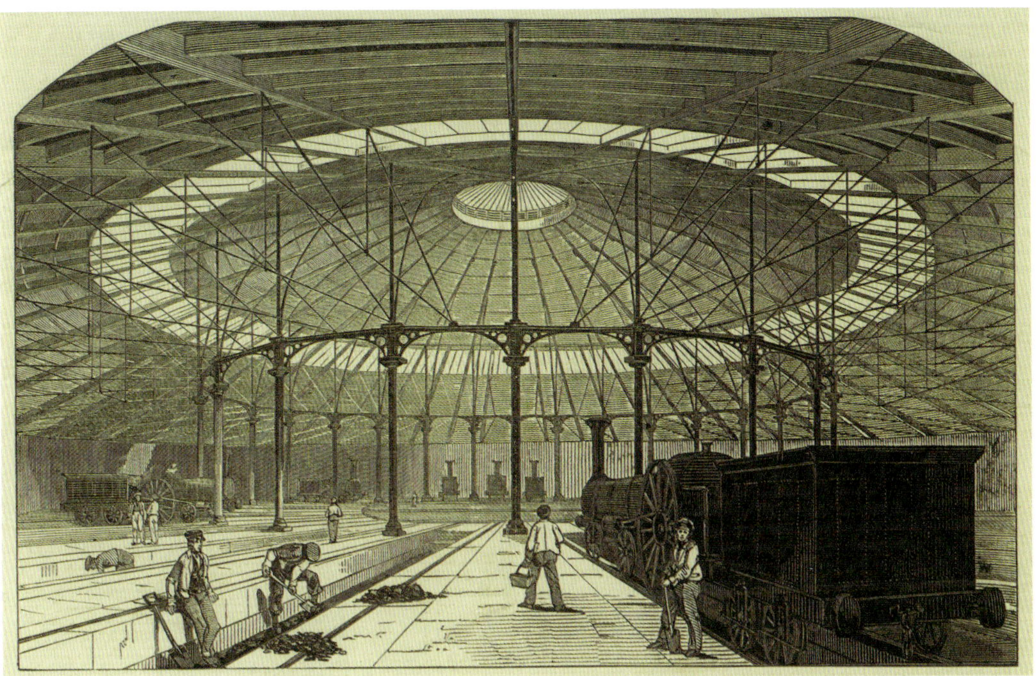

Fig. 11
The 'roundhouse' at Camden (1847), in London, designed by R. B. Dockray and Robert Stephenson, for the London and Birmingham Railway, was another of the noteworthy round train sheds.

these structures of the Victorian age that *The Building News* was able to remark in 1875 that 'railway termini and hotels are to the nineteenth century what monasteries and cathedrals were to the thirteenth…They are truly the only real representative building[s] we possess'. The 'sheds' of the principal Victorian stations, which housed the platforms where trains alighted passengers, were one of the technical wonders of the age. Alongside bridges, these structures captured the promise and possibilities of iron construction in Victorian architecture. Noted for their exploitation of iron truss and arch technology, station sheds achieved some truly novel structural and spatial effects.

An early example of note was Liverpool Lime Street, as rebuilt by the engineers Richard Turner and Joseph Lock in 1849–50. It achieved a clear span of 153 feet (47m) by utilising a truss system known as a 'sickle girder'. This was surpassed at Birmingham New Street in 1854, by Edward Cowper of Fox, Henderson & Co., with a span of 211 feet (64m), again exploiting lightweight iron truss technology. Other examples include the stations at Charing Cross (1860–3) and Cannon Street (1866), both in London, for the South Eastern Railway company. These had single-arch spans of 164 feet (50m) and 187 feet (57m) respectively. The Birmingham record, however, was only broken by W. H. Barlow's famous shed at St Pancras, London (1866–8), for the Midland Railway Company **[12a]**. At 245½ feet (74.8m), covering six platforms at a total length of 690 feet (210.5m), it would remain the largest single-span structure in the world until the Jersey City station was opened by the Pennsylvania Railroad in the United States in 1888, with a span of just over 300ft (91m). The massive, riveted wrought-iron ribs of the St Pancras shed's roof (twenty-four in total) rise 105 feet (32m) above platform level,

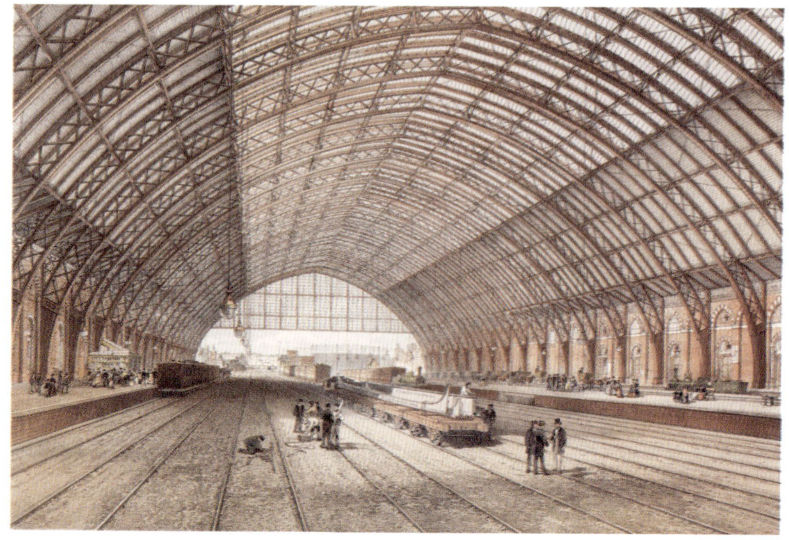

Fig. 12a

The magnificent iron-work structure (1866–8) of William Henry Barlow's train shed at St Pancras train terminus, London, then the largest single-span structure in the world.

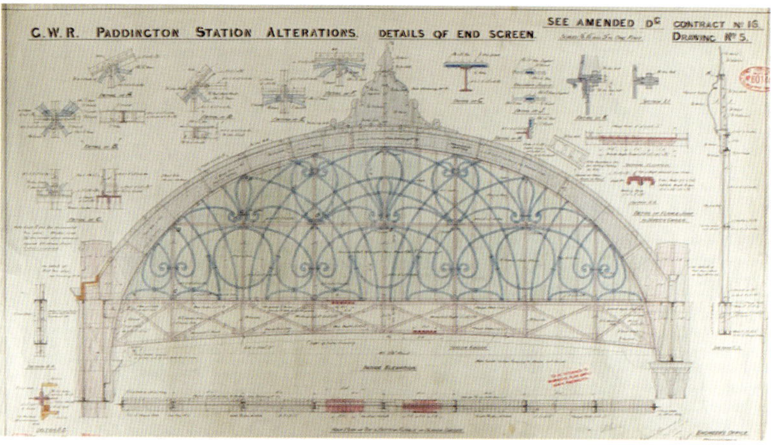

Fig. 12b

Detail working drawing, end screen to train shed, Paddington Station, London, by Isambard Kingdom Brunel and Matthew Digby Wyatt. Although a later drawing for alteration and repair (1914) purposes, it shows clearly the decorative effects achieved by Wyatt through the application of wrought-iron bar work.

coming to a slight point at the centre. These were manufactured in Derby by the Butterley Company, and brought down on the Midland's own lines.

The architectural effect of train station sheds, which in principle were purely perfunctory structures, fomented considerable debate. Some, such as John Ruskin and A. W. N. Pugin, among others, viewed them not as 'architecture' but as straightforward works of engineering. Such views reflected the so-called iron problem in Victorian architecture, being a criticism levelled at all manner of novel structural systems invented during the period, particularly where iron-work was exposed or 'expressive'. Buildings in this category, apart from stations, included factories, market halls, and exhibition spaces. Perhaps the most famous such structure was the Crystal Palace, erected in Hyde Park, London, for the Great Exhibition of 1851 (see Chapter 2). Engineers were sensitive to such criticisms, and genuinely keen to address this 'problem'. Brunel, for instance, worked with architect Matthew Digby Wyatt in giving his iron shed at Paddington Station, London (1852–4), an ornamental character **[12b]**. Here Wyatt incorporated Renaissance, Moorish, and anthemion inspired motifs into the column capitals, along the principal flanges of the main structural girders, and on the end screens of the station, giving the impression of a coherent design. Such tactics were employed in part to put commuters at ease with what would have seemed at first an unfamiliar if not frightening spatial experience. On the other hand, they gestured towards a totalising aesthetic intent, leading to calls for such ironwork to aspire to more abstracted, linear, and geometricised formations appropriate to iron's inherent material properties.[6]

There were also attempts at giving the exterior of railway stations a degree of architectural flare. Architects were not always involved. For instance, Brunel was responsible for the Tudor Gothic front at Bristol Temple Meads station, for the Great Western Railway, in 1841. Four years later he did the same for the Bristol & Exeter Railway, only metres away. There was also Euston Arch, from the very beginning of the Victorian era, by Philip Hardwick, who was an architect. Its heavy Greek countenance, although not universally admired, was certainly striking, disguising the hyper modernity of the railway infrastructure behind the cultured gravitas of classical antiquity. In some instances the novelty of railway infrastructure was openly celebrated. A good example is the brick front to the Great Northern Railway terminus at King's Cross, in London (1851–2), by Lewis Cubitt. This showcased rather than concealed the building's huge, twin-arched iron structure within **[13a]**. Whether Pugin would have approved or not, this was its own kind of structural honesty.

But the most interesting and spectacular train stations of the Victorian period were located abroad. In the first rank are the Victoria (1878–88) and Churchgate (1894–6) termini, both in Bombay (Mumbai), by the architectural engineer F. W. Stevens **[13b]**. Taking inspiration from G. G. Scott's hotel front at St Pancras Station in London, both buildings bristle with Gothicised and Indic ornament of every conceivable description, making for two of the largest and most extraordinary Gothic Revival confections ever erected. As such they were conspicuous symbols of the command Britain exercised over the region, being key nodal points in the extensive network of railways that snaked their way through 25,000 miles of the Indian Subcontinent. Further east, in Australasia, are the two 'imperial Baroque' specimens of Flinders Street Station, Melbourne (1899–1910), by James Fawcett and H. C. P. Ashworth, and Dunedin Railway Station, New Zealand (1904–6), by George A. Troup **[14a]**. These structures stood as emblems of a new age of mass communication, where buildings of this type and scale were considered landmarks of progress and modernity. In this respect, railway stations, both in Britain and in the wider British world, were much more than stand-alone works of architecture and engineering. As funnels in and out of the Victorian transportation network, their presence monumentalised the accelerated forces of social, commercial, and political connectivity that characterised the Victorian age.

Alongside major termini often sat large-scale commuter hotels. Most large towns and cities had one or more such buildings, especially as extended rail networks began making travel cheaper and easier. In some cases, these hotels, which were usually built and operated by rail companies, defined entire station complexes, as in the case of G. G. Scott's

Fig. 13a

Anon., *Arrival of Queen Victoria at King's Cross Station*, watercolour, c.1852. The structure was designed by Lewis Cubitt.

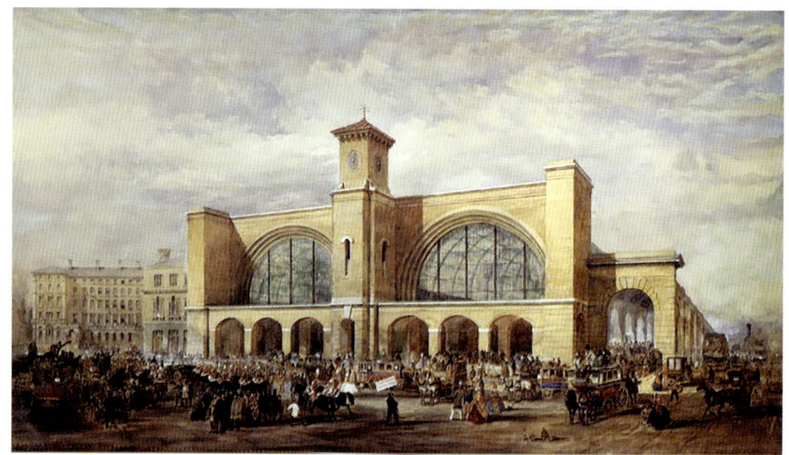

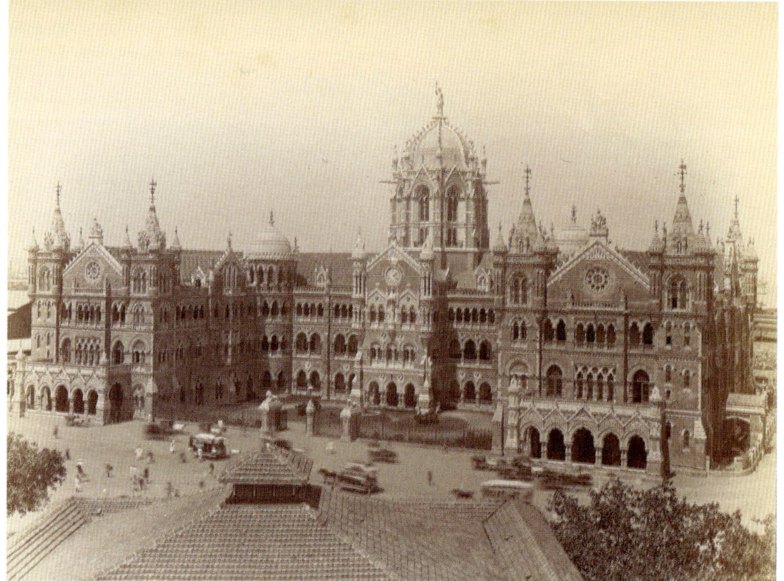

Fig. 13b

Victoria Terminus (1878–88), Bombay (Mumbai), India, by F. W. Stevens.

Midland Grand Hotel at St Pancras in London (1868–77) **[37]**. Considered next to the Royal Courts of Justice on the Strand (see Chapter 4), Scott's Midland Grand is one of the largest and grandest buildings ever erected in the Gothic Revival style. Equivalent to six stories in height, with a clock tower soaring 240 feet (73m) above street level, the building was nothing if not conspicuous, dominating its urban surrounds. Designed in a rich, polychromatic style, and built using the latest in technology and materials, it displays formal influences from England, France, the Low Countries, and Italy, typical of the High Victorian movement. But, again, it was not just in Britain that such railway infrastructure could be found. Across the Atlantic, in Canada, a similarly spectacular brand of railway hotel was rising. Often set in stunning and dramatic locations, and designed in variations of the so-called Château Style, these formed part of the Canadian Pacific Railway network. Two outstanding examples are the

Fig. 14a
Dunedin Railway Station, New Zealand (1904–6), by George A. Troup.

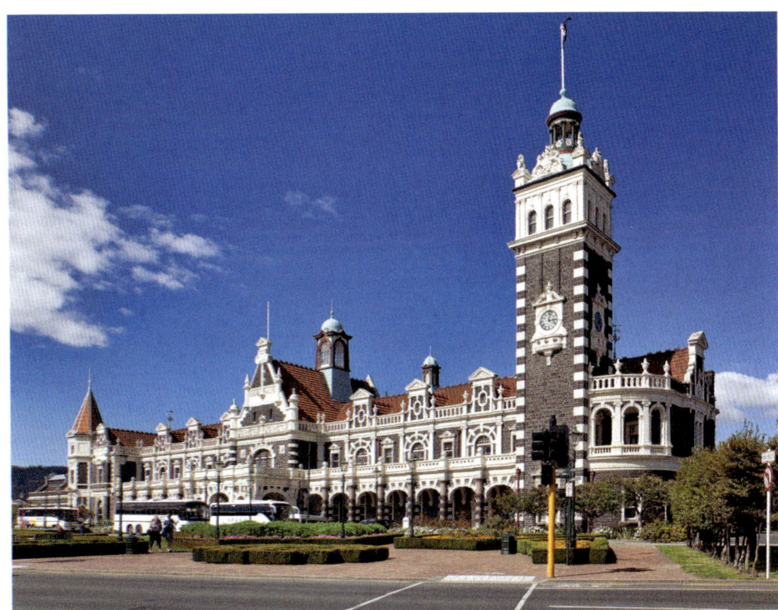

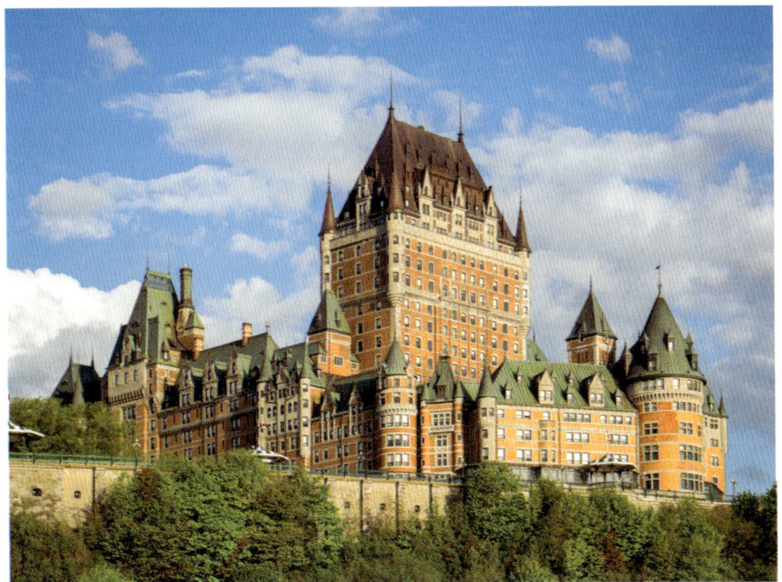

Fig. 14b
French influence: Château Frontenac (1892–3), railway hotel, Quebec City, Canada, by Bruce Price.

Château Frontenac (1892–3), in Quebec City, by Bruce Price, and the Empress Hotel (1904–6), in Victoria, British Columbia, by Francis Mawson Rattenbury **[14b]**. Buildings of this kind were designed to capture something of the novelty and romance of the railway age, drawing on the historical allusions of colonial French culture.

Docks and Shipping Facilities

There are other structures that one could point to concerning the Victorian transportation revolution. For instance, much like the locomotive, the advent of the steamship witnessed increases in the speed and reliability of the oversea movement of people and goods. The increased activity, along with the growth in industrial processes, around mechanised shipping led to the emergence of vast landscapes comprising port and docking facilities for the processing, storage, and transhipment of cargo, as well as ever larger passenger terminals. Developments of this kind were also concerned with obtaining greater degrees of security, whether from fire or theft. By the beginning of the nineteenth century London had massively upgraded its docking facilities with the construction of the East and West India Docks (1802–6) and St Katherine's Dock (1827–8). Then, in the 1880s, came the Royal Victoria and Royal Albert docks, and the Tilbury Docks, further towards the mouth of the river Thames **[15]**. In Liverpool there were the Royal Albert (1846), Huskisson (1852), and Canada (1859) docks, among others, adding to what was already one of the most extensive wet-dock systems in the world. Enclosed by brick and cast-iron warehouses, and covering some 7.5 acres, the Albert Docks incorporated the latest in hydraulic technology for ease of loading and unloading ships. Their designer, the engineer Jesse Hartley, was also alert to the need for integrating transportation links from the docks via rail, canal, and road. Again, as with railway infrastructure, some attempt was made at giving the equipment associated with docks a degree of architectural flare, as seen in the extraordinary medieval fort-like hydraulic accumulator tower (*c.*1859) at the Canada Dock in Liverpool, also by Hartley **[16a]**.

Further afield, but no less integrated into British imperial maritime trading networks, were the Bombay docks. Following the opening of the Suez Canal in 1869, Bombay quickly became British India's principal port. The Sassoon Dock, first of the new wet docks, was built in 1875, followed by the Prince's and Victoria Docks in 1880 and 1888. Extensive storage and transhipping facilities were installed during this period, helping establish the Indian cotton trade, with substantial links to Manchester. Smaller-scale enterprises also invested heavily in docking facilities. The Jardine, Matheson & Co. depot at East Point in Hong Kong, for instance, reveals how such industrialised landscapes had become commonplace in various parts of the British empire by the 1850s, in this case to facilitate the hugely lucrative China Trade, including the smuggling of opium **[16b]**. One of the features of such landscapes was their reliance on maritime trade links for gathering the best-quality materials for construction purposes, especially for building godowns for the secure storage of goods.

Landscapes of Colonial Industry and Extraction

Through such infrastructure communities were connected and commodities transferred in previously unimaginable ways. It led to different kinds of larger-scale industrialised landscapes around the British empire, and beyond. We have already heard something about dock, warehouse, and transhipment facilities, but this also came in the form of broad-acre agriculture (especially grazing and grain production) and natural resource extraction, including mining and timber-getting.[7] Alongside these were other industries associated with the full or partial processing of raw materials, from palm oil and rubber to cotton, sugar, and tobacco. Plantation and cash crop

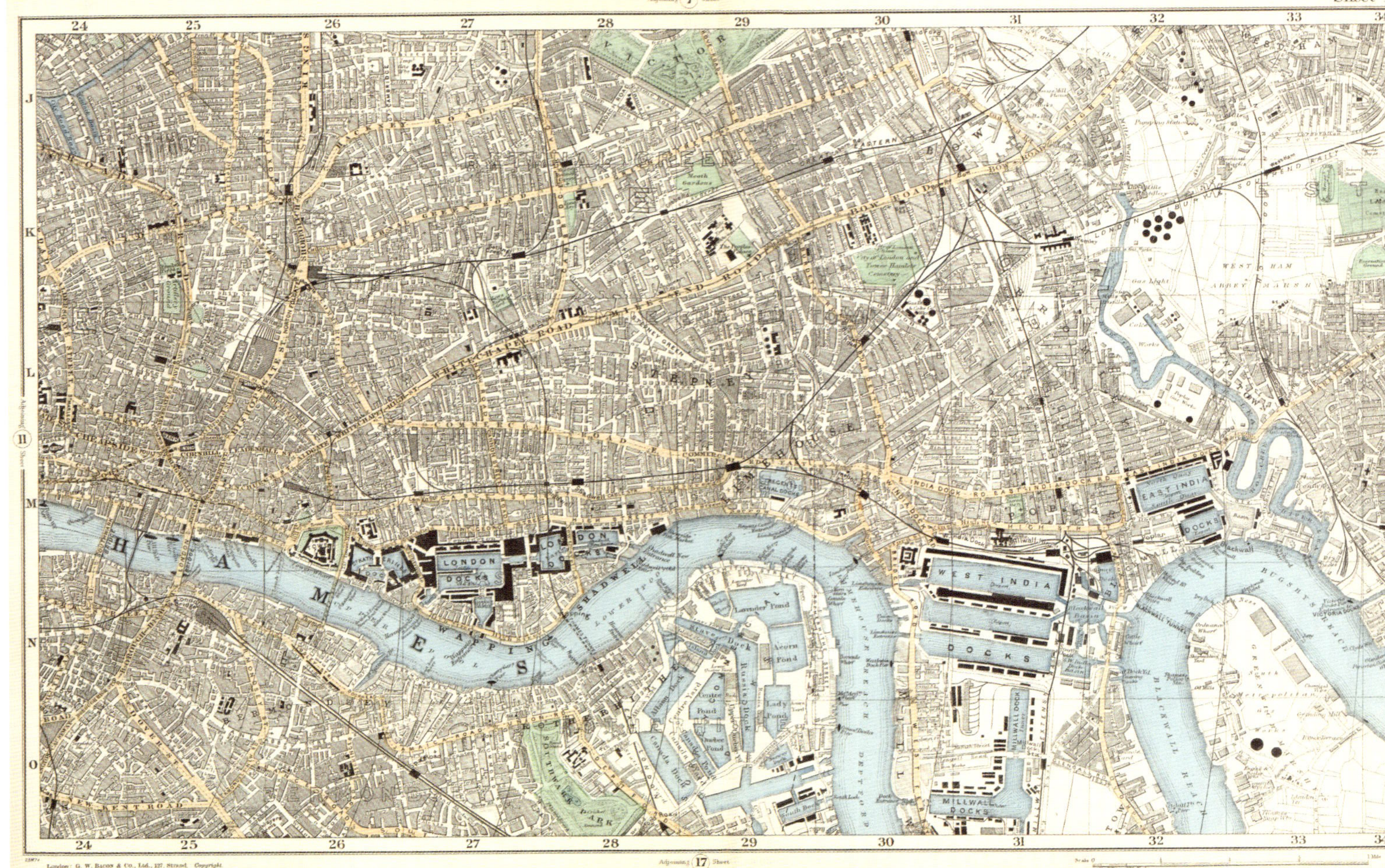
Sheet 12
Adjoining 7 Sheet
Adjoining 13 Sheet
Adjoining 11 Sheet
Adjoining 17 Sheet
STEPNEY
EAST INDIA DOCKS
WEST INDIA DOCKS
MILLWALL DOCK
MILLWALL DOCKS
BLACKWALL REACH
LONDON DOCKS
THAMES
WAPPING
SHADWELL
SOUTHWARK PARK
Lavender Pond
Acorn Pond
Lady Pond
Russia Dock
Canada Dock
VICTORIA DOCKS
London: G. W. Bacon & Co., Ltd., 127, Strand. Copyright.

Fig. 15

Detail of map, London docks (1903), from *Bacon's New Large-Scale Atlas of London and Suburbs* (1903). Here can be seen the extent of London's wet-dock development by the end of the nineteenth century.

industries of this kind were often located in the tropical zones of empire, such as Sub-Saharan West Africa, India, and Southeast Asia, and concerned exploitative working practices, including indentured labour. Elsewhere industrialisation involved the growing, slaughter, and packing of livestock on a scale inconceivable in Britain.

This is partly explained by the fact that between 1870 and 1914 Britain became heavily dependent on imported foodstuffs, particularly cereals. It was also reliant for much of its timber requirements on external sources, not only the Baltics but also British North America. For instance, by the close of the nineteenth century much of Britain's wheat supply was coming from the North American prairies, produced and ferried across the Atlantic by steamship; while by 1890 nearly 2 million frozen sheep carcases were arriving annually from as far away as New Zealand.[8] Timber increasingly came from places such as New Brunswick, Burma, and Australasia. All this had significant implications for what is referred to today as Britain's exported production footprint, including those 'reciprocal landscapes' altered and degraded through processes of industrial extraction.[9] The structures that

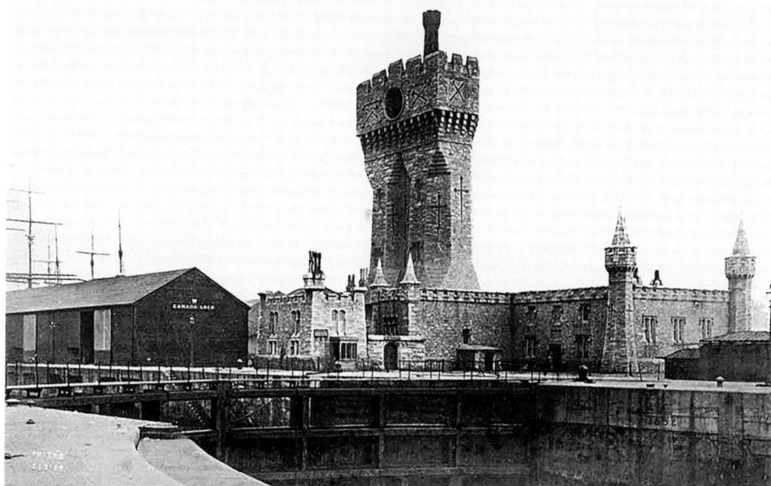

Fig. 16a

Hydraulic tower and power station at Canada Dock, Liverpool (*c.*1859), by Jesse Harley.

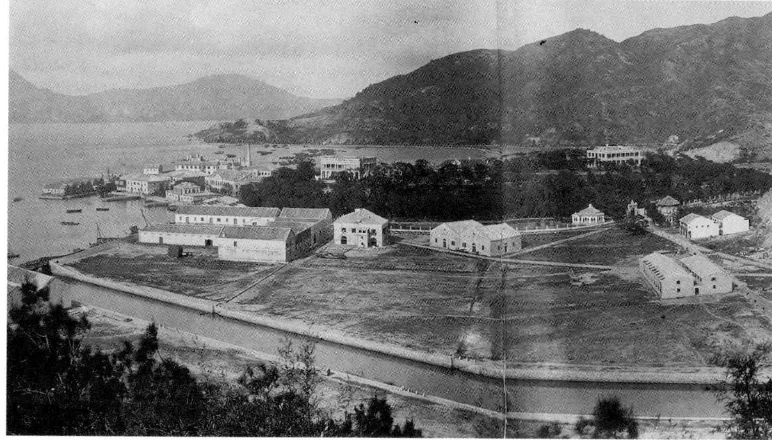

Fig. 16b

The industrialised landscape at the Jardine, Matheson & Co. depot, East Point, Hong Kong (photo *c.*1869).

facilitated these types of colonial development are therefore an important aspect of the Victorian built environment.

Broad-acre cereal cropping witnessed the emergence of the steam-powered grain elevator as a distinct industrial building type on the prairie lands of North America in the second half of the nineteenth century. As far as the Canadian prairies were concerned, these structures—comprising a tall, somewhat narrow wooden shed, clad in timber or corrugated iron, and housing elevator equipment—were linked to railway extension across Canada in the 1880s, in particular the Canadian Pacific Railway. They were designed to transfer grain efficiently and with speed from grain pits and silos into train boxcars for transportation to major transhipping ports such as Port Arthur and Fort William at Thunder Bay on Lake Superior, then by steamer across the Atlantic to markets in Britain **[17a]**. In time these elevators became larger and larger, with ever-greater capacity. By 1911 there were fifteen elevator terminals operating at the Thunder Bay ports, with a combined capacity of 16 million bushels, bestowing upon Canada the epithet 'the breadbasket of empire'. Indeed, with nearly 10 million acres under cultivation by that time, the prairies had been ecologically transformed. This process led not only to the near extinction of the great bison herds by horse-mounted Indian and Euroamerican commercial hunting practices, utilising modern firearms, but also to environmental degradation **[Map 3]**.[10]

Timber was another of the colonial world's foremost commodities. Further east, in New Brunswick, the abundant coniferous forests had been exploited since the late eighteenth century but had acquired new levels of industrial output by the 1850s.[11] It was a similar scene in parts of Asia and the Australasian colonies. There the extraction of old-growth eucalyptus forests (or kauri in New Zealand) supplied the timber for rapacious colonial urban development, as well as other specific needs. Kauri, huon pine (Tasmania), and teak (Burma) were much sought after for ship building. During the Victorian period timber-getting and sawing became major industries, giving rise to their own building typology in the form of the sawmill and its accompanying timber yard. The mills themselves were usually lightweight structures in wood, clad in bark, timber slabs, or corrugated iron sheeting, and designed to provide cover for the industrial sawing machinery housed inside. In New Brunswick they were often located along principal waterways, from which they gathered logs floated downstream from felling areas. The highest concentration was at the mouth of the St John River, but entire 'sawmill villages' could be found in many other locations, such as that at Boiestown **[17b]**. For such high-volume throughput, steam power was necessarily required. By the 1850s the larger mills were operating numerous gang and circular saws simultaneously, capable of cutting in excess of 60,000 feet of timber in under 12 hours. In the United Kingdom, too, sawing, planing, and moulding mills were established to process raw timber imports. The plant of Martin & Son in Dublin **[18a]** is indicative in terms of size and scope of activity, as was that of Peto Brothers in Pimlico, London. The expanding colonial frontier represented by these activities not only brought colonial settlers into contact (and conflict) with indigenous peoples, but also led to widespread habitat destruction. In New Brunswick the debris from

Fig. 17a

Grain elevators with horse-drawn wagons waiting, Barons, Alberta, Canada (1913).

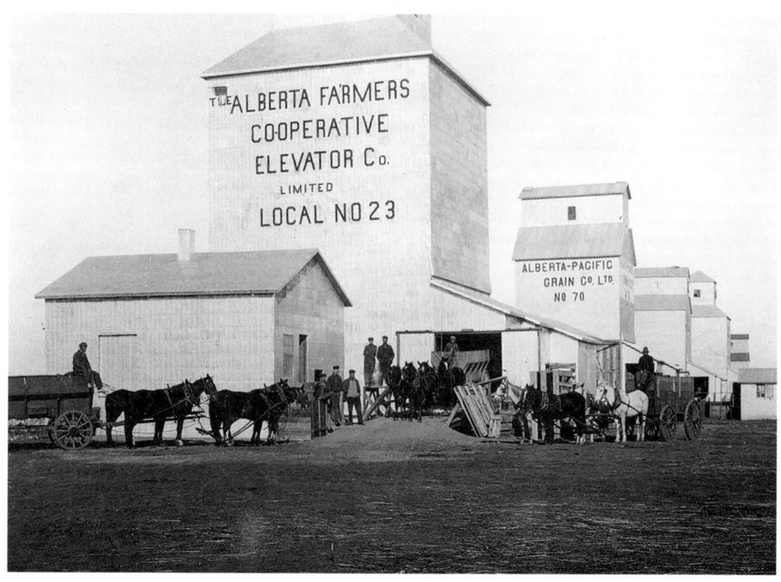

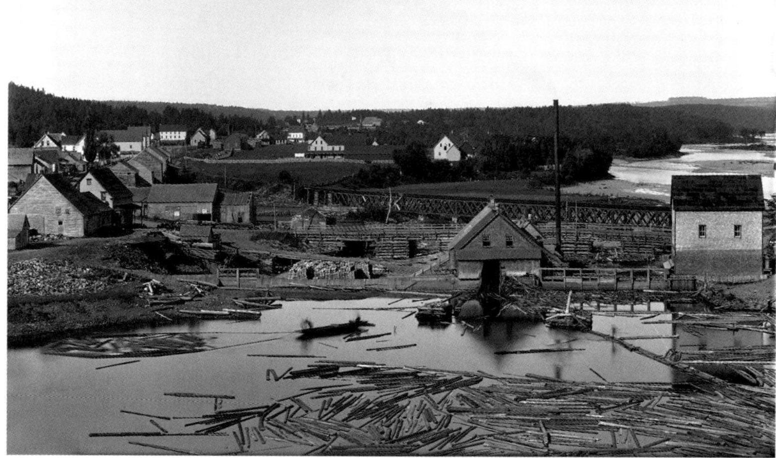

Fig. 17b

Lumber mills along the Southwest Miramichi River at Boiestown, New Brunswick, Canada (*c*.1890).

milling ended up lodging along the banks of waterways, with the sawdust sinking to the bottom of rivers, disturbing their ecology.

Mining, too, was big business. In Australasia alone it attracted hundreds of thousands of immigrants from across the globe, including tens of thousands of Chinese. The gold rush in the colony of Victoria during the early 1850s is among the best-known examples of such a mining boom, but there were others in Queensland and Western Australia, in the 1860s and 1890s, and across the Tasman Sea in Otago, New Zealand, in 1861. The enterprise was marked by incessant digging, with the larger operations discernible by their conspicuous surface works, including cast-iron (poppet) headframes similar to those used for coal mining in Britain, which towered tens of feet above the ground **[18b]**. Grouped around these, especially after steam power was introduced, were often large timber or brick structures to house engines for pumping water and hauling and crushing rock. These, too, were marked out in the landscape by their tall smokestacks. One consequence of shaft mining for gold was the appearance of mullock heaps (digging refuse), leading to the creation around mining districts of vast lunar-like landscapes. The scene illustrated here was typical of concentrated diggings, such as those around Ballarat, Bendigo, and Castlemaine on the Victorian goldfields, or in British Columbia and South Africa from the 1860s through to the 1890s.

Coming off the back of this activity, quite literally, was wool production for British and European markets. In Australia, as the historian James Anthony Froude once remarked, 'the fable of Midas is reversed, food does

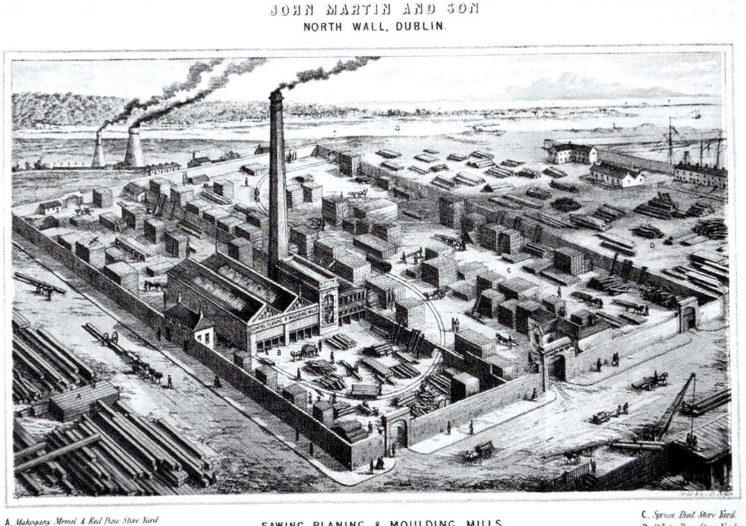

Fig. 18a
Timber processing mill, John Martin & Son, Dublin (*Dublin Builder*, 1860).

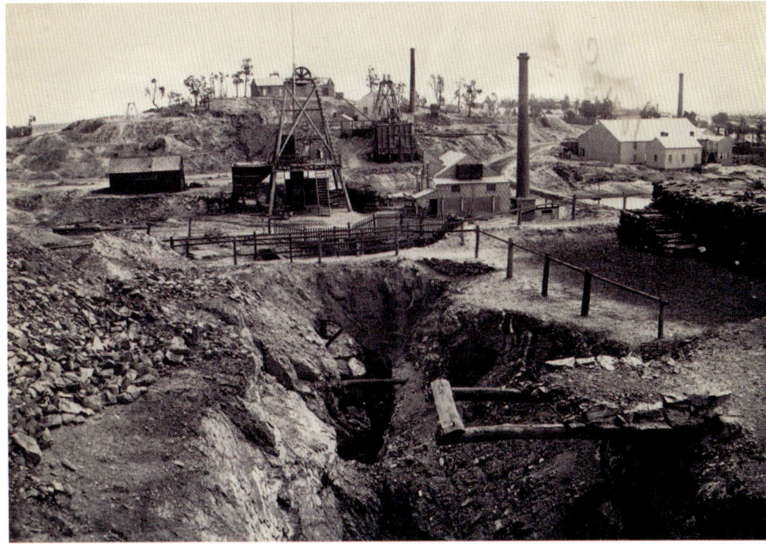

Fig. 18b
View of gold diggings at Victoria Hill, Bendigo (1876), Victoria, Australia.

not turn to gold, but the gold with which the earth is teeming converts itself into farms and vineyards, into flocks and herds'.[12] By the 1890s the country was grazing over 100 million sheep, approximately half the ovine population of the entire southern hemisphere. For the most part these were grazed on tracts of leasehold crown land known as 'runs'. These runs formed the basis of huge pastoral stations. Located primarily in the Western (Port Phillip) and Riverina districts of colonial Victoria and New South Wales, these stations comprised tens of thousands of acres each, and were often accumulated by 'squatters' (pastoralists) into holdings consisting of hundreds of thousands, even millions of acres. It was not unusual for such holdings to run 100,000–200,000 sheep each, producing 5,000–10,000 bales of wool per annum. A similar pattern of development emerged in New Zealand, with pastoralists from Australia crossing the Tasman Sea to set up runs in the South Island, near the settlements of Canterbury and Otago.

As in Canada, this type of agricultural colonisation brought with it land clearance and animal husbandry practices that were devastating to native ecosystems, in the process disrupting sustainable indigenous environmental management customs. A range of specialised infrastructures came with the process, of which the woolshed was the most iconic. Built mainly throughout the second half of the nineteenth century, and continually modernised and extended, these were effectively shearing and fleece processing and packing plants, operating at times on an industrial scale. They were usually erected by specialist builders, and sometimes designed by architects. Varying in size, they were constructed using local timbers, and clad initially in weatherboards, then corrugated iron. Modulated and easily stackable, corrugated iron sheeting made good ballast in ships coming from Britain, and was widely used in the building industry throughout the British colonial world. In the south some woolsheds were made of more sturdy stuff, such as brick or stone. Woolsheds could be very large, with huge areas set aside for sweating and catching pens, and boards (platforms) big enough to make space for 40–70 shearing stands. Among the larger ones in Australia were Kinchega (1875), Tubbo (*c.*1860–1906), Toganmain (1875), and Urangeline (1864–78) in the Riverina; and Terinallum (1850) and East Loddon (*c.*1871), in the Western District **[19a]**. In New Zealand there is the outstanding specimen at Morven Hills, North Otago (*c.*1873). By the 1880s steam power was introduced, enabling the mechanisation of the industry via mechanical handpieces. Huge, warehouse-like structures known as wool stores were required at the major ports for classing, storing, and transhipping the wool. A good early example is the three-storey C. J. Dennys & Co. wool store (1872) in Geelong, Victoria, erected in local bluestone (basalt).

Related to wool was meat production. As early as the 1860s the demand for meat in the United Kingdom was already outstripping supply. The need was first met via tinned exports from the southern hemisphere, from Australia and New Zealand, then jerked and dead meat exports from Argentina. The breakthrough came with the invention of steam-powered refrigeration machines for long-distance transport, enabling the trade in frozen meat to flourish.[13] Places such as Australia and New Zealand were now well-placed to take advantage of this innovation. To give some perspective, in 1881 New Zealand's population was half a million, while the number

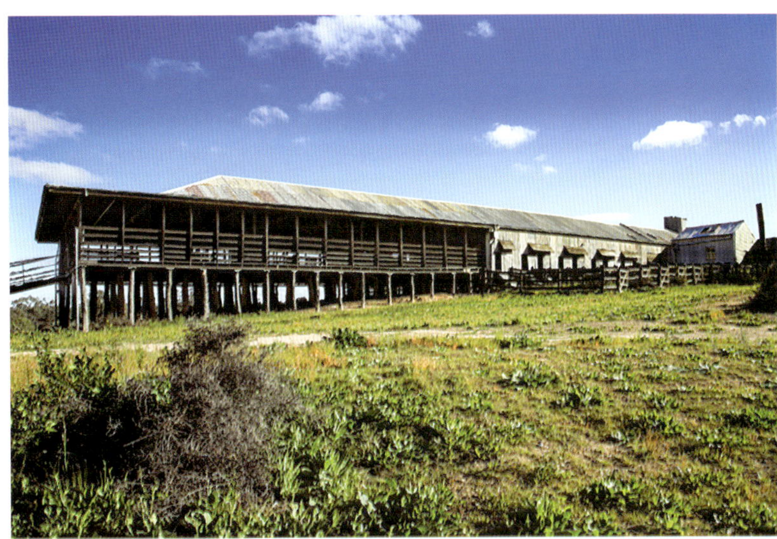

Fig. 19a

Kinchega woolshed (1875), western New South Wales, Australia.

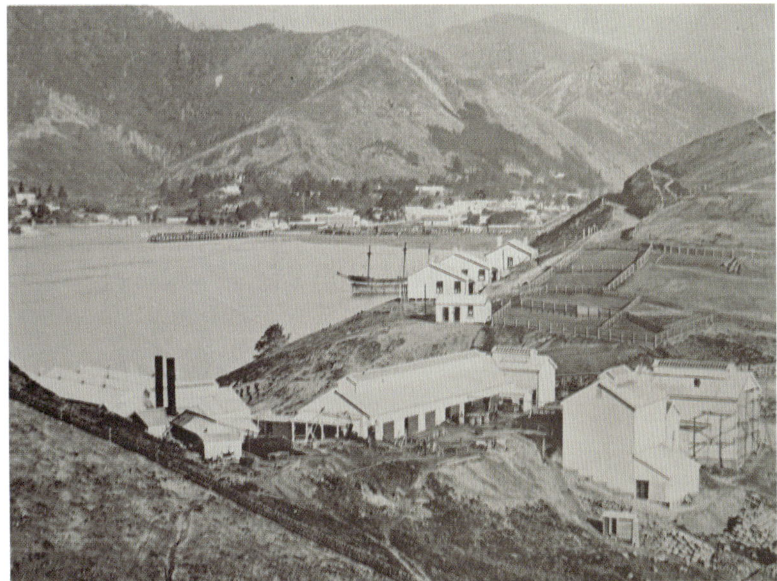

Fig. 19b

Complex of buildings and holding pens at Picton freezing works, Christchurch Meat Co., Picton, New Zealand (*c.*1900).

of sheep it contained approached 13 million. By 1911 thirty-six factories for freezing beef and mutton had been established in Australia, and twenty-eight in New Zealand. This included 111 warehouses built in the United Kingdom to receive and store this meat.[14] The impact on the built environment was significant. Freezing works were dotted mainly along the eastern seaboard of Australia during this period, in the colonies of Queensland, New South Wales, and Victoria. In New Zealand they sprang up in Dunedin, Christchurch, and Wellington. One of the biggest was the Nelson Brothers Freezing Works in Tomoana (near Hawkes Bay), with a storage capacity of 160,000 carcases. Like most such works, the plant comprised a series of huge corrugated iron-clad sheds, connected along a processing chain. At its peak the Nelson Brothers works was over 100 acres in extent **[19b]**.

There are other industries one could point to in this regard, including sugar milling in the British West Indies and rubber and palm oil production in Southeast Asia. As discussed further below, colonial industries led to new forms of urban development, but were more immediately responsible for the rolling out of an industrial infrastructure that characterised, transformed, and even scarred the non-European world.

Cities and the Urban Scene

Remarkable urban transformation was a distinguishing and much discussed feature of the Victorian age. Indeed, the Victorians may be credited with creating a type of civilisation more 'thoroughly of the town' than any other in human history.[15] In the push to modernise, as well as to relieve the worst effects of overcrowding, Britain's urban transformation was often fast, unplanned, and destructive. Yet, there was a clear aspiration for something better. Unsurprisingly, appeals to 'improvement' were to be heard often and everywhere. We have encountered something of the uneasy pace of this transformation already. But what were the Victorian city's defining characteristics? How did it *un*make and *re*make itself against a backdrop of such dramatic social and technological upheaval? Here I only wish to highlight some of the more salient aspects of what is evidently a very complex phenomenon. Therefore, I shall start with a few basic statistics. In England and Wales alone, those living in urban settings with a population of 2,500 people or more had reached over 50 per cent by 1851, and nearly 80 per cent by 1901. The comparable figure was approximately 35 per cent in 1801. Birmingham, Manchester, and Liverpool had all achieved populations of over 100,000 by the 1820s, and were joined by the likes of Bristol, Newcastle, Leeds, and Sheffield in the 1840s. London of course stood alone with over 2 million by this time. Scotland's two principal cities, Glasgow and Edinburgh, went from having between 50,000–100,000 residents each in 1801, to 250,000 and 100,000 respectively by 1841. Even in Ireland, a largely rural province ravaged by famine in the 1840s, the urbanised population grew in the latter nineteenth century, reaching 33.5 per cent by 1911. Dublin was the largest city with around 250,000 residents in 1881, then Belfast with a little over 100,000, and Cork with some 80,000. All the while the population in Britain as a whole went from 10.5 million in 1801 to 37 million in 1901. As can be appreciated, such growth in the urbanised population put considerable strain on the infrastructure of Britain's existing towns and cities.

At one level it was hoped that the evolving urbanism of the period would usher in and thus configure a new social order based on capitalist enterprise, industrial development, and private interest: the idea of the liberal, *laissez-faire* state made manifest. But this did not preclude more communally based notions of civic-mindedness. In fact, in most cases, this was encouraged through the idea of civic identity and pride. This was the Victorian city at its most vigorous and confident. At another level, however, and alongside the worthy and oftentimes grand developments enacted in the name of public amenity (the libraries, hospitals, schools, theatres, museums, mechanics' institutes, and enhanced commercial facilities, not to mention road widening and advances in transportation), sat equally spectacular squalor, poverty, and disease, and in certain colonial settings, racialised discrimination. The 'slum' was of course a common feature of most Victorian cities, as the literature and images of the period by those such as Charles Dickens, Luke Fildes, and Gustave Doré so vividly portray. The Victorians were slow, perhaps too slow, to remedy these defects, often leaving it to private philanthropic initiative. Consequently, and with the demands of the Chartists (1838–48) raising alarm, the spectre of the city as a site of popular radicalism and potential unrest stalked the British political imagination. In this respect the Victorian city was messy, both physically and conceptually. It was a place of seeming contradiction and collision; of fear, disorientation, even oppression; an unprecedented live experiment framed by its inherent oppositions and apparent indifference towards controlling or containing itself. But above all the Victorian city was energetic, both frantic and full of movement, as well as a tremendous consumer of manpower and resources.

Destroying and Rebuilding the City

An account of the Victorian city might normally begin with discussion of good and bad in Victorian urban development, either the progress brought by industrial urbanism, or the social ills that came in its wake. But I want to begin instead with the idea of destruction. For although a lot was built during the Victorian age, a lot was also destroyed. We do not often think of the Victorians as great destroyers, but they were, and their greatest exertions in this regard are to be found at the scale of the urban. Thus, *de*struction and *con*struction were different sides of the same coin for the Victorians in their attempts at remaking the city. For instance, the greatly increased internal traffic of people and goods in Victorian Britain's expanding cities necessarily required expensive schemes for street widening and realignment, not to mention the flattening of entire neighbourhoods for the penetration of rail lines and termini. Such 'beneficial demolitions' came in the guise of so-called metropolitan improvements. They were undoubtedly aimed at 'improvement', and most were, but they also came at a cost, both socially and in terms of built heritage. Those who bore the brunt of such destruction were predominantly the working class. Through parliamentary acts allowing compulsory acquisition, inner-city estates that contained working-class accommodation, many of which were considered slums, were condemned and bought by railway companies, with the inhabitants summarily evicted, often at very short notice. A conservative estimate puts the displaced, in London alone, at nearly 80,000 between 1853 and 1901. In the case of the Midland Railway Company, the proposers of which razed Somers, Camden, and Agar towns in the mid-1860s for the St Pancras terminus and goods station on Euston Road, a total of 32,000 were made homeless. As the 'restless foot of local improvement' came down on the working poor, there was very little in the way of legislation to compel companies to rehouse them. This would not change until the 1880s, and even then loopholes were exploited.[16]

In this respect, the railway was the single most important agent in the transformation of the Victorian urban environment. By 1900, between 5 and 9 per cent of the central areas of cities were owned and occupied by railway companies, carving up and re-zoning cities in ways previously unimagined. As mentioned, outside the centre, additional areas were overtaken by marshalling yards, locomotive and carriage works and sheds, and link and cut-off lines. In Glasgow alone, the combined yards and sidings occupied over 820 acres by this time, an area equal to three-quarters of the entire city in 1840. The improvements they brought were often greeted in the press with enthusiasm, labelled as a necessary 'cleansing' of the city of 'nurseries' or 'rookeries' of vice, crime, and disease-ridden poverty. But the problem was only transposed, and usually nearby, as displaced tenants migrated locally. Some likened the spectacle of railway development to a kind of natural disaster. Described as a 'great earthquake' by Dickens in *Dombey and Son* (1848), we hear of the 'deep pits and trenches', as well as the 'enormous heaps of earth and clay thrown up', while all around stood buildings 'undermined and shaking, propped by great beams of wood'. Emerging from these infernal crevices could be seen 'fragments of unfinished walls and arches, and piles of scaffolding, and wildernesses of bricks, and giant forms of cranes, and tripods'.

These disruptions did not begin and end with the railways, however. The general scene extended to clearances of a different kind, such as the nuisance of inner-city slaughterhouses and livestock markets, like London's Hungerford, demolished in 1862. Indeed, market halls in general found themselves increasingly at the centre of urban renewal schemes in Victorian towns and cities, such as Kirkgate in Leeds (1855) and Market Place in Stockport (1860–1). The desire was to modernise market spaces, bringing them further under municipal control, thus making for more ordered and hygienic environments. Adopting the latest in architectural technology, materials such as cast iron, encaustic tiles, and plate glass were seen as part of this new regulatory regime, allowing for greater levels of light, ventilation, and cleanliness. In the case of the Columbia Market, Bethnal Green, there was a social agenda, too. Sponsored by the banking heiress Angela Burdett Coutts, and named after her founding of the bishopric of British Columbia (1857), the idea was to obtain not only better-quality food but also a better grade of costermonger to serve the 'deserving poor' of this notoriously rundown area of London. In clearing 2 acres of existing urban fabric to make way for an extraordinary Gothic pile, it was reckoned 'impossible for the coarsest and most ignorant minds to be in constant familiarity with graceful forms without profit of elevation and refinement' **[20]**.[17] The minds of such people would not be influenced, however, and the scheme was a failure. In an attempt to beautify the city, parliamentary acts also allowed for the removal of great swathes of domestic housing in and around key sites such as Westminster Abbey and the Houses of Parliament, including those cleared along Parliament Street and Old Palace Yard in the 1890s, making way for the open spaces and vistas we enjoy today. Indeed, street clearances in general accounted for the dislodgment of nearly 100,000 people in London between 1830 and 1880.

Subterranean improvements likewise unsettled the city. Under the guise of enhanced sanitation, monumental sewage works required clearance and mass excavations of a similar kind. Such works had become a matter of urgency given the number of people beginning to cram within the creaking

Fig. 20

Columbia Market, Bethnal Green (1864–9), London, sponsored by the banking heiress Angela Burdett Coutts.

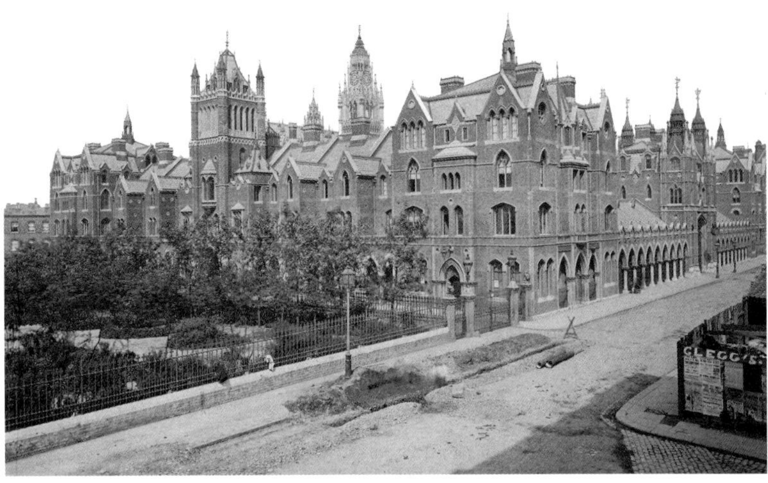

and dilapidated fabric of Britain's towns and cities. Their overflowing excrement led not only to unacceptable levels of contamination and pollution, but also to outbreaks of deadly disease, especially cholera and typhus. Many of the rivers that ran through Britain's industrial cities—the Irwell in Manchester, the Tame in Birmingham, the Mersey in Liverpool, the Aire in Leeds, and of course the Thames in London—became clogged with refuse. By all accounts the stench was horrendous, as London's 'great stink' of 1858 proved. The London sewer system, engineered by Joseph Bazalgette to remedy the problem, and built ostensibly between 1858 and 1865, must therefore be considered one of the great construction events of the Victorian age **[21a]**. Despite being mostly invisible, it meandered its way beneath the city for nearly 2,000 kilometres. Where it did emerge it took the form of steam-powered pumping stations which were required to raise water levels at certain points in order to keep the effluent flowing. The stations at Crossness (1859–65) and Abbey Mills (1865–8), for instance, are interesting pieces of architecture in their own right **[41a]**.

Perhaps the most famous destruction–construction project of the Victorian age was the London Metropolitan Railway, otherwise known as the 'underground' or 'tube'. Contemporary images of the works associated with this enterprise have the appearance of bomb sites, eerily prophetic of the 1940–1 blitz **[21b]**. There is something of the city as perpetual ruin in this.[18] The scene was both chaotic and catastrophic, as building after building fell to make way for new developments. Commercial improvements, too, were part of the story. John Summerson has observed, for instance, how from the 1840s to the 1870s the 'almost uniformly Georgian and domestic' scene of the old City of London was largely demolished to make way for smart-looking bank and insurance company buildings, including a new

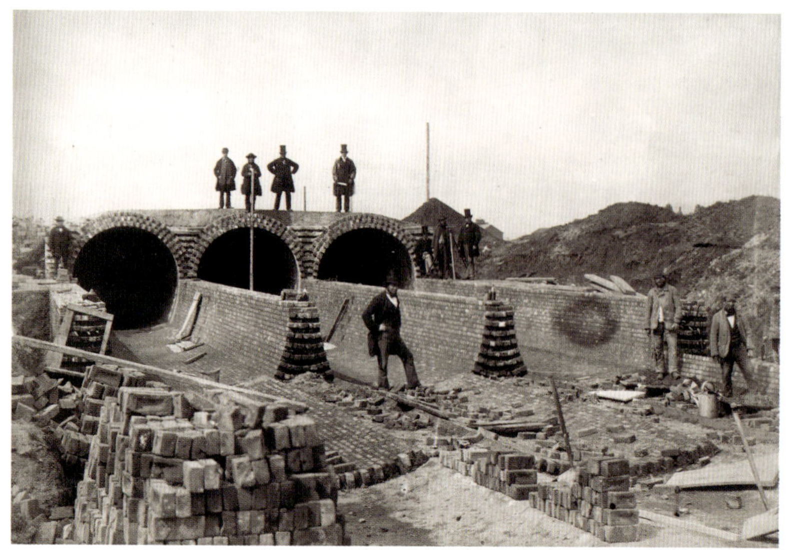

Fig. 21a

Construction of Northern outfall sewer below London's Abbey Mills pumping station (1862). Joseph Bazalgette can be seen at top right of the image.

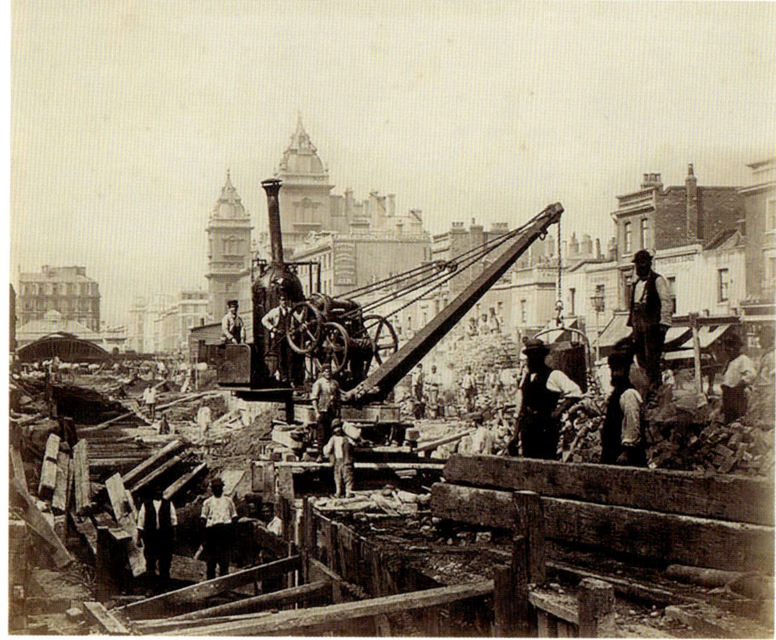

Fig. 21b

Railway construction workers on Praed Street, Paddington, building the London underground railway link between Paddington and Blackfriars. They adopt the 'cut-and-cover' method used before the development of the tunnelling shield devised by James Henry Greathead. The towers of the Great Western Railway's Paddington terminus hotel loom large in the background.

Royal Exchange (1842–4) by William Tite **[22]**.[19] Other modern conveniences followed, such as gas street lighting. The extraordinary photographs of 1870s Manchester by James Mudd show modern development of this kind advancing through the old city like a steadily moving lava flow, slowly gouging a path across the pre-modern, pre-industrial urban landscape **[23a]**. Here the modern city was being forged in unrelenting, unsentimental fashion. Very little it seemed could resist the forces of improvement.

Indeed, Manchester might be pointed to as the quintessential modern city remade. For a time at least, its factories and warehouses, rising like prototype skyscrapers, were where the future could be glimpsed. Ominous

Fig. 22

The new Royal Exchange, Threadneedle Street (1842–4), City of London, by William Tite.

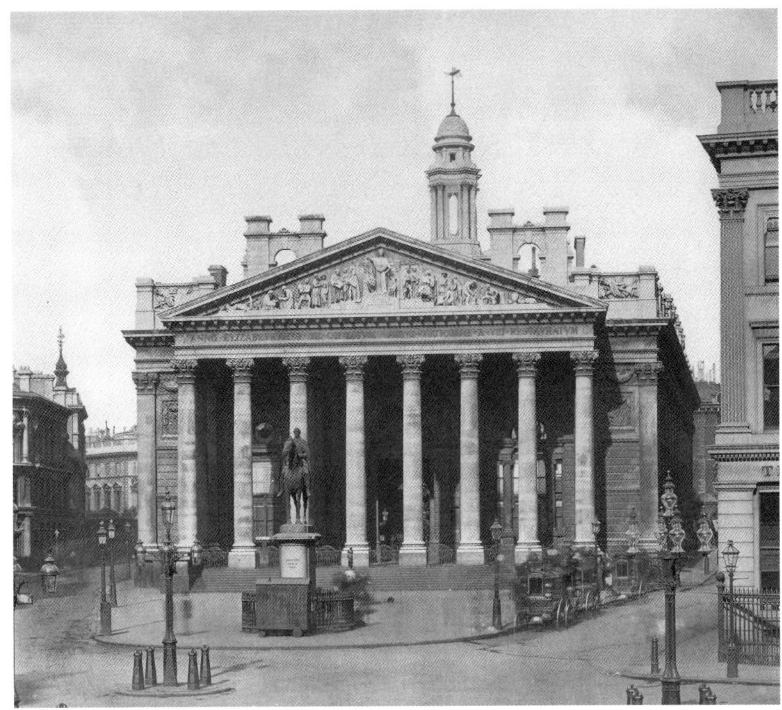

Fig. 23a

Remaking the city—contrast between old and new. James Mudd's 'Royal Exchange and Deakin's Entire', from 'Ancient and Modern Manchester' (1875).

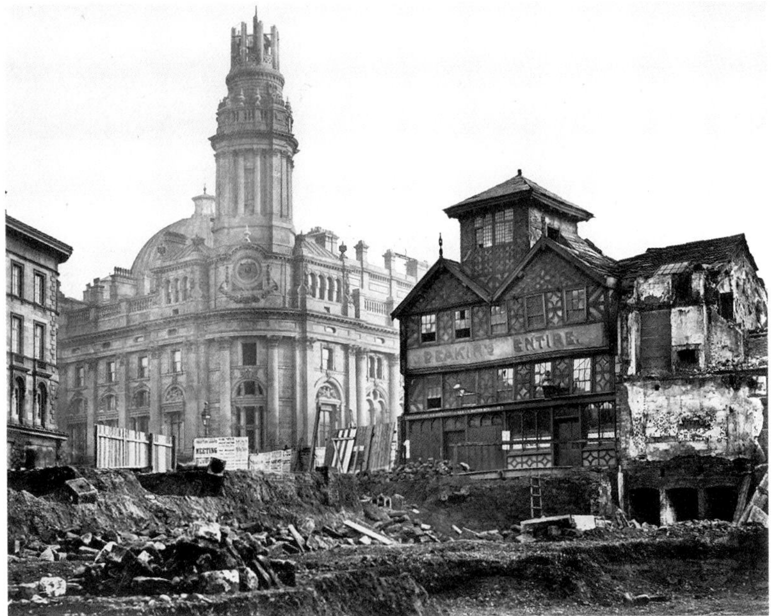

and beguiling in equal measure, they captured not only the imagination of visitors, but also the spirit of 'Free Trade' Britain. Beginning their march from Ancoats across to Piccadilly in the city's north-east as early as the late eighteenth century, these buildings, including the planning rationale they embodied, brought newly systematised modes of urban development. This involved the question of how the advent of machines would ultimately shape the buildings and experiences of Britain's cities.[20] Textile manufacturing from huge cotton imports—initially from slave plantations in the southern United States, then India—was the impetus, and the substantial profits generated had transformed both Manchester's and Britain's wider political landscape by the beginning of the Victorian age. As a result, Manchester's population grew rapidly, too rapidly, with dire consequences, as the accounts of Friedrich Engels, James Phillips Kay, and Henry Gaulter testify. By 1801 it contained over 70,000 souls; by 1831, 142,000; and by 1851, some 400,000. Again, the flipside to the rational, gridded planning of factory space was the prevalence of inadequate, insanitary, and unplanned workers' housing.

In the factories, at least, brick and cast iron were used in a truly modern sense, in which economies of finance, space, and labour intersected in brutally efficient ways. The need for effective fireproofing was also a factor. Such spaces were deeply integrated with, and in many respects co-productive of, the wider networks of rail and canal infrastructure mentioned above. Fuel and raw material were moved in, manufactured products moved out. Driven by the accelerated power of coal, which conveniently came from mines in nearby Lancashire, the steam-operated machinery of Manchester's factories spewed out smoke and soot from its more than 500 chimneys in quantities that bewildered and even terrified onlookers. Described wearily by Ruskin as the 'storm cloud of the nineteenth century', this putrid emanation was prone to drift as far as the Lake District, over 70 miles to the north.

The tremendous wealth generated from this enterprise fostered an industrial bourgeois class that oversaw a renewed sense of civic virtue, grounded in notions of liberal politics and trade. Apart from the new town hall (see Chapter 4) and the Royal Exchange, the most potent architectural symbols of this urban vision were the warehouses in the Piccadilly area of the city, on Portland and Mosley streets especially. Fashioned like great Renaissance palazzi over four or five storeys, these hulking buildings dominated their urban surrounds, serving a multitude of functions, from retail shops and offices to department stores and workshops for the finishing of textile products **[23b]**. Initially composed in brick, by the 1850s many were faced in stone. Their large, arched openings at street level also allowed for the expansive use of plate glass, thus facilitating new forms of consumer experience. In this respect, Manchester's warehouses were understood as a form of architectural representation whereby the city's new industrialists might fancy themselves modern Renaissance merchant-princes.[21]

Similar stories of urban redevelopment and renewal can be found in numerous other Victorian cities. There is the example of Birmingham under the leadership of Joseph Chamberlain, for instance, whose City Improvement Scheme of the 1870s—informed by a 'civic gospel' of public-spirited capitalism, and backed by a largely Nonconformist cadre of leading business-

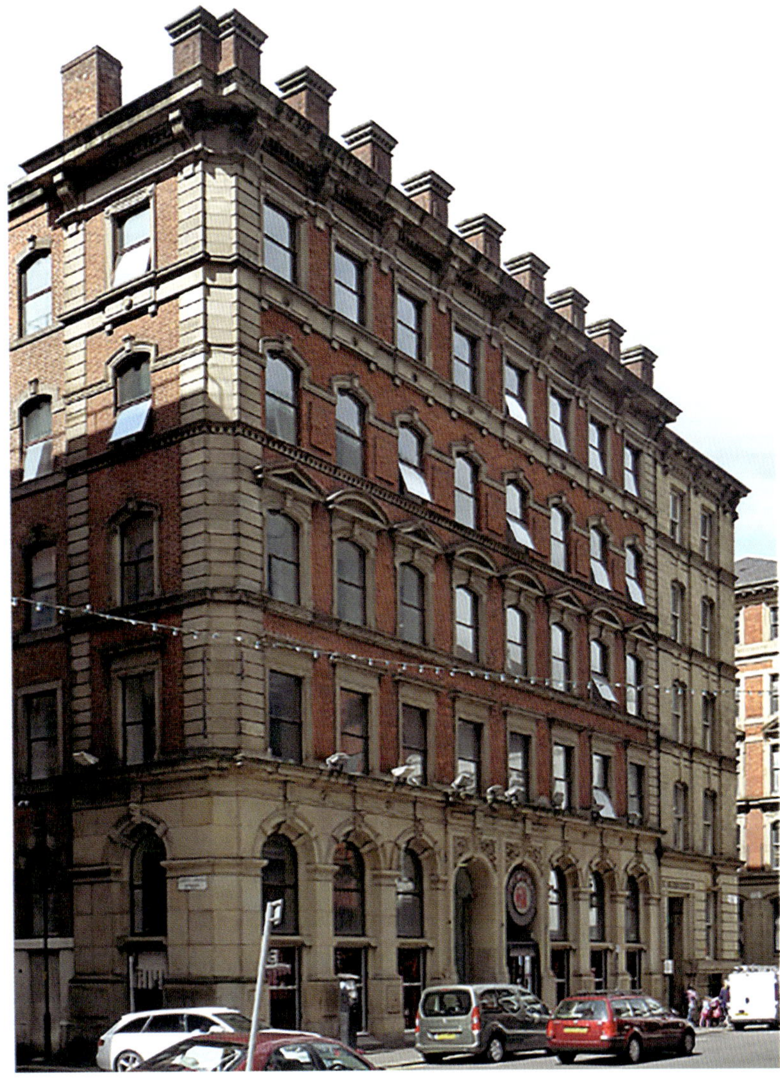

Fig. 23b

Manchester warehouses, 14–16 Charlotte Street, Manchester (*c.*1856–8), by Edward Walters.

men—led to the municipalisation of gas and water services; the building of libraries, schools, and other public amenities; the opening up and pushing through of parks and new streets; and extensive slum clearances. Before this there was the City of Glasgow Improvements Act of 1866, which ultimately saw much of central Glasgow demolished to make way for the formation of thirty-ninc new streets, and the alteration of twelve old ones. By 1876 over 25,000 people had been displaced in the process.[22] This kind of redevelopment also led to new forms of commercial zoning, as local authorities got to grips with modern planning; while technologies such as gas (then electric) street lighting, the telegraph, the hydraulic lift, and better and cleaner pavements led to new ways of seeing, communicating, and moving through the city. It also made it safer for women.

Slums and the Urban Poor

Initiatives of this kind highlighted the plight of the urban poor. The latter Victorian period, in particular, is replete with accounts of the conditions of the working classes in British cities caused by such overcrowding and substandard accommodation. These provided a grim catalogue of the appalling moral and physical decrepitude of many of those living and working in Britain's large industrial towns and cities, heightening public awareness with a view to initiating action. Most cities contained one or more slums of this kind. Manchester had Angel Meadow and Little Ireland, Liverpool Little Scotland, while Glasgow had Blackfriars. Some of the more famous accounts chronicling these areas included those by James Philips Kay (1832) and Engels (1844) in Manchester, and Henry Mayhew (1851) and Andrew Mearns (1883) in London. There were also scientific surveys designed to obtain a better understanding of the precise conditions and causes of poverty in Britain's larger cities, such as Charles Booth's *Life and Labour of the People in London* (1886–1903), noted for its revealing colour-coded maps of class distribution **[24a&b]**. Public inquiries followed as feelings of guilt and fear mounted among Britain's political class. All the while the critique of the Victorian city as a largely senseless, modern-day 'mammon' became louder. It was now a blight on the collective conscience, and, as Thomas Carlyle remarked acerbically, a place that not merely broke but ground to dust the nation's social contract.

Most if not all such accounts pointed to the buildings and spaces associated with the urban poor, disclosing to many (if they were not already aware) a most shocking state of affairs. Although sensationalist, Mearns's *The Bitter Cry of Outcast London* captured the scene:

> Few...have any conception of what these pestilential human rookeries are, where tens of thousands are crowded together amidst horrors which call to mind what we have heard of the middle passage of the slave ship. To get to them you have to penetrate courts reeking with poisonous and malodorous gases[,]...sewage and refuse scattered in all directions and often flowing beneath your feet...You have to ascend rotten staircases, which threaten to give way beneath every step...You have to grope your way along dark and filthy passages swarming with vermin. Then, if you are not driven back by the intolerable stench, you may gain admittance to the dens in which these thousands of beings...herd together.

Here the city and its architecture are presented as a type of death trap, with the extended structure of the slum acting like a great vice of depravity from which there appeared to be no escape.[23]

For some, like William Booth, founder of the Salvation Army, these horrors had wider implications. At one level, they resonated with late Victorian notions (and prejudices) concerning the civilisational 'darkness' and 'savagery' of equatorial Africa; at another, the remedy was to be sought in the colonies, where such poor wretches might best be relocated. Either way, this was 'darkest England', a cancer at the heart of the imperial organism, and one that required immediate treatment.[24] Relief came, or was at least proposed, in the form of the Royal Commission on the Housing of the Working Classes (1884). This not only invigorated existing acts concerned with working-class accommodation in Britain's industrial cities, such as the Torrens (1868) and Cross (1875) acts, but also ushered in the new Housing of the Working Classes Act (1885). Importantly, it also led to the Local Government Act of 1888, instigating the formation of the London County

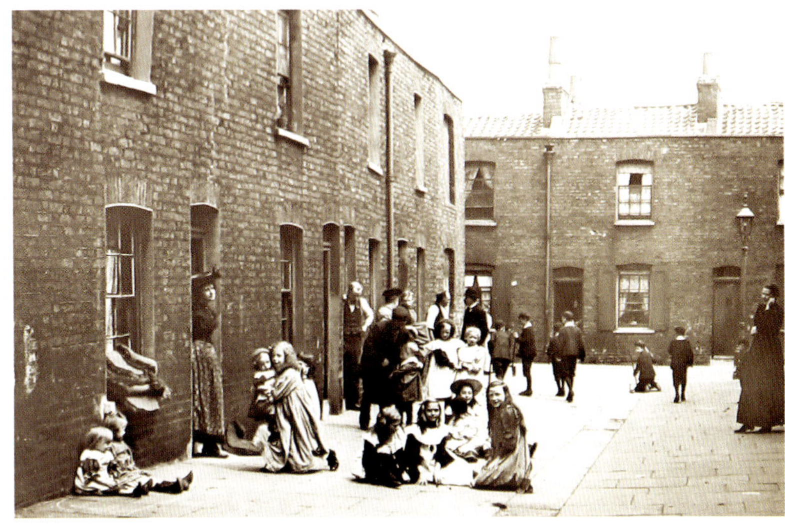

Fig. 24a

Slum housing, South London (1897).

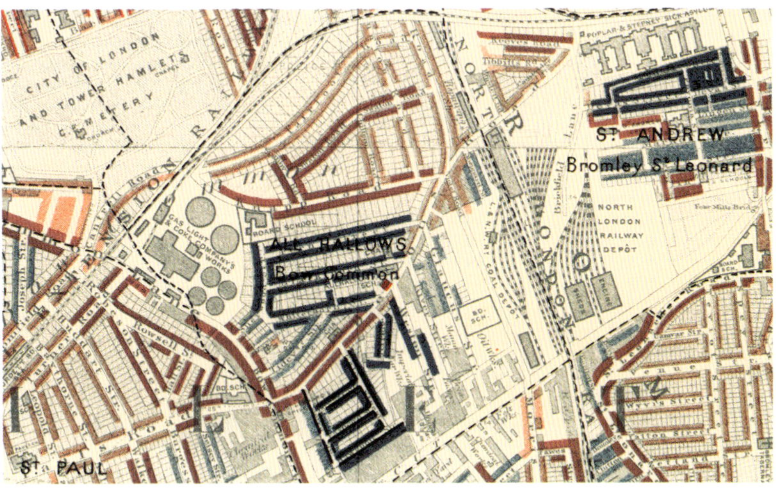

Fig. 24b

Charles Booth, *Map Descriptive of London Poverty, 1898–9*, detail of 'Sheet 1 – Eastern District' showing Bromley. The rows of houses in black represent 'Vicious—semi-criminal', while those in maroon and pink indicate 'Some comfortable, others poor' and 'Fairly comfortable' respectively.

Council. Such acts gave local authorities the power not only to clear slums but to borrow money to erect better planned working-class housing. The impact of these measures was mixed, however.

It is little wonder, therefore, that the wholesale clearance of slums, when it happened, was a cause for near universal celebration. But the problem persisted. The increasingly cramped, insanitary, and polluted environs of inner cities during the latter Victorian period, along with the desire for greater privacy, precipitated an exodus into the suburbs. There more space and light could be found, not to mention greenery. This changed both the demographic and morphological configuration of most larger towns and cities in Britain, both exacerbating and reinforcing the functional and socially segregated patterns of urban growth characteristic of the Victorian city. Although some working- and artisan-class residents could find a way out to better accommodation by the 1880s, thanks to the imposition of cheap commuter fares on railway companies, the bulk of the flight was from among the burgeoning middle classes who were taking up residence in detached or semi-detached villas on the outskirts of cities (see Chapter 8). In reference to the discussion above, suburban development of this kind was made possible in part by improvements in transport technology—not only the advent of regular horse-drawn omnibus services, and later electrified tram and light-rail networks, but also better roads, which facilitated private carriages. To work in the city but live outside was a realisable ambition for many by the turn of the twentieth century.

In London, although the wealthy chose to remain centrally in places such as Mayfair, the middle classes went out to Highgate, Hampstead, Putney, Wimbledon and Wandsworth, some 5 to 8 miles from the city centre. Earlier, in Manchester, there was the suburban 'park' concept, seen in examples such as Victoria, Ellesmere, and Fielden parks from around mid-century, with the Altrincham and Wilmslow commuter lines extending outer-city development further **[25]**; while Birmingham's middle classes poured into Edgbaston, Harborne, and Moseley. Those of Leeds moved to Headingly, while Edinburgh's aspirant middle classes, if not already in the New Town, relocated to Marchmont, Bruntsfield, and Morningside.

The problems associated within the Victorian city inevitably led to visionary, even utopian, proposals of model towns for the labouring classes. Some of the more practical solutions were in fact realised in places such as Saltaire (1851), Port Sunlight (1888–90), and Bournville (1895–1900), made possible with the backing of enlightened industrialists. It would also lead to the Garden City and wider town-planning movements of the late nineteenth and early twentieth centuries, exemplified in Hampstead Garden Suburb, which proved hugely influential (see Chapter 8). These conceived of the city in an organic sense, almost as a living creature, which had 'veins', 'arteries', and 'lungs', which needed to 'breathe', and around which entities 'circulated'. This was the city as 'healthful' environment. From this would emerge a more abstract set of planning principles represented in such noted publications as Ebenezer Howard's *To-morrow: A Peaceful Path for Real Reform* (1898), where urban, district, and region-wide zoning were understood as operating in tandem. One concept associated with this thinking was a green buffer or 'belt' around cities, which remains with us to this day.

Colonial Urbanism

With increases in outward migration from the United Kingdom and elsewhere during the late Victorian period, colonial cities thrived. In some instances, and especially in relation to resource booms such as mining, it was not unknown for large conurbations to spring up almost overnight. Many colonial cities started from virtually nothing, or only small, pre-existing settlements, indigenous or otherwise. By 1900 some could boast populations numbering in the hundreds of thousands. For instance, Singapore and Hong Kong had over 500,000 and 200,000 respectively; Montreal, Toronto, Sydney, Melbourne, and Johannesburg likewise ranged between 200,000 and 500,000; while smaller cities, such as Adelaide, Brisbane, Wellington, Auckland, and Cape Town, had populations of between 47,000 and 162,000.[25] Prominent South Asian cities, such as Madras and Bombay, which mostly comprised indigenous inhabitants, had reached 500,000 and 770,000 respectively by this time, with Calcutta topping out at over 1 million.

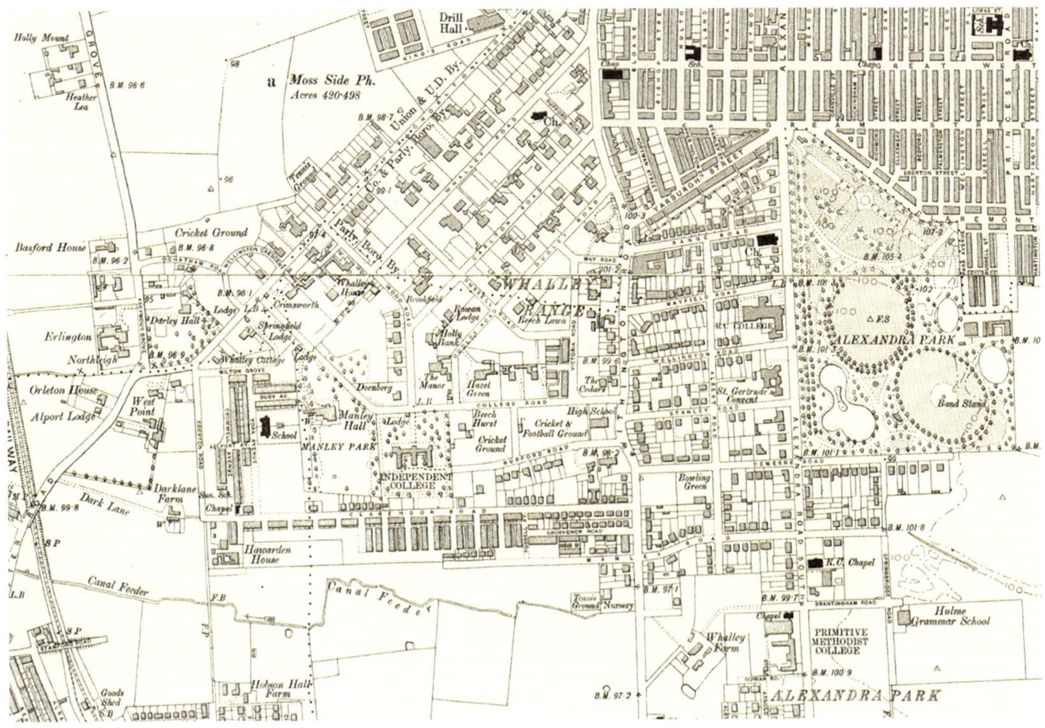

Fig. 25

Suburban development at Moss Side and Whalley Range (Manchester), detail of Ordinance Survey map (*c.*1885).

Like colonial expansion and settlement itself, this kind urbanism had distinct yet overlapping political and economic dimensions. It was political in the sense that it was concerned with territorial acquisition and control, whereby towns and cities, strategically located, became the largest and most conspicuous forms of spatial domination, and from where government was administered. It was economic in that colonial cities became centres for the management of extractive developmental practices (mining, forestry, broad-acre and plantation agriculture), where the people, institutions, and technologies that facilitated these practices were concentrated, including banks, insurance companies, agency houses, and shipping firms. Thus, at a local level, such cities organised, managed, and lived off the surpluses of their hinterlands; at a regional and wider global level, they redirected those surpluses to other colonial cities and back to the metropolis. In this sense, Britain's colonial cities should not be considered from a 'home' perspective as merely distant places—somehow detached, in far-off parts of the world (although they certainly were)—but as extended outposts of the metropolis itself, like vital and interdependent appendages of a larger, living organism.

To be sure, much urban development in the colonies was substantially different from that in Britain. This was owing to the vast variations in climate and culture that could be experienced across the British world. At the same time, however, such urbanism was in many ways similar, and occasionally identical. Generally, the most common pattern for such development, and the one in which many of the buildings discussed in this book were located, was the grid-iron plan. This was repeated often and everywhere across the British empire, both before and during the Victorian period. Although such orthogonal planning could be found in parts of the British Isles, it was rarely if ever the basis for whole-city design. It was used most prominently in seventeenth-century plantation Ireland, and famously as the foundation of James Craig's plan for Edinburgh New Town in 1766. Abroad, its origins lay in the so-called Grand Modell of colonial urban planning, dating back to the seventeenth century, which was itself inspired by sixteenth-century Spain's 'Laws of the Indies'. In the early British empire this approach was adopted for planning towns and cities in the Americas, such as Philadelphia (1682), Kingston (1690s), and Savannah (1734). By the nineteenth century, however, it had become synonymous with 'systematic colonisation', where settlement was geared towards permanent and ordered existence, leading to self-sufficiency and responsible government.

A legacy of Enlightenment rationality, the Cartesian logic that underpinned this 'model' was itself symptomatic of a wider spatial reasoning that lay at the foundation of methods used for surveying and distributing land in British colonial contexts. One of the best-known examples is the plan for Adelaide (*c.*1839) in the colony of South Australia **[26]**. Proposed by Colonel William Light, it was based on wide, orthogonal streets, separated in two parts by the river Torrens. Strategically interspersed throughout were public squares, with the whole surrounded by an early type of green belt. Other examples include the settlements of Port Phillip (Melbourne, 1837), Wellington (1841), Christchurch (1848), and Johannesburg (1887). Like large, urban-scale ledgers, these plans were imposed on the landscape, often-times regardless of topography, and were marked by their methodical enumeration and subdivision, with wide open streets for a more healthful environment. Garden city principles followed in time, as the perimeters of these grids were hemmed in with urban parks and gardens, not to mention spacious suburbs. The names given to streets and roads, too, often relating to key figures and events at 'home' or in the colony, played a crucial role in place-making and constructing narratives of imperial identity.

Indeed, urban patterning of this kind could occur on the smallest scale. During the 1850s gold rush in the colony of Victoria (Australia), for instance, settlement initially followed the positioning of mining claims. But as these settlements grew, ordered grid formations soon took over, making for a dual urban structure. This 'two-type' structure became a particular type of 'gold rush urbanism', characteristic of many such mining towns during the Victorian era, including Castlemaine, Stawell, Bendigo, Ballarat, and Tarnagulla.[26] Such urbanism—developed around deep, narrow plots—also resulted in a built environment whereby individual buildings were forced to address the street, usually at one end, encouraging a type of 'façadism' **[27a&b]**. So-called Boom Town development in colonial cities such as Melbourne, Perth, and Johannesburg during the 1880s and 1890s was symptomatic of this phenomenon, where real estate speculation, combined with conditions of intense capitalist economic growth, led developers to vie with one another architecturally. Through this type of urbanism, the wealth and prosperity of these colonies was showcased in an eclectic and splendiferous, if at times garish, manner.

Fig. 26

Colonel William Light's plan for Adelaide (*c*.1839), South Australia.

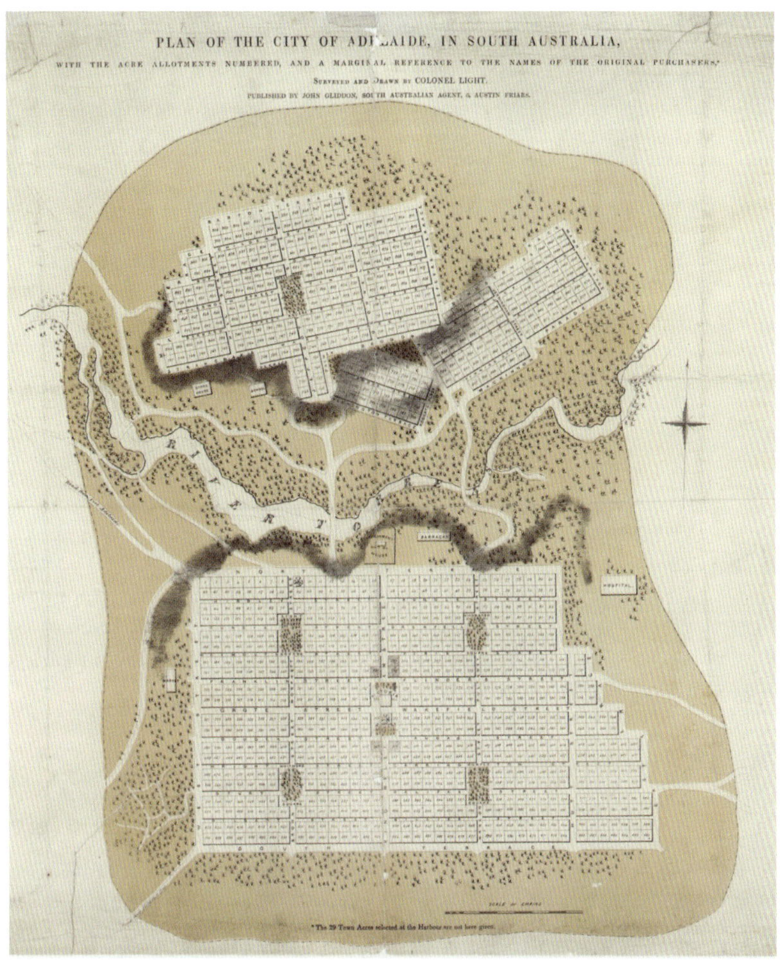

It was a different story in other parts of the British empire, however. Many colonial cities, especially in Sub-Saharan Africa and subcontinental Asia, had sizable majority indigenous and/or non-European migrant populations. This posed a 'management' problem for the minority colonial authorities, especially when it came to perceived issues of security and public health. In India, for example, outside the major port cities, the principal form of urbanism initially came in the shape of military forts and cantonments. These were located strategically, often nearby existing 'native' or 'old' towns and cities. They were usually designed by military engineers, and, like the plans mentioned above, were strictly orthogonal in formation. In time these grew to have so-called civil lines (i.e., civilian administrative districts), which were also planned in this way, sometimes being an extension or outgrowth of the cantonment. These not only accommodated civilian officials in isolated bungalows, but also contained civic infrastructure such as courthouses, government offices, schools, hospitals, police stations, churches, recreational facilities, and so on **[28a]**.

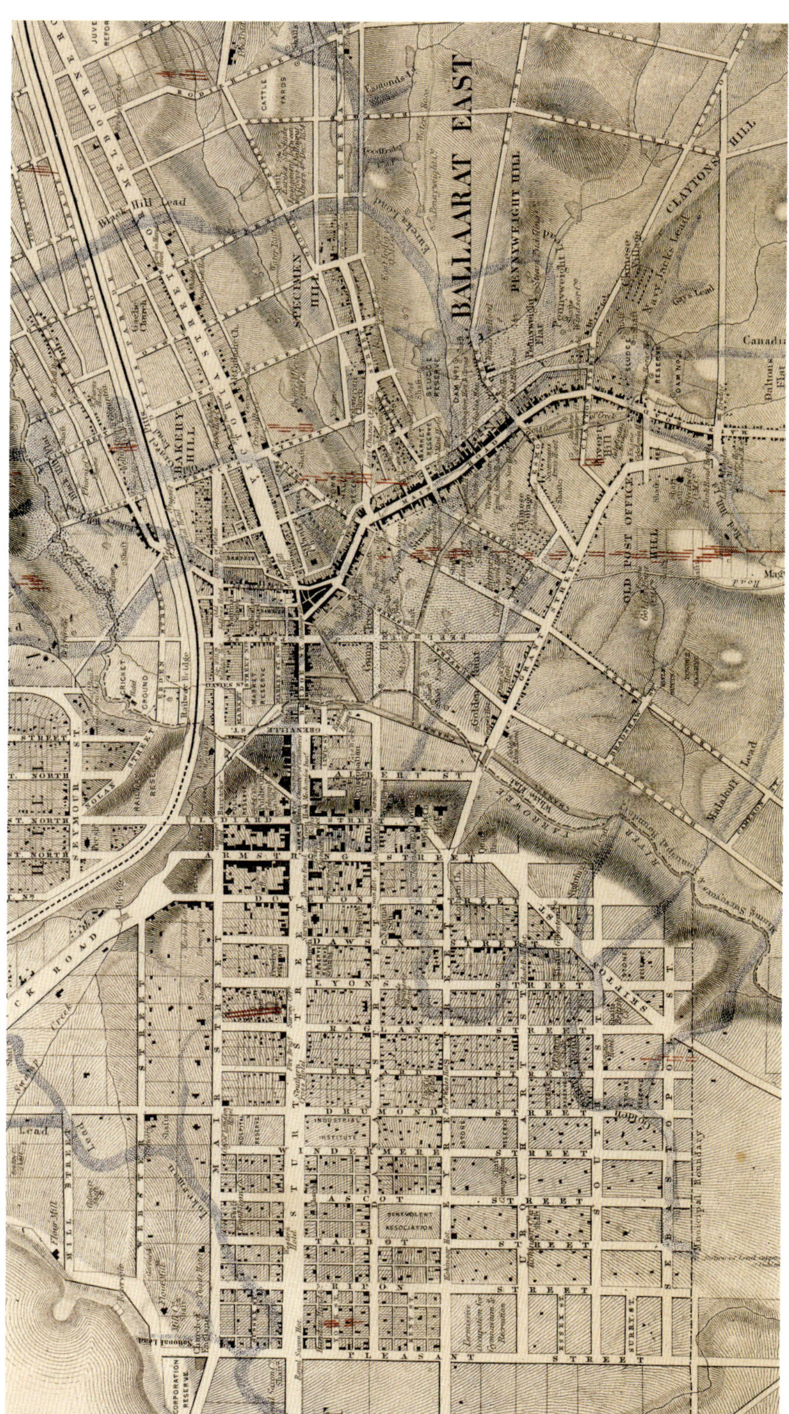

Fig. 27a

Map of the Victorian goldfields city of Ballarat (1861), Australia. Here the original diggings settlement, with its irregular street pattern, can be seen at the middle top. This later joined with and developed into the gridiron on the bottom.

Fig. 27b

Gold-rush urbanism: streetscape from Bakery Hill, Ballarat (*c.*1880).

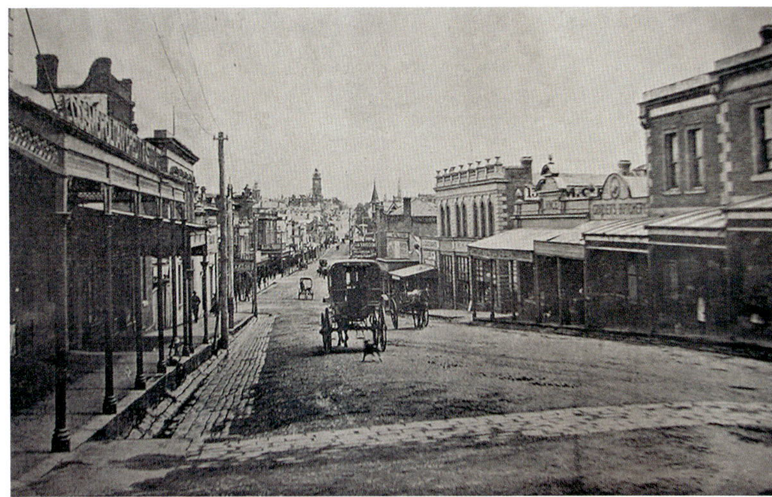

Fig. 28a

British colonial bungalows within the Civil Lines at Barrackpore (1870), India.

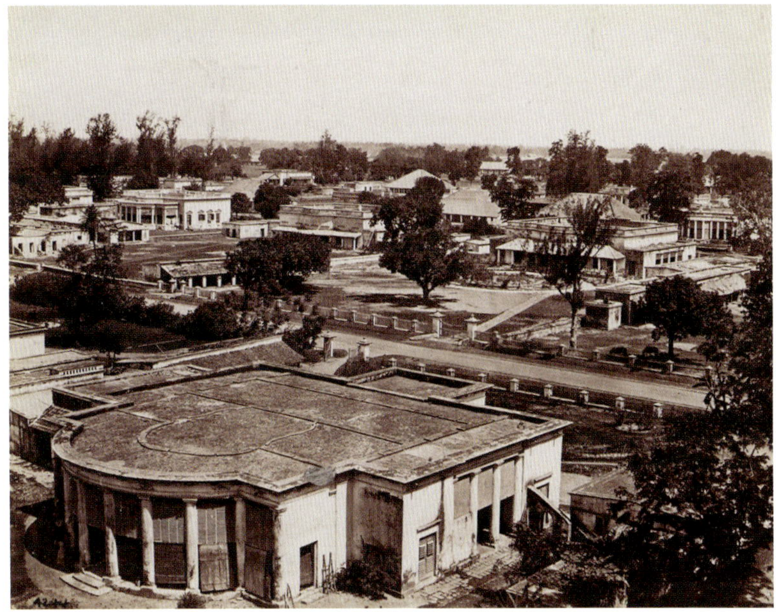

However, and particularly during the Victorian period, concerns over defence and public health were combined with racial prejudice, leading to segregation along ethnic lines. Apart from widespread views endemic of European cultural superiority, these segregation practices were informed, initially at least, by erroneous beliefs concerning the spread of diseases such as malaria, which were thought to be transmitted via bad air or 'miasma'. Following the Indian Rebellion of 1857, over 100 such cantonments were created, governed by the newly constituted Cantonment Acts (from 1864). All these settlements displayed in one way or another forms of spatial separation and isolation in their urban arrangement, such as Allahabad and Agra in northern India, and Bangalore in the south. This model was exported to southern Africa in the 1870s and 1880s, primarily in the guise of corporate

Fig. 28b

Segregation—race and class: Chinese shophouses (fore and middle ground), Taipingshan district, Hong Kong (1870s), with detached colonial villas on the Peak in the background.

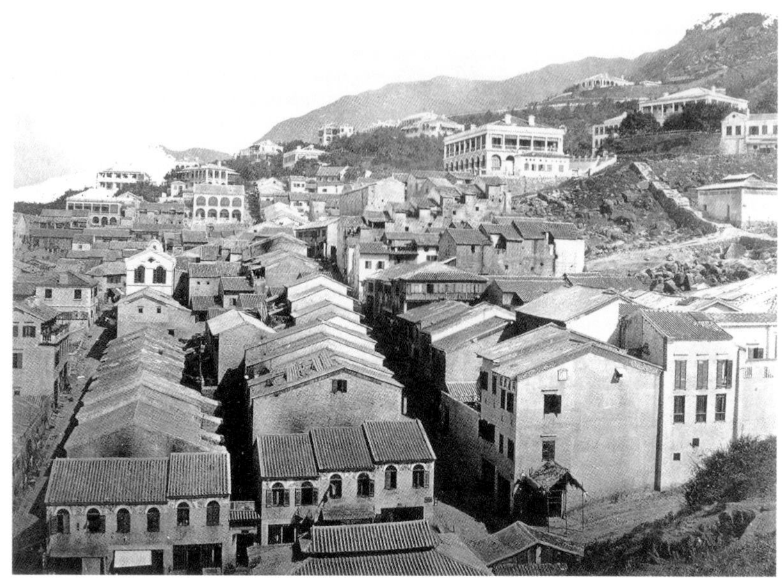

townships associated with gold and diamond mining. In such places indentured Indian, Chinese, and indigenous workers were housed in shoddily built, restricted, and heavily surveilled barrack compounds, where their criminality was presumed, contributing to the biopolitical production of race that defined the Apartheid era of the twentieth century.[27]

In other parts of Asia, such as Hong Kong, the drive for improved sanitation had equally pernicious consequences. As a major British military outpost, on a relatively small and rocky island, both security and disease prevention were paramount. Thus, in the city of Victoria, slums containing the majority Chinese immigrant population were considered not only incubators of disease, but also hotbeds of moral decrepitude and potential dissent. In stark contrast to the mostly European villas erected on higher ground, and away from the more ordered and spacious civic and commercial infrastructure of the city centre, these slums comprised mainly cramped *tong lau*-style housing **[28b]**. Much like in British India, they were the result of a combination of economic and racist forces that corralled Chinese coolie labourers into tightly bounded districts of the city, such as Taipingshan. As in London, districts such as this would be swept away entirely, making room for alternative and better planned urban development.

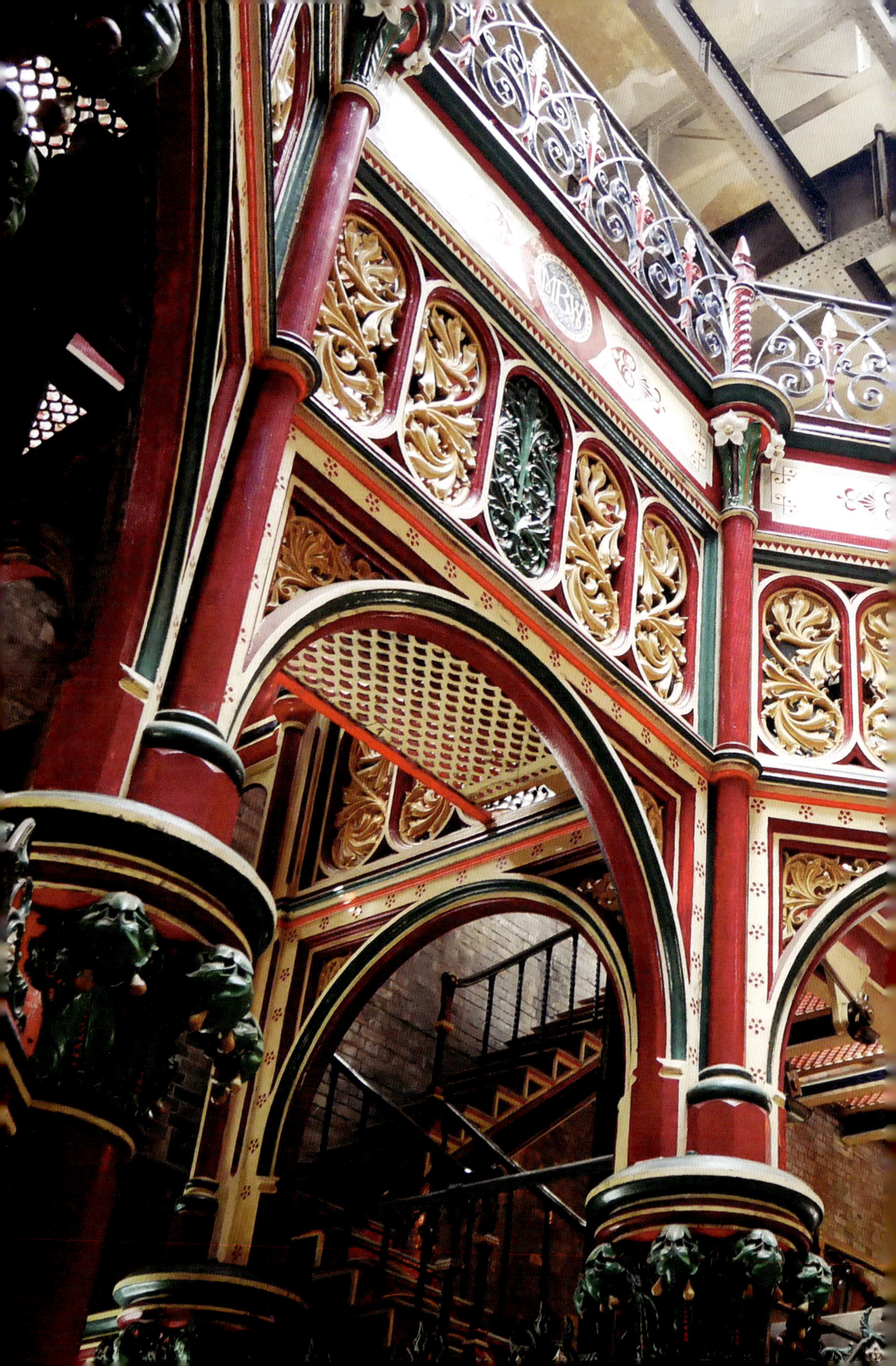
MBW

Material Abundance: Energy and the New Building Ecology

2

When Victoria came to the throne in 1837, the nature and array of materials available to architects was not a great deal different from what it had been 20 years earlier. This was an intellectual constraint as much as a practical and technological one. Not only did common building materials range little beyond what was used consistently in previous centuries (brick, stone, timber, etc.), but architects themselves had yet to conceive of architecture much beyond the use of such materials. This is both what the wider industry could provide and what clients expected. To be sure, advanced factory and warehouse buildings had begun adapting iron construction techniques for fireproofing purposes, but architecture proper had yet to respond. The transportation of heavy building materials prior to the advent of extended canal and rail networks was also prohibitively expensive. However, by mid-century the situation had changed markedly. As one enthusiastic 'progressive' observed at the time, such were the advancements that had been made in Britain's economic and industrial development by 1851, that, on almost every conceivable indicator, the nation's output had increased several-fold relative to population growth, including architectural production.[1] The consumption of building materials, such as timber and bricks, not to mention iron, had gone up anywhere between two to five times, with over 2.1bn bricks reportedly having been used in England and Wales in 1847 alone (compared to around 700m in 1800).[2]

But the transformation went beyond sheer quantity. There was a qualitative difference, too. What a casual observer of architecture would have discerned between the years from about 1840 to 1870 was a precipitous increase in the frequency of industrially manufactured materials such as terracotta, encaustic tiling, cast iron, plate glass, and machine-produced bricks. This also included mechanically procured natural materials such as stone, marble, granite, and timber. By the 1850s, claimed A. J. B. Beresford Hope, architects were 'vying with each other' to see who could include the most 'red brick, and yellow brick, and black brick, most granite, serpentine, and encaustic tiles all over their buildings'.[3] The other noticeable difference in the architecture of this period compared to that of previous generations was innovation in infrastructure relating to services such as heating, gas, water,

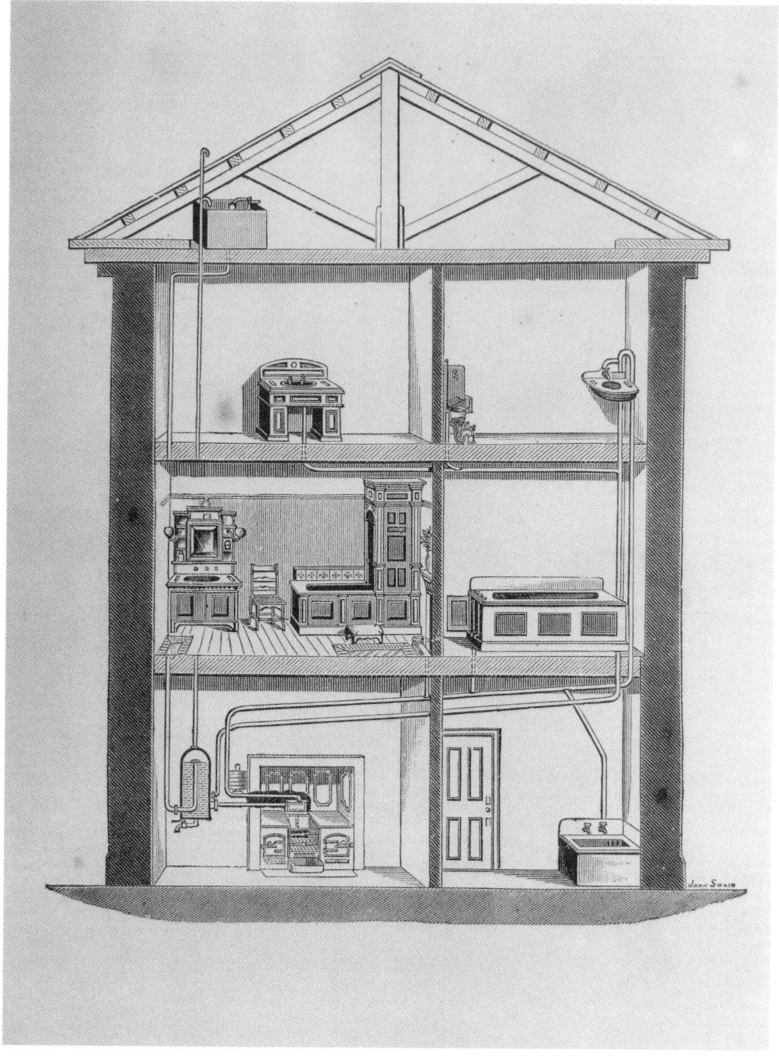

Fig. 29

Technical systems developments: cut-away section of house showing integrated services, in this case hot-water apparatus. Illustrated catalogue, Llewellins & James, founders and general engineers, Bristol (1889).

and sanitation. As the century wore on, the appearance of electrical and communications wiring in the fabric of buildings, along with ever-more complex means of tempering their internal environments—the origins of what today is referred to as HVAC (heating, ventilation, and air conditioning) systems—would have become apparent through the installation of vents, ducts, radiators, and electric lighting **[29]**. Concrete, too, had become much more prevalent by century's end. Thus, what made a building 'modern' in the minds of architects during the period was not just a matter of aesthetics, but also, and perhaps primarily, of specification and performance.

There is something of a chicken-and-egg conundrum here. As discussed in the previous chapter, industrialisation, in the form of technological innovation, brought with it an incredible array of new possibilities for architecture in terms of product design and material invention. However, was the advent of these products purely demand driven (in an endogenous sense), or did the appearance of new materials and processes (for other reasons) inspire new ways of conceiving architecture, thus creating its own, previously unrecognised forms of demand? In other words, did a positive feedback loop exist between technological development and product demand in the Victorian building world? This may be something of a moot point, but it does highlight the entwinement between architecture, engineering, and technology in the Victorian imagination. Leading architects of the age understood this pact with 'science', even if some wished to downplay its effects. Moreover, how such a relationship created the conditions for 'emergent' innovation of various kinds is important to how we understand Victorian architecture and its comparatively changeful disposition over time. For instance, in 1852 *The Builder* proclaimed how, 'the coloured and glazed bricks now manufactured offer materials for adaptation;...[and] examples of ornament in baked earth...should show architects that there is an unworked field open to them for the display of artistic talent and ingenuity'.[4] These sentiments were foreshadowed not only in Beresford Hope's comment two years earlier that the 'aesthetic possibilities' now available would enable the interior effect of All Saints', Margaret Street, to be one of 'construction' rather than surface decoration, but also by George Edmund Street a little while later who noted that architects now had 'no excuse' not to innovate.[5]

The answer to the question concerning architecture's relationship to technology lies somewhat beneath appearances, and underneath discourses concerning style and taste. Although, according to the dynamic of this feedback loop, design intent on the part of architects slowly absorbed technological innovation, re-presenting it in aesthetic form, it is important to consider how such innovation was made possible in the first place, and why it resulted in a new kind of material abundance. The 'palette' of materials architects had at their disposal by 1860 was the direct result of a peculiar form of economy. I shall return to the connection between 'design' and technology below, but for now let us ponder the effects of this economy on the trajectory of Victorian architectural design. This will require us to think about architecture from a material perspective first and foremost, taking into account the processes of production and procurement in product manufacture and distribution, including new scales of efficiency brought about by Britain's evolving capitalist economy. This will also help us evaluate Victorian architecture from an environmental impact point of view.

New Materials, New Possibilities

As we saw in the previous chapter, by mid-century Britain had all but transformed from an organic, sustainable economy (based largely on readily available and replaceable sources of energy, such as human/animal power and wood/plant matter for fuel) to a fossil-fuel-driven, consumptive one, based primarily on the extraction and burning of coal. What emerged from this transformation were new conditions of energy and movement, or motive force, that fundamentally reshaped life in Britain, and eventually the wider world. This can be understood as a new and particularly disruptive type of thermo-industrialism which had direct consequences for the built environment. The transition was of course uneven and its effects patchy, especially in those places initially beyond the limits of modern transport infrastructure, but ultimately it revolutionised the Victorian building industry. It had wider social and political implications, too, as the ability to direct energy sources in unprecedented ways enabled new and conspicuous levels of scale and prestige in the built environment that, in far exceeding necessary expenditure, symbolised evolving power relations within Victorian society. In this respect, the surpluses accrued owing to intensified energy expenditure, such as extraordinary financial accumulation, considerably enhanced architectural opportunity. In other words, a grand town hall or elaborate commercial premises signified more than civic or commercial dignity and independence; it also embodied control over resources and the organisation of labour. To understand the impact of this new economy requires us to rethink the history of buildings from the perspective of energy security as a key catalyst of societal change.

Brick

A good place to start such an analysis is with manufactured earth or fictile products for architectural purposes. Here we may include bricks, encaustic tiles, and terracotta and faience/majolica ware, as well as smaller but less widespread products, such as modern 'opus sectile'. These are all characteristic elements of Victorian architecture. Bricks are particularly interesting as they have been a mainstay of architecture, the world over, for many thousands of years. But the way they were produced changed radically during the Victorian period. There were a number of reasons for the prevalence of brick in Victorian architecture, including a new appreciation for medieval brickwork by architects (discussed in the following chapter). But two of the principal reasons for this prevalence were novel techniques of mechanised mass production and the lifting of the brick tax in 1850. Experiments in the former were spurred by new enthusiasms for brick technology unleashed by the latter, so that by 1856 there were more than 250 patents extant for brick-making machinery **[30]**. Although production by mechanisation did not lower brick prices as much as initially anticipated, over time, and especially at scale, machinery was able to increase output substantially while reducing costs per unit.

This new technology—including pug and rolling mills, pressing machines, and larger, more modern kilns—also allowed for greater quality control and product range. By 1868, the Manchester Society of Architects was able to declare, after some years of debate and scientific examination, that hand-made bricks, compared to their machine-made equivalents, could no longer be relied upon for high-end architectural affect. Moreover, the widespread adoption of coal as fuel in the industry enabled a precision approach to firing which brought out a fuller and more consistent variety of colours. Add to this an ever-expanding rail network, and quality, mass-produced bricks in a range of shapes and colours could be obtained at distance, with speed, at competitive prices. For example, even into the 1870s, good facing bricks used in urban and suburban developments in Dublin were being imported all the way from Bridgwater and Staffordshire in England, and later Belfast. Even though the expense for these was comparatively high, their quality, and the fact that Ireland did not initially have a mechanised brick industry, meant

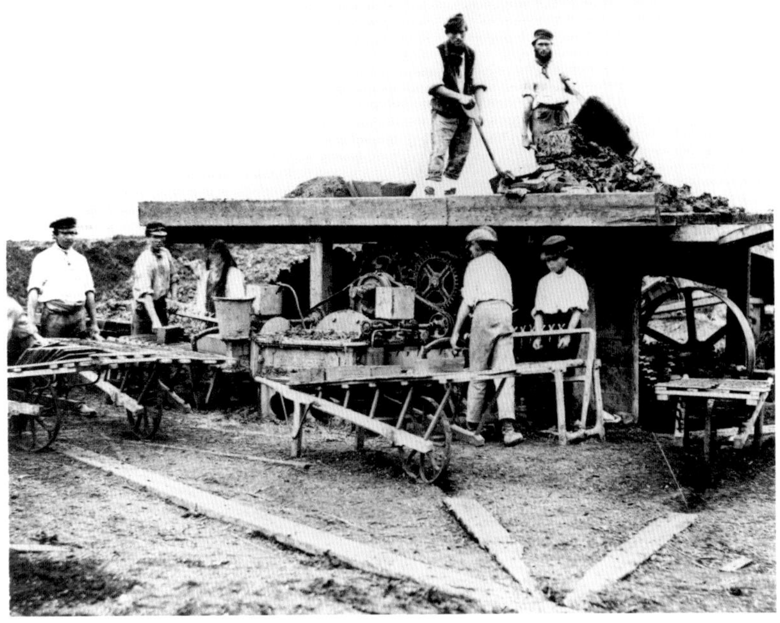

Fig. 30

Railway navvies working a brickmaking machine during the construction of the Midland Railway's St Pancras Station, London (photo 1865).

that it was considered worthwhile.[6] In a burgeoning middle-class housing market, quality and effect clearly trumped cheapness and ready access to inferior products.

Advances of this kind were slower to arrive in farer-flung colonial settings, however. Initially, lack of investment and smaller economies of scale meant that industries for local, hand-made products remained essential in such places. But with the influx of mechanical technology used for mining, along with rapidly growing populations and expanding rail networks, by the 1870s and 1880s large-scale mechanisation had been achieved in many parts of the Greater British world. This included the appearance of continuous and modern down-draught kilns, which could be found operating in Canada and Australia by this time. An example of such technology transfer was the Brunswick Brick Manufactory in Melbourne, which had a coal-fired Hoffman kiln in operation by 1870, with brick-making machinery imported from Britain, producing 15,000 bricks per day.[7] Thus, the full-scale industrialisation of brick manufacturing through the middle decades of the nineteenth century had a clear and near immediate impact on architecture, with even traditionally self-sufficient markets such as London regularly importing bricks from a radius of 80 to 100 miles. The result was that probably more bricks were laid during the Victorian period than in all previous periods put together.

Terracotta

Much the same can be said for industrialised terracotta and tile manufacturing. As with large-scale brick production in many parts of Britain, the architectural terracotta industry grew up alongside coal mining, where iron-rich, carboniferous clays and marls were to be found between coal measures, particularly in the north of England and Wales. The iron oxide content of these materials is what gave terracotta, upon firing, its distinctive earthy-red colour. The clay deposits around Ruabon in Wales were particularly prized for this purpose. When processed and fired properly, these products were all but weatherproof. Moreover, their near-vitrified surface made terracotta products—whether tiles, architectural elements, or ornament—essentially self-cleaning. This led to a rise in popularity for the product among Victorian architects from about the 1870s, where it was seen as a cheaper and more pollution-resistant substitute for stone. Architectural terracotta of course came not only in red, but in a range of natural colours (depending on the clay and how it was fired), including bone and 'buff' through to brown, grey, and blue. In its glazed form (faience), it was considered suitable for both inside and out.

Conspicuous examples of its large-scale use in Britain are to be found in the major buildings of Alfred Waterhouse, including the Natural History Museum (1865–80) and Prudential Assurance Building (1885–1901), both in London, as well as his Refuge Assurance Company Offices in Manchester (1891–5). Indeed, among the first large-scale architectural applications of terracotta was across the road from the Natural History Museum, at the South Kensington Museum (1859–72) **[155b]**, and up the way at the Royal Albert Hall (1867–71), both by 'Cole Circle' affiliates Francis Fowke, Godfrey Sykes, and Henry Y. D. Scott. Other outstanding examples include Aston Webb and E. Ingress Bell's Victoria Law Courts, Birmingham (1887–91), for its extensive use of Ruabon red terracotta, and the Russell Hotel, London, by Charles Fitzroy Doll, with its distinctive *thé-au-lait* ('milky tea') colouring **[31a&b]**. Terracotta's popularity as a practical, hard-wearing architectural

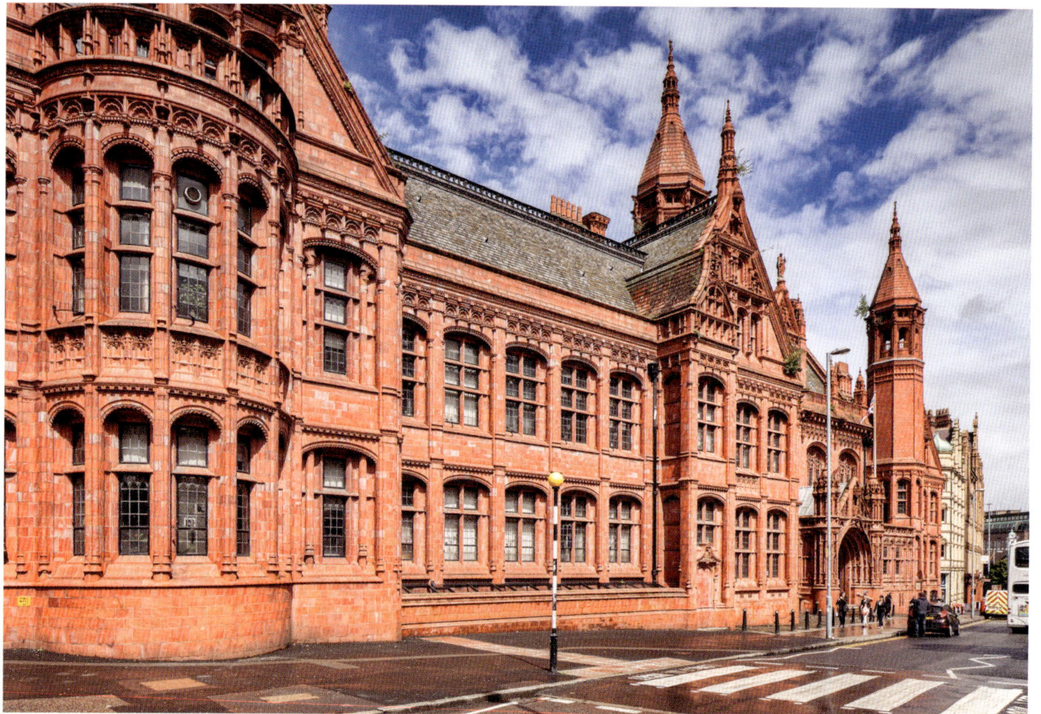

Fig. 31a

Materials revolution—terracotta: Victoria Law Courts, Corporation Street, Birmingham (1887–91), by Aston Webb and E. Ingress Bell.

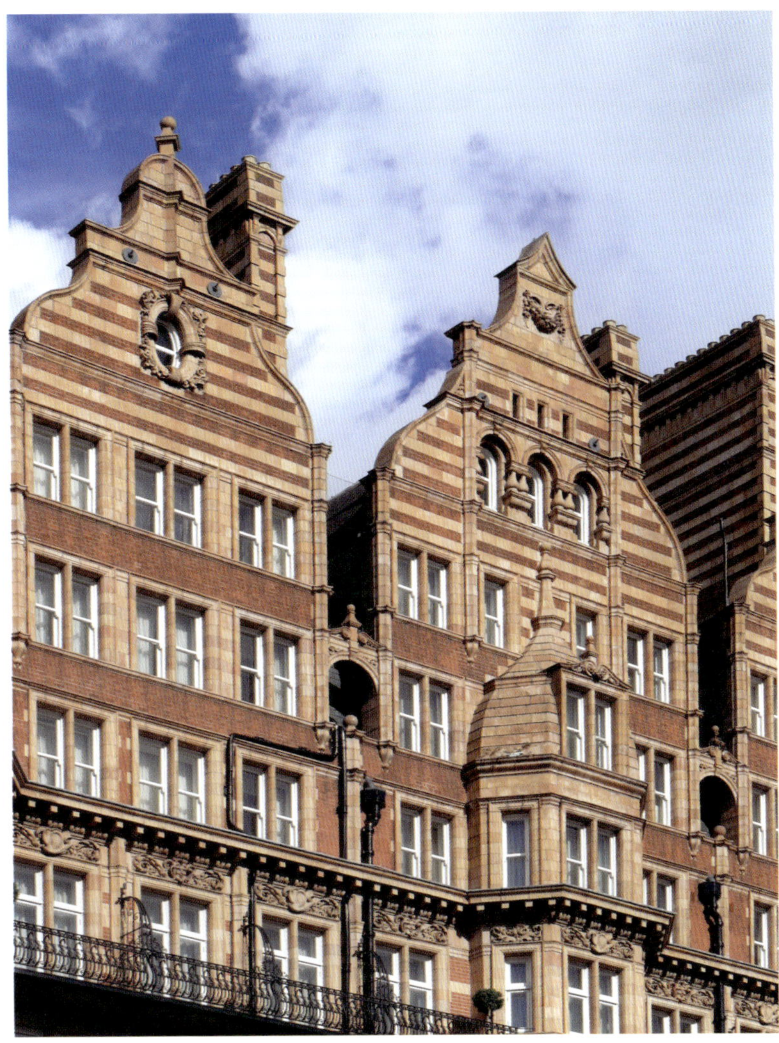

Fig. 31b
Russell Hotel, Russell Square (1898–1900), London, by Charles Fitzroy Doll.

material continued in some parts of Britain well into the Edwardian period, found in the magnificent Baroque-style warehouse buildings by Harry Fairhurst in Manchester, which make effective use of orange terracotta, seen at India House (1906) and Lancaster House (1905–10). In the eyes of some architects, Waterhouse included, precision manufactured products like machine-made bricks and architectural terracotta lent buildings a certain up-to-date quality, or what was otherwise considered an air of 'modernity'.[8] Among the biggest producers of the period were Gibbs & Canning (Tamworth, Staffs.), Doulton & Co. (London), and Hatherns (Loughborough). The premises of some of these companies acted as giant billboards for their products, such as the impressive High Victorian confection of Doulton's pottery in Lambeth (1876–8), south London, studded as its façades were with the firm's own terracotta componentry **[32]**.

The production of much basic architectural terracotta during the late Victorian period was associated with pre-existing brickworks, as they

Fig. 32

Showrooms and studios building (1876–7), Doulton & Co. pottery works, Lambeth, London, by Tarring & Son, and Wilkinson.

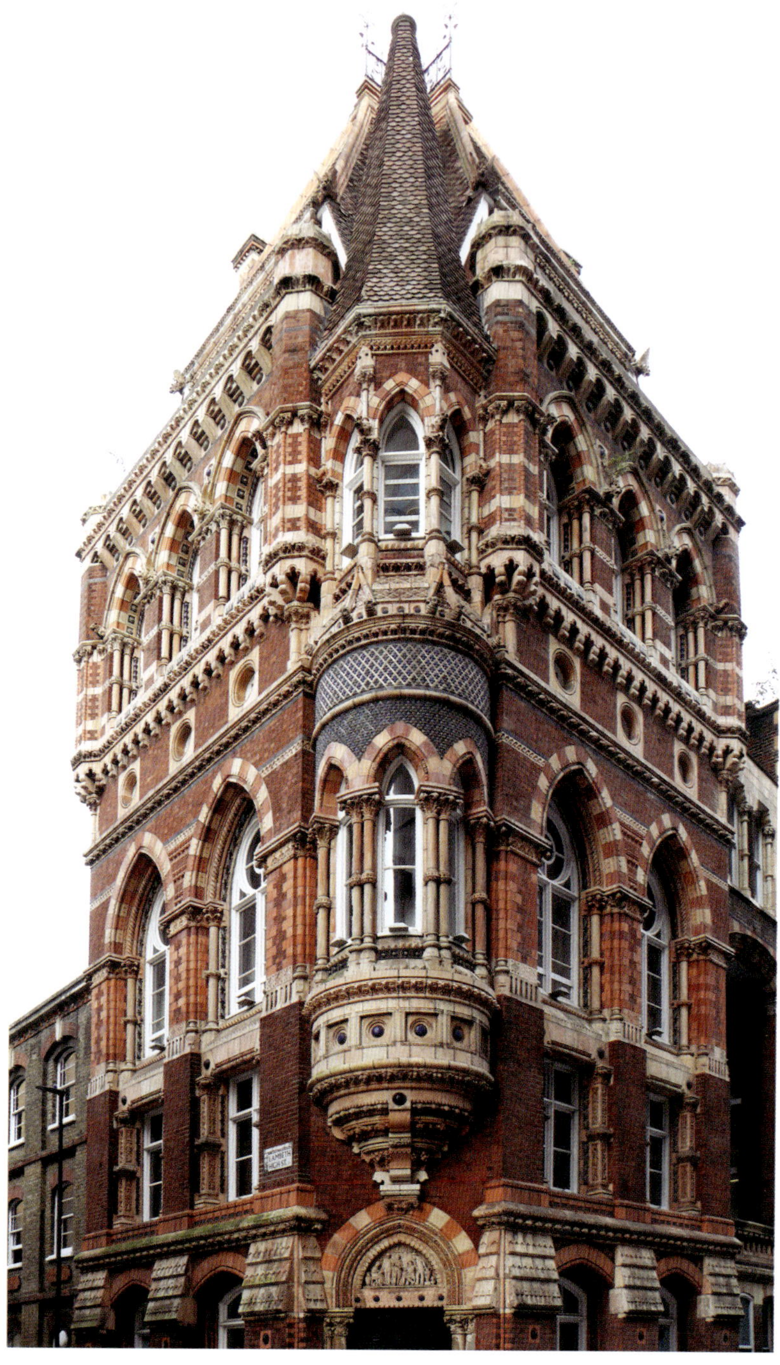

expanded into terracotta manufacturing. Again, as with mass-produced bricks, such production, through the assistance of mechanised processes, including repetitive moulding for standard components, along with developments in coal-fired kiln technology, connected the terracotta industry to national markets via the ever-expanding national rail network. Lending itself readily to the plastic arts, terracotta could also adapt, through artisan skill, to wider decorative demands, including elaborate ornamentation. Thus, almost from the outset of the industry, decorative terracotta production was associated with the new 'industrial' schools of art and design, in London and elsewhere. It was Doultons, for instance, through efforts at the Lambeth School of Art, that produced the extraordinary Jubilee fountain for the Glasgow International Exhibition in 1888, demonstrating the versatility of terracotta treated artistically. A taste for the material soon found its way across the Atlantic, to the United States, where landmark buildings such as the Museum of Fine Arts, Boston (1870–6), formed a bridge from British markets into North America, including the transfer of expertise and skilled artisanship.[9] Twenty years later Louis Sullivan would famously encrust both the Wainwright Building, St Louis (1890–1), and the Guaranty Building, Buffalo (1894–5), in this material.

Encaustic Tiles

The manufacturing of encaustic tiles was another key industry in the development of Victorian architecture. Based primarily in Staffordshire, near ready supplies of coal and good clay, the technique in its modern form was revived and patented by Samuel Wright in 1830. By the second half of the nineteenth century, however, the manufacture of encaustic tiles came to be dominated by a small number of large-scale, industrial producers, the most noted of which were Minton, Hollins & Co. (Stoke-on-Trent) and Maw & Co. (Jackfield, Salop.). These companies delivered not just across Britain, but around the world. The invention of new machinery in the mid-1850s based on the dry or 'dust pressing' method enabled huge increases in output, with the work of two to three men (attending the machine) achieving as much as 60 to 100 men by hand. It was said that one, well-operated tile-making machine could produce as many as 15,000 six-inch tiles in the same time it took a skilled labourer to produce approximately 200. Encaustic simply means 'burnt in', and so the process of producing a hard and durable ceramic tile, with a variety of patterns fired into its surface, and for a very competitive price, became a mainstay of Victorian architecture and design.

The impact of these developments was profound. As Zerah Colburn put it before a meeting of the Society of Arts in 1865: 'The architect...is more or less bound in his designs by commercial considerations; and to give him a known material at a cost commercially within the limits of general application, where previously it could only be sparingly employed, is virtually to give him a new material.'[10] With the help of influential critics and purveyors of 'taste', such as Charles Locke Eastlake, and the promotion of such products through widely publicised international exhibition circuits, the manufactured encaustic tile became *de rigueur*. Thus, encaustic tiling for general use, particularly in domestic settings, had become ubiquitous by the latter half of the nineteenth century. The product's widespread adoption in civic architecture also became normal, whether in the numerous town halls going up across Britain, or in colonial legislatures abroad. Among the more impressive examples in Britain, and those that set something of a benchmark for the product's use, include the Houses of Parliament (1837–67)

[57b], St George's Hall, Liverpool (1841–56), and the Foreign and India offices, London (1861–73). It is also important to note that students of design at this time were systematically exposed to these innovations, especially at South Kensington, which had its own museum of construction materials, many of which were for modern use.[11]

But the one area of architecture where the encaustic tile came into its own was in church design. With the rapid and continued growth in population throughout the course of the nineteenth century, both in Britain and the wider British world, there was an equivalent spurt in the erection of new churches. By some estimates, around 1,700 new churches were erected (with 7,000 restored) in England and Wales alone between 1840 and 1876. For those denominations concerned with decorative effect for sacramental purposes, such as Anglicans and Roman Catholics, the opportunity afforded by a material such as encaustic tiling was embraced with enthusiasm. Indeed, some of the greatest ecclesiastical architects of the period, including A. W. N. Pugin, William Butterfield, and G. E. Street, worked with tile manufacturers to achieve the best and most 'authentic' results. Therefore, to find encaustic tiles, of one form or another, on either the floor or walls (or both) of a church from this period was a very common sight, and may even be considered one of the defining features of Victorian church architecture.

Importantly, this phenomenon is evident almost as much in the British colonial world as in Britain. With a desire to emulate 'true' ecclesiological principles in colonial church design, much that was considered standard practice at 'home' was replicated as far as possible abroad, including in the realm of church furnishings. Therefore, to enter a church in a colonial town or city and find English (and later locally) manufactured encaustic tiles was a relatively common occurrence. Early examples of English tile use abroad can be found at St Anne's Chapel, New Brunswick (1846–7); the Afghan Memorial Church, Bombay (1847–65); and the church of St John the Baptist, Buckland, in Tasmania (1847–8). Larger, more elaborate designs include Christchurch Cathedral, New Zealand (1862–1904); St Patrick's Cathedral, Dublin (restored 1845–52); and St Paul's Cathedral, Melbourne (1880–91) **[33]**. Indeed, once fashionable, encaustic tiles (and terracotta) could be found in all manner of buildings in colonial settings, including major civic structures, banks, courthouses, hotels, theatres, pubs, as well as domestic environments, with the likes of Mintons and Maw & Co. maintaining a large foreign export trade. We find them in sizable quantities, for instance, in the Parliament buildings at Melbourne (1856–92) and Ottawa (1859–76); Fernberg house, Queensland (now Government House, 1865–88); the so-called 'Cathedral Room' at the old English, Scottish & Australian Bank (1880–3), Melbourne; Lanarch Castle, Otago, New Zealand (1871–87), and many more. They proved particularly popular in nineteenth-century Bombay, where they graced the floors of numerous institutions, including the Law Courts (1871–9), the David Sassoon Library (1867–73), and the University (1878).

In considering all of this, we must also take account of the power and reach of new forms of advertising, including the spectacle of commodity display associated with exhibition culture which burgeoned in Europe, Britain, and elsewhere from the late 1840s. The invention of the steam rotary press, along with type-setting innovations such as improved letterpress

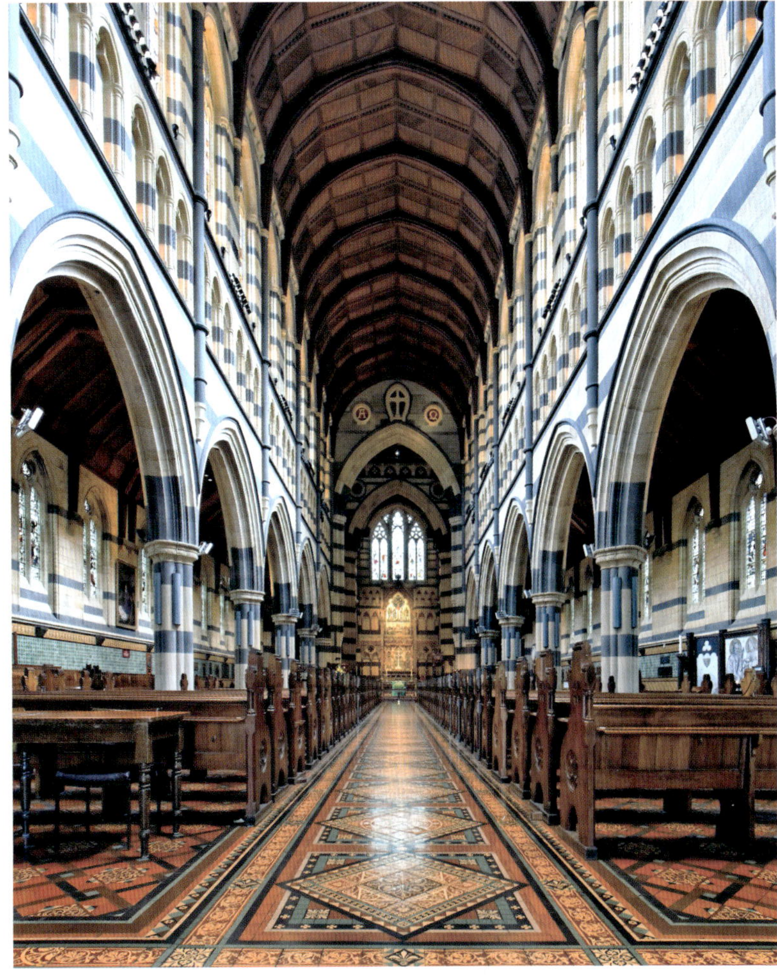

Fig. 33

Global spread of British-made encaustic tiles: interior, St Paul's Cathedral (Anglican), Melbourne (1880–1931), Australia. Original design by William Butterfield.

techniques and chromolithography, allowing for sophisticated (and thus alluring) combinations of text and image, revolutionised how manufacturers could present their wares in ever-expanding markets, including the production of illustrated catalogues. These innovations, along with those mentioned above, established a production ecology that thoroughly entwined fossil-fuel consumption, mass production, mechanisation, transportation, and marketing that made the Victorian building world what it was. Without these forces acting in tandem, it is hard to imagine what Victorian architecture would (or indeed could) have looked like.

King Coal: The Energy Factor

In order to understand this new architectural ecology and its effects on the built environment, it is important to appreciate the energy context from which it emerged. As discussed in Chapter 1, this context was neither accidental nor inevitable; nor, for those interested in the history of architecture, should it be taken for granted. Rather, it was one that was wholly recognised, planned, and legislated for. It allowed a fossil-fuel, steam-driven energy 'regime' to rise to dominance in nineteenth-century Britain, the incentives for which were compelled by the logic of industrial capitalism. This is important because it asks us to consider architecture as the outcome of energetic processes the consequences of which resonated well beyond buildings themselves, and remain with us to this day.

From the early eighteenth century onwards, coal became increasingly important as a source of energy in Britain. Initially used as a substitute for wood, it quickly proved its effectiveness at intense heat transfer. Coal's high energy density per unit mass meant that, once conditions for its controlled and efficient combustion had been established, it would become the principal energy source for industrialisation. Such had coal's dominance become by the mid-nineteenth century that in 1865, at the height of Victorian industrial transformation, the noted English economist Stanley Jevons declared it 'all-powerful'. It stood, declared Jevons, 'not beside but entirely above all other commodities', becoming the 'motive power' that underpinned the British economy.[12] Therefore, when one speaks of an 'age of coal', as Jevons does, one is effectively announcing the appearance in the Victorian period of what today would be called the 'carbon economy'.[13]

By the 1850s, coal represented an incredible 92 per cent of all annual energy use per capita in England and Wales, compared to just 10 per cent in the 1560s, and 40 per cent by the first decade of the eighteenth century. More striking still is the jump from 61 per cent in the 1750s, the very beginning of that technological transformation referred to as the Industrial Revolution.[14] This reliance on coal as a key energy input during the Victorian period has significant consequences for how we understand buildings as material objects. It cuts to the very essence (i.e., ontology) of architecture, inviting us to ask what Victorian architecture *is* as a matter of substance. Therefore, when considering the relationship between architecture and energy with respect to materiality, it is not style, theory, or patronage we must focus on, but process.

A New Material Substance

In elaborating this relationship, it is important to take a step back and ask a more fundamental, first-order question. Returning to the manufacture of bricks, this would entail examining what constitutes a brick. Although the bricks in two different buildings may look superficially similar or the same, it is possible they differ radically in terms of the way they were produced. How do such bricks differ in terms of substance? This concerns the difference between a hand-made unfired/wood-fired product versus a machine-made coal-fired one. It is this basic difference in nature that fundamentally distinguishes much so-called Victorian architecture (i.e., post-1830) from that which preceded it, despite whatever stylistic continuities may be evident. This fundamental distinction in materiality is one in which energy inputs were crucial.

As the Manchester Society of Architects report on brickwork revealed, the mechanical production of bricks had not only increased output substantially by the 1860s, it had also facilitated a supply of better-quality bricks, made to reliable standards of form, colour, density, hardness, and non-porosity (compared to the patchy quality of hand-made equivalents). Consequently, a substantive and measurable difference began to open up between hand-made and machine-produced bricks in Victorian Britain. Moreover, developments in coal-fired kiln technology made for greater scales of efficiency in terms of evenness and thoroughness of burn, producing less wastage in the process. These transformations led in turn to an equal divergence between hand- and machine-made products with respect to their aesthetic attributes, as bricks became smoother, more consistent, and 'truer' (or could be ordered as such). This new and somewhat alien degree of precision was of course something that critics of mechanised brick production were at pains to highlight. Victorian architects thus saw and appreciated (or not) these changes as they occurred.

But in order to affect such change, energy inputs were high, or at least much higher than previously. The location of brickworks along railway lines, and often in conjunction with coal pits, facilitated transportation of both energy and finished products, putting such works across the country in reasonable economic striking distance of major markets in the industrial North, the South East, and elsewhere. Although, in many cases, transporting bricks further added to the cost at point of delivery, it was generally considered a price worth paying. This applies especially to the growing taste among Victorian architects (and their clients) for polychromatic effect, requiring a variety of different coloured bricks from a number of locations. Consider, for instance, William Butterfield's insistence on using quality black bricks from Cowbridge in Wales on All Saints', Margaret Street in London (1849–59), for an astonishing £4 per 1,000 (compared to around £1 for ordinary hand-made stocks, or £2 for ordinary manufactured) **[34a]**. To be sure, a demand for hand-made bricks never ceased, especially for local markets, and disagreements over the best methods of machine production continued. Nevertheless, by the close of the nineteenth century, mechanisation of the industry, in one form or another, was all but complete.

The implications that coal-fired mechanisation had for the building industry in nineteenth-century Britain were evident across the sector, not just in brick production. There would have been no 'iron problem' in 1850s British architectural discourse, for instance, without iron; and there would have been no iron (in any significant quantity, at least) without efficient production processes driven by industrial-scale, coal-fired furnace technology. Nor would there have been any concern over the potential social and psychological malaise caused by mass production in architecture (i.e., the loss of handcraft traditions, etc.) without the advances in mechanisation that resulted from the efficient harnessing of steam power, itself only made possible (again, on any significant scale) by the effective transferral of heat energy through the controlled combustion of coal. Nor would there have been any talk of making use of richer and harder-wearing materials such as marble and granite, to any extent in Victorian architecture, without vast improvements in speedy and efficient steam-powered transportation technology and steam-driven cutting and

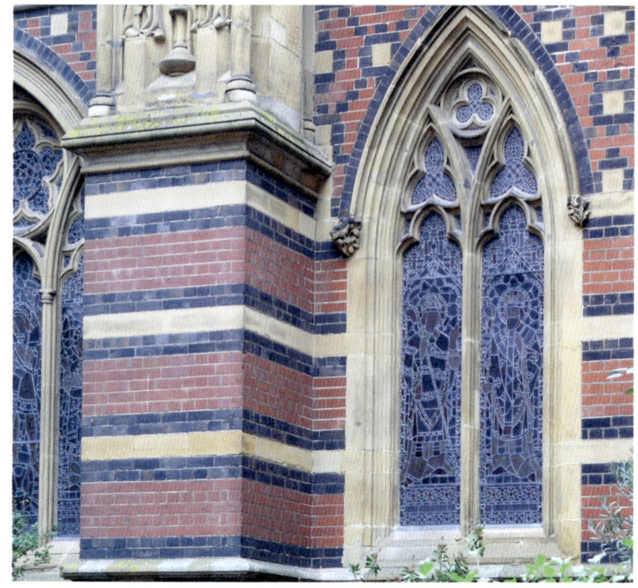

Fig. 34a

Detail, exterior nave wall, All Saints', Margaret Street (1849–53), London, by William Butterfield. Here Butterfield has used black bricks manufactured at Cowbridge in Wales.

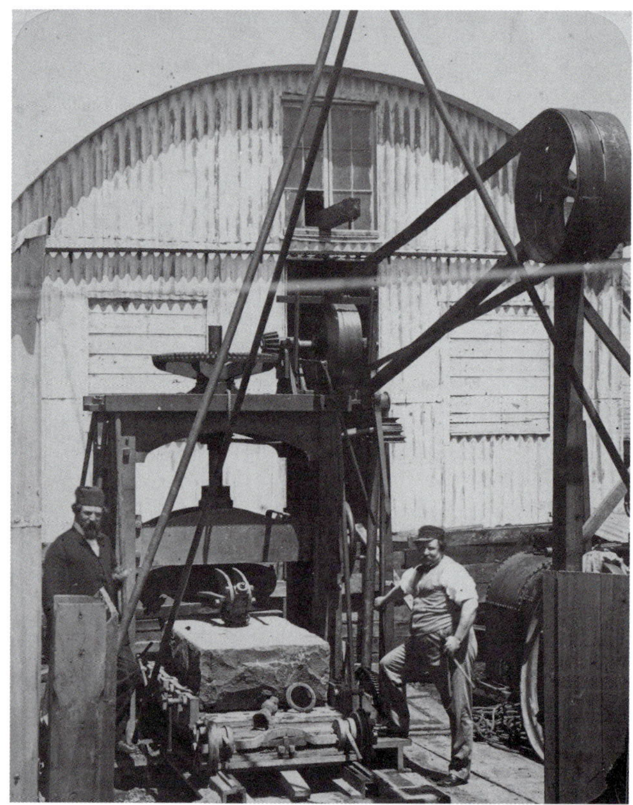

Fig. 34b

Stone dressing machine by Rentsch & Riegg in use at Thomas Glaister & Co. (*c.*1866), Melbourne, Australia.

polishing machinery **[34b]**. One might go so far as to say that the very idea of what today is termed 'High Victorian' would not have arisen without easy and relatively cheap access to modern transport infrastructure. As George Edmund Street so aptly observed, this infrastructure gave the professional architect every opportunity to familiarise himself with Continental art.[15] Moreover, once the inspiration of Continental art had been realised, its effective and widespread dissemination within the British architectural community through illustrated, high-volume book and periodical production would likewise not have been possible without the steam-powered rotary press, and the coming of the so-called second print revolution.[16]

Technological Zoning and Rotary Force

Therefore, and notwithstanding dissenting practices within movements such as the Arts and Crafts, many of the peculiarities we observe in Victorian architecture (or at least what made them possible)—the vastly increased scale, precision, material complexity, and frequency of buildings of all kinds—relate more to this condition of materiality, and the processes and procedures that governed it, than to debates over style or meaning in architecture **[35]**. Critical to the functioning of this material domain was the operation of 'technological zones'. Such zones were both physical and intellectual spaces in which technological practices, procedures, or forms of knowledge not only coalesced through cumulative degrees of productive co-dependency (say, between coal mine, railway, steam engine, and industrial furnace), but also where the differences between these were reduced and common standards established.[17] Zoning of this kind is typical of industrial regimes, where fields of qualification necessarily emerge that connect producers and consumers, knitting them into a steadily increasing regulatory framework in which industrial products and processes may be assessed and compared, and through which certain economic and political strategies can be reliably planned for and realised. The increasing standards, quality, and scale observable in Victorian architecture were a result of the performance of 'zones' of this kind. This was supported by the intellectual superstructure of the rapidly evolving sciences of geology and cartography, which came together in identifying and mapping key mineral resources, not just in Britain but across the world, in the process magnifying British industrial and political power.

The effective moment of this key transformation in the British economy was *c*.1830, with the reliable application of steam-powered locomotion, especially rotary force. Owing to the proliferation of industrial processes and networks of transportation that ensued, mainstream architectural practice became a vastly different phenomenon. Over a relatively short period of time, architectural offices became noticeably larger, more organised and technologically orientated, having transformed almost beyond recognition by century's end. Therefore, although it would be wrong to suggest that architectural design was driven primarily by technological innovation, it

Fig. 35

Granary on Welsh Back, Bristol (1869), by Ponton & Gough. The scale and material diversity of buildings increased dramatically during the Victorian period.

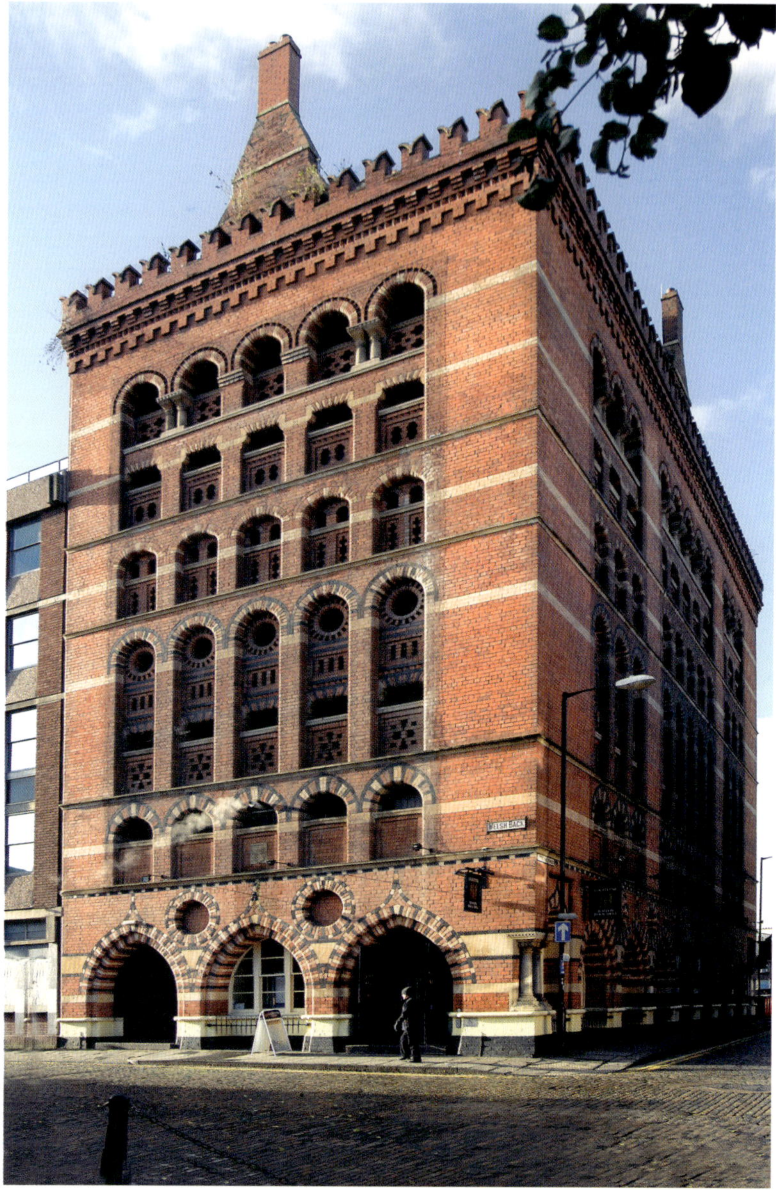

would be equally misleading to insist that such innovations were largely incidental to the design process. Architects were very much aware of the industrial transformations occurring around them, and, on the whole, not only were keen to incorporate them but also assisted in their development. As Street observed, 'architecture cannot be the best which is content to forego the use of the greatest mechanical advantages and inventions'.[18] Those architects that would succeed in this brave new world needed to adapt. After all, remarked Viollet-le-Duc, 'we possess immense resources provided by industry and ease of transportation'. It was considered remiss by many not to make use of these. Some well-known architects, such as William Butterfield, were of course still concerned to employ local materials when they could. But Butterfield also understood the value of using what the 'nineteenth century...provides'. As we have seen, others like Alfred Waterhouse fully embraced this new industrial regime and the opportunities for architectural innovation it afforded.

The Victorian building world was therefore a by-product in many ways of the advent of this system and its ecology of energy extraction, transportation, and consumption. This also had indirect consequences on architecture during the period. Consider, for instance, G. F. Bodley's design for All Saints, Selsley, in Gloucestershire (1861–2). Coming back to the idea of surplus for a moment, it could be argued that the church as it appears was largely made possible by the wealth accumulated by its patron, the textile magnate Samuel Stephens Marling, whose Ebley Mill had benefited substantially from the introduction of the power loom from the 1840s. As the church's design evolved in 1858–9, exceeding its modest budget, Marling ploughed nearly £2,000 of his own money into it.[19] This enabled Bodley's vision to be realised, connecting the church's very existence to the energy-intense processes of the mill in the valley below.

Carbon Economies of Architecture

A useful way to consider what this might mean architecturally, and thus allow us to comprehend better the radical distinction between Victorian architecture and its preceding manifestations, is to think about building assemblage via 'embodied energy', or what is otherwise referred to as a building's carbon footprint.

Embodied energy may be taken specifically as the sum of the energy requirements associated, directly or indirectly, with the delivery of a good or service. This includes the energy embodied in individual building components, such as the energy required to extract raw materials (i.e., to quarry stone, or excavate marl and clay), process them, assemble them into usable products, and then transport them to site, as well as the energy required to assemble those same components once on site, including labour. This applies especially to those industries discussed above, which, producing manufactured and thus 'artificial' building materials, contained increasing amounts of embodied energy. But it is important to remember that the processing of natural materials, such as stone and timber, was also caught up in this procurement revolution. Most timber for construction purposes in the British Isles came from abroad during the Victorian period, where it was shipped in, either from established colonial markets such as New Brunswick, or from other parts of America and Northern Europe, then processed in large, steam-driven sawing, planning, and moulding mills (see Chapter 1). Indeed, by the 1860s systematic knowledge of colonial timbers and their properties had been accumulated at institutions such as the museum of construction and building materials in South Kensington. Traditional handcraft occupations such as joinery were affected significantly by the increased introduction of efficient machinery from the 1820s, as demand and competition rose. By the 1870s, the productivity and flexibility of such machinery was being proven by its ability to handle a variety of colonial timbers then available to British consumers, demonstrated, for instance, at the workshops of Peto Brothers in Pimlico. Even within local colonial contexts, such as the Tasman region of Australia and New Zealand, sawn and pre-fabricated timber products circulated freely among colonies owing to market forces, even reaching as far as California.

It is also easy to forget just how much the development of the Victorian stone industry relied on such technologies and networks. As a result, its products contained ever-more embodied energy. A hitherto near unobtainable array of decorative and common building stones, not just from within Britain, but from across Europe and the Mediterranean basin, appeared rather suddenly in quantities and of a quality and at a cost that made them available for general use for the first time. With the reopening of ancient Mediterranean quarries, advertisements begin to appear from the late 1840s and early 1850s in the professional press, notifying architects, sculptors, and builders of new and more regular supplies of marble. Again, these developments were dependent upon a particular input of energy, whether in terms of new steam-driven cutting and polishing technology, or reliable steamship transportation, or indeed, the laying out of higher-speed and higher-capacity rail networks. This applied as much to marble and granite as to other common building stones. For instance, the dressing of Portland stone for many of London's grand civic and commercial buildings was increasingly carried out using machinery, at first steam-driven and later electrical. Indeed, as Beresford Hope observed as early as 1861: '[t]he application of coloured material—marble, brick, and so on—both to the main features and the decorative details of buildings, is every day coming into vogue with a fullness which never could have been compassed while the steam-engine was still unknown'.[20] This helped facilitate the construction of buildings that he was directly involved with, such as the church, vicarage, and choir school at All Saints', Margaret Street. Abroad, in places like Australia, commercial quarries had begun employing steam-driven haulage equipment by the 1880s, which was particularly useful in working hard and dense material such as 'bluestone' (basalt) used extensively in Victoria, for both buildings and civil infrastructure.

Therefore, what really distinguishes Victorian architecture vis-à-vis the new carbon economy is that it is fundamentally, and at base, an architecture of energy and movement—if not the first architecture of energy and movement, then at least the most vigorous and disruptive that the world had yet experienced. Architectural production during this period may, on the whole, be considered the by-product of steam-powered motive force on a previously unimagined scale: materials coming from far away, procured under increasingly mechanised conditions, entailing the consumption of fossil-fuel energy in huge quantities. When we consider further what we call 'Victorian architecture' in this context, we must understand it as a peculiar outcome of this technological shift.

But there were exceptions to this general trend, some of which are quite notable. One such is British India. As examples illustrated throughout this book reveal, a lot of magnificent architecture was produced in India during the Victorian period, by a variety of actors, both foreign and indigenous. Although the rolling out of the subcontinental railway network enabled increased capacities for long-distance haulage, labour was abundant and cheap in India compared with that in Britain. Pressure to mechanise the building industry was therefore nothing like as acute. The ready availability

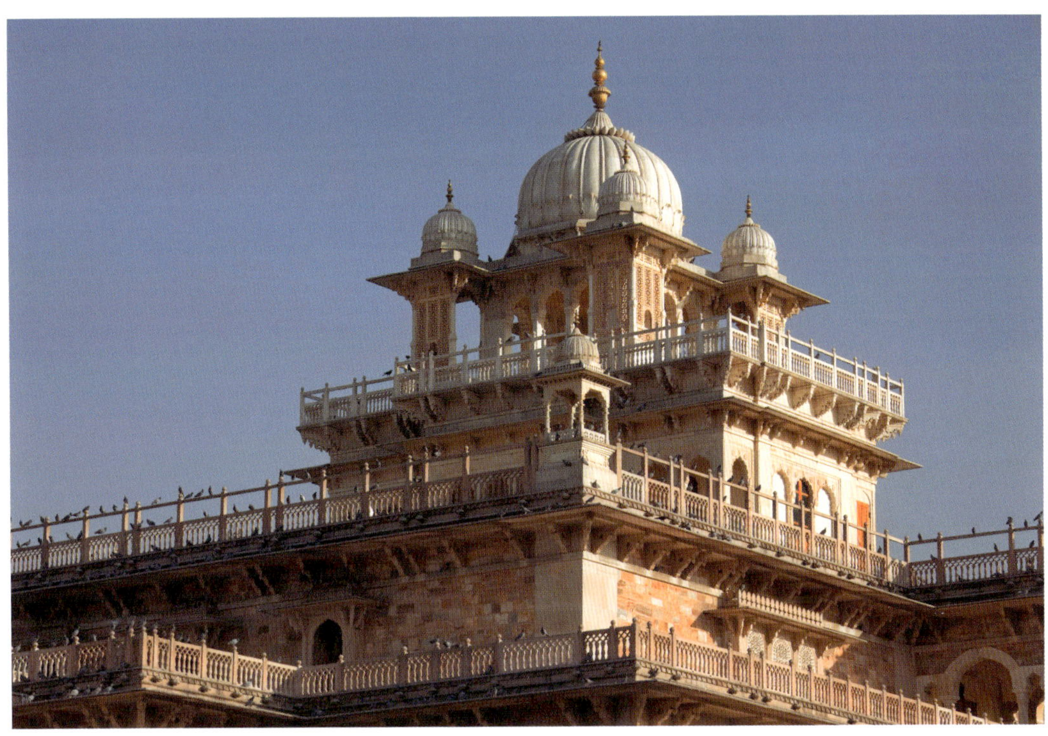

Fig. 36

Sustaining local craft traditions—Indo-Saracenic architecture: Albert Hall Museum, Jaipur (1900), in Rajasthan, India, by Swinton Jacob.

of indigenous skilled craftsmen in many parts of India (stone carvers, etc.) also meant that detailed decorative work on buildings could be carried out generously and reliably. We see this perhaps most clearly with so-called Indo-Saracenic architecture, mostly produced for the civic realm by the ruling British Raj **[36]**. The energy-to-production ratio was clearly different in these cases, but not inconsequential, and it is still useful to think of such buildings from a thermodynamic perspective, for they had various impacts politically, culturally, and environmentally. Nevertheless, by the turn of the century specialist stone-cutting machinery was being imported from Britain for the construction of major public works, such as the Victoria Memorial (1906–21) in Calcutta, including the haulage of the stone all the way from the Makrana quarries (near Jaipur) some 1,000 miles away.

While this general technological shift (and its consequences) is observable in all manner of building types and practices throughout Britain and its empire—more or less from warehouses and factories, to the grandest civic structures and domestic dwellings—a representative example is St Pancras Station in London (1866–77) **[37]**. As the London terminus of the Midland Railway Company, the materials for both the main hotel building (by G. G. Scott) and the adjoining train shed (by W. H. Barlow) came from across Britain, but largely from the Midlands. The facing portion of the 60 million bricks used in the station's construction were produced at major industrial brickworks in Nottingham and Leicestershire, while the stone used included Red Mansfield (Notts.), Ketton and Ancaster, with Shap and Peterhead varieties of granite. The ironwork came from the Butterley Company in Ripley (Derbys.), while slate roofing was

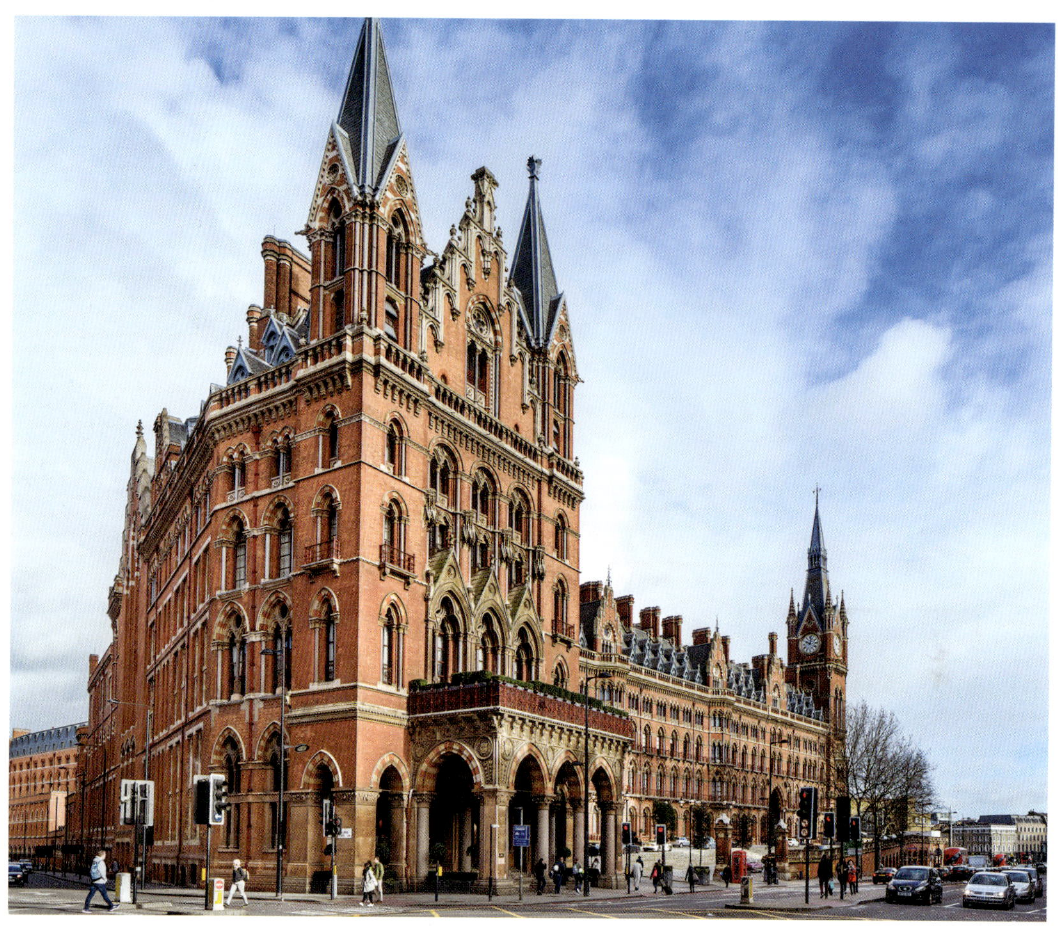

Fig. 37
Midland Grand Hotel, St Pancras Station, London (1866–1877), by George Gilbert Scott.

brought from Wales and Charnwood (Lincs.). Coal-fired industrial machinery and processes were employed throughout, even for the common bricks used in the building's substructure, which were produced at a rate of 60,000 per day, using extrusion machines and a Hoffmann kiln. In this respect the St Pancras Station complex—in both its material variety and consequent aesthetic quality—was the veritable embodiment of industrial 'zoning' and its networked connectivity.

None of this is necessarily to suggest that the connection between architecture and energy was merely taken for granted, or viewed uncritically, in the Victorian age. The associations between fossil fuel consumption, industrial production, and architecture were, as mentioned, well understood. Indeed, a more universal awareness of the potential long-term dangers of carbon-dioxide pollution had been under discussion for quite some time, as the engineer and inventor Charles Babbage observed as early as 1832. Some were extremely wary of these connections and their effects. For John Ruskin, the mining and combustion of coal had not only clear environmental impacts concerning the atmosphere, but also manifold moral consequences with respect to idleness (vital force versus mechanical force), rampant consumerism, and the disciplining of desire. The calamitous effects of this pol-

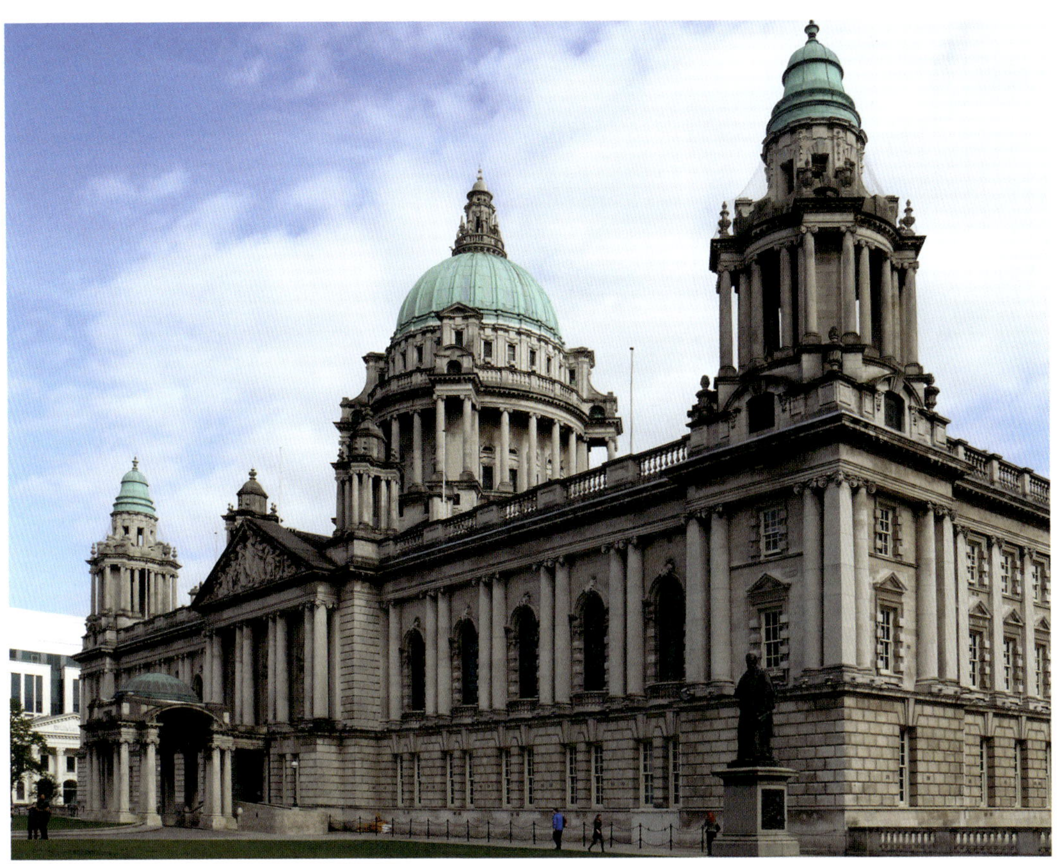

Fig. 38

Belfast City Hall, Belfast (1899–1906), Ireland (now Northern Ireland), by Alfred Brumwell Thomas.

lution, including its associated 'plague winds', were what Ruskin later called the 'storm cloud of the nineteenth century'.[21] Later, misgivings over industrial manufacturing and its effects on craftsmanship would become the *cause célèbre* of William Morris and friends, as the Arts and Crafts movement sought to strike a pose against the regrettable consequences of the new energy-rich, carbon-based economy. Traditional trades within the building industry often went on strike in protest against these consequences, particularly in relation to industrialised labour-saving technologies. We see this as late as 1900, for instance, with the anger expressed by stone masons working on Belfast City Hall (1899–1906) over the architect's proposal to use modern stone-cutting machinery **[38]**.

But none of this changed the facts, and the doubting of Ruskin and others was largely a pushing against the insuperable tide of technological progress. A new architectural reality had evolved. Increasingly fast, linear, punctiform, and thus efficient systems of modern production characterised this new carbon-rich economy, as large amounts of machine-processed material were procured and transported from point to point via rail and steamer, not only increasing quality and quantity, but also reducing time and cost. Therefore, in order to make full sense of what happened to architecture during the Victorian period, understanding the relationship between energy inputs and materiality is crucial.

Iron Age: Applied Science and Engineering

In 1863 Viollet-le-Duc noted that architecture belonged 'almost as much to science as to art'. This reminds us that not only science in the abstract, but science as applied to the practical challenges confronting humankind, was axiomatic to the Victorian frame of mind. The popularisation of scientific discourse and its methods was a general characteristic of Victorian society, as dissemination of knowledge through increased learning and publication, as well as via exhibitions, museums, libraries, and other institutions, brought science and its discoveries to public attention. This was part of a wider agenda in Victorian Britain to promote didactic utility within the public realm. Over time new levels of scientific literacy emerged, leading to new forms of political economy that tended to view both nature and society through the principles of scientific thought.

At one level, these tendencies were observable in the idea of the museum as a space of science in its own right, where its educational potential acquired new and urgent meaning (see Chapter 7). But the relationship between architecture and science perhaps took its most conspicuous form in the rise of engineering as a profession, to the point where civil and structural engineers commonly engaged in building design. Although architects grumbled about this, claiming that it was debasing architecture as an art, it occurred most often in contexts where professional architectural expertise was in short supply, and especially in colonial contexts where a military presence was strong. There are many instances of buildings (in some cases rather grand buildings) designed by royal engineering corps, especially in British India, and where engineers were embedded in public works departments. Indeed, the diffusion of industrial technology through the outward movement of British-trained engineers is what made imperialism (as a mechanism of spatial conquest) possible to a large degree.[22]

Iron Cages and Glass Boxes: Forms of Progress

Underpinning this general scientific thrust was that ever-present appeal to 'progress' in the Victorian imagination. The idea of progress was a powerful motivating factor in the 'age of improvement', and the application of scientific knowledge as a spur to technical innovation was understood as being among the primary means by which society could advance, both intellectually and materially. To many, belief in the power of science was tantamount to an article of faith. Through this the Victorians sought to bring new degrees of order to their domain. This concerned not only understanding better the mechanics of worldly phenomena (whether natural or anthropogenic), but exercising greater control over those phenomena in ways that were measured and empirical. In this regard, knowledge and understanding led not only to innovation and development but also to new regimes of evidence-based regulation and thus productive efficiency, particularly in the realms of industry and management. Again, ever-greater inputs of energy were central to realising the potential of such innovation, as powerful machinery was devised with the motive force of steam in mind. Moreover, the application of such knowledge, and its associated technical triumphalism, was one of the primary means by which Britain was able to extend its reach and influence abroad.

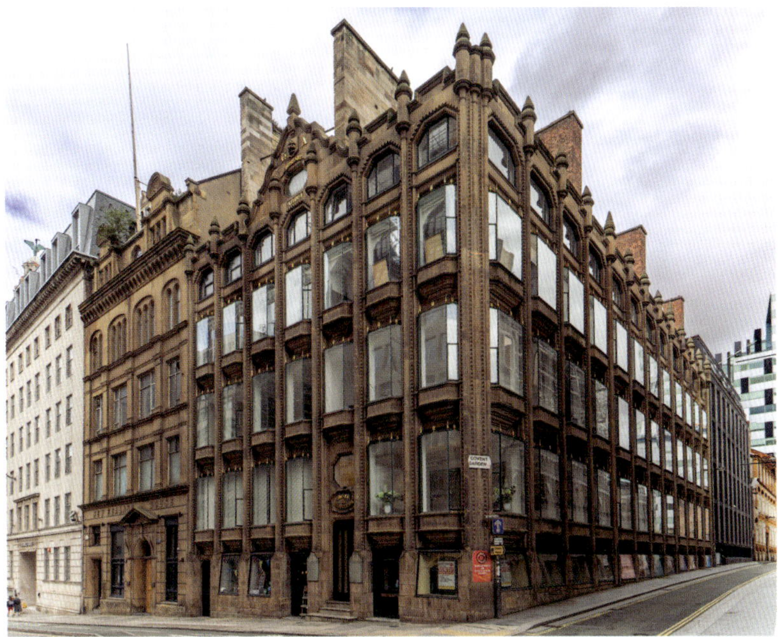

Fig. 39
Extensive use of plate glass at Oriel Chambers, Water Street (1864), Liverpool, by Peter Ellis.

This applied scientific approach, incentivised as it was by market-based capitalist imperatives, is readily observable in the Victorian brick, terracotta, and tile manufacturing industries mentioned above, where the desire to invent, improve, and rationalise products, as well as increase productivity through mechanisation, transformed procedures of material procurement. For instance, the desire to create and patent high-volume mixing, moulding, and pressing machinery in these industries demonstrated relatively high (and consistent) levels of applied scientific understanding in the development of new technology. Reporting on improvements in these industries, whether in the professional press or at learned societies, was often accompanied by no small amount of discussion concerning observation and experimentation which were seen as leading to technical breakthroughs (or failures, as the case may have been). This suggests not just that there was a push for industrial capacity in such industries, but that there was a verifiable scientific basis to them. This level of scientific regulation also helped establish industry standards and thus 'zoning' of the type already mentioned.

Glass production, too, was drawn into these processes. Although most Victorian glass was hand blown, including that for the Crystal Palace, plate glass, owing to its thickness and therefore weight, required mechanised forms of rolling and polishing. Its increased availability from 1845 transformed the streetscape of many British towns and cities, as shopfronts could now utilise great expanses of clear, uninterrupted glass (transparent walls, effectively) to display their wares to best effect **[39]**. Scientific inquiry into the chemical composition and industrial manufacture of colour also brought new levels of intensity and fixity with regard to both materials and applied surface decoration. We see this in developments in everything from stained-glass technology to wallpaper design. Amid the interminable 'fog' that cloaked so many cities and towns in the Victorian world, bright colour was considered one way of punching through the deadening atmospheric effects of industrial existence (both visually and morally). These developments enhanced the peculiar material qualities of Victorian architecture.

Perhaps the one material that symbolised this transformation more than any other, for good or ill, was iron. Some of the practical and cultural implications associated with iron in British architecture were discussed in Chapter 1, and the nexus between the rise to prominence of this material and the new energy revolution has been mentioned. In many ways, industrially manufactured structural and decorative ironwork may be taken as wholly symbolic of the new relationship between architecture, science, and energy in Victorian Britain. In its sheer novelty and artificiality, it excited and horrified Victorian architects in equal measure. The development of the iron industry and its application to architecture in Britain over the course of the century prior to 1850 was itself based in scientific discovery, and many saw it as the domain of the engineer as opposed to the architect. It had been used mainly in combination with brick as a means of developing fireproof construction in factory buildings, as seen at Shrewsbury flax mill (1797), or the rope house at Dartmouth dockyard (1812). Again, iron thus presented something of a 'problem' for the architectural profession. Indeed, it was in the constructive ambiguity between the perceived responsibilities of architect and engineer that the use of iron achieved its earliest and most spectacular potential in market halls and train stations, and where applied scientific knowledge was crucial.

Famously, the Crystal Palace, home to the Great Exhibition of 1851, captured all this promise and anxiety in a single structure **[40a&b]**. An astonishing building in mostly iron and glass, the Crystal Palace—both in its purpose, and as a material construct—symbolised modernity and the potential of industry to transform the world via 'commercial intercourse'. Its utopic aura, much commented on at the time, held out the apparent limitless possibilities that industrial production and technical precision could bring to architecture, even if some of the processes employed during its erection were not as industrialised as initially intended. Indeed, if Matthew Digby Wyatt, pointing to the 'wondrous' engineering accomplishments behind modern bridge design, had asked what such developments promised for architecture, then the Crystal Palace provided something of an answer. But it was a bracing experience. The fact that it was not only designed by the informally educated horticulturalist and engineer Joseph Paxton, inspired by his previous efforts at Chatsworth with the 'Great' conservatory (1836–40), but also realised by one of the leading engineers and contractors of the period, Charles Fox (of Fox, Henderson & Co.), struck a raw nerve with many in the architectural profession. Perhaps the building's most provocative lesson was its demonstration of the benefits of prefabricated assemblage, which seemed to vindicate efforts towards further industrialisation, modularisation, and specialisation in the building industry. From Wardian cases, to terrariums, to conservatories, to giant exhibition spaces, Victorian technologies of the transferable glass container had achieved their ultimate manifestation in the Crystal Palace as 'hothouse'. The science behind the building as such even extended to its interior decoration scheme, where Owen Jones, following colour theories proposed by the chemists George Field and Michel-Eugène Chevreul, painted the iron structure in combinations of red, yellow, and blue.

Fig. 40a

Crystal Palace (1851), home to the Great Exhibition of 1851, Hyde Park, London, by Joseph Paxton with Fox Henderson & Co.

Fig. 40b

Details of transept roof, Crystal Palace, Hyde Park, London.

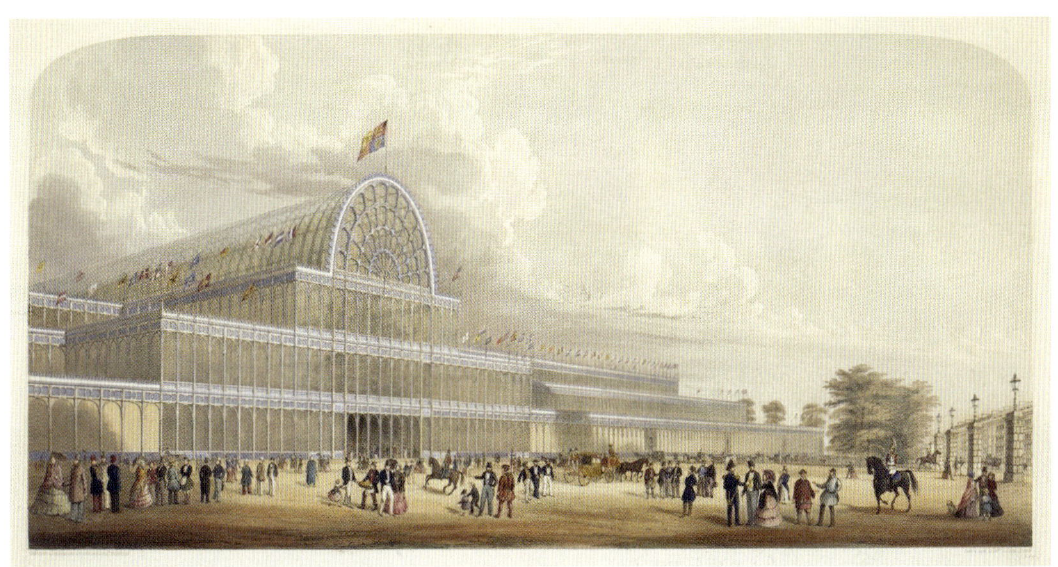

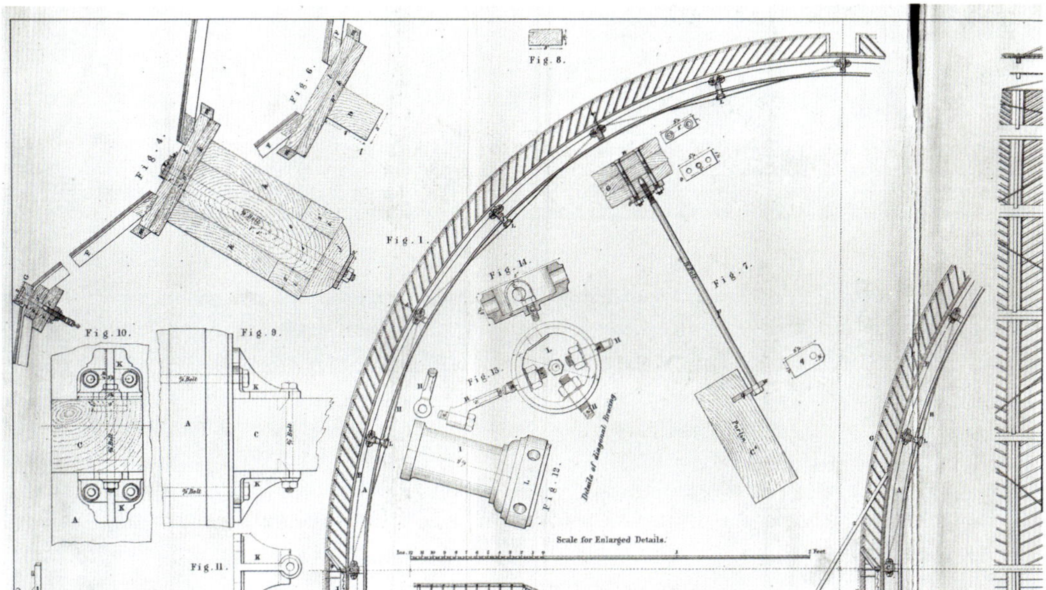

Although never fully accepted in some circles, iron, and eventually steel, would be adopted by the profession. Despite the controversy that attended them, buildings like the Crystal Palace helped smooth the way. Used in an appropriate manner, iron could, it was argued, not only enhance the underlying structural strength and flexibility of a building, but also add to its

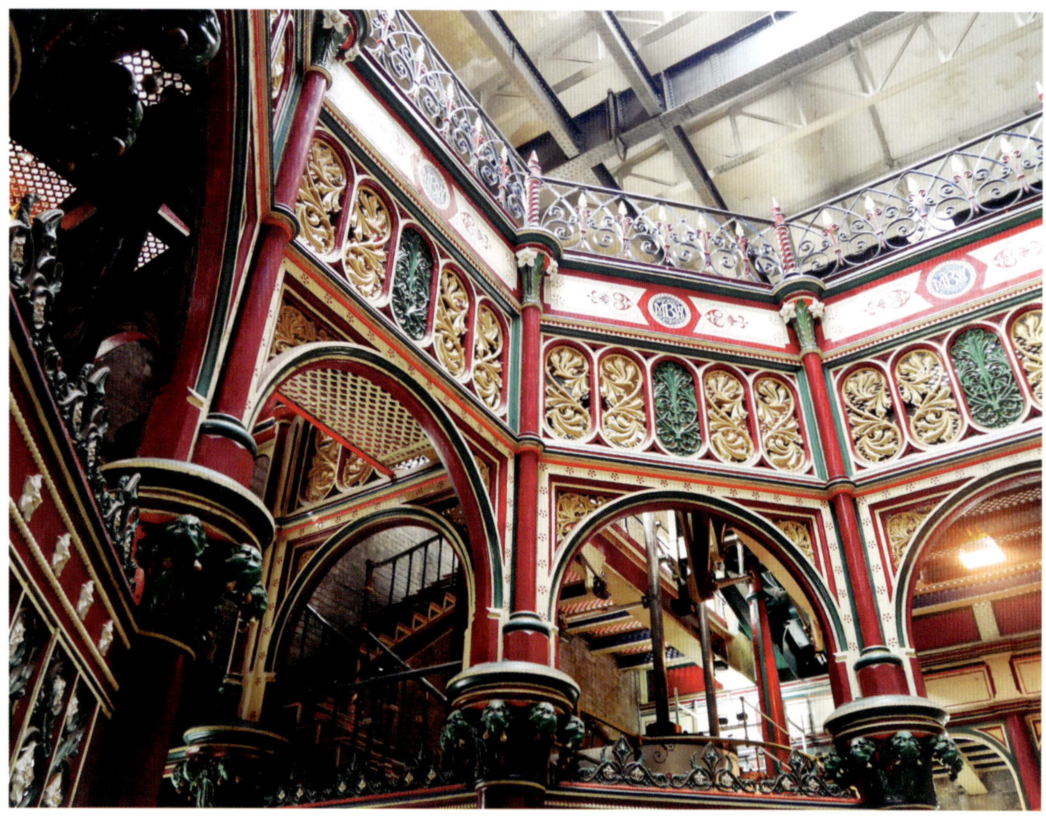

Fig. 41a

Ornamental cast-iron interior, Crossness pumping station, Kent (1859–65), by Charles Henry Driver and Joseph Bazalgette.

beauty. Even buildings that were understood as having wholly perfunctory or even insalubrious purposes, such as sewerage pumping stations, could acquire new levels of artistic pretension through the employment of prefabricated cast iron, with that at Crossness, outer London (1859–65), being among the more famous examples **[41a]**. Indeed, the manufacture of architectural components in iron led to experiments in the prefabrication of entire buildings during the Victorian period, as seen, for instance, with the façade of the Gardner & Son department store in Jamaica Street, Glasgow (1855), by John Baird **[41b]**, or the many cast-iron-fronted buildings that rose in North American cities, as in Montreal and New York in the 1860s and 1870s.[23] As discussed in the previous chapter, prefabricated iron buildings were even flat-packed and shipped abroad. Market halls, kiosks, bandstands, fountains, and even churches were sent around the world this way, many to communities across Britain's empire. Iron foundries in Britain, such as Saracen of W. MacFarlane & Co. in Glasgow and Andrew Handyside & Co. of Derby, became leaders in producing and exporting iron décor and street furniture, including benches and lampposts **[4]**. Such buildings were also coveted by wealthy and powerful Africans, such as the Efik king Eyamba V, of Calabar (*Akwa Akpa*), south-east Nigeria, where they were absorbed into the Efik political economy as status symbols.[24] Moreover, for some, iron was considered to have genuine artistic potential, as structures like the trading hall at the London Coal Exchange (1847–9), or the atrium

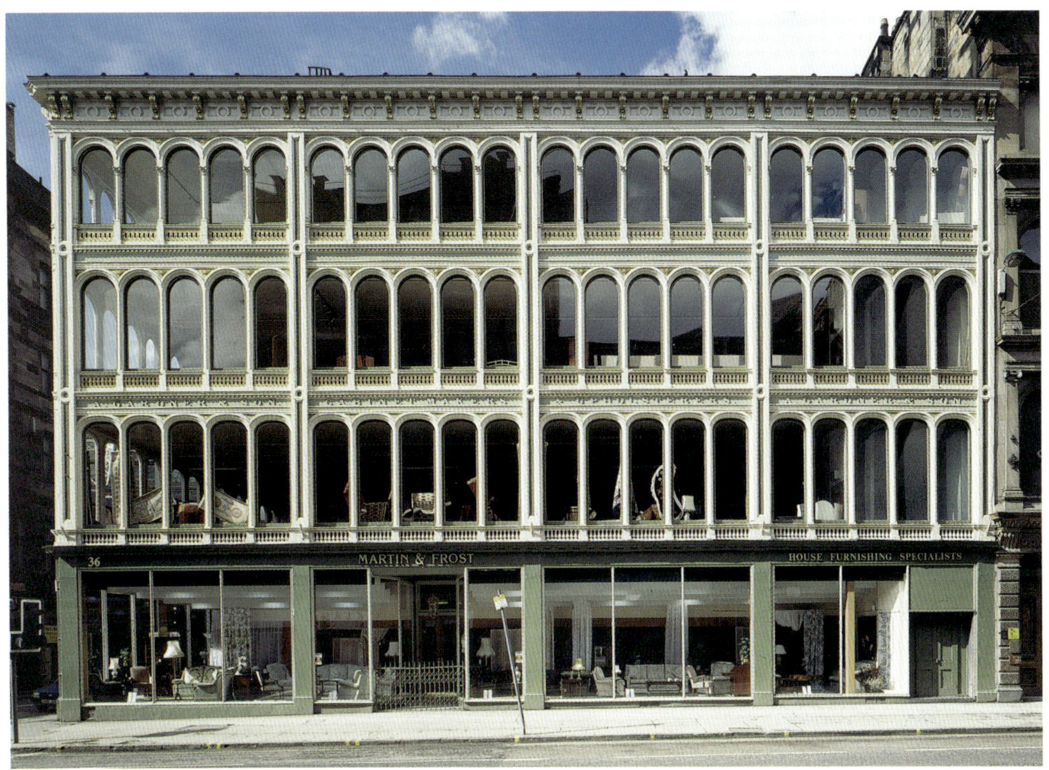

Fig. 41b
Cast-iron front: Gardner & Son department store, Jamaica Street, Glasgow (1855), by John Baird.

of the Oxford Natural History Museum (1855–60), were inclined to demonstrate **[146b]**. But the debate over how it should sit alongside more traditional materials, or achieve an aesthetic potential 'true' to its own integrity, was never fully resolved.

James Bunning's Coal Exchange building is an interesting case in point. Not only did it exemplify these tensions in the stark material and aesthetic disparity between interior and exterior, but it also, in terms of function, played a crucial role in regulating the market for industrialisation's key energy source. The cage-like countenance of the cast-iron trading hall (or court), with its ribbed dome in glass hovering high above, had the appearance of a building within a building, and one that could hardly have been suspected as one approached from the street **[42]**. The marvellous structural capacities of this iron, all 3,000 tons of it, forged in the coal-fired furnaces of Dewers on Old Street, embodied its own synergies with regard to the nation's Promethean, fossil-fuel economy. In case this was not so obvious, the hall's design motifs and applied décor, including images of fossilised ferns based on collections at the British Museum, alongside displays of botanical specimens, highlighted in plain sight the origins of coal in the tropical forests of the Carboniferous era that once blanketed much of the British Isles. Added to this were arabesque panels containing images in enamel of Britain's principal collieries. In a way, this united the building's function and decoration in bringing a popular scientific and industrial viewpoint (structurally and representationally) to what was otherwise a perfunctory business premises.[25]

Fig. 42
Interior illustration of the Coal Exchange (1849), Lower Thames Street, London, by James Bunning.

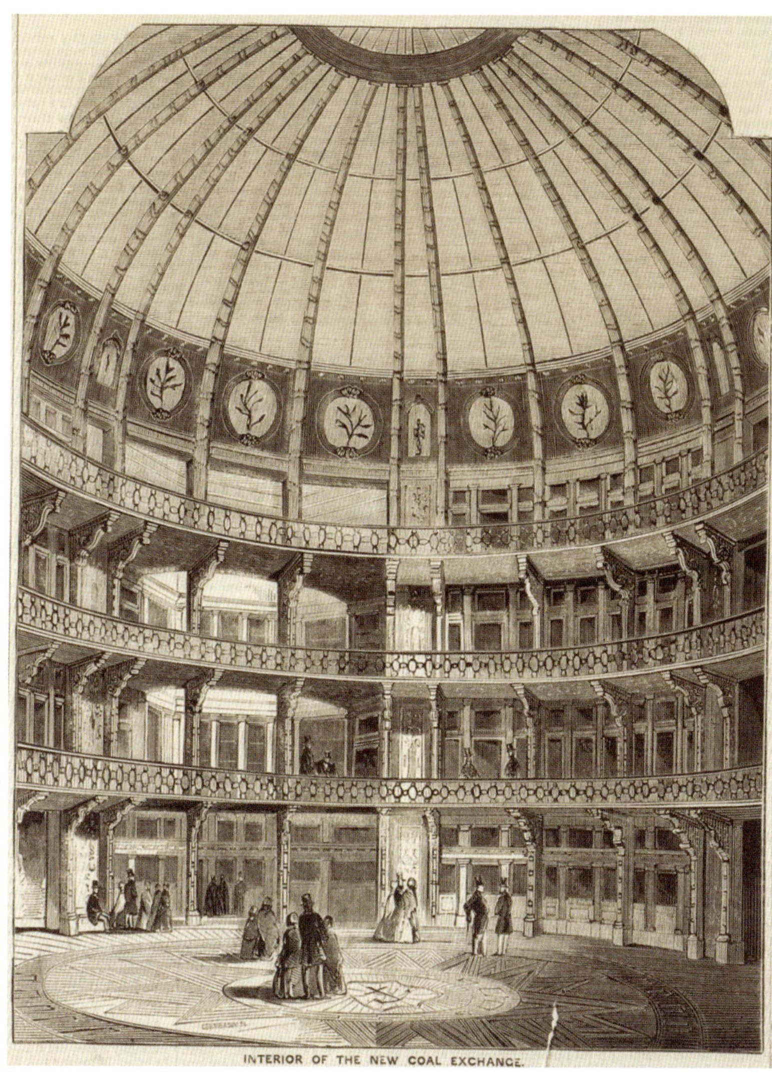

'King Coal's palace', as it was colloquially known, therefore held particular symbolic force in both its demonstration and facilitation of coal's incredible transformative power. Just as Britain's rapidly expanding rail network symbolised the security of heat energy via coal, so the Coal Exchange signified the political economy that underpinned this energy regime and its consumptive proclivities. In this one building's form, the scientific, architectural, and energetic concerns of Victorian society were inextricably entwined. This is important, for as Henry-Russell Hitchcock observed, the London Coal Exchange opened the way, conceptually, to structures like the atrium of the Oxford Natural History Museum more so than those such as the Crystal Palace or King's Cross station.

Controlled Environments: The New Architecture and Its Implications

These relationships between science, energy, and political economy were played out in other significant architectural projects at this time. Principal among these was the rebuilding of the Houses of Parliament following its destruction by fire in October 1834. As recent scholarship has shown, this endeavour was as much a technical and scientific problem as it was an aesthetic one. The question of style was of course important in such a significant building, and the way its architects Charles Barry and A. W. N. Pugin negotiated this was central to the nation's projection of itself. But how decisions were reached regarding the selection of materials and environmental controls in the building, including lighting and ventilation, were equally important for the way they captured the perceived legislative needs of a modern industrial society, and one at the centre of a global empire. This necessarily engaged the creation and application of scientific knowledge in Victorian society, and who had the authority to invoke it, when and where. As the building of the Houses of Parliament unfolded through the 1840s and 1850s, application of such knowledge became increasingly important, if fraught. From the geological insights employed in selecting building stone, to the elaborate simulated and *in situ* experiments conducted in devising the mechanical ventilation and artificial lighting systems, the new Houses of Parliament revealed the co-productive nature of the 'science of architecture' during this period. To be sure, these processes exposed a contested domain of knowledge production, often divided along social lines. Perceived as dangerous and radical by some, this knowledge both challenged and changed ideas concerning political conduct at Westminster, associated as it was with cultures of reform in Victorian Britain.

Landmark buildings that one can point to in this regard include the Reform Club, Pall Mall (1838–40), by Charles Barry, and Pentonville Model Prison (1840–2), by the engineer Joshua Jebb. As will be discussed further in Chapter 6, these buildings were considered 'mechanical' or machine-like in their way, even as forms of artificial organism, highlighting the technical and scientifically derived infrastructures that formed the basis of their performance as inhabited spaces. The Reform Club was kitted out not only with an elaborate, vented gas lighting system, but also with a steam-driven, ducted heating and ventilation apparatus. Likewise, the carefully engineered systems at Pentonville all but entirely mechanised and depersonalised the experience of incarceration, including the delivery of meals. Other notable structures that had built-in atmospheric control systems were the new British Library reading room (1852–7), by Robert Smirke, and Waterhouse's Natural History Museum. Ironically, the need for such control, especially ventilation, was a result of increased levels of pollution caused precisely by mass industrialisation. Later in the century these techniques evolved to enable so-called compact or 'deep-plan' structures that did not rely on passive, cross-ventilation but were instead designed with the increasing effectiveness and capacity of mechanical systems to artificially heat, cool, and clean air.

These systems had antecedents in the late eighteenth and early nineteenth centuries, as concepts were steadily developed and tested, but did not become either generally accepted or reliable technology until around the middle of the nineteenth century. Alongside these developments came inbuilt notions of structural and material obsolescence, as the increasingly complex and professionalised interface between engineering and economics factored time as a long-term value problem. In this sense, buildings, especially commercial ones, were now measured and understood at least partly as capital assets.[26] Moreover, biopolitical notions of 'efficiency' emerged, including social imperialism, in which techniques of spatial design and management became increasingly focused on bureaucratic productivity. What today would be called 'healthful' environments were planned, where precise levels of ventilation, communication, and illumination were specified, allowing for greater levels of wellbeing and thus powers of concentration among clerical staff. These innovations, implemented in view of the administrative advantages they would accrue via their combined effect, were understood as technologies that increased 'states of productive attention', especially electric lighting.[27] They not only created better working conditions but also facilitated instantaneous communication, both around individual buildings and beyond. However, implicit in each was the assumption that technologically assisted services, along with their social and political implications concerning environmental control and governmentality, could be secured as required through ever-cheaper and more reliable sources of energy.

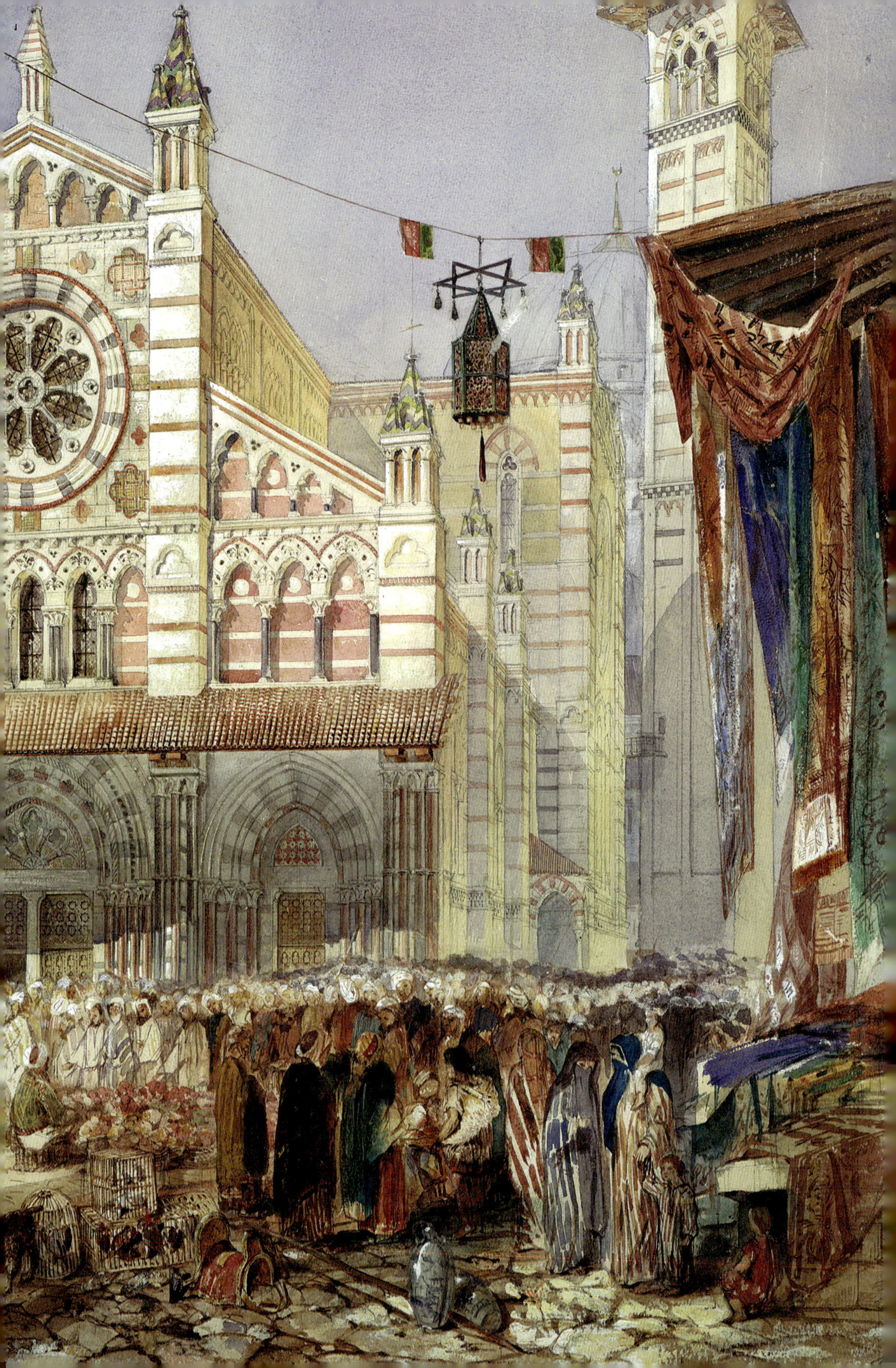

3 The Quest for Modernity: Theory and Style

Architects, critics, and historians during the Victorian period were concerned with the intellectual dimensions of the built environment. It is important to remember that like all periods and movements in the history of architecture, there were leaders and there were followers. While leaders—whether critics or designers—often engaged in debate over the state of architecture (lecturing, writing down their thoughts, and offering alternative means of development), followers were content to seize upon any 'style' that emerged from this process, reproducing it on demand. This was normal in Victorian Britain. Trainee architects under the pupillage (i.e., apprenticeship) system were initially inculcated in one or more styles by their masters, through drawing, before entering private practice on their own. Only later did schools of architecture, such as the Architectural Association, London (est. 1847), and the Liverpool School of Architecture and Applied Arts (est. 1894), instruct student architects specifically in drawing techniques, accompanied by a degree of theoretical pedagogy. We must be careful, therefore, not to overstate the pervasiveness of theoretical thinking in architecture during the Victorian period.

Nevertheless, in studying Victorian architecture closely, we can see clearly how it was shaped by a lively, and sometimes acrimonious, theoretical discussion over what style of architecture was considered best suited to the needs of a modern, 'civilised' nation state. These debates revolved largely around Classical versus Medieval forms of architecture, with one or other in the ascendency. The ensuing 'battle' over style that engulfed architectural practice through the middle decades of the nineteenth century was prefigured in certain ways, with staging posts marking its escalation along the way. One such was the standoff in Oxford between the Taylor Institution (1841–4), designed by the aging Classicist C. R. Cockerell, and the Martyrs' Memorial (1841–3), by the young Gothic enthusiast, George Gilbert Scott **[43a]**. These structures stood only metres apart, as if taunting one another from either side of Magdalen Street: the one standing for time-honoured tradition, the other for the possibility of a new way forward. The brewing tension over style represented by these two, very different structures was exacerbated through the rise in the 1840s of professional architectural literature, in the form of journals, magazines, books, and other special interest publications. The advent of the steam rotary press, along with the lowering and eventual abolition of taxes on paper, allowed architectural debate to

Fig. 43a

Stand-off—Magdalen Street, Oxford: Taylor Institution (1841–4), by C. R. Cockerell, and the Martyrs' Memorial (1841–3), by George Gilbert Scott.

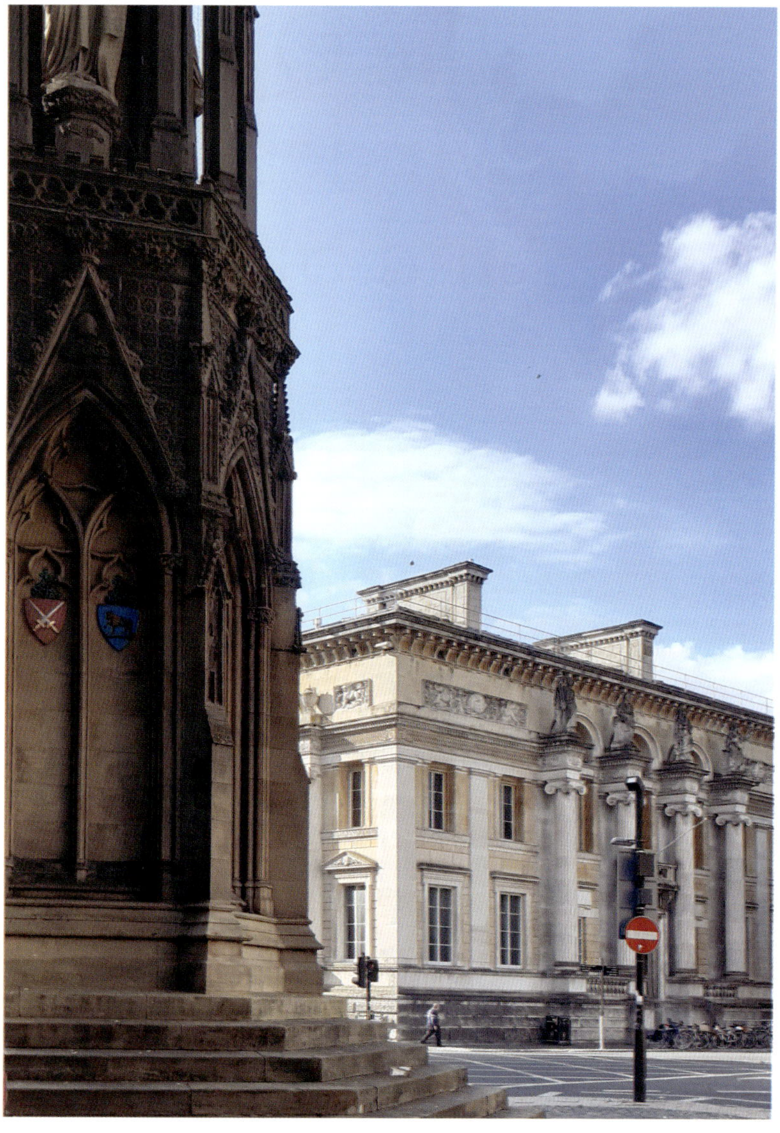

engage a much wider audience. Ideas concerning architecture were therefore central to the evolution of the Victorian built environment.

It is important to emphasise, however, that there was no single moment when thinking on architecture transitioned from being 'Georgian', or 'Regency', to 'Victorian'. Coming into the Victorian period the world of British architecture was still largely dominated by theories pertaining to the Classical tradition. This was underpinned by an elite cultural worldview that was more than just architectural.[1] To be sure, what became known as the Gothic Revival (or 'Gothick' as it was initially termed) had already made significant inroads in British architectural discourse and practice, associated as it was with broader theories of the picturesque, Romanticism, and antiquarianism. But when it came to the design and erection of major buildings, institutional or civic, one or other form of Classicism prevailed. As we shall see, the rebuilding of the Houses of Parliament in a Gothic style at this early stage was the exception (a rather prominent one) that proved the general rule that Classicism was considered the hallmark of civilised European society.

Although perhaps the deepest fault line in Victorian architectural theory, the tussle between the Gothic and the Classical was but one among numerous such skirmishes, and there were many. Therefore, I will not attempt here to cover every intellectual ripple that broke over the surface of Victorian architecture. Instead, I will focus on the main lines of debate and influence. My aim is to delineate the principal contours of Victorian architectural thinking, while capturing something of its complexity.

Classical Continuity: History and Tradition

Despite the deep and solid foundations of Classicism in Britain, it had begun to bifurcate by the early nineteenth century. The 'rediscovery' of Ancient Greece through grand touring, archaeology, and publication (prints and books) steadily impacted on ideas regarding 'civilisation' and pan-European culture through the latter half of the eighteenth century. Hellenic idealism emerged partly in response to the perceived inadequacies that had begun to taint the values and institutions of the Romano-Christian tradition in Western culture, as intellectuals sought new, more 'original', and thus purer civilisational roots, especially in the face of societal disruption and change.[2] This was aided by the fact that the educated classes in Britain were already familiar with the ancient world through their study of Greek and Latin in school and at university, facilitating a focus on the achievements of the Greco-Roman past and modern society's relationship to it. At the time, this Hellenism equated to ideals of beauty and perfection found only, it was believed, in ancient Greek buildings. This idealism was enveloped to some extent in the romance of what the architect William Wilkins described as 'Athenian magnificence'. Moreover, Joseph Gwilt claimed in his *Encyclopaedia of Architecture* (1842) that the new taste for Greek architecture had introduced a much-needed 'chasteness and purity' into British architecture, an influence considered more in keeping with the 'refined' Anglo-Saxon temperament.[3] Thus, although Rome had long held a special place in the cultural imagination of the educated elite in Britain, Athens was catching up.

The revival of Greek taste in British art and architectural design perhaps left its greatest impression following the transferal of the Parthenon marbles by Lord Elgin from Athens to London in 1803. The stimulus these great sculptures affected upon artistic production at the time, especially after they went on display in 1807, witnessed a marked increase in the frequency of Greek-style buildings in the rural and urban landscapes of modern Britain. Publications, too, exerted a powerful influence. Volume One of James 'Athenian' Stuart and Nicholas Revett's *The Antiquities of Athens* had first appeared as far back as 1762. But the publication of the final three volumes much later, with the fourth only materialising in 1816, allowed the Greek Revival to draw upon a live scholarly tradition. This was augmented by a spate of additional publications, including the *Antiquities of Magna Graecia* (1807) and *Atheniensia*

(1816), by William Wilkins; *The Temple of Jupiter Olympius at Agrigentum* (1830), by C. R. Cockerell; and F. C. Penrose's *An Investigation of the Principles of Athenian Architecture* (1851). Distinguished architects of the Regency period, such as Wilkins, Decimus Burton, John Nash, John Soane, Cockerell, and Robert Smirke, all produced noteworthy buildings in a neo-Greek mode, some with more fidelity than others. Here we may point to Wilkins's projects for Downing College, Cambridge (1807–20), and University College London (with J. P. Gandy-Deering, 1827–8); Soane's 'wall' façade to the Bank of England (1823–6); Nash's Carlton House Terrace, London (1827–9); and Smirke's British Museum (1823–47) **[43b]**.

The Greek Revival was felt particularly intensely in Scotland, and especially in Edinburgh, the so-called 'Athens of the North'. There, architects—engaged by both the picturesque topography of the city (often likened to that of Athens itself) and its celebrated reputation as a centre of intellectual progressiveness (i.e., Scottish Enlightenment)—were inspired to create the 'Periclean dream' anew, through the erection of civic institutions and public monuments in a distinct Greek Revival style. Plans included a proposal to build a replica of the Parthenon atop Calton Hill, to a design by C. R. Cockerell and William H. Playfair, in memory of those who had fallen in the Napoleonic Wars (1803–15). Begun in 1822, this particular venture remained unfinished, however, and stands to this day as a conspicuous modern ruin. But many other notable Greek Revival buildings were completed in Edinburgh. These may be counted among the very finest of Greek Revival structures produced anywhere in the world at the time, and include Thomas Hamilton's Royal High School (1825–9) and Burns Monument (1830), on Calton Hill, and Playfair's Royal Scottish Academy (1822–6) **[44]** and Surgeon's Hall (1829–33).

These developments are important because they demonstrate how the long-standing inspiration that British architecture drew from the Classical traditions of ancient Greece and Rome, as well as their mediation through

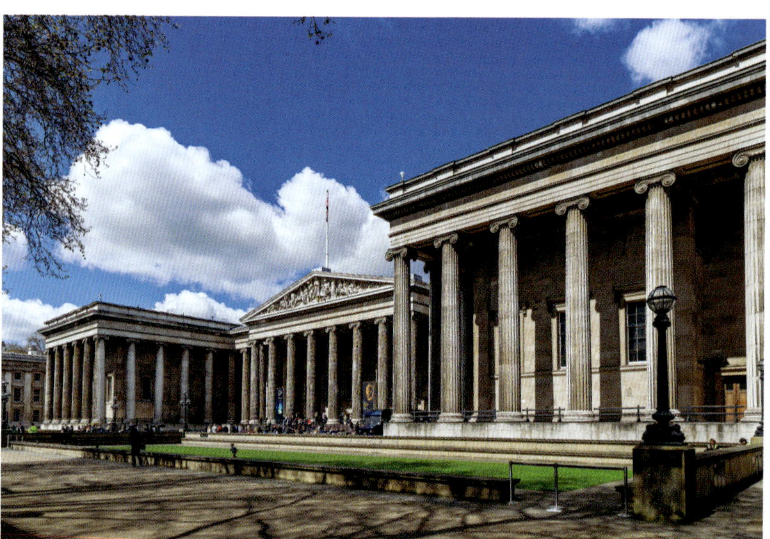

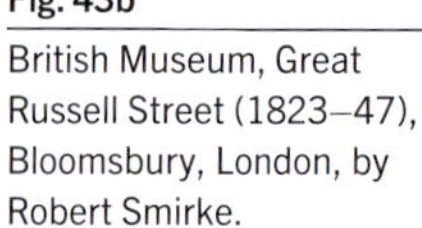

Fig. 43b

British Museum, Great Russell Street (1823–47), Bloomsbury, London, by Robert Smirke.

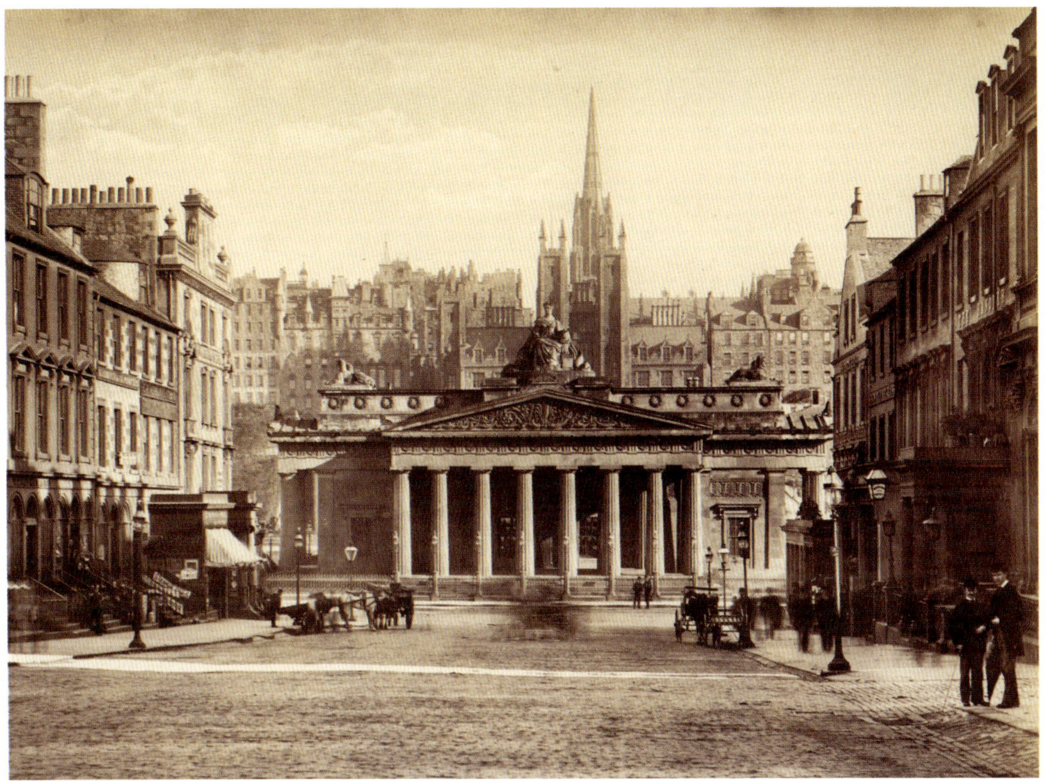

Fig. 44

View looking south down Hanover Street, Edinburgh, to the Neo-Greek splendour of the Royal Scottish Academy (formerly Royal Institution), by William Playfair. The twin Gothic towers of New (theological) College (1845–50), also by Playfair, can be seen beyond, and the spire of Victoria Hall (Presbyterian church, 1842–4), by J. Gillespie Graham, beyond that.

the Renaissance, remained a dominant intellectual force coming into the Victorian period. Many such notable buildings were either designed or completed during this time, including the British Museum (not finished until 1847) and Birmingham town hall (1832–61). Other notable buildings in the style from this period include Euston station Arch (propylaeum), London (1836–9), St George's Hall, Liverpool (1842–54) **[45]**, and the Scottish National Gallery, Edinburgh (1850–7). Leading architects, such as Cockerell, Smirke, Charles Barry and T. L. Donaldson, continued to advocate for the Classical style well into Victoria's reign.

Morality and Meaning: The Burdens of Truth

Charles Robert Cockerell was among Britain's most knowledgeable authorities on ancient Greek and Roman architecture. His ideas on the universal validity of the Classical tradition reached a wide professional audience through his Royal Academy lectures between 1841 and 1856, which were reported regularly in the influential architecture magazine, *The Builder* (est. 1842). Although Cockerell had many misgivings over the use and abuse of the Classical style in contemporary British design, he nevertheless focused his students' attention on what he saw as the underlying principles that governed ancient form-giving, consisting primarily of order, geometry, proportion, and mass. In essence, these constituted stability, in turn revealing (and thus perpetuating) a certain 'truth' in good design. Employed correctly, these principles, as facilitated through close and faithful study of the

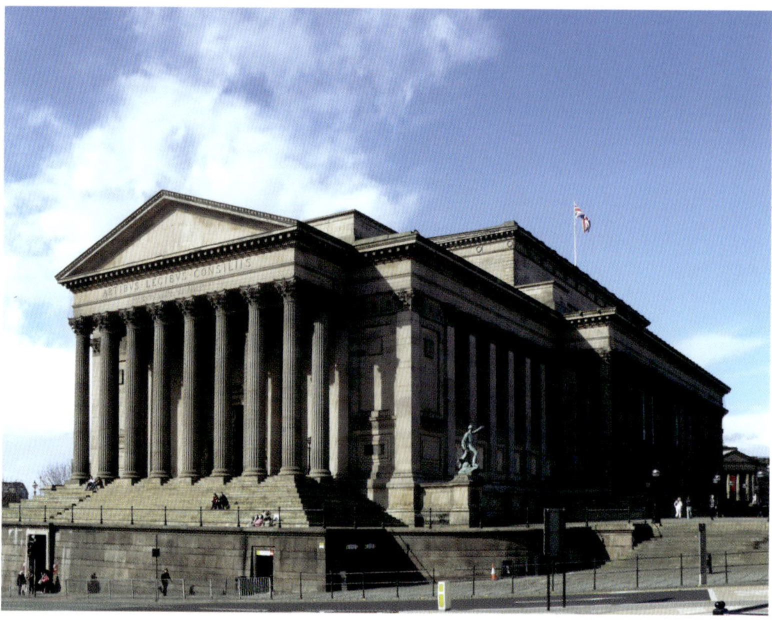

Fig. 45

St George's Hall, Liverpool (1842–54), by H. L. Elmes and C. R. Cockerell.

Classical orders, had the potential to connect architecture meaningfully with the past.

In this sense, Cockerell stressed that architecture 'belonged' to history, and if 'calculated for endurance to the future she *must* be founded on the principles of the past'.[4] Such thinking was intended to imbue the Classical orders with continued relevance beyond matters of mere 'style'. It also connected architecture with notions such as morality, social order, and identity, including the God-given perfection of the human body. Thus, built form was a true mark of accumulated wisdom and 'civilisation'; as Cockerell had learned from the Greeks, architecture was essentially a manifestation of culture. As will be discussed further in a moment, one can see how such a theory aligned with wider social and political ideas regarding constitutional stability and European civilisational order as time-honoured 'constructs'. Architecture's past was the theoretical justification for building in the present; history *was* theory.

But there was an important if somewhat veiled undercurrent at work in this. At the foundation of architecture was an ever-growing emphasis on the value of accuracy and truth. This was associated with the rise of serious, scientific antiquarianism in Britain, which, in its modern form, was a product of eighteenth-century Enlightenment rationalism. What came with this was a new archaeological bent in the analysis and understanding of historic buildings, and how this knowledge might be applied in producing a better and more principled kind of architecture. There was, of course, something of a myth of purity in this, which was connected in its own way to a particular romantic idealism. Nevertheless, the search for new, elemental truths in architecture would come to overlap neatly with the widespread renewal of Christian values in British society during the late eighteenth and early nineteenth centuries, particularly among Evangelicals. This included new emphases on moral and ethical probity which seeped deep into the body politic.[5] Moments of political reckoning, too, such as the Reform Act of 1832 and the Chartist movement, had fomented a mood of change and uncertainty. Theories of architecture during this period should not be intellectually dissociated from these tectonic cultural shifts. Thus, in architecture and its attendant theorisation there was the inherent possibility of something 'revealed', whether it be the mysterious workings of the Almighty, or critical insights from the ancient past.

William Whewell, Robert Willis, and the New Scientific Method

It was around this time (the 1830s and 1840s) that influential architectural thinkers such as William Whewell and Robert Willis emerged to take the understanding of architecture to new levels of scientific attainment. These were men of a particular scientific bent. There was Joseph Gwilt, older than Whewell and Willis, who had already shown a concern for the comprehension of mathematics and geometry as applied to architecture in his *Rudiments of Architecture* (1826) and *Encyclopaedia*. But Whewell and Willis were of a different order. Both were also concerned more with Gothic architecture than Classical. Dedicated interest in medieval architecture had been growing throughout the course of the late eighteenth and early nineteenth centuries in Britain, connected to Romanticism and ideas of national origins. To be sure, antiquarians had been busy documenting great church and cathedral buildings for quite some time, and it would not be long before the novels of Walter Scott, such as *Ivanhoe* (1819), made all things medieval fashionable. But behind this lay an increasing desire to understand Gothic architecture properly, and to dissect it analytically as a process of design and construction, including the presentation of certain 'facts' concerning its history. From this came such influential publications as Thomas Rickman's *An Attempt to Discriminate the Styles of English Architecture* (1817), A. C. Pugin's *Specimens of Gothic Architecture* (1821), and John Britton's *The Architectural Antiquities of Great Britain* (1826), which provided something of a basis for a more 'correct' form of Gothic Revival architecture, especially as they appeared on the cusp of a new church-building age in Britain. Rickman's treatise was also significant for its breaking down of Gothic architecture into phased periods of development corresponding to distinct formal traits ('Norman', 'Early English', 'Decorated', and 'Perpendicular'), revealing the emergence of a certain taxonomic understanding of built form. This demonstrated a need for constructing a consensus-building vocabulary for the analysis of architecture which was itself informed by strategies of knowledge production in contemporary scientific discourse.

Both Whewell and Willis took this endeavour seriously, contributing significantly to the analytic vocabulary of architecture. As both would go on to hold chair professorships at the University of Cambridge in science-related subjects, scientific method percolated freely through their architectural thinking, in the process lending the study of historic architecture a degree of authority it had previously lacked. For Willis, evidence-based measurement was considered key in building up a more scientific picture of what architecture was and how it changed over time. This rather instrumental approach allowed for more accurate and reliable (i.e., rational) comparison between different periods of architectural development. Drawing on modern scientific terminology, such an inductive approach relied on the compilation and classification of what Willis referred to as 'specimens' of observed architectural detail, such as vaulting patterns or window tracery, from which certain general rules about the history of architecture might be inferred. Like great static machines, Gothic churches were therefore seen to comprise a series of interdependent members of construction, evincing a theory of structure Willis called 'membrology'. This approach was couched within an evolving discourse concerning the significance of measurement to faithful knowledge production in Victorian Britain, which, like concerns over taxonomic classification in Rickman, aligned with evolving societal values relating to matters of truth, accountability, and natural hierarchies.[6]

Whewell's approach, on the other hand, was more philosophical. Affected appreciably by German Idealist thinking which was exerting its influence in Britain, Whewell had greater sympathy than Willis for the representational capacities of architecture. Where Willis was primarily focused on the 'mechanical' side of architecture's development, largely ignoring its 'decorative' dimension, Whewell understood that architecture was animated just as much by cultural concerns, and that it could be seen as the embodiment of an idea. To his mind notions of the vertical and Gothic architecture were inextricably linked. Through such a connection, Gothic architecture spoke to certain self-evident truths about Christianity, 'exhibiting in the leading lines of its members, and the aspiring summits of its edifices, forms "whose silent finger points to heaven"'.[7] Such an understanding is what Whewell described as the 'philosophical investigation' of architecture's 'principles', which he believed was necessary for a complete apprehension of architectural change through time.[8]

A. W. N. Pugin and the Medieval Ascendency

Whewell and Willis, and the antiquarian and philosophical traditions they epitomised, may be seen as representing two aspects of a 'modern' understanding of architecture that intersected neatly with the rise of the mature Gothic Revival in Britain around the mid-1830s. It was at this point that the Gothic began to challenge seriously for the first time Classical orthodoxies in British architecture, on a broad front, both religious and secular. Although the revival of Gothic (or 'Gothick') forms in architecture had been long underway, it was figures such as A. W. N. Pugin, and organisations like the Ecclesiological Society, that translated historical perspectives on architecture into clear and urgent theories for practice. This was the Victorian Gothic Revival's 'big bang' moment. Pugin was a trailblazer in this regard. His own buildings led by example (see Chapter 5), but two of his publications in particular had a considerable impact on the way architects reformed the principles upon which buildings were designed, and the perceived role that architecture was understood to play in shaping society at large. Both were highly polemical in nature, appealing strongly to Christian sentiment.

The first of these publications, to give it its full title, was *Contrasts: or, A Parallel Between the Noble Edifices of the Middle Ages, and Corresponding Buildings of the Present Day; Shewing the Present Decay of Taste*, published in 1836. In many ways, the title spoke for itself, prefiguring the trenchant nature of the content within. The main text amounted to thirty-five pages of passionate, morally inflected prose. Through its unflinching, rhetorical force, its aim was to jolt architects (and no doubt their clients) from what its author saw as their unfeeling and irreligious ignorance. To aid in this endeavour, Pugin included twelve whole-page illustrations (plates), each containing two examples of old and new 'contrasted', which captured in a visually striking way the difference between good and bad design.

Pugin, like Whewell, was inclined to emphasise the psychological dimensions of architecture, focusing on the relationship between ideas and form. The principal 'idea' in the book was the righteousness of true Christian faith: the liturgy and lessons in devotion that were writ large through its great historic monuments, particularly those of the medieval past. In this sense, Pugin saw architecture as a type of moral machinery. Yet, concerned as he was with veracity, Pugin also stressed that his conclusions were derived from a careful and serious observation of extant buildings and ancient Catholic liturgy, invoked as hard evidence of correctness in design—a commitment elaborated in his *Glossary of Ecclesiastical Ornament and Costume* of 1844. His basic argument was that, having strayed from the foundational principles of faithful building design, architecture in Britain had deteriorated to a point of utter debasement. Being a Roman Catholic, to which faith he converted in 1834, Pugin blamed this decline on the Protestant Reformation, which, he believed, had irrevocably fractured Christian Europe's great unifying vision, with devastating consequences for 'true art'. The result was that both architecture and modern society had reverted to a type of shallow and utilitarian 'Paganism'. Although Pugin was against bad architecture in all its forms, including 'carpenter's Gothic', Classicism was his primary target, which promoted what he saw as a creed of deceit through structural discord and superficial décor.

The one aspect of his polemic that seemed to cut through most forcefully, however, was the readily comprehensible notion that good architecture was founded not on the whims of stylistic 'fashion' but on 'sincerity and reality'. For Pugin, it was the pursuit of such Christian values through design that were best calculated to 'advancing the cause of truth over that of error'. Here was the idea that architecture must, above all, be an exercise in integrity; indeed, that the 'great test' of beauty in this regard was the 'fitness of the design to the purpose for which it is intended'. In other words, that the form and use of a building ought to correspond to such an extent that 'the spectator may at once perceive the purpose for which it was erected'. This is what he would later refer to as the 'propriety' fundamental to all good design.

At the core of this zero-sum moral equation was the powerful if not explosive insinuation that architecture was a reflection—indeed, a kind of ethical barometer—of the social condition of those who created it (i.e., modern Britain). This thinly veiled rebuke came across even more clearly in the second, much expanded, edition of the book which appeared in 1841. In this version additional plates were inserted, including the now famous ones depicting a 'contrast' between a fictitious English town in 1440 and 1840, and 'Residences for the Poor', comparing an 1830s workhouse with a medieval alms-house **[46a]**. These effectively highlighted the apparent decline not only in beauty, taste, and wellbeing in Britain, but also in morality. Not surprisingly, most of the buildings on the adverse side of these comparisons

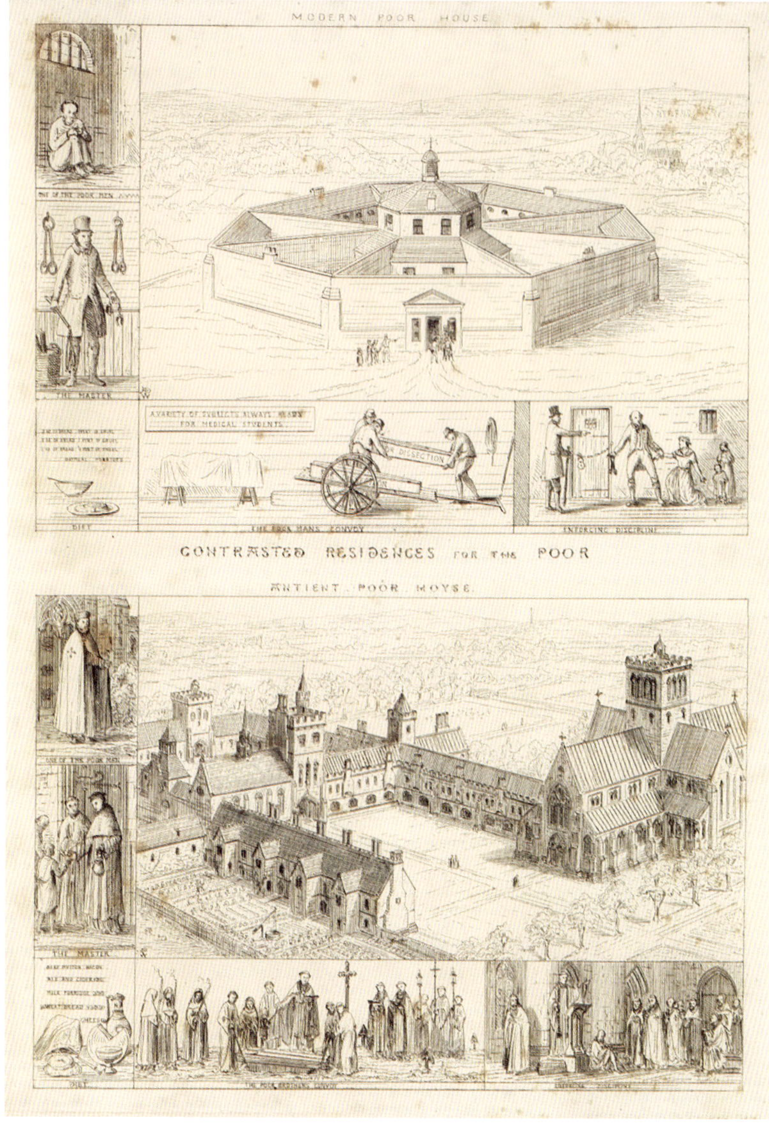

Fig. 46a

'Contrasted Residences for the Poor', from A. W. N. Pugin, *Contrasts; or, A Parallel between the Noble Edifices*...(1841).

were forms of derived Classicism. These insights of Pugin instantly and permanently changed the terms of architectural debate, both in Britain and throughout much of the Anglophone world.[9]

These themes were picked up and amplified in Pugin's second major publication, *The True Principles of Pointed or Christian Architecture* (1841). Here he laid down what he considered to be the two 'great rules' of architectural design: 'that there should be no features about a building which are not necessary for convenience, construction, or propriety', and 'that all ornament should consist of enrichment of the essential construction of the building'. Like the two great commandments upon which Christian law hung (Matthew 22:40), these were Pugin's response to what he saw as the

Fig. 46b

Page showing illustrations that highlight 'true' design from false, in A. W. N. Pugin, *The True Principles of Pointed or Christian Architecture* (London, 1841). The top illustration shows the essential form of a finial; the bottom one, the double and 'dishonest' structure of the dome of St Paul's Cathedral, London.

CHRISTIAN ARCHITECTURE. 9

by the majority of persons as mere ornamental excrescences, introduced solely for picturesque effect. The very reverse of these is the case; and I shall be able to show you that their introduction is warranted by the soundest principles of construction and design. They should be regarded as answering a double intention, both mystical and natural: their mystical intention is, like other vertical lines and terminations of Christian architecture, to represent an emblem of the Resurrection; their natural intention is that of an upper weathering, to throw off rain. The most useful covering for this purpose, and the one that would naturally suggest itself, is of the form represented in the annexed figure: only let this *essential form* be *decorated* with a finial and crockets, and we have at once a perfect pinnacle. Now the square piers of which these floriated tops form the terminations are all erected to answer a useful purpose; when they rise

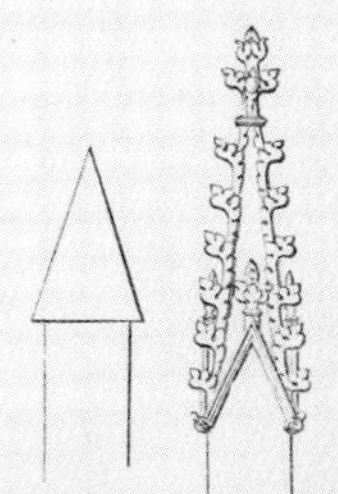

nexed section, the upper part of St. Paul's is mere imposing show, constructed at a vast expense without any legitimate reason.

From the various symptoms of decline which I have shown to have existed in the later pointed works, I feel convinced that Christian architecture had gone its length, and it must necessarily have destroyed itself by departing from its own principles in the pursuit of novelty, or it must have fallen back on its pure and ancient models. This is quite borne out by existing facts. Now that the pointed style is reviving, we cannot successfully suggest any thing new, but are obliged to return to the spirit of the ancient work.

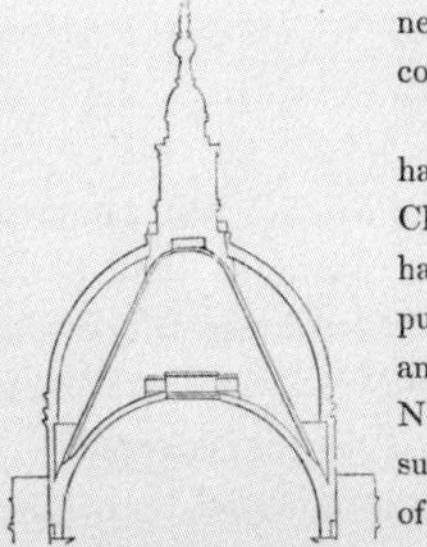

Section of the Dome of St. Paul's.

Indeed, if we view pointed architecture in its true light as Christian art, as the faith itself *is perfect, so are the principles on which it is founded.* We may indeed improve in mechanical contrivances to expedite its execution, we may even increase its scale and grandeur; but we can *never successfully deviate one tittle from the spirit and principles* of pointed architecture. We must rest content to *follow,* not to *lead;* we may indeed widen the road which our Catholic forefathers formed, but we can never depart from their track without a certainty of failure being the result of our presumption.

carelessness and confusion of his own day. In one form or another, they were to resonate profoundly through architectural discourse for much of the nineteenth century. Again, as with *Contrasts*, the primary meta-themes here were the dual principles of honesty and truth; that architecture should make no attempt to conceal or deceive **[46b]**. Importantly, embedded within this theory of propriety was an argument for adhering to 'national' precedent. This clearly had implications for how architecture could be understood in relation to identity, a concern that would gather pace in the decades succeeding the appearance of *True Principles*. Indeed, the relationship between identity and built form would become one of British architecture's most vigorously defended (and contested) symbolic registers, shaping such infamous and long-running controversies as the 'Battle of the Styles' (see Chapter 4).

The Camdenians and the Advent of Ecclesiology

A major obstacle faced by Pugin was his Roman Catholicism. Although Roman Catholic civil disabilities had been relieved ('emancipated') in the United Kingdom through act of parliament in 1829, much social prejudice remained. This made many suspicious of Pugin's motives, let alone his brand of architecture, which some were inclined to view as 'popish'. This was especially the case among Evangelicals, particularly Nonconformists. Although many recognised the underlying religious and moral justifications of Pugin's arguments, his polemics required support from a trusted quarter if they were to gain wider traction. As it happened, this provision came from the established Church of England, which was then going through its own reformist convulsions in the guise of the Oxford Movement. This process of Anglican renewal was based largely on a reinvigoration of theology, doctrine, and teaching, led by a number of Oxford clerics, including John Henry Newman, Edward Pusey, and John Keble. It was part of a wider reformist agenda within the Church that saw it as a rather moribund institution coming into the second quarter of the nineteenth century, and in dire need of reconstitution. Reform of the institution itself was one thing, and government would see to that through the Ecclesiastical Commissioners, but the spiritual side sought inspiration in first principles, looking back to earliest (so-called 'primitive') times for guidance on the fundamentals of 'Catholic' faith. This renewed focus on the liturgical functions of the Church necessarily had an architectural dimension. How, it was now asked, should space be formed, used, and also decorated according to the 'true' rites of Christian worship?

What emerged from this concern were powerful, special interest organisations dedicated to a better understanding of church architecture. The first of these was the Oxford Society for Promoting the Study of Gothic Architecture, establish in February 1839. It was followed very shortly afterwards by the Cambridge Camden Society, founded by two Trinity College undergraduates, John Mason Neale and Benjamin Webb. It was hoped the advent of such organisations would amplify the morally resolute tone that now characterised the Gothic Revival, and it did. But it was the latter of these organisations that had the greatest impact on church design and restoration, not only in Britain but across the wider English-speaking world. Essentially, the ambition was to elevate church design and liturgical arrangement to a level of seriousness not seen since the Middle Ages. In this respect, the Society's stated aims were clear: 'the theory and practice of ecclesiological architecture; the investigation of Church Antiquities; the connection of Architecture with Ritual; the science of Symbolism: the principles of Church Arrangement; Church Musick and all the Decorative Arts'. Their basic rules pertaining to church design were equally explicit: let 'the bones...be constructed before the flesh which covers them. Chancel and nave, altar and font, secured, any thing [*sic*] else may be boldly added'. Although this led initially to accusations of copyism, knowing what a church *was* became the first, unconditional step on the way to a better, more religious, and liturgically literate society.

The term 'ecclesiological' is key here. The Camden Society's initial adherence to the perceived conventions of English medieval church architecture led to the development of an approach known as 'ecclesiology'. Corresponding with their stated aims above, what this essentially amounted to was a form of antiquarian study that yielded authoritative rules for design based on ancient (i.e., early Medieval) precedent. It was according to the diktats of this new 'science' that the Society's ideas concerning 'correctness' in Anglican church architecture gained sway. Through publications such as the *Transactions of the Cambridge Camden Society*, *The Ecclesiologist* (from 1841), and *Instrumenta Ecclesiastica*, the views of the Camden Society were widely disseminated, particularly among architects and the clerical elite, both at 'home' and abroad **[47]**. Remaining true to their ideal, the Society would later change its name to the Ecclesiological Society (1845), removing itself from Cambridge to London. This new-found seriousness connected the activities of the Society to the ideas of Pugin, thus enabling a conduit through which his basic precepts—propriety, truth, and the axiomatic rela-

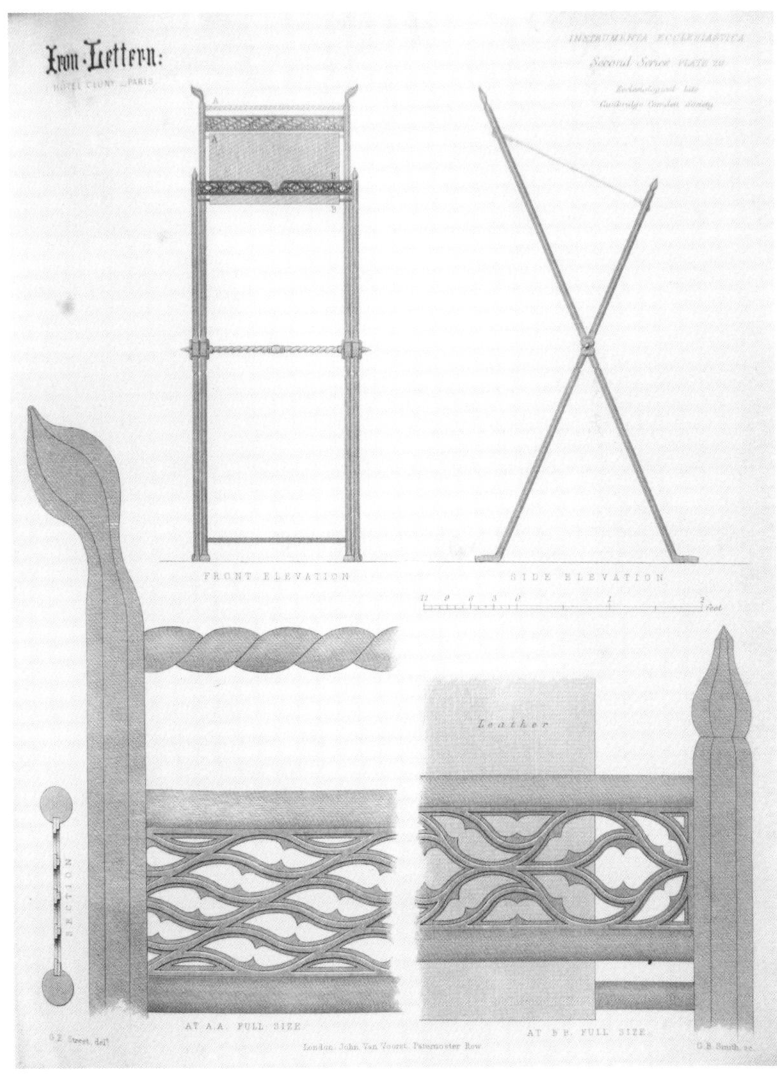

Fig. 47

Elevations and details of foldable iron lectern, from *Instrumenta Ecclesiastica* (1856), published by the Ecclesiological Society. This publication was designed to offer, and make widely available, 'correct' working models for ecclesiastical buildings and furnishings.

tionship between Gothic architecture and Christian values—could begin flowing into the wider world of church design in Britain.

Indeed, much like Pugin, the Ecclesiological Society's view on the fundamentals of 'correct' church design were nothing if not puritanical, and enforced with an unrelenting and at times cruel authoritarian zeal. For a moment their power within the confines of the established Church seemed almost limitless, with their influence extending to the most minute detail, whether on matters concerning furnishing, stained glass, decorative sculpture, church plate, or even embroidered altar frontals. The regeneration of interest in architectural symbolism was also one of their pet enterprises, injecting something of a new intellectual earnestness into discussion and debate around sacramentality and 'æstheticks' in church design—an agenda that was well calibrated to the needs of a literary culture inclined to 'read' meaning into the world around it (see Chapter 5). On this matter the Ecclesiologists found it necessary in 1843 to translate and reissue an edition of William Durand of Mede's thirteenth-century treatise on church symbolism, *Rationale Divinorum Officiorum* (*c.*1290), prefaced with a 135-page 'introductory essay' by Neale and Webb on the significance of this all-important principle.[10]

The Theory of Development: Time and Change

The other aspect of the Ecclesiologists' remit was to influence church building not only 'at home' but also 'in the Colonies'. This endeavour would come to affect what is perhaps the Society's greatest intellectual legacy: the idea of 'development'. I will discuss this idea further in Chapter 5, but let us observe for now that the idea of development was one that drew its power from resonance with the most profound scientific, philosophical, and theological questions of the day. These questions equated broadly with the concept of evolution, or mutation through time. The rising influence of natural theology in the curricula at Oxford and Cambridge in the early decades of the nineteenth century, along with its steady infusion into the minds of the reading public, left its mark on a generation of intellectuals, including architects. The quasi-evolutionary theses of scientists, philosophers, and theologians such as William Paley, Charles Lyell, William Buckland, John Henry Newman, and Robert Chambers, not to mention the startling evidence of industrial 'progress' that was visible all around, began to shape this generation's view of the physical, social, and historic structures of the phenomenal world. The notion of 'development' was one that a number of key figures in the world of British architecture wrote about in the 1840s and 1850s, including G. G. Scott, A. J. B. Beresford Hope, E. A. Freeman, and George Edmund Street. The basic idea was that change, or the intrinsic evolution of architectural form and structure, was not only a good thing, but also a natural one, associated as it was with an invigorating force that kept architecture a 'living' art. These ideas helped shape appreciably what later became known as the 'High' Victorian movement in British architecture (*c.*1850–70).

In the minds of those who formulated it, this idea was essentially a rejection of style for style's sake in favour of a deeper, more synthetic approach to architectural design. The foundational premise of the developmental thesis as it applied to architecture was that, if true principles (*à la* Pugin and the Ecclesiologists) were followed at all times, then modern architects were free to seek inspiration from wherever they saw fit, within the Christian world and beyond. The caveat was that this ought to be within the confines of the pointed arch, but could incorporate features from other traditions, such as the horizontal 'repose' (sense of weight and solidity) of Classical architecture. At one level, this eschewing of a parochial perspective on architectural design coincided with English architects' new-found interest in Continental ecclesiology, especially French and Italian. Such an approach, it was believed, would breathe new life into modern British architecture, allowing it to evolve in novel and interesting ways, without deviating from standards of integrity, or having to resort to the repetitiveness of 'pure' or narrowly defined national styles.

The history of architecture, too, was increasingly influenced by this changed context, with writers and critics such as E. A. Freeman, A. J. B. Beresford Hope, and James Parker encouraging a developmental perspective. Taking such a view of 'history' was of course operative in the sense that it, too, was attempting to influence contemporary practice. For the likes of Parker, the new geological sciences, including stratigraphy, provided an entirely novel conceptual language for understanding architectural change through time, in which the idea of stone was key. In this schema, and taking his cue from Buckland, the revelation of vast geological periods observable in the earth's crust provided crucial historiographic insights, pointing to a 'development' from one medieval stylistic phase to another, from 'Norman' to 'Third Pointed'. Taking a different tack, and before Parker, Freeman proposed a parallel history based on cultural rather than natural development that sought to explain the rise and superiority of Gothic architecture **[48]**.[11] His essential thesis, in line with a number of other theorists at the time, was that architecture should be understood as a manifestation of the ethos (i.e., 'spirit') of the culture from which it emanated, and, like so many 'species' in competition, was capable of not only development but also stasis, even decay. In these ideas the historical understanding of built form was infused with a sense of urgency in suggesting that architecture had always evolved, and must continue to do so.

But when it came to practicalities, there were other considerations to bear in mind. Ecclesiologists were keen to point out that, although an Englishman abroad might well prefer the architecture of his own country, in particular 'English Pointed', it could not be condoned as 'the model for every church in any climate'. Adaptive modification, or what became known as 'appropriateness', was vital to the successful transmission of British architecture into the colonial world. If, it was declared, the question of 'ecclesiological developements [*sic*]' was now pertinent, then British architects must 'develope aright'. As discussed further in Chapter 5, this concerned how, for instance, a church building in a foreign land could best respond to prevailing conditions, not only of climate but also of materials **[49a]**. Considering the privation associated with most foreign missionary environments, it was even conceded that if a 'church be of mud, it may still be a church'.[12] Again,

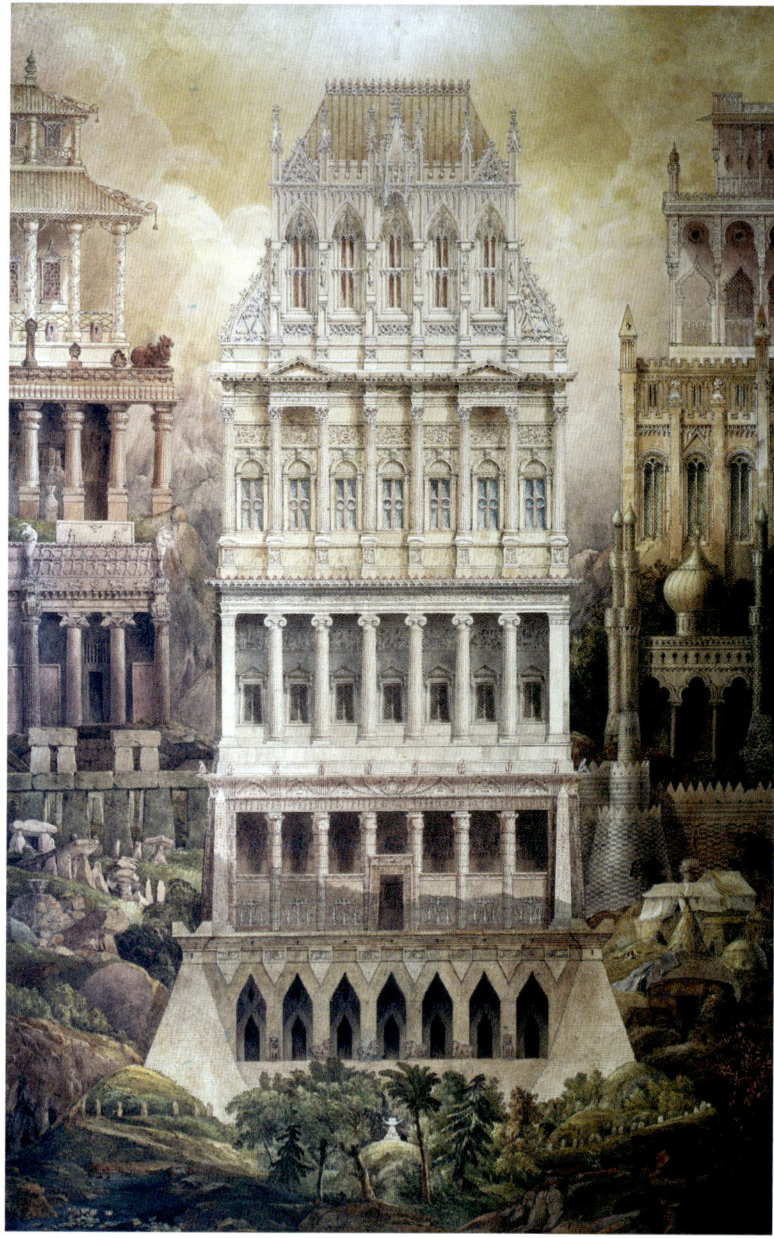

Fig. 48

J. M. Gandy, *Comparative Architecture* (1836). Gandy's image conveys a connotation of the 'stratification' of architectural style through time, with the concocted edifices emerging from the geological substrate of the earth itself.

this spoke to the imperative of fundamental liturgical considerations over merely aesthetic ones in architectural design.

This line of reasoning was pursued by Beresford Hope, who, like Freeman, extended it beyond climate into the realm of culture. His notion of progression by eclecticism—or 'development' by another name—encouraged a cross-fertilisation of styles and forms that would reflect the increasing reality of Britain's position in the world as the metropolis of a burgeoning global

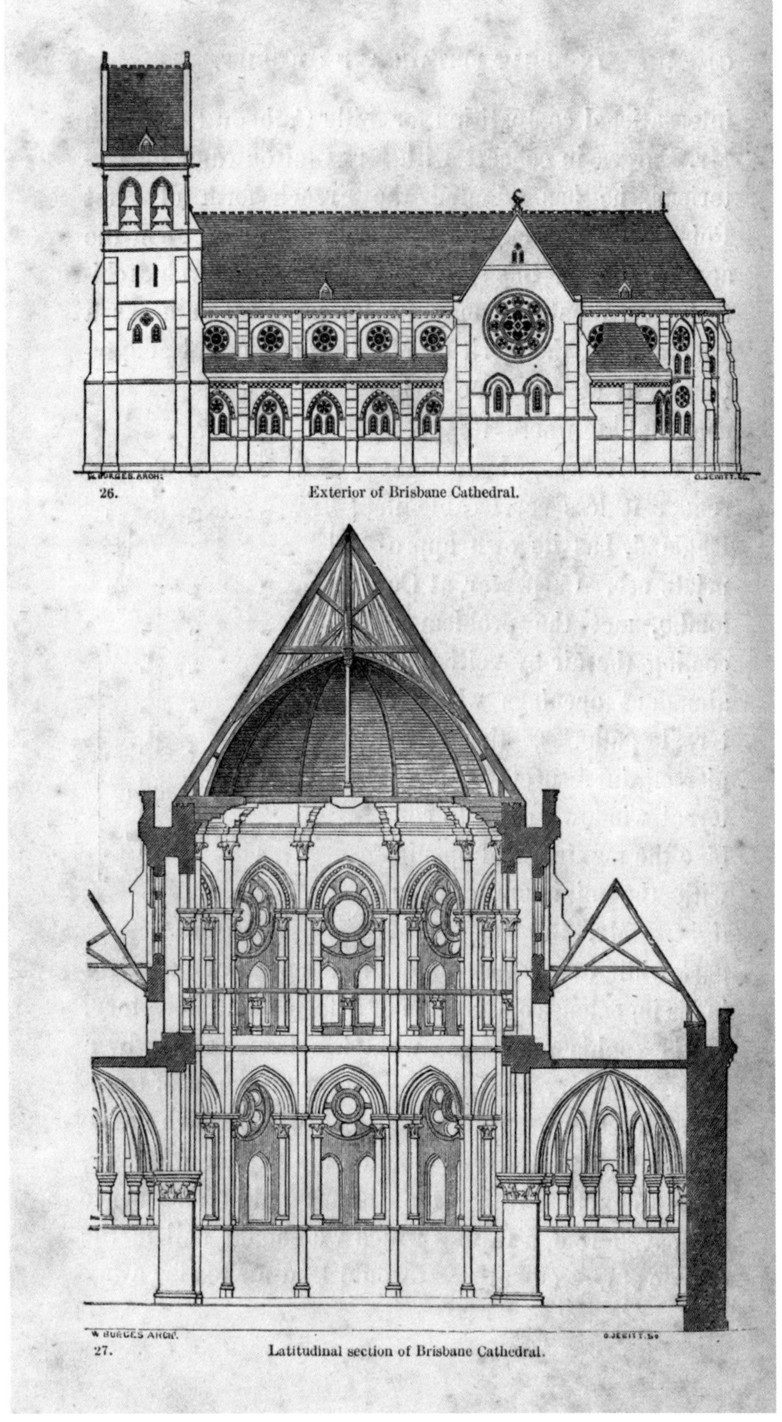

Fig. 49a

Elevation and section drawings of William Burges's unexecuted design for Brisbane Cathedral (1860), Australia, from A. J. B. Beresford Hope's *The English Cathedral of the Nineteenth Century* (1861).

empire. 'We must not for this discovery confine ourselves to England or to the Western Church,' he implored:

> we must penetrate to the East and her venerable heredity uses...we must be as familiar with San Clemente, Santa Sophia, and the church of the Holy Sepulchre, as with Heckington and York Minster...We should remember that Great Britain reigns over the torrid and the hyperborean zone, that she will soon have to rear temples of the True Faith in Benares and Labrador, Newfoundland and Cathay.[13]

But this, as Beresford Hope would later make clear, was no call for random eclecticism, less still a pitch for architectural relativism. On the contrary; such architecture should progress, ideally, from an Early English base, or perhaps from an early French or Italian one, depending upon location and climate **[49b]**.[14]

However, such a theory posited the architecture of European, and specifically English, civilisation at the heart of what was considered truly

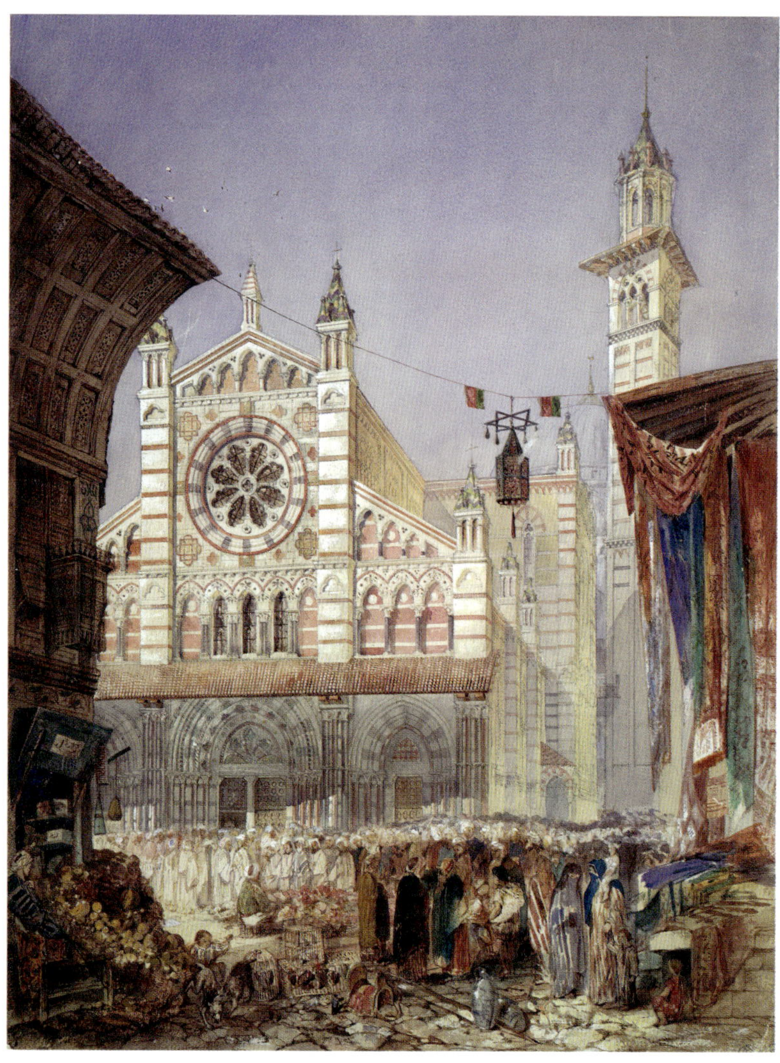

Fig. 49b
Cultural and climatic adaptation: William Burges's unexecuted design for the Crimean War Memorial Church (1851), Constantinople (Istanbul), Turkey.

progressive, suggesting the architecture of other, 'lesser' civilisations as suitable only for secondary purposes, if at all. This kind of thinking had its corollary in the views of British architects and critics on non-Western architecture in general, including that of James Fergusson, John Ruskin, and Freeman, as being essentially static or debased, despite whatever beauty it may have possessed at first glance. Ironically, Fergusson, although producing the first great histories (in the modern sense) of the indigenous architecture of the Indian Subcontinent, proclaiming its sublime magnificence, was nevertheless quick to condemn it as not only inferior to the great Western traditions of Greece and Rome, but also the product of a civilisation in a state of social and intellectual decline. Profoundly immersed in an Enlightenment worldview, with its unwavering belief in Western superiority and standards of comparison, the likes of Fergusson could only see non-European architecture in ultimately negative terms. What such thinking highlighted, apart from anything else, was an underlying racism. This was part of the Victorians' narrative understanding of the historical development of architecture, globally considered, and how their own history and accomplishments were seen to fit within it.

This musing over architectural development in diverse global contexts betrays this theory's indebtedness to the fact that Britain was the metropolis of a worldwide empire, demonstrating the two-way exchange that gave the idea its apparent legitimacy. This confirms that Victorian architecture relied to a certain extent on an imperial horizon, even when not explicitly stated.[15] Even John Ruskin's hugely influential *The Stones of Venice* (see below) can be interpreted in this way, as an allusory warning concerning the potential fate of modern Britain, with medieval Venice once having been a small island state in command of a mercantile empire. Colonial architecture itself was of course directly informed by the outward transmission of such ideas, and there were many designers and theorists, both in Britain and abroad, who gave considerable thought to how basic European forms could be adapted to foreign, climatically extreme conditions. Without this diffusion and exchange of knowledge and ideas, one cannot be certain that the theory of 'development' would have arisen in quite the manner that it did, let alone have achieved global influence.

John Ruskin and Nature's Lesson

The historical and theological implications of sciences such as geology and palaeontology were profound, especially for the way they challenged conventional notions of biblical time in the Victorian imagination. Creation was no longer seen as a sudden, unique event but one that was progressive, over eons. Geological strata, and the remnants of organic matter they contained, such as fossils, demonstrated successive cycles of decay and renewal, indicating an evolutionary process from simple to complex life forms **[50]**. For some, this exploded the 'myth' of biblical history, thus undermining Old Testament truths; for others, it was still God's work.

We have already seen this in relation to James Parker, but such themes were especially present in the ruminations of John Ruskin, the most eloquent and influential architectural critic of the age. Among the more compelling features of Ruskin's voluminous writing on architecture, and

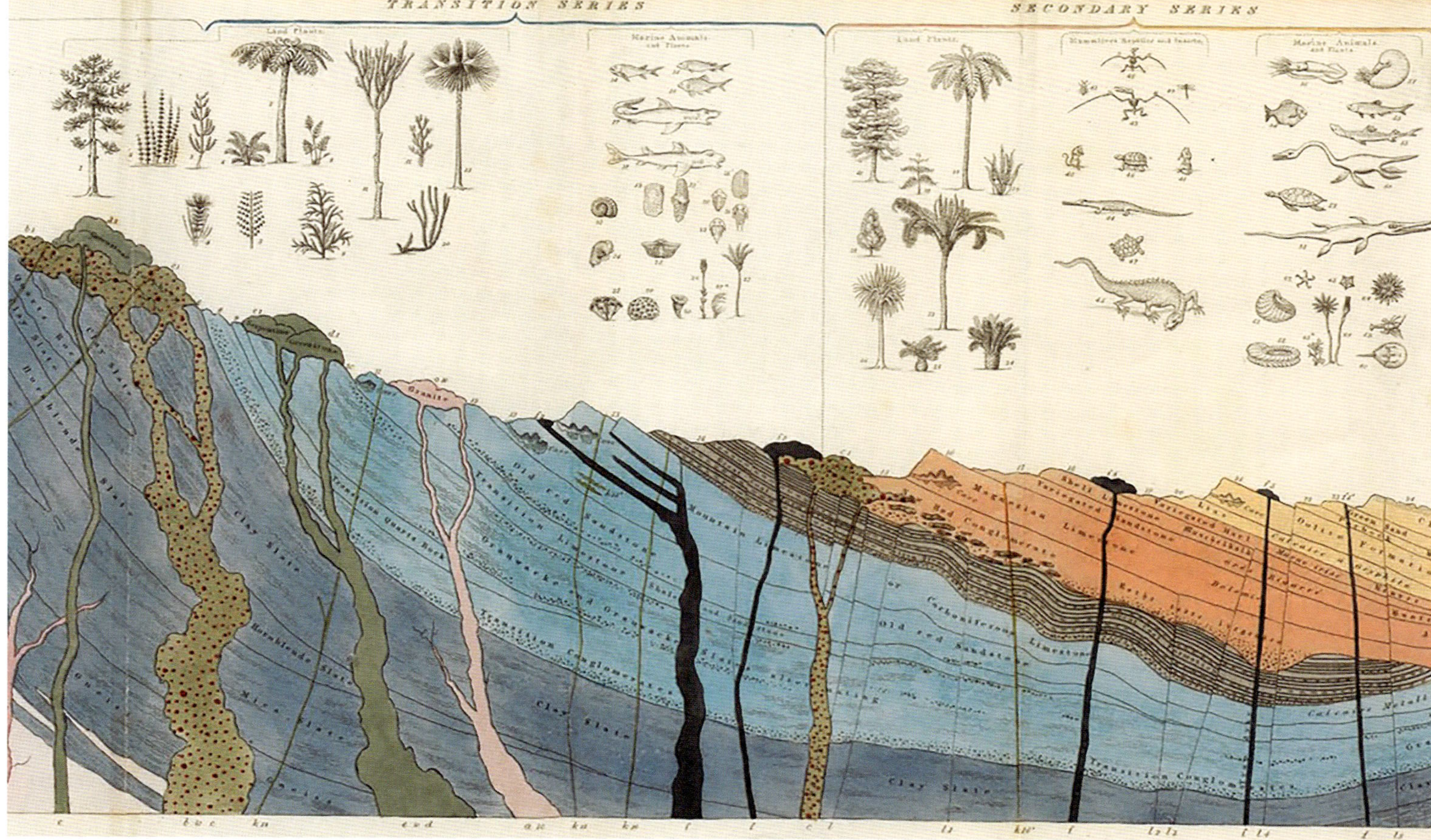
TRANSITION SERIES
SECONDARY SERIES
Land Plants
Marine Animals and Plants
Land Plants
Mammifers Reptiles and Insects
Marine Animals and Plants
Granite
Clay Slate
Hornblende Slate
Mica Slate
Transition Quartz Rock
Old red Sandstone
Transition Limestone
Greywacke and Greywacke Slate
Transition Conglomerate
Mountain Limestone
Carboniferous Limestone
Old red Sandstone
Red Conglomerate
Magnesian Limestone
Shell Limestone
Variegated Sandstone
Variegated Marl
Lias
Oolite Formation
Green Sand
Chalk
Clay Slate

Fig. 50

'Ideal Section of a Portion of the Earth's Crust', from William Buckland, *Geology and Mineralogy Considered with Reference to Natural Theology* (1836), vol. 2.

one that architects took to heart, was its appeal to nature. It was through the example of 'Nature'—as demonstrable evidence of the 'great Builder' (i.e., God) at work—that certain eternal truths in architecture only were not revealed but might also be encouraged. Again, this reflected a propensity among educated Victorians to read meaning into the world around them. For Ruskin, buildings were among the most conspicuous (and thus intellectually and emotionally affective) of anthropogenic constructs. Although Ruskin famously rejected the instrumentalisation of his ideas, architects were nonetheless keen to draw lessons from his eulogies, particularly from the best-selling *The Seven Lamps of Architecture* (1849) and the multi-volume *The Stones of Venice* (1851–3). These publications derived their power from implied rather than specific religious explication, with Ruskin's Evangelical upbringing inclining him to decode the world in typological fashion, presenting it as a hypostasis of God. Style, process, and technique thus became irresistible semantic vehicles for the interpretation of built form as both the embodiment and revelation of a higher purpose. Gothic and other medieval forms of architecture were seen as best reflecting these immutable truths.

Ruskin's sermonising, along with its means of understanding the world as divine 'plan', was familiar and thus attractive to many of his readers. What they primarily took from his writing was a broadly applicable ethical message concerning what constituted good architecture, with the added implication that it ought to move, excite, and inspire. This is what separated Ruskin from his contemporaries. As John Steegman has observed, it was not enough for the Gwilts and Fergussons of this world to be respected and much read if they could not stir the emotions.[16] One of Ruskin's most profound utterances in this regard was his essay in the second volume of *The Stones of Venice*, entitled 'The Nature of Gothic'. In this Ruskin sought to identify an underlying 'spirit' of Gothic architecture: what he otherwise termed its 'Gothicness'. In a similar way to Freeman, he linked what he saw as 'certain mental tendencies' in medieval craftsmen with the architecture they produced. Animating this phenomenon, and essential to it, were 'various moral and imaginative elements' peculiar to what he perceived as the indelible 'fellowship' between true Gothic art and 'Northern hearts'. This identitarian aspect to Ruskin's theory in turn rested upon particular characteristics, such as 'Savageness', 'Love of Change', a 'Disturbed Imagination', and perhaps most importantly, 'Love of Nature'. In this last lay an especial 'truthfulness'. Through nature man was connected to God, by which he could access truth and find redemption. Good architecture was an embodiment of this message.

At a more fundamental level, Ruskin divided what he called the 'practical duty' of building into two branches: 'acting and talking'. Buildings such as churches, monuments, temples, and public edifices not merely provided shelter but were 'books of history', communicating their intent 'clearly and forcibly'. This is where the caricatured notion, long associated with Ruskin, that buildings are 'sermons in stone' stems from. Sometimes these edicts could be quite specific, as in his call in *The Seven Lamps* for the decoration of a future 'India House', where relevant historic scenes of British imperial command, as well as 'oriental' materials and motifs, could be employed in enabling its architecture to be a living record **[51]**. This line of thinking had

Fig. 51

Buildings as 'books of history': Façade detail, T. N. Deane and Benjamin Woodward's unbuilt proposal for the new Foreign Office (*The Builder*, Oct. 1857), London, with relief sculpture depicting, among other things, scenes of contemporary warfare.

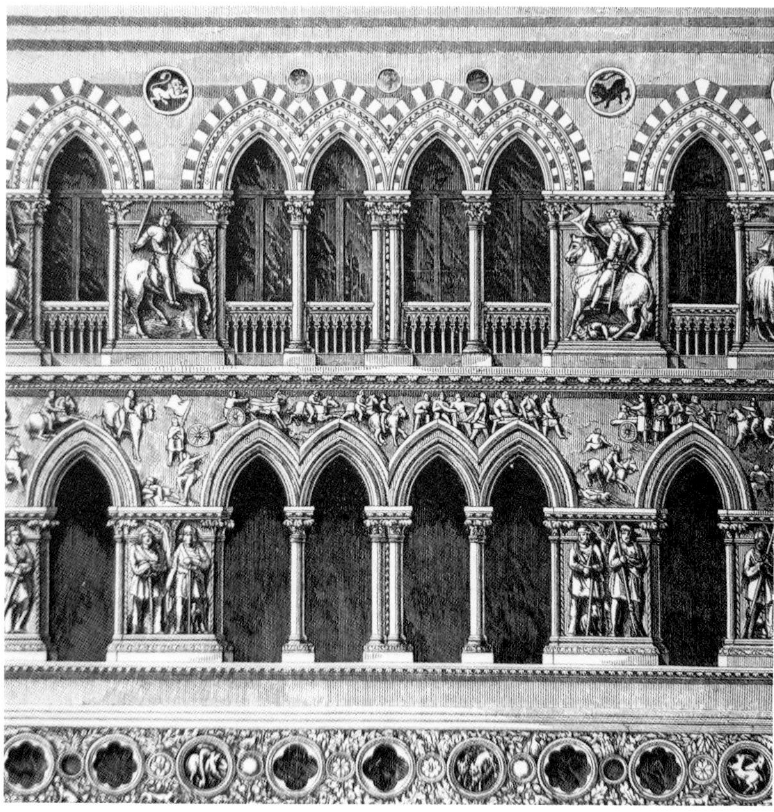

its corollary in the rise of the penny press and illustrated newspapers in Britain from about the 1840s, which represented the steady democratisation of the media and its means of communication.[17] Thus, like a great three-dimensional book, buildings, especially those associated with public purpose, had the capacity to communicate local, regional, and national narratives in a similar way through their ornamentation.

Despite some of his observations being rather fanciful, Ruskin's influence in this respect was tremendous, and its visible effects on the world of Victorian architecture were palpable. The attachment of these ideas to style may initially have fallen on deaf ears (even rankled) in some quarters, especially in the context of the vexed religious politics of the early 1850s, but they did eventually assist in softening sterner Protestant suspicions over Gothic as indelibly popish. Through persuasive prose, and his rare interpretative genius, Ruskin was able to show medieval architecture as essentially Protestant long before Protestantism.

For Ruskin, one of nature's most captivating and enduring beauties was colour. Although the use of colour in architecture, along with its theorisation, had a reasonably long history in early nineteenth-century Britain, including in debates on its use in ancient Classical architecture, it was Ruskin, perhaps more than anyone else, who popularised the idea of polychromy in contemporary architectural design. The principles of colour were ordained in nature, he believed, and, because of this, buildings ought to be understood as a 'kind of organised creature; in colouring which we must look to the single and separately organised creatures of Nature'.[18] This reasoning extended to the inanimate world, too, including the earth itself. Geological formations, such as variegated marbles, were laden with revelatory power for Ruskin **[52a]**. 'Another singular point in the business', he insisted, was

> that these stones which men have been cutting into slabs, for thousands of years, to ornament their principal buildings with, . . . are precisely those on which the signs and brands of these earth-agonies have been chiefly struck; and there is not a purple vein nor flaming zone in them, which is not the record of their ancient torture.[19]

Mysterious and beguiling, marble, Ruskin insisted, was therefore 'one of the most *marked* pieces of purpose in the creation' **[52b]**.[20] The architecture of medieval Italy was prized by Ruskin precisely because its architects appeared to recognise this quality.

Present here was the concept of geological or *deep* time. Ruskin may have said that colour in architecture ought to be independent of form, but he was innately appreciative of the fact that a building was a 'constructed' accretion, and one that revealed this explicitly through its design, structure, and surface formation. If a building did not so much 'evolve' in this sense, it at least demonstrated a time- (and thus effort-) laden process of lamination. Being a conservative, Ruskin was somewhat suspicious of progressive ideas such as 'development', but he nevertheless recognised the synergies between architecture and the 'building up' of geological features and strata in the observable world. Given that other leading theorists, either in Britain or known to British architects, such as Gottfried Semper and Viollet-le-Duc, drew on geological metaphor, the idea, for a time at least, was both pervasive and influential. In this sense, via Ruskin and others, architecture had fundamentally superseded its own internal logic, responding not merely to the arc of human history but to that of the wider universe scientifically understood. In this sense, certain features of Victorian architecture were peculiarly and self-consciously modern.

These ideas of truth, sincerity, and nature that had come through and informed architectural theory left a powerful legacy in British architecture. In practice, and especially through the middle decades of the nineteenth century, they led to various approaches concerning the relationship between colour and structure in architecture. The latter of these loosely became known as 'constructional polychromy', being one of the defining features of High Victorian architecture. Devotees of Ruskin, such as G. E. Street, who also studied the medieval buildings of northern Italy, were convinced that colour, in the form of stone, brick, and certain manufactured materials, including terracotta, would not only brighten Britain's dull, soot-laden streets, thus injecting new life into towns and cities, but could also be used to delineate the main structural lines and forces in a building. This was perceived as signalling a fundamental integrity, or what architects liked to call 'reality'.

In his influential publication, *Brick and Marble in the Middle Ages*, first published in 1855 (revised and reissued 1874), Street commented frequently on the character and quality of the humble brick in Italian buildings. He

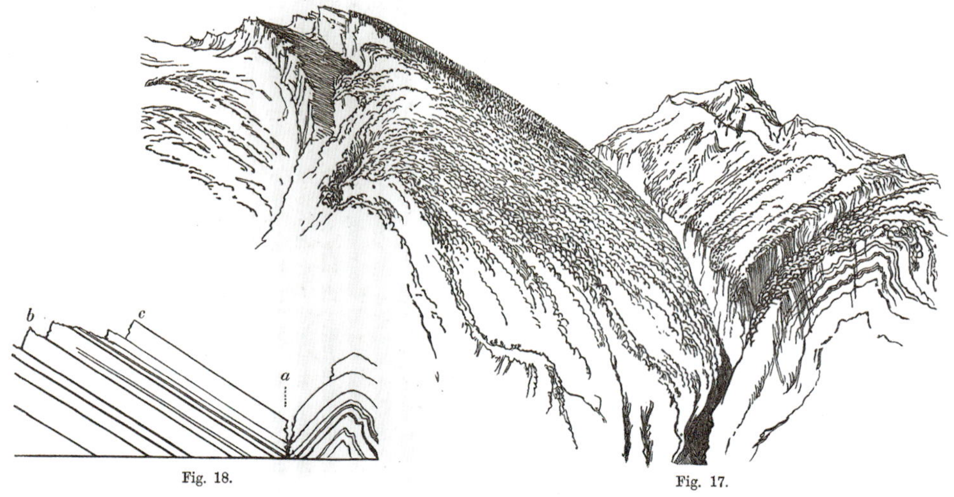

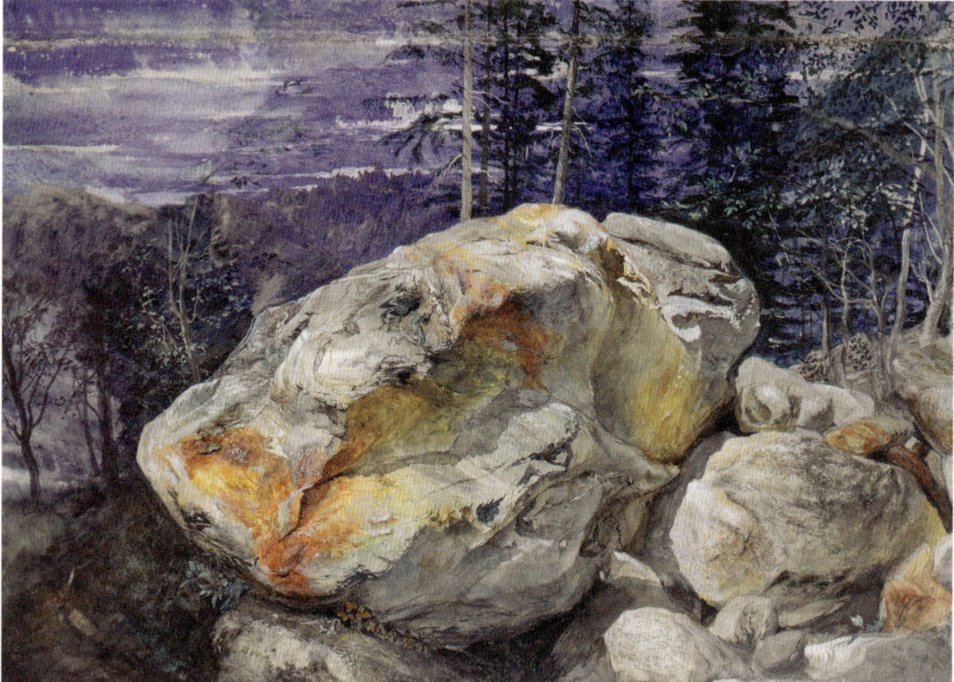

Fig. 52a

Illustrations of the Gorge of Ardon, Valais, Switzerland, from John Ruskin's *Modern Painters* (1856).

Fig. 52b

John Ruskin, *Fragment of the Alps* (c.1855). Pencil, watercolour and gouache.

noted the material's extensive use throughout the north of the country, including its full and uninhibited exposure on the facades and interiors of many structures. The use of brick in this regard was especially poignant for the way it demonstrated structural polychromy, or what he termed 'colour in construction'. Brick provided a relatively cheap and easy way of achieving this effect, and was perfectly suited to modern architectural needs.[21] For Street, this was a means of achieving a new and peculiarly modern form of architecture. Polychromy in this regard was enthusiastically

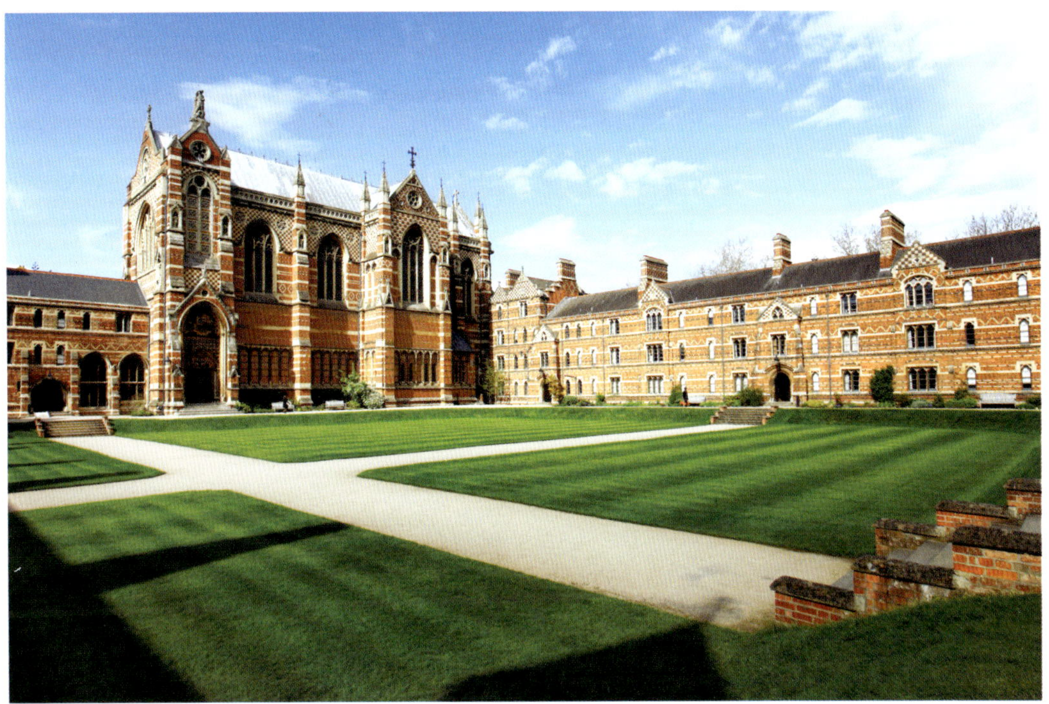

Fig. 53

The effects of Continental European influence, theories of development, and a widening material palette. Keble College, Oxford (1867–83), by William Butterfield.

adopted by many of Britain's leading practitioners of the day, including William White, S. S. Teulon, J. L. Pearson, Deane & Woodward, William Butterfield, G. G. Scott, and of course Street himself (see Chapter 5). The architecture of Butterfield, especially, captured the visual impact and intensity that this kind of architecture could achieve, evidenced in such (in) famous buildings as All Saints', Margaret Street (London), and Keble College, Oxford **[53]**. Not liked by everyone (indeed, derided by some), they nevertheless attracted attention, and remain indicative of one of the most inventive and intellectually charged phases in the history of Victorian architecture.

Against the Grain: James Fergusson and Alexander Thomson

By this time the Gothic Revival had made significant inroads into British architectural practice, especially in ecclesiastical architecture. Not everyone agreed with the supposed irrefutability of the Gothic thesis, however. The 'Battle of the Styles' proved that. Moreover, certain leading theorists and historians, such as James Fergusson and Robert Kerr, remained unpersuaded by the moralising zeal of the 'goths'. Fergusson, as someone laden with a scientific frame of mind, turned the Gothic Revivalists' key arguments against them, reasoning that the 'system' of design they advocated was as 'false' as anything they themselves rejected. His basic contention was that the Pugin-inspired revival was a type of forgery, steeped in practices of copyism and deception. This was an old accusation, admittedly, and one that was rather cynically made, but one that nevertheless had the irritating propensity to stick. It rankled especially given that the Gothic Revival had moved a long way since the earliest utterances of Pugin. Indeed, Fergusson gave the game away when in his *A History of the Modern Styles of Architecture* (1862) he asked, with no small amount of Protestant exasperation, 'why should we be asked to ignore all the progress made in the enlightenment during the past four centuries?' Where had all the 'common-sense' in art gone, he grumbled.

Fergusson's views on architecture were informed by his unwavering commitment to the precepts of modern scientific inquiry. More so than Rickman, or even Willis, he was inclined to affirm a strict classificatory basis to the interpretation of architectural form, an approach that predictably drew criticism from Ruskin. Grounded in empirical schema such as observation, cataloguing, and categorical organisation, Fergusson's system reflected, among other things, a uniformitarian conception similar to that of geological change. Thus, if the 'common-sense' in architecture was something of a plea to contemporary architects to appreciate professional practice as a type of 'science', first and foremost, then his appeal to lithic conceptions of development posited the history of architecture firmly within a scientific purview. In this respect, Fergusson was one of the principal inheritors (and thus advocates) of the 'scientific method' in architectural research espoused by the likes of Willis and Whewell. Ironically, and despite the clear disparity between their views, what united the likes of Fergusson and the Gothic Revivalists, apart from an interest in geology, was a typically Victorian search for 'truth', whether moral or objective.

But there were others who had even stronger moral and spiritual objections to the Gothic Revival. We have already touched on the fact that Evangelical and Nonconformist Christians rejected it, initially at least, because of its apparent associations with 'popery'. The Scottish architect Alexander Thomson was one such principled objector. Being an elder of the United Presbyterian Church of Scotland, he was imbued with particularly hard-line Protestant sensibilities. Like Ruskin, Thomson tended to view the world around him as encoded with religious portent. Architecturally, this translated into ideas such as the notion that stone signified 'imperishable thoughts', including truth and justice. The emphasis laid on the Old Testament by his religion enabled him to see in ancient Egyptian, and especially Greek, architecture an uncanny sense of poise and harmony, which, to his mind, reflected divine beauty. Waxing lyrical over the Parthenon in Athens (and quoting Revelation 21:2), for instance, he stated emphatically how such a 'group of beautiful forms' could only be God-given. Architecture of this kind was merely 'pagan' in a limited cultural sense; in Thomson's universe, where the creative force of the Almighty was omnipotent, it was considered sacred.

Drawing on Edmund Burke's theories of the sublime, and finding inspiration in the work of artists such as John Martin, J. M. W. Turner, and Thomas Cole, Thomson's Protestant mindset was able to channel the righteous power of God through architecture, both past and present. Indeed, Martin's terrifying images of divine wrath held special appeal for Thomson, and it is little wonder that his own buildings bore more than a passing resemblance to those in Martin's paintings **[54]**. After all, it was Burke who said that the highest illustrations of the sublime were to be found in

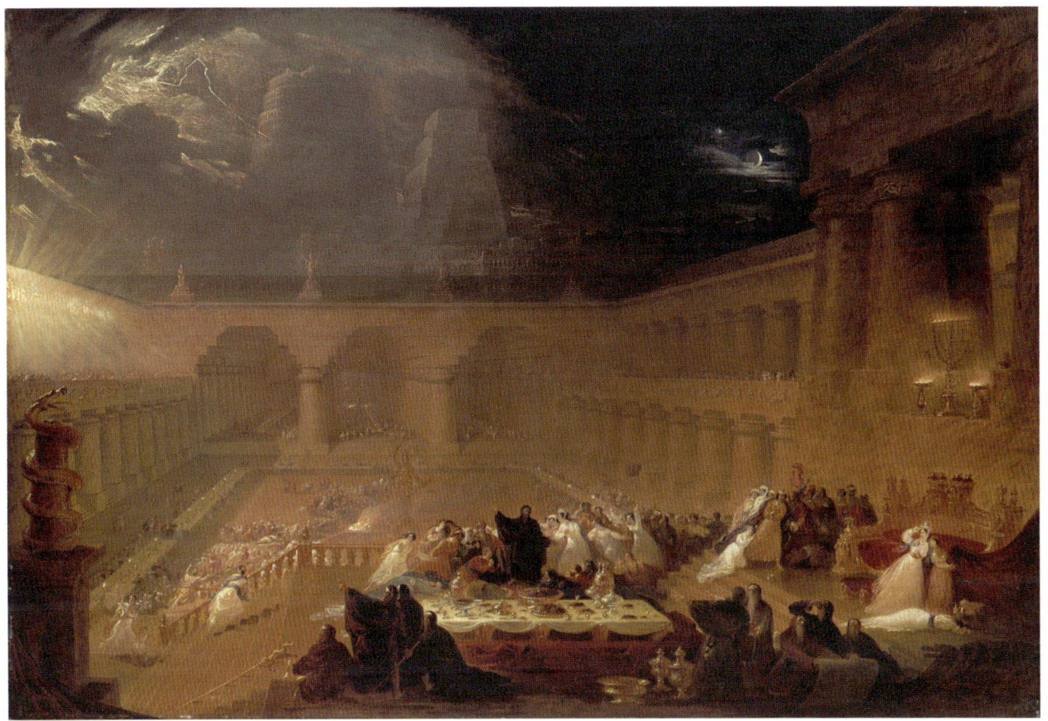

Fig. 54
John Martin, *Belshazzar's Feast* (1820). Oil on canvas.

'Scripture alone', whenever God was seen to appear or speak. It is for this reason that Thomson was able to condemn so confidently as nonsense the assertion that only Gothic architecture could be considered 'Christian', jibing G. G. Scott directly over his designs for Glasgow University. His rejection of Gothic also stemmed from his suspicion of all arcuated forms of architecture as inherently degenerate, having characterised European building culture prior to the Protestant Reformation.

'Constructive Utility': Decorative Arts and Industrial Design

A certain utilitarian instinct lay behind these reactions to the Gothic Revival, which was itself characteristically Victorian. Among the most articulate and organised advocates of this utilitarian strain in Victorian design thinking were those associated with the so-called Cole Circle of industrial designers, architects, and educators. This 'circle' included, among others, the architects Owen Jones, Matthew Digby Wyatt, and Francis Fowke; the painters Richard Redgrave and William Dyce; the designer Christopher Dresser; and the German art theorist Gottfried Semper. They were all connected in this way through Henry Cole, the influential career civil servant and, along with Prince Albert, prime mover behind the Great Exhibition of 1851. The kinds of buildings they were associated with included the South Kensington Museum (1855–7), the Royal Albert Hall (1867–71), and, of course, the Crystal Palace.

In attempting to improve design standards in post-Exhibition Britain, which were widely criticised at the time, this group sought to devise a wholly reformed, more contemporary approach to the conception of art and architecture. In so doing, their views reflected a new moral purpose in early Victorian political culture for ideas of public duty, including increased bureaucratic professionalism and systematic management.[22] Their initiative—broadly referred to now as the Design Reform Movement—was part of the ongoing effort to institute practical art training in Britain, which first emerged with the Government School of Design, established at Somerset House in 1837, before relocating to South Kensington in the 1850s. Taking an instrumentalist perspective, and moving beyond high or 'fine' art, Cole and his colleagues were concerned with the unique possibilities offered by the embrace of art and science through industrial technology, thus giving 'designed' manufactures a greater role in the industrial and economic (and therefore material) advancement of the nation. In this respect, and largely opposed to the likes of Ruskin, they were advocates for the burgeoning capitalist system in Britain as a fundamental 'condition' of the age.

Members of the group had begun expressing views on these matters some time before the Great Exhibition, through the *Journal of Design and Manufactures*, founded by Cole and Wyatt in 1849. Their efforts were partly in aid of extending quality, design-based products to the masses, but also to encourage a new regime of tasteful design founded upon the principles of usefulness, or what was otherwise termed 'constructive utility'. In this schema, excessive, purposeless, or frivolous ornament was to be eschewed. Indeed, in the final assessment of the manufactures on display at the Great Exhibition, it was those produced in the non-European world, in places like Egypt and India, that were seen as best in uniting design, utility, and true beauty. Exposing something of a crisis in British manufacturing, such products were seen as holding the key to the Cole Circle's own moral basis for good design, what they later identified as 'universal principles'. Nothing less than the artistic prestige of the nation was at stake.

Where this group and its theorising did overlap with that of Ruskin and other Gothic Revivalists, however, was in an appeal to nature. Their 'universal principles' were best observed, in model form, in the way nature structured itself. This did not entail imitation of natural phenomena, such as copying flowers or foliage, but in understanding how the underlying constitution of the natural world could be applied, abstractly, in the invention of ornamental art. This point was perhaps best captured by William Dyce, a leading teacher at the Government School of Design. The real purpose of ornamental art, he argued, was to

> impress on the creations of human ingenuity somewhat of the *cosmetic* art of nature... [T]he very word 'cosmetic', if used in its original acceptation, as 'that which beautifies', or 'adorns', suggests to us the elevated character of the study of ornament. The word is derived from the Greek verb *κόσμεῖν*, which signifies to 'adorn'; and from this same root the Greeks formed their word *κόσμος*, 'the world', or 'the universe',—as if in thinking of the world, the idea of it uppermost in their minds was its ornate character... [T]he object of the ornamentist is not to make mere copies of natural objects... His purpose is to adorn the contrivances of mechanical and architectural skill by the application of those principles of decoration, and of those forms and modes of beauty, which nature herself has employed in adorning the structure of the world.[23]

When it came to architecture specifically, Matthew Digby Wyatt was clear on what this principle demanded, that 'all decoration' must undergo what he called a process of 'conventionalizing'. What he meant was that the 'duty' of the architect was to 'symbolize rather than to express, and to strive to convey an idea of particulars and qualities only, instead of to make a necessarily imperfect reproduction'.[24]

In this sense, as Semper had recognised, ornamental art (as opposed to fine art) should be considered a type of practical science.[25] This notion was codified by Owen Jones in 1856, in his now famous *The Grammar of Ornament*, where he laid down some thirty-seven 'propositions' for good design. These included: '1. The Decorative Arts arise from, and should properly be attendant upon, Architecture'; and '3. As Architecture, so all works of the Decorative Arts, should possess fitness, proportion, harmony, the result of all which is repose'; or, the rather Puginian, '5. Construction should be decorated. Decoration should never be purposely constructed. That which is beautiful is true; that which is true must be beautiful.' Perhaps most importantly for architecture, however, we have '2. Architecture is the material expression of the wants, the faculties, and the sentiments, of the age in which it is created. Style in Architecture is the peculiar form that expression takes under the influence of climate and materials at command.' This last proposition referred directly back to the group's embracing of the techno-capitalist realities of British society. But lessons could be learned from the past, too, or even from other cultures, and Jones favoured oriental, especially Islamic, design for what he perceived as its abstract, integrated (as opposed to additive) approach. The basic strategy was to modernise the nation's decorative arts industry, leading to a competitive market for British manufactured commodity goods.

William Morris and the Arts and Crafts Movement

But there was a backlash against this kind of capitalist techno-abstraction, and it came in the form of the design philosophy known as Arts and Crafts. William Morris was its leading figure, and his ideas, which were rather simple and straightforward at heart, revolutionised the world of British design during the course of the late nineteenth and early twentieth centuries. A one-time aspiring architect, having entered the office of G. E. Street in 1856, he went on to found 'the Firm' (Morris, Marshall, Faulkner & Co.) in 1861, which dedicated itself to the production of decorative arts, including interior furnishings and stained glass. Through this he was connected to the Pre-Raphaelite Brotherhood of artists and designers, including Dante Gabriel Rossetti, William Holman Hunt, John Everett Millais, Edward Burne-Jones, and William De Morgan. The Firm's guiding principle was the production of 'work of a genuine and beautiful character', hand-crafted, and based on a broad medieval aesthetic. Personality-wise, Morris was known to be a rather strong-willed, tempestuous individual. He was also quite excitable, and at times depressive. But, significantly, and maybe because of this, he had an acute admiration for simplicity, which manifested itself as an appreciation for those now familiar concepts of honesty in design and truth to materials, which he gleaned from the likes of Pugin, and to a lesser extent Owen Jones.

Among the more important things to note about Morris is that there existed a potent and, indeed, self-righteous connection between his artistic and political beliefs. A disciple of Ruskin, he had absorbed the humanitarian and quasi-socialist agendas underpinning that writer's theories on art and architecture, particularly those views concerning mechanical production and handicraft. So enamoured was Morris of Ruskin that he described his essay 'The Nature of Gothic' as 'one of the very few necessary and inevitable utterances of the century'. He would later reprint it through his own publishing enterprise, the Kelmscott Press (1892). He observed that what struck him and his fellow travellers most forcefully about Ruskin's writing was its 'ethical and political' rather than artistic dimensions. Beyond Ruskin, he was enthralled by the socialist philosophies he encountered through his expanding circle of friends and acquaintances, as well as in the writing of Carlyle, Robert Owen, Charles Fourier, and later Karl Marx and Sergius Stepniak.

With such ideas swirling in his head, Morris concluded that, with the 'new birth' of art there had to be a definite and corresponding rise in the condition of the worker in British society, and that emphasis must be placed on the dignity of labour and the implementation of quality handcraftsmanship. He had been inspired to this end while at Oxford, where he and Burne-Jones had immersed themselves in Celtic and Norse mythology, in medieval romances and chronicles, in Chaucer, and in nineteenth-century poetry, especially Shelley, Keats, and Tennyson. Thus, bursting with idealism, as well as seething with anger over the state of British society, they proposed to launch a 'crusade and Holy War against the age'. To Morris, the medieval past was the age that best captured those principles he wished to emulate. In this respect, he was a child of the Gothic Revival, simultaneously looking back while pressing forward.

Morris's strong idealism agitated him into action. For unlike Ruskin, who merely sermonised, Morris was keen to get his hands dirty. His first serious venture into architecture, Red House (1859–60), designed with his friend Philip Webb, who he had met while in Street's office, perhaps best represents Morris's attitude towards total design **[55]**. More will be said about this landmark building in Chapter 8; suffice it to say that the principle behind the building, and thus the architectural theory of the Arts and Crafts in general, was simplicity, convenience, and function. In every conceivable way, architecture, including all its internal fittings and arrangements, ought to be guided by these key principles. Indeed, Morris had said that he 'learned' to think of architecture as the 'union of the arts, mutually helpful and harmoniously subordinated one to another ... [W]e cannot escape it ..., it means the moulding and altering to human needs of the very face of the earth itself'.[26] To this end the planning of Red House revolves almost entirely around its use, and its assembly demonstrates a near fanatical engagement with the idea of handicraft and on-site workmanship. In this respect, Morris was able to do what Ruskin could not, linking ideas concerning cultural production with material practice and a revolutionary politic.

Although clearly a brand of Modern Gothic, Red House avoided 'stylism' by opting instead for a much freer interpretation of medieval tendencies

Fig. 55

Red House, Bexleyheath (1859–60), London, by Philip Webb and William Morris.

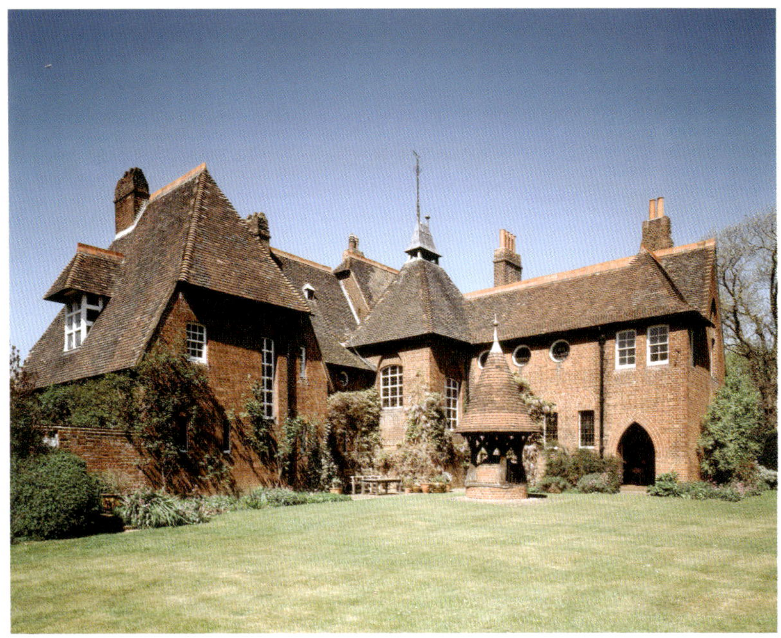

in architecture. One of Morris's greatest concerns for the house was that it not only be built of locally sourced, undisguised materials (hence the raw, handmade red brick), but also be in dialogue with its surrounds. The philosophy behind its design was both inspired by and spilled out into its location, including its garden. Morris's efforts at Red House show that his affection for the Gothic was not academic, but rather sprang from a kind of emotive attachment to the 'spirit' of Gothic. To be sure, he was stirred by great works of medieval art, but what appealed to him most of all were lower works of medieval art and architecture, those unselfconscious, simple, 'folksy' medieval buildings such as cottages, alms-houses, and barns (the Great Coxwell Barn in Gloucestershire was a favourite). These buildings were seen to have something of the everyday about them, buildings that were in a sense 'vernacular'. After all, Morris had claimed, 'simplicity of life, even the barest, is not a misery, but the very foundation of refinement'.[27] This is partly why he so admired the smaller domestic dwellings of Butterfield and Street, such as Coalpit Heath vicarage, Avon (1844–6), and Laverstoke parsonage, Hampshire (1858), which influenced his vision for Red House.

However, being more of a 'sentimental socialist', as Friedrich Engels had once dismissed him, Morris became caught in an ethical quandary of his own making. Despite aspiring to bring quality, handcrafted design to the masses (as part of his art-based revolution), his products found their way more readily into the homes of the capitalist bourgeois elite, making both him and his vision seem hypocritical. He was of course aware of this inconsistency, and it exercised his conscience. But it was something he had difficulty overcoming, and to this day both his 'style' and his products are still considered firmly middle class. Despite this, his ideas on architecture would go on to inspire and influence future generations, including W. R. Lethaby, C. F. A. Voysey, Barry Parker, Raymond Unwin, Charles

Rennie Mackintosh, Robert Lorimer, and C. R. Ashbee in Britain; Harold Desbrowe-Annear, W. L. Vernon, and James Chapman-Taylor in Australasia; Charles Summer Greene, Frank Lloyd Wright, and Eden Smith in North America; Herbert Baker and the Cape Dutch Revival in South Africa, and many more besides. The list is almost endless. Moreover, Morris's influence lived on in other ways, through the activism of organisations such as the Society for the Protection of Ancient Buildings (SPAB), which he founded in 1877.

Considering architectural theory in the Victorian era, we might also highlight here the determined shift back to Classicism in the latter part of the century into the Edwardian period. This was associated with a concerted effort to connect a notion of home-grown, 'vernacular' Classicism with ideas of cultural, racial, and imperial identity, based on the precedent of architects such as Christopher Wren, Nicholas Hawksmoor, and John Vanbrugh. This I shall cover in the following chapter.

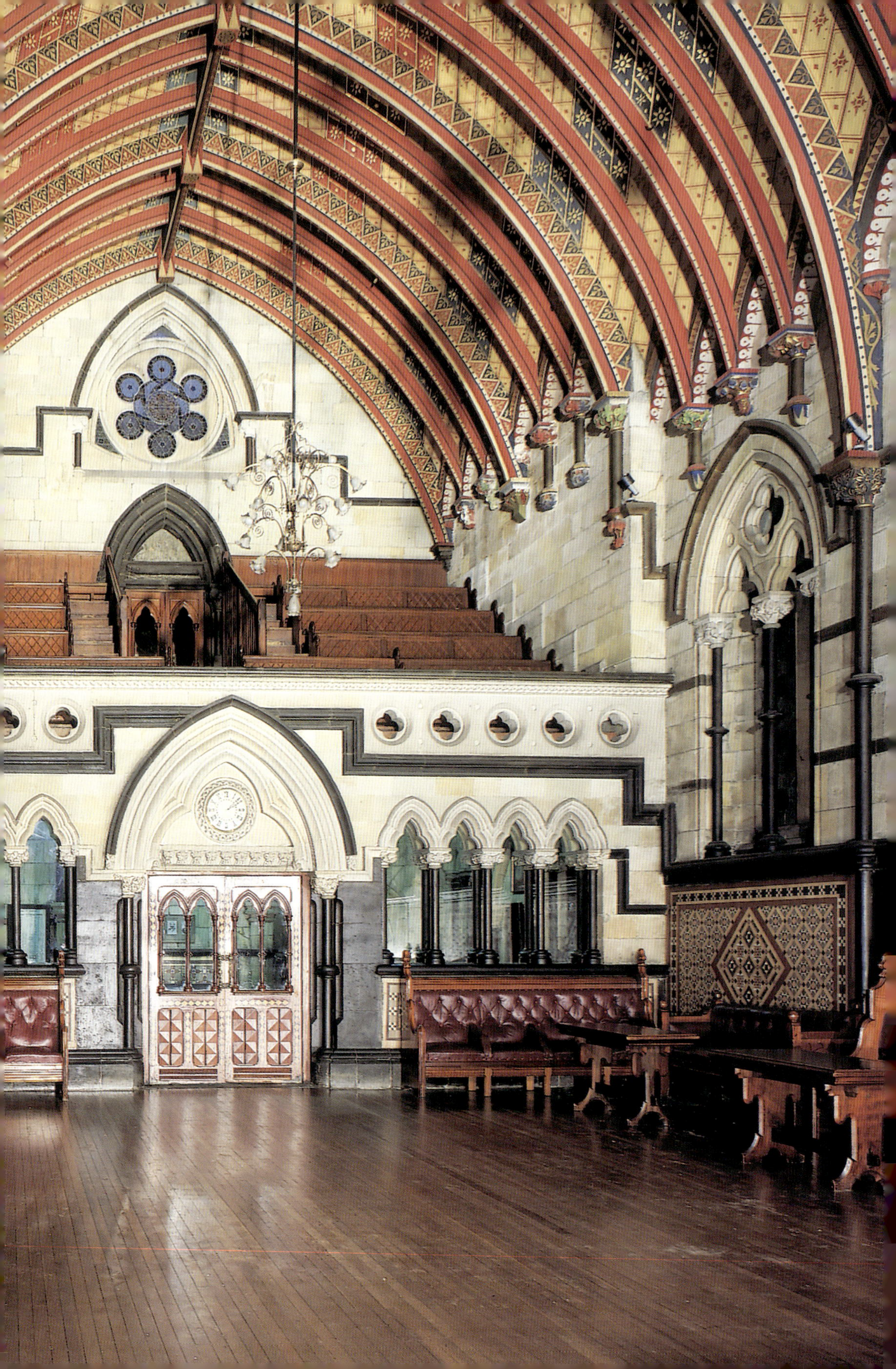

4 Building the State: Architectures of Power and Pride

The Victorian era coincided with the great age of European nation building. It was the period during which France experienced the turbulent birth of its second and third republics, a united Italy emerged from its Risorgimento, and an integrated German empire rose out of victory in the Franco-Prussian War (1870–1). It was also the period that witnessed the ascent of the United States of America to geopolitical pre-eminence following the conclusion of its Civil War in 1865. Although the United Kingdom of Great Britain and Ireland had been a stable nation state since the 1801 Act of Union, it nevertheless experienced the tumults of industrialisation and societal reform through the first half of the nineteenth century, including the challenge of how to cohere as a 'nation' across its four constituent ethnic communities (English, Irish, Scottish, and Welsh). Through this process Britain emerged as an increasingly modern, democratic, and technologically advanced country, with an ever-stronger sense of collective identity and purpose.

The world's nation states vied with one another economically, politically, and militarily. In Europe, especially, their newly forged identities were in part a measure of their distinction from one another, tainted as this was with unflattering comparison and more than a tinge of xenophobia. It needs recalling that Britain and much of Europe had been at war with Napoleonic France during the opening decades of the nineteenth century. Although Britain and its allies were ultimately victorious, a great deal of blood was spilled and treasure consumed in prosecuting the war, leaving Britain and its economy rattled. Other nations were keen to enter the race for global dominance, including Russia. Thus was born the age of Great Power rivalry, leading ultimately to the battlefields of the First World War. Amidst this international competition Britain strove to extend its commerce and project its power worldwide. Renewed prosperity, coupled with a sense of cultural and technical achievement, inspired confidence, not just at home, but also abroad, as Britain leveraged its global empire. This was an age not only of revolution, of capitalism, and nationalism, but of imperialism, too.

Architecture inevitably came to reflect ideas of modern nationhood. Britain's political and economic elite required buildings from which to operate that set a stage equal to their perceived civilisational superiority. This mentality spurred debate over the architectural style of new government buildings, from the Houses of Parliament, to government departments on Whitehall, to provincial town halls, in both Britain and the colonies. As we shall see, such architecture was concerned with constructing a type of governmental imaginary in which to build bureaucratic infrastructure was in effect to build the state, whether locally, nationally, or indeed globally.[1] Identity in this respect was complex and multivalent in nineteenth-century Britain. Although it naturally included what it meant to be British, it was also heavily embroidered with local and regional identities. One could identify as being British as well as English, Welsh, Scottish, or Irish; or might be further inclined to identify foremost with a particular city or region.

Out of this evolving identity arose new forms of decentralised local government, leading to the erection of grand town halls that were seen as symbols of new-found civic pride. Such buildings were emblematic of not only industrial might, but also the growing political power of the manufacturing middle classes. Tectonic shifts in wealth, power, and class were underway in Victorian Britain. By the last quarter of the nineteenth century, this applied also to the extremities of the British world, especially in crown colonies and across the settler dominions. In these places migrants increasingly saw themselves as 'Australian', 'New Zealand', or 'Canadian' as much as British, with these different guises understood as interchangeable. This led to new kinds of state building through architecture, which sought to fuse wider cultural affiliation with local and ever-growing nationalist sentiment. Even in places where British rule was not particularly welcome, and where it experienced resistance, British colonial authorities continued to erect buildings of state that spoke to perceived universalist notions of European power, identity, and cultural superiority.

Mother of Parliaments: Nationhood and the New Palace of Westminster

The accretion of ancient and modern structures that comprised the complex of buildings known as the Houses of Parliament in London was destroyed almost entirely by fire on the evening of 16 October 1834. Only Westminster Hall and parts of St Stephen's chapel survived. Although this event occurred just a few years before Victoria's accession to the throne, the process that governed the structure's rebuilding was very Victorian. For instance, it was framed within the political and professional context of an architectural competition, a procedure that, despite detractors, became something of a mainstay in the erection of substantial buildings in Victorian Britain, particularly those where the expenditure of taxpayers' money was involved. This was in many respects a precautionary measure, and therefore rather typical of the Victorian ruling elite's sense of prudence and their ever-watchful eye for retrenchment in the confines of governmental reform. Cronyism and 'old corruption' had been increasingly blamed for bad architecture in Britain, so a concerted effort was made to seek the best architect, with the best design, as objectively as possible.

Built into the competition brief was a requirement to accommodate an appeal to national identity through built form. If the liberties secured under the parliamentary system were considered a source of national pride, so too, it was claimed, should be the buildings in which those liberties were enshrined. The instructions to competitors were clear in making such connections.

Considering the immediate urban context, and conscious of the rich history of English constitutionalism dating back to the Middle Ages in such documents as Magna Carta, the Royal Commission appointed to oversee the process announced to competitors that the new building must be in either a Gothic or an Elizabethan style. This had much to do with the 'genius' of the location, associated as it was not just with Westminster Hall and the adjacent abbey, but also with the ancient royal palace that once occupied the site. Thus, from among ninety-seven entries, it was a design by Charles Barry in a late, Perpendicular-style Gothic that emerged victorious **[56; see also 3]**.

Barry solicited the assistance of the young and supremely talented Gothic enthusiast A. W. N. Pugin to help realise his vision. It was a fortuitous moment, for Pugin had only recently come to attention through the publication of his inflammatory polemic *Contrasts* (see Chapter 3). With Barry as master planner and lead architect, Pugin was tasked with devising the myriad Gothic details that would be required to bring the building to life, and to make it a coherent work of architecture. It would take Pugin some fifteen years, and thousands of drawings, in assisting Barry to complete this undertaking, culminating in his efforts to design the interior for the House of Lords **[57a]**. What emerged was a true 'palace', indeed a total work of art. Steeped in the romance of the Middle Ages, and driven by a furious passion for bringing his ideas to reality, Pugin, with Barry's oversight, left little to chance. Every detail was accounted for, including fittings, furniture, textiles, stained glass, and other decorative elements, both inside and out. As noted in Chapter 2, so important was the new parliament building—as the presiding mind of the nation, and the 'instrument' that facilitated its good governance—that the very latest technological innovations were incorporated from the outset. This included not only advances in ventilation, heating, lighting, acoustics, but also the sourcing and scientific testing of building materials. The harmonious performance of these various elements was understood as corollary to that of a well-oiled machine; or, to invoke a contemporary biological metaphor, the 'healthful' functioning of the Victorian body politic.

The rebuilding of the Houses of Parliament unfolded against the backdrop of the rise to prominence of the Gothic Revival in Britain, and the idea that the Gothic was an indigenous and therefore historically 'national' form of architecture—a view espoused by Pugin himself. Moreover, with political conceptions of the 'Gothick' passed down from the eighteenth century, the idea of a Gothic parliament building, dripping with romantic monarchical and libertarian associations, was something that both Whig and Tory found appealing. Not everyone was satisfied, though. There were those, especially among the older generation of architects and politicians, who remained wary of Gothic, and who believed that only Classical architecture was capable of symbolising stable, orderly, and 'civilised' government. Previous architects, such as William Kent, the Adam brothers, and John Soane, had all envisaged the British parliament as a grand Classical pile. Some detractors even argued for the removal of the new building to an entirely different site, away from the filth and bustle of the city, to take advantage of fresh air, light, and greenery. This tension over style provoked the first skirmishes in a rather bitter and

PALACE OF WESTMINSTER.

A

B

C

D

E

F

WESTMINSTER HALL

ST. STEPHENS PORCH

STAR CHAMBER COURT

COURT OF CLOISTERS

ST. STEPHENS COURT

CHANCELLORS COURT

JUDGES COURT

PEERS COURT

ROYAL COURT

COMMONS COURT

COMMONS OFFICE COURT

PEERS OFFICE COURT

SPEAKERS COURT

THE QUEENS ROBING ROOM

THE ROYAL GALLERY

THE VICTORIA HALL

PEERS LOBBY

COMMONS LOBBY

CENTRAL HALL

WEST DIVISION LOBBY

EAST DIVISION LOBBY

CHANCELLORS CORRIDOR

CHAIRMANS CORRIDOR

PEERS CORRIDOR

COMMONS CORRIDOR

BLACK RODS CORRIDOR

PEERS LIBRARY CORRIDOR

PEERS COMMITTEE ROOM CORRIDOR

COMMONS COMMITTEE ROOM CORRIDOR

COMMONS LIBRARY CORRIDOR

SPEAKERS PRIVATE CORRIDOR

SUITE OF PEERS LIBRARIES

PEERS COMMITTEE ROOMS

PAINTED CHAMBER

SELECT COMMONS COMMITTEE ROOM

SUITE OF COMMONS LIBRARIES

PLAN OF THE PRINCIPAL FLOOR

Scale of 50 0 50 100 150 200 250 300 350 Feet

Fig. 56

Plan, ground floor, new Palace of Westminster (Houses of Parliament), Westminster (*c.*1843), office of Charles Barry. (A) Victoria Tower; (B) House of Lords; (C) Central Hall; (D) St Stephen's Hall; (E) Westminster Hall; (F) House of Commons.

protracted dispute among architects, politicians, and other interested parties during the middle decades of the nineteenth century that became known as the 'Battle of the Styles'.

With the myriad applications that such a building placed before them, MPs were keen to take advantage by considering how it might operate as a vehicle for communicating Britain's national story. To this end, the Royal Commission for Promoting and Encouraging the Fine Arts in the Decoration of the New Houses of Parliament was established in November 1841. Led by the Prince Consort, Charles Eastlake, Robert Peel, and a number of other distinguished peers and statesmen, the Commission's aim was not only to make suggestions for the embellishment of the new Palace, but also to elevate the moral and intellectual character of the nation through the instructive and inspirational capacities of art. Fundamental to this aim was the political economy of state patronage through artistic endeavour. Indeed, so essential was this considered to be, that Eastlake opined, 'always being open to the public', the building ought to contain through its decoration 'a selection of subjects from British history, especially such as relate to warlike achievements, the vastness of the empire, and great commercial and civil events...calculated to inspire the citizens with loyalty, patriotism, and enterprise'. Thus, reconstructing the Houses of Parliament (both as a building and as a receptacle for art) presented an opportunity not only to create and showcase national talent but also to represent national honour and achievement.

In the end it would not be until 1867 that the new Houses of Parliament were practically complete. Following Pugin's untimely death in 1852,

Fig. 57a

Interior, House of Lords, Houses of Parliament, London (1837–67). Architectural detailing, including Sovereign's Throne, to designs by A. W. N. Pugin.

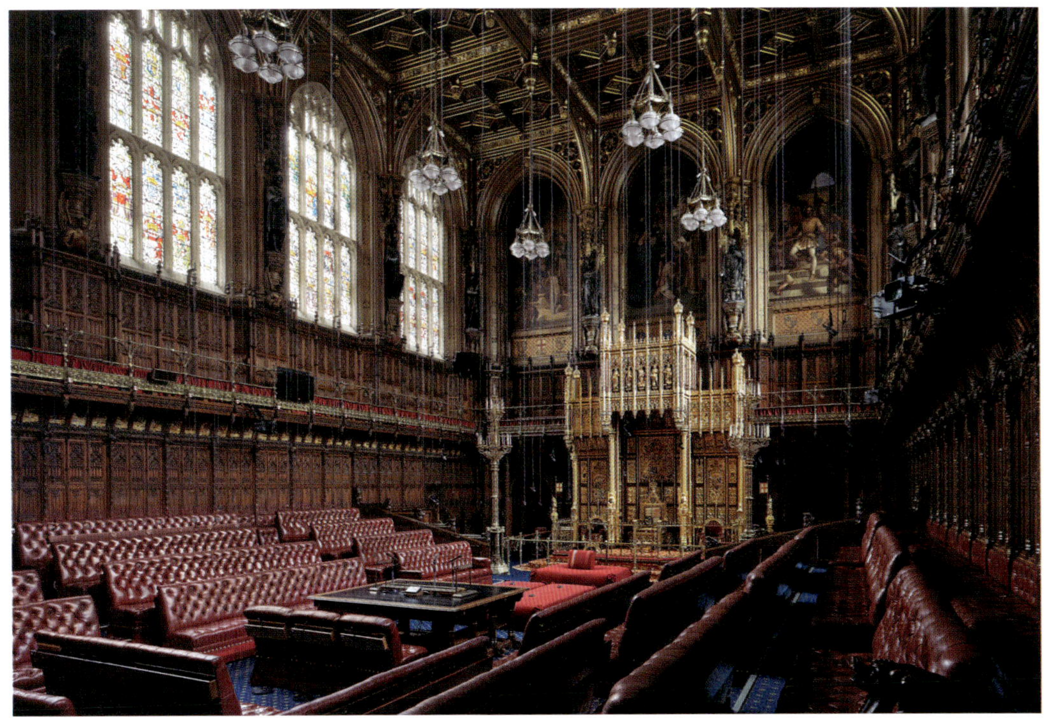

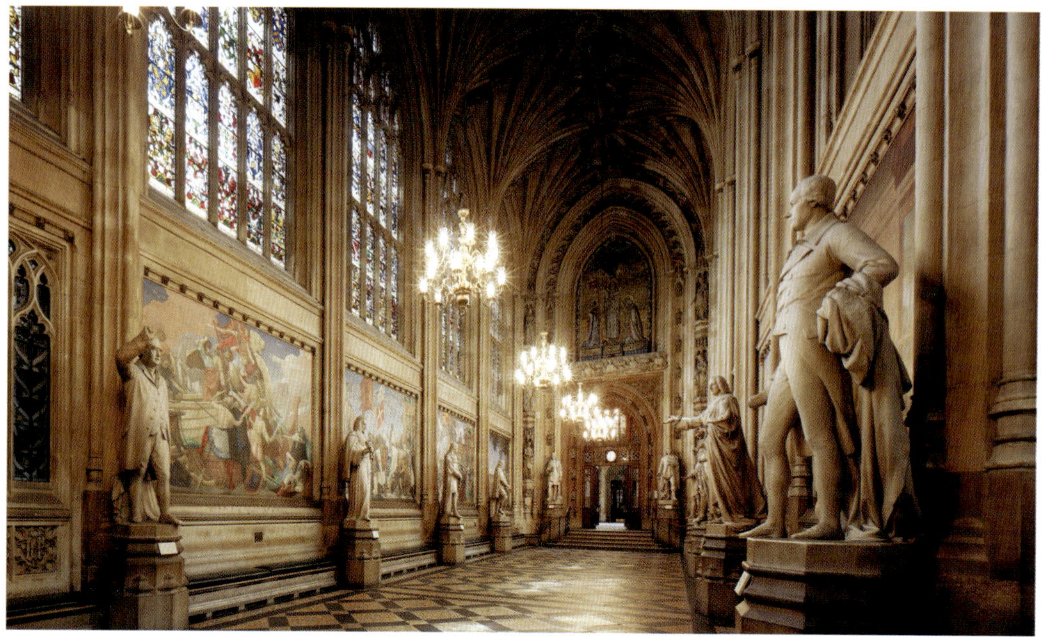

Fig. 57b

St Stephen's Hall, Houses of Parliament, London, showing incorporation of narrative murals and figurative sculpture.

followed by Barry's in 1860, the project was taken through to completion by Barry's son, Edward Middleton Barry. But it was initially thanks to Pugin, and the legion of other artists who followed in his wake, that nationally inspired art would eventually come to characterise the interiors of the building, ranging from murals, to full-figure sculpture, to carvings of every description, in both wood and stone **[57b]**. It included great scenes from the battles of Waterloo (1815) and Trafalgar (1805), along with numerous other figures and events from across British history. Whether these efforts constituted a 'national school' of art is a moot point, for upon entering the building the visitor was impressed with a near overwhelming spectacle of national myth making, the accumulated effect of which allowed the building to perform its didactic function as intended. Despite this, it is no small irony that Pugin—that most ardent and inspired of Gothic revivalists—understood fully the building's conceptual flaws, particularly in an age that demanded new levels of architectural integrity. 'All Grecian, sir', he is said to have remarked to a friend; 'Tudor details on a classic body'.

Projecting State Power: Government Offices in an Age of Empire

In 1856, amidst the construction of the Houses of Parliament, a proposal to erect another great building of state was initiated. This time it was for new Foreign and War office buildings; the location, across Parliament Square on Whitehall. It was in the context of this project that the Battle of the Styles came to its ignominious head. Being the largest and most prestigious commission in British architecture since the Houses of Parliament, these new buildings were a potentially hazardous venture. Therefore, as with their illustrious predecessor, a competition was held in order to obtain a suitable design. Two hundred and eighteen entries were received, from British architects and others, with first prize awarded to two Classically inspired designs by the little-known partnership of H. E. Coe and H. H. Hofland (Foreign Office) and Henry B. Garling (War Office).

But political machinations were waiting in the wings. Considerable debate in the media, coupled with growing official indifference, caused this first phase to end in October 1857 with no action being taken. An incoming Tory government (February 1858) appointed a parliamentary select committee to investigate the matter, chaired by the Conservative MP and president of the Ecclesiological Society, A. J. B. Beresford Hope. Criticising the 'injustices' of the competition, the committee recommended that the judges' decision be overturned. This naturally provoked vitriol from within the architectural profession concerning the merits of competition. In the event, the War Office component was shelved and George Gilbert Scott, along with his Gothic design, was summarily awarded the commission in November 1858 **[58a]**. He had initially only received third prize for his Foreign Office entry. To complicate matters further, the Indian 'mutiny', or great Sepoy Revolt, had broken out in March 1857. It was not quelled until the middle of 1858, amidst the opening stages of the project's development. Following this event, in January 1859, a new India Office component was added, taking the place of the War Office.

Rumbling beneath all this was the question of style. Would the new building(s) be Gothic or Classical? The advocates for a Classical design were inclined to uphold traditional associations between civil society and architecture. They believed the new building should emulate the works of those great English masters such as Jones, Wren, Gibbs, Vanbrugh, and Hawksmoor, as well as those eminent examples of 'acknowledged beauty' along Whitehall, such as the Banqueting House (1619–22) and Horse Guards (1750–9). The regular and orderly principles of Classical architecture were thus seen as symbolising civilised values including order, economy, and secular probity. But for Scott and his supporters, Gothic architecture provided a way through what they saw as the regimented monotony of Classicism. The ability of Gothic to adapt to contemporary circumstances, coupled with its distinctly native associations, legitimated its transition from the religious to the secular domain.

But there were larger considerations. The buildings in which the Foreign and War office departments of government had been located (a group of shabby eighteenth-century terraced houses on Downing Street) were widely viewed as embarrassing for a nation that reckoned itself a great imperial power. A building that spoke to this political reality was now demanded. Indeed, as Charles Edward Trevelyan, a leading politician and one-time administrator of the East India Company, observed:

> I consider that we have a very important national duty to perform in this respect; this city [London] is something more than the mother of arts and eloquence; she is the mother of nations; we [the British] are peopling two continents, the Western and the Southern Continent, and we are organising, Christianising and civilising large portions of two ancient continents, Africa and Asia; and it is not right that when the inhabitants of those countries come to the metropolis, they should see nothing worthy of its ancient renown.[2]

Trevelyan's experiences in India had no doubt revealed to him the role that architecture could play in the service of the state. Like the buildings in

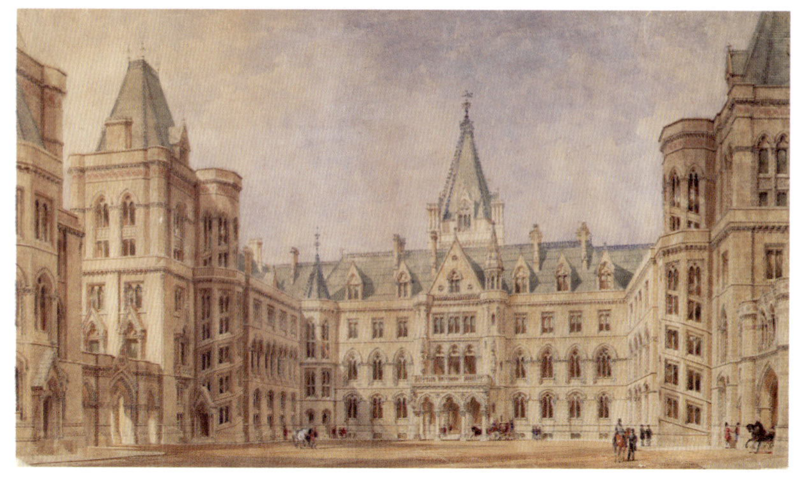

Fig. 58a
Revised design for new Foreign and India offices (*c.*1858), Westminster, London, by George Gilbert Scott. Perspective of court looking west (towards St James's Park).

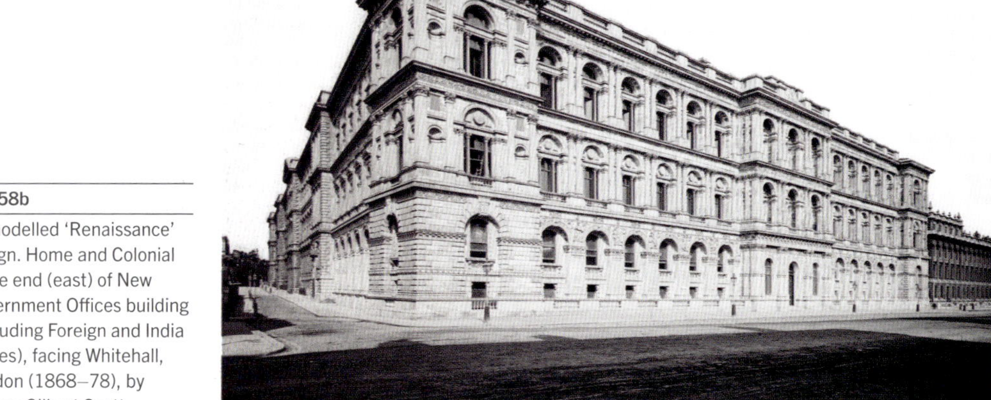

Fig. 58b
Remodelled 'Renaissance' design. Home and Colonial office end (east) of New Government Offices building (including Foreign and India offices), facing Whitehall, London (1868–78), by George Gilbert Scott.

which he had worked in Madras and Calcutta, he could readily imagine the new government offices teeming with the servants of a reformed bureaucratic and imperial state. In the 'official mind', architecture was seen as playing an increasingly important role as one of the most imposing and visually prominent markers of cultural expression.

There was a problem, however. Lord Palmerston, who had little sympathy for Gothic architecture, returned to power at the head of a new Liberal government in June 1859. Ultimately, Scott was forced to jettison his Gothic design for a Classical one, much to his dismay. After an initial scrap with Palmerston, Scott acquiesced, as the commission was simply too prestigious to forego. His initial effort was a 'Byzantine' compromise, which was also rejected. He later returned with a Renaissance palazzo-style design, which was accepted. The affair ended a little over two years later, in July 1861, with the House of Commons voting in favour of Scott's revised Renaissance proposal, resulting in the building we see today **[58b]**. This includes the new Home and Colonial offices which were added to the structure in the 1870s, also designed by Scott.

Despite the discontent over style, what is clear on the finished building are the references it makes to Britain's place and influence in the world. Both inside and out, it is emblazoned with relief sculpture and statuary depicting not only British history, but also, and most explicitly, Britain's colonial expansion. With respect to the India Office, which involved the design input of Matthew Digby Wyatt, we see statues of former governors general of British India, as well as those Indian princes who remained loyal to Britain during the Sepoy Revolt. We also see motifs referring to Mughal royalty (peacock), the Star of India (awarded for distinguished military service during the Revolt), and other indigenous animals, such as cows, tigers, and elephants. Inside, the great 'Durbar Court' is dripping with narrative-based sculpture referring, again, to British involvement in India, including key moments in Britain's subjugation of the Subcontinent. The Home and Colonial office buildings were also decorated with murals and sculpture that made reference to the geographical extent of British rule, including reliefs at street level depicting Africa, North America, and Australasia.

'All-Pervading Style'? The Rise of Secular Gothic

The 'battle' over style was, for a moment at least, all-consuming within the Victorian architectural establishment. Architects wrote and argued passionately about it, as did many outside the profession. It was a constant theme in the architectural press through the middle decades of the century, and was often reported in the media more widely, especially when public building projects came under scrutiny. As seen with the two landmark buildings just discussed, the debate hinged on the appropriateness of Gothic architecture for secular purposes. In the case of the new Foreign Office project, it even instigated something of a media storm, with the likes of E. A. Freeman, Beresford Hope, John Henry Parker, William Tite, and Robert Kerr, among others, weighing in on one side or the other. What this demonstrated above all was that, despite the gains that had been made by the Gothic Revival up to 1860, the profession remained divided on the matter of Gothic architecture's limitations as a universally applicable style.

The reality was that Classicism endured as the style of choice for civic architecture in Britain. Nevertheless, it was generally conceded by the late 1850s that Gothic could be used for such purposes. It had already leapt the ecclesiastical divide, having appeared in a range of commercial, domestic, and educational buildings. Prominent contemporary examples included Midland House, Birmingham (1857), by J. H. Chamberlain; the Crown Life Office, New Bridge Street, London (1858), by Benjamin Woodward; and the stained-glass studios of Lavers & Barraud, Endell Street, London (1859), by R. J. Withers, not to mention the Natural History Museum in Oxford, by Deane and Woodward, begun in 1855 (see Chapter 7) **[59a&b]**. Its appeal in the commercial sector, traditionally dominated by Classicism, would also find its way to the colonies, as the English, Scottish & Australian Bank (1880–3) and (old) Stock Exchange (1888) buildings on Collins Street, Melbourne, illustrate **[60]**. Although efforts of this kind were inspired by the writings of Ruskin and Street, and later by books such as T. G. Jackson's *Modern Gothic Architecture* (1873), it was Scott who did most to promote the cause of 'secular Gothic' at this critical juncture, producing one of the most forceful and coherent defences of it during the Victorian period.

First published in 1857, Scott's *Remarks on Secular & Domestic Architecture, Present and Future* appeared precisely at the moment the debate over the new government offices in Whitehall was entering full swing. It was not so much a theory as a general thesis concerning the secular merits of 'pointed' architecture, and how adopting this style on a 'principled system' would remedy what Scott saw as the meanness of contemporary architecture. Hitting out at the Gothic Revival's critics, he began with the rather mundane but signally utilitarian point that 'the revival of Pointed architecture' was not a backward-looking antiquarian enterprise, but that the Gothic was in fact '[a style] pre-eminently free, comprehensive, and practical; ready to adapt itself to every change in the habits of society, to embrace every new material or system of construction'. He then progressed by appealing to Victorian logic, arguing that:

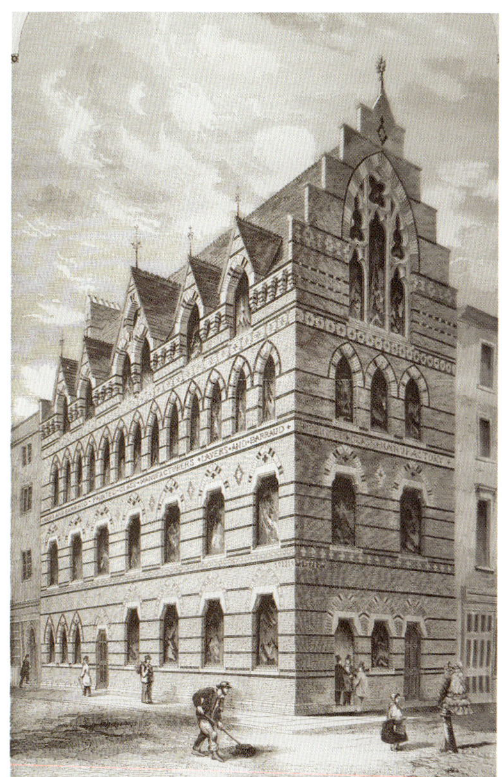

Fig. 59a

Lavers & Barraud stained glass manufactures, Endell Street (1858–9), London, by R. J. Withers.

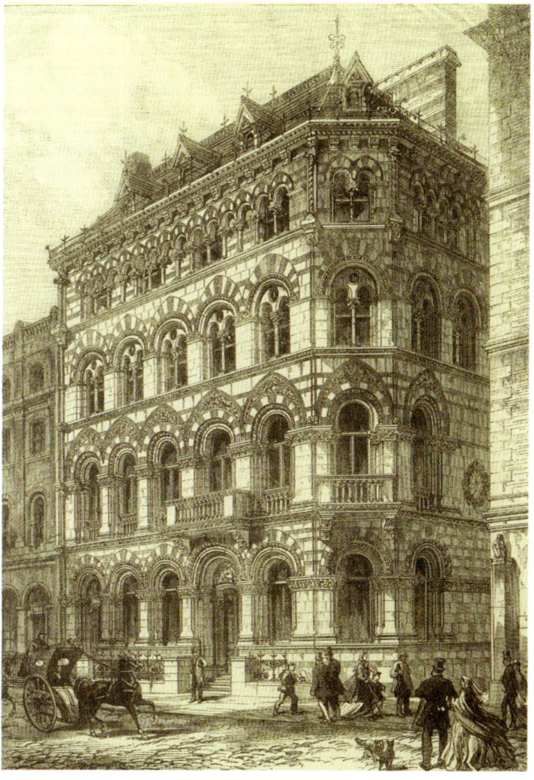

Fig. 59b

Crown Life Assurance Company offices, New Bridge Street (1858), London, by T. N. Deane and Benjamin Woodward.

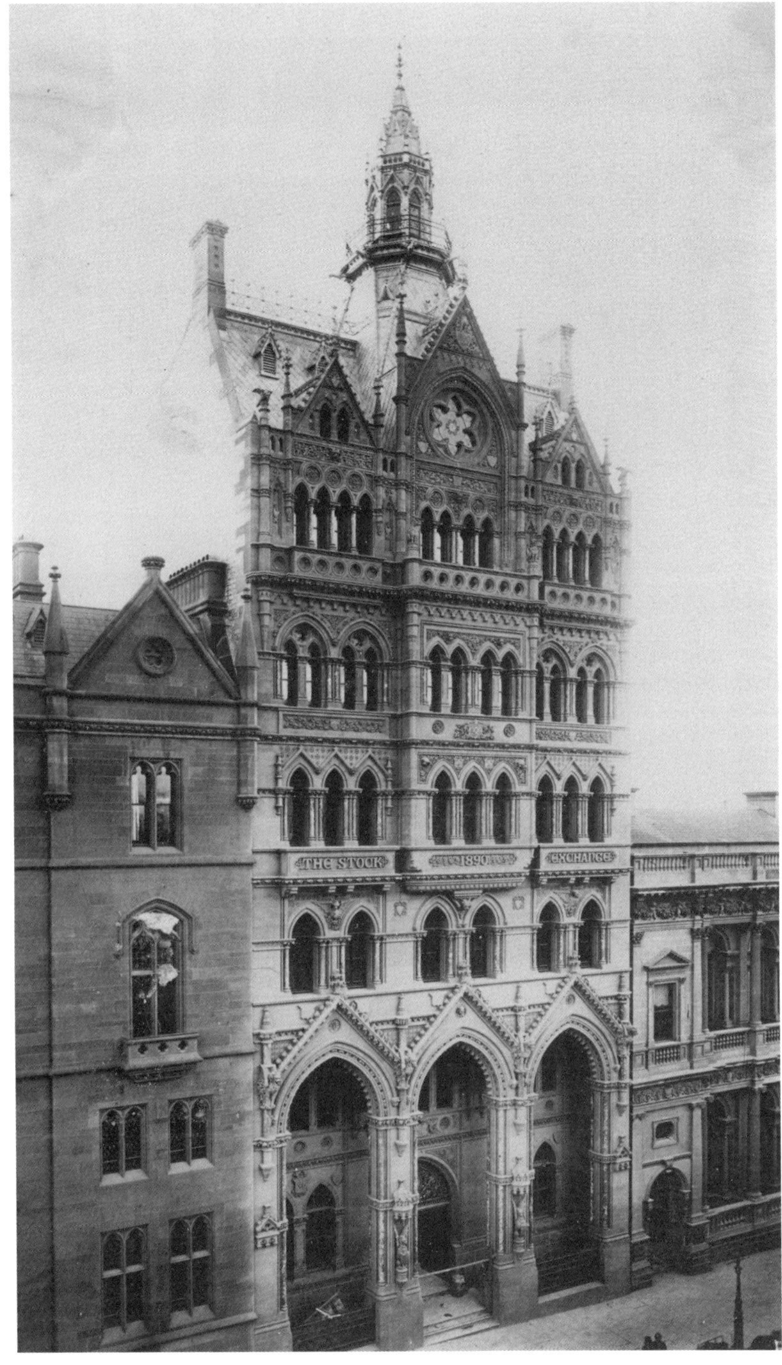

Fig. 60

(Old) Stock Exchange, Collins Street, Melbourne (1888), Australia, by William Pitt.

Our architecture...must be universal in its applicability. The style which is best for the church, must be equally so for the palace, the court of justice, the market, and the dwelling-house. It must embrace also engineering works,—as bridges, viaducts, and railway constructions. It must influence the character of our commercial structures, as warehouses and factories, and our agricultural buildings and labourers' cottages...Each must have its own forms and characteristics, yet a bond of union pervade the whole which will make it clear that all belong to one commanding, comprehensive, and all-pervading style.[3]

With Scott being one of the profession's leaders, *Remarks* was an influential publication, legitimising once and for all the merits of secular Gothic. To some extent it echoed claims made by George Edmund Street several years earlier in relation to the Natural History Museum at Oxford, where he observed that Gothic was 'indigenous, natural, real, and suitable', while Classicism ran contrary to 'natural principles', being 'unsuited in its effects to English habits, and its design to our English climate'.[4] But others, as we have seen, disagreed, including Alexander Thomson, James Fergusson, and T. L. Donaldson, who were hardly inclined to back down. The battle raged on.

It rumbled across the United Kingdom into the wider British world, manifesting in the design of local government buildings such as town halls, colonial legislatures, and courthouses. Indeed, one of the first grand municipal buildings to strike back in favour of the Gothic following the demise of Scott's original Foreign Office design was the Assize Courts in Manchester (1859–64), by Alfred Waterhouse **[61]**. Commissioned via open architectural competition, a procedure that was fast becoming the wearisome norm for civic infrastructure of this kind, the building proved the case for both the

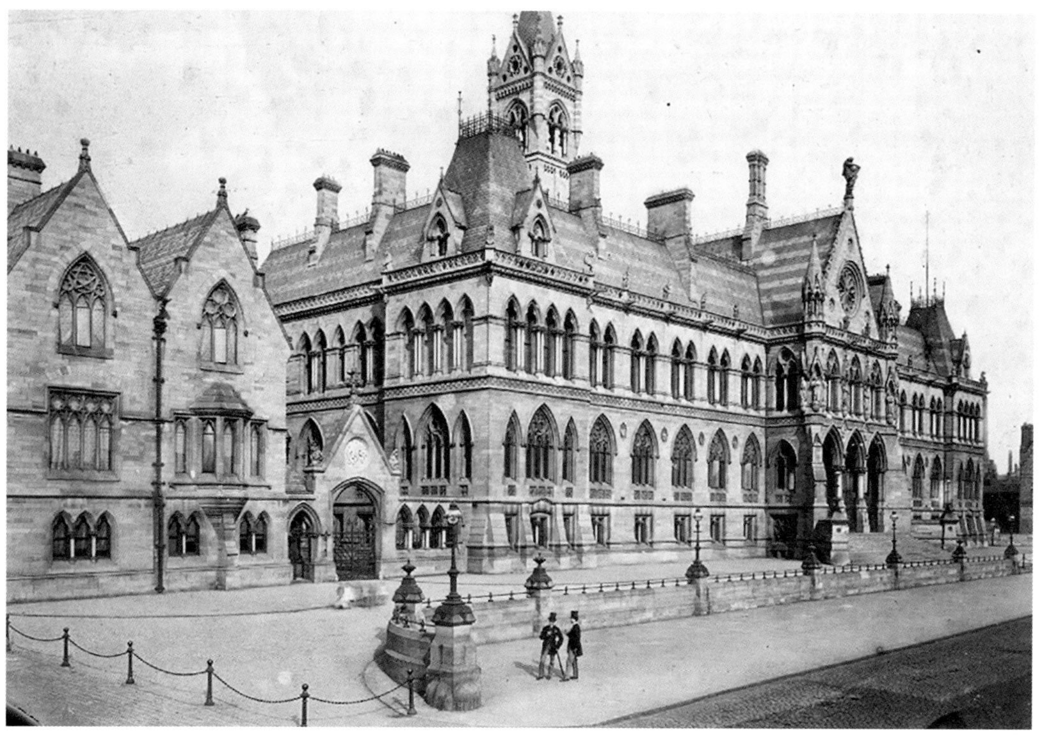

Fig. 61

Gothic triumphant? Assize Courts, Manchester (1859–64), by Alfred Waterhouse. Demolished 1957.

practicality and suitability of modern Gothic for secular purposes, particularly in large buildings. For Waterhouse, this was a matter of propriety. Having studied the arguments in Scott's *Remarks*, and recently visited the great secular Gothic buildings of Belgium's leading cities, he was convinced of the style's applicability to contemporary circumstances. In this respect, Gothic was seen to appeal to ideas of both functionality and historic nationalism. Although somewhat derivative of Scott's ill-fated Foreign Office proposal, Waterhouse's brilliant, picturesque handling of mass and form at the Manchester Assize Courts—set off by his skilful rendition of a robust, broad-based Ruskinian Gothic—made for one of the most impressive High Victorian buildings of the period. It was widely admired, by both critics and those who used it, including Ruskin, with *The Times* going so far as to describe it as one of 'the best courts of law in the world'.

The building represented a culmination point in the trend towards specialist courthouse design in Britain, signifying a new and more clearly defined relationship between the State, the law, and its legal subjects. From about this time onwards, courts of law became increasingly conspicuous landmark structures in mediating this evolving relationship in the Victorian urban realm, often occupying sites of civic prominence. Upon completion, the Manchester Assize Courts stood as the most sophisticated and convenient purpose-built facility for the administration of law in Britain, setting new standards for the provision of legal infrastructure.[5] This included the clear separation of functions in its planning for professional and security reasons, based on the 'concentric circle scheme', which placed the courts and hall in the centre and the offices and other subsidiary spaces to the exterior, with both served by a ring of corridors.[6] In achieving these standards, in such an unapologetically conspicuous manner, Waterhouse's court building was calculated to enhance the renewed sense of civic identity and reformed social values that came with Manchester's rapid urbanisation. In so doing, it monumentalised the aspirational vision of that city's manufacturing elite for a different and more modern kind of public sphere.

The triumph of the Manchester Assize Courts soon led to the erection of a number of other great symbolic court buildings in Britain, including the Royal Courts of Justice in London (1874–82), by G. E. Street, and the Victorian Law Courts in Birmingham (1887–91), by Aston Webb and E. Ingress Bell **[31a]**. The association between the law and medieval styles of architecture represented by these structures soon found its way overseas, into the wider British world, carried by émigré architects. One such is the Supreme Court building in Auckland, New Zealand (1865–9), by Edward Rumsey, who was a one-time pupil of Scott **[62a]**. Other examples include the Canadian Supreme Court, Ottawa (1874), by T. S. Scott, and the High Court in Bombay (1871–8) by James A. Fuller. Even in smaller, local courthouses the Gothic Revival left its mark, seen for instance in the Melbourne suburbs of Prahran (1886) and Carlton (1887) **[62b]**.

But it was Street's Royal Courts of Justice that was the most celebrated building **[63a]**. Given the date of its initial design (1866), this structure was, like Waterhouse's Assize Courts, perceived as a great victory for the secular Gothic cause, despite the fact that its completion some 20 years later effectively sounded the style's death knell for secular purposes as it ebbed

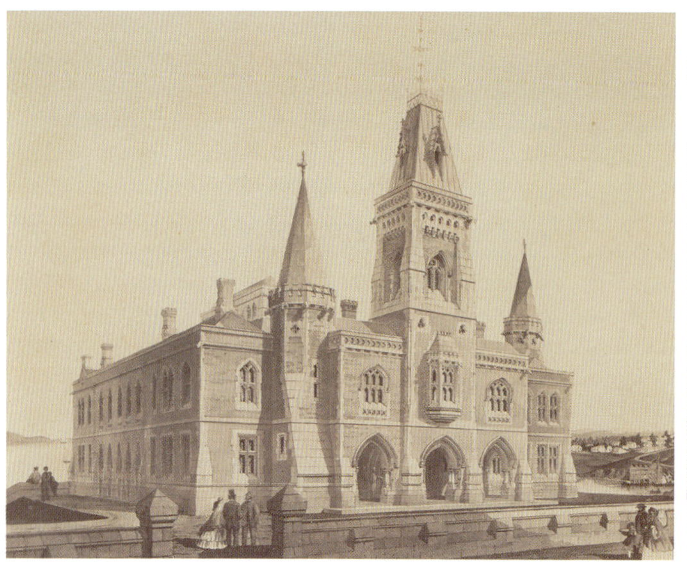

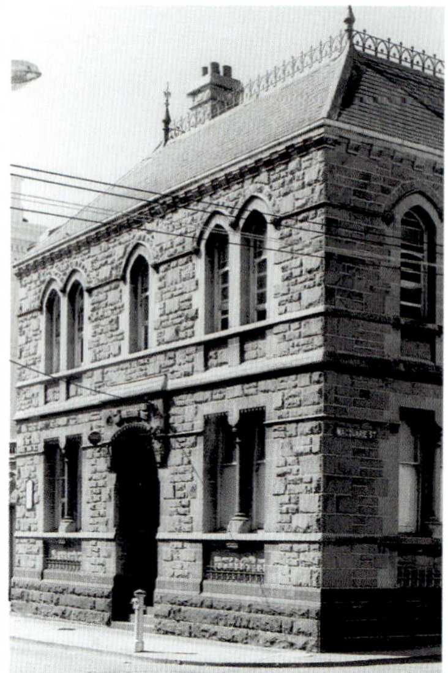

Fig. 62a

Design for Supreme Court, Auckland (built 1865–9), New Zealand, by Edward Rumsey.

Fig. 62b

Courthouse and Police Station (old), Grenville Street façade, Prahran (1886), Melbourne, Australia.

from vogue. Functionality and the efficient administration of justice were necessarily key, but so too was the idea of judicial dignity. Combined, these embodied the significance of the reformed English legal system. Moreover, romantic associations concerning architectural style and the origins of English law were never far from view, highlighting once again the connection between architecture and identity within the wider context of the 'battle' over style. In this case, the building's architecture (and that proposed in every other of the competition entries) appealed to the court's origins at Westminster Hall. Its most remarkable feature, the 230ft long (82ft high) central hall, had clear and appropriate connotations with the nave of a great medieval cathedral **[63b]**.

Civic Pride and the Town Hall Tradition in Britain

The one building that perhaps best captured the aspiring civic mindedness of the industrial city was Manchester Town Hall (1868–77) **[64]**. Also designed by Waterhouse—who was, after all, a local Nonconformist (Quaker) with extensive connections among the area's manufacturing elite—it was widely regarded as a symbol of the city's rise to economic and political pre-eminence. Ranging over six floors, on a site exceeding some 7,000 square metres, with a usable floor space of 6 million square feet, it was not only a huge structure for its time, but also the largest and most complete building of its kind in Europe. As long-time local MP John Bright observed at the time of its inauguration, it was 'truly a municipal palace...Whether you look at its great proportions outside or its internal decorations,...there is nothing like it that I know of in any part of the United Kingdom'.[7] As the mayor, then the bishop, of Manchester spoke in turn, pride in the city and its achievements was positively reinforced. Indeed, the following day Manchester's working classes, also feeling immense satisfaction at the raising of this great

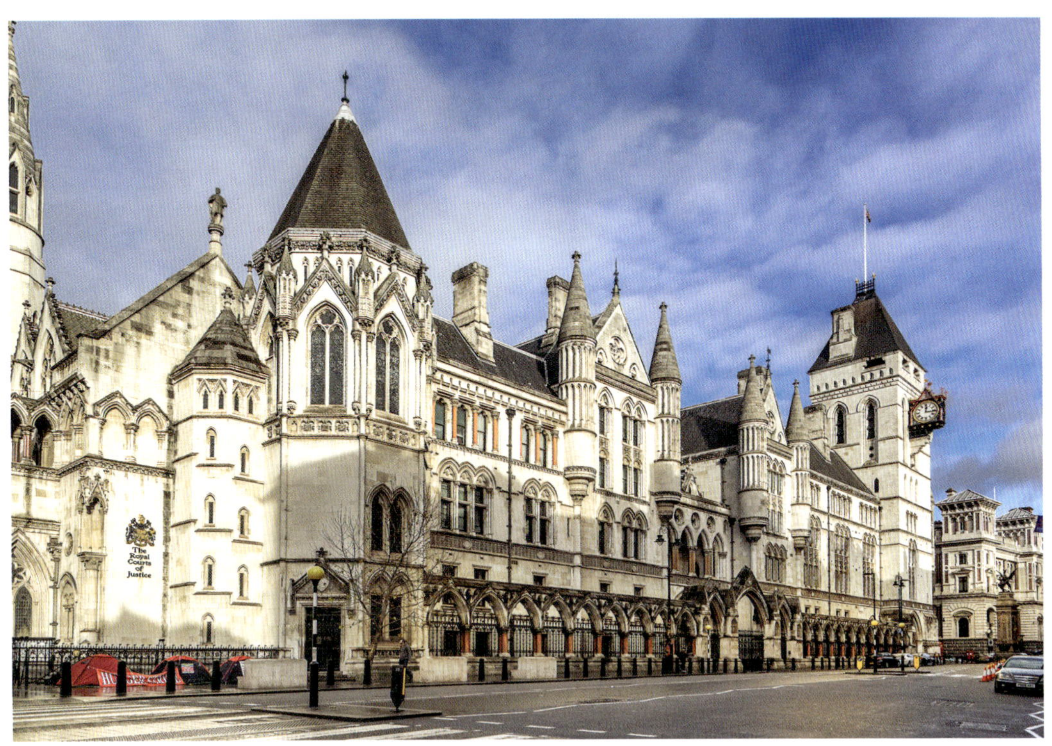

Fig. 63a

Royal Courts of Justice, Strand, London (designed 1866, built 1874–82), by George Edmund Street.

monument to their city's success (and the hard work they themselves had put into it), marched by the building in a spectacular, 40,000-strong 'procession of the trades'.

Built largely of brick, encased in a veneer of light brown Spinkwell sandstone from quarries near Bradford, its most imposing feature is the 98-metre-high clock tower, facing Albert Square, one of the most distinguished public spaces in the city. Designed in a different but no less robust Gothic style to that of the Assize Courts, and costing nearly £800,000 (£70 million in today's money) to complete, it also took its cue from the great medieval town halls of Northern Europe. But it was not its striking appearance as such that won Waterhouse the commission, although this aspect of the design was certainly considered adequate. Rather, it was his genius for planning **[65a]**. He only received fourth place in the second stage of the competition, but the judges determined that, all things considered, his was the best design, especially the attention he accorded practical considerations such as 'ease of access, and supply of light and ventilation'. The difficulty that Waterhouse and the other competitors had to overcome was the awkward triangular site, which necessitated a clever solution to the building's internal arrangements. In achieving this, Waterhouse proposed the employment of continuous, single-loaded corridors to the interior perimeter of the structure. With attention to such detail, including an awareness for the latest in building technology, materials, and services, Waterhouse produced in Manchester Town Hall one of the outstanding 'modern Gothic' structures of the age.

Fig. 63b

Great Hall, Royal Courts of Justice, London.

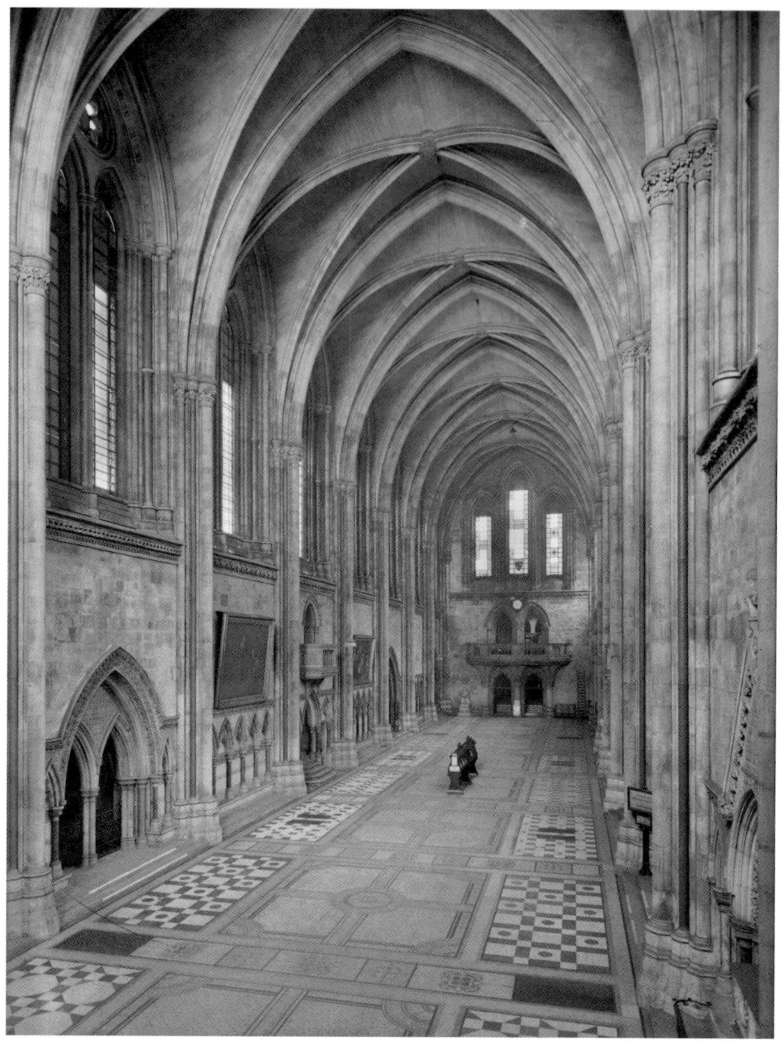

As mentioned, buildings of this nature in Victorian Britain—in terms of scale, elaboration, and cost—were more than just symbols of a new-found civic pride. They served an urgent practical purpose, too. With corporate government becoming increasingly specialised and bureaucratic, larger and more sophisticated facilities for local administration were required. The Victorian town hall was the most conspicuous emblem of this burgeoning bureaucratic burden, symbolic in its own way of the rise of local representative government (or, in this case, the entrenchment of bourgeois capitalist interests) during the period. But these buildings also sought to peg ideas of local identity to larger regional, national, and even imperial frames of reference. How they communicated this as monumental works of art became a question not only of civic patriotism but of how 'their story' fitted into and enhanced the evolving national narrative, even if that story was at times inconsistent or open to challenge. Again, considering Manchester Town Hall, there is much in the way of decoration that is

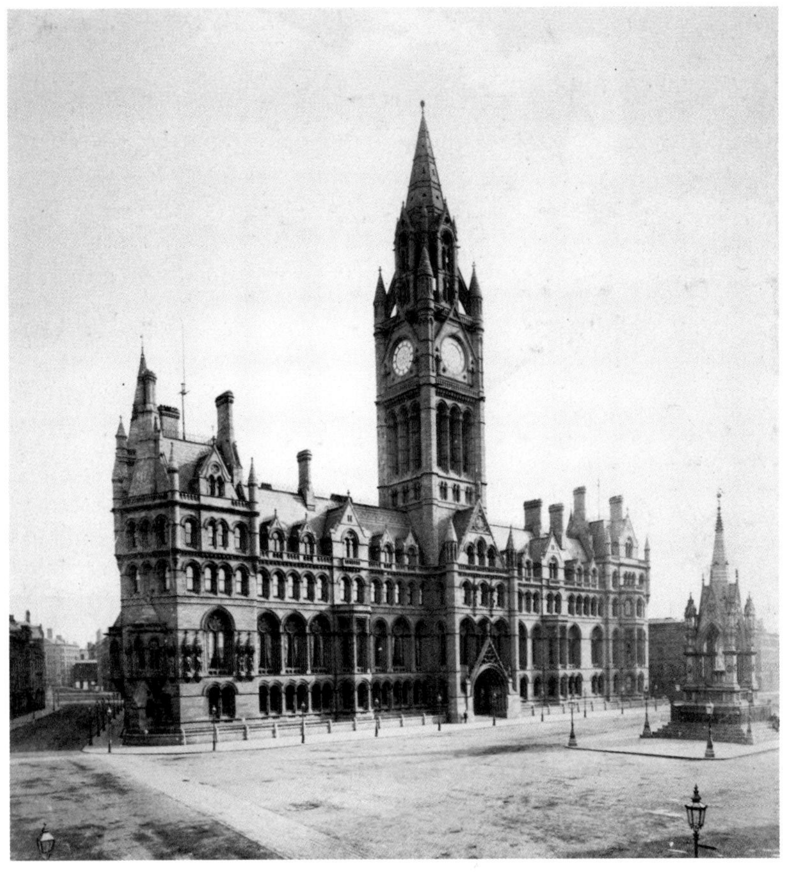

Fig. 64

Provincial pride: Manchester Town Hall (1868–77), by Alfred Waterhouse. The Manchester Albert Memorial by Thomas Worthington can be seen at lower right.

both local and regional, especially the series of murals in the public hall by Ford Madox Brown charting the rise of Manchester and its associated industries. The charming bee emblem that can be found throughout the building also alludes to the idea of industry, as do more specific references to cotton.

But mid-nineteenth-century Manchester understood itself as a city of national and international import and influence. The town hall's inauguration was reported and celebrated both nationally and internationally. The exterior was emblazoned with statues of many of England's great kings and queens, placing the city at the heart of a reflexive national narrative. Moreover, in the hall, on the ceiling above Brown's murals, could be found heraldic devices of the numerous countries that Manchester traded with, including many in the British colonial world. The architecture itself sought to embody this expanding narrative. For instance, the three spiral staircases that mark the internal corners of the triangular plan comprise granites from the different 'nations' of the United Kingdom (excluding Wales), making for 'English', 'Irish', and 'Scotch' features within the building's fabric **[65b]**. It seemed highly appropriate, too, that the 'white rock' stone used throughout the building's interior came from among coal measures, the very energy source upon which Manchester's industrial economy was founded. Indeed,

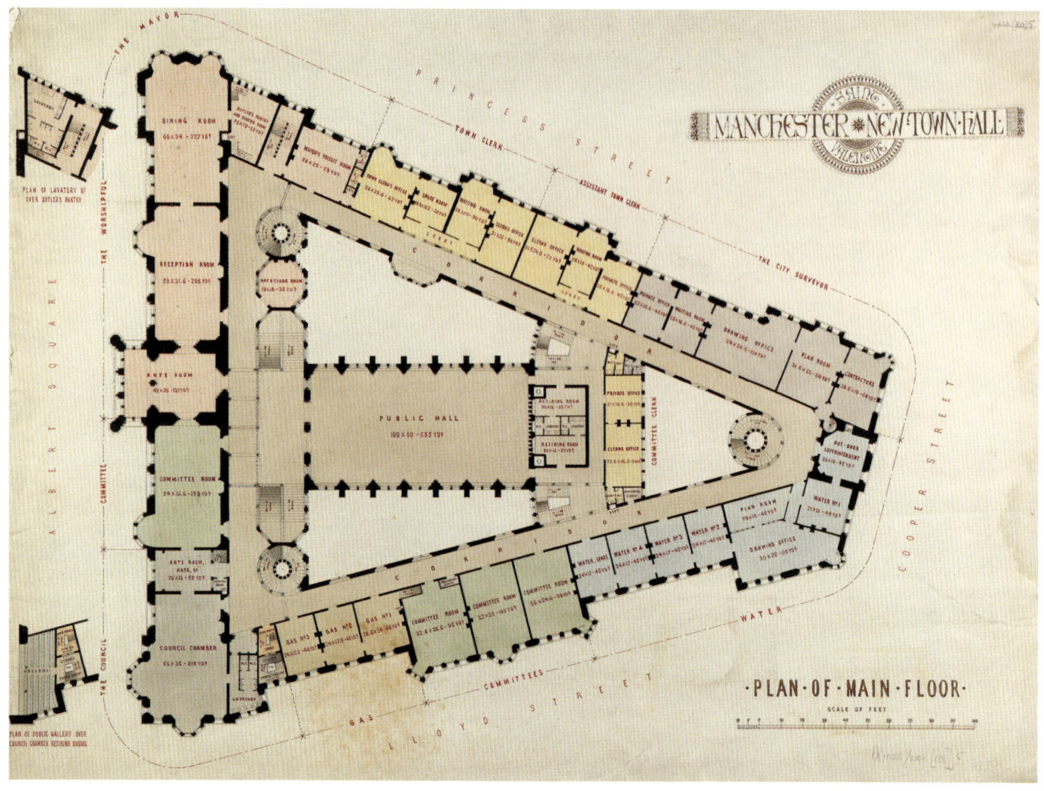

Fig. 65a

Main-floor plan, Manchester Town Hall, competition entry (1868), Alfred Waterhouse.

the architectonic imaginary that underpinned the application of Gothic architecture, including the procurement and production of materials, was not only the embodiment of an industrial mindset but also symbolised the idea of the building as a kind of machine.[8] As one of the building's chroniclers observed, it was a Gothic 'suffused with the feeling and spirit of the present age'.[9] In showcasing their credentials in this way, buildings such as the Assize Courts and Town Hall in Manchester helped 'invent' a new tradition of civic modernity in Victorian Britain.

Many distinguished buildings of this kind rose across the United Kingdom during the period, especially from the 1850s onwards. Some of the grandest were in fact Classical, such as St George's Hall in Liverpool (1841–56), by H. L. Elmes and C. R. Cockerell; Leeds Town Hall (1853–8), by Cuthbert Brodrick **[66]**; Todmorden Town Hall (1860–75), by John Gibson; or, slightly later, Birmingham Council House (1874–9), by Yeoville Thomason, and Paisley Town Hall (1879–82), by W. H. Lynn. Again, the dilemma of style was at stake in deciding what kind of architectural statement best represented urban identity and authority in modern Britain, with Classicism retaining something of its traditional influence. Outstanding examples in the Gothic style we might point to include Chester Town Hall (1865–9), by W. H. Lynn; Rochdale Town Hall (1866–71), by W. H. Crossland (new tower added by Waterhouse in 1885) **[67a]**; City Hall in Bradford (1869–73) **[68]**, by Lockwood and Mawson; Preston Town Hall (1862–7), by G. G. Scott; and the colossal Middlesbrough Town Hall (1883–8), by

Fig. 65b

One of three internal spiral staircases at Manchester Town Hall, showcasing regional stone.

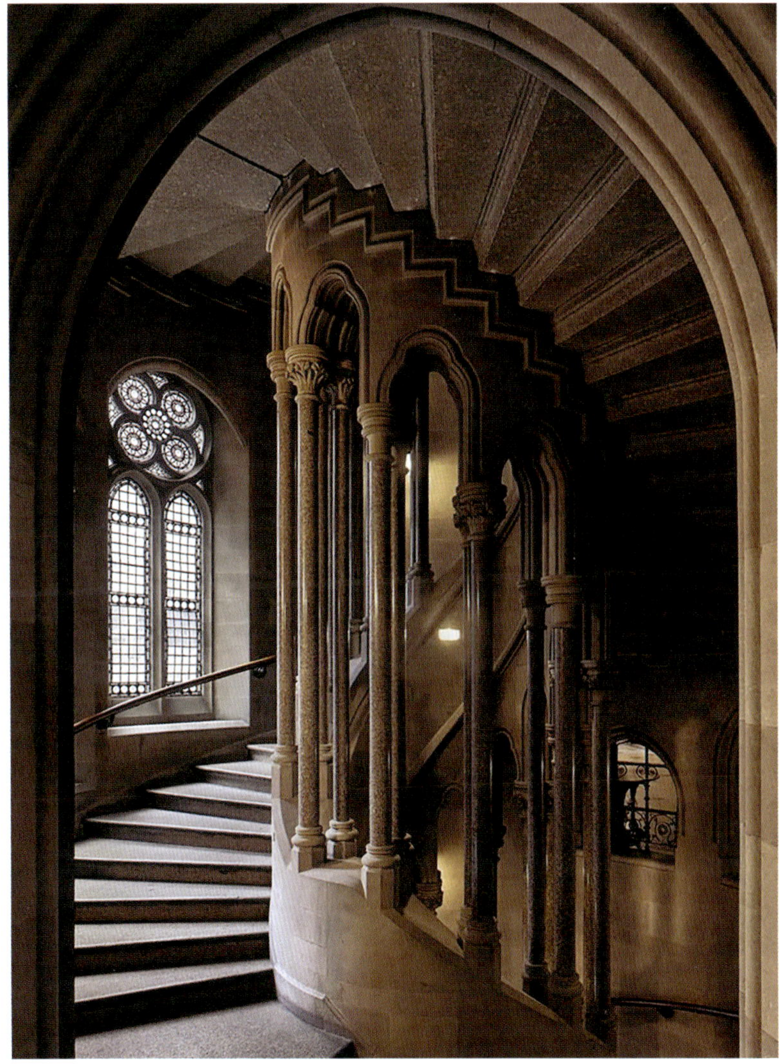

G. G. Hoskins. In Scotland there was the Town House, Inverness (1872–8), by William Lawrie, with its Scots Baronial flourishes, and the Municipal Buildings, Perth (1878–81), by Andrew Heiton **[67b]**; while in Wales we have Abergavenny Town Hall (1869–71), by Willson & Willcox. The tower at Bradford made direct allusion to the Palazzo Vecchio in Florence. As one pundit observed, this was 'thoroughly in harmony with the genius of self-government and the commercial spirit,' adding that Gothic was 'the chosen style of free and popular communities'.[10]

As noted in Chapter 3, Ruskin had insisted upon the communicative capacity of good architecture. The Gothic Revival guild hall at Northampton (1861–4, extended 1889–92), by E. W. Godwin, is perhaps the best example of Ruskinian principles applied to municipal architecture, with Godwin himself later claiming that it was founded 'entirely on the *Stones of Venice*' **[69a]**. Rendered in a neat yet powerful High Victorian Gothic, with a

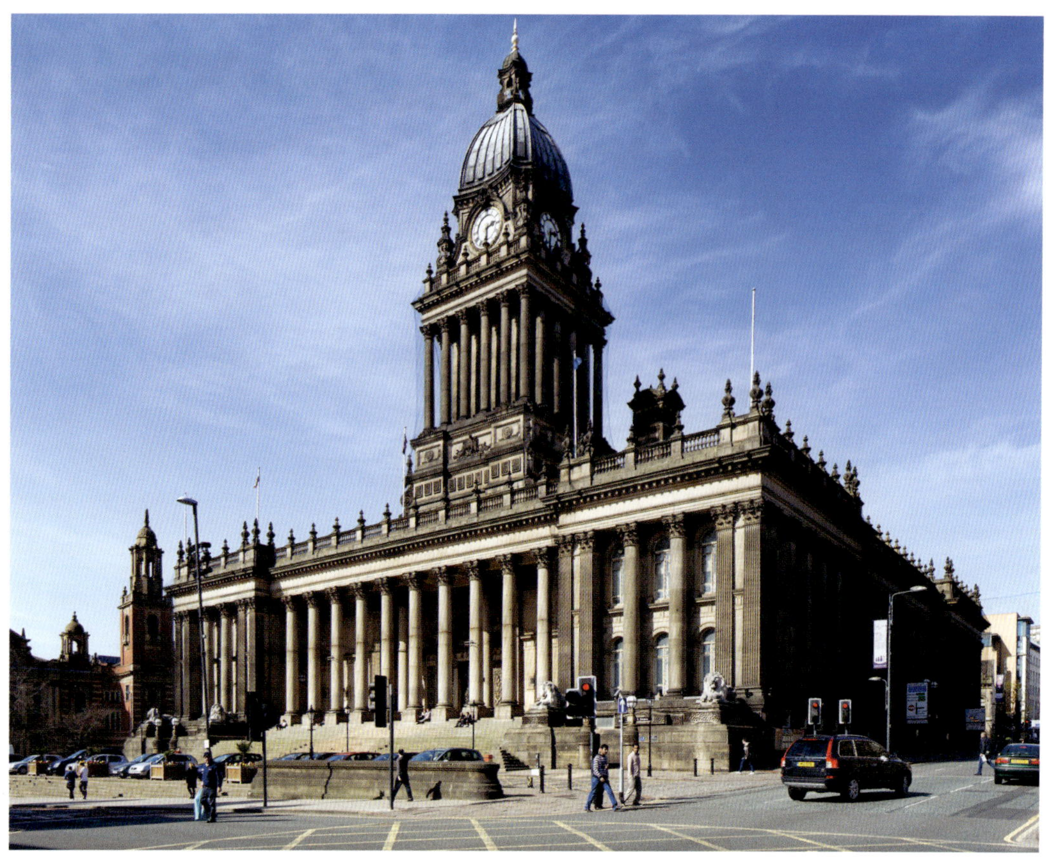

Fig. 66

Leeds Town Hall (1853–8), West Yorkshire, by Cuthbert Brodrick.

strong horizontal emphasis articulated by coloured stone banding and heavy string coursing, it too may be seen as part of that tradition initiated by the Oxford Natural History Museum, and the unrealised designs for the Foreign Office competition by the likes of Scott and Deane & Woodward. By this time the identitarian resonances of modern Gothic were well understood. But emerging here also was the allusion to the medieval town hall tradition of the Low Countries and Germany that would achieve full force at Manchester. In order to enhance the building's messaging Godwin deployed the power of sculpture. Taking his cue directly from Ruskin, he was clear in observing how sculpture, if 'treated properly', would 'cut the histories of our cities and of our civil and religious freedom at the corner of the street', conveying 'some valuable lesson to the passerby'.[11] As with Manchester town hall, and many other structures like it, what we see is a desire to set local events within a wider narrative frame. Arrayed across the upper level are various kings and queens of England, bringing the nation's regal lineage down to the present with Queen Victoria; below are tympana containing scenes from local history with wider significance, in bold relief, such as the trial of Thomas Becket and the erection of an Eleanor cross **[69b]**. In this scenography local and national were fused and employed in aid of building a reformed landscape of devolved, representative government.

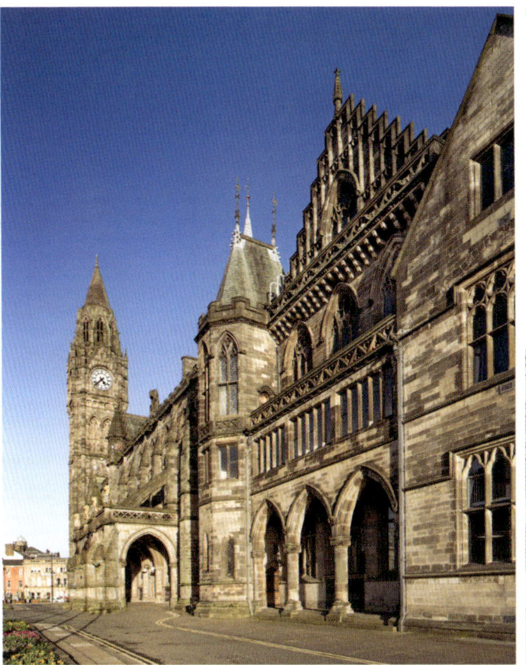

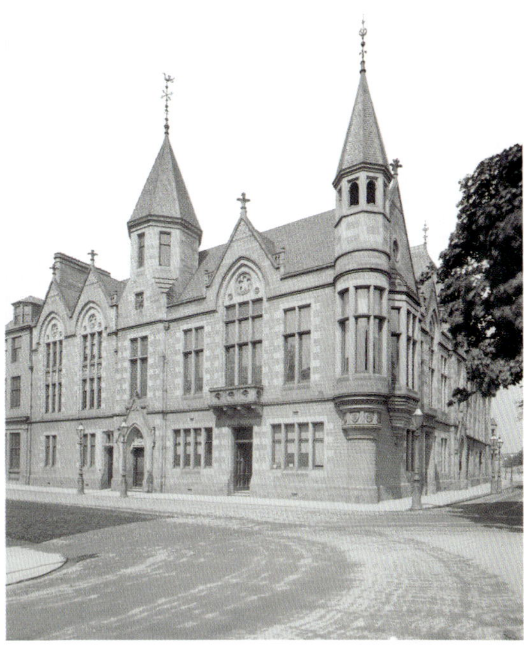

Fig. 67a

Rochdale Town Hall (1866–71), The Esplanade, Rochdale, by W. H. Crossland (tower added by Waterhouse in 1885).

Fig. 67b

Municipal Buildings (1878–81), High Street, Perth, by Andrew Heiton.

Monumental Government Architecture in the British Colonial World

The same scenes played out in the wider British world. In certain places, such as the settler colonies in Australia, Canada, South Africa, and New Zealand, a desire for local government arose early. This was not only a matter of practicality, but also an attempt to appease colonial nationalist sentiment, which became increasingly strident in the late nineteenth century. The lessons of the American Revolution still loomed large in the rear-view mirror of British imperial politics, and the need to maintain loyalty (and territory) in an increasingly unstable and perilous international order was considered paramount. What emerged from this were colonial legislatures that required appropriate accommodation.

One of the first, large-scale projects of this kind during the Victorian period was the erection of a parliament building in Melbourne (1856–92), in the newly minted colony of Victoria (1851) **[70a]**. As observed in Chapter 1, the settlement of Melbourne grew rapidly off the back of the early 1850s gold rush. For a burgeoning metropolis of a 'far away' British community, an architectural statement equal to its wealth and aspirations for self-determination was demanded. Yet, for such a young community, looking back to the motherland for inspiration was something of a reflex. Indeed, considering the symbolic rise of provincial government in Britain, the building's architect (Peter Kerr of the Melbourne-based firm Knight & Kerr) looked directly to the emerging town hall tradition, producing a design heavily influenced by the monumental Classicism of Leeds Town Hall.[12] This is somewhat ironic given that Kerr himself, before emigrating to Australia in 1852, not only knew and admired Pugin, but had worked in the

Fig. 68

City Hall, Bradford (1869–73), by Lockwood and Mawson.

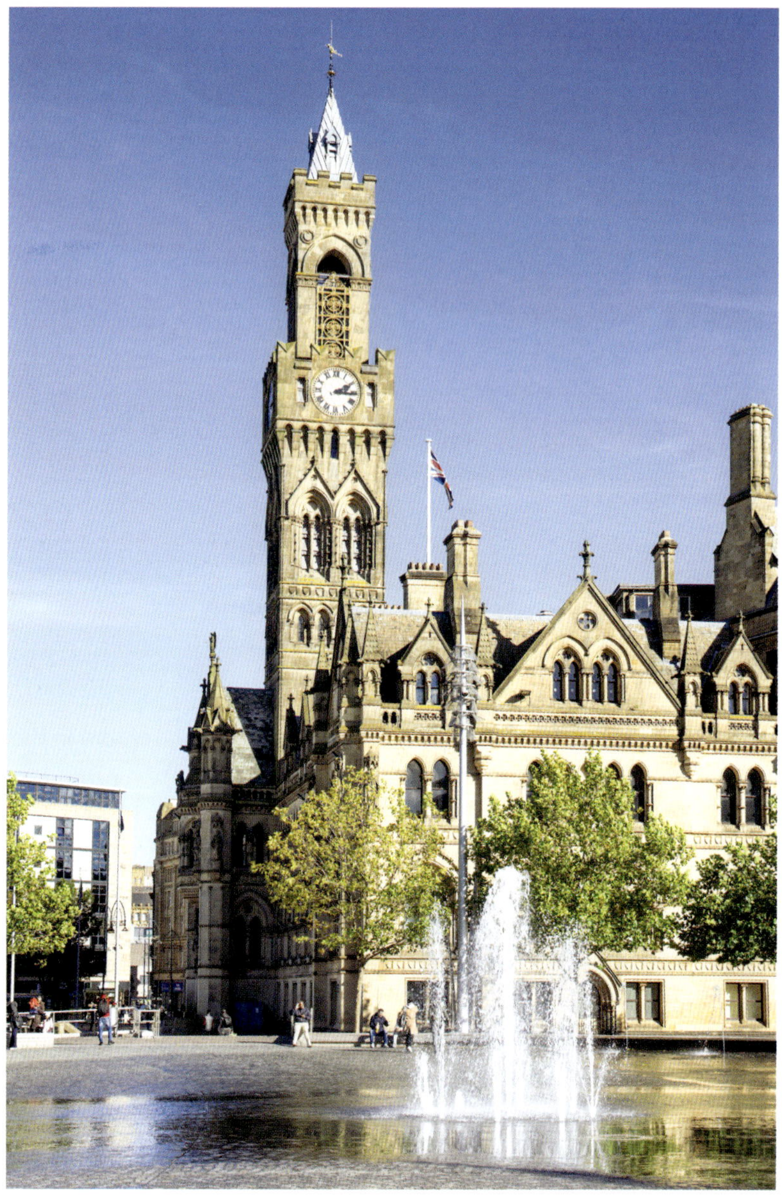

offices of Charles Barry on the Houses of Parliament. But the idea of erecting such a landmark civic building in 1850s Melbourne in a Gothic Revival style would have been rejected, despite the precedent set in the imperial capital. Monumental Classicism signalled not only authority, but civility, too. Through architects such as the precocious J. J. Clark, Melbourne would go on to set an early standard for Neoclassical architecture in the colonies, evidenced in the Italianate splendour of the new Treasury Building (1858–62), adjacent Parliament House.

French Second Empire and Italianate Classical government houses, town halls, and municipal offices would come to grace cities, suburbs, and

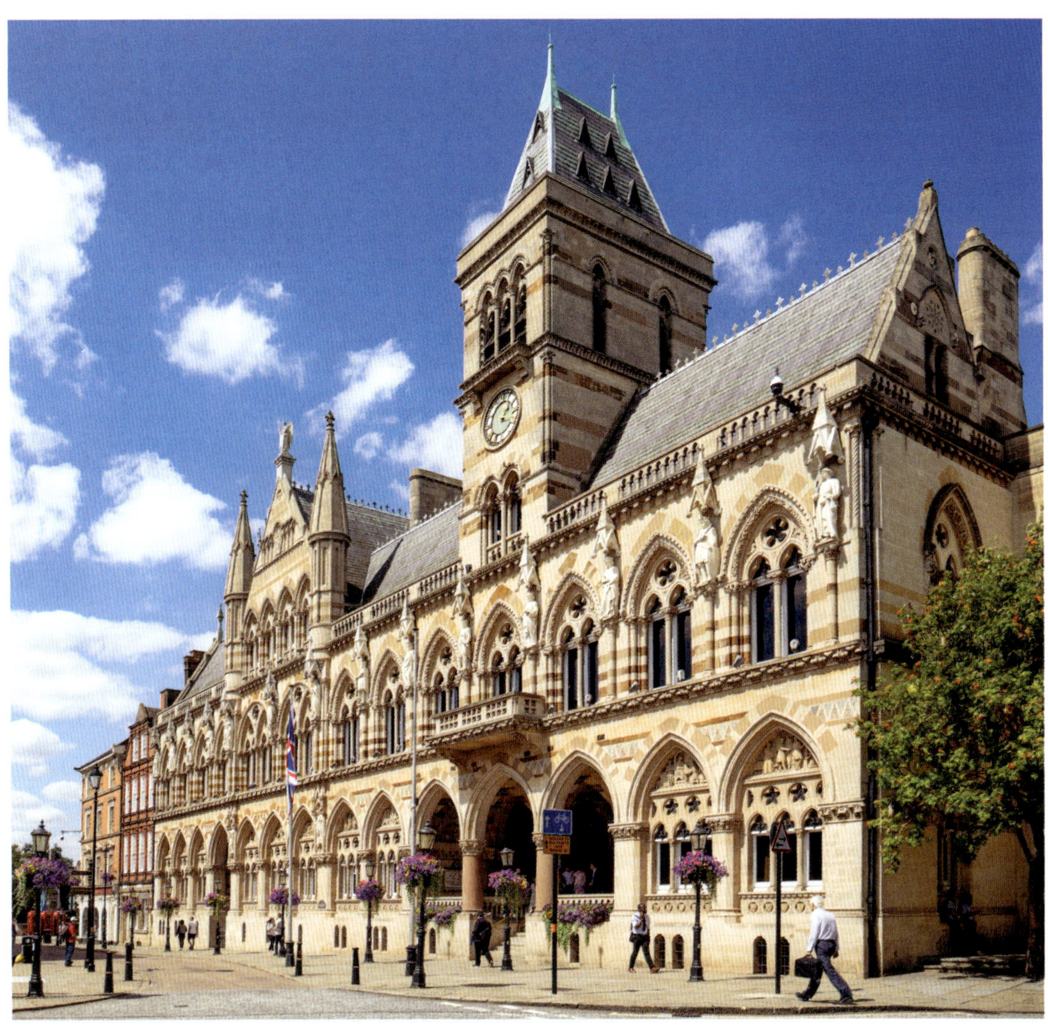

Fig. 69a

Northampton Guildhall (1861–4, extended 1889–92), by E. W. Godwin.

towns right across the length and breadth of the Australian colonies, and beyond, becoming something of a lingua franca for colonial governance. Variations on the Italianate style were the most common, as seen in Melbourne and its suburbs. There were numerous other regional examples, too, with nearly every town and city exhibiting such a structure, however small. Outstanding examples of the genre include Government House, Victoria (1871–6), by William Wardell, and the Treasury Building in Brisbane (1883–5), by Clark. Across the Indian Ocean stood the rather grandiose example of the Town Hall in Cape Town (1905), by Reid & Green. French influence was more apparent in the town halls at Sydney (1869–78) and the central Victorian gold-mining city of Bendigo (1859–72). There were places in the empire where French cultural influence was particularly strong, as in Montreal (Québec, Canada), where the Hotel de Ville (1872–8) was modelled on its Parisian counterpart **[70b]**. Although such buildings embodied and expressed the liberal ideal of local representative govern-

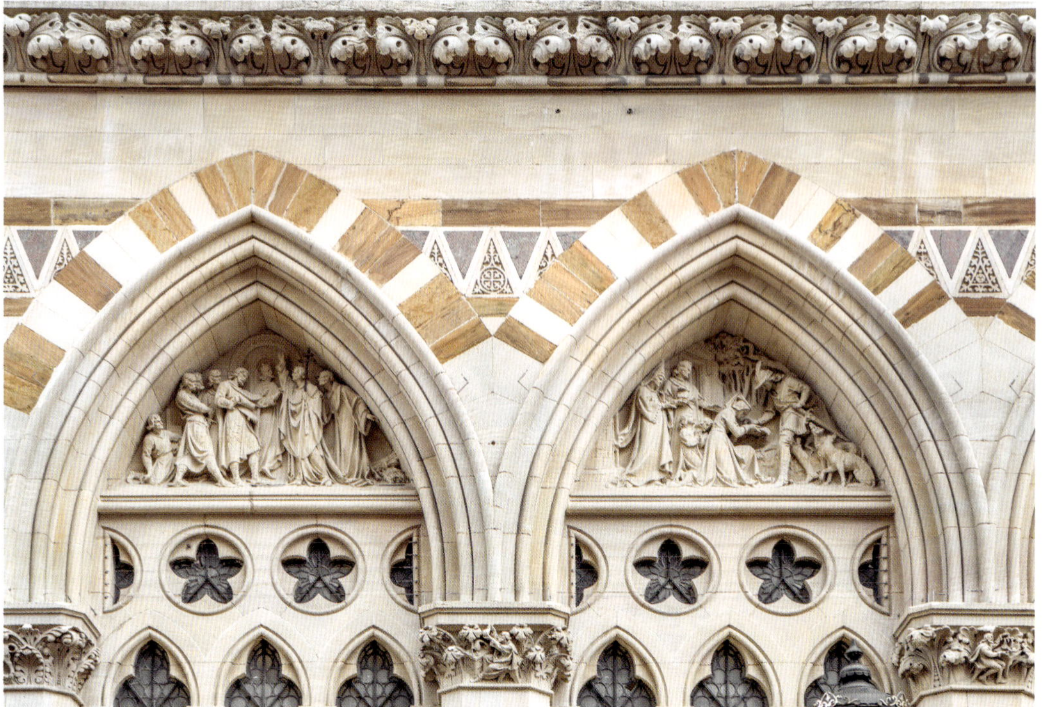

Fig. 69b

Detail, façade, Northampton Guildhall, showing relief sculpture.

ment, they also revealed the need to impose upon the landscape a common fabric of colonial order.

But the Gothic was not ignored in these contexts, even finding its way to the tropics. In Port of Spain, Trinidad, for instance, there was the Police Headquarters building (1876), designed in a striking Ruskinian-Italianate Gothic; while in Bridgetown, Barbados, the so-called Public Buildings (1870–4) were raised in a rather heavy, climatically adapted Gothic, with the west block sporting a clock tower that echoed its illustrious precursor in Westminster **[71a]**. Designed by John Bourne of the Public Works Department, and incorporating arcading to shield its interiors from direct sunlight, it was built to house the local assembly and other government offices, including that of the Colonial Secretary. In this vein we might also point to the Town Hall in Colombo (*c.*1873), Sri Lanka, by the Public Works Department architect James Smither, with its contextually sensitive Mediterranean-style Gothic inflections. In Canada we find yet another twist on Victorian medievalism in Toronto Town Hall (1889–98), by E. J. Lennox **[71b]**. Here the increasingly assertive influence of Canada's much larger, culturally ebullient neighbour, the United States, is evident in the Romanesque language of one of their greatest nineteenth-century architects, H. H. Richardson. This American influence, especially its Beaux-Arts traditions as filtered through French experience, would heavily

Fig. 70a

Parliament House, Melbourne (1856–92), Australia, by Peter Kerr.

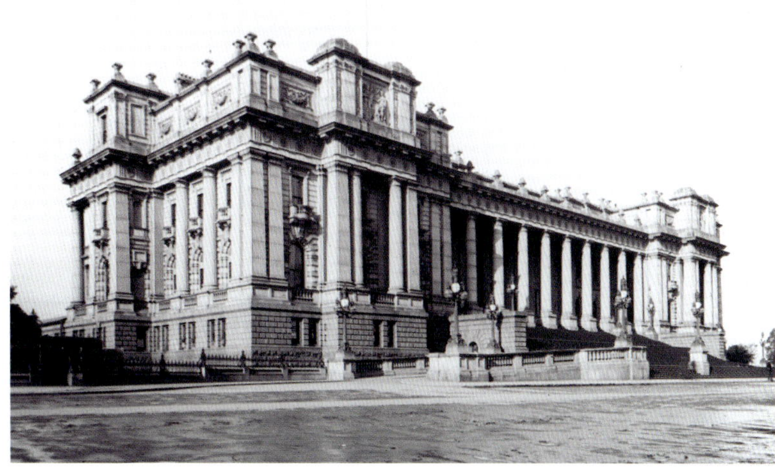

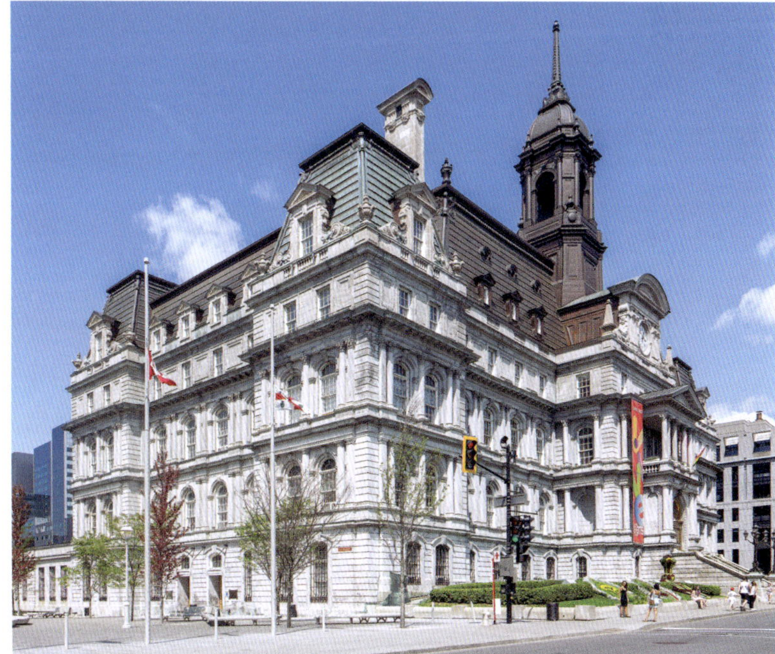

Fig. 70b

Hôtel de Ville (1872–8), Place Vauquelin, Montreal, Canada, by Henri-Maurice Perrault and A. C. Hutchison.

inflect architecture in Canada's major metropolitan centres during the late Victorian and early Edwardian periods. Still, despite the clear stimulus of Richardson in the case of Toronto, one cannot help but see echoes of Waterhouse and Manchester.

Indeed, it was in Canada that one of the greatest of all colonial legislatures in the Gothic Revival style was built **[72]**. Located in Ottawa, the

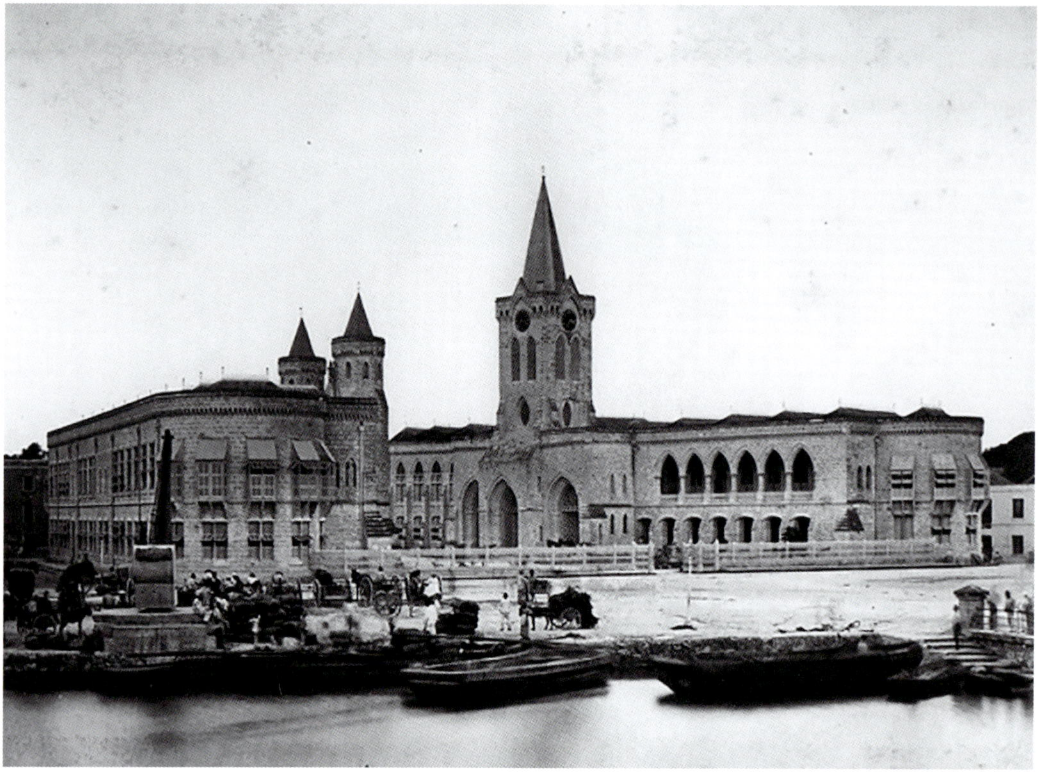

Fig. 71a

Tropical Gothic. Public Buildings (1870–4), Bridgetown, Barbados, by Superintendent of Public Works, John F. Bourne.

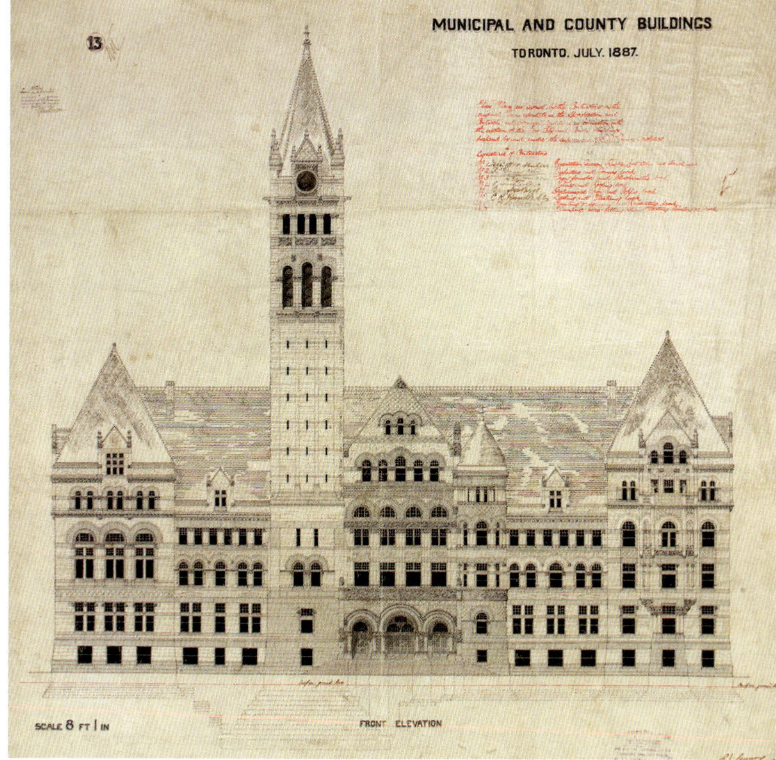

Fig. 71b

Design drawing (1887), main façade, Toronto Town Hall (Municipal Buildings), Toronto, Canada, by E. J. Lennox.

newly selected capital of the United Province of Canada, the Canadian Parliament Buildings were among the highest-profile projects in furtherance of the secular Gothic cause. Not surprisingly, the design was arrived at by international competition. The complex of buildings that resulted comprised a majestic Centre Block (1859–66, burned and replaced 1916–27) and attached Library (1859–77) by Thomas Fuller and Chilion Jones, with flanking East and West Blocks (1859–65) by Thomas Stent and Augustus Laver. Jones was Canadian-born, the others were recent arrivals from England. Interestingly, Stent and Laver would go on to receive second prize for their Gothic design in the 1862 competition for a new parliament building in Sydney. The winning design, also Gothic (by W. H. Lynn of Dublin), was never built, however. Although the pursuit of the Gothic Revival in the colonies was an extension of architectural developments in Britain, it also concerned questions of identity. In the Canadian context the use of Gothic was seen, in part at least, as a conscious act of imperial consolidation, providing an important contrast with Classical sources that were preferred in the neighbouring republican United States. In this respect the colonies often led the way with large-scale experiments in secular Gothic building design. As the architectural historian Henry-Russell Hitchcock would later observe of the Canadian parliament building, 'the variety of form, the gusto of the detail, and the urbanistic scale of

Fig. 72

Canadian Parliament Buildings, Ottawa (1859–65), Canada, by Thomas Fuller, Chilion Jones, Thomas Stent, and Augustus Laver.

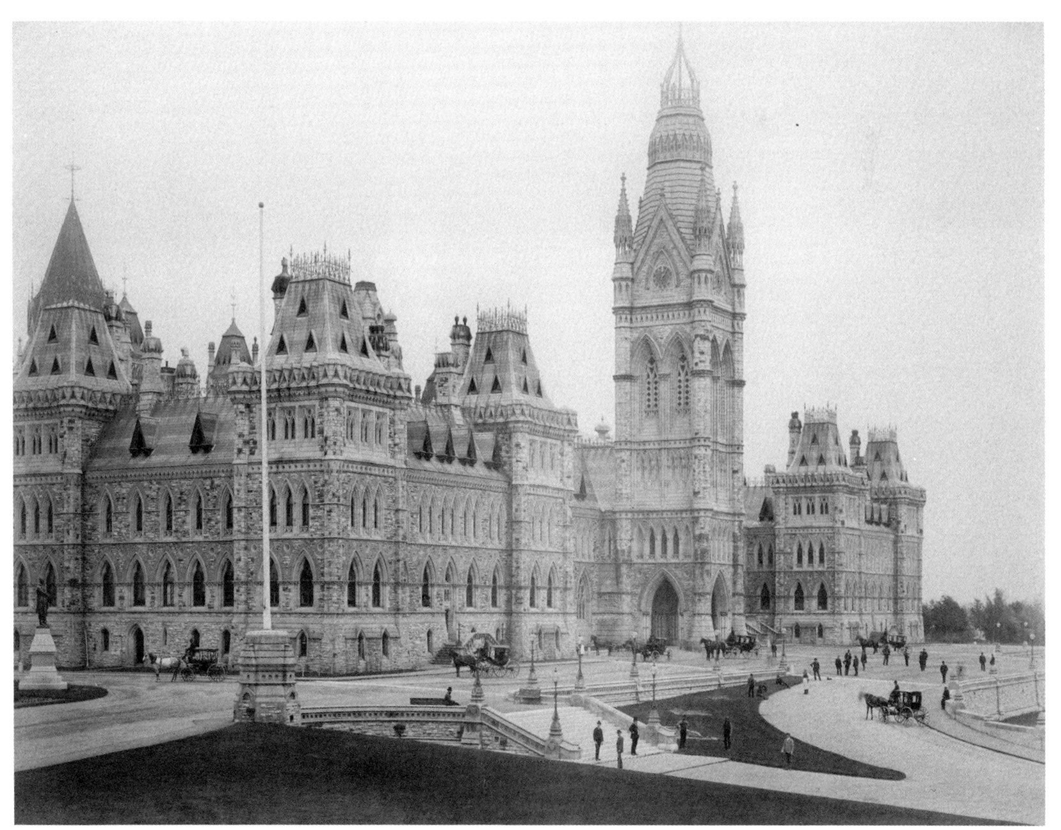

this project made [it] a major monumental group unrivalled for extent and complexity of organization in England'.[13]

Adaptation and Hybridisation

The scope for urbanism offered by the Gothic Revival led to intriguing outcomes elsewhere in the British colonial world. This is partly explained by the freedom architects had to act in such places, where in many cases little or no civic infrastructure existed, and where planning decisions were largely unimpeded by extant urban fabric. Two good examples are the settlements of Canterbury, in New Zealand, and modern Bombay, in India.

At Canterbury it was the Pugin-inspired Benjamin Mountfort who was commissioned to design the Provincial Council Buildings, Christchurch, completed in three stages between 1857 and 1865 **[73a]**. Given the time period, as well as the religious foundation of Canterbury as an Anglican settlement, there was a natural preference for the Gothic. Starting off as a picturesque array of timber structures, Mountfort formed the complex around a cloistered quadrangle, including offices, library, and a debating chamber. As the settlement grew, and further resources became available, more permanent structures were added in masonry, including a central tower in bands of red scoria and local grey stone. The *piéce de rèsistance*, however, was the magnificent stone council chamber added in 1864, rendered in a simple yet sturdy High Victorian Gothic. This was quite a sophisticated work of architecture, with rich polychrome interior, extensive use of stained glass, and an unusual ridge and furrow ceiling **[73b]**. Mountfort's invention at Canterbury, some 12,000 miles from his native Birmingham,

Fig. 73a
Provincial Council Buildings (1857–65), Christchurch, Canterbury, New Zealand, by Benjamin Mountfort.

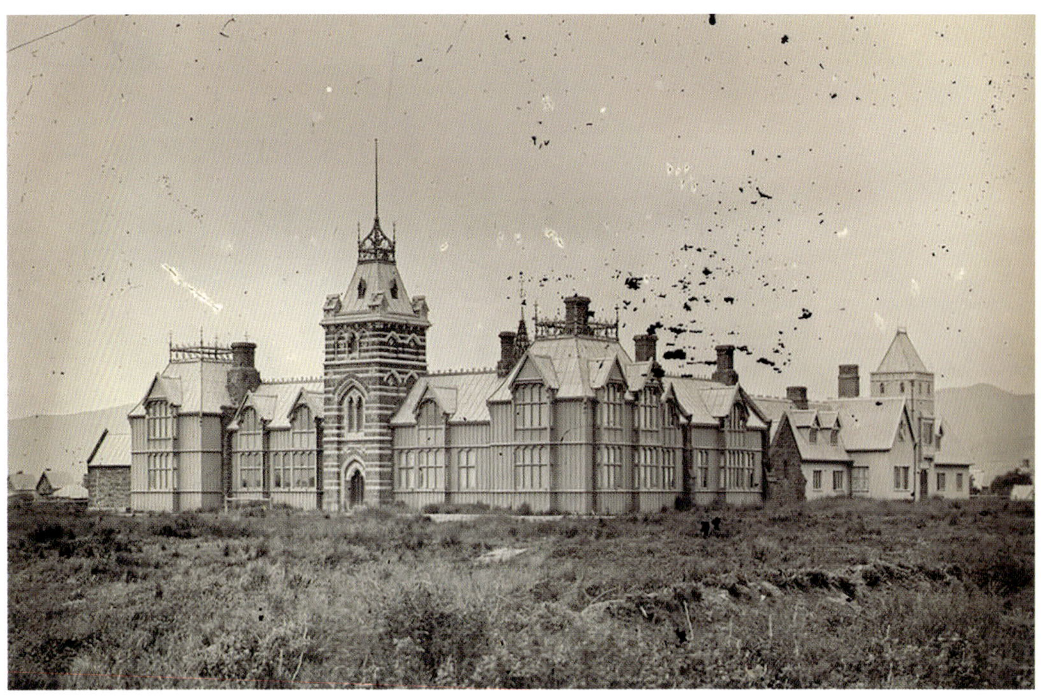

Fig. 73b

Interior, Council Chamber, Provincial Council Buildings, Christchurch.

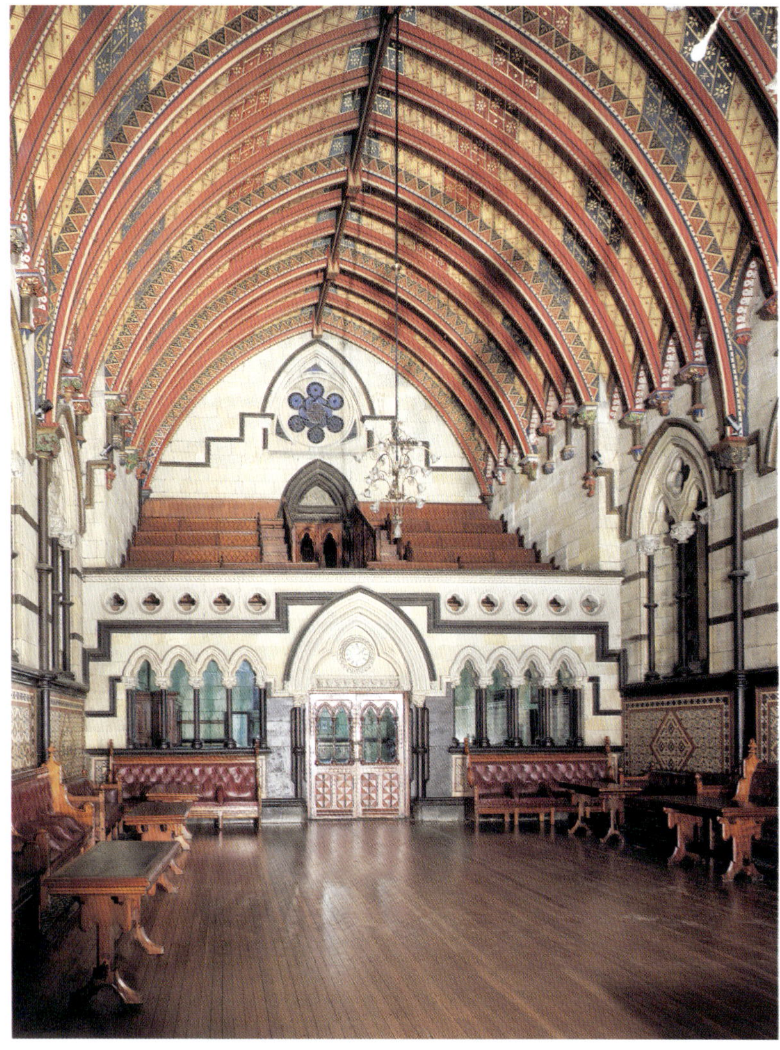

demonstrated that distance was no impediment for skilled émigré architects working to Victorian design principles rather than simply (and superficially) adapting historical styles to new environments. It also demonstrates once again the desire on the part of British colonials to import and impose English forms of governance, and to solidify these through ever-more permanent and substantial structures. Mountfort would later add a museum (1869–82) and two schools—Christ's College (1857–86), and Canterbury College (1876–96)—to the evolving Gothic townscape of Christchurch.

One of the most spectacular set-pieces of Gothic Revival urbanism in the world during this period, however, was Bombay—the so-called *Urbs Prima in Indis*. Acquired initially from the Portuguese through Charles II's marriage to Catarina de Bragança in 1661, the city experienced an economic boom during the 1860s through trade in cotton, facilitated by Civil War shortages in the United States. The opening of the Suez Canal in 1869 also enabled the city to exploit its strategic geographic location as a key Asian port. The result was a dazzling array of Ruskinian-style structures designed and built between the late 1860s and early 1890s. Marked by their polychrome vitality, these buildings adopted Southern rather than Northern European medieval forms, largely in response to the climate. The 'eastern' context was considered conducive to a Venetian-inspired aesthetic, described by *The Building News* as a 'free treatment of Early Gothic with an Oriental feeling'. Despite the call by some to adhere to unadulterated European forms as an index to imperial power (i.e., Roman), this kind of architecture signalled a shift in official thinking toward a hybrid style that attempted to root British rule in regional traditions.

Most prominent among these buildings in Bombay were the Public Works Office (1867–74) **[74]**, the High Court (1870–8), the New Post Office (1871–4), and Elphinstone College (1871). Apart from the new university designed by G. G. Scott (see Chapter 6), these buildings were the initiative of local military engineers-cum-architects, such as Col. Henry St Clair Wilkins and Col. J. A. Fuller. They were assisted in the endeavour by the philanthropic largesse of the local Parsi community. As such, the advent of this architecture is part of what has been referred to as a 'joint enterprise' between the colonial authorities and local elites, where the mutual commercial and political interests of both were clearly aligned.[14] Later examples include the stunning Municipal Buildings (1888–93) **[75a]**, opposite Victoria Terminus, by F. W. Stevens (see Chapter 1) **[13b]**.

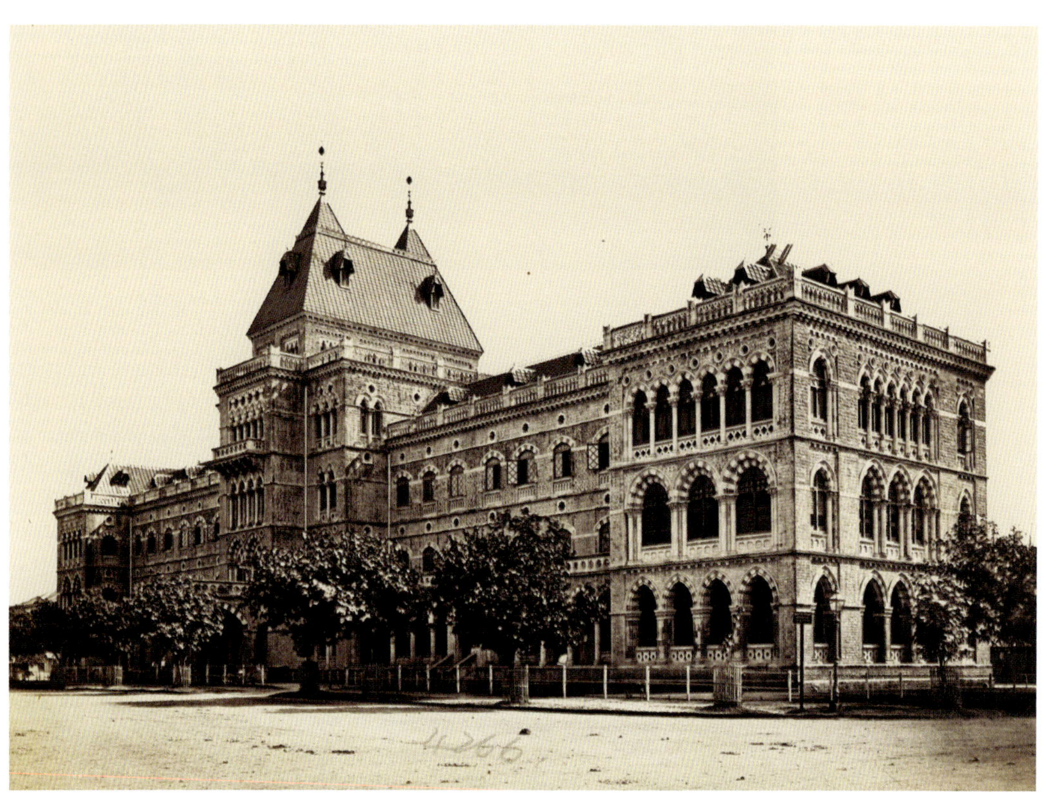

Fig. 74

Public Works Office (1867–74), Bombay (Mumbai), by Col. Henry St Clair Wilkins.

Fig. 75a

Municipal Buildings (1888–93), Bombay (Mumbai), by F. W. Stevens.

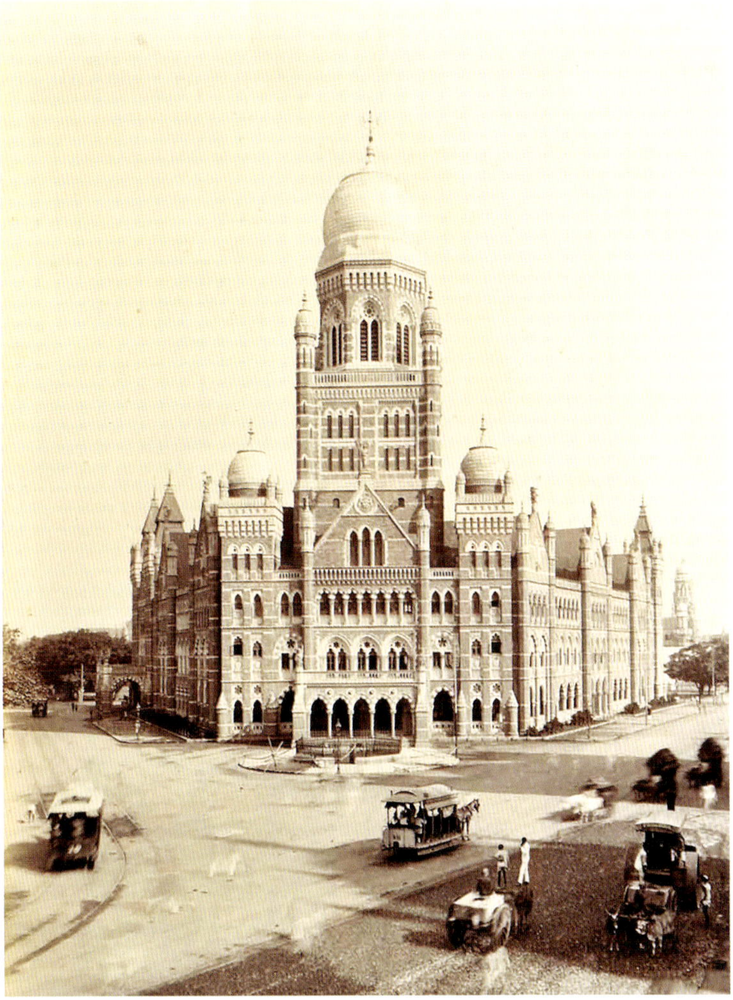

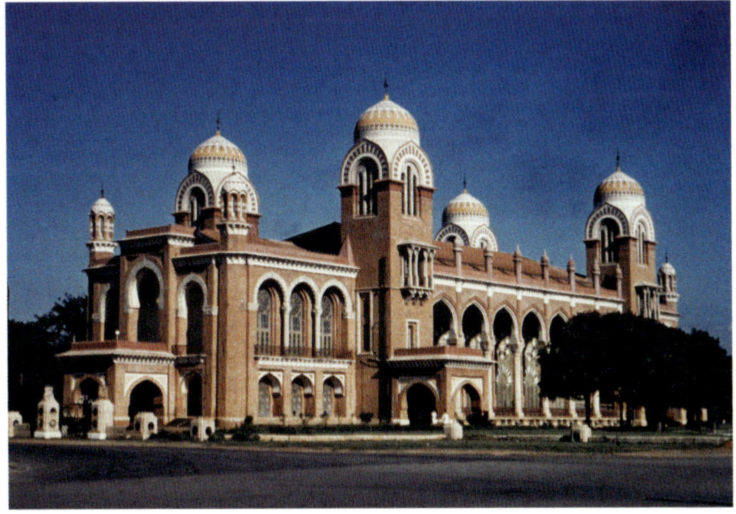

Fig. 75b

University Senate House (1874–9), Madras (Chennai), by Robert F. Chisholm.

However, unlike the evolving democratic tradition in Britain, rule in India was based on the imposition of authoritarian government, backed by military force. This was the condition that characterised imperial power relations between Westminster and 'dependent' colonies throughout the British world during the Victorian era. Even so, events such as the Sepoy Revolt (or 'mutiny') of 1857 shocked Victorian sensibilities, leading to questions over the benefits let alone merits of overseas empire. The drain on resources and potential for corruption were simply too high, claimed some; while others bemoaned the 'civilising mission' as a thankless task. But far from abandoning India, the perceived necessity to stay on and reform imperial government was seen, in a very Victorian way, as a grave if inspired responsibility. Internal debate directed a reassessment of how colonial rule operated, not just bureaucratically but also symbolically. In the case of India, this resulted in the transfer of dominion from the East India Company to the British Crown following the return to civil order in 1858, accompanied by a declaration to the people of India from Queen Victoria herself.

This shift in both the substance and optics of power had a direct effect on architecture. Although the British continued to see themselves as modern Romans, they nevertheless began to construct a notion of empire in which they were not mere conquerors but indigenous rulers, linked directly to the Mughals and therefore India's own past. If British imperial authority in the post-Revolt era was to be seen as legitimate, then it had to be effected within categories and structures rooted in Indic culture. This ushered in the period of British government in India known as the Raj. Indeed, British architects, artists, and engineers with experience of India had begun to make this very argument in the years following the new political reality, especially for buildings associated with the state. In 1873, for instance, William Emerson (later president of the RIBA), like the artist and educator J. L. Kipling before him, protested that the British should follow the example of those who they had supplanted as its rulers. The Mughals, advised Emerson, had 'seized upon the art indigenous to the countries conquered, adapting it to suit their own needs and ideas'.[15]

For those on the ground, such as Lord Napier, governor of Madras, the appeal of indigenous architecture in this respect was increasingly obvious. Although, following Fergusson (see Chapter 3), he rejected the potential of Hindu architecture, he remained impressed by Muslim—or so-called Saracenic—architecture, which he thought was not only beautiful but also scientific (and thus economical) in its use of the pointed arch. In this respect, much like Beresford Hope's notion of 'development by eclecticism', Napier could see the possibility for synthesis with European architectural traditions, especially medieval. The domes as used by Mughal architects were considered particularly suitable for covering large spaces in modern buildings, such as railway stations, theatres, galleries, museums, and public halls. In a lecture before the Madras University senate in 1869, he remarked:

> We have arrived at a most important period in the history of architecture in this country, and it will be decided in the course of the next five or ten years whether we are to have a style suited to the requirements of this country, or whether we are to be the mere copyists of every bubble which breaks on the surface of European art, and import our

architecture, with our beer and our hats, by every mail-steamer which leaves the shores of England.[16]

These concerns were a part of an increasingly vigorous debate similar to the Battle of the Styles in Britain regarding the search for an architectural language suitable to a modern bureaucratic world order. At base was a vision for how such an architecture might identify and thus symbolise reformed colonial governance in India, amounting to what the architect John Begg later referred to as an 'imperial' style. It led to the emergence of an architectural idiom known as the Indo-Saracenic, which was effectively a grafting of Indic details and motifs onto buildings based on modern European planning and construction principles. As a style, it became widespread during the late nineteenth and early twentieth centuries, given its own aesthetic lexicon by the British military engineer Swinton Jacob through publication of his *Jeypore Portfolio of Architectural Details* (1880–1913).

Ultimately, the Indo-Saracenic was a mixture of European architectural modernity, an Arts and Crafts concern for skilled workmanship, overlaid with the appropriation of indigenous design aesthetics as a form of political rhetoric. The city of Madras under the governorship of Napier became an early experimental centre for the application of this hybrid architecture. The key protagonists were architects and military engineers including R. F. Chisholm, J. W. Bassington, and Henry Irwin who designed such buildings as the Revenue Board (1870–1), the University Senate House (1874–9) **[75b]**, the new Law Courts (1888–92), and the Post and Telegraph Offices (1874–84). Other architects who promoted the style across British India, encompassing Burma and the Malay States, included William Emerson, Charles Mant, George Wittet, Frederick Stevens, and A. B. Hubback, in places as geographically disperse as Bombay, Hyderabad, Jaipur, Allahabad, Madras, Dhaka, and Kuala Lumpur. Indeed, in Lahore the efforts of locally trained indigenous architects were on display, such as the designs of Bhai Ram Sing for the Lahore Museum (1893) and the University of the Punjab (1905).

Public Art: Architecture, Sculpture, and National Commemoration

By the mid-nineteenth century Britain had developed a practice of commemorating leading national figures in monumental form. This tradition emerged in particular from the carnage of the Napoleonic Wars, where there was an attempt to memorialise various battles and feats of heroism associated with the ultimate yet costly victory of Britain and its allies. Some that made it beyond the drawing board include those dedicated to specific military heroes, such as that to Lord Horatio Nelson, in the form of Nelson's Column (1840–67), in Trafalgar Square. Existing monuments were also appropriated for the purpose, such as Wellington Arch, Hyde Park, which was topped in 1846 with a bronze equestrian statue of the Duke of Wellington. Other noteworthy monuments in this 'heroic' tradition include that in Edinburgh (1840–5), to the great Scottish novelist Sir Walter Scott, with its striking 61m-high Gothic steeple by George Meikle Kemp, and the extraordinary Wallace Monument (1861–9), near Stirling, by J. T. Rochead **[76]**.

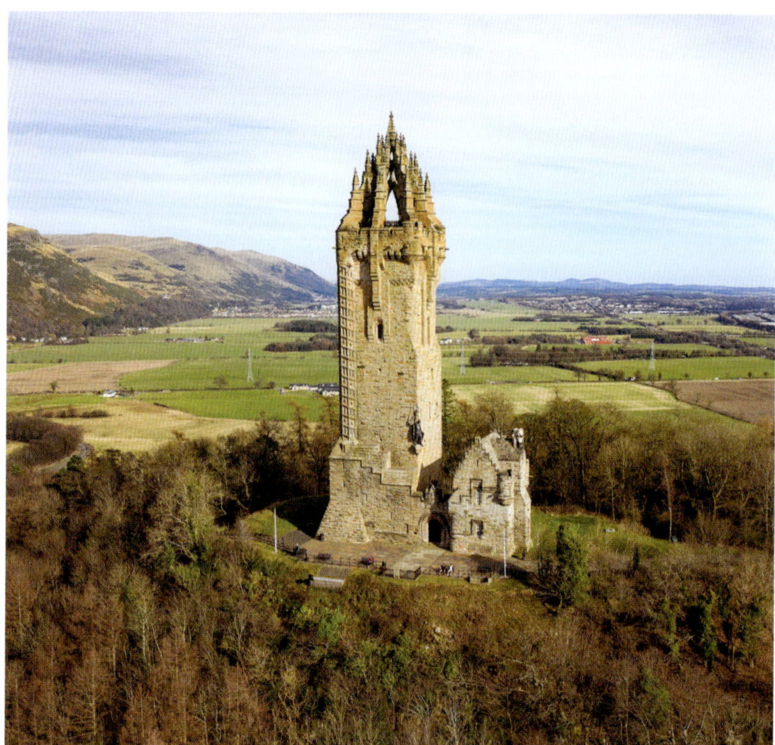

Fig. 76
The expression of national and regional identity: Wallace Monument (1861–9), near Stirling, Scotland, by J. T. Rochead.

But undoubtedly the greatest monument of this type was that dedicated to the Prince Consort, commonly known as the Albert Memorial.

Located at the south-western edge of Hyde Park in London, the Albert Memorial is one of the most important and ambitious undertakings in the history of public art in Britain **[77]**. Many memorials to the Prince would be erected across the length and breadth of the land, including a large and elaborate one in Manchester **[64]**. However, it was the one in London that was officially designated 'national'. Designed by G. G. Scott, the commission for which came his way via limited competition, its construction involved a wide array of artists, including leading sculptors, metal workers, and mosaicists. It took 13 years to build (1863–76), at a cost of some £143,000, of which the government pledged a substantial amount (at least £50,000), with the rest raised through public subscription. Although erected to the memory of one man, the Albert Memorial has always been appreciated in considerably broader terms. Indeed, from the very outset it was intended as an 'illustration' of the many objects to which the Prince devoted his energies, not least the Great Exhibition of 1851. Through its intricate decorative schema, it sought to represent nothing less than the values and ideals of its time. Under its glittering baldachin Queen Victoria's late husband, Albert, was enshrined not in any restricted personal sense (merely as someone of high social standing), but in a manner that presented him as an exalted individual, as someone who had attained belated 'hero' status for his service to the nation.

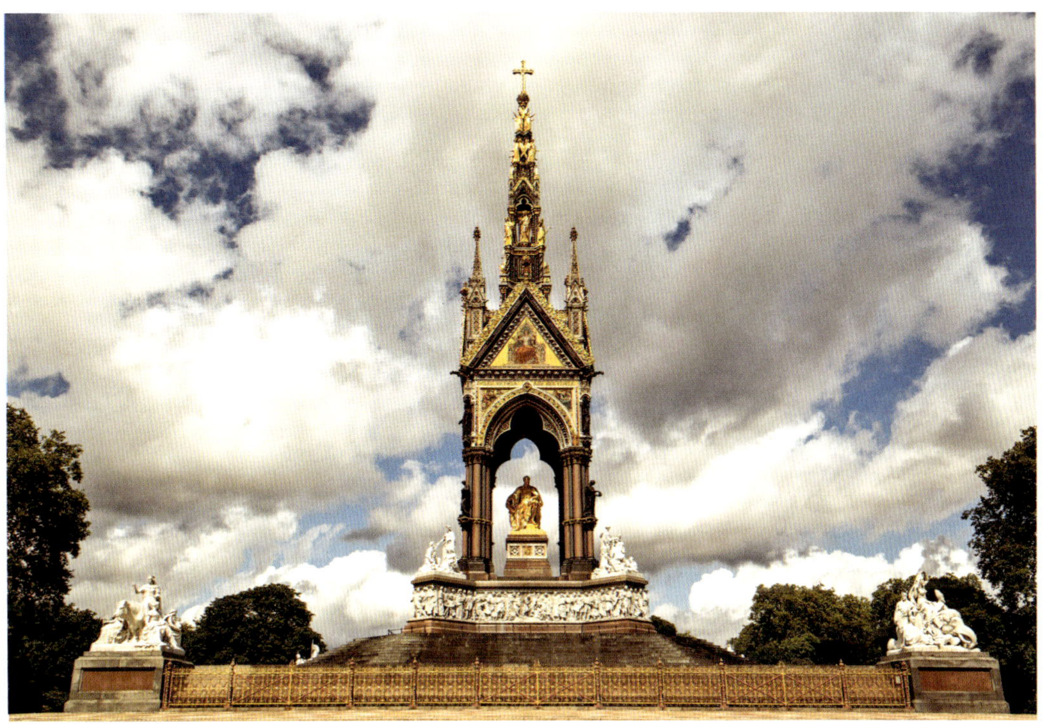

Fig. 77

Albert Memorial (1863–76), Hyde Park, London, by George Gilbert Scott.

For this reason, the Albert Memorial was designed to reflect certain, generally acknowledged national traits and feats of cultural, scientific, and artistic achievement. Through Scott's endeavour to communicate these ideas as directly as possible (again, an example of Victorian artistic didacticism), the monument in its completed form gives us a good sense of how the respectable, educated classes in mid-nineteenth-century Britain perceived both themselves and their country: energetic, adventurous, technologically advanced, and progressive; yet civilised, learned, morally astute, and, above all, pious. Underpinning this panoply of attributes was the leitmotif of Britain as a nation of distinction and global pre-eminence. In this sense, the Albert Memorial's aesthetic, didactic, and triumphalist intentions were deliberately orchestrated to coincide in what has been described as its over-arching iconography of 'piety, progress, and power'.[17] It represents Britain at the height of its self-assuredness as a nation—a confidence that, ironically, had begun to wane by the time of its completion. In its formal exuberance and polychrome richness the memorial not only typifies the mid-Victorian love of colour, but also stands as an index to the variety of materials then accessible through modern manufacturing techniques, such as wrought iron-work and polished granite, not to mention the coal-fired technologies employed in enabling its assemblage.

Arguably the most captivating aspect of the memorial are the large sculptural groups at its outer base depicting the 'four quarters' of the globe. It is well known that these groups, in their reference to diverse geographical regions through caricatures of different animals and peoples, were understood as invoking the 'international' dimension of the Great Exhibition. But, like many motifs on the memorial, they were open to varied interpretation. As the Great Exhibition was an exercise in international competition and rivalry as much as anything else, these sculptures also alluded to Britain's standing in the world as a great imperial power, implying the extent of its dominion. It would seem no accident, for instance, that the key figure representing 'Asia' was a 'sultana' of the Indian Subcontinent, atop an Indian elephant. As a monument funded by both government and the wider public, the Albert Memorial therefore embodied a sense of collective endeavour on the part of Britain and its people, culminating in what one noted artist later described as a 'great national effort'.[18]

Classicism Resurgent: The Edwardian Baroque and Imperialism

Towards the end of the century British architecture witnessed a swing back to Classicism. Although, as we have seen, the appeal of Classicism did not evaporate entirely during the height of the Gothic Revival, especially with respect to secular buildings, it came back with renewed vigour from around the middle of the 1880s. This time, however, it took a rather distinct form. This was not a simple rehash of what had come before, but instead a desire to promote a uniquely national or 'English' form of the style. It was inspired in large part by a resuscitation of the reputation of Christopher Wren, an architect who by this time was widely regarded as the nation's greatest. Monuments such as St Paul's Cathedral (1675–1710), Hampton Court Palace (1690), and Greenwich Royal Naval Hospital (1696–1716) were seen as holding special appeal. Alongside Wren, architects also began to re-evaluate the works of other great 'Renaissance' masters of local pedigree, such as Inigo Jones, Nicholas Hawksmoor, John Vanbrugh, Thomas Archer, and William Chambers. By the 1890s this new-found admiration for the English Classical tradition, particularly that of the seventeenth and early eighteenth centuries, resulted in a full-blown Renaissance Revival, or what is now more commonly referred to as the Edwardian Baroque.

This plea for a home-grown, 'vernacular' Classicism came with added social and political baggage, however. In short, the achievements of Jones, Wren, and their followers were understood as a reflection of the achievement and thus greatness of the nation at large. The sentiment was captured in a lecture on English Renaissance architecture, delivered at the Architectural Association school of architecture in 1889, by John Brydon, one of the leading lights of the movement:

> The seventeenth century...had been a wonderful century; the country had made immense advances in all that makes for the greatness of a nation. It was no longer a question of England and Scotland, but of Great Britain...The East India Company had been incorporated, and made great progress in the formation of what ultimately became our Empire in the East. England's Colonial Empire had been founded by the settlements in the Carolinas and the New England States,—the beginning of that Greater Britain which has come to be such a factor in the civilisation of the world...Through sixty years of it all, Wren worked away at his architecture...With the death of Wren may be said to have closed the Early English Renaissance, which had lasted about one hundred years. It had now become firmly established as the national style,—the vernacular of the country...We must recognise that we are here in the presence of an English Classical style as truly the embodiment of the civilisation and the life of the people..., a living, working, architec-

tural reality, as much a part of England as its literature or its great school of painting…, the nearest to us in time and in similitude of requirements…[19]

Reaching across the ages, Brydon attempts to argue here that the seventeenth and nineteenth centuries were related to one another in terms of vision, ambition, and development. His lecture also reveals an understanding of Britain's historic, political, and economic rise in the world, and how this had become a fundamental part of contemporary British life, invoking the by then well-worn notion of 'Greater Britain' as a type of globally continuous cultural configuration. In this sense the lecture mirrored contemporary rhetorical methods in which a chronology of historic events or moments were strung together in such a way as to stimulate and legitimise an identity-centred understanding of the past in hock to present needs. In so doing, it helped set the tone for discussion of English Renaissance architecture through its carefully modulated language concerning ideas of Englishness. Between Brydon's lecture and the death of Queen Victoria (1901), a number of serious and scholarly publications appeared that were dedicated specifically to the period of architectural production highlighted by Brydon, including W. J. Loftie's *Inigo Jones and Wren* (1893), Reginald Blomfield's *A History of Renaissance Architecture in England 1500–1800* (1897), and John Belcher and Mervyn Macartney's *Later Renaissance Architecture in England* (1898–1901).

This aesthetic manoeuvring is perhaps best understood in the context of Britain's perceived standing in world affairs at the time. Anxiety over the nation's position had steadily intensified since the 1870s. Once all powerful, Britain now faced multiple and potentially intractable challenges. Economic and agricultural depression, followed by the grim realisation that the nation was losing its grip on industrial supremacy, heightened feelings of vulnerability and decline. Added to this was the rise of competing global superpowers, such as Germany, Russia, and the United States. 'Great Power' rivalry now threatened Britain's continued success. One response to these challenges was for politicians to look to leverage Britain's global empire as a means of reasserting the nation's economic and political influence. This led, among other things, to what became known as the 'New Imperialism' in British cultural life. It was amid this tumult of insecurity that ideas of empire, nationhood, and identity were recast in the service of making Britain great again, with the effects felt across every facet of society, including in architecture.

Indeed, coming into the 1880s there was an increasing degree of disgruntlement among leading architects concerning the direction in which British architecture was heading. The eclectic cul-de-sac into which it had seemingly cornered itself was coming to be viewed as a sign of national weakness. To some, a more resolute expression was required to restore order, clarity, and a new kind of 'strength' in British architecture—an architecture that would address the growing tide of national doubt. The resulting Edwardian Baroque style became popular among Britain's leading architects, such as Aston Webb, John Belcher, William Young, John Brydon, Richard Norman Shaw, Herbert Baker, and Reginald Blomfield, among others, shaping appreciably the architecture of the period, particularly in grand civic,

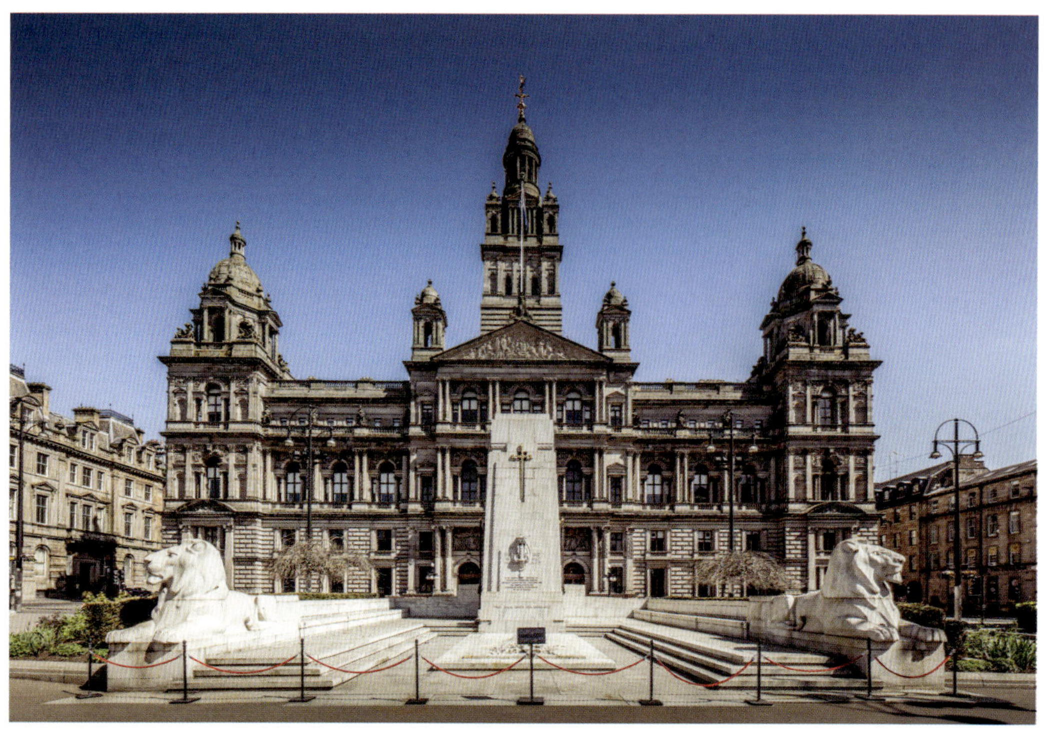

Fig. 78
Glasgow City Chambers (1882–8), by William Young.

corporate, and institutional structures, both in Britain and the wider British world.

The earliest, tentative manifestation of the style, already replete with imperial connotations, is identifiable in Glasgow City Chambers (1882–8), by William Young, with its boldly articulated classical façade and Baroque-style flourishes, including decorative sculpture depicting ideas of Greater Britain **[78]**. One can also point to John Brydon's slightly more sober but no less 'Renaissance' Old Vestry Hall, Chelsea (1885–7). A little later came Brydon's extension to the Guildhall in Bath (1891–3) and Edward Mountford's town hall in Battersea (1891–3). But the most magnificent early rendition of the style was John Belcher's Chartered Accountants' Hall (1890–3), off Moorgate in London, which set the tone for future developments. This led to some of the greatest set-piece projects in the genre, such as Belfast City Hall (1898–1906), by A. Brumwell Thomas; the War Office (1899–1906), on Whitehall, by Young; and Colchester Town Hall (1897–1902), by Belcher **[79a&b]**,Others that one could point to include the New Government Offices (1899–1908/17), by Brydon, and Admiralty Arch (1908–13), London, by Aston Webb. Indeed, coming back to ideas of law and order, Edward Mountford's Central Criminal Court, Old Bailey, London (1902–7), signalled through its reassuringly assertive forms the fundamental constitutional basis of the 'rule of law'. The vigorous but ordered classicism of the Edwardian Baroque, with the weight of cultural authority that lay behind it, both ancient and modern, seemed particularly suited to the dynamics of law in action. As

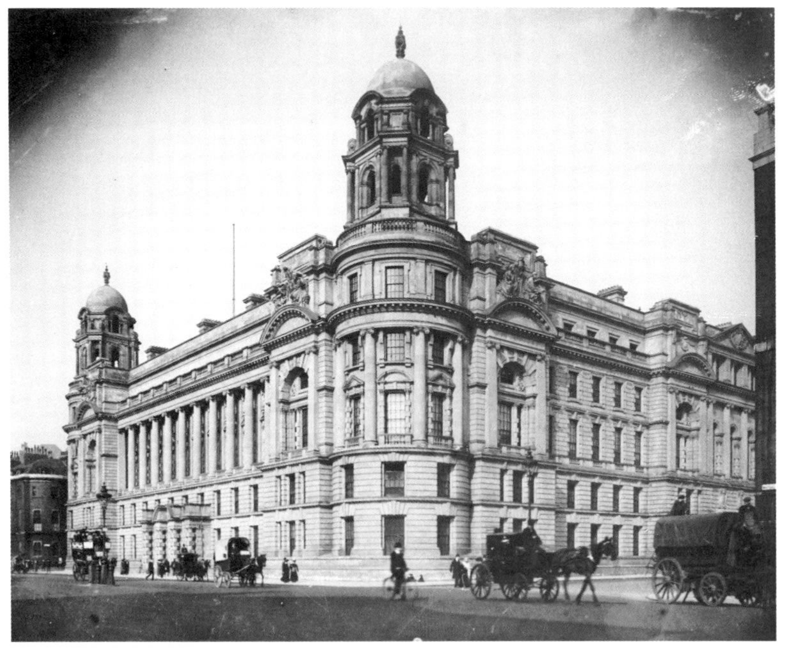

Fig. 79a

Revived baroque splendour. War Office, Whitehall (1899–1906), London, by William Young.

The Building News remarked at the time, the demand for something monumental in this regard had 'been boldly and honestly met'.[20] Importantly, all of these buildings display full-blown Edwardian Baroque features, to varying degrees, such as pronounced rustication, overwrought keystones, extensive use of Gibbs surrounds, giant-order columns/pilasters, segmental aedicule motifs, corner turrets, and, in some cases, highly articulated Baroque-style domes in the manner of Wren.

The nationally inspired classicism of the Edwardian Baroque was associated by many with notions of Anglo-Saxon masculinity. This came mainly via references to the perceived intellectual 'clarity' of English Classicism, along with its comparatively reserved yet sturdy composition. Thus, by the time we reach the first decade of the twentieth century, a forthright, sober, and 'manly' form of architecture that reflected those self-same, no-nonsense characteristics of the British nation and its people was the order of the day. Keeping the Old Bailey in mind, this was considered especially apposite in buildings associated with the administration of law and order, as the outward expression of a modern, 'efficient' state. Buildings such as those mentioned above were understood as having a semiotic dimension that enabled them to 'perform' (as a type of spectacle or urban theatre) the idea of 'government'.[21] Here the massing of buildings, or what was referred to as the 'Grand Manner', was also considered important in terms of providing an image of strength and clarity of form.

But English variants of the idiom were not the only ones adopted. Despite the rhetoric concerning identity, some architects, such as Edwin

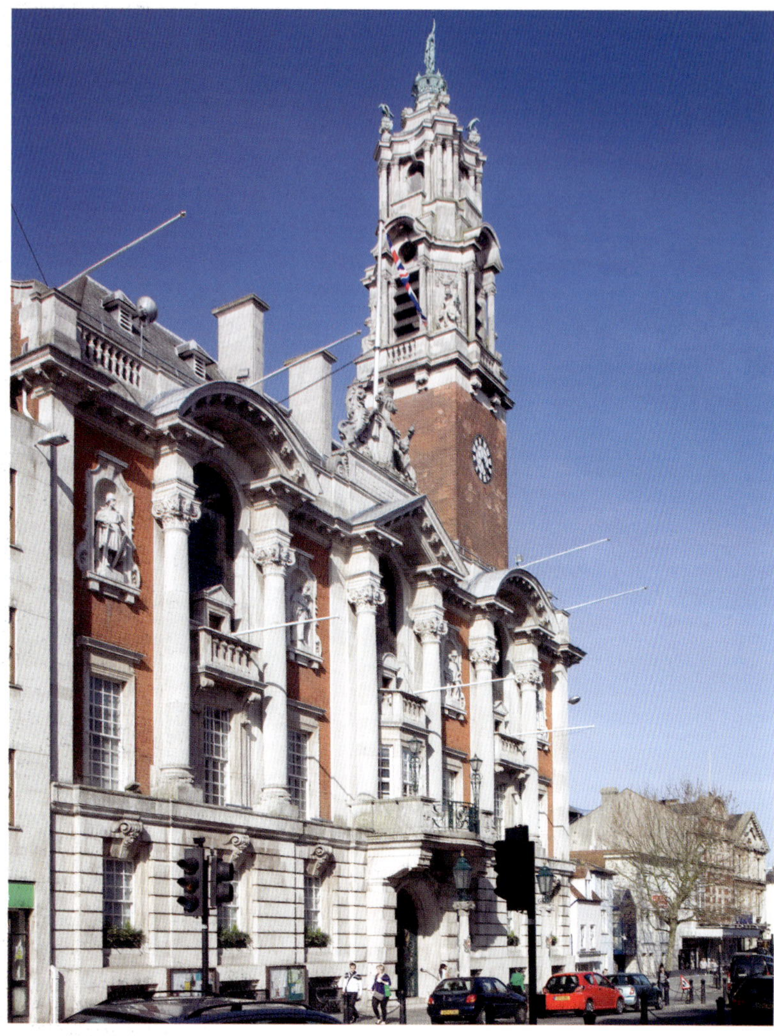

Fig. 79b

Colchester Town Hall (1897–1902), Essex, by John Belcher.

Richards, preferred to look to the Continent for inspiration, in particular French and German Baroque architecture. We see this influence clearly in his design (with Henry Lanchester) for Cardiff City Hall and Law Courts (1897–1906), as well as in his competition entry for the London County Hall of 1907. It was also at this time that planning principles derived from the French Beaux Arts tradition began to exert ever-greater influence on British architectural design, especially in relation to large commercial and institutional buildings. Having visited the imperial capitals of Continental Europe for inspiration, it is hardly surprising that such influence crept into Webb's designs for the Victoria Memorial, especially the re-facing of Buckingham Palace (1912–13).

In any case, government architecture in Britain spanning the decades either side of 1900 was based on a reasonably strong vision of what institutional architecture of this type could, and preferably should, be. In this

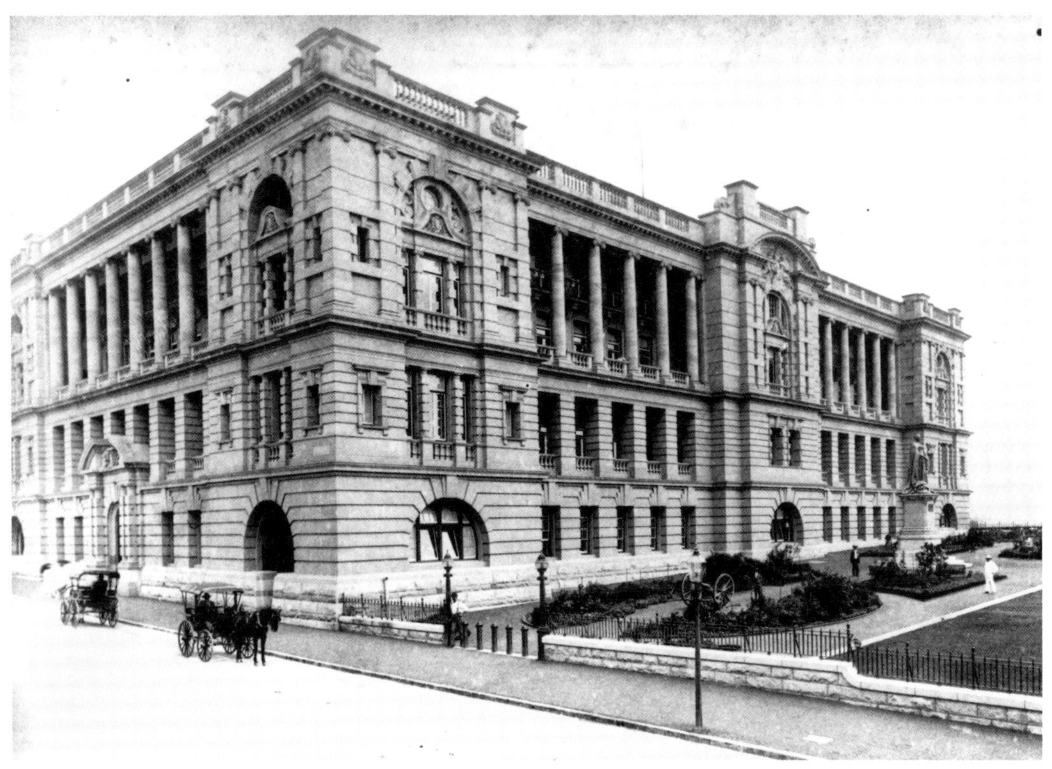

Fig. 80
Executive Building (1900–5), Brisbane, Queensland, Australia, by Thomas Pye.

respect it applied equally to 'Greater Britain', where we see it popping up in various parts of the wider British world, particularly in the so-called white settler dominions of Australia, New Zealand, Canada, and South Africa. Here the aspirations of imperial continuity represented by such architecture were fully realised. Notable examples include the Executive Building (1900–5), in Brisbane, Australia, by Thomas Pye **[80]**; the Public Trust Offices (1906–9), Wellington, New Zealand, by John Campbell; Durban Town Hall (1905–10), South Africa, by Stanley Hudson; the Legislative Building (1908–12), in Regina, Saskatchewan (Canada), by E. & W. S. Maxwell; and even the Supreme Court (1899–1912) in Hong Kong by Aston Webb and E. Ingress Bell **[81a&b]**. Indeed, notions of British cultural connectivity and world order embodied in this kind of architecture were perhaps best represented in buildings associated with communications technology, such as post and telegraph offices. Here we need only compare Henry Tanner's design for the General Post Office in London (1907–10) with those in Auckland and Wellington (both 1910–12) by John Campbell, in conjunction with the New Zealand Public Works Department. The synergies in appearance were deliberate. The latter even included a large sculpture above its main entrance of two figures and a globe entitled 'The Girdled Earth'. Executed by the noted British sculptor Alfred Drury, these burly looking female personifications—one holding a

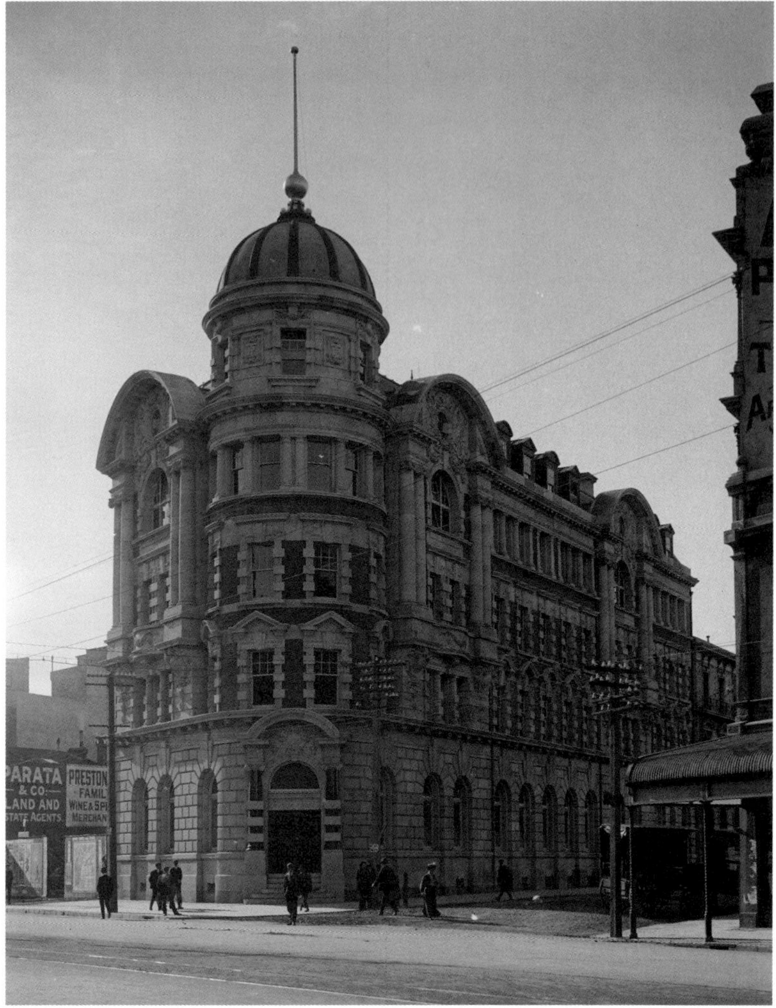

Fig. 81a

Public Trust Offices (1906–9), Wellington, New Zealand, by John Campbell.

locomotive, the other a ship (in bronze)—were indicative of the two chief modes of transporting the king's mail, whose cypher appeared in relief on a cartouche at the base. Flanked either side by two additional figures representing 'Telegraphy' and 'Letter Delivery', it is hard to resist the conclusion that seen together these sculptures were allegorical of the need to secure Britain's 'all red' lines of communication across the globe, thus ensuring British imperial stability.

It is often quipped that, for all its bombast and vast political dominion during the heady days of empire, Britain never managed to invent an 'imperial style' of architecture. Nevertheless, and notwithstanding competitor

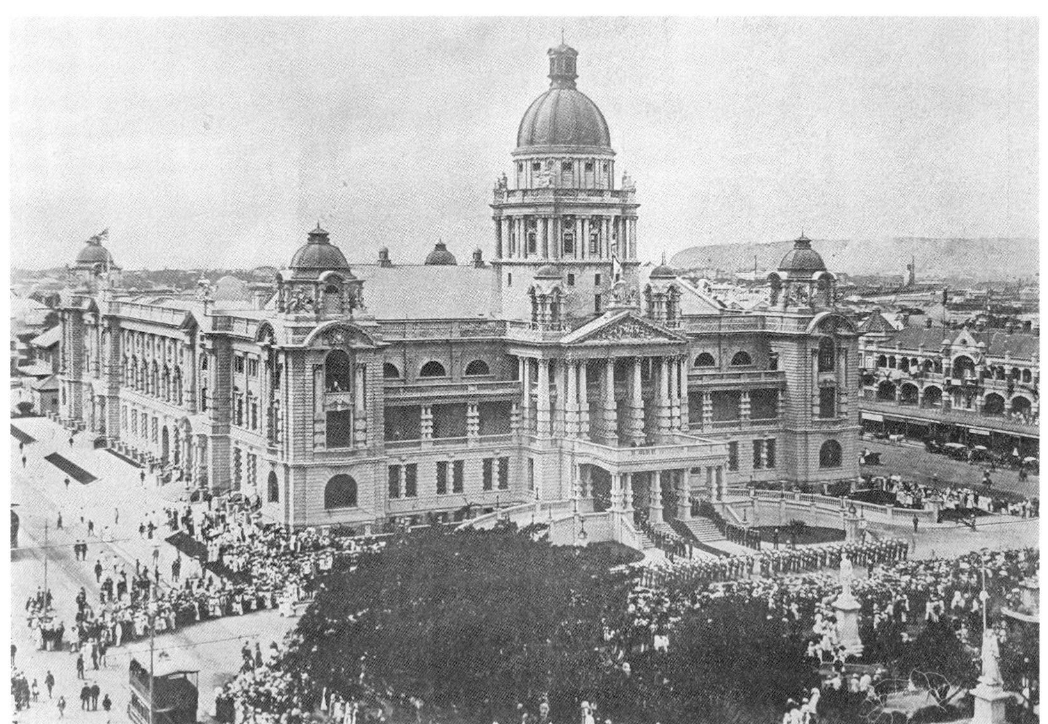

Fig. 81b

Durban Town Hall (1905–10), Durban, South Africa, by Stanley Hudson.

styles for the title such as the Indo-Saracenic, the Edwardian Baroque was the closest Britain came to achieving this. Appropriately enough, it was in the domain of state and civic architecture that it realised its most strident articulation, contributing significantly to 'building the state', across the length and breadth of the British world.

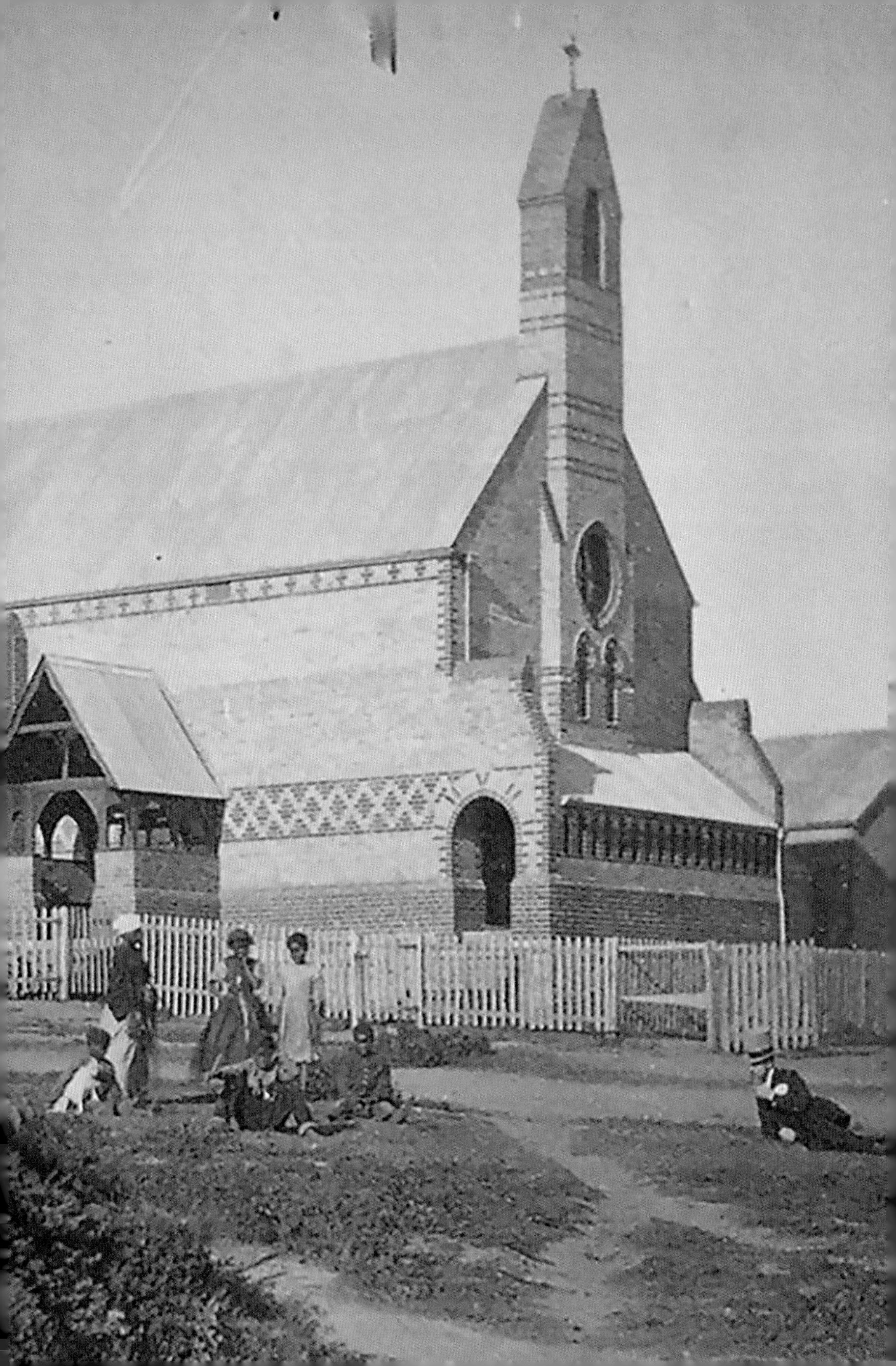

5

New Jerusalems: Fabricating Faith in the Victorian World

In the Introduction I observed that building typology would play only a minor role in the way this history of Victorian architecture was structured. Buildings for worship and religious contemplation, in particular churches and chapels, are possibly one exception. This is because they represent a very common and conspicuous manifestation of the deep-seated cultural condition of religiosity in Victorian society. It needs recalling that unprecedented numbers of churches, chapels, church schools, parsonages, convents, and other religious buildings were erected during the Victorian period. They were also given more attention in the press than any other building type.[1] As noted in Chapter 3, so central were structures of this kind to the Victorians' vision of the built environment that they could make, or even break, an architect's career.

In order to understand Victorian Britons it is necessary to appreciate the social, cultural, and thus political force that Christianity was in their conception of the moral universe. So much of their worldview was refracted through the ethical prism of religious teaching, either directly or indirectly. We see it in their instinctive sense of duty, their desire for social and material improvement, as well as in their unabashed disposition to intervene out of a self-righteous belief in their own cultural (and spiritual) superiority. What we now recognise as the socio-religious character of Victorian society had steadily built through the late eighteenth and early nineteenth centuries. Stemming from the Protestant evangelical revival, including the rise of Nonconformist values and piety, and through the spiritual renewal of the established Church in England, religious sentiment of this kind became manifest in the renovation of social mores and a revived call to 'seriousness'. Even in those much-vaunted ideals of courage and self-sacrifice, or through contested forms of cultural imperialism, the precepts of Christianity (and the example of Christ himself) were very much to the fore. Many Britons also perceived their nation's rise in the world as a matter of divine providence.

Although society in Britain and in many of its former colonies has become ever more secular since Victorian times, we should never forget that ecclesiastical architecture, for the reasons mentioned above, was once a highly significant and symbolically powerful building typology. This was the case in both Britain and the wider British world. In so many ways the image of the 'village church'—as a time-honoured, romantic ideal—came to stand in for the essence of what it meant to be Anglo-British, invoked often in art and literature. Most towns and cities across Britain and its former colonial empire, particularly in the so-called white settler dominions, had one or more Christian churches (and still do) that, with their spires reaching for the heavens, dominated their surrounds, marking out the character of British society globally. To this extent, the British world was a Christian world.

This was not only the result of increased migration and trade, but also because of a dramatic surge in church extension and missionary enterprise. Even much closer to 'home', in Continental Europe, concerted efforts were made during this period to raise the profile of the English Church in key strategic locations. Nonconformist churches were active, too, with missionary work becoming an increasingly important aspect of their 'calling'. Despite the insistence on the part of many Christian denominations in maintaining their independence from government (i.e., enlarging the 'kingdom of God', rather than that of 'man'), their activities nevertheless extended the frontiers of Western knowledge and civilisation into the non-European world, often softening the way for harder forms of colonialism that followed.

As the Victorian world continued to expand, its architecture inevitably impinged upon the lives of non-European indigenous peoples, leading in many cases to Christian conversion. Despite this, the majority of Britain's indigenous colonial 'subjects' remained either untouched by or resistant to Christianity, especially in Asia. In these places other religions were predominant, including Hinduism, Islam, Sikhism, and Buddhism. These were ancient religions, with their own, long-standing architectural traditions. But this does not render them entirely irrelevant to a study such as this. Admittedly, there were very few buildings in Britain at the time associated with these religions, the most notable being the Shah Jahan Mosque, Woking (1889), by William Isaac Chambers. More were designed by British, European, and indigenous architects in British territory abroad, in places such as Burma and Malaysia. Arguably, these structures are part of the history of Victorian architecture, broadly conceived. To this may be added Jewish synagogues, particularly in Britain, of which many were erected during the period, including the magnificent New West End Synagogue, London (1877–9), or the Princes Road Synagogue, Liverpool (1872–4), both by George Audsley. One might also include here Parsi fire temples erected in the late nineteenth century in cities such as Bombay.[2] But as this chapter deals with Christianity and the Victorian church, I make this observation only in passing.

Prevailing Trends in Church Architecture: A. W. N. Pugin and His Influence

The history of church architecture during the Victorian period is, in part at least, a history of the Gothic Revival. As we shall see, not all churches built during this time were Gothic in style. Classicism still prevailed in certain quarters, especially among Nonconformist and Dissenting denominations. There was also the legacy of the 1818 Church Building Act, which, although emphasising Gothic as a cheap and practical alternative, still saw numerous 'Commissioners' Churches' erected in a Classical style. From the 1840s, however, Gothic was very much in the ascendency. Most of the thousands of new churches, and many of the new chapels, erected from this moment onward would be in one or other medieval style. The reasons for this are partly explained in Chapter 3, but it needs recalling here that the rise of the Gothic Revival in British church architecture involved a series of intersecting factors. These included the spectacular growth in Britain's population, particularly in urban centres, requiring additional space for religious worship; the coming of the Gothic Revival into its theoretical maturity around the late 1830s, and how this was understood to align with new modes of practice, making for a more coherent and thereby convincing justification for Christian usage; and the considerable influence of certain practitioners and advocacy organisations—such as A. W. N. Pugin, George Gilbert Scott, and the Cambridge Camden Society, not to mention the Nonconformist architect F. J. Jobson—upon a younger generation of British architects.

Let us begin with Pugin. As certain esteemed practitioners who followed in his wake freely acknowledged, Pugin may be considered the 'father' of the Victorian Gothic Revival. Although his career as a practitioner lasted less than twenty years, Pugin left an important if limited legacy of built work. It was limited mainly because his feverish activity resulted in his premature death in 1852 at the relatively young age of forty, widely attributed to exhaustion. Moreover, the centuries-long legal restrictions (effective ban) on Roman Catholicism in much of the British Isles owing to the Protestant Reformation were only 'relieved' by Parliament in 1829. This meant that there were comparatively few practicing Catholics in England at the time—around 300,000 in 1844, or 1.8 per cent of the population[3]—and therefore fewer opportunities for building new Catholic churches. Nevertheless, Pugin was soon inundated with commissions, especially as Irish immigrants escaping famine poured into Britain's industrial cities in the 1840s.

Given his strong religious convictions, Pugin confined himself largely to working with Catholic patrons. Indeed, a number of his early church commissions came from Ireland where there was a larger resident Catholic population with an operating episcopal hierarchy. Some of these churches, including cathedrals, have since been assessed as rather primitive structures, such as the Church of the Assumption at Bree (1838), or St Mary's, Tagoat (1843). Funds were scarce, but it must be remembered that Pugin, in line with his own principles, sought to relate his Irish commissions to their historic medieval context, which he claimed was 'rude and simple'. In England, too, simplicity was required in a number of contexts with constrained means. We see the results of this, for instance, at St Chad's Cathedral, Birmingham (1839), with its rather slender, planar massing inspired by the hall church tradition of northern Germany. The best of Pugin's churches, however, such as the small but perfect St Mary's, Warwick Bridge, Cumbria (1840–1), or the exquisite St Giles', Cheadle, in Staffordshire (1841–6), were all but flawless exemplars of what a principled and truly 'Christian' church ought to be **[82]**.

Whether large or small, simple or more elaborate, 'proper' church buildings, according to Pugin, had to follow fundamental design rules, espoused in his forceful polemic *True Principles of Pointed or Christian Architecture* (1841). These rules were understood in relation to the social and material context of a given commission, including his two most basic diktats: the use

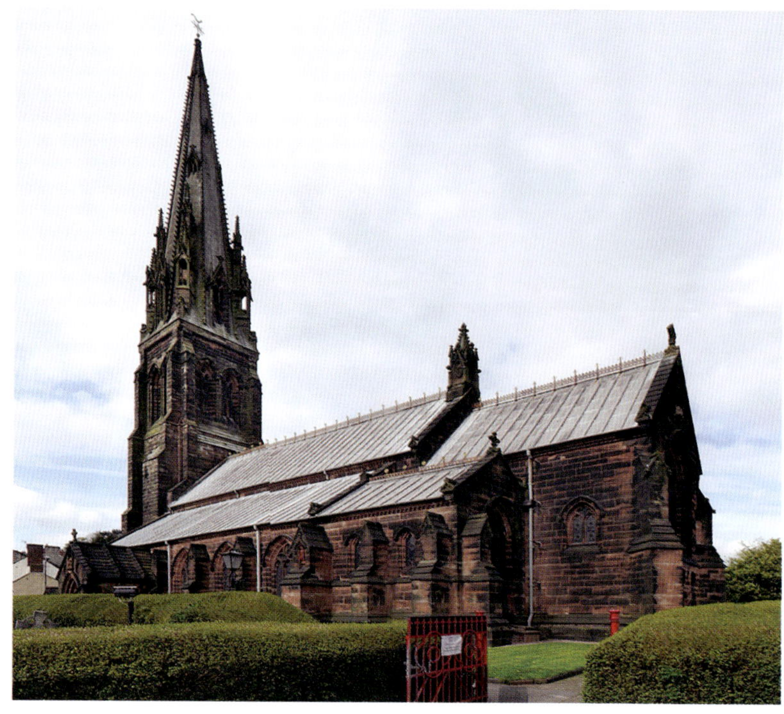

Fig. 82
St Giles', Cheadle (1841–6), Staffordshire, by A. W. N. Pugin.

of 'real' materials; and honesty in construction. It was the application of these principles, in a self-conscious and disciplined way, that alone would lead to a church architecture of integrity (i.e., of material, spiritual, and ethical consistency). Importantly, these principles were not abstract but contingent, to be framed in a distinctly national (i.e., English) version of Gothic architecture, in line with Sarum Use liturgy.

St Giles' gave Pugin his greatest opportunity to showcase what these principles looked like in practice. It may be considered one of the most influential and therefore significant buildings of the Victorian age. Designed in 1840, and erected between 1841 and 1846, St Giles' was commissioned by the powerful Catholic aristocrat, the sixteenth Earl of Shrewsbury. It came with a substantial budget, allowing Pugin to indulge his ambitions. What the building demonstrated most clearly was a seriousness for archaeological accuracy based on historic precedent: that this was not only desirable, but possible. In plan it followed a simple yet time-honoured layout of liturgically derived spatial components, including distinct nave, chancel (with aisles), sacristy, porch, and tower **[83a]**. In terms of décor, a medieval exuberance was brought to bear. As with the Houses of Parliament, we find not only elaborate carving inside and out, including beautiful Decorated window tracery, but also many elements of Pugin's own design, such as luxuriously coloured encaustic tiles, stencilling, metalwork, wallpaper, and numerous other interior furnishings, becoming ever more elaborate towards the east end. The stained glass, too, was produced to designs by Pugin. In achieving this effect Pugin was not afraid to employ modern, industrial processes, engaging firms such as Mintons (tiles) and Hardman & Co (metalwork), all

Fig. 83a

Plan, St Giles', Cheadle.

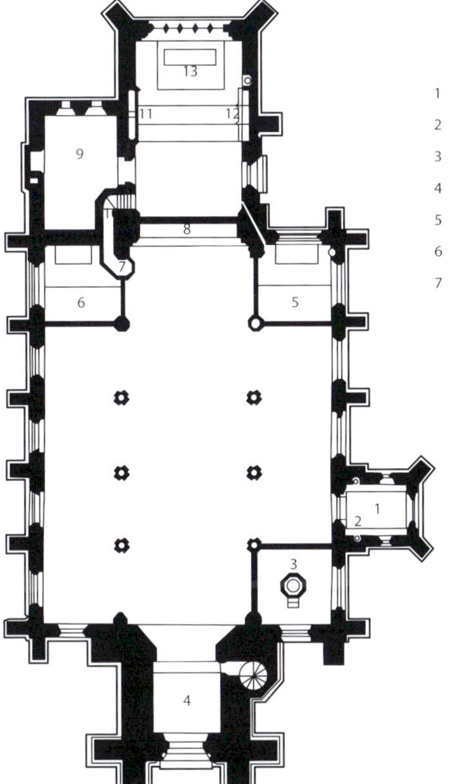

Fig. 83b

Interior, St Giles', Cheadle, looking down nave towards the chancel.

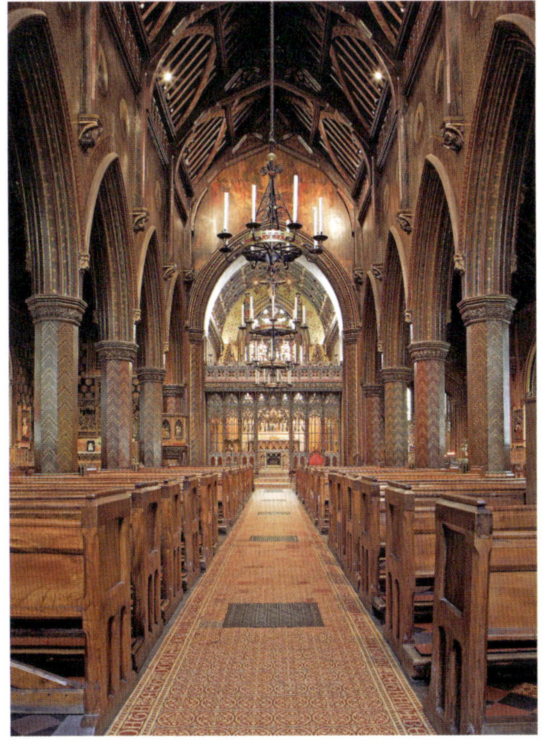

in aid of deploying architecture as a form of religious technology **[83b]**.[4] Although it looked like a medieval parish church, St Giles' was no copy. Its convincing appearance nevertheless did much to bolster its credentials as a modern yet 'truthful' work of ecclesiastical architecture.

This concern for proper church architecture followed Roman Catholics more or less wherever they went, including into the wider British world. Through emancipation, enhanced seminary education, and the ultramontanist efforts of organisations such as the Association for the Propagation of the Faith (*Propaganda Fide*), plans to extend the presence of the Catholic faith in Britain's colonies through missionary work was underway by the early part of the nineteenth century. Initially, the Australian colonies were targeted owing partly to their increasingly large Irish immigrant population (convicts, and those escaping poverty and starvation). Following the erection of the Roman Catholic diocese of Hobart Town in 1842, covering virtually all of what was Van Diemen's Land (now Tasmania), Robert William Willson, a close friend of Pugin's, was installed as bishop. Pugin supplied Willson with designs for everything from church plate, vestments, and stained glass, through to head-stones and fonts, including two complete designs for parish churches that would become St Paul's, Oatlands (1850–1), and St Patrick's, Colebrook (1855–7), both masterful specimens in the Gothic Revival idiom **[84]**.

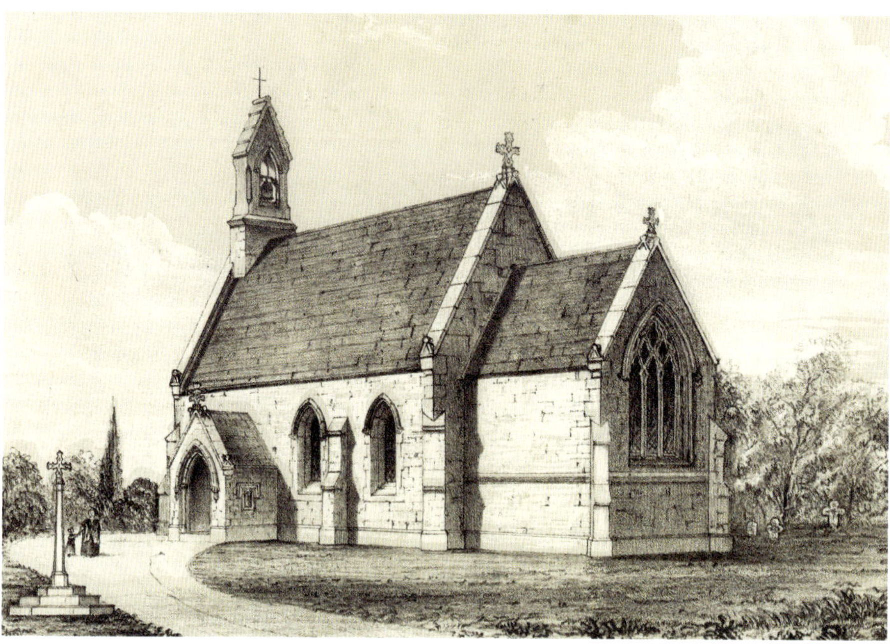

Fig. 84

Gothic dream in the antipodes. St Paul's, Oatlands (1850–1), in Tasmania, Australia, by A. W. N. Pugin.

Pugin was equally keen to assist Willson's colleague in Sydney, bishop John Bede Polding, to whom he also sent a number of church designs, including that for St Benedict's, Chippendale (1842). The vision was extended by Pugin's admirers. Following the appointment of James Goold as bishop of Melbourne (1848), church plans by Charles Hansom were sent from England.

These resulted in a number of modest but ecclesiologically sophisticated churches across the colony of Victoria, in new settlements such as Port Fairy, Portland, Keilor, Kilmore, Kyneton, and Ballarat. Irish Catholic architects also emigrated to Canada, extending Pugin's influence there. Principal among these was Joseph Connolly, who arrived in 1873, having trained in the Dublin office of the 'Irish Pugin', J. J. McCarthy. Connolly's churches—often for Irish clients—clearly reflect Puginian principles, including St Patrick's, Hamilton (1875–6), and St Peter's Cathedral, Ontario (1880–1958).

Perfection and Beauty: The Church of England, Home and Abroad

Not surprisingly, Pugin's strident Catholicism did not endear him to other Christian denominations in Britain, most of which were Protestant in constitution. John Ruskin despised him, and even the established Church of England, which had become more tolerant of 'high' (i.e., Anglo-Catholic) doctrine since the advent of the Oxford Movement, approached his views with caution. But the irresistible moral and spiritual logic of Pugin's principles cut through, especially in an age that reckoned itself pious. They were taken up and repackaged initially by the Cambridge Camden Society (est. 1839), which presented them as the material counterpart of Tractarian theology, and thus essential to 'proper' Christian architecture. It argued that, as part of Anglican renewal, the liturgical machinery of the ancient, pre-Romanised 'catholick' church ought to be appreciated afresh. Moreover, and following Pugin's lead, these liturgical practices were seen as best represented in medieval architecture, particularly in the earlier phases of Gothic, identified as 'Early English' and 'Decorated', or 'First' and 'Second' pointed.

Along with its sister organisation, the Oxford Society for Promoting the Study of Gothic Architecture (Oxford Architectural Society), the Ecclesiological Society—as the Camden Society became known from 1845—promulgated its new ideas on 'correct' church design through a series of influential publications. These included their long-running bi-monthly periodical, *The Ecclesiologist*, and a series of pamphlets with titles such as *A Few Words to Church-builders* (1841), and *A Few Words to Church Wardens on Churches and Church Ornamentation* (1842). The pamphlets in particular were practical publications aimed at those responsible for architectural patronage and 'discipline', such as priests, wardens, and parish vestries. Somewhat like Pugin's *True Principles*, these texts sought to lay down the fundamentals of church design and restoration, spelling out through clear headings and simple diagrams the key components of a correct church. Here one could find not only their most famous diktat, 'There are two parts, and only two parts, which are absolutely essential to a church—chancel and nave', but advice on a long list of other features including aisles, porches, towers, general orientation, and the elevation of chancels, to individual items such as fonts, pulpits, pews, the use of bells, the reredos, and the placement and decoration of the altar. Stated here also was the Society's disdain for galleries.

The views put forward in these publications, along with the Society itself, soon became influential, to the point where they all but totally transformed

Anglican church design in the space of a few years. A considerable number of old and dilapidated churches were also given a new lease of life through the Society's initiatives for restoration. Although controversial on archaeological grounds, this initiative salvaged (some claimed disfigured) many hundreds of otherwise abandoned, underutilised, or 'wrongly' administered buildings. There was of course a degree of resistance to all this, being seen by some, especially those from within the Evangelical wing of the Church, as a Trojan horse of 'Romanism'.[5] Architects, too, such as George Gilbert Scott, bemoaned what they saw as the Society's unjustly pernickety and at times prejudicial criticism. Despite this, the longer-term success of the Camdenian reforms demonstrated the power of the widespread desire for spiritual renewal within the established Church, and beyond, including the yearning to reconnect with foundational principles.

This influence initially fostered what A. J. B. Beresford Hope called an 'Anglo-Parochial' phase in Anglican ecclesiology, leading to a focus on strict English precedent for which the Society was eventually accused of 'copyism'. We see this, perhaps most famously, in George Edmund Street's church of St Peter, Treverbyn, in Cornwall (1848–50), which is almost an exact replica of a small, medieval parish church erected using local materials. Not every architect was persuaded by the pursuit of such rugged authenticity, however. Others, such as R. C. Carpenter, sought a more synthetic approach based on knowledge of approved English sources, evident in his modish church of St Mary Magdalene, Munster Square, in London (1849–52). Others still, like Scott, or the young Henry Woodyer, took a rather safe Puginian line in designing churches in a predominantly plain yet correct English Decorated style, not only in homage to Pugin's principles, or to seek the approbation of the Camdenians, but also to satisfy the rather conservative tastes of their clientele. Scott soon became one of Britain's greatest and most prolific church architects, going on to design set-piece masterworks of the genre, such as All Souls', Halifax, in Yorkshire (1856–9) **[85a&b]**.

Colonial Extension, and Beyond

It was around this time that the perceived need to promote Christianity as a plank in British imperial policy took root in the 'official mind' of the ruling classes. The growing and intense religiosity of Victorian society necessarily affected the way Britain perceived its moral 'obligation' to the wider world, particularly with respect to its own colonial empire. Lack of achievement in this regard had been widely criticised. Although architectural knowledge was thin on the ground initially, ever greater numbers of architects emigrated to Britain's colonies, taking their expertise with them. Given the ascendency of the Gothic Revival in ecclesiastical architecture at the time, it increasingly took precedent in the colonies too. Publications, including guides, glossaries, and pattern books, steadily made their way to these locations, carried not only by professional architects but also by clergymen. Architects in Britain, including Scott, also sent plans for new church buildings to friends, family, or indeed anyone else who required them. As the settler colonies in particular became more populous and wealthy, so too did their aspirations for architectural pretension. The hope was that what had been achieved in the Old World could be replicated in the New.

Fig. 85a

All Souls', Halifax, Yorkshire (1856–9), by George Gilbert Scott.

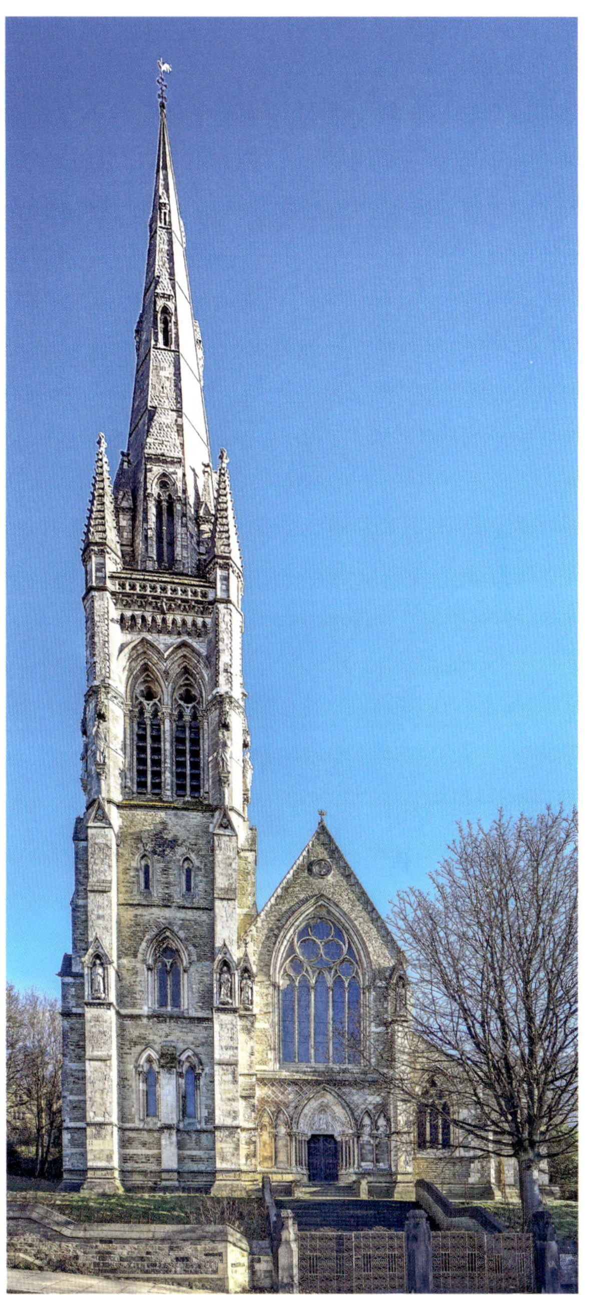

There was no small amount of religious politics at play here. Among those who made the journey were a young and more spiritually focused breed of clergyman, determined to do God's work. Mostly Oxbridge-educated, they had strong ties to both the Oxford Architectural and Cambridge Camden societies. Some were even accomplished amateur architects, which proved useful given the dearth of professional design skill they encountered upon arrival. They saw it as their responsibility to promulgate

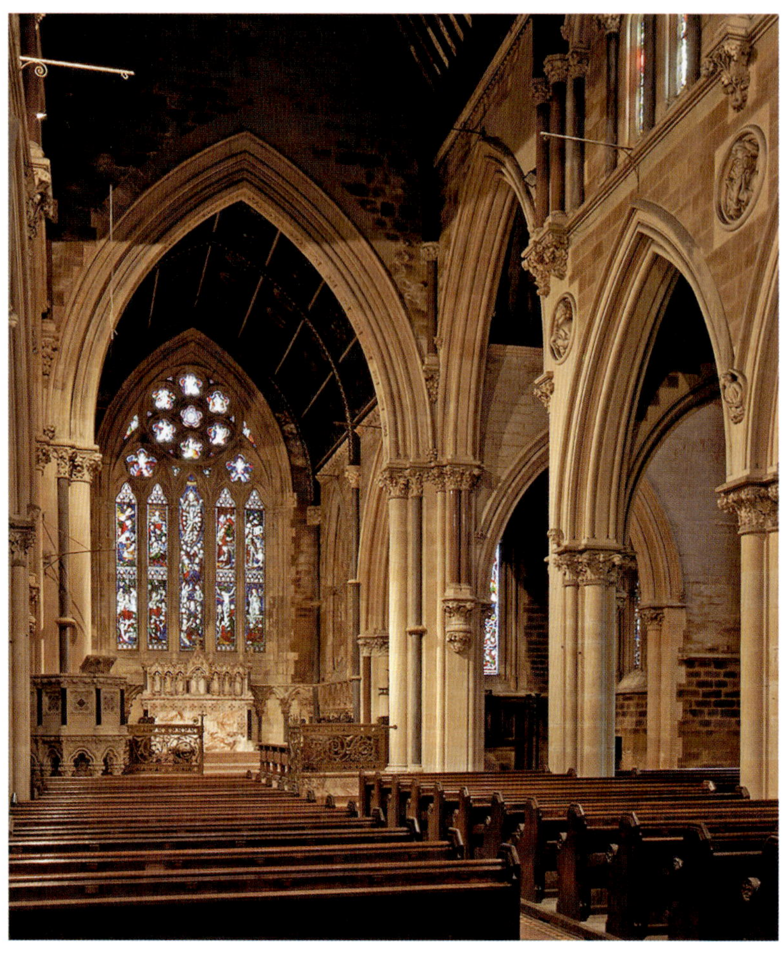

Fig. 85b
Interior, All Souls', looking towards chancel.

correct church architecture in an effort to usher in a novel regime of orderliness and propriety, in lands that were widely viewed as 'wilderness'. This included a sense of urgency towards evangelising the indigenous peoples of the non-European world, who were not to be neglected in this project to elevate and fortify the moral fibre of empire. Among the earliest proponents of this vision for extending Anglican ecclesiology abroad was the Rev. F. H. Cox in Tasmania. Here the Ecclesiological Society proved particularly useful, sending three church designs to Tasmania in the form of drawings and models produced by R. C. Carpenter, one of which became the parish church of St John the Baptist (1847), Prosser Plains **[86]**.

This approach, which exploited a growing network of Anglican ties throughout the ever-expanding British world, became something of a pattern. In time, the Ecclesiological and Oxford Architectural societies would produce a series of publications on designs for churches and ecclesiastical furnishings, for use in colonial contexts, the best-known collection of which was *Instrumenta Ecclesiastica* (1847–56). Assistance was offered directly to colonial bishops and clergymen, such as to G. A. Selwyn in New Zealand, John Medley in New Brunswick (Canada), and James Chapman in Sri Lanka.

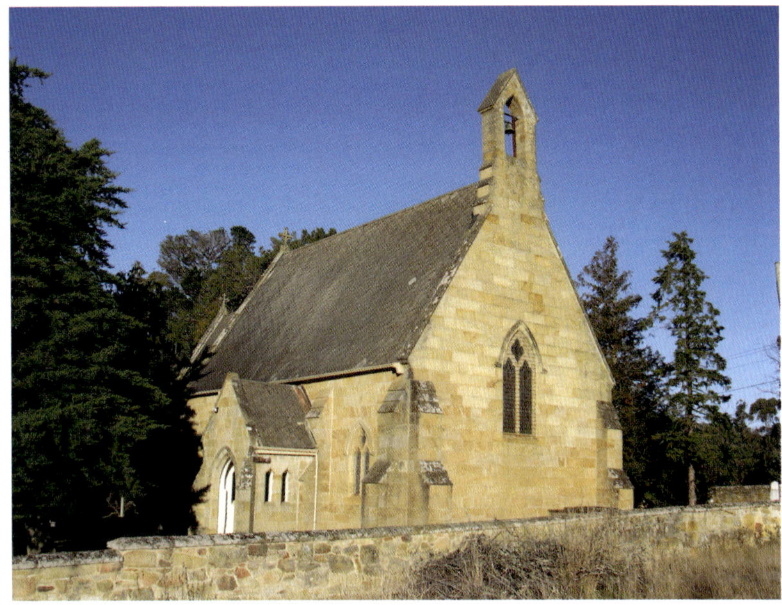

Fig. 86

Ecclesiological 'correctness' abroad. St John the Baptist (1847), Prosser Plains, in Tasmania, Australia, by R. C. Carpenter.

Naturally, these ideas also found their way into other non-European, anglophone contexts, such as the United States of America, where architects such as Frank Wills, Richard Upjohn, and John Notman (all British immigrants) extended ecclesiological principles among the Episcopalian community. Indeed, when asked how many churches around the world had been affected by the ideas of the Ecclesiological Society, John Mason Neale, one of its founding members, is reputed to have replied: 'It would be as difficult almost as to count the stars on a clear frosty night.'[6] Benjamin Webb, being more specific, was able to report that up to the year 1852 advice had been given to 'the Canadas, Bombay, Ceylon, Sierra Leone, the Mauritius, the Himalaya, Tasmania, Guinea, Australia and New Zealand, Newfoundland and Hong Kong'.

Networking of this kind was not solely the preserve of the Tractarian wing of the Church. Evangelicals, too, through the auspices of the Church Missionary Society, worked their contacts both within Britain and across the empire to establish principles and strategies for dealing with built infrastructure in the mission field, especially with respect to native agency (see below).

Ecclesiological Developments and Modern Church Design

The 'Anglo-parochial' phase in Anglican ecclesiology slowly gave way to expanded horizons at the close of the 1840s, with the Ecclesiological Society, among others, encouraging architects to look to Continental Europe for inspiration. There were a small number of existing church buildings in Britain that already pointed in the direction of this inspiration, such as Christ Church, Streatham (1840–1), by James Wilde, but these were exceptional. As growing numbers of articles on the subject began to appear in leading periodicals, and opportunities for first-hand observation through greater accessibility to travel increased, British architects began to infuse their designs with non-English features in aid of a more modern and flexible

Gothic architecture. This is where ideas concerning 'development' and structural polychromy discussed in Chapter 3 had their greatest impact. Architects widened their palette of materials, providing justifications for the use of brick, coloured stone, and manufactured products such as terracotta and encaustic tiles. They also considered alternative models for design, such as devising an appropriate ecclesiology for populous urban settings.[7] At this point ecclesiastical architects became specifically interested in Italian, French, and German medieval architecture, not only for its polychrome effect but also for its spatial conception and formal massing.

Fig. 87a

All Saints', Margaret Street (1849–53), London, by William Butterfield.

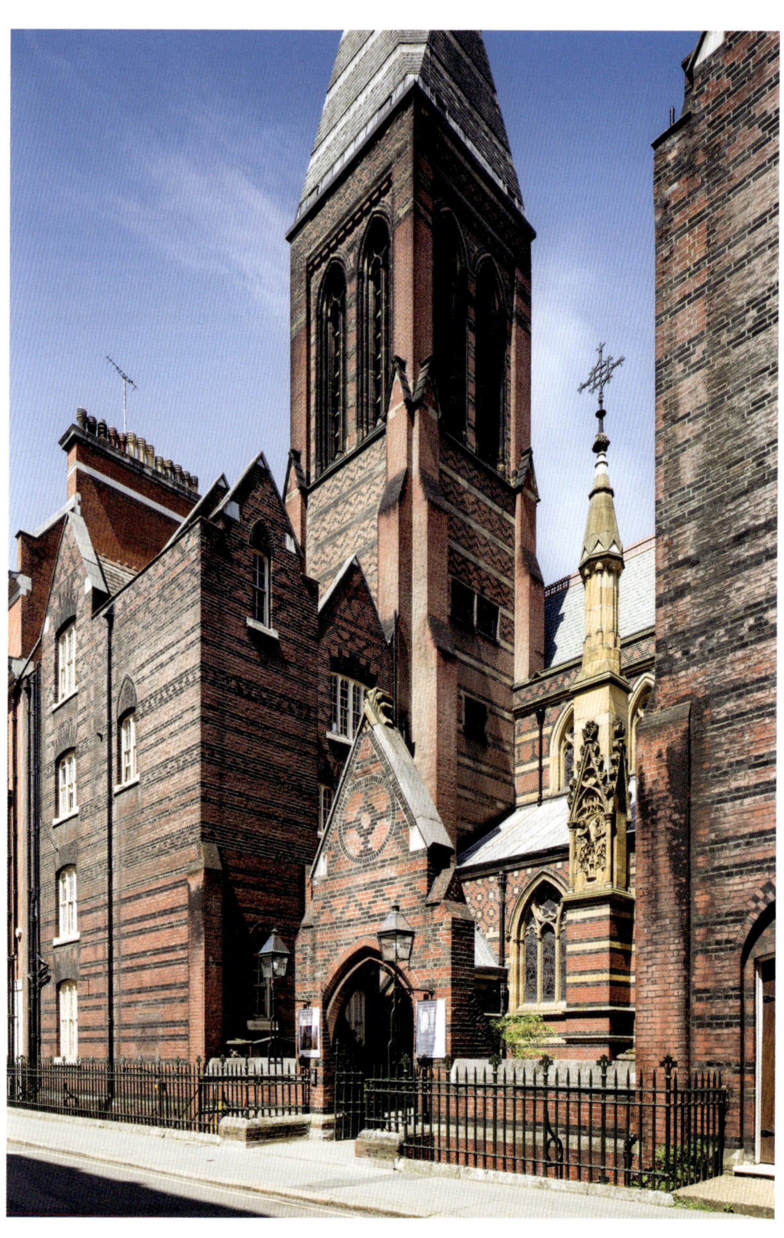

This inspiration, combined with a renewed appreciation for the simple and massive forms of Romanesque and Early English Gothic architecture, affected church design markedly in Britain. It led to a 'muscular' phase in which a primitivist aesthetic of powerful geometries, broad planar surfaces, and bold detailing became *de rigueur*. Intellectually, Ruskin set the tone with the 'Lamp of Power' in his *Seven Lamps of Architecture* (1849), in which qualities such as mass, bulk, weight, breadth, and vigour were extolled. Others, such as Edward Garbett and Beresford Hope, cited these qualities as facilitating a new kind of sublimity, grounded in the inspiration of nature.[8] Others still sought to provide workable prototypes, as in George Truefitt's *Designs for Country Churches* (1850). There was, as the historian Henry-Russell Hitchcock put it, a 'strident plasticity' evident in the buildings of the age. The architecture that resulted is what we now call 'High Victorian'. It was an architecture deemed suitable for an age primed to confront the combined challenges of industrialisation, mass urbanisation, and the spectre of irreligion and moral degradation among the working classes, not to mention global expansion into unfamiliar, even hostile lands.

One of the earliest and most influential church buildings to emerge from this phase in English ecclesiology was All Saints', Margaret Street, in London (1849–53) **[87a&b]**. Designed by William Butterfield, one of the most talented architects of his (or any) generation, it was largely financed by Beresford Hope, a linchpin of the Ecclesiological Society, and someone with whom Butterfield had close relations. Together they produced a truly

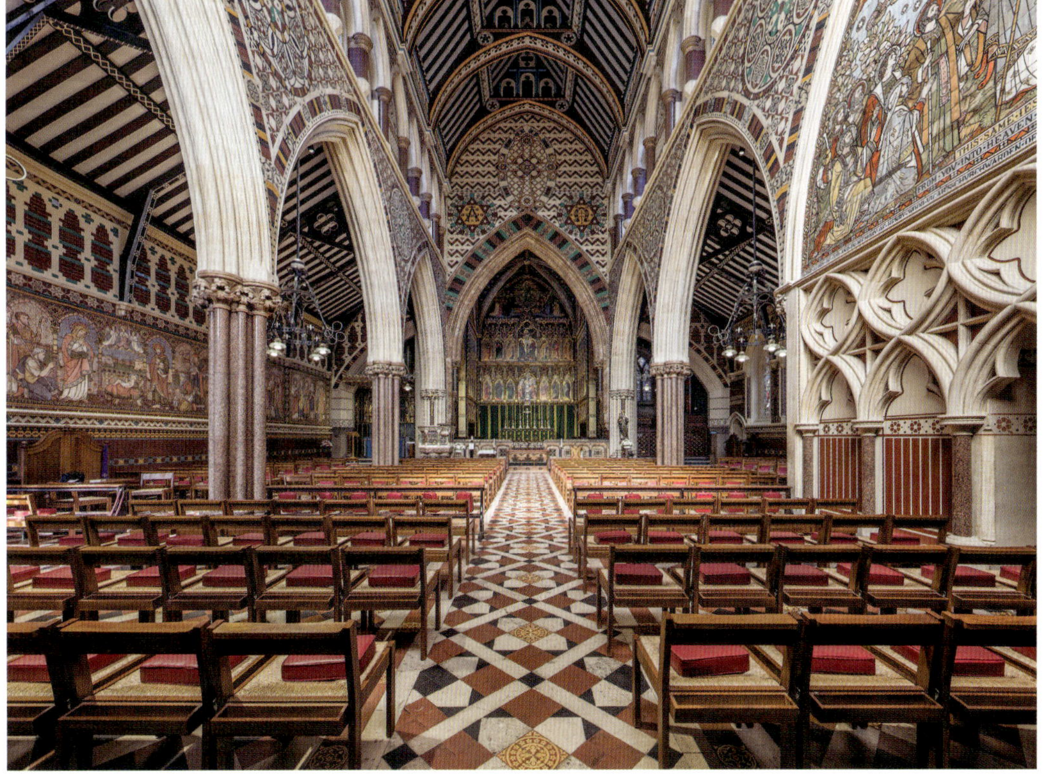

Fig. 87b

Explosion of colour: interior, All Saints', looking towards chancel.

original work, 'correct' in every way, but strikingly unusual in terms of both its accommodation within a restricted urban site and its unflinching embrace of Continental-style architectural polychromy. And all this within a Decorated Gothic frame. Both inside and out it is a riot of colour, making the most of an extraordinary array of natural and industrially manufactured materials. There are elements of German and Italian medieval architecture observable in the tower, chancel vaulting, and pulpit, but the combination is entirely novel. Like Pugin's St Giles', All Saints' made quite a stir within the British architectural fraternity. There could scarcely have been a more shocking (some said 'ugly') yet satisfyingly modern church, adapted in every way to the conditions of the age. In this respect it heralded a new frontier in British ecclesiastical design, showcasing what a town church could be.

By the mid to late 1850s the 'mania' for structural polychromy had caught on, helped in no small measure by the repeal of the brick tax in 1850. The architects touched most by it were those who emerged into the profession in the 1840s, such as G. E. Street, G. F. Bodley, William White, Henry Woodyer, and John Loughborough Pearson. Some of these restless young designers, such as Bodley, Street, and White, passed through G. G. Scott's office, as either pupils or improvers, while Woodyer was a product of

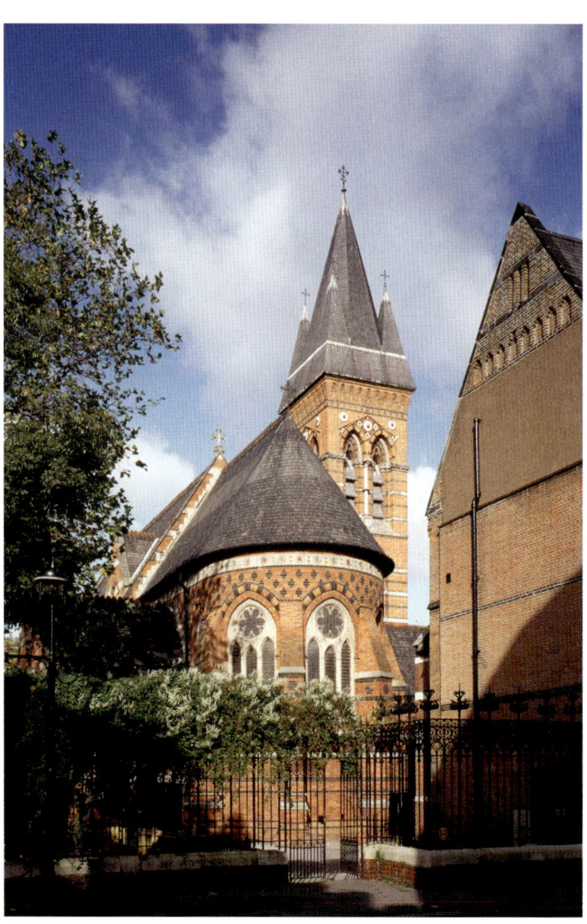

Fig. 88a

St James the Less, Pimlico (1859–61), London, by George Edmund Street.

Butterfield. These architects, increasingly frustrated by the strict discipline of ecclesiology, saw themselves as raising a new standard for architectural design in Britain, and understood what they were doing as a conspicuous break with hitherto established aesthetic convention.

For his part, Street produced a string of churches showcasing this novel mode, including All Saints', Boyne Hill, Berkshire (1854–7) **[95]**; SS. Philip and James, Oxford (1859–65); and, later, St Mary Magdalene, Paddington (1867–77). All of these show clear Continental influence, in both their formation and their use of materials, including structural polychromy. Foremost among Street's churches, however, is St James the Less, Pimlico, in London (1859–61) **[88a]**. In it we see the influence of French and German medieval architecture acting on the building's formal composition, particularly in the spire, apsidal east end, and use of plate tracery; while Street's love of Italy and admiration for Ruskin comes through in the dazzling polychrome surfaces and naturalistic carving. Even in some of his smaller country churches, where polychromy is less pronounced, as at St John the Evangelist, Howsham, in Yorkshire (1859–60), or St Mary the Virgin, Fawley (1865–6), Continental influence remains potent **[88b]**. Likewise, the churches of White demonstrate the extent

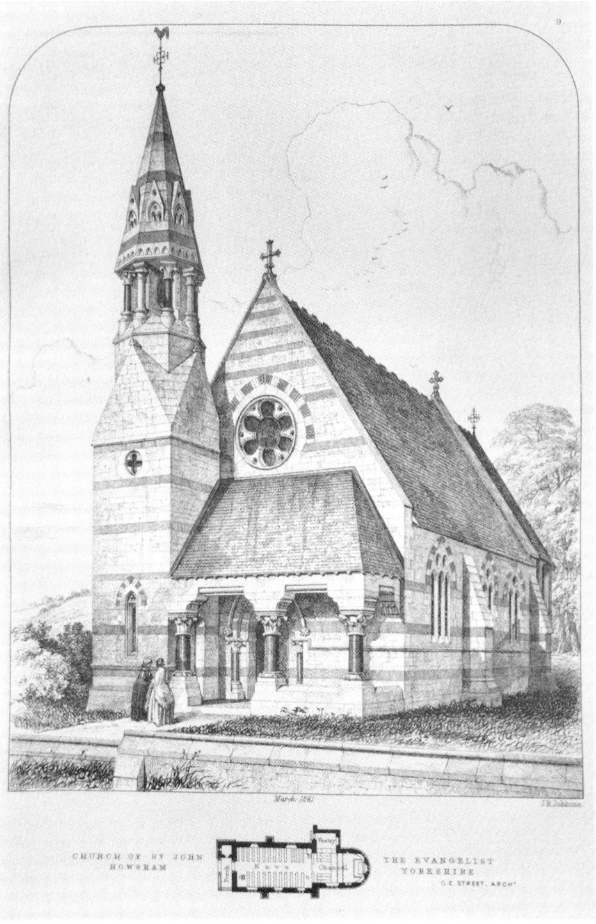

Fig. 88b

St John the Evangelist, Howsham (1859–60), Yorkshire, by George Edmund Street.

to which these effects could be taken in terms of variation and subtlety. Two are St Michael and All Angels, Lyndhurst (1858–69), and St Saviour's, Aberdeen Park, Islington (1863–9), where powerful massing and coloured brickwork combine to make striking (and very modern) ecclesiological statements. Although this group of architects worked primarily for High Church clientele, it should be noted that Broad Church and Evangelical Anglicans were not immune from this craze, as the impressive polychrome interiors of St George's, Campden Hill (1864–5), by Bassett Keeling, and St Simon Zelotes, Chelsea (1858–9), by James Peacock, amply demonstrate.

Such developments naturally found their way to the colonies. However, due to the persistence of conservative taste in colonial society, along with the unevenness of technology transfer, the filtering through of such innovations took time. But this was not because colonial architects lacked ability or vision. 'Modern Gothic' ecclesiology in brick did catch on, as the examples of All Saints', Dunedin (1865–73), by William Clayton; St Peter's church on Carleton Street, Toronto (1864), by Henry Langley; or indeed St Philip's mission church in Fingo, Grahamstown (1863–7), by William White, illustrate **[89a]**. The results could be quite spectacular. For instance, inspired by the writing of Ruskin and Street, and having returned from his own tour of Northern Italy in 1865, the Melbourne-based Cornish architect Joseph Reed produced St Jude's, Carlton (1866–74), with its vivid combination of polychrome brick and stone **[89b]**.

Fig. 89a

Exporting the polychrome revolution. St Philip's mission church (1863–7), Fingo, Grahamstown, South Africa, by William White. The labour of local black converts was used to erect the church in an effort to impart skills applicable to colonial assimilation.

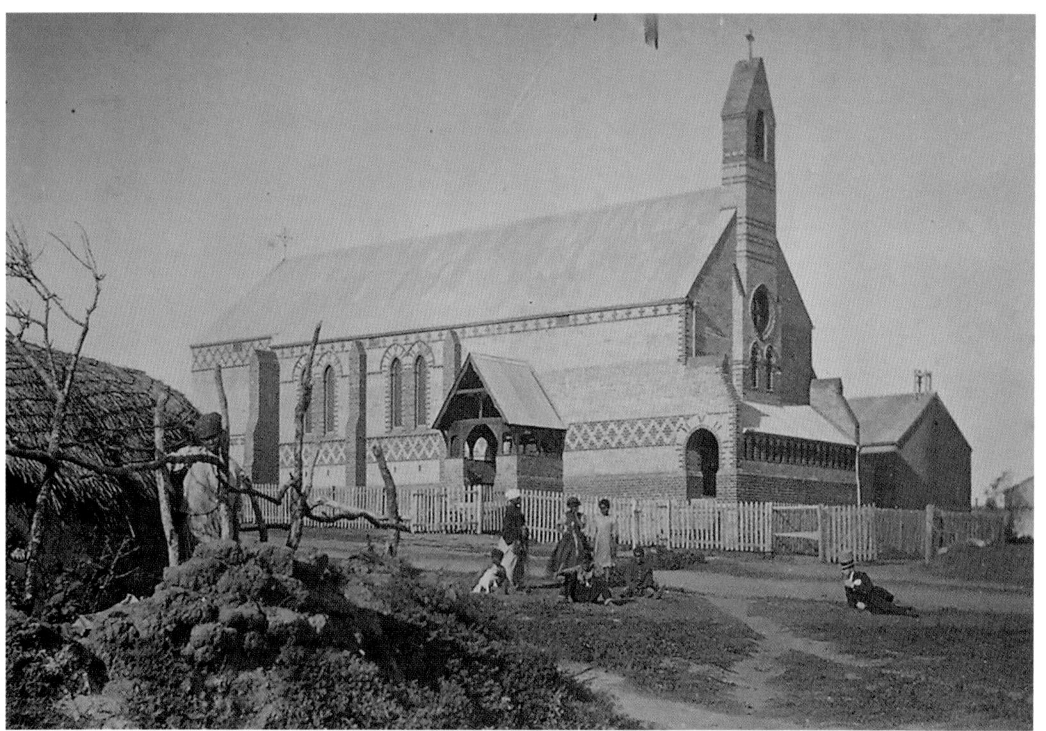

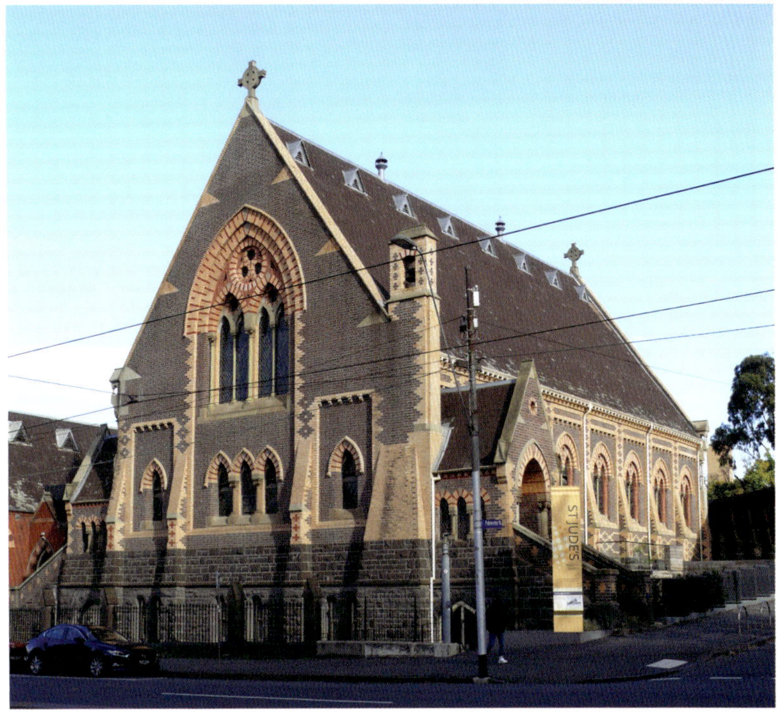

Fig. 89b

St Jude's, Carlton (1866–74), in Melbourne, Australia, by Joseph Reed.

Back in Britain, other architects, including William Burges, Pearson, and Bodley, took a different tack, focusing less on constructional polychromy and more on composition and arrangement. Burges, in particular, was critical of what he saw as the excesses of Victorian polychromy. An admirer of Viollet-le-Duc, he favoured the chromatically muted yet structurally assertive forms of thirteenth-century French Gothic. His ability as a designer allowed him to take this inspiration and meld it into something of tremendous strength and beauty. As a result, Burges's churches ripple with a physical immediacy rarely matched in Victorian architecture. We see this, for instance, at St Fin Barre Cathedral, Cork, in Ireland (1865–78) **[90a]**, as well as at his two most noteworthy ecclesiastical commissions in Yorkshire for the 1st Marquess of Ripon: Christ the Consoler, Skelton-on-Ure (1870–6), and St Mary, Studley Royal (1870–2) **[90b]**. Each captures in its own way a palpable sense of compressive force through the sculptural dynamism and taut muscularity apparent in their rich, compact, and boldly carved detailing. Pearson's smaller rural churches of the late 1850s and early 1860s, such as St Leonard's, Scorborough (1857–9); St Peter's, Daylesford (1859–61); and Christ Church, Appleton-le-Moors (1863–6), also show strong Early French influence, as do his major urban churches of the same period, such as St Peter's, Vauxhall, in London (1863–4) **[91a]**. Bodley, too, bought wholeheartedly into this modern Gothic, exemplified, for instance, at All Saints', Selsley, in Gloucestershire (1861–2) **[91b]**.

The enthusiasm for thirteenth-century French Gothic had wide appeal among Victorian ecclesiastical architects. As Charles Eastlake observed in

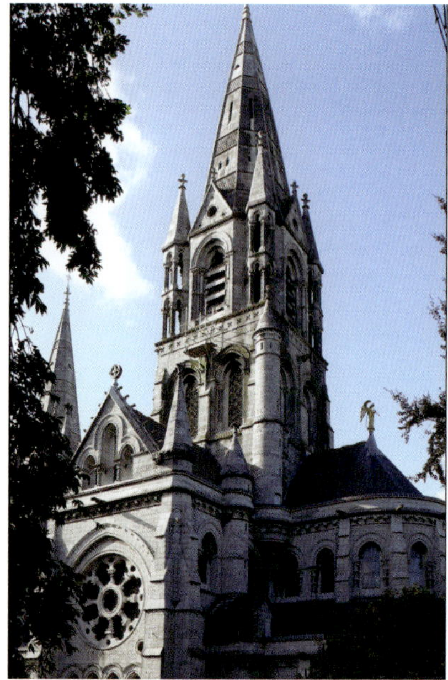

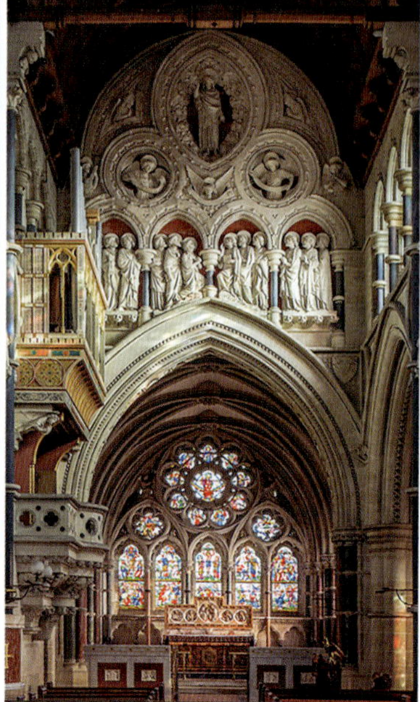

Fig. 90a

The muscular churches of William Burges: St Fin Barre Cathedral, Cork (1865–78), in Ireland.

Fig. 90b

Interior, Christ the Consoler, Skelton-on-Ure (1870–6), Yorkshire, by William Burges.

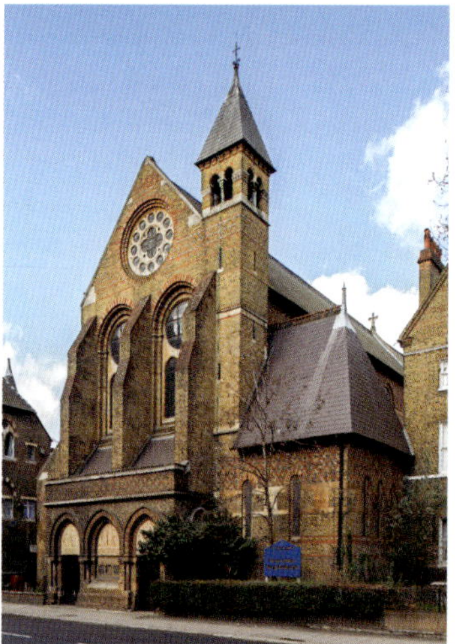

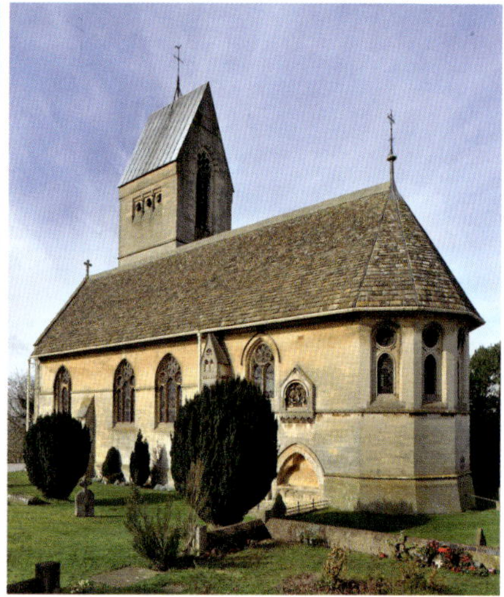

Fig. 91a

St Peter's, Vauxhall (1863–4), London, by John Loughborough Pearson.

Fig. 91b

All Saints', Selsley (1861–2), in Gloucestershire, by George Frederick Bodley (photo Geoff Brandwood).

his *A History of the Gothic Revival* in 1872, it was 'for some years decidedly in the ascendant'.[9] It continued to exert its influence in the work of Pearson, evident at St Augustine's, Kilburn (1871–8), and his magnificent cathedral at Truro, in Cornwall (1880–1910) **[92]**; while in Edinburgh it shone through at Christ Church, Morningside (1875–8), by Hippolyte Blanc. Even among that older generation of British architects, which included the likes of Scott and the rather more eccentric S. S. Teulon, French influence left its mark. In the case of Scott, we see it clearly at St Michael and All Angels, Leafield (1859), and, in a more refined mode, in his chapels at Exeter College, Oxford (1854–60), and St John's College, Cambridge (1863–9) **[93]**. For Teulon, it

Fig. 92

French influence: Truro Cathedral, Cornwall (1880–1910), by John Loughborough Pearson.

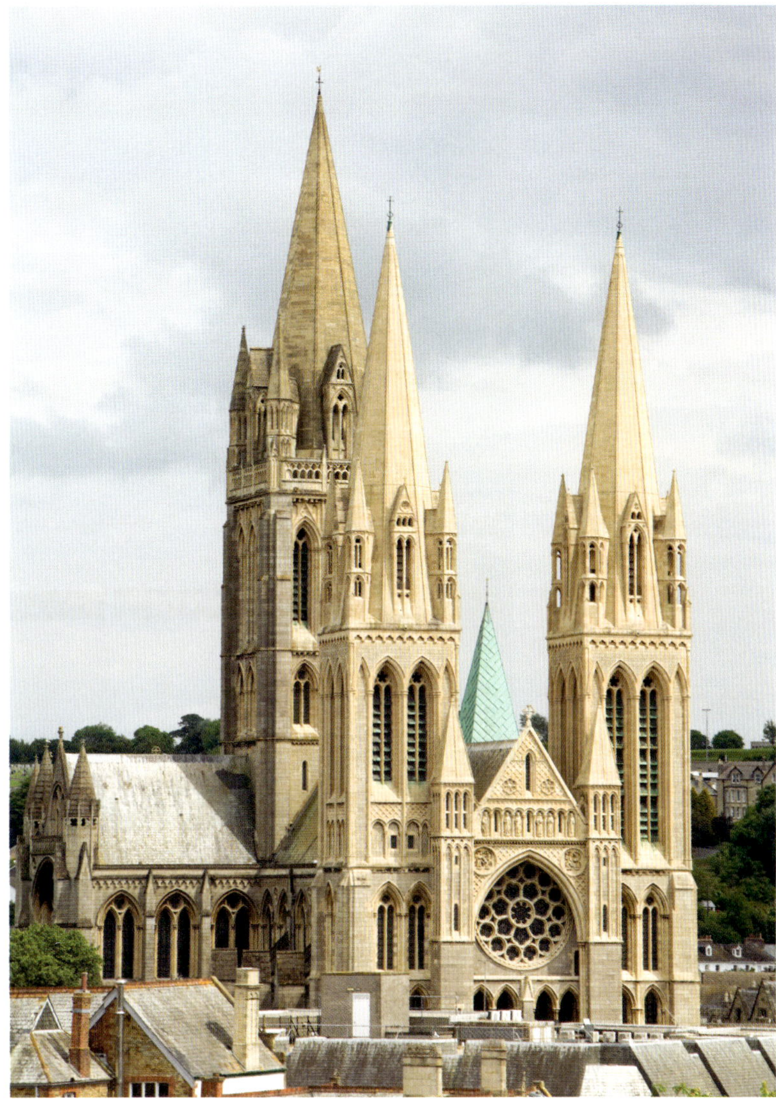

manifests in the church of St John the Baptist, Burrington, Lincolnshire (1856–7), St Thomas's, Agar Town, London (1863–4), and the much larger St Stephen's, Hampstead (1866–9) **[94a]**.

The churches of English architects could also be found throughout Continental Europe at this time, especially among British resident communities. With numerous regions in Europe under weak governance, at war, or in revolutionary tumult by mid-century, Protestants on both sides of the Atlantic sensed an opportunity to challenge the Church of Rome on its own turf, as well as push at the western edges of the Muslim Ottoman empire. Into this 'field' of strained Anglican extension we find architects such as Street at work. He produced masterful essays in High Victorian ecclesiology for both the English and American Episcopalian communities in Rome: All Saints', Via del Babuino (1880–7), and St Paul's

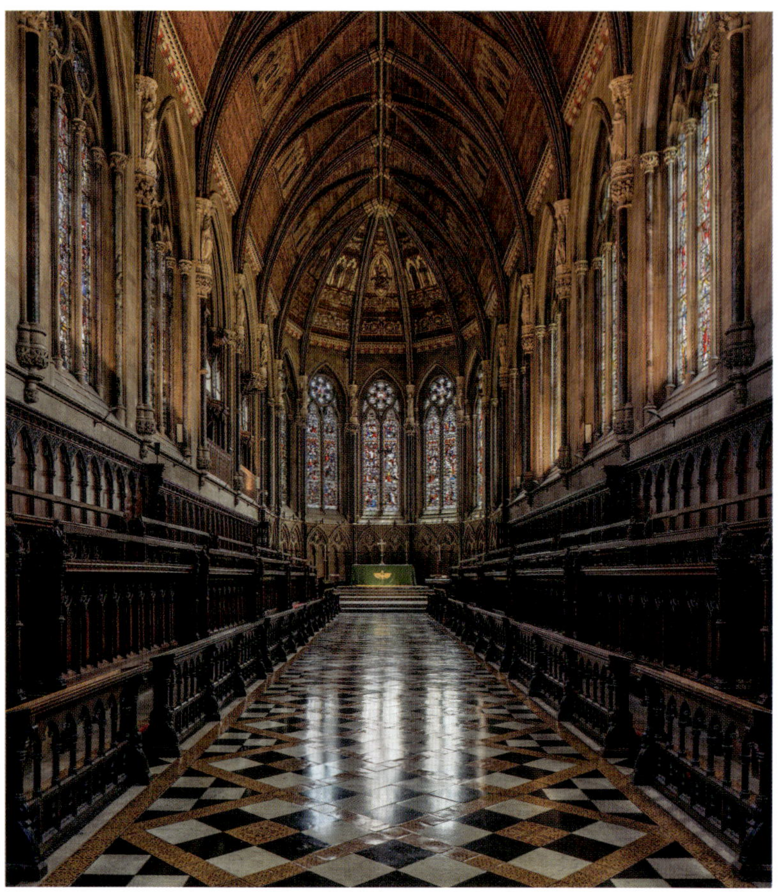

Fig. 93

Interior, St John's College Chapel, Cambridge (1863–9), by George Gilbert Scott (photo David Iliff).

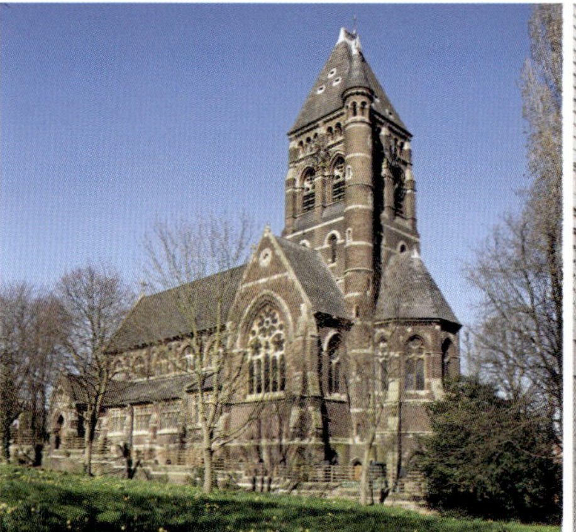

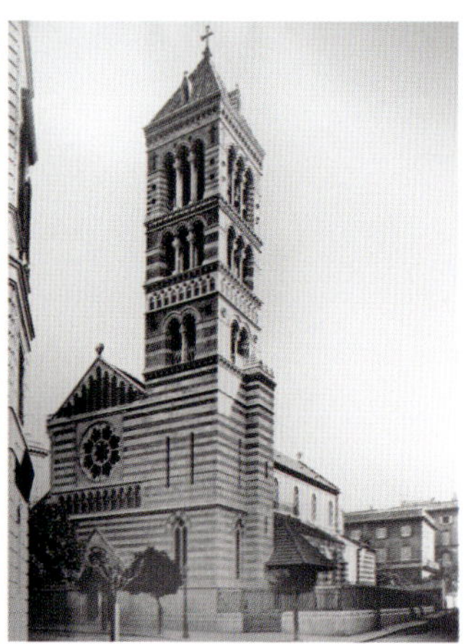

Fig. 94a

St Stephen's, Hampstead (1866–9), London, by Samuel Sanders Teulon.

Fig. 94b

St Paul's Within-the-Walls, Via Nazionale (1872–6), Rome, by George Edmund Street.

Within-the-Walls, on Via Nazionale (1872–6) **[94b]**. Only a few years earlier he had designed the resolutely muscular Crimean War Memorial Church (1864–8), Istanbul, as a 'mission' church for the English. In this Street had superseded Burges and his equally spectacular design for the same building. Although unbuilt, Burges's design, with its heavy countenance and rich polychrome appearance, was considered a masterstroke of 'adapted' ecclesiology **[49b]**.

Sacramentalism, Affective Spaces, and the Involvement of Women

Something that was increasingly discernible at the time, especially in the context of Tractarianism and the rise of the reformed High Church movement, was the attention given to ideas of sacramentalism in church design. This concerned what a church building was understood to mean, symbolically. It is important to remember that clergymen—who, apart from anything else, were patrons of church architecture—also imbibed modern science and its developmental theses, leading them to perceive 'design' throughout the universe as a type of divine plan.[10] This was the fundamental premise of so-called natural theology. As far as Christian architecture was concerned, the translation of such ideas into built form had medieval roots. But by the Victorian period it had acquired a peculiar nineteenth-century twist owing to the existential challenge thrown up by modern science and the need to absorb and rationalise its key findings. Natural theology relied much on the authority of scholars such as William Paley, Robert Chambers, and William Buckland, whose way of thinking about creation helped theologians navigate the polarising extremes of the 'Genesis vs geology' debates, as well as the implications of Darwin's theory of natural selection (evolution).

Symbolic Forms

Some of the theory surrounding this concept is elaborated in Chapter 3, in particular that concerning the impact on architectural thought of the geological sciences and evolutionary biology. Strictly speaking, sacramentality was taken by ecclesiologists to mean 'the idea that, by the outward and visible form, is signified something inward and spiritual'. In other words, that the 'material fabrick [of a church] symbolizes, embodies, figures, represents, expresses, answers to, some abstract meaning'.[11] This idea also owed something to the Victorian propensity to read meaning into the world, and to imbue art with didactic intent.

It could take different forms, from the loosely metaphorical, through the iconographic, to the strictly symbolic, as in the representational embodiment of liturgy. For those like Ruskin, architecture had certain poetic possibilities in this regard, principally in reference to God's presence. With respect to Creation, for instance, and in particular the expository power of geology, he observed how

> ...it is perfectly natural that the different kinds of stone used in [a wall's] successive courses should be of different colours...They are, in the first place, a kind of expression of the growth or age of the wall, like the rings in the wood of a tree....they are valuable in their suggestion of the natural courses of rocks and beds of the earth itself.

This was part of Ruskin's concept of the 'wall veil' which was influential in Victorian church design. We see it in the work of his devotees, such as G. E. Street, in the chancel at All Saints', Boyne Hill, and at St James the Less, Pimlico **[95]**. Figurations of this kind were pleasing to ecclesiologists. Indeed, specific materials were indicative of this sacramental idealism,

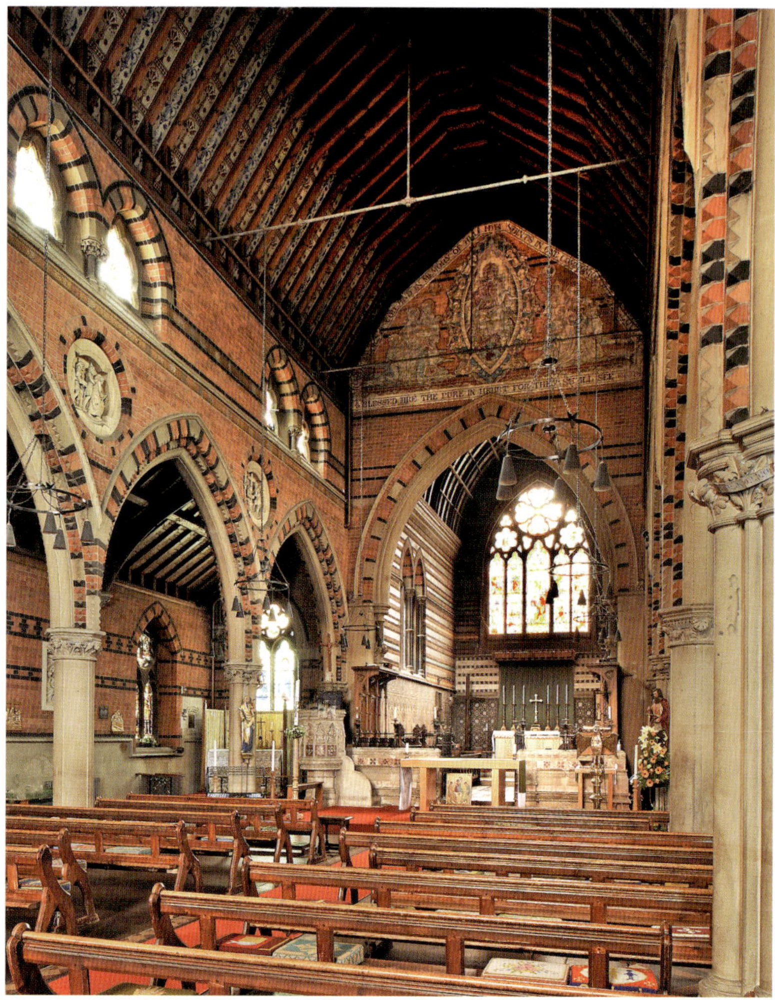

Fig. 95

Interior, nave and chancel, All Saints', Boyne Hill (1854–7), Berkshire, by George Edmund Street (photo Geoff Brandwood).

especially variegated marbles and stone containing fossils, emphasising historical narrative.[12]

Affective Spaces

One of the understated but no less important functions of this type of architecture was its evocation of an emotional response in worshipers. Victorian religious architecture was designed to be *affective* in this way, 'to move as well as to teach'.[13] The introduction of dazzling colour was intended to contribute to an overwhelming sensory encounter, heightening religious sentiment. This tactic could rely as much on sound, or even smell, as it did on sight, making for a fully 'immersive' experience. For example, the revival at this time of choral and organ music, along with the restoration in some settings of long-since-abandoned liturgical practices, such as the burning of incense, enhanced the spatial and olfactory dimensions of worship considerably. But it was not only in High Church environments that this applied. In Evangelical settings, the alluring capacity of sight was downplayed for its

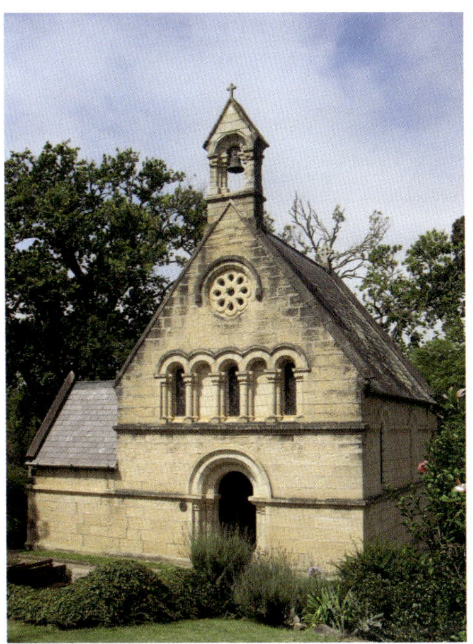

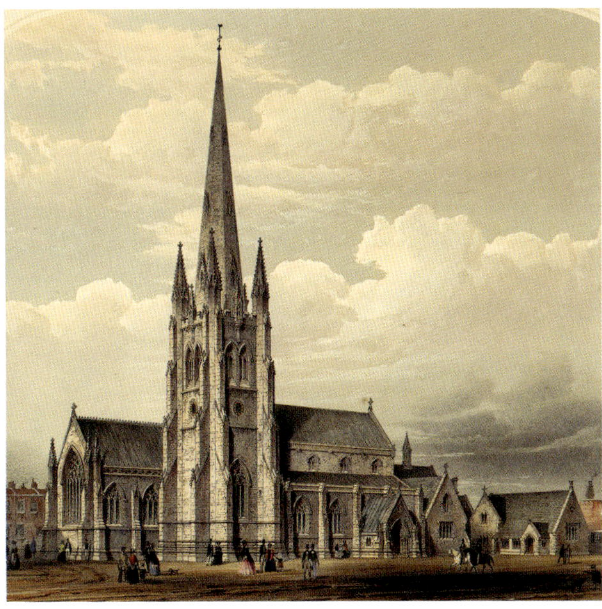

Fig. 96a

Holy Trinity, Belvidere (1851–3), South Africa. Adapted plan by Sophia (Sophy) Gray.

Fig. 96b

St Stephen's, Rochester Row, Westminster (1847–50), by Benjamin Ferrey.

perceived corrupting influence, with sound—as in hearing the Word loud and clear—elevated in its place. This had its own emotive affect. Moreover, the deliberate evocation of mystery, through the re-introduction of rood screens, of which Pugin was an advocate, was designed to trigger an emotive response through an engagement with notions of sacred space. But the spectacle of such devotion could go too far, even in the eyes of High churchmen. William Butterfield for one complained about this occasionally, equating the express appeal to 'feelings' in some ecclesiastical architecture with subjectivity, sensationalism, and even moral decay.[14]

Women and Victorian Religious Buildings

Although there were vanishingly few female 'architects' at the time, and those who played such a role did so either on an amateur basis or alongside their husbands, women were nonetheless important in various ways as patrons or advisors in the design process. Involvement in church and chapel design was considered especially appropriate for women in Victorian society owing to their supposed superior moral and spiritual virtue. There is the noted case of Sarah Losh at St Mary's, Wreay (1840–2), a small but neat neo-Romanesque structure in the Lake District, as well as the numerous churches by Sophy Gray in South Africa. Indeed, the first Anglican bishop of Cape Town, Robert Gray, relied almost entirely on his wife Sophy to adapt and reconfigure plans they brought from England, some by William Butterfield. It is believed that between 1847 and 1871 Sophy was involved in the design of over 100 buildings. This highlights the important role that women played in the realisation of ecclesiastical architecture under certain circumstances. Notable churches by Sophy include St Paul's, Rondebosch, Cape Town (1848–72); Holy Trinity, Belvidere (1851–3) **[96a]**; St Saviour's, Claremont (begun 1849); and St Mark's, George (1849–50).

Memorial chapels were often the locus of female involvement, where a grieving widow might take a special interest in overseeing affairs. This was the case with Emily Meynell Ingram at Bodley's exquisite Holy Angels, Hoar Cross, in Staffordshire (1872–6). In terms of patronage, one could point to the Monk sisters who were behind Street's St James the Less as a memorial to their father, the Rev. James Henry Monk, bishop of Gloucester. There is also the indomitable figure of Angela Burdett Coutts (1814–1906), the banking heiress once described by Edward VII as being (next to his mother) 'the most remarkable woman in the country'. She contributed significantly to architectural projects, including churches. Her deep personal piety, combined with a compassionate concern for the alleviation of poverty, compelled her in 1846 to fund the erection of a church, with school, at 'Devil's Acre', one of West London's most deprived and dangerous slums. This church, which had a distinct missionary dimension, would become St Stephen's, Rochester Row, Westminster (1847–50), among the highest-profile projects of its day **[96b]**.

Much like the famous fictional character of Ethel May in Charlotte Yonge's *The Daisy Chain* (1853/6), Burdett Coutts exerted her influence over the project from the off, choosing its architect, style, and orientation, as well as the subject matter of its stained-glass windows, and many other items besides. The architect was Benjamin Ferrey, one of the 'approved' designers of the Ecclesiological Society; the style, a rather conventional but nonetheless elegant Puginian Decorated Gothic. Although Burdett Coutts did not 'design' St Stephen's, it is clear that she was a patron in full knowledge of and control over proceedings, often to the architect's frustration.[15] In pursuing management of the project with such determination, Burdett Coutts displayed 'masculine signifiers of strength and power' that were considered unsuitable for a gentlewoman of her time, despite the fact she was an adherent to the patriarchal order of Victorian society.[16] Indeed, the increasing and energetic involvement of leisured and unmarried women in the affairs of the Church of England during this period was often viewed by its misogynist critics as presenting an unacceptable challenge to conventional Victorian values concerning a woman's rightful place in the patriarchal structures of family and society. Connections were also made between increased ritualism and effeminacy in the Church, where women's apparent concern for decoration, guided by their susceptibility to emotive impulse, was seen as a corrupting influence.[17]

It is not only churches that ought to be considered in this context. Houses of religious orders—what are otherwise referred to as convents and monasteries—were also a feature of the Victorian religious landscape. Notable among these are the convents designed by Pugin from the late 1830s, including Mercy Convent, Handsworth (1840–1), and Mount Vernon convent in Liverpool (1840–3); or, later, Teignmouth Abbey (1863) by George Goldie. Sometimes the inhabitants of these cloistered sanctuaries were involved in their design. There is evidence, for instance, that this occurred at Mercy Convent, Handsworth, where Mother Catherine McAuley clashed with Pugin over certain aspects of planning, ultimately imposing her will in certain areas, with the sisters later making subsequent alterations.[18] It is also the case that the design for the convent of the Anglican sisterhood of

St Margaret at East Grinstead, Sussex (1865–75), by G. E. Street, was influenced by its mother superior, Alice Crocker, who took command of the project in 1866 following the death of the sisterhood's founder, John Mason Neale.[19] Besides this, the convent became an important centre for ecclesiastical embroidery, with its products, especially altar frontals, ending up in churches all over the country. Like many other such institutions in Victorian Britain, it played an important role in education, nursing, and general mission work, all of which were seen as respectable outlets for unmarried female exertion at the time.

Later Developments

Although the 'muscular', Continental characteristics of High Victorian architecture continued to exert their influence well into the 1870s, and beyond, by the early 1860s some architects had begun taking things in a different direction. This has been described as a turn to 'refinement'.[20] This concerned reconsideration of the applicability of indigenous English forms in ecclesiastical design, especially the beauty and charm of Decorated Gothic. Leading the way was G. F. Bodley, with projects such as All Saints', Jesus Lane, in Cambridge (1862–71), and St John the Baptist, Tuebrook, Liverpool (1867–70) **[97a]**. Here we see not only more delicate and unpretentious English Gothic exteriors, but also a decided shift towards an

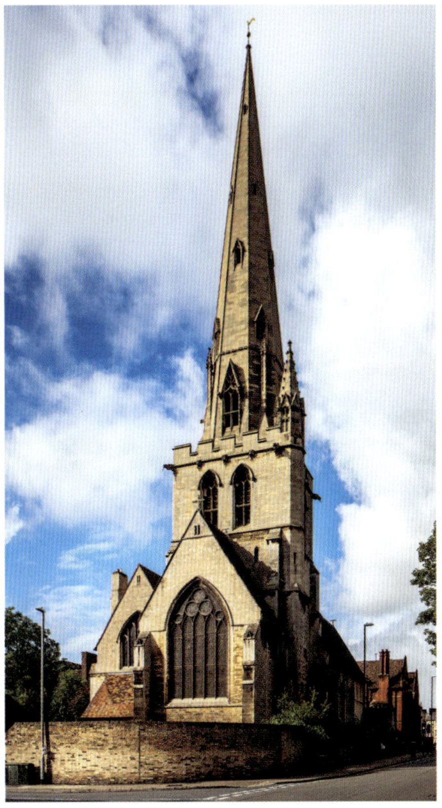

Fig. 97a

Movement away from High Victorianism. All Saints', Jesus Lane (1862–71), Cambridge, by George Frederick Bodley.

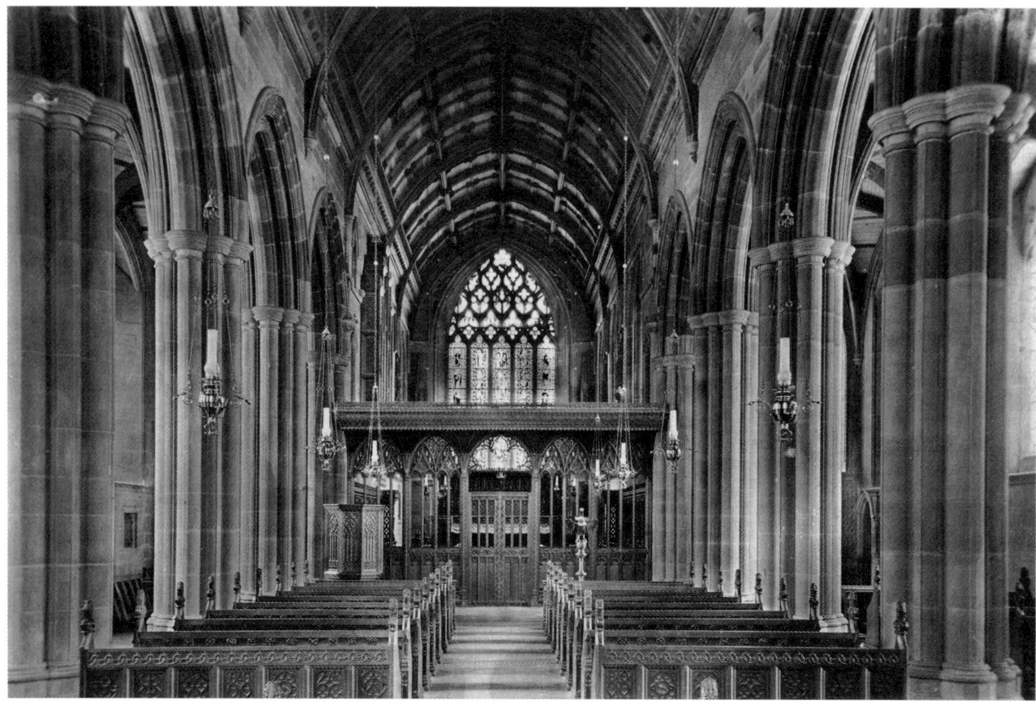

Fig. 97b

St Mary, Sledmere, in Yorkshire (1893–8), by Temple Moore.

Aesthetic Movement approach to interior ornamentation, with its softer yet holistic English sensibility, including stained glass by Pre-Raphaelite artists William Morris, Edward Burne-Jones, and Ford Madox Brown. Advocates of this approach, such as Alphonse Warrington Taylor and the Ecclesiologists, also saw this shift in relation to a resurgent appeal to notions of national identity.[21]

This swing back to an English aesthetic soon gained momentum in elite Anglican circles, associated as it was with the entrenchment of Anglo-Catholicism. It led, among other things, to a predilection for larger and more slender, open-planned spaces in church design, modelled in part on the ecclesiastical architecture of medieval mendicant friars (Franciscan, Dominican, and Augustinian). There was also an increasing delicacy and finesse when it came to ornamental decoration. These new spatial requirements were sought owing to the increased need for urban churches in late nineteenth-century Britain, especially ones that would hold larger and more socially diverse congregations. Later periods of Gothic architecture were also preferred, such as 'Third Pointed' or English Perpendicular. Both these qualities are observable, for instance, in St Paul's, Wimbledon Park, London (1888–96), by J. T. Micklethwaite. Although initiated by the likes of Bodley, Pearson, and James Brooks, this period in English church design is associated more with a later generation of architects, including not only Micklethwaite but also J. D. Sedding, George Gilbert Scott Jr, Temple Moore, R. N. Shaw, and Ninian Comper. The churches produced by these architects—like that of St Agnes, Kennington Park, London (1874–91), by Scott Jr; or St Mary, Sledmere, in Yorkshire (1893–8), by Moore—were very much a retort against High Victorianism **[97b]**. Among the crowning glories of this late period of the Gothic Revival in Britain is the Anglican cathedral in Liverpool (1904–78), by Giles Gilbert Scott, grandson of George Gilbert Snr.

Emerging out of this aesthetic shift, particularly from the work of Shaw and Sedding, came an evolving Arts and Crafts ideal in church design. This was not a major movement, and remained limited to a handful of architects, but it nonetheless produced intriguing results, some of which display distinct proto-Modernist tendencies. We see this not only at C. R. Mackintosh's Queen's Cross Church in Glasgow (1898–9), for instance, but also at All Saints' church, Brockhampton, Herefordshire (1901–2), by William Lethaby **[98]**. These architects were two of Britain's foremost designers of the late nineteenth and early twentieth centuries. Mackintosh's church is marked by a clear Art Nouveau propensity, both in detail and overall massing, while the interior of Lethaby's presents a clean, abstracted monumentality that belies its modest size. In different ways both buildings heralded a shift to what would ultimately become a more self-consciously Modernist approach in the second quarter of the twentieth century.

Roman Catholic church design towards the end of the nineteenth century also witnessed change in terms of stylistic preference. Despite Pugin's railing against Classicism, we do find isolated but significant examples of its continued use, as at Brompton Oratory, in London (1880–4), by Herbert Gribble. This may be put down to the founders' desire to make a statement concerning the Oratory's fealty to the Church of Rome, as well as to John Henry Newman's ultimate distaste for Gothic architecture. It also had something to do with making the Roman Catholic Church conspicuous

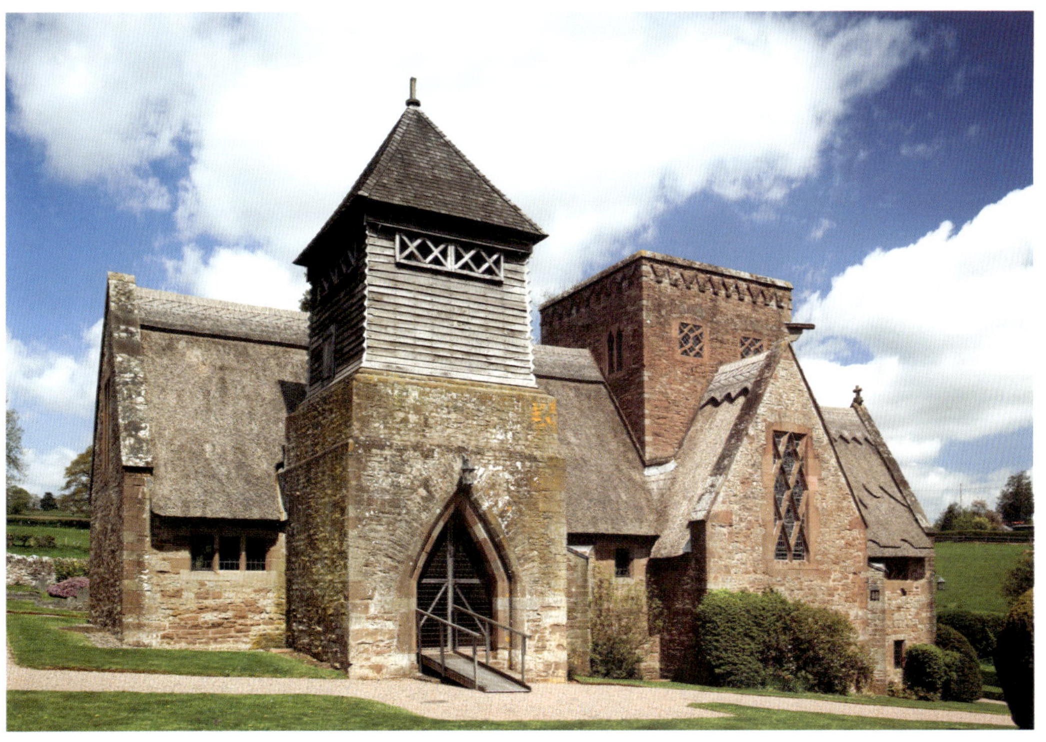

Fig. 98

Arts and Crafts: All Saints', Brockhampton (1901–2), Herefordshire, by William Lethaby.

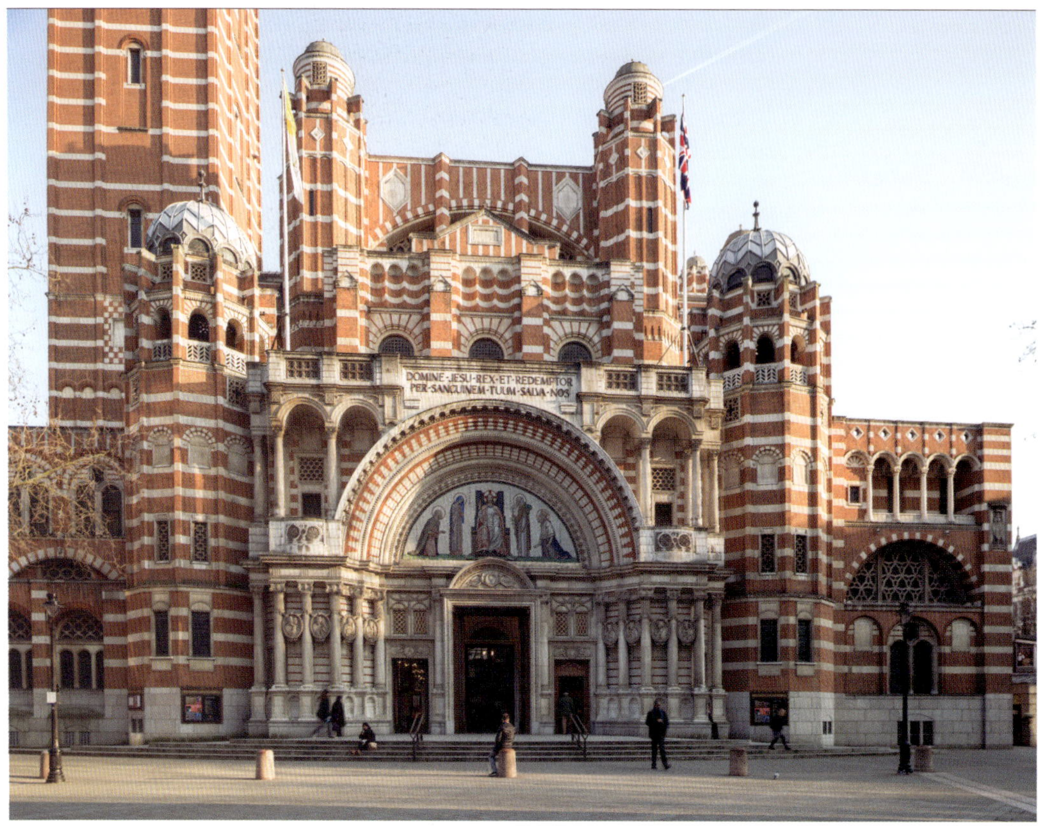

Fig. 99

Westminster Roman Catholic Cathedral (1895–1903), London, by John Francis Bentley.

again. This is evident in the most significant and interesting Roman Catholic church erected at the time, Westminster Cathedral (1895–1903), by John Francis Bentley **[99]**. Neither Gothic nor Classical, it was Byzantine instead. Distinguished by its soaring campanile, dazzling polychrome façade, and incredibly sumptuous interiors, it recalls the early Christian churches of Ravenna, Venice, and Pavia. Cardinal Vaughan, who oversaw the design, initially hoped for a building based on 'the ancient Basilican or primitive form of Christian architecture', preferably St Peter's in Rome. But Bentley sought inspiration in Hagia Sophia in Constantinople. Given that London was the capital of a global empire, his reasoning was that a 'cathedral of the world-metropolis should be of a type rather *international* than limited by any national and perhaps insular characteristic'.[22] In this respect Westminster Cathedral not only sought to distinguish itself architecturally from the nearby abbey, but also had imperial pretensions, considering itself—much like Hagia Sophia—the 'mother' church of a Christian empire.

Adapting in the Wider World: The Theory and Practice of Acclimatisation

One of the key concerns attending the extension of European religious architecture into the wider world during the Victorian period was the necessity for adaptation. Theories about how best to adapt such architecture, especially

Gothic, to the extreme conditions experienced in much of Britain's empire (both hot and cold climates) were at the heart of mid-nineteenth-century ecclesiology. Informed by both building science and architectural theory, thinking along these lines yielded some unique if unexpected results. Initially, this tactic was pushed by the Cambridge Camden Society, which discussed the subject at length in the pages of *The Ecclesiologist*, considering it fundamental to the advancement of 'colonial ecclesiology' (see Chapter 3). Connected to wider debates then current in British architecture, such as the theory of 'development', discussions around adaptation looked to a new, vital, and ultimately flexible future for modern church design.

In practice the issues focused on pragmatic concerns, such as how climatic limitations affected the size, shape, and materiality of buildings, as well as certain cultural considerations. The latter of these included the best way of presenting Christian architecture to non-Christian ('heathen') audiences, which involved spatial arrangements that maintained liturgical 'discipline' while accommodating pre-existing cultural and religious customs. Two main approaches for adapting Gothic forms to extreme climatic conditions were devised: the *speluncar*, or 'cave-like', approach that relied on thermal mass (heavy, thick walls with few openings to shut out heat and cold), and the so-called 'draught-admitting', which was essentially a passive cooling approach reliant on cross-ventilation (open, lightweight structure with large windows and shading devices). Oftentimes, however, a combination of these was used. Indeed, for Europeans in remote locations, as in the case of missionaries entering upon a field for the very first time, temporary portable structures such as tents were considered permissible, so long as they were arranged 'correctly'. An example of such a makeshift structure was that erected in 1863 by the Universities' Mission to Central Africa, at Morambala (*Morumbala*), in the Shiré Highlands in what is modern-day Malawi. Based on indigenous construction technology, it was built using a combination of elephant grass and local timbers **[100a]**. This form of 'appropriateness', although temporary, proved especially useful in circumstances where missionary work was either itinerate or vulnerable to the vagaries of shifting political frontiers.

At the more substantial end of this approach is All Saints' Cathedral in Allahabad, India (1870–87) **[101]**. Designed by William Emerson, it is marked by its heavy French character, with plate rather than English mullioned tracery, including Mughal-inspired *jali* screens. The windows are small and accompanied by deep arcaded eaves at clerestory level, making for a dark and cool interior. In many respects, Allahabad was the culmination of numerous similar proposals for 'torrid zones' put forward in the 1840s and 1850s, such as R. C. Carpenter's design for Colombo Cathedral, Sri Lanka (1847), or Burges's unrealised proposal for a cathedral in Brisbane (1860) **[49a]**. In these designs we see the beginnings of how these theories were developed in practice, demonstrating ways in which an ecclesiastical building could remain fundamentally 'church-like' while insulating itself from the worst effects of the surrounding environment. Another example is the remarkable mission church of St Barnabas, Norfolk Island (1875–80), in the South Pacific, by T. G. Jackson, with its compact 'speluncar' construction **[100b]**.

As timber was more readily accessible than either stone or brick in some colonial contexts, especially early on, it led to entirely new species of Gothic

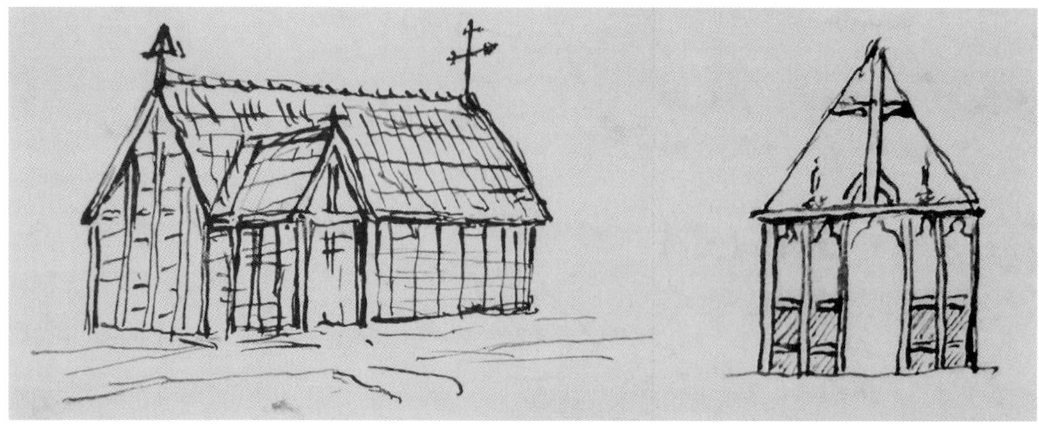

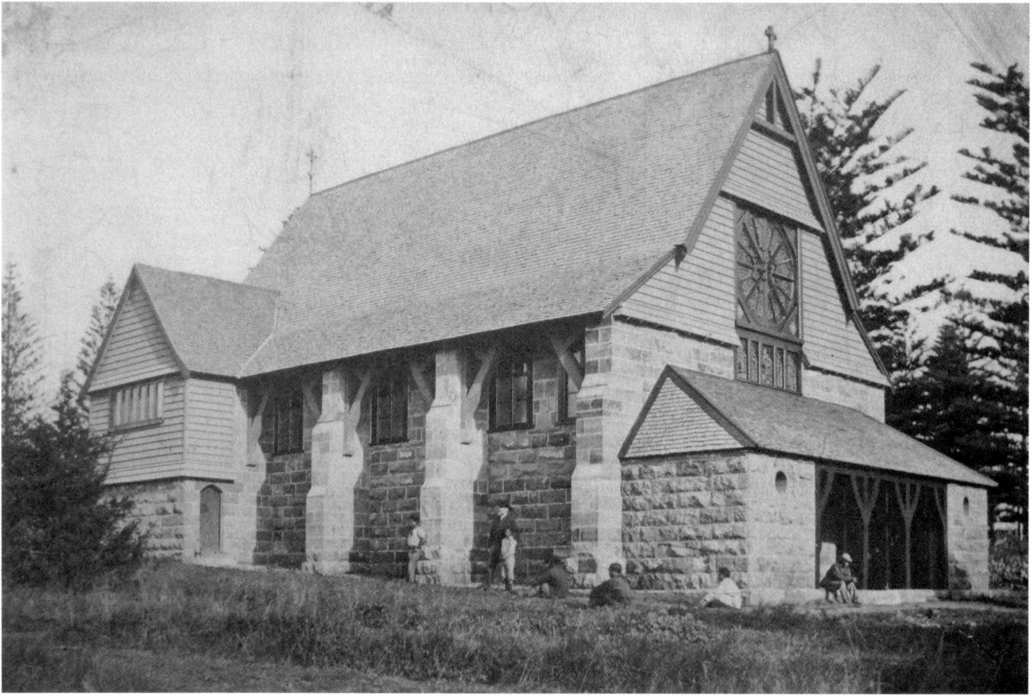

Fig. 100a

Colonial ecclesiology. Mission church made of elephant grass (1863), Universities' Mission to Central Africa, Morambala (*Morumbala*), Shiré Highlands, Malawi.

Fig. 100b

St Barnabas', Norfolk Island (1875–80), South Pacific, by Thomas Graham Jackson.

Revival architecture. This is observable in Canada, for instance, in the efforts of clergymen and architects such as William Grey, William Hay, and later Edward Medley **[102]**. Perhaps the most spectacular variant of this approach is that found in New Zealand. Initiated under the close supervision of bishop G. A. Selwyn, timber churches in the so-called 'Selwyn Gothic' style were developed as a response to the windswept and earthquake-prone environments experienced by Anglican missionaries. Although the earliest exemplars were humble structures, such as the chapel at St John's College, Bishop's Auckland (1847), it culminated in the truly magnificent specimens of St Paul's, Wellington (1865–6), by Frederick Thatcher, and St Mary's Pro-Cathedral, Auckland (1886–98), by Benjamin Mountfort, both built entirely of native woods **[103a]**. 'Carpenter Gothic' of this kind also migrated

Fig. 101

Climatic adaptation: All Saints' Cathedral, Allahabad (1870–87), India, by William Emerson.

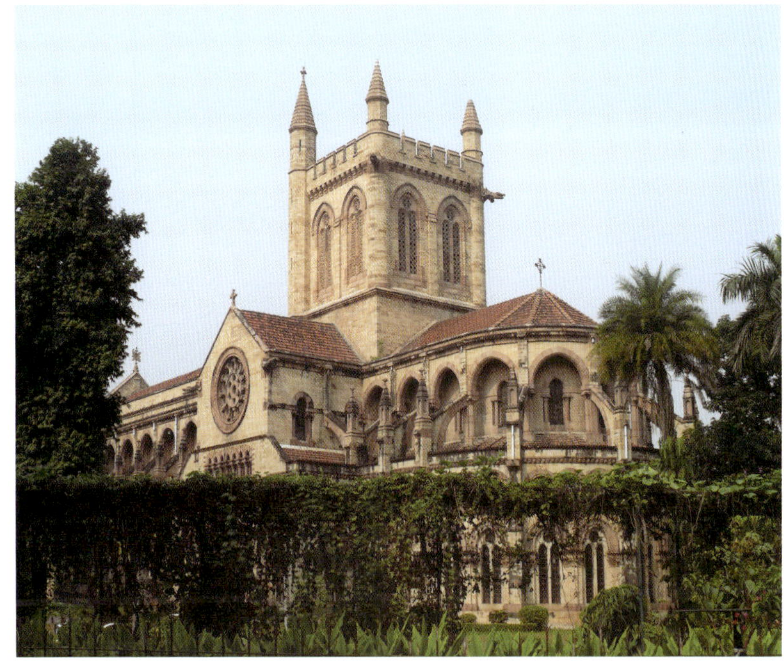

Fig. 102

Timber ecclesiology. Christ Church, St Stephen, New Brunswick (1863–4), Canada, by Edward Medley (photo Peter Coffman).

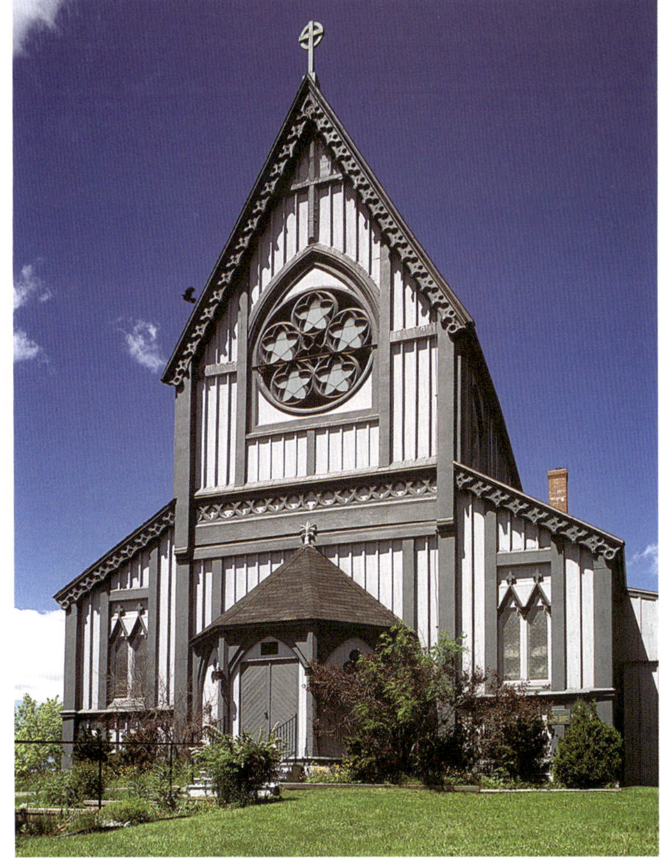

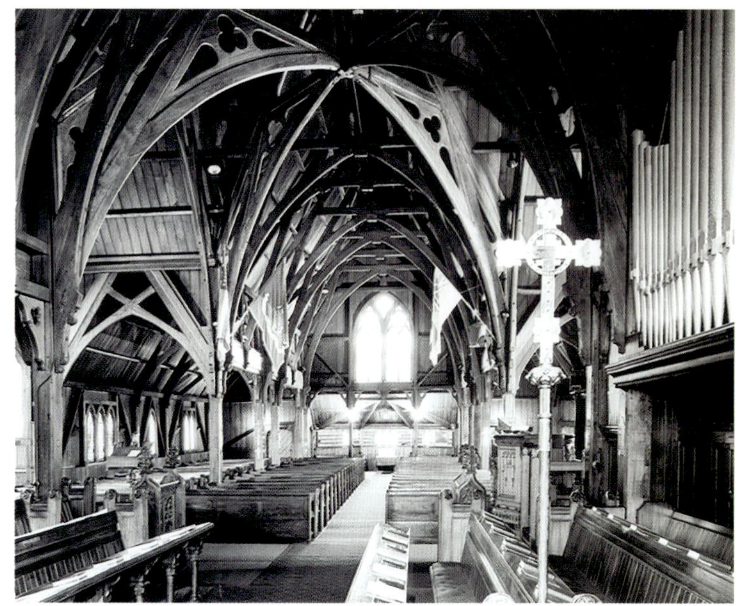

Fig. 103a

St Paul's, Wellington (1865–6), New Zealand, by Frederick Thatcher.

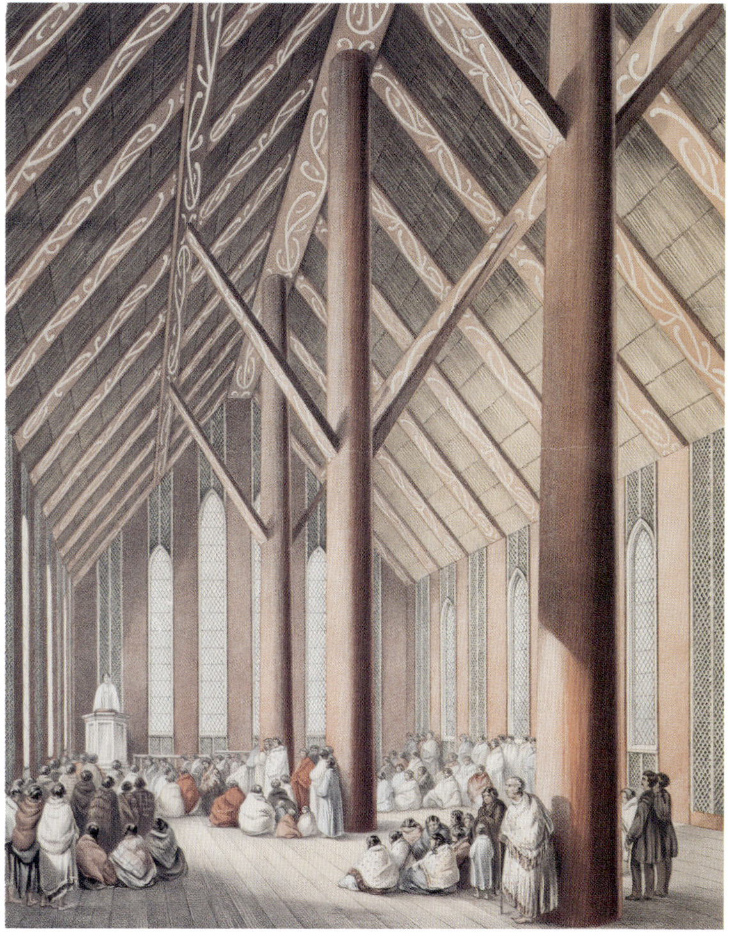

Fig. 103b

Indigenous influences. Rangiātea church, Ōtaki (1848–54), New Zealand.

further south, into the United States, evidenced in the early churches of keen ecclesiologists such as Upjohn. We see it at St Mary's, Raleigh, North Carolina (1855–7), for instance, and in other specimens inspired by models contained in Upjohn's *Rural Architecture* (1852), such as St John Chrysostom, in Delafield, Wisconsin (1853), by Ralston Cox.

This attitude towards adaptation led in some quarters to types of ecclesiastical architecture being developed that encouraged the cross-fertilisation—deliberate hybridisation, even—of European and indigenous forms. This was a process familiar to Roman Catholic missionaries, known as 'inculturation', which had been extant for centuries in places such as colonial America. In the British context, it came to the fore in places like Stone Town, Zanzibar, in the design for Christ Church Cathedral (1873–80), erected by the Universities' Mission to Central Africa, with its intriguing amalgam of Arabic and Christian forms. We see it also among the first Church Missionary Society churches erected in West Africa, in Yorubaland, modern-day Nigeria, as well as at Namirembe, in Uganda, culminating in the extraordinary 'fourth' cathedral of St Paul (1900–4), with its mudbrick walls and distinctive Buganda-style thatched roof. Indeed, the Church Missionary Society was among the earliest to adopt this strategy, promoting it as a specific missionary tactic. The roof at Rangiātea church, Ōtaki (1848–54), in New Zealand, rested upon a huge ridge beam of totara (signifying the one true Christian God), which was in turn supported by three massive tree trunks of the same timber (signifying the Holy Trinity) **[103b]**. The rafters were decorated with a sacred motif known as the *mangōpare* (hammerhead shark pattern), while the walls were hung with woven *tukutuku* panels signifying the Milky Way (the heavens). A number of such 'native chapels' were built in the north island of New Zealand in the 1840s and 1850s. Among the largest and most magnificent was that referred to as Manutūkē IIB (1849–63), fabricated almost entirely by Christianised Māori craftsmen.[23]

Viewed in the round, developments in colonial ecclesiology led to some of the most ambitious church projects attempted anywhere in the world, involving some of the biggest names in Victorian architecture. If G. G. Scott's hybrid timber and stone design for Christchurch Cathedral, New Zealand (1862), had been built as originally planned—or, for that matter, William Butterfield's proposed cathedrals in Melbourne (1880) and Adelaide (1868), or James Trubshawe's grand polychromatic vision for Bombay (1865)—they would have been among the most innovative and spectacular of the period. Those that were built largely as designed include Scott's cathedrals in St John's, Newfoundland (1847–1905) **[104a]**, and Grahamstown, South Africa (1861–1912); those by Frank Wills (with Butterfield) in Fredericton (1845–53) and Montreal (1857–60), Canada; William Hay's in Bermuda (1844–68); and Bodley's in Hobart, Tasmania (1868–1936). Roman Catholics would not be outdone. Vying with Anglican buildings for beauty and scale, if not surpassing them, are William Wardell's truly impressive cathedrals of St Patrick's, Melbourne, and St Mary's, Sydney (1868–2000) **[104b]**, not to mention Joseph Connolly's Church of Our Lady, Guelph (1876–88), in Canada. These last two were buildings on a scale comparable with the great cathedrals of Europe.

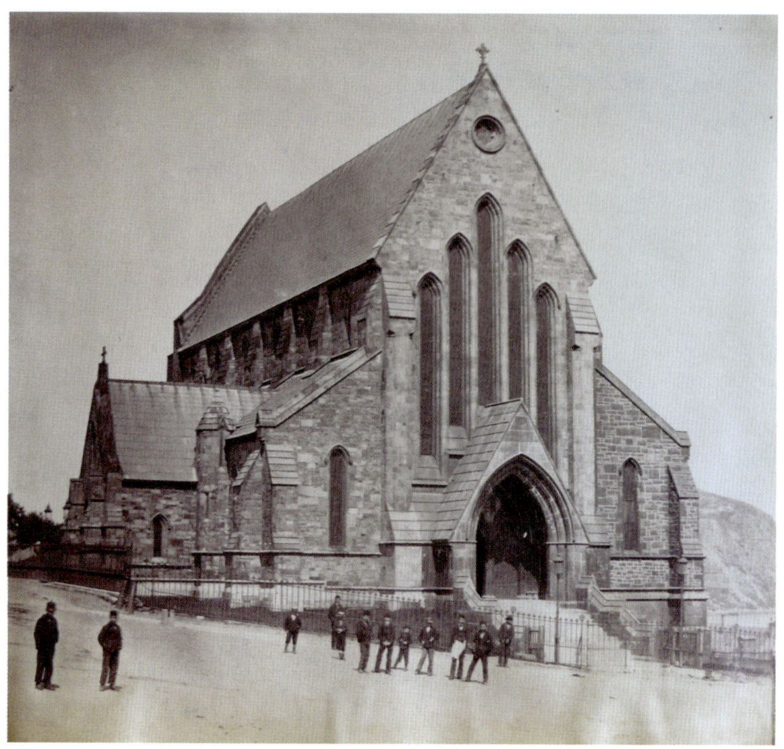

Fig. 104a

St John's Cathedral, Newfoundland (1847–1905), now Canada, by George Gilbert Scott.

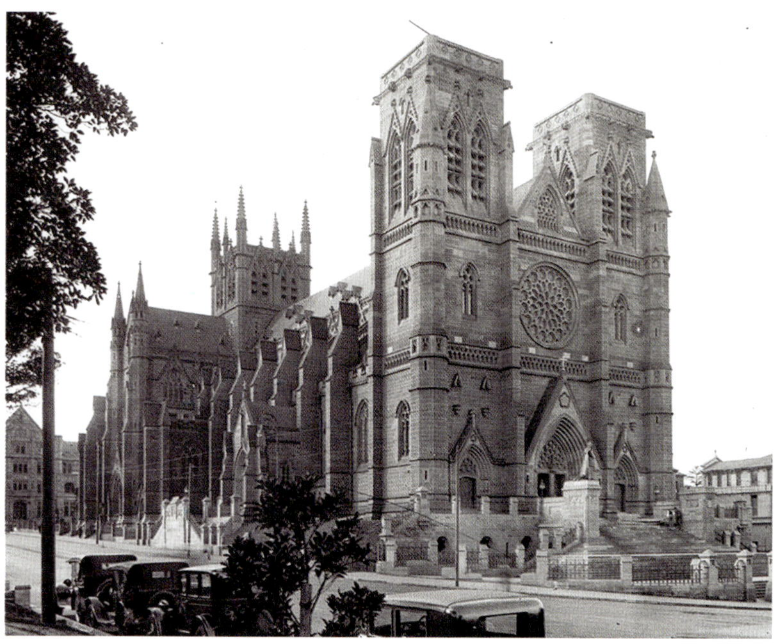

Fig. 104b

St Mary's Cathedral, Sydney (1868–2000), Australia, by William Wardell.

Righteous Forms: Nonconformist and Dissenting Church Architecture

With the repeal by parliament of the Test and Corporation Acts in 1828, followed by the overturning of other discriminatory religious laws, Nonconformist and Dissenting religious communities in the United Kingdom were finally given rights equal to those of their established co-religionists. These communities largely consisted of Methodists, Baptists, Congregationalists, Quakers, Unitarians, and various forms of Presbyterianism, as well as smaller sects, such as the Catholic Apostolic Church. The rise to political and economic importance of these communities is a fundamental feature of Victorian society. Having either emerged out of or been reinvigorated by the eighteenth-century Evangelical revival, they were strongly associated with family values and public propriety, including temperance, frugality, and prudence. They were also heavily involved in the anti-slavery and abolitionist movements. Naturally, given the strong Protestant and British libertarian ideals that combined to shape their religious attitudes, notions of individual conscience, freedom, and responsibility lay at the foundation of their worldview.

It is easy to forget the significant presence these communities had. The church/chapel distinction was a fundamental social dividing line in the United Kingdom during the nineteenth century.[24] By the 1850s Nonconformist numbers had swelled considerably, making up around half of all Sunday churchgoers in England (according to the 1851 religious census). Confident in their righteousness, these communities felt a compelling sense of mission in elevating the moral and spiritual constitution of the nation and wider world. The Wesleyan and Baptist missionary societies, the London Missionary Society (Congregationalist), and the Salvation Army, among others, operated throughout Britain's industrial conurbations and colonial empire, bringing with them a particular brand of Protestant moral, spiritual, and educational 'improvement'.

These communities had a considerable impact on Victorian religious architecture. Indeed, the increased physical presence of chapels was a conspicuous challenge to the established Church as the 'national' church. Nonconformist and Dissenting churches largely rejected the hierarchical structures and authority embedded in the ordinances of the established Church. They took different views on matters of theology and religious truth, which, in relation to their assertive Protestant outlook, led to characteristic building types and spaces. Emphasis was placed on open, auditory-style spaces for effective vocal transmission, as well as ancillary halls and classrooms for communal and educational activities. To enforce the symbolic primacy of the 'word', the pulpit in most Nonconformist chapels and meeting houses was in a very conspicuous, centrally located, and often elevated position, usually occupying the place where the chancel would be in an ancient medieval, Anglican, or Roman Catholic church. Because of their abstemious inclinations, many Nonconformist and Dissenting traditions eschewed excessive (sometimes all) decoration, which was perceived as needless at best, 'popish' at worst. In this, such churches had something in common with the Evangelical wing of the Church of England through a shared Calvinist/

Arminian ethos. This often led to rather austere, even secular-like spaces in comparison to the typical Anglican or Roman Catholic church built during the Victorian period, as other types, such as town halls and theatres, were looked to as models, and new materials such as iron commonly used.

Although the use of the pointed arch in Nonconformist and Dissenting chapel and meeting-house architecture was not unheard of prior to the Victorian period, the most common style adopted had been a restrained, often astylar Classicism. This was not only a vestige of seventeenth-century Puritanism, but also a way for Nonconformists to distinguish their type of worship from other, more established Christian denominations, particularly in the wake of Roman Catholic emancipation, the rise of Pugin, and the advent of Anglican 'ecclesiology'. It was also a legacy of their historic inclination for unpretentiousness and to be inconspicuous. As there were almost no aesthetic (and very few spatial) requirements for Nonconformist and Dissenter chapel and meeting-house architecture, it was often derided as boorish. As one critic wrote, 'Popery is the religion of cathedrals, Protestantism of houses, and Dissenterism of barns'.[25] But this tactic was a shorthand way for such churches to distance themselves from the 'taint' of popery, which was commonly associated with the 'idolatrous' spectacle of worship, and a way to signal their rejection of traditional hierarchy. Because of this, such groups often attracted suspicions of republicanism.

In the immediate aftermath of Pugin's murmurings on the Catholicity of Gothic forms, and the connections he made (for the worse) between Protestantism and Classicism, an antipathy naturally prevailed among many Nonconformists towards Gothic architecture. Moreover, at work was the self-consciously 'rational' basis of Protestant religion adhered to by Nonconformists. Through architecture, this manifested as a way for those among the ministerial ranks of these churches to allude to their classical learning. As the magnetic Baptist preacher Charles Haddon Spurgeon would later observe, 'Greek was, with Hebrew, the only sacred language cherished by Christians'.

Among the earliest buildings of this tradition include those by the West Yorkshire joiner-turned-architect James Simpson, who designed the Centenary Wesleyan Methodist Chapel in York (1839–40). This building, with its prominent Portico and plain Ionic columns, set a dignified standard. Internally, it possessed those qualities originally sought after by the Methodist preaching tradition, with a large, open space surrounded by raked galleries (to augment capacity), with a focus on the pulpit, which was raised on a rostrum at one end of the chapel. The interior decoration was also minimal, with plain timber panelling and basic Classical plaster mouldings, mostly in muted tones. Other examples from this period include the temple-like structures for Congregationalists erected on East Parade, Leeds (1839–41), by Moffat and Hurst, and Albion Street, Hull (1842), by H. F. Lockwood. Equally formidable was the Wesleyan Chapel, Great Thornton Street, Hull (1842), also by Lockwood (& Mawson) **[105a]**, and the Great George Street Congregational Chapel, Liverpool (1840–1), by Joseph Franklin. The former of these was described by Henry-Russell Hitchcock as 'perhaps the handsomest church begun in ... 1841 by any other architect than Pugin'.[26] All these buildings were conspicuous, sporting large

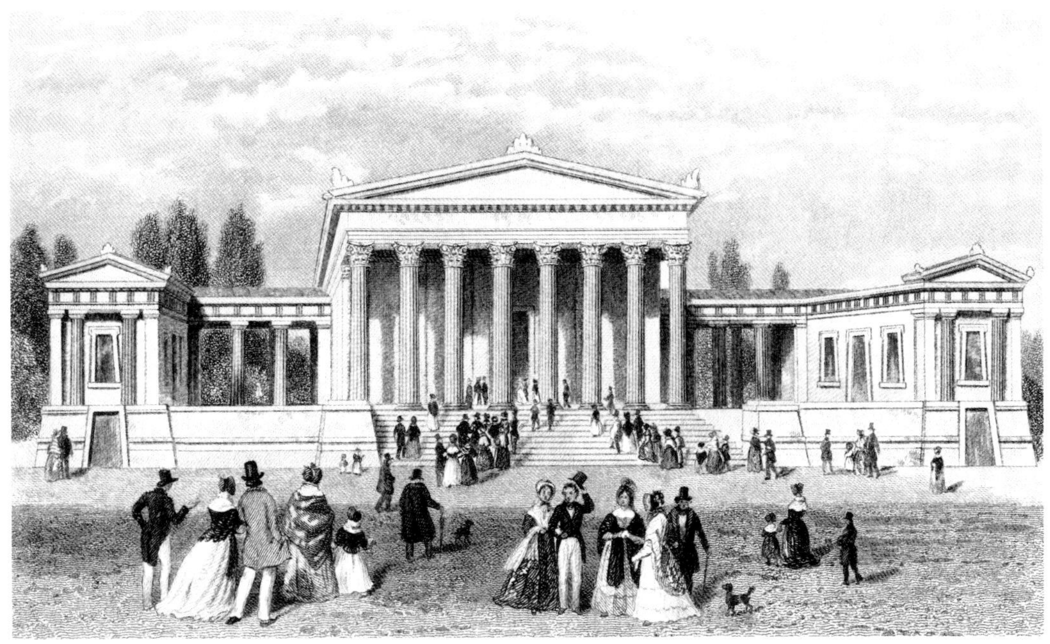

Fig. 105a

Wesleyan Chapel, Great Thornton Street, Hull (1842), by H. F. Lockwood of Lockwood & Mawson.

and prominent Classical porticoes with fluted columns. To these might be added the Apostle's chapel in Bristol (1839–40), by R. S. Pope, with its fine hexastyle portico and Corinthian columns. This not only revealed something of the debt the architects of these buildings owed to the Classicising vision of Continental architects such as K. F. Schinkel, but was also a sign of the growing size, pride, and societal influence these denominations had now acquired.

This architecture's focus on congregational and communal gathering as opposed to sacramental observance is what distinguished it from much Anglican and all Roman Catholic architecture of the period. With expansion came a revived interest among Nonconformists in ever-larger, centralised spatial configurations, such as circles, ovals, Greek crosses, and hexagons, or a combination thereof. Some of this interest stemmed from Protestant traditions in Continental architecture, in places such as Germany and Scandinavia. Arrangements of this kind not only made for better auditory conditions, but also, from a planning perspective, facilitated the incorporation of ancillary spaces such as halls and classrooms.

Despite initial reservations over Pugin and the Ecclesiologists, Nonconformist and Dissenting congregations increasingly turned to Gothic forms from the 1840s. To be sure, some groups had never really shied away from them, such as Unitarians, seen at Upper Brook Street Chapel, Manchester (1837–9), or Dukinfield Chapel, Cheshire (1839–40). Indeed, in an apparent effort to counter the casual association between Protestantism and arid rationalism, the Unitarians challenged the Ecclesiologists directly with chapels that not only looked like 'correct' churches, but also facilitated more liturgically orientated forms of worship. This effort was spurred by the

Dissenters' Chapels Act (1844), which extended property rights to Unitarians in England. The chapel at Gee Cross, in Hyde, Cheshire (1846–8), by Bowman & Crowther, for instance, is one of the most spectacular outcomes of this reform **[105b]**.

But it was the appearance of several key publications on chapel and school design from the late 1840s that transformed the scene for Nonconformists. First came James Blackburn's article in the *Congregational Year Book* of 1847, entitled 'Remarks on Ecclesiastical Architecture as Applied to Nonconformist Chapels', which pointed to the possibilities of Gothic as both flexible and economical. Then came the influential *Chapel and School Architecture* by Frederick James Jobson in 1850, the result of the newly formed Wesleyan 'Model Plan Committee' (est. 1846). This, like Blackburn's article, found that building in the Gothic style was comparatively cheap, especially now that the initial shock of Pugin's ideas had passed. Jobson's book was essentially a plea for Gothic architecture, lamenting as he did the 'unsightly forms' of much traditional Methodist architecture. His starting position was that even Protestants owed something to the 'outward associations' of God's worship. No longer burdened by original Puritan objection, and safe in the knowledge that 'extremes' could be avoided, 'Truth

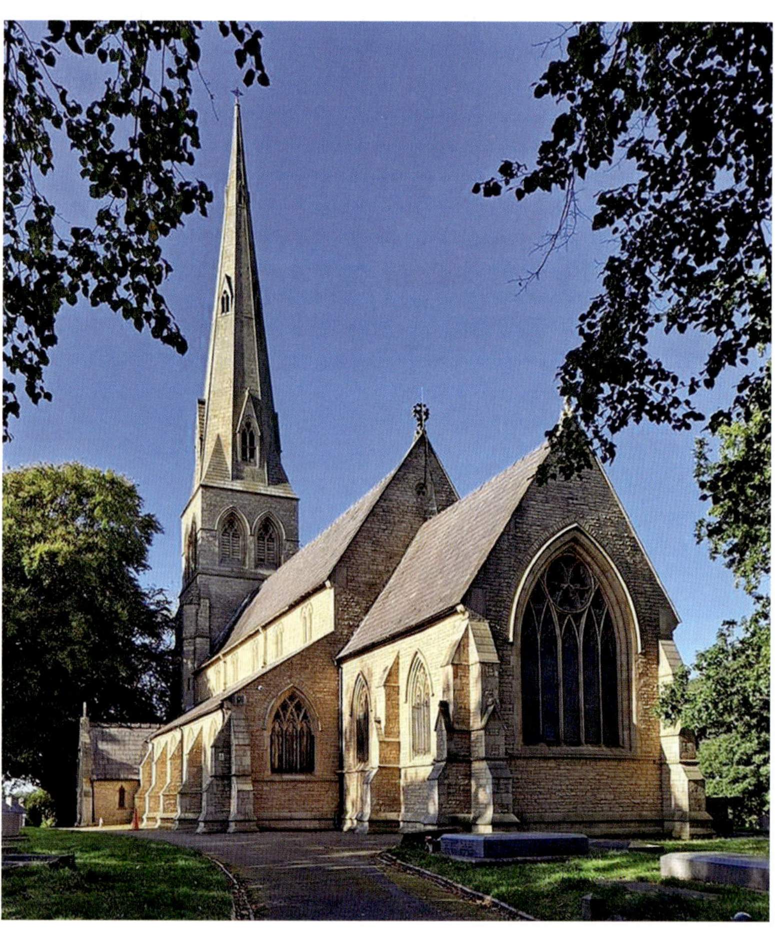

Fig. 105b

Unitarian chapel at Gee Cross, Hyde (1846–8), Cheshire, by Bowman & Crowther.

in Architecture', declared Jobson, need not be associated 'with Error in Religion'.[27] As Ruskin's *Seven Lamps of Architecture* had relayed so eloquently, ideas concerning structural honesty clearly had a legitimacy and appeal beyond the partisan polemics of Pugin. To illustrate the point, Jobson's book contained a design for a simple 'Village Chapel', looking, externally at least, like something that might easily pass for a small and correct Anglican church.

In 1865 came George Bidlake's pattern book *Sketches of Churches Designed for the Use of Nonconformists*. Although this contained numerous Gothic designs, it also had many Classical, demonstrating that Classical architecture remained viable, if not desirable, for such groups. This architectural 'pluralism' may be put down to the continued efforts of Nonconformists and Dissenters to distinguish themselves from other denominations in local areas, as well as competitor institutions such as pubs. Thus, by the 1860s we see a variety of forms and styles emerging. These ranged from impressive Classical buildings, such as the Methodist chapels in Market Rasen, Lincolnshire (1863), and Oxford Street, Harrogate (1861–3), through to the huge, Romanesque-style Congregationalist chapel at Westminster (1863–5), to the octagonally planned Gothic chapels in Harcourt (1855–6), Carlisle (1860), and Tufnell Park, London (1865–8) **[106]**.

Bidlake's book was followed by James Cubitt's *Church Design for Congregations: Its Development and Possibilities* in 1870. Full of intriguing, even daring, suggestions, this guide called for a more adventurous age in Nonconformist chapel design. For Cubitt, this meant novel forms of

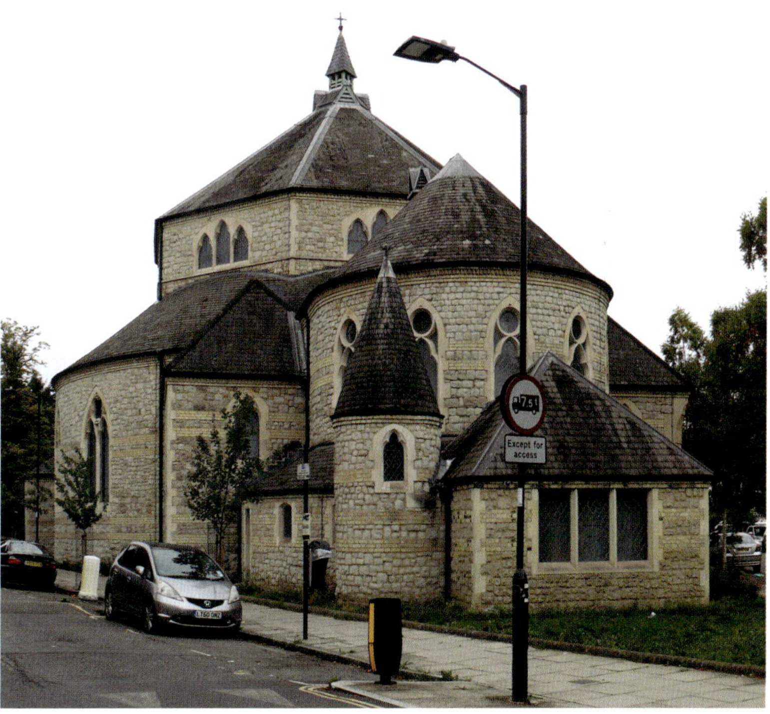

Fig. 106

Congregationalist chapel, Tufnell Park, London (1865–8), by George Truefitt.

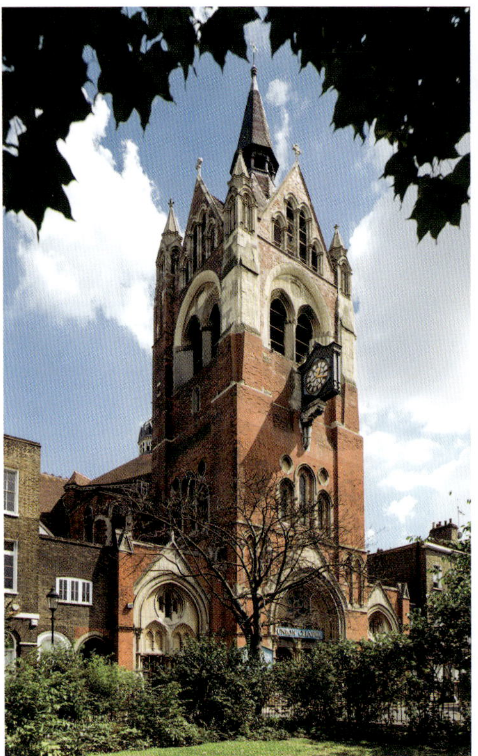

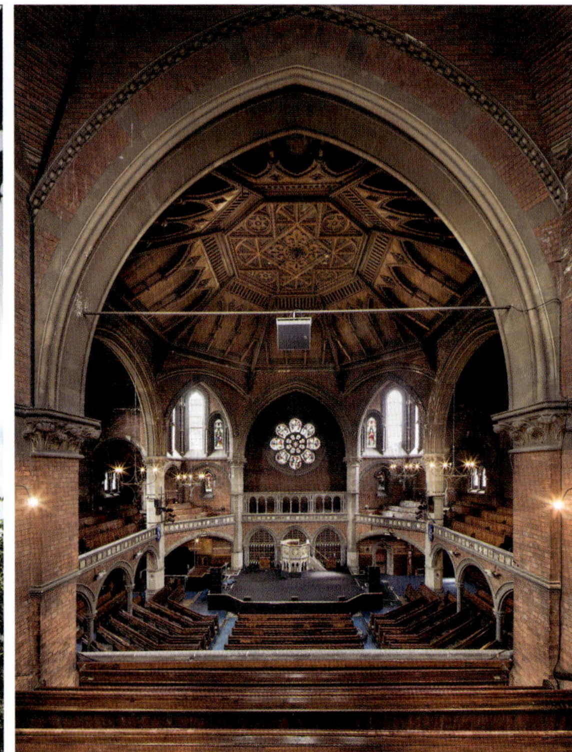

Fig. 107a

Union Chapel, Islington, North London (1875–89), by James Cubitt.

Fig. 107b

Interior of the Union Chapel, showing huge centralised congregational space.

'character and fitness', meeting the needs of modern, industrialised society. To be sure, some architects, like the young Alfred Waterhouse (himself a Quaker), had already been thinking along these lines. In his design for the Great Ancoats Street Congregationalist chapel in Manchester (1865), for instance, we see a modern polychrome exterior enveloping a centralised wedge-shaped plan which accommodated over 1,000 worshipers. But it was Cubitt himself who would be responsible for one of the most extraordinary religious buildings erected in the Victorian period: the Union Chapel in Islington, North London (1875–7, tower 1881–9) **[107a]**.

Built for the local Congregationalist community, this building, in terms of technological advancement, had more in common with modern hospitals, prisons, and schools of the period than churches. It was designed with user comfort in mind, including adequate sightlines, lighting, acoustics, heating, and ventilation, with built-in systems and underfloor ducting for this purpose. The layout reflects Cubitt's interest in centrally planned spaces for worship, and its style and materiality (red brick, terracotta, and stone) the influence of the Gothic Revival. We can also see ideas from his *Church Design* coming through, especially in the appeal for modern architects to take lessons from the centrally planned, columnless spaces of early Christian and mosque architecture in the Levant. Such precedents, Cubitt claimed, were the most suitable for Protestant worship, and required that modern architects overcome their hang-ups regarding architectural purity if true progress was to be achieved.[28] An intentionally rich work of architecture, Union Chapel contained sculptured decoration by Thomas Earp and stained glass by Frederick Drake of Exeter. The end result, with its huge, cavernous chapel (seating 3,500), supported on a massive, pointed-arch arcade with octagonal dome above, is truly impressive **[107b]**.

Indeed, by the 1880s any misgivings regarding the Gothic among Nonconformists seem to have evaporated. Perhaps the most astonishing example of what could be achieved by this time was the Thomas Coats Memorial Baptist Church, Paisley (1885–94), by Hippolyte Blanc, colloquially referred to as the Baptist 'cathedral' of Europe, costing over £100,000 to erect **[108]**.

Presbyterianism in Scotland and Ulster

In Scotland the Gothic Revival also had a significant impact among Presbyterians. Following the Protestant Reformation there remained a rich, indigenous legacy of medieval architecture for Scottish architects to draw upon. This heritage had been turned over to the Church of Scotland, providing opportunities for liturgical repurposing. However, the split within the established Church of Scotland in 1843, known as the Disruption, led to a major breakaway denomination in the form of the Free Presbyterian Church. Four years later, in 1847, earlier and much smaller secessionist movements combined to form the United Presbyterian Church. For ideological and financial reasons, these three separate churches took different views on matters concerning architecture. In the case of the breakaway 'free' churches,

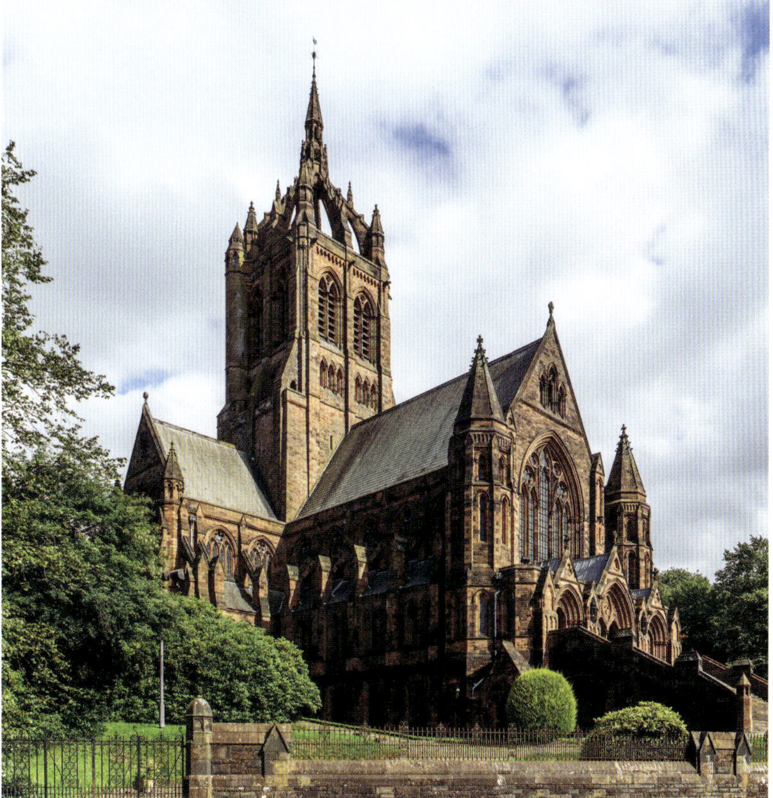

Fig. 108
Thomas Coats Memorial Baptist Church, Paisley (1885–94), by Hippolyte Blanc.

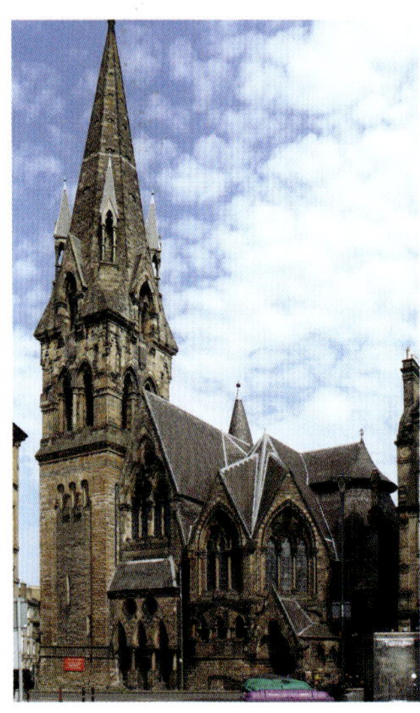

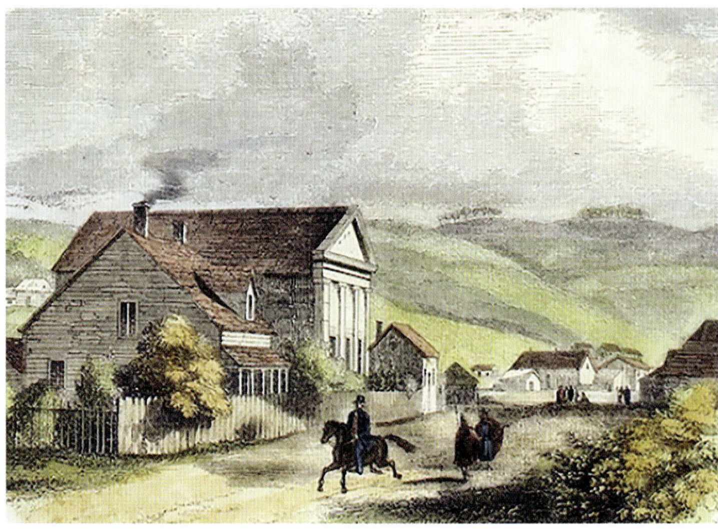

Fig. 109a

Barclay Church, Edinburgh (1862–4), by F. T. Pilkington.

Fig. 109b

Primitive origins. Methodist chapel, Manners Street (1845), in Wellington, New Zealand.

this meant the formidable task of raising funds and starting from scratch.[29] Within the established Church of Scotland (far older and wealthier), there was a steady move towards a more solemn and decorous form of worship, with increasingly elaborate variants of Romanesque and Gothic deemed appropriate. This led, in some instances, to the return of chancels, choirs, and even altars, in a tradition that had eschewed such 'distractions' for centuries.

Gothic forms also crept into the newly founded Free Church, which still cleaved heavily to its strict Calvinist roots. A good example is Mayfield Salisbury Church, Edinburgh (1878–95), by Blanc. Similarly, in Northern Ireland, where Presbyterianism had remained strong since the Scottish plantation of Ulster in the seventeenth century, the Gothic Revival left its mark. It had a major impact on important church buildings in the latter part of the nineteenth century and early twentieth, including St Enoch's, Carlisle Circus, Belfast (1870–2), by A. T. Jackson, and the Fisherwick Presbyterian Church (1901–5), in the same city, by Robert Young, with its extraordinary Tudor Gothic exterior. But among the most impressive examples of Presbyterian Gothic is Barclay Church (1862–4), in Edinburgh, by the eccentric Scottish architect F. T. Pilkington **[109a]**. Rising like a great geological feature some 250 feet above the slopes of Bruntsfield, this building is characterised by its craggy massing and overwrought detailing, including naturalistic sculpture. Its compressive muscularity is comparable to that of Burges, entirely appropriate for a building the congregation of which began life as a mission among the doughty working-class residents of Tollcross.

The United Presbyterians veered in a different direction. Initially, at least, their churches were modelled on prominent public buildings, such as town halls, with Neoclassicism as the preferred style. It was from this tradition that the religious architecture of Alexander Thomson emerged (see Chapter 3). Here we may point to his distinctive and rather idiosyncratic churches on Caledonia Road (1856–7), St Vincent Street (1859) **[2]**, and at

Queen's Park (1869), all in his native city of Glasgow. In accordance with the United Presbyterians' strict Calvinist theology, the interiors of Thomson's churches are based on the auditory model, with a focus on the pulpit for the proclamation of God's word. Outstanding examples in this tradition include Wellington Church (1883–4), Glasgow, by Thomas Lennox Watson.

Presbyterian and Nonconformist Churches in the Colonies

Nonconformists and Scottish Presbyterians also emigrated to Britain's colonies in large numbers. It needs recalling at this point that although the Church of England was the established church in England, it was not in other parts of Britain, nor especially in most colonies where a pluralist settlement was maintained among competing denominations. This had a direct impact on the built environment where the Anglican church was not necessarily the largest or most prominent place of worship in town, if one existed at all. Like their Roman Catholic and Anglican counterparts, Dissenting and Nonconformist communities were equally keen to erect places of worship once settled, creating their own versions of the 'New Jerusalem' on earth.

Initially, those built specifically for congregational worship were often austere, such as the Wesleyan Methodist chapel on Hindley Street, Adelaide, in South Australia (1838), or that on Manners Street, Wellington, in New Zealand (1845) **[109b]**. The latter of these had some architectural pretensions with its appliqué classical pilasters, but remained on the whole very simple. Limited resources and knowhow, along with the oftentimes itinerant nature of early settlement, meant that some resorted to ordering prefabricated buildings from Britain, such as the very basic Presbyterian church at Numbaa, New South Wales (1854), produced and sent by Edwin Maw of Liverpool.[30] The prefabrication and shipment of entire church buildings, or parts thereof, from Britain to the colonies was not uncommon in the nineteenth century.

But once the lessons of the Gothic Revival absorbed by Nonconformists in Britain had found their way to the colonies, the new style was adopted with enthusiasm. To be sure, plain buildings were still erected, especially in remote rural areas. However, by the 1860s and 1870s, nearly all the major Nonconformist denominations were beginning to build, or had already built, churches in one or other medieval style. Among Presbyterians Romanesque was often favoured because of its perceived absence of Roman Catholic allusion, although Gothic was far from shunned, especially after about 1860. In some cases the use of Gothic occurred even earlier. Evidence for this is to be found at Grahamstown, South Africa, in Thornley Smith's design for the Commemoration Methodist Chapel (1845–50). Far from sophisticated ('sham Gothic' by Puginian standards), it nevertheless demonstrates that, as in England, Nonconformity was open to Gothic forms. The Eastern Cape was a place where strong Protestant ideals prevailed among the so-called 1820 Settlers, who had been encouraged to migrate by the British government as frontier colonisers in an effort to quell and ultimately subdue the indigenous Xhosa people. Church architecture—both in its service to European settlers and as a missionary aid—was understood as vital to this colonialist endeavour.

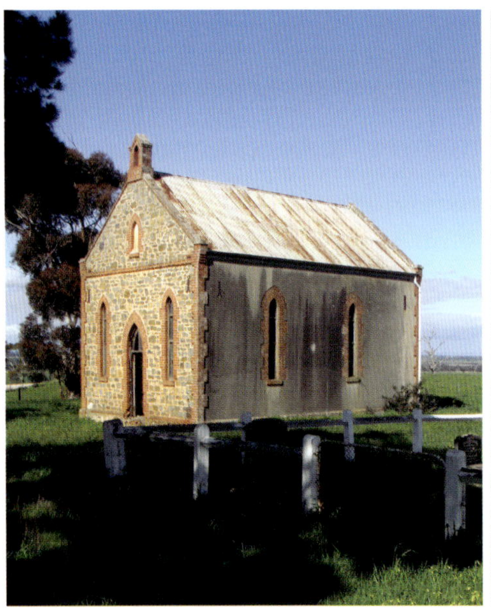

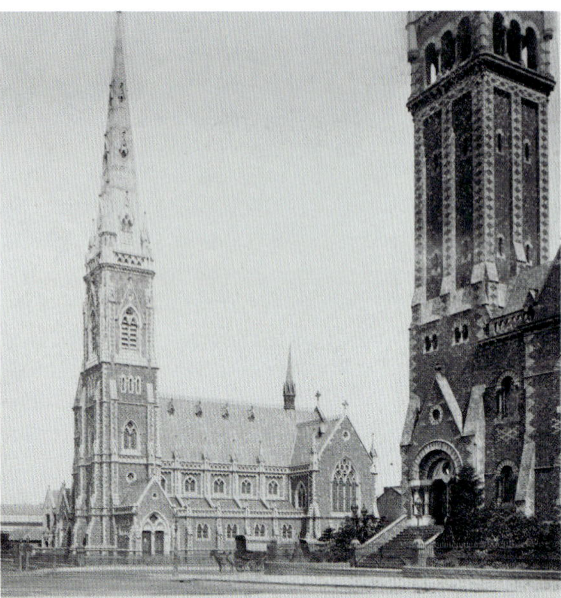

Fig. 110a

Wesleyan Methodist chapel, Sandergrove, South Australia (1867).

Fig. 110b

St Michael's (1866–7) and the Scots' Church (1869–74), Collins Street, Melbourne, Australia, both by Joseph Reed.

In more rural locations, even the tiniest of buildings sought degrees of architectural pretension, such as the Wesleyan Methodist chapel at Sandergrove, South Australia (1867) **[110a]**, or the more elaborate, but no less diminutive, Teviot Presbyterian church in Roxburgh, New Zealand (1880). In the larger towns and cities, especially where wealth existed through agriculture and natural resource extraction, more elaborate structures were possible. As noted in Chapter 1, Melbourne is a case in point, having grown rich off the early 1850s gold rush. Here, facing each other across Russell Street, on the south-western edge of Eastern Hill, are St Michael's (Unitarian) and the Scots' Church (Presbyterian) **[110b]**. These buildings were completed in 1875, by the same architect: one in a rich polychromatic, neo-Lombardic style, the other in a rather heavy, nondescript, decorated Gothic. At the time, these buildings were comparable, if not superior, to the nearby Anglican church of St Paul's on Flinders Street. This pattern of denominational representation through church architecture was repeated in towns and cities across Australia, and many other parts of Britain's colonial empire, in one or other medieval style.

Examples in suburban Melbourne include the Congregational Church at Kew (1860), by Charles Vickers; the Wesleyan Methodist church in Brunswick (1872), by Percy Oakden; and the Wesleyan Methodist church in Auburn (1888–91), by Alfred Dunn. Major inland settlements, too, such as Bendigo and Ballarat, had erected impressive Methodist churches in a polychrome Gothic style by the 1870s, the intense colouration of which is partly explained by the red duplex soils found on the adjacent goldfields. Across the Tasman Sea was the muscular Trinity Congregational Church, Christchurch (1873–5), by Mountfort, and the First (Presbyterian) Church in Dunedin (1868–73), by the Scottish émigré architect R. A. Lawson, who had moved from Australia to New Zealand in 1862 **[111a]**. Rendered in an

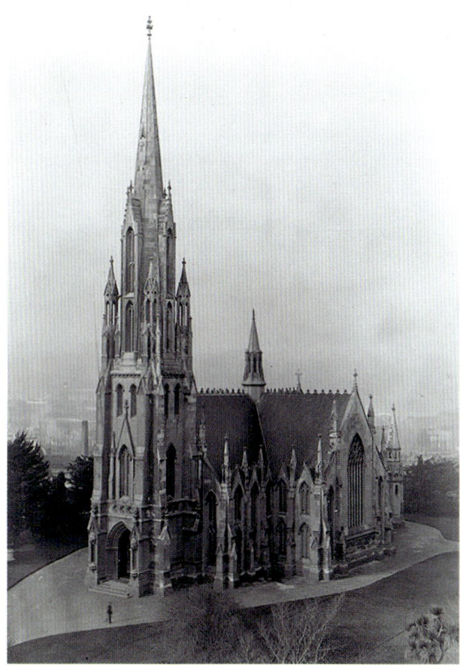

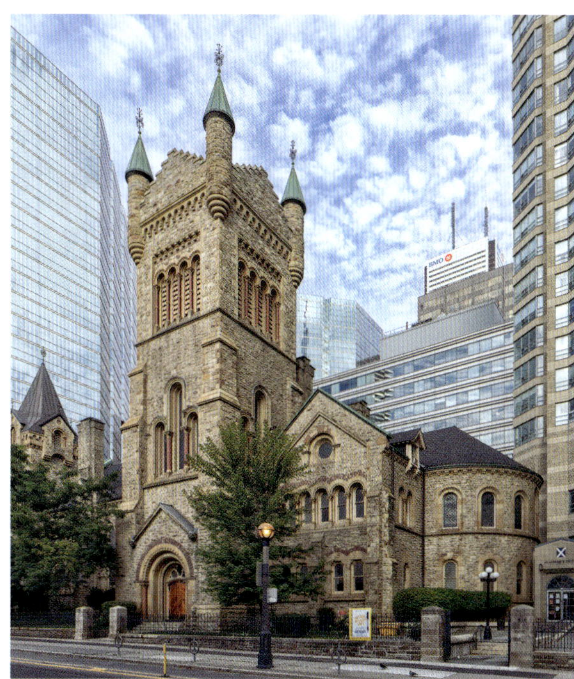

Fig. 111a

First (Presbyterian) Church, Dunedin (1868–73), New Zealand, by R. A. Lawson.

Fig. 111b

St Andrew's (Presbyterian), King Street (1876), in Toronto, Canada, by William G. Storm.

elaborate Decorated Gothic, this building was diametrically opposed to the stylistic diktats of Alexander Thomson back in Scotland, demonstrating the extent to which the design of Christian architecture in the British world had been captured by Gothic sentiment, even among hard-line Protestant communities.

In Canada, the most spectacular specimens of this phenomenon came in the form of Henry Langley's Metropolitan Methodist Church in Toronto (1868–72), and Alexander Dunlop's 'St James' Methodist Church, Montreal (1887–9), with its distinct French Gothic architecture. Envisaged on a huge scale, they were capable of accommodating over two thousand worshippers, challenging the Anglican cathedrals of both cities. Langley also helped to realise the aspirations of Baptist congregations through his designs for the New Baptist Church, Port Hope (1867), and the Jarvis Street Church, Toronto (1874). Likewise, Presbyterians were forging ahead with distinctive and impressive designs of their own. A standout example is the intriguing St Andrew's, King Street, in Toronto (1876) **[111b]**. This is rendered in a peculiar Romanesque-cum-Scottish Baronial style, referred to as 'Norman Scottish' by its architect, William Storm. This style was chosen to distinguish the building not only from other Christian denominations in the city, but also from the other half of its own, now divided community, which had chosen Decorated Gothic.[31] In such competitive and often acrimonious contexts, politics and architecture were never far apart.

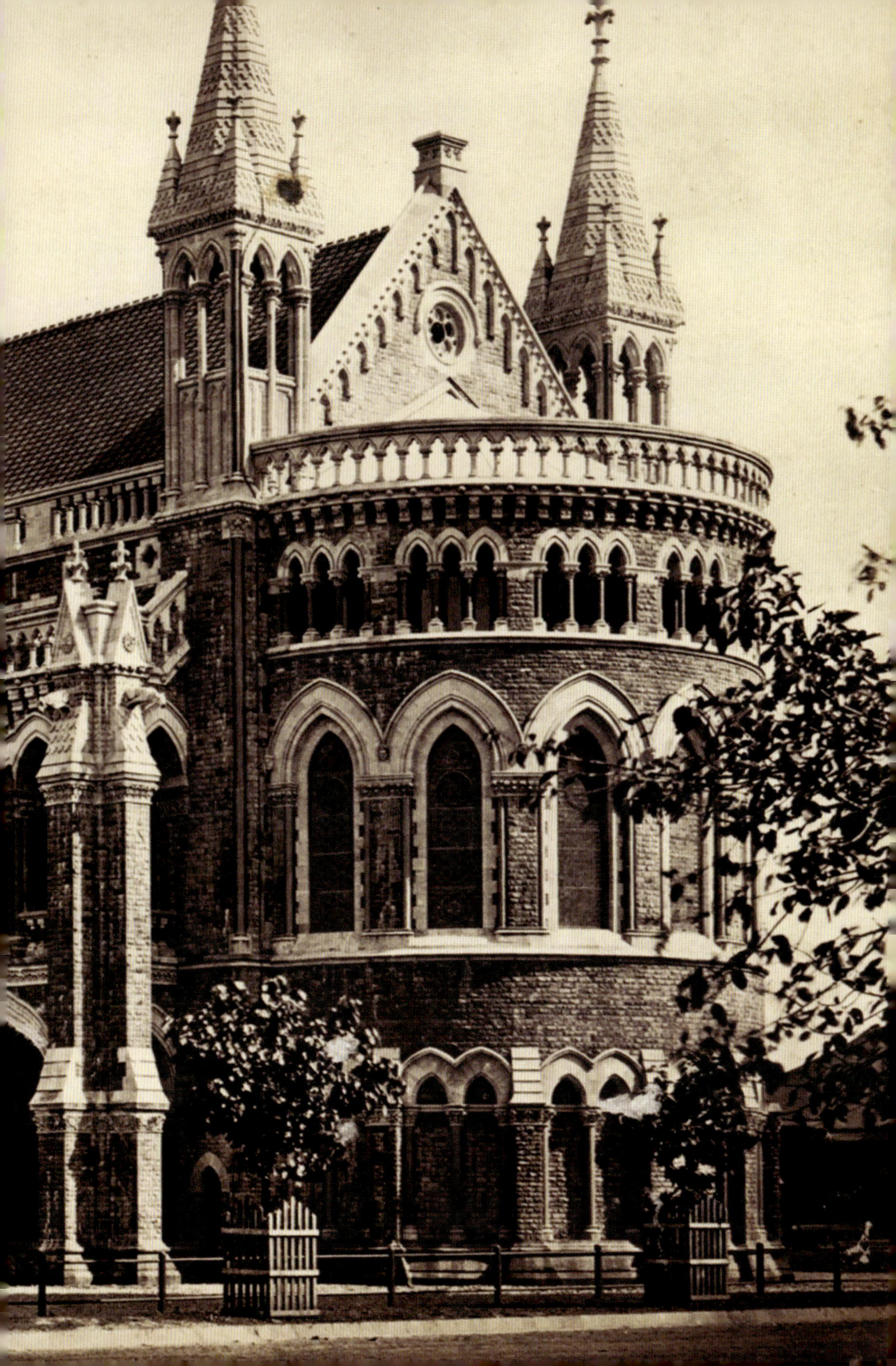

Correction, Reform, Discipline: Shaping Institutional Architectures

6

Advances in science and technology opened up further possibilities for reform in Victorian society. To be sure, the 'age of reform', as it has since become known, began well before this time. But it might be said that the Victorians were the first generation to profit fully from the effects of initiatives set in motion between *c*.1815 and 1832, and were keen to build upon them and to institutionalise their ethical and practical implications. Matters of 'propriety' would gain almost spiritual status during the period. 'Old formula, old opinions' and 'hoary systems' of corruption, clientelism, dogma, abuse, and monopoly that were seen to characterise the Augustan age in Britain were busily cast asunder.

It is perhaps easy to overstate the effects of these reforms. After all, we have already seen how the social problems the Victorians faced, particularly among the working and destitute classes, remained doggedly persistent. But there is little doubt that the flowering of a new age of liberalism—social, political, and economic; in the reform of parliament, the law, the church, and education—was well underway. Coming in the wake of the repeal of the Test and Corporation Act (1828), the Catholic Emancipation Act (1829), and the great Reform Act (1832) was the repeal of the Corn Laws and Navigation Acts, in 1846 and 1849 respectively; the Northcote-Trevelyan reform of the civil service (1854); the Second Reform Act (1867), which effectively doubled the electorate in England and Wales; the Elementary Education Act (1870), providing for compulsory non-denominational education for children between 5 and 13 years of age; the admission of 'dissenters' into the universities of Oxford and Cambridge (1871); the Married Women's Property acts (1870–82), granting women the right of legal independence from their husbands; and the Housing of the Working Classes Act (1885), to name but a few. These were major societal reforms. Even in the case of the construction industry this reforming spirit had already seen the advent of the Institution of Civil Engineers in 1818 (incorporated 1828), followed by the Institute of British Architects (1834), which received its royal charter in 1837. These organisations were established to give these now recognised 'professions' a more organised, regulated, and thus integral basis.

The mantras of 'progress' and 'improvement' were to be heard everywhere. The political economy associated with notions such as honesty, integrity, impartiality, and increased equality, as matters of principle, were steadily built into the Victorian values system. Although we today may query the outcomes associated with such efforts, they were nonetheless among the first serious and systematic attempts at creating the open and democratic society we enjoy today. Indeed, the desire for systems reform as such ran deep in the Victorian social and political imagination, and it is hard to overstate its pervasiveness. We see it in almost every quarter of society, no matter how obscure or unappealing its object of inquiry may have been. Accompanying this was a new kind of therapeutic humanism. This was most evident in areas of society where practices of punishment, confinement, and care were active, such as in prisons, asylums, schools, and even hospitals. Through a renewed interest in the power of psychology, coupled with quasi-Christian notions of redemption, it was believed that 'misfits' and miscreants could be 'reformed' and rehabilitated, not merely locked up or punished. The ill, and those under intellectual instruction, through degrees of systematised action (often backed by scientific experimentation and evidence), could be moulded and brought to health. To be sure, Victorian punishments could be harsh. Capital and corporal punishment were in place and actively employed, but the crimes for which the death penalty could be applied reduced significantly during the period, with public execution banned entirely in 1868 (for treason in 1870).

This reformist agenda had quite a significant impact on the built environment. With legal and prison reforms came new modes of incarceration that saw the advent of distinctly more 'efficient' types of prison architecture. Changes in attitude towards the poor resulted in the rise of the workhouse system, with its ill-fabled infrastructure appearing across the length and breadth of the country. Developments in psychology and medicine led to new therapies and treatments that led in turn to new spatial configurations in hospitals and asylums. The 1870 Education Act witnessed the need for extensive educational facilities in the form of school buildings, which opened a debate over what a 'school' was and how it ought to be arranged. These building types, and the activities that took place within them, were concerned in some form or other with the Victorians' renewed desire to quarantine abnormality, and to impose degrees of discipline, or 'correction', upon subjects of actual or potential disorder, oftentimes strictly. This reflected the need of the educated political classes to objectify procedure in ways that were quantifiable, fostering new types of institutional(ised) culture.

Buildings as Machines

Before considering further some of the building categories affected by these changes, it is first useful to ponder the idea of architecture as machine in the Victorian imagination. With the industrial revolution in full swing by the time Victoria came to the throne in 1837, it is perhaps not surprising that buildings of various kinds began to be looked upon as mechanical phenomena. As noted in Chapter 2, new and improved service technologies—gas, heating, drainage, ventilation, electricity, etc.—gave modern buildings an inhabited mechanical presence. Some of this was visible (vents and radiators), reminding the occupants that such services were in evidence, contributing to their comfort. But much of it was hidden, in walls and other concealed spaces throughout the building, sometimes ingeniously. The sounds these services made—the dissipation of air, the hissing of gasoliers, and the expansion of heating pipes and radiators—heightened this presence, as a building whirred into 'life'. Thus, the notion of buildings as 'machines' in this sense had metaphorical parallels with historic discourses concerning both natural and anthropogenic objects as 'organisms', or those displaying organism-like characteristics. In factory settings, this experience could be extreme, with entire spaces often taken up with actual machines, operating very loudly, and either manufacturing products themselves, or moving these around and between spaces, both inside the factory and beyond. The Victorians appreciated the character and capabilities of architecture in this regard, with such buildings sometimes causing confusion, even alarm.

Understandably, there was something of a perceptual overlay between the increasing use of iron in buildings during the Victorian period and the presence of iron machinery. In this context, iron and mechanisation were synonymous, with iron componentry in buildings often being (or observed as) operable. In Chapter 1, for instance, we saw how locomotive machinery in the form of trains was associated closely with iron construction in station architecture. Moreover, there was an idea prevalent at the time that buildings were types of 'engine' for producing particular outcomes, especially as the tasks they housed became increasingly complex and specialised. The mid to late nineteenth century was also the age of increased machine-aided prefabrication, where buildings (comprising assembled elements), often in cast iron, were flat packed and moved great distances, to places as far afield as Africa, Asia, Australia, and New Zealand.

A crucial link between architecture, mechanics, and efficiency was therefore established, leading to a kind of 'mechanisation of design thinking'.[1] Pegged to ideas such as utilitarianism and optimal functionality, the notion that a 'good' building ought to embody a sense of its own operability was normalised. This type of thinking also emerged through a latent machine aesthetic associated with certain 'modern' styles of architecture. For instance, through an array of intersecting concerns—from mechanical ways of knowing and seeing, to a thoroughly industrialising mentality among governing elites—the Gothic architecture of Manchester Town Hall both embodied and reflected (abstractly, but also literally in its detailing) a deeply ingrained 'machine' ideology.[2] We may also recall from the previous chapter how certain religious buildings, especially churches, were increasingly understood in these terms, as their liturgically geared decoration and spatial organisation were likened to the 'machinery' of devotion. This also occurred during a period of thoroughgoing ecclesiastical reform.

This thinking applied especially to the rebuilding of the Houses of Parliament. The application of the latest in science and technology would bring forth, it was reckoned, an appropriate legislature for the modern age, and for the world's leading industrial nation and centre of a vast global empire. Attention to issues such as lighting, acoustics, and ventilation, through applied science, were therefore paramount. These were seen, for better or worse, as the key to conditioning and thus improving the environments in which MPs governed the nation. What came with this was the parallel intuition that the procedures of governance, as well as MPs themselves, might also be 'reformed' in corresponding ways to suit this new modernising agenda.[3] The novelty of this approach naturally made it politically contentious. But these were issues that Barry and his associates, such as the Edinburgh chemist David Boswell Reid, took seriously and often debated during processes of experimentation with regard to the building's performance, including its mechanical ventilation (air-conditioning) system.

It was a similar situation at the Reform Club (1837–41), in London, also designed by Charles Barry. This was described as a kind of organism. For instance, the French architectural journalist César Daly noted with some enthusiasm how

> [t]his edifice is not an inert mass of stone, brick, and iron; it is almost a living body, with its circulatory and nervous systems. In these walls, so motionless to the eye, circulate in fact gases, vapours, fluids, liquids; on exploring them one discovers flues, conduits, wires—the arteries, veins, and nerves of this new organic being—by which are carried warmth in winter, fresh air in summer, and in every season, light—warm water—cold water—food—and all the numerous accessories which a high civilisation demands.[4]

Thus, despite its demure Italianate palazzo exterior, within the building was a vital entity **[112a]**. The metaphor may have been organic, but the structure was machine-like in every respect. Its most revealing quarter in this regard

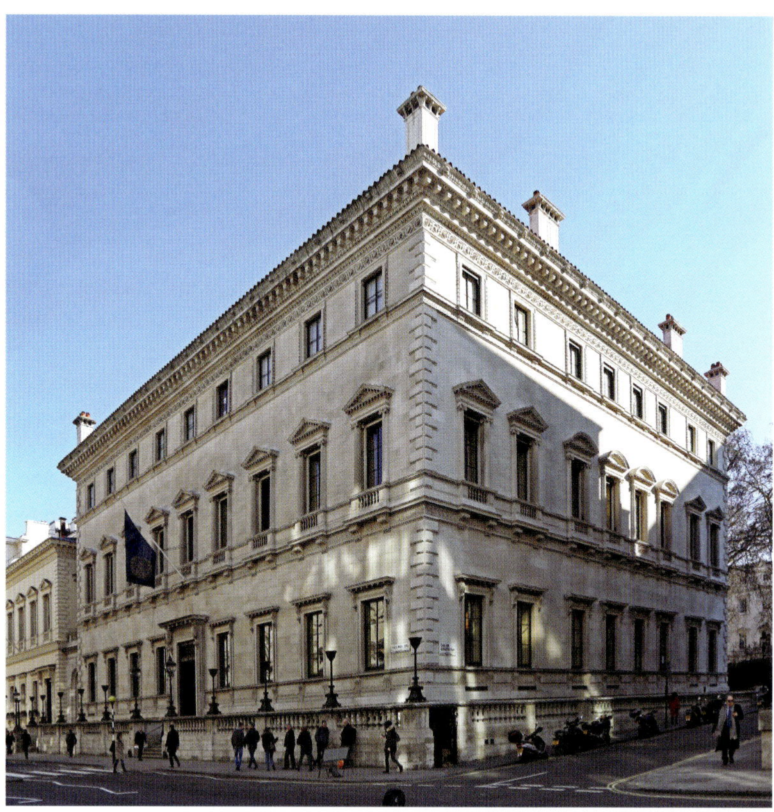

Fig. 112a
The Reform Club, Pall Mall (1837–41), London, by Charles Barry.

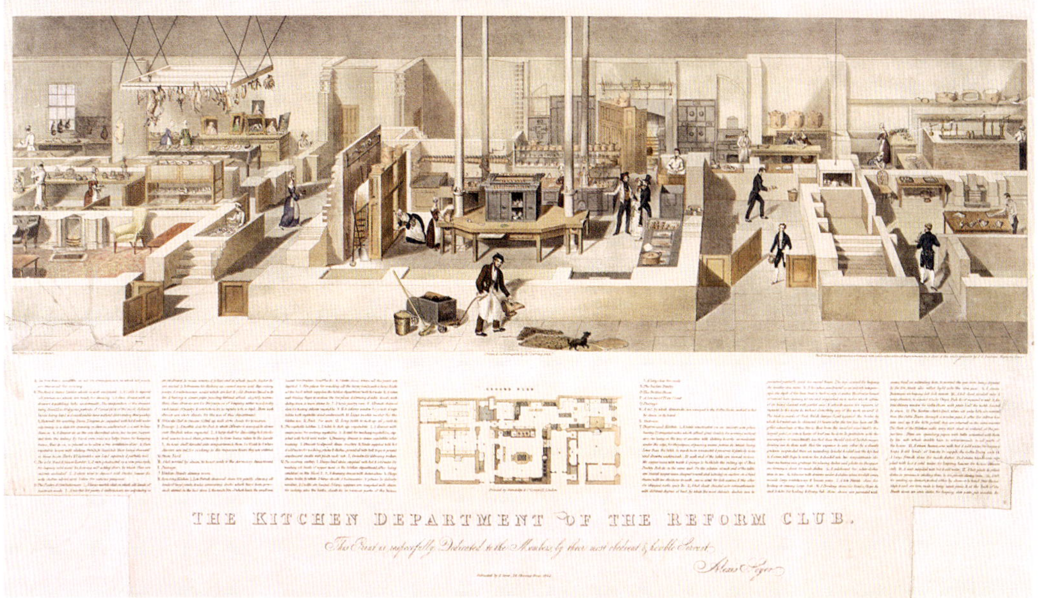

Fig. 112b

Food production machine. The 'Kitchen Department', Reform Club, overseen by chef Alexis Soyer.

was the famous kitchen overseen by the French chef extraordinaire, Alexis Soyer **[112b]**. Here could be found every conceivable device in aid of culinary innovation, from mechanical rotisseries to moving furnaces to dumbwaiters. Mechanisation in the service of comfort was the aim, synonymous with what Daly himself labelled 'progressive architecture'.

These two buildings, and the ways in which they were perceived, provide us with insights into how architecture was understood as inherently capable of acting upon its occupants, 'processing' and 'conditioning' them in various ways. If, as Ruskin had insisted, buildings spoke (see Chapter 3), then they also breathed and moved. When united with a political economy concerned with reform, architecture was itself viewed as a technology in aid of facilitating vast and unprecedented societal change. From this fundamental premise would emerge refined institutional strategies for social manipulation and control.

Carceral Spaces: From Prisons to Workhouses

One of the most fertile domains for architecture to exert its effect in this way was in the reform of disorderly and undisciplined minds. Such minds were considered increasingly problematic during the Victorian period as concerns over morality, social conformity, criminality, and political stability were heightened in a context where diagnostic notions of congenital degeneracy, mental deficiency, and 'feeble-mindedness', not to mention environmental deprivation (i.e., urban slums), were identified as sites for inspection and treatment. Whether criminally inclined, indolent, ignorant, or just insane, these minds might now be 'corrected', not only via scientific means but also through the novel application of space. In this sense, space was seen as both a tool for 'safe' segregation and a medium of clinical observation and intervention.

Prisons

The one typology where we see this mode of thinking applied most starkly is prison architecture. There had been a relatively long and well-developed discourse on the redemptive capacities of incarceration in Britain and its wider European context stretching back many decades. At the basis of this reformative agenda was the idea that the character of offenders could be shifted from vice to virtue, and that architecture would aid this process. The Victorians did not invent this idea, but they refined it. Initially, the formula behind these reforms was articulated in the Penitentiary Act of 1779, and subsequent acts of 1781 and 1784, where solitary confinement, accompanied by well-regulated labour and religious instruction, were identified as the remedy. This led to the evolution of a new, state-controlled system, which saw a spate of 'reformed prisons' erected in numerous counties following the acts, the most celebrated of which were those built in the 1780s in Gloucestershire by the architect William Blackburn. In these prisons, and others like them, concerns for a healthy and strictly ordered environment were paramount. It was through such architectural configurations that the idea of the prison as a type of mechanical apparatus originated.

By the 1830s dozens of prisons along these reformed lines had been built throughout the country, establishing a more centralised and regulated national system. Their architecture had already begun to incorporate those planning features associated with new regimes of surveillance. This included layouts with orthogonal, rationally planned spaces, open work and exercise yards, and observational arrangements that facilitated long and direct lines of sight for warders. The principle behind this planning was derived from Jeremy Bentham's 'Panopticon' concept of continuous surveillance in carceral settings, whereby a prisoner was unable to determine when, by whom, or even from where he was being observed. This was designed to enact a type of psychological constraint (torture, even) that rendered its physical equivalent unnecessary. In theory, the prisoner—or the person/body under 'correction'—was led to believe that he was being watched constantly. Not knowing one way or the other was supposed to induce a form of docility, deterring undesirable behaviour that could lead to punishment, and thus rendering the subject compliant. Based on utilitarian assumptions, one can see how this spatial regime was intended to make the process of confinement, and attempts at prisoner reform, more efficient and effective. In this context, architecture was understood in terms of its potential as a medium for 'processing'—through confinement, discipline, and moral instruction—the criminally minded.

The most famous example of this system in action was the Pentonville 'model' prison in north London, designed by Joshua Jebb, and built between 1840 and 1842. It was based on the 'separate system'. This was the notion that seclusion through the forced separation of prisoners—in effect, a form of solitary confinement—was conducive to introspection and thus character reform. The prison comprised 520 individual cells, each practically isolated and self-contained **[113a&b]**. The cells were serviced by a purposely designed gas and water plumbing system networked throughout the entire building, supplied by on-site water tanks and a gas factory. Light penetrated each cell through a small, louvered window placed just high enough to prevent

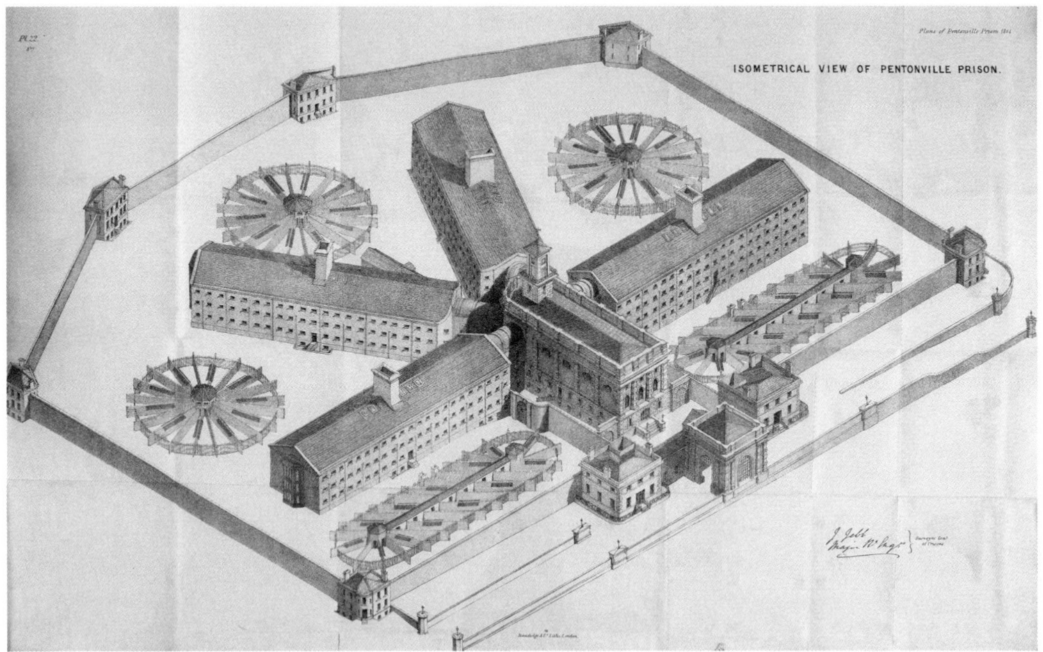

Fig. 113a

Isometric view of Pentonville Prison, Islington (1840–2), north London, by Joshua Jebb.

the inmate from engaging with the outside world. Jebb also considered the circulation of air via a carefully calibrated 'thermo-ventilation' system. Designed around the 'ascending air' method developed by Hadens of Trowbridge, it utilised the principle of convection whereby vitiated air was extracted at the top of the building while fresh air was drawn in from below, warming it when necessary by passing it over coal-fired hot-water stoves located in the basement of each block **[114]**. Access to individual cells was controlled by double doors with a 2 foot cavity between them. The outermost door had a metal 'inspection slide' that permitted warders to look in without being seen, while a small in-built trapdoor allowed food to be inserted. Indeed, mealtimes in the prison, which required the simultaneous feeding of all 520 prisoners, were facilitated by an elaborate mechanical system of pulleys, conveyors, and trollies, distributing food in a cacophony of movement and noise. So precision-based was this 'machine', that the entire operation of feeding the prisoners could be accomplished in less than 10 minutes.

As the overall planning of the prison illustrates, these systems were aided by the radial arrangement of the four cell blocks, with long, straight corridors converging at a central point in front of the administration block. This radically enhanced the surveillance potential of the building, effectively allowing a handful of warders to supervise the entire internal circulation space of the prison simultaneously. In this way the 'model' prison at Pentonville was a deliberately centralised, mechanised, and thus depersonalised experiment in total environmental control. Each individual 'cell' was akin to a 'chrysalis within which the transmutation of the criminal mind' was intended to take place.[5]

With Jebb as Surveyor General of Prisons, and the New Gaol Act of 1839 (and later 1865) enshrining the separate system in law, the Pentonville model

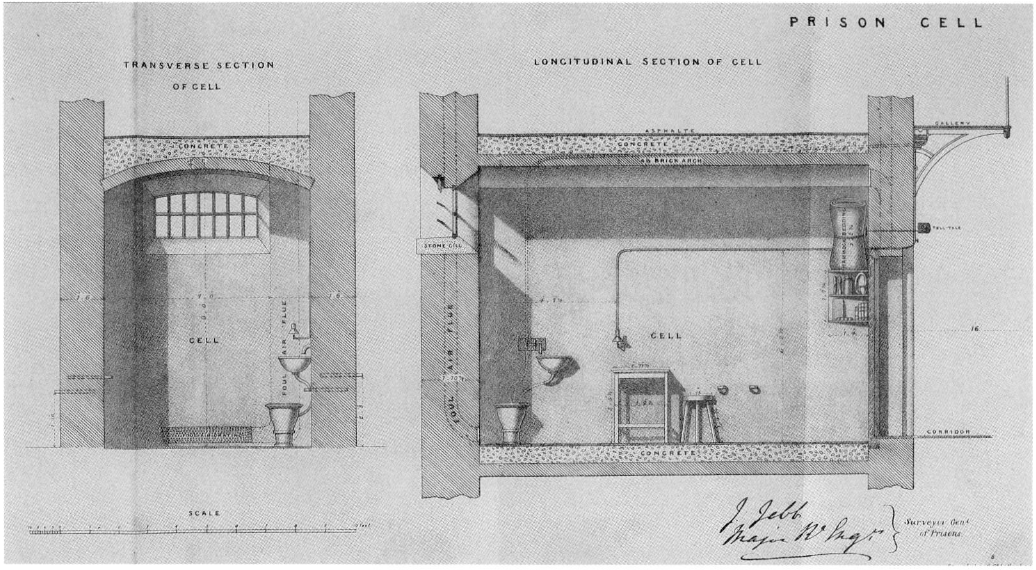

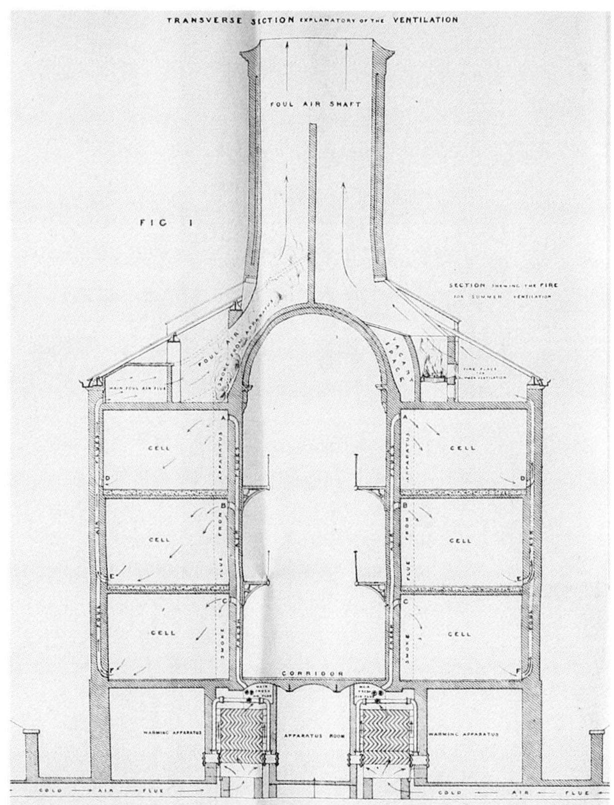

Fig. 113b

Processing of prisoners. The single or 'separate' cell unit at Pentonville Prison (transverse and longitudinal sections).

Fig. 114

Transverse section through cell block at Pentonville Prison, showing how the stack ventilation system works, drawing in cool air from the bottom and expelling vitiated or 'foul' air at the top.

became the basis of reformed prison design throughout much of the country up until the 1880s. Apart from the separate system of incarceration, the radial plan upon which the model was based proved particularly influential. No less than nineteen county and borough prisons were built in this way

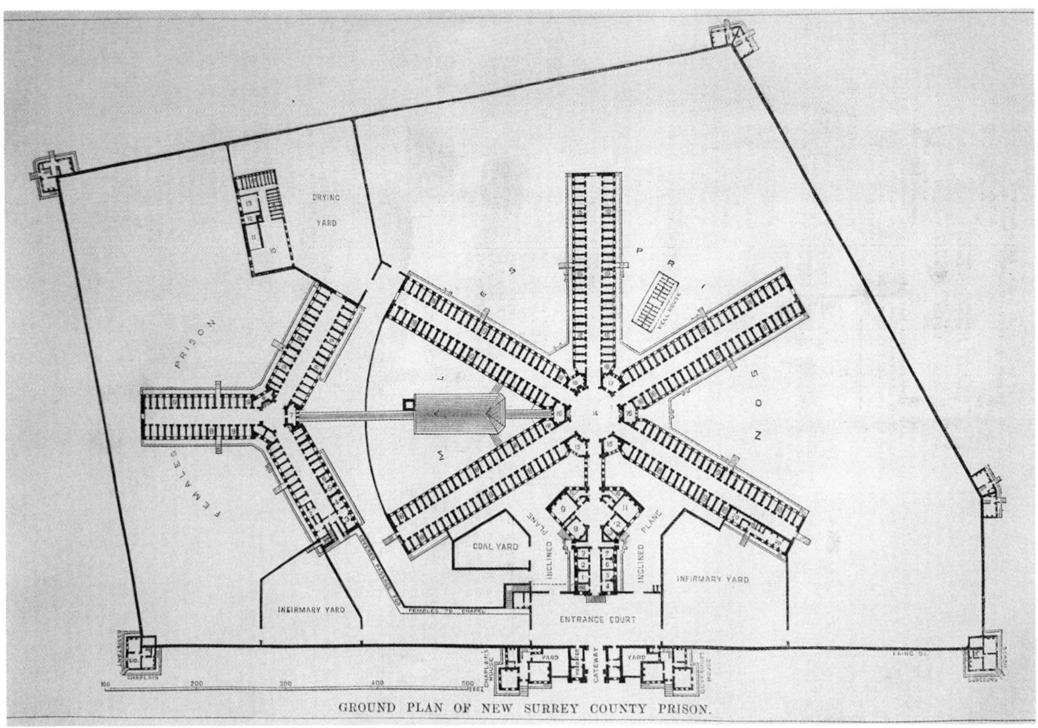

Fig. 115

Plan of Wandsworth Prison, Surrey (1849–51), south London, by Joshua Jebb. An example of the 'separate system' on the favoured radial-plan model.

between 1842 and 1877, including HMPs Leeds (1843–7), Winchester (1846–9), Wandsworth (1849–51) **[115]**, and Lincoln (1868–72). Generally the architecture of these buildings was very severe, in keeping with their intended purpose. But the main entrance facades were often dressed up in a more architecturally pretentious manner, frequently in heavy if picturesque castellated form.

The model quickly spread to Scotland and throughout other parts of Europe. In the United States something like it had already been implemented in landmark prison buildings, such as those designed by John de Haviland in Cherry Hill (1821–9) and Pittsburgh (1829–32), based on the English radial model. The model was also exported to parts of the British empire. Prime examples include the 'separate' prisons erected at the penal colonies of Port Arthur (1848–55), in Van Dieman's Land (Tasmania) **[116a&b]**, and Fremantle (1852–9), Western Australia. At Port Arthur a simple cruciform variant of the radial layout was adopted, containing seventy individual cells, a chapel, and exercise yards, all surrounded by a high masonry wall. It was erected by the convicts themselves, as was that at Fremantle. Through the export of such technology, so far afield, a double 'isolation' was enforced: that of the separate system itself, along with being sent to the extremities of the known world, never to return. In Singapore a different system prevailed. There Indian and Chinese convicts, who were deployed extensively in the construction of public infrastructure, were appointed their own warders as an inducement towards good behaviour. They, too, built their own prison at Bras Basah between 1841 and 1860, which also housed the colonial public works department.

Fig. 116a

Exporting the 'system' abroad. Plan and section(s) of Separate Prison at Port Arthur convict prison (1848–55), in Van Dieman's Land (Tasmania), Australia.

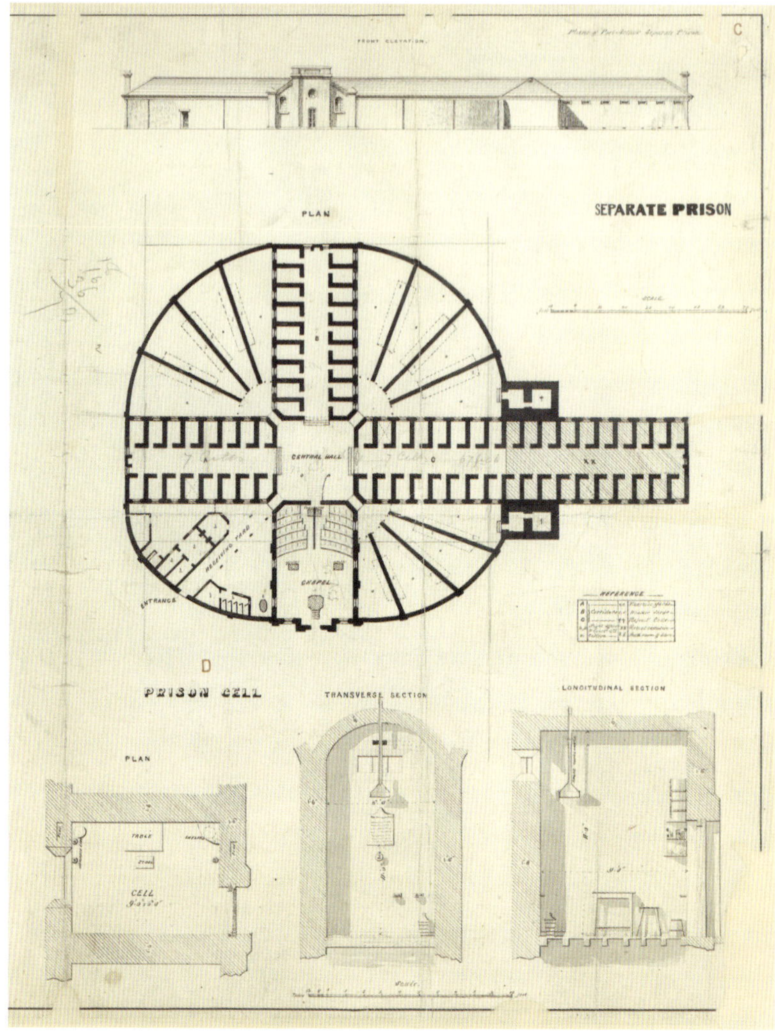

As the science of criminal psychology advanced, the belief in the possibility of reforming the criminal mind waned. With the realisation that criminality was not merely environmentally induced but apparently congenital, the notion of incarceration and harsh punishment as forms of deterrent returned to prominence. In this respect, the 'criminal classes' were seen as a 'race' apart, indelibly degenerate and a danger to society. Edmund Du Cane, who accepted this line of reasoning, and who had previously served five years in west Australia as director of convict labour at the Swan River colony, was appointed in 1869 as Jebb's successor to the general surveyorship of English prisons. Orchestrated by Du Cane, Wormwood Scrubs prison, Hammersmith (1874–91) perhaps best represents this new thinking in built form. Here the concept of central inspection via the radial plan is jettisoned in favour of a parallel block arrangement. In all other respects, however, the architecture and its accommodation was as draconian as its predecessors.

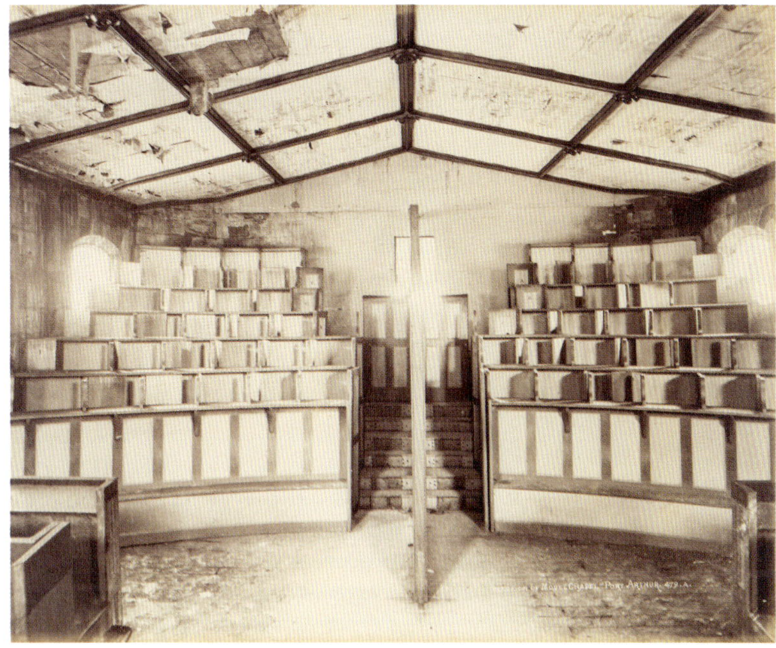

Fig. 116b

Model chapel, Port Arthur, Tasmania (photo *c.*1880). The chapel was designed in such a way that inmates were unable to converse with one another, thus maintaining their separation.

Workhouses

The principles underpinning reformed prison architecture were detectable in other building types concerned with the organisation and conditioning of citizen subjects. As the planning of such buildings was steadily refined over time, the inherent assumption was that a carefully distributed architecture would operate as a countervailing device against the effects of neglect, perversion, and degeneracy. One such type was the notorious workhouse.

Workhouses had a fearsome reputation, by design. In effect, they were open or voluntary prisons, and places where only those who were desperate—usually owing to homelessness, disability, and/or abject hunger (i.e., the destitute)—would willingly admit themselves. The conditions within were hardly better than prisons. Indeed, much like the new prisons, the workhouse system was founded along utilitarian lines, the basic premise of which was not only to categorise but also to stigmatise those who entered. Some were lucky enough to be designated as 'deserving poor', such as the old and infirm (considered 'first-class'); others, especially able-bodied men ('second-class'), were viewed as not merely unfortunate but somehow defective. Those in this latter category were deemed fundamentally immoral (or 'demoralised,' to use the contemporary term), requiring both correction and moral improvement.

This architectural solution to poverty emerged out of the 1832 Royal Commission established to investigate the workings of England's poor laws. It was headed by the English Utilitarian social reformer Edwin Chadwick, and resulted in the Poor Law Amendment Act of 1834. The existing laws, which dated back to the sixteenth century and were administered individually within each of England's some 15,000 parishes, were, by the early nineteenth century, criticised for their practical inefficiency and openness to abuse. The giving of what was known as 'outdoor assistance' (the doling out of aid in the form of money, food, or fuel to poor people) came to be viewed negatively as enabling pauperisation. The principal charge was that no incentive existed for such people to seek employment and, through this, to 'improve' themselves. Thus, a system of centrally (i.e., nationally) administered workhouse 'unions' were established to take the place of doling out aid piecemeal. In Scotland, 'Poor Houses', as they were commonly known, were similarly grouped and administered under 'Combinations'.

To be effective, the workhouse had to be seen as a deterrent and place of last resort. They were places where relief could be found in the form of free food and shelter, but where what one received was so meagre that it caused distress. In no way could workhouses be seen as comfortable, either psychologically, emotionally, or physically. This managed 'distress' was choreographed in several ways. To begin with, when people entered, including families, they were separated. Ostensibly, there was no contact at all between men, women, and children. This spatial segregation was considered a form of 'appropriate' treatment, with clinical overtones, as a barrier against contagion and in order to deter pauperism. Like prison, the inmates were forced to get up at five or six o'clock every morning to work around 10 hours a day doing menial tasks such as breaking rocks, grinding corn, crushing bones, or making sacks. If this were not enough to shatter their spirits, they were fed the most basic of foodstuffs, such as gruel (thinned-down porridge), which kept them on the borderline of nourishment. The dormitories, which could contain up to dozens of people, where poorly lit and heated. It would seem hardly surprising, therefore, that in some workhouses the mortality rate was reported to be as high as 40 per cent.

By 1841 there were 340 such establishments in existence throughout England. There was some diversity of architectural style, but most were plain in the extreme, tending towards an astylar Classicism **[117]**. This was intended to reflect and facilitate the oppressive regime within. The young

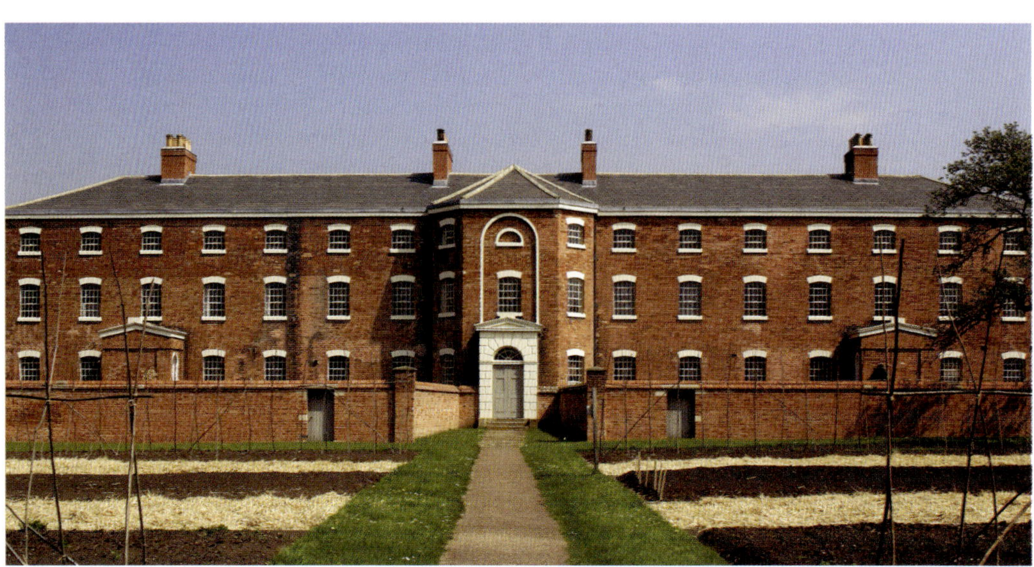

Fig. 117
Austerity: Thurgarton Hundred workhouse (later Southwell Union), Upton (1824), Nottinghamshire, by William Nicholson. Thurgarton set the tone for many workhouse buildings coming into the Victorian period.

G. G. Scott and his partner, W. B. Moffatt, were among those who designed some of the earliest workhouses. But it was the official architect to the Poor Law Commission, the inexperienced Sampson Kempthorne, who later emigrated to New Zealand to assist bishop G. A. Selwyn with church designs (see Chapter 5), who devised the infamous 'model' plans. The idea behind Kempthorne's plans was simple if menacing. As the Assistant Commissioner, Francis Head, explained:

> The principle behind a poorhouse is this, build poor men's cottages; but instead of having one long street, bend it into a quadrangle, which forms also a prison, having within itself an area…which the board can introduce any system it may choose.[6]

This basic formula resulted in the quadrangular and hexagonal plans for which Kempthorne became known **[118a]**. Much like the model prisons, they were devised with administrative blocks located at the head or in the centre of the plan, or both, around which were arrayed the living and work spaces of the inmates. Most also included a chapel space for moral and religious instruction. What strikes one as characteristic is the division of space and austerity of design. The plan had to reflect the functional requirement of the workhouse in terms of the segregation of inmates and their strict supervision. In one form or other, these structures were organised around separate sections for men, women, and children, as well as a clear vantage point from where the master of the house could survey the entire premises **[118b]**. This arrangement symbolised the centrality of authority, both institutional and governmental, reflecting what has been termed the workhouse's 'moral geometry'.[7]

The system did not go uncriticised for its seeming cruelty. We may recall, for instance, that a Kempthorne-type configuration formed the adverse side

Fig. 118a

Model plans. 'Perspective View of a Workhouse for 300 Paupers', by Sampson Kempthorne, from *First Annual report of the Poor Law Commissioners for England and Wales* (1835).

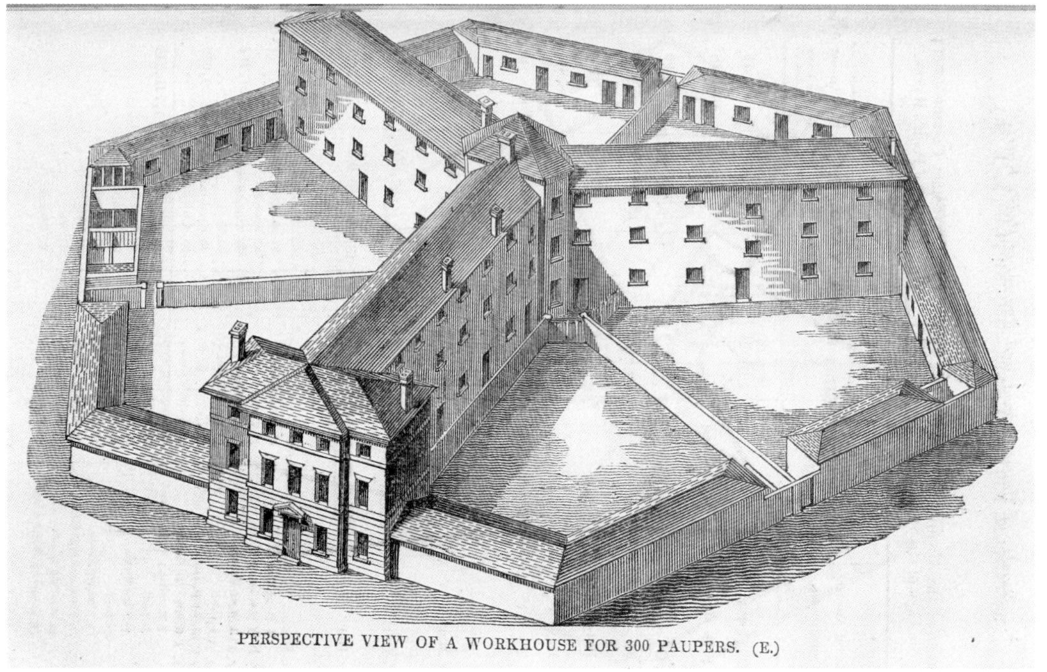

Fig. 118b

Alternative plan, 'Workhouse for 300 Paupers' (1835), by Sampson Kempthorne.

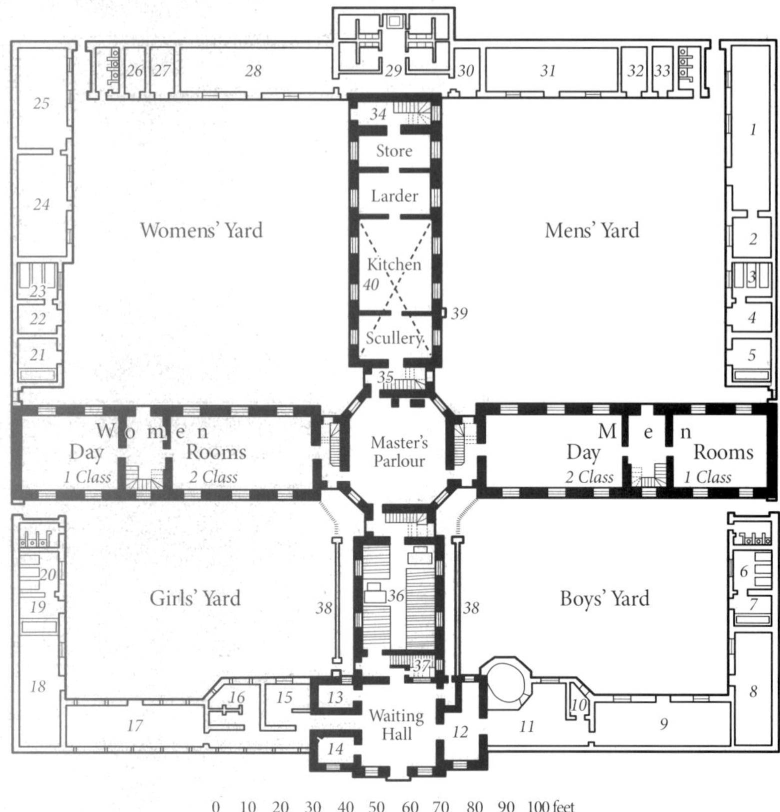

1 Work Room
2 Store
3 Receiving Wards, 3 beds
4 Bath
5 Washing Room
6 Receiving Ward, 3 beds
7 Washing Room
8 Work Room
9 Flour and Mill Room
10 Coals
11 Bakehouse
12 Bread Room
13 Searching Room
14 Porter's Room
15 Store
16 Potatoes
17 Coals
18 Work Room
19 Washing Room
20 Receiving Ward, 3 beds
21 Washing Room
22 Bath
23 Receiving Ward, 3 beds
24 Laundry
25 Wash House
26 Dead House
27 Refectory Ward
28 Work Room
29 Piggery
30 Slaughter House
31 Work Room
32 Refectory Ward
33 Dead House
34 Women's Stairs to Dining Hall
35 Mens' Stairs to ditto
36 Boys' and Girls' School and Dining Room
37 Delivery
38 Passage
39 Well
40 Cellar under ground

in one of A. W. N. Pugin's famous 'contrasted' images of residences for the poor in 1841 **[46b]**. Anti-Poor Law protestors also agitated against the system. Ironically, when Francis Head moved to his next posting as governor of Upper Canada in 1836, local church organisations, fearful that he would implement the draconian workhouse system there, moved to create their own, more humane 'houses of industry', examples of which were erected in Toronto (1837) **[119a]**, Kingston (1850), and Waterloo (1869). In Britain, workhouses became steadily more commodious and architecturally decorative as the century wore on, especially their central administration blocks. Architectural firms began to specialise in their construction, and it is clear that more and better design initiatives were implemented, within the constraints of Poor Law propriety. Examples include the Hampstead Workhouse (1849–50), by H. E. Kendall; the Birmingham Union Workhouse (1850–2),

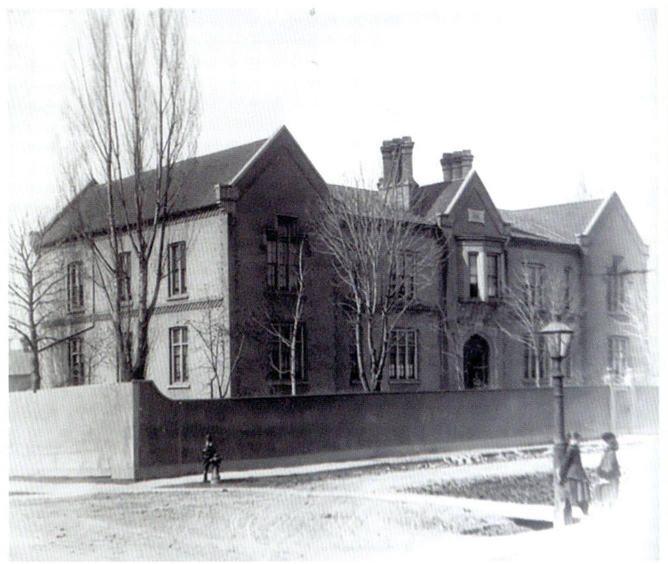

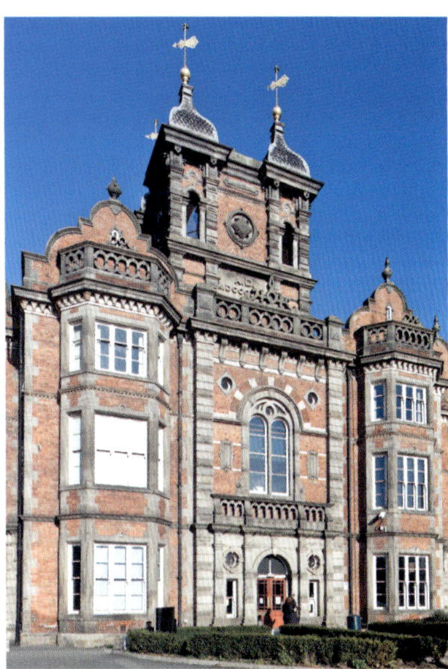

Fig. 119a

'House of Industry' (workhouse), Elm Street (1848), Toronto, Canada, by William Thomas.

Fig. 119b

Architectural pretence. Leeds Union Workhouse (1858), Leeds, by Perkin & Backhouse.

by Bateman & Dury; and the Leeds Union Workhouse (1858), by Perkin & Backhouse **[119b]**. By this time the Kempthorne plans had been largely abandoned, with the pavilion system, as developed in hospital architecture, widely adopted for accommodation blocks, as seen at Lambeth Workhouse, in London (1871–4), by Thomas Aldwinckle.

Educational Architecture: Habits of Mind and Body

Schooling in Victorian Britain, and therefore the evolution of school buildings, is a complex and varied topic. This is not to mention buildings for higher education, such as universities, women's colleges, specialist art colleges, or places of practical learning for working-class people, including industrial schools and mechanics' institutes. Quite a number of these were built during the period, with mechanics' institutes alone numbering 600 by 1850. Art schools, too, were a unique and interesting subset within the Victorian educational sector, often producing landmark buildings, such as Charles Rennie Mackintosh's art school in Glasgow (1897–1909). Given the emphasis of this chapter, I will focus primarily on certain educational reforms aimed at the intellectual, moral, and physical regeneration and well-being of children, and the role architecture played in enabling this ambition. Here I will consider the links between the arrangement of space, ideas of aesthetic presentation, and the deep-seated cultural and political desire to institute new regimes of behavioural conditioning, regulation, and improvement.

To some extent, schools have always been concerned with shaping and disciplining the minds of children. In the Victorian period, however, this idea became strictly formalised, even codified. In the schooling system that pre-dated state provision in Britain (1870–2), religion also played a central role in overseeing and administering educational provision, whether Presbyterian, Anglican, Roman Catholic, or some other denomination. This 'voluntary' system was fees based, thus limiting access; or partly grant funded by the state, as in the case of National Schools (Church of England) for poorer children. In 1870, recognising the limitations of such provision, a new and more comprehensive state system of education was enacted through parliament. Known as the Elementary Education Act, it received royal assent in August that year. It was a transformative piece of legislation. Its purpose was to supply a basic, non-sectarian, and standardised level of education for children between the ages of 5 and 13 in England and Wales. Section 74 of the act mandated compulsion of attendance, but enforcement of this varied in practice. Although Scotland had a public education system predating political union with England and Wales by nearly a century, it too had a similar act passed in 1872, wresting control from the Church of Scotland. A slew of subsequent acts of parliament up to the end of the nineteenth century steadily increased the age of compulsion, further restricted child employment, and abolished school fees. In Ireland, although a national board for elementary education had been established as early as 1831, schooling there was not compulsory until the 1890s.

The Act was devised for a number of reasons. Following the 1867 Reform Act, which extended the franchise into parts of the male working-class population, it was felt that if representative government was to function effectively, a certain level of education among the voting public was desirable, if not essential. In the context of growing international competition and rivalry, it was also deemed necessary to raise the level of educational attainment in order that Britain keep pace with other industrialised nations, especially Germany. As W. E. Forster, sponsor of the original parliamentary Bill observed, the nation was threatened by 'invading armies of ignorance, misery, and destitution [which] swarm in upon us like insects[,]...feed[ing] on the trees of our commercial prosperity'.[8] In addition to these reasons, it was also reckoned by the elite within British society that education, in providing some degree of aspiration and opportunity, would go some way towards quelling revolutionary tendencies that had built up among the lower classes through the middle decades of the nineteenth century.

By the 1860s, the winds of change had already blown through the voluntary sector, especially in relation to 'public' schooling (i.e., private fee-paying). This included esteemed establishments such as Eton, Winchester, Harrow, and Rugby. The Arnoldian reform of the sector—after the initiatives of Dr Thomas Arnold, headmaster at Rugby School in the 1830s—saw systematic modifications around the conditioning of the whole student through enhanced disciplinary codes and the imposition of outdoor activity, such as games and sport. The intention was to produce not only capable, morally attuned minds, but also strong and healthy bodies, with ideas of responsibility, resilience, and self-restraint at its core. What came with this new 'ethos', and ultimately what helped enable it, was considerable expansion in both provision and buildings. Particular attention was paid to sporting facilities, new, more hygienic spaces for learning, better accommodation (for boarders), and the provision of moral instruction via religion through the erection of chapels. With the identity of the Victorian public school having coalesced by the 1870s and 1880s, 'ancient' models, such as Eton and Winchester, were turned to for precedent in terms of planning, including the ubiquitous use of monastic-style quadrangles and the Gothic-cum-

Tudor aesthetic that characterised the architecture of many such schools. Despite certain notable exceptions, such as Wellington College (1856–9), with its neo-Wrenian Classicism, the 'image' of this type of school was largely fixed by the late nineteenth century. An early example is Lancing College (1854–8), West Sussex, by R. C. Carpenter (chapel 1868–75, by R. H. Carpenter and William Slater), with its double-quadrangle core and Gothic Revival architecture **[120a]**; or, later, on a more extensive scale, Christ's Hospital, Horsham (1897–1902), by Aston Webb & E. Ingress Bell, with its large central quadrangle and ebullient Tudoresque styling **[120b]**.

Meanwhile, what emerged in the new state sector was both similar and different. First, there was the establishment of local 'school boards' for purposes of administration. These boards—in England, Wales, and Scotland—were charged with erecting the necessary infrastructure, including new school buildings, to be funded by the rate-paying public. From the off, the planning of this essentially new building type was a matter of debate. Initially, school board architects worked from known traditions of school design in the voluntary sector. This included grouping large classrooms, over a number of levels, separated by sex and to some extent age. But this arrangement soon proved inadequate, as the new school inspection regime that came with the boards reported that levels of concentration, discipline, and therefore the inculcation of basic pedagogic principles were lacking in most instances. A new approach was required. Some of the architects of the new board schools travelled abroad to investigate alternative arrangements. Attention soon focused on the so-called Prussian model of German educational architecture, which allowed for an array of smaller, individual classrooms linked along a connecting corridor. This system was perceived as allowing for more concentrated forms of instruction, efficient circulation, and the enabling of greater levels of order among pupils. Grafted onto this basic model were other innovations, such as the inclusion of a central hall and raked galleries, which originated in the theories of the Scottish educationalist David Stow.

In London, for instance, this basic model was fully integrated by the 1880s. Through the appointment of an official board architect, E. R. Robson, a degree of relative consistency was brought to bear in relation to planning. We see the archetype in its mature from in some of Robson's own designs for London Board Schools, such as that at Latchmere Road, Battersea (1889), with its central hall surrounded by classrooms, linked via a corridor. Since the model had first been suggested by T. Roger Smith in his design for Jonson Street School, Stepney (1871), other board schools adopted variants of the 'separate-classroom' arrangement, large and small, including West Street, Hackney (1873); Aldenham Street, Camden (1874); and Cobbold Road, Chelsea (1900) **[121a&b]**. The model soon spread across England and Wales, and even abroad. In Manchester, for instance, where the cause of the new state system was embraced with enthusiasm, the local board built thirty-nine such schools before 1902; Leeds built sixty-one, with their local architect, Richard Adams, accounting for thirty-five of them **[122]**. Good examples include the Varna Street School, Manchester (1896–7), by Pots, Son & Pickup; and Conway Road, Birmingham (1900), by Martin & Martin. The separate-classroom model also prevailed in the voluntary sector, with many of the new (and most of the old) public schools

Fig. 120a

Medieval paradise. Aerial view of R. C. Carpenter's proposal for St Mary and St Nicholas College, Lancing, Sussex (*Illustrated London News*, Jan. 1856).

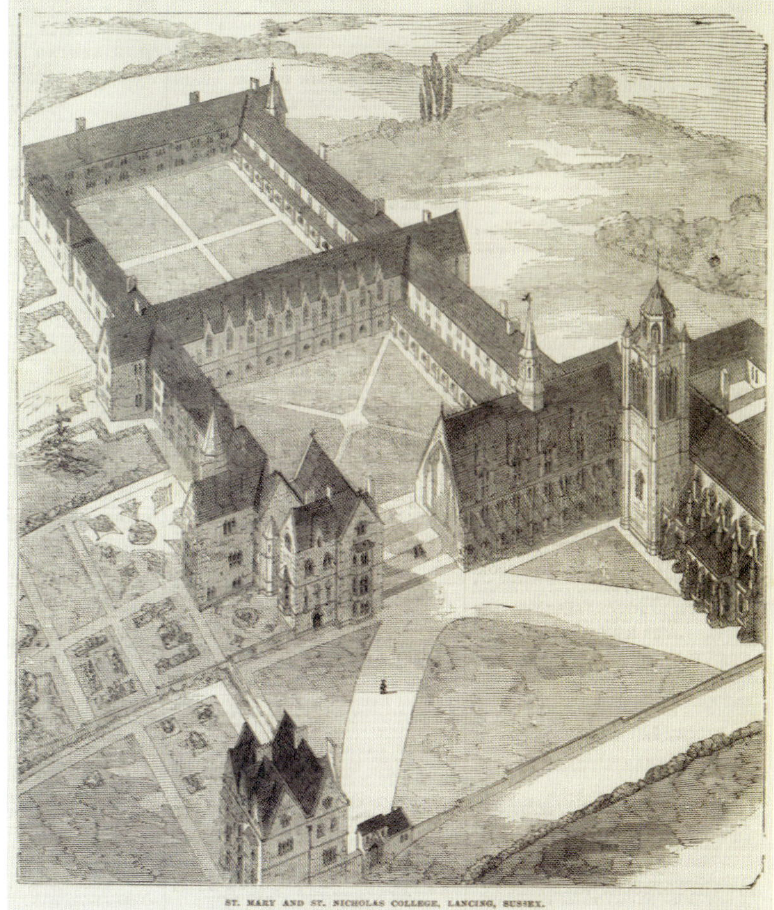

Fig. 120b

Christ's Hospital, Horsham (1897–1902), by Aston Webb & E. Ingress Bell.

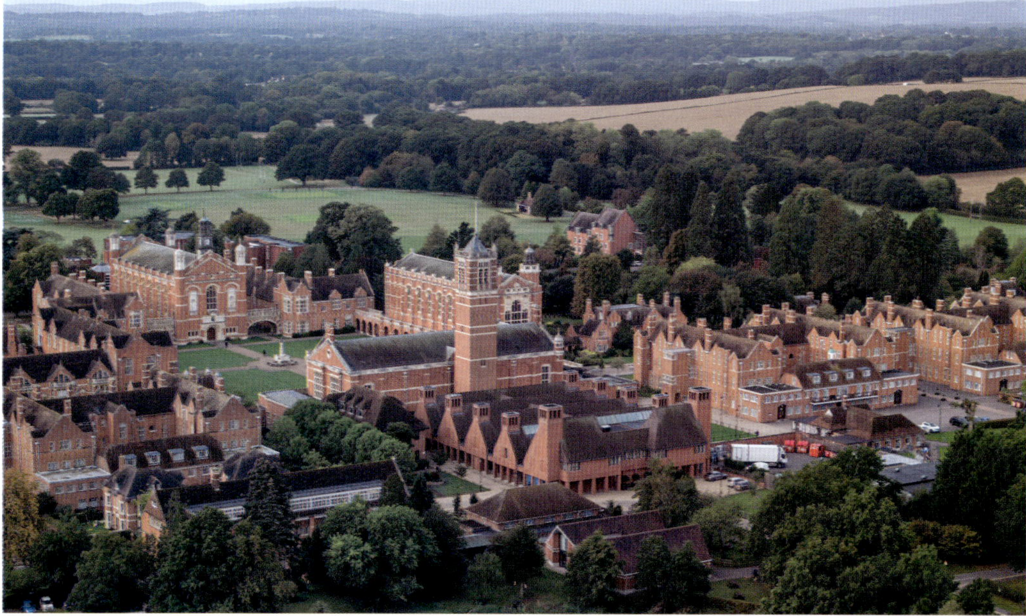

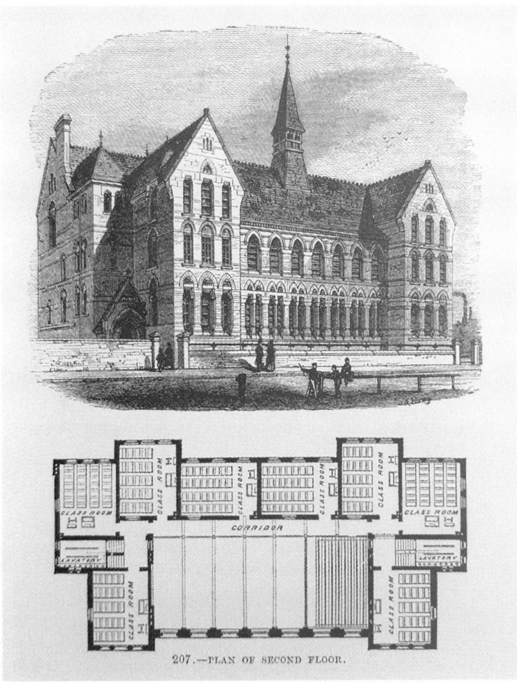

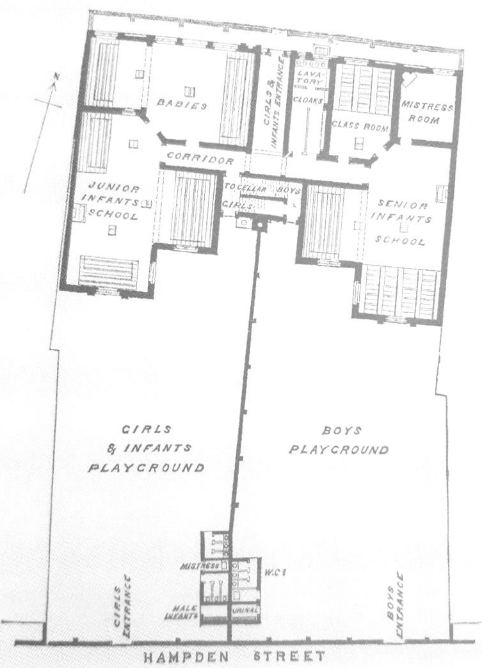

Fig. 121a

T. Roger Smith's design for Jonson Street School, Stepney (1871), London, based on German models.

Fig. 121b

Aldenham Street Board School, Camden (1874), London, by E. R. Robson.

embracing it to varying degrees. For instance, Alfred Waterhouse's design for the new St Paul's School, Hammersmith, in the early 1880s shows the extent of its influence.

Sending children to school was about more than just inculcating knowledge, however. As Robson himself admitted, school planning had by now become a 'science'. What this meant was that designing a school was also an exercise in how best to condition pupils socially, and the 'apparatus' required. This moral-cum-psychological dimension was summed up by Robson when he declared that the 'school-architect' was designing for

> children whose manners, morals, habits of order, cleanliness, and punctuality, temper, love of study and of the school, cannot fail to be in no inconsiderable degree affected by the attractive or repulsive situation, appearance, out-door convenience and in-door comfort, of the place where they are to spend a large part of the most impressionable period of their lives.[9]

Part of this 'appearance' had to do with the affect that the form and countenance of the building conveyed. This idea we have already encountered in relation to the new public schools, where a certain image of what such a school ought to be was communicated through its architecture. It was the same in the state sector. To this end, most school boards opted for a rather minimal, but not mean, brand of architecture in brick, in one or other historical style. Gothic and Renaissance styles soon took precedence. Although Gothic was seen by some as having residual and therefore inappropriate religious connotations for a non-sectarian system, it prevailed in Manchester until the 1890s, where the local board favoured a stripped-down Gothic for

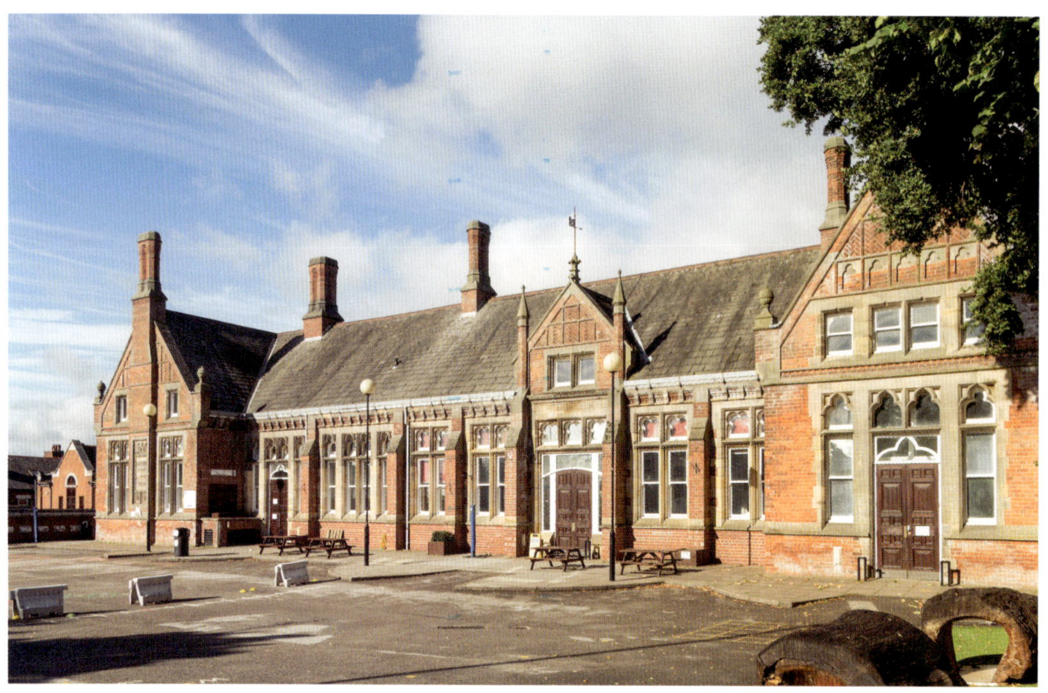

Fig. 122
Chapeltown Board School, Leeds (1878), Yorkshire, by Richard Adams.

many of its school buildings, such as those at Every Street (1876), by William Davies, and Upper Jackson Street (1883), by Royle & Bennett **[123a]**. This reflected something of the civic architectural identity that the Gothic had acquired in Manchester through such landmark buildings as the Town Hall and Assize Courts (see Chapter 4). In London, however, Queen Anne was the preferred style. Chosen for the quaint allusion of its historic national associations, it became all but characteristic of the London School Board during this period **[123b]**. To this extent, such buildings, believed Robson, were to be 'sermons in brick'. Thus, assured in their red, yellow, or brown (or combination thereof) stock brick facades, and towering as they did three or four storeys above their urban surrounds, each stood '"like a tall sentinel at his post", keeping watch over the interests of the generation that is to replace our own', recalled the social reformer Charles Booth.[10]

Inside, this noble mission was facilitated by the incorporation, by design, of principles concerning the latest in techniques of ventilation, lighting, and hygiene. Combined with the new separate-classroom system, board schools were therefore to be thoroughly 'modern' buildings. As in the voluntary system, this was understood in the context of 'conditioning' both the minds and bodies of pupils, and was applied to the smallest detail, including separate entrances for girls and boys. In relation to desks and furniture, it was observed that 'public interests and educational advantages' were to be held in consideration at all times. 'Anything', Robson noted, 'which contributes to proper physical training and to the development of a robust, healthy, and vigorous people cannot be deemed a minor or unimportant matter'. School furniture, therefore, had to take account of efficiencies in terms of strict functionality. In the case of desk design, correct posture, comfort, and visi-

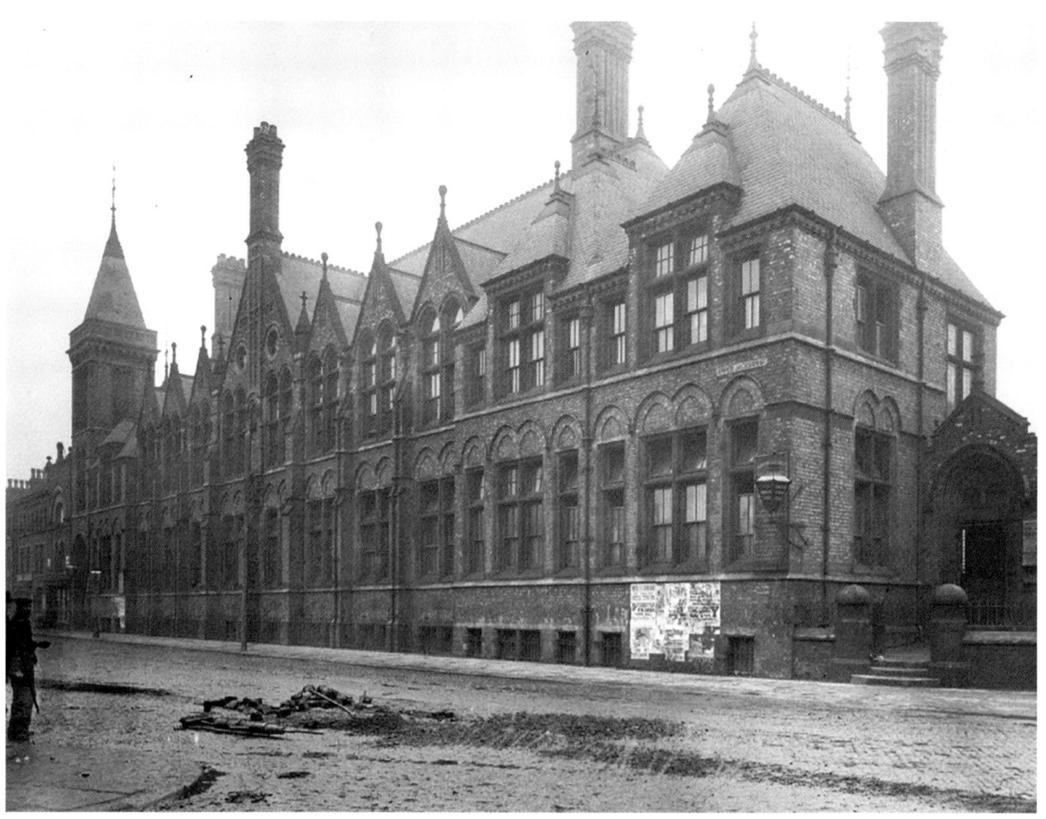

Fig. 123a

Upper Jackson Street Board School, Hulme, Manchester, by Royle & Bennett.

bility were key for the encouragement (if not enforcement) of 'regular and orderly' conduct **[124a]**. Again, German models were looked to. In this sense, the new classroom and its 'machinery' for learning was akin to a great contraption for manufacturing a better, smarter, and more resilient child-citizen.

As the nineteenth century wore on, these ideas played into concerns over national decline in the context of Great Power rivalry. The new citizen that the new schools were tasked with producing was now concerned with competitive national 'efficiency'. Glaring weaknesses exposed in the populace, especially the urban, owing to decades of poverty, malnourishment, and environmental degradation had created a physically and intellectually 'stunted' nation. Schools had to get better at rectifying this potentially disastrous situation, as Britain saw itself slipping behind in key areas of science, trade, and the military. In this respect, schools were now seen as 'tools' of social regeneration. In the voluntary sector, the craze for games and sport had been concerned with producing a 'fitter' specimen for serving king, country, and empire, but now a more academically focused curriculum was required. For schools of all types, corridors and smaller classrooms were implemented as ways of minimising disruption and facilitating focused learning; larger widows became *de rigueur* not only for more light and better ventilation, but to aid powers of productive attention **[124b]**; and more efficient, centralised heating systems were installed for a warmer and more comfortable work environment. In the state sector especially, better exercise spaces and

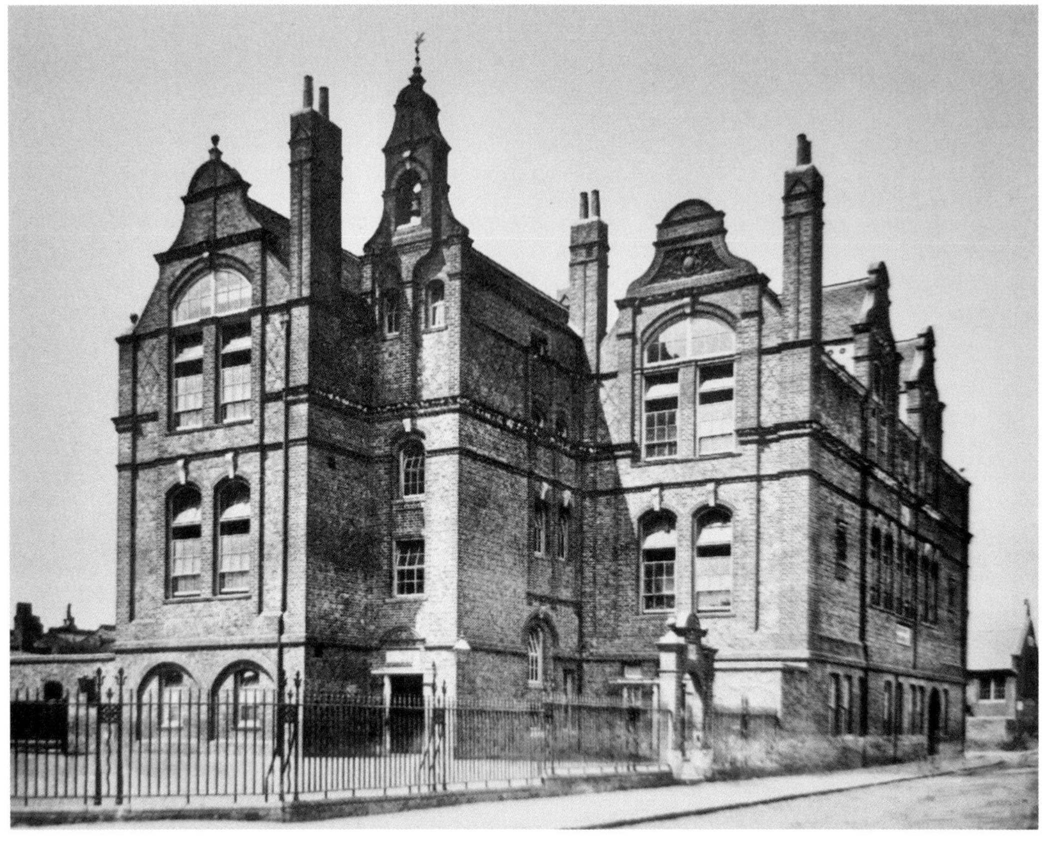

Fig. 123b
The Queen Anne aesthetic: Bonner Street Board School, Hackney (1875), London, by E. R. Robson.

associated management were introduced for elevating baseline physical fitness. At work here was a bio-political regime through which pupils would be 'moulded' according to a new and urgent set of national and imperial ideals.

Schools in the Wider British World

Abroad, similar patterns to those in Britain prevailed. Initially, as with voluntary schools throughout much of the United Kingdom, these were often religious and denominationally based, with small numbers attending. The first buildings were nearly always rudimentary, including the use of makeshift structures such as tents. Some were prefabricated in iron and sent from Britain. Indeed, missionaries played a key role in establishing basic, Western-style education in many parts of the wider British world. They were particularly active in places like Sub-Saharan Africa, British North America, and Australasia, where their focus was on converting, educating, and in many cases Westernising indigenous peoples. But they catered to settler colonial communities as well. Anglicans, Catholics, Methodists, and Presbyterians, among others, were all involved. Through this, notions of 'godliness and good learning', wedded to concepts of 'muscular Christianity', were inculcated. An early example of such an institution was St John's College, Auckland, founded in 1847 by the Anglican bishop of New Zealand, G. A. Selwyn **[125a]**. Writing to a friend in 1843, Selwyn noted how the

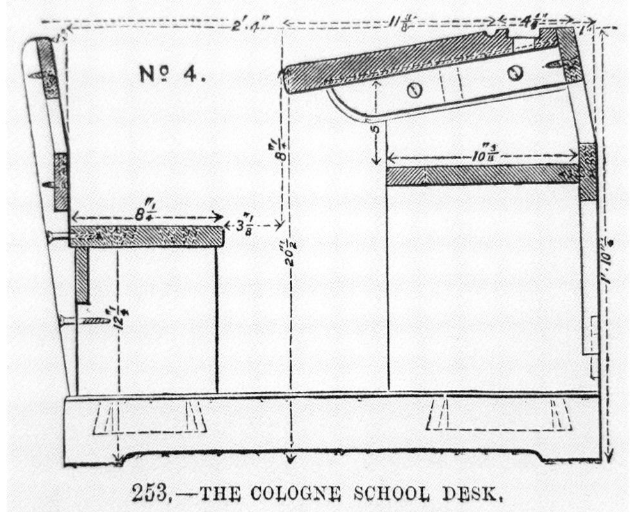

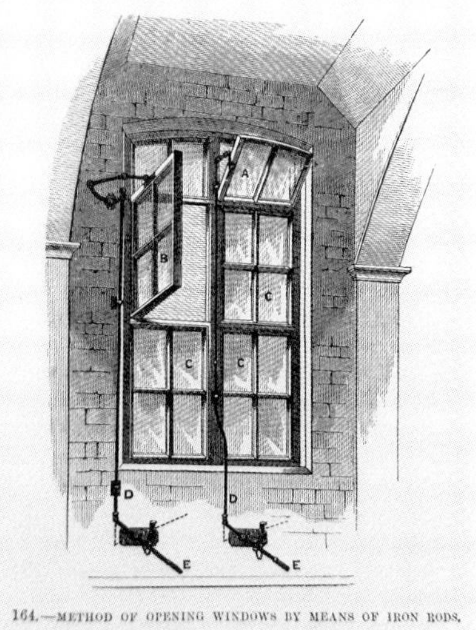

Fig. 124a

Illustrations from E. R. Robson's *School Architecture* (1874). Technical drawing, showing relative measurements, of the 'Cologne School Desk'.

Fig. 124b

Example of school window operable using iron rods.

school would be conducted upon the plan of Eton. It was a similar scenario at Bishop's College, Rondebosch (near Cape Town), in South Africa (est. 1849), except there the model was the 'new' communal system at Radley College, Oxfordshire. In some places, such as in the Australian colonies and Canada, state-funded non-sectarian systems were already active from the 1840s and 1850s. In such places indigenous children were separated. As in Britain, the basic aim was to instil good 'habits' of behaviour, including Christian values, and to promote assimilation in the case of indigenous children.

Given the context (remote from 'home' and alien), it is hardly surprising that familiar forms were turned to. Those carrying moral, religious, and historic connotations especially, such as Gothic and Tudor, were employed extensively. Considering the colony of Victoria in Australia, for instance, we see this not only in the buildings of private denominational schools, such as Melbourne (1856) and Geelong (1857) Church of England Grammar schools, or indeed the Roman Catholic Loreto College in Ballarat (1875), but also in state school buildings. With the passing of the 1872 Education Act in the Victorian parliament, the latter type became far more common. As in Britain, economy was paramount. Styles ranged from very plain Tudoresque to Gothic Revival, mostly in polychrome brick, and sometimes with stone detailing. Examples typical of the type include school No. 112, Carlton (1877), by Reed & Barnes; school No. 2605, also in Carlton (1884), by J. H. Kelleher; and school Nos. 210, Eaglehawk, and 307, North Melbourne (1882), both by H. R. Bastow, architect to the Victorian education department **[125b]**. In adopting the Gothic Revival, these schools tended to follow Manchester's lead rather than London's. The Robson planning reforms eventually filtered through, too, with many features similar to those found in Britain. A comparable approach was taken in other parts of Australia. Here we may point to the Model School in Burra, South Australia (1878), for instance. Also in South Australia, at Poonindie, we find an example of a 'native training institution', at which indigenous people, having been forcibly removed from their tribal settings, were educated and taught trade skills with a view to

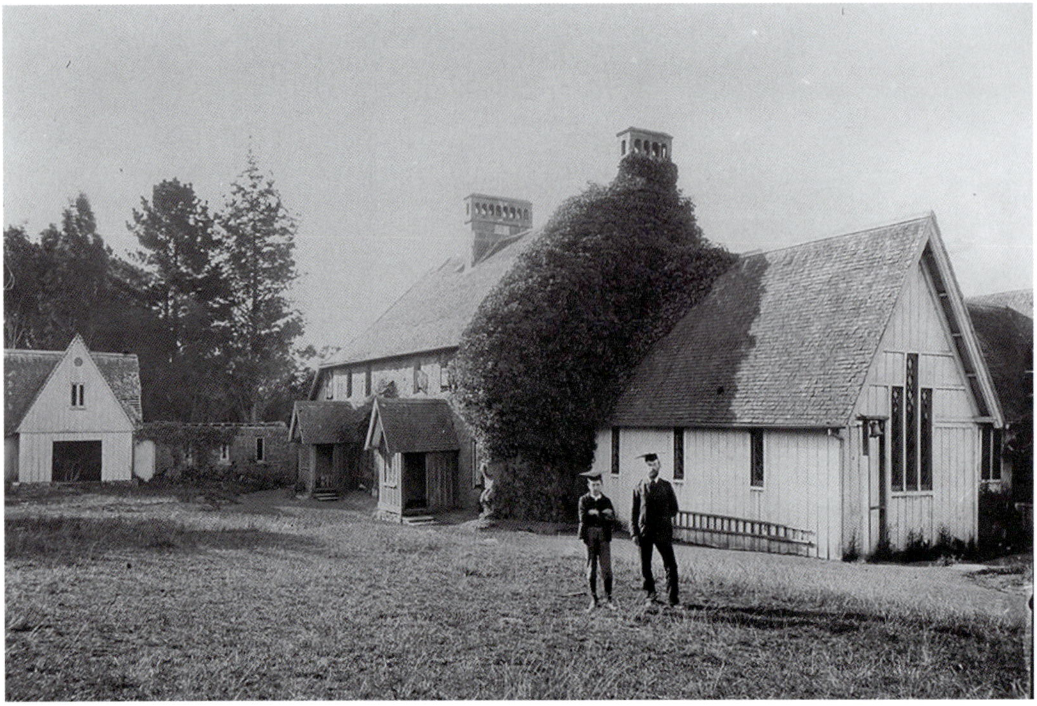

Fig. 125a

St John's College, Auckland, New Zealand, founded 1847. Photograph (1890) looking north-west showing the library (right), a scholar, and headmaster (Thomas King).

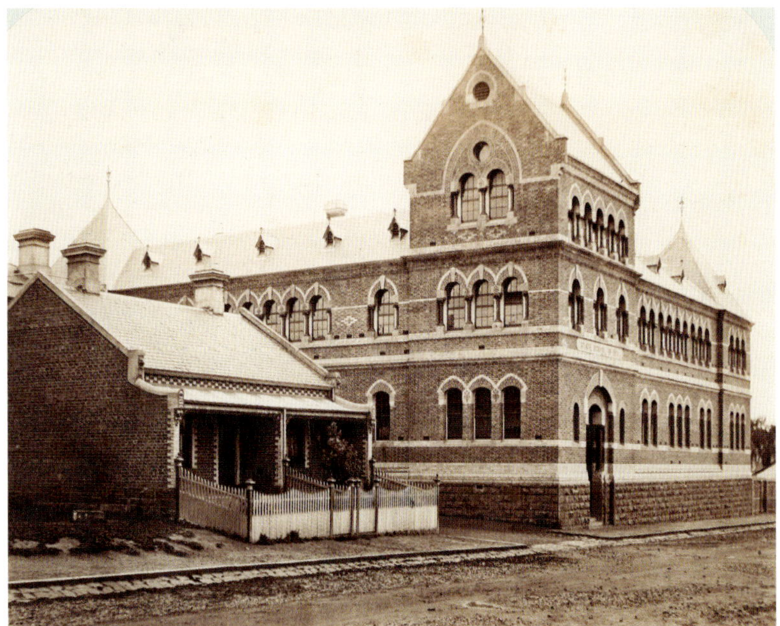

Fig. 125b

Cambridge Street school, Collingwood (1877), Melbourne, Australia, by H. R. Bastow.

assimilation **[126]**. The school room-cum-chapel (1855) here demonstrated the reach of medievalising tendencies in British educational architecture.

In British India the hybrid approach of the Indo-Saracenic was encouraged (see Chapter 4). The leading private schools there of the Victorian era were partly understood as institutions for inculcating Western knowledge and mores, thus creating a new, more sympathetic Indian elite. Distinguished among this class of building were Kolhapur High School (1873) and Mayo College, Ajmer (1875), the so-called 'Eton of the East', both by Major Charles Mant. Spatially, however, these buildings were very much imports, with Mayo College adopting what appears to have been the classic Scottish 'burgh school' model. Such architecture, despite its appearance, was active in facilitating new disciplinary regimes through its enforcing a type of spatial arrangement that was both peculiar and alien.

Higher Education Facilities

The Victorian period was of course one that saw the origins of the modern university sector as we know it today. A growing population, alongside the rise of professionalism and the need for specialist technical knowledge in the context of industrialisation, meant that higher forms of education were required more than ever. The ancient universities of England, Scotland, and Ireland had serviced what need there had been prior to this moment, with the founding of a small number of additional ones in the early nineteenth century, including University College, London (1826), and Durham University (1832). In the establishment of such full-blown institutions, the colonies were rather ahead of the mother country, with universities appearing in Toronto, Sydney, Melbourne, Bombay, Calcutta, and Madras in the 1850s. Although a new university was created by act of parliament in Aberdeen in 1860 from the existing King's and Marischal colleges, new 'universities' in England usually began life as civic colleges of specialist or further education, before later receiving royal charters as universities. Such institutions had appeared in

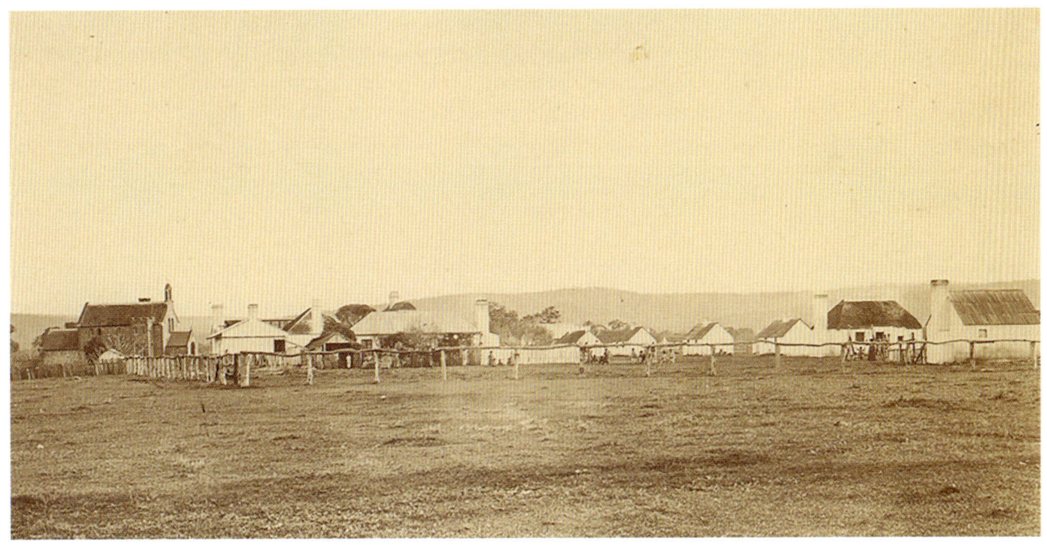

Fig. 126
'Native training institution' (mission school), Poonindie, South Australia, est. 1850. Note the Romanesque-style chapel at far left.

Birmingham (1843), Manchester (1851), Newcastle (1871), Aberystwyth (1872), Leeds (1875), Nottingham and Sheffield (1879), and Liverpool (1882), among other locations, resulting in the rise of the so-called Victorian 'redbrick' university.[11] Central to the rise of this new higher education phenomenon was philanthropy, mostly from industrial magnates and businessmen, who ploughed millions into its realisation.

Buildings and infrastructure were a major part of this. Alfred Waterhouse's rebuilding of Owens College (1871–3), the forerunner to Manchester University, was rather typical in the sense that more modern, coherently planned, and better-equipped spaces and facilities were at the heart of what such an institution ought to be, including state-of-the-art laboratories and extensive library facilities **[127a]**. In such educational settings one could also detect appeals to 'discipline'. At the missionary training centre of St Augustine's College, Canterbury (1845–8), for instance, William Butterfield, under instruction from the college authorities, deliberately created a Spartan environment in order to condition and thus prepare students for what lay ahead.[12] Moreover, as with wider school reforms, universities and colleges of further education were expanded and rebuilt in the context of perceived industrial decline in Britain, where inculcating new forms of technocratic knowledge was understood as fundamental to the 'efficiency' movement.

Stylistically there was a broad desire to emulate ancient English, even European, precedent. Naturally, the Gothic-cum-Tudor aesthetic, with its apparent connotations of lofty learning, was popular. Waterhouse's work at Owens was original yet familiar in this regard. Earlier we find the transmittance of this inherent symbolism in Pugin's design for St Patrick's College, Maynooth, a new quadrangle to which he added in 1846–52. There was also Queen's College, Cork (1846), by Thomas Deane and Benjamin Woodward, newly established under the Queen's Colleges (Ireland) Act of 1845, which included institutions at Galway (now University College) and Belfast (now Queen's University), which drew influence in particular from Oxbridge collegiate models **[127b]**. Indeed, Oxford and Cambridge themselves underwent considerable expansion and rebuilding during this period, with numerous structures added by the likes of G. G. Scott, Alfred Waterhouse, and T. G. Jackson. Some of these were in a traditional Gothic or Tudor style, others in something more akin to the Renaissance Revival. In some cases entire new colleges were got up, such as the brilliant polychrome Gothic Revival of William Butterfield's Keble College, Oxford (1867–83) **[53]**, or Waterhouse's more monochrome, domestic-scale Gothic at Girton College, Cambridge (begun 1872).

As mentioned, in the British colonial world there was the prominent example of the University of Sydney (est. 1850), the main buildings for which were erected between 1855 and 1862 to the designs of the English émigré architect Edmund Blacket **[128a]**. Likewise, these were in a Tudor Gothic style typical of Oxbridge collegiate architecture, with the Great Hall recalling the medieval grandeur of Westminster Hall in London. A similar approach was taken at Melbourne. Perhaps the finest example of such architecture, however, is to be found at the University of Bombay (1869–78), with its carefully considered 'Eastern' variant of the Gothic Revival by G. G. Scott

Fig. 127a

Owens College (1871–3), later Manchester University, Manchester, by Alfred Waterhouse.

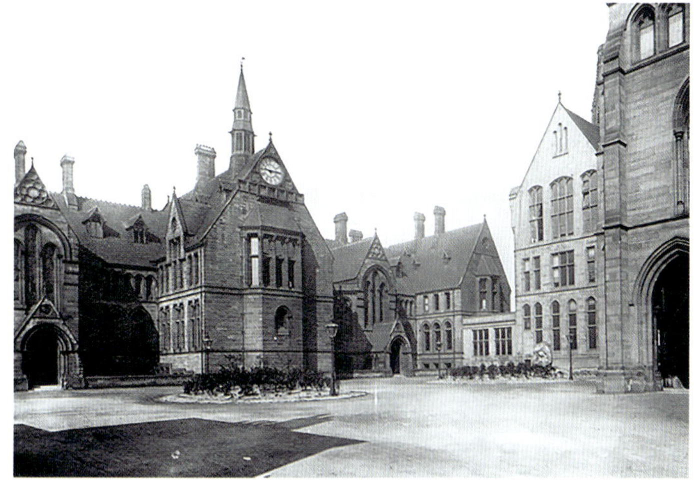

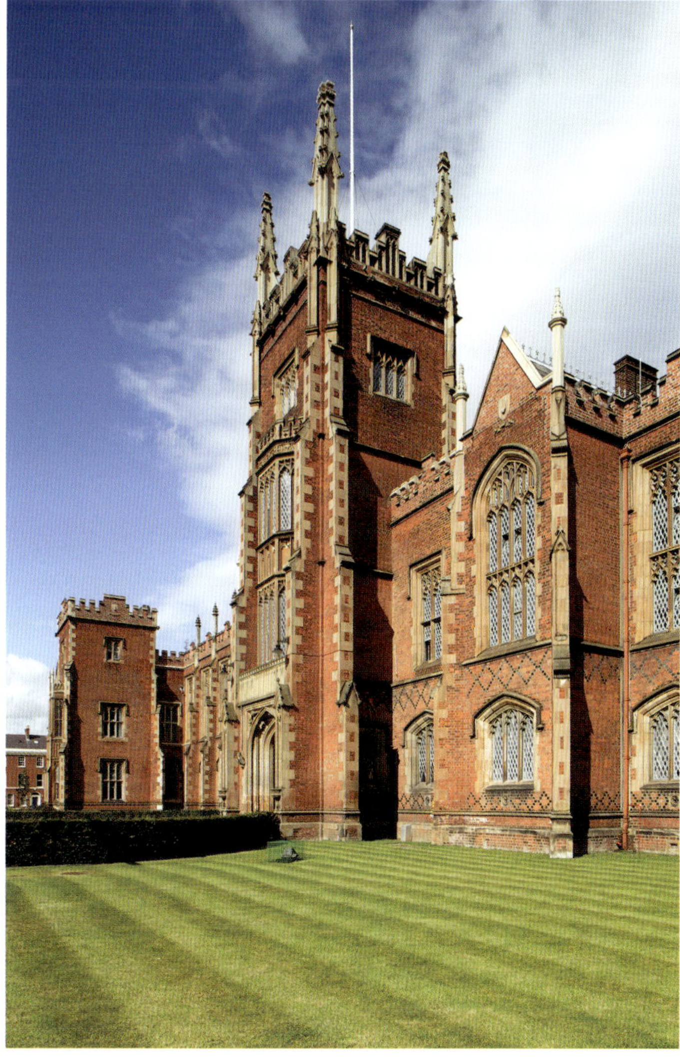

Fig. 127b

Queen's College (now University), Belfast (1849), by Charles Lanyon.

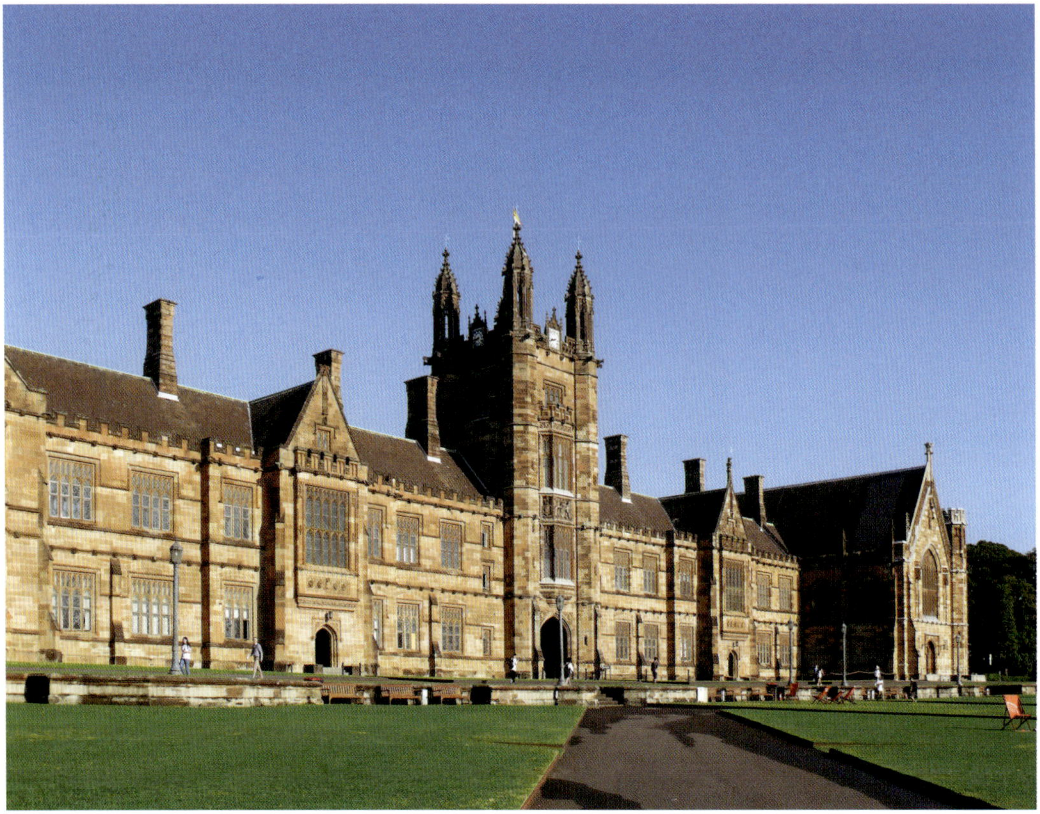

Fig. 128a

Great Hall, University of Sydney (1855–62), Australia, by Edmund Blacket.

Fig. 128b

Hall, University of Bombay (1869–78), India, by George Gilbert Scott, with some local amendments by George Twigge-Molecey and Walter Paris.

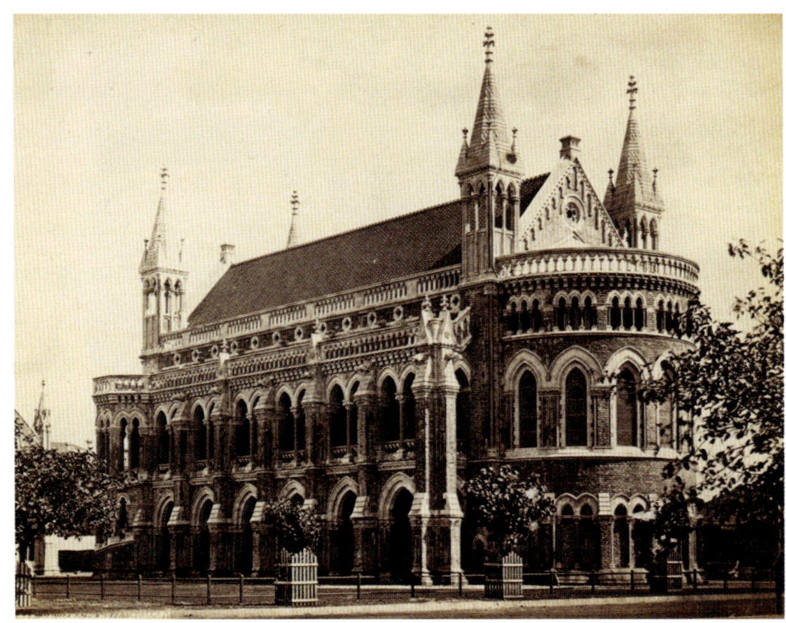

[128b]. This amazing ensemble of buildings was largely funded by wealthy Parsi businessmen and philanthropists in Bombay, highlighting the so-called 'joint enterprise' between the mutual interests of these communities and the colonial authorities. The colonial university system also supported the creation of a network of knowledge enhancement and exchange that advantaged the British world.

Alternatives to the Gothic-cum-Tudor model could be found, too. Among the first structures at McGill University, Montreal, for instance, was the Arts Building (1843), by John Ostell, in a stripped-back Neo-Grecian style **[129a]**. Scottish influences were carried abroad by the large numbers of Scotsmen who populated the empire. For example, the main buildings at the University of Otago in Dunedin, New Zealand (1878–83) recalled G. G. Scott's rebuilding of the University of Glasgow in the early 1870s, especially the distinguished clock tower. A similar experiment was undertaken at the Presbyterian Ormond College (1879–93), University of Melbourne. Here one might also mention Theological Hall (1879) at Queen's University in Kingston, Ontario, which opted for an earlier Romanesque-style architecture **[129b]**. Indeed, by the time we reach the 1870s and 1880s, greater diversity in university architecture is generally evident. At the University of Adelaide, for instance, the Mitchell Building (1879–82) by William McMinn displays distinct High Victorian overtones in its polychrome eclecticism. These institutions were founded in a climate of burgeoning colonial confidence, representing a degree of colonial self-consciousness and rivalry.

Fig. 129a

Arts Building (1843), McGill University, Montreal, Canada, by John Ostell.

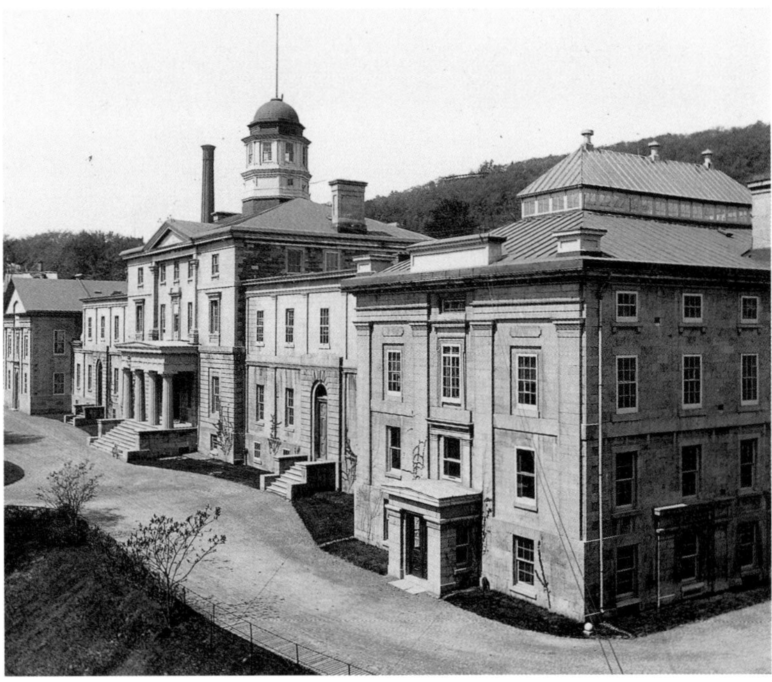

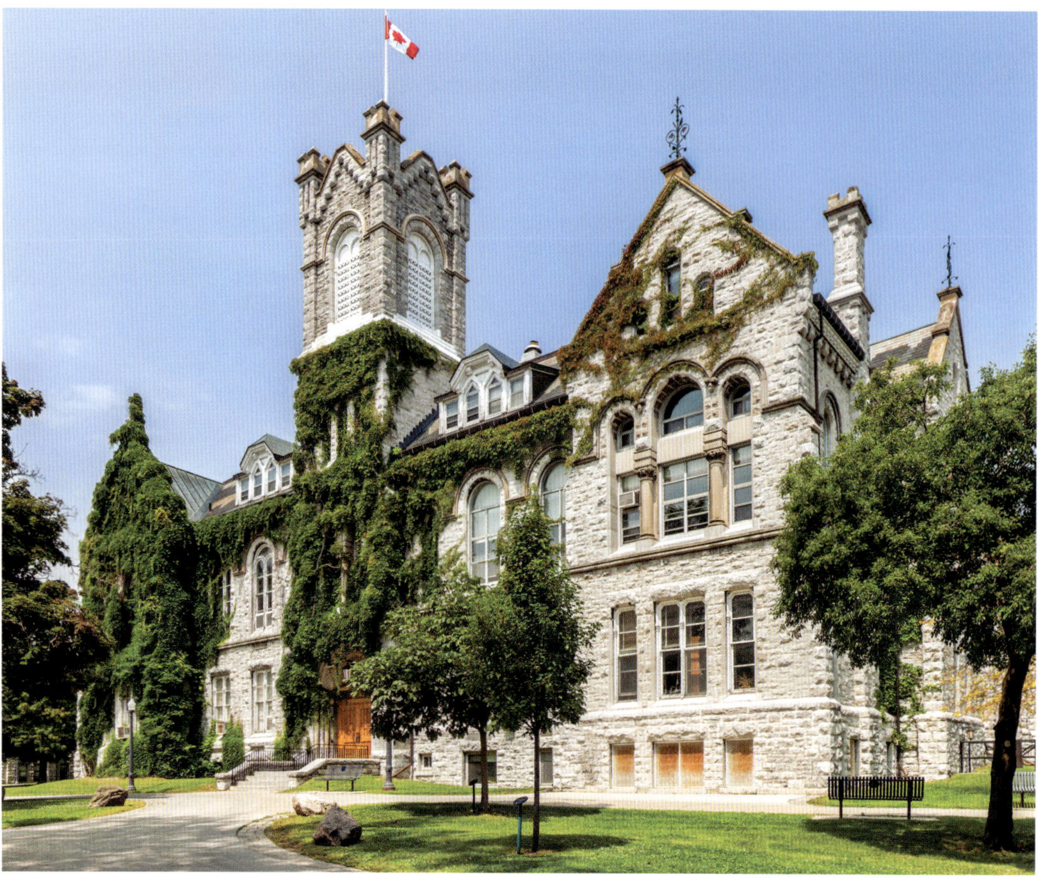

Fig. 129b

Theological Hall (1879), Queen's University, Kingston, Ontario, in Canada, by Gordon & Helliwell.

Architectures of Health: Curing and Conditioning the Sick

During the Victorian period tremendous changes took place not only in the organisation and sanitation of such facilities but also in their design. In the case of hospital architecture, much of this was down to the vision and effort of Florence Nightingale, but other pioneers were involved, such as the Scottish surgeon John Roberton, and the campaigning editor of *The Builder*, George Godwin (a friend of Nightingale's).[13] The reforms in hospital planning and hygiene that these campaigners initiated were all aimed at systematising and streamlining regimes of treatment and care. Combined, the principles they introduced dominated hospital design and management well into the twentieth century. Some of these remain with us to this day, such as Nightingale's insistence on the mandatory washing of hands.

These reforms were made famous by Nightingale's views on modern nursing practices. A close associate of Edwin Chadwick, Nightingale came to prominence during the Crimean War in the mid-1850s. By mistakenly invoking the 'miasma' or zymotic theory of disease transmission (i.e., bad air), she was nevertheless able to show that the horrendous casualty rates of the war were not down to deaths on the battlefield, or by wounds, but by disease and infection transmitted while wounded soldiers were convalescing in military hospitals. So moved was she by the plight of British soldiers, she took it upon herself to corral a group of over fifty nurses to go to Crimea in an effort to reorganise and cleanse the filthy and chaotic conditions. For this she is credited as the 'mother' of modern nursing. Indeed, in developing the modern pie chart ('rose' diagram), Nightingale was able to show in dramatic fashion the comparative causes of mortality in the initial stages of the war, in the process making a significant contribution to the visualisation of statistics.

Along with the insights and assistance of Roberton and Godwin, Nightingale essentially revolutionised modern hospital care by completely rationalising and regimenting it, including implementing very strict rules concerning sanitation and round-the-clock inspection. Nursing staff in particular were to be 'trained', becoming professional and disciplined in ways hitherto unknown. In so doing, hospitals could be made to run as clockwork, effectively machine-like. Science and clinical knowledge were brought to bear at every juncture. Nothing was left to chance, nothing unattended. All was to be exposed and expunged. As Nightingale later observed, it was strange for her to have to point out that the 'very first requirement in a Hospital' is that it 'should do the sick no harm'.[14]

With this idea in mind, Roberton, Nightingale, Godwin, and others insisted that patient wards in hospitals ought to be modelled on what was known as the 'pavilion system', being the provision of elongated, single-volume spaces that could be opened either side along their major axis. This was advised on the grounds that it would not only allow copious amounts of light into the space but, most importantly of all, allow for cross ventilation to clear out the foul air and therefore prevent (it was believed) the spread of disease. Indeed, Nightingale wrote a widely acclaimed, critical account of hospital design and management based on her experiences in the Crimea and elsewhere, entitled *Notes on Hospitals* (1859, enlarged 1863). Perusing the content pages of this book one gets a very clear idea of Nightingale's thinking, with subjects such as 'defective means of ventilation and warming', 'defects in drainage, water-closets, etc.', and 'defective hospital kitchens', among others. In Britain, the pavilion system—based on hospitals in France such as Lariboisière in Paris (1846–54), and the military hospital at Vincennes (1858)—would eventually become known as the 'Nightingale ward'.

Apart from the basic principle of having open, cross-ventilated wards, hospitals ought to separate (even isolate) specific functions from one another, such as kitchens, sanitary compartments, accommodation, sick wards, linen storage, etc., rather than lumping all these together. Nightingale, with several of her architect and social reforming friends, including Godwin's campaigns in *The Builder*, fought hard to have these principles adopted in the building of British hospitals, ultimately with great success. In fact, virtually every hospital built in Britain from about the 1860s up until around the turn of the twentieth century incorporated their ideas on the pavilion system. Early prominent examples included Blackburn Infirmary (1859–61), by James Turnbull; Buckinghamshire Infirmary (1861–2), by David Brandon **[130a]**; Herbert Military Hospital, Woolwich (1861–5), by Cpt. Douglas Galton; and Leeds General Infirmary (1864–8), by G. G. Scott. Later came St Thomas's Hospital, London (1868–71), by Henry Currey; the Royal Infirmary, Edinburgh (1872–9), by David Bryce; and University

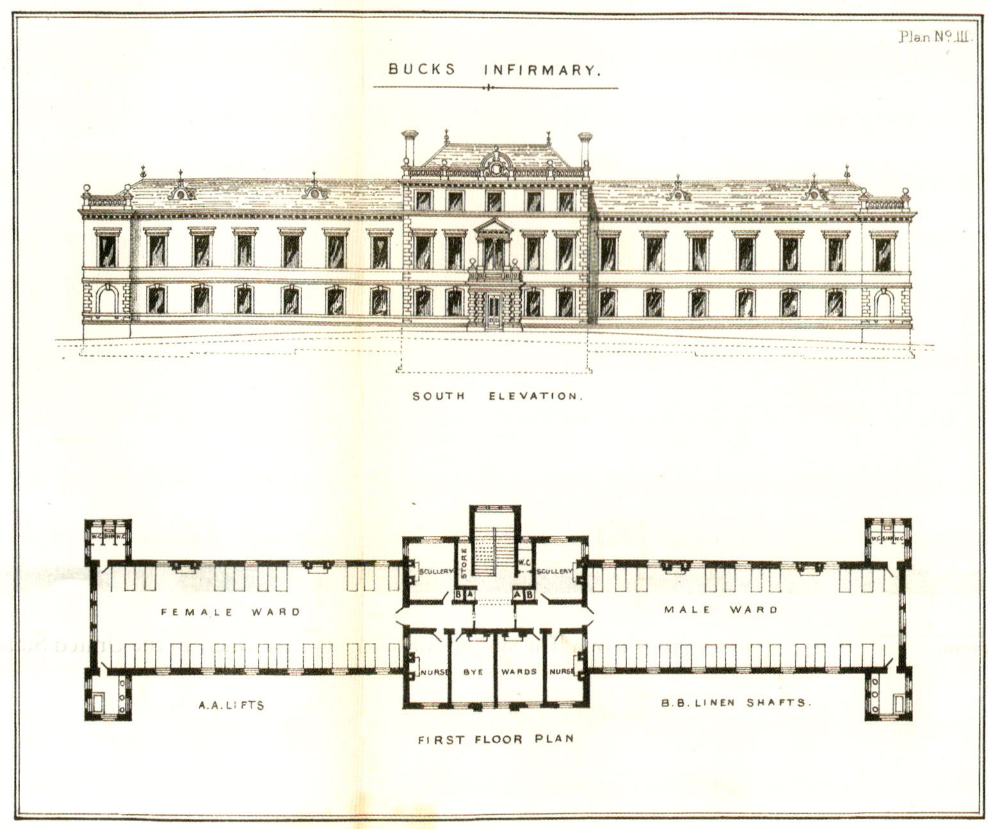

Fig. 130a

Elevation and plan, Buckinghamshire Infirmary (1861–2), by David Brandon.

College Hospital, London (1897–1906), by Alfred Waterhouse, the latter with its novel cruciform plan.

The concept naturally migrated overseas, into the wider British world. In tropical contexts, the pavilion system was adopted in an effort to combat elevated levels of miasma ('bad air') that was understood (until the advent of germ theory) as being responsible for high mortality rates, especially among European soldiers. Controlling disease was clearly important for effective imperial administration.[15] Examples include the Sir Takhtasinhji Hospital, Bhavnagar, India (*c.*1879), by William Emerson; the Prince Alfred Hospital, Sydney, Australia (1876–82), by Mansfield Bros.; the Military Hospital at Valletta, in Malta (*c.*1884), by E. Ingress Bell and Maj.-Gen. Andrew Clarke; and the Royal Victoria Hospital in Montreal (1887–93), by Henry Saxon Snell **[130b]**. Indeed, Snell represented what had become by this time a new breed of specialist healthcare architect. Ranging over three to five storeys, his design for the hospital at Montreal incorporated the pavilion ward system throughout, where patients could be separated according to illness, sex, and age.[16] The building's form was based on the Scots Baronial aesthetic of the Royal Infirmary in Edinburgh, which is not entirely surprising given that the project's principal donors were prominent Scottish businessmen in Canada, including Donald Alexander Smith, 1st

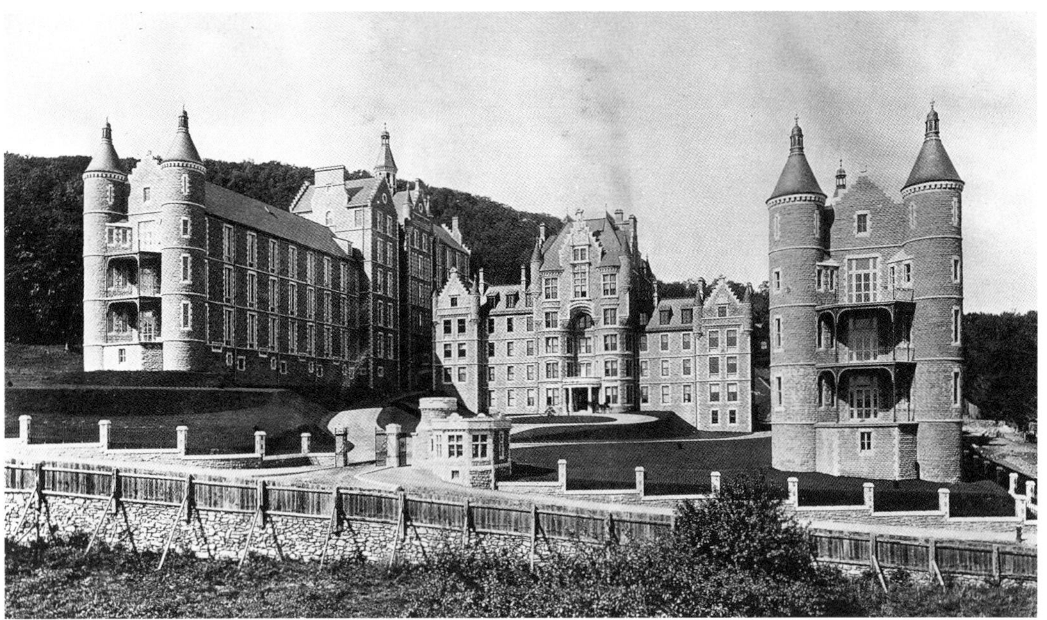

Fig. 130b
Royal Victoria Hospital, Montreal (1887–93), Canada, by Henry Saxon Snell.

baron Strathcona. The system was also adopted widely in the United States, with the Johns Hopkins Hospital, Baltimore (1877–89), designed by surgeon J. S. Billing with assistance from the architect J. R. Niernsee, being a prime example.

There were also important contributions made by indigenous, non-European architects in this area, such as the civil engineer Khan Bahadur Muncherji Cowasji Murzban. During his employment at the Bombay public works department, Murzban designed a number of indigenous medical and educational facilities under the collaborative 'joint enterprise' initiative established between the colonial authorities and local Parsi philanthropists. Counted among these facilities are the Pestanji Hormusji Cama Hospital for Women and Children (1883–6) **[131]**, the Bomanji Edalji Allbless Obstetrics Hospital (1891), and the Parsi Lying-in Hospital (1895). These buildings are exquisite if somewhat idiosyncratic renditions of that rather heavy, polychrome Gothic style typical of late-nineteenth-century public works architecture in Bombay, adapted to the climate. Rather than merely aping stylistic trends emanating from Europe, however, this architecture was understood as a response to the Parsi community's own reformed attitudes towards enlightened modernity through modern medicine.[17]

The demise of the pavilion system came with the advent of mechanical ventilation in hospital design. This was in part necessary for the purification of air from external sources, which in urban areas was heavily polluted. The Royal Victoria Hospital, Belfast (1899–1903), by Henman & Cooper of Birmingham, with assistance from the engineers Henry Lea and Samuel Cleland Davidson, was the first to operate this model based on a densely compact, single-storey, top-lit plan **[132a]**. Like a great machine for air-conditioning, the ducted system, with huge, slow-turning axial flow fans which functioned on residual steam from the hospital's laundry, forced fil-

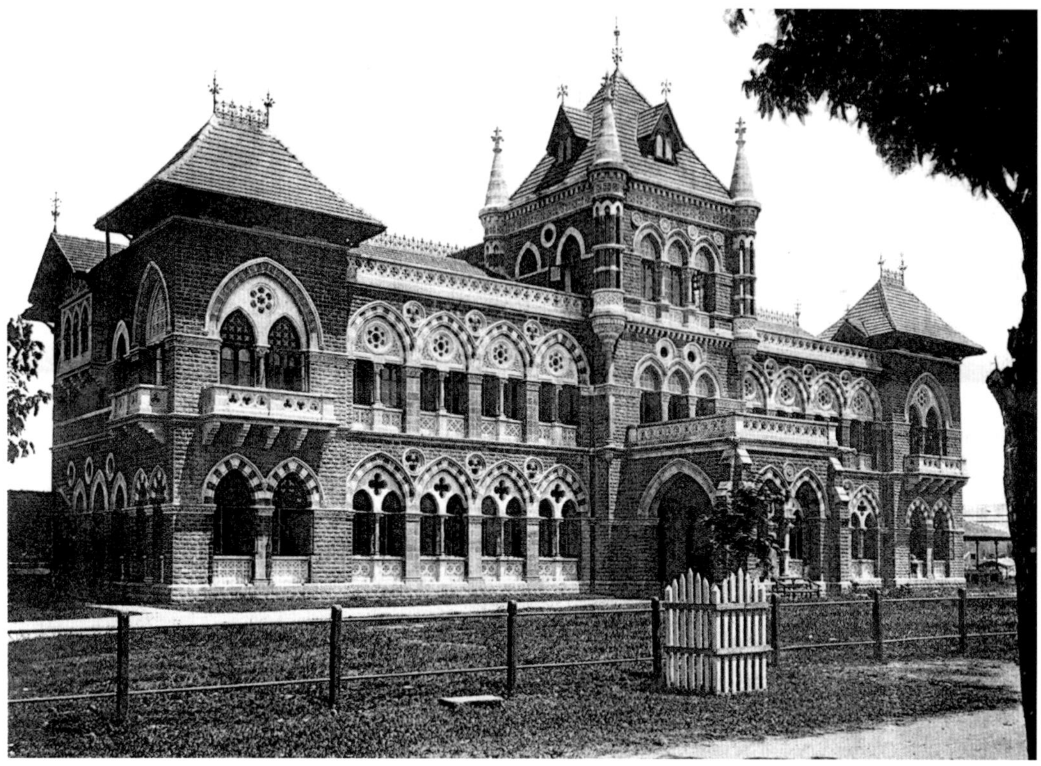

Fig. 131
Pestanji Hormusji Cama Hospital for Women and Children (1883–6), Bombay (Mumbai), India, by Khan Bahadur Muncherji Cowasji Murzban.

tered air through the building via strategically located registers and slots, before leaving through vertical risers in the roof. Such an arrangement made for more efficient use of space, as well as thermal insulation, becoming the basis for hospital design in the twentieth century.

Asylums

Asylums had a similar clinical and therapeutic purpose to hospitals, and their buildings shared many characteristics in common. Prior to the 1845 Lunatics Act (1857 in Scotland), the mentally ill in Britain were not catered for particularly well. The science of psychiatry had yet to develop, and most 'lunatics' were, on the whole, either confined in smaller licensed institutions, or often ended up misallocated in places such as workhouses or even prisons. Following the Lunatics Act, however, a spate of state-funded asylums were built throughout Britain and the wider British world, especially for so-called pauper lunatics. This reform was part of wider advances in institutional knowledge and culture in Victorian Britain. But the advance of modern medical psychiatry, with its clinical diagnosis of 'deviance', was also something of a socially and professionally manufactured phenomenon, set against the backdrop of industrialisation, political reform, and the evolution of a mature market economy. The new forms of official bureaucratisation that followed aided in the distinction and categorisation of problematic sections of the population, setting them aside physically and symbolically as being in need of 'efficient' segregation, control, and treatment. The rise of a culture concerning the therapeutic medicalisation of the 'insane' thus

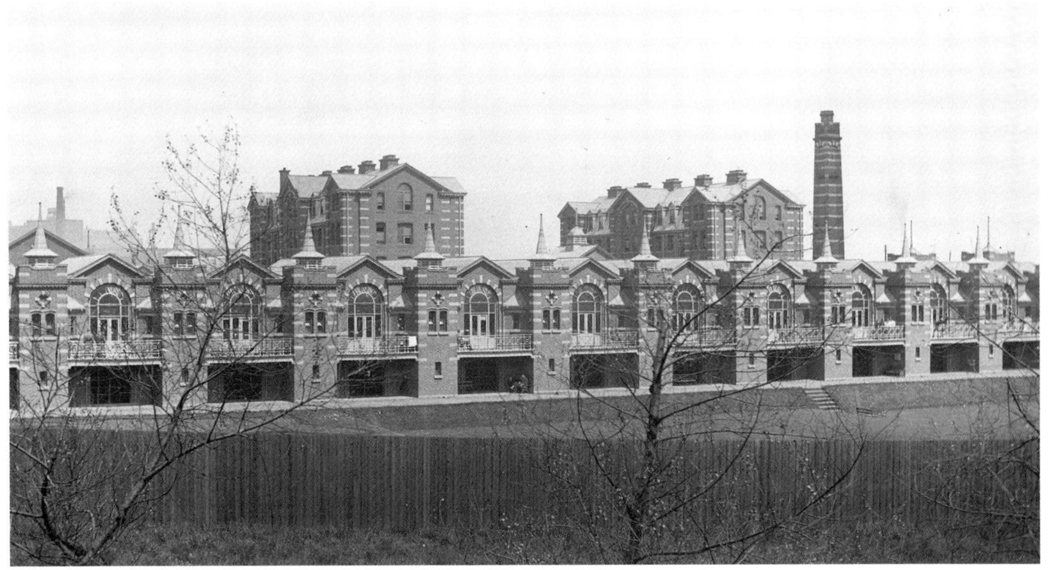

Fig. 132a

Royal Victoria Hospital, Belfast (1899–1903), by Henman & Cooper.

involved specialist claims over prescription and intervention, characterised by the assertion of professional understanding. This enabled the steady institutionalisation of the whole category of 'madness', including its architectural (i.e., spatial) ramifications. This, as some scholars have claimed, led directly to the advent of the asylum.[18]

Between 1847 and 1914, over eighty purpose-built asylums for the 'insane and idiotic' were erected in England and Wales alone. Typically, the Victorian asylum aimed at creating a healthful environment, of 'attractive' architecture situated in open, well-planted grounds, and, where possible, located in rural or semi-rural surroundings. Such care was taken that the grounds of many of these asylums, whether pauper or private (middling class), were arranged by professional landscape designers, horticulturalists, and nurserymen, and often likened to the estates of large country houses. They were also based on the principle of 'non-restraint', and concerned with the moral as opposed to physical 'management' of patients. Indeed, by 1847 manuals on how to build asylums, and best treat those within, were being published by leading physicians, such as Edward Charlesworth's *Remarks on the Treatment of the Insane* (1828) and John Conolly's *The Construction and Government of Lunatic Asylums* (1847). As Conolly observed, unlike so many previous institutions, the new asylum type was concerned with 'the recovery of the curable, and the improvement of the incurable', not to mention the 'comfort and happiness of all patients'. This, he added, ought to be kept in mind at all times by architects charged with the design of such buildings, amounting in effect to an environmental determinist approach to the treatment of insanity.[19] His recommendations would take the asylum as Britons knew it from a building that resembled a prison to one that was akin to a hospital. The government's Lunacy Commission, partly in response to Conolly's criticism of it, would later publish advice for architects based on his views in the form of a pamphlet entitled *Suggestions for the (1) Sites: (2) Construction and Arrangement of Buildings: (3) Plans: of Lunatic Asylums*

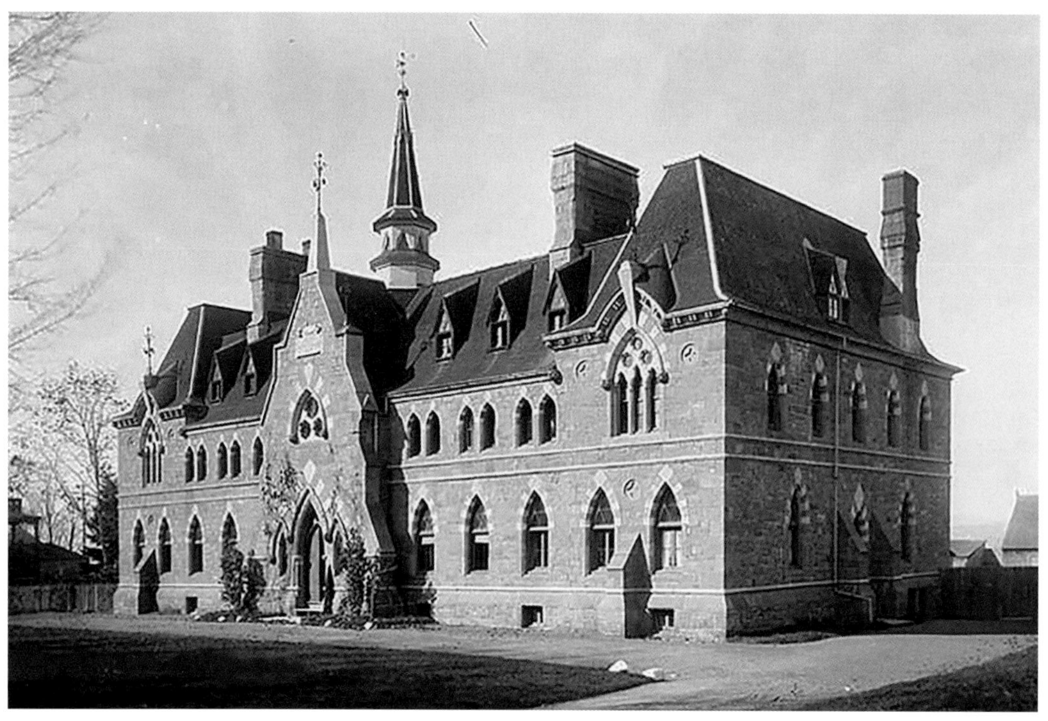

Fig. 132b

Finlay Asylum, Quebec City (1860–2), Canada, by Stent & Laver.

(1856, 1870). It is clear in these instructions that the asylum is posited as an apparatus of conversion and therapy as opposed to a place merely to remove and house the insane.

Like so many of the institutions we have considered so far in this chapter, whether prisons, workhouses, schools, or hospitals, the planning of Victorian asylum buildings was dictated by the judicious use of corridors, often long and straight, connected to an administrative or service core. This not only had obvious surveillance implications, but also assisted greatly in the rationalisation and therefore functionality (i.e., operability) of the space, giving the structure a purpose-driven, institutional character. The asylum's facilitation of confinement, circulation, and inspection as such, through which claims for 'new' possibilities in treatment were constituted and justified, made for a kind of 'corridoric machine'.[20] It was claimed, for instance, that the new Middlesex Asylum at Colney Hatch (1849–51), by W. B. Thomas, contained no less than six miles of accumulated corridor space. Clarity and intent of movement in this respect was key to the Victorian asylum's projected ambition.

There are many such asylum buildings one can point to that illustrate these Victorian reforms. Most major cities had several in their vicinity by the close of the nineteenth century, servicing a spectrum of conditions, including for the criminally insane. They also ranged in size, from a few hundred patients up to a few thousand. Noted architects were involved, such as G. G. Scott and Arthur Blomfield, among others. Commission by competition was also common; but, as with other specific building types, specialist architects soon emerged, including G. T. Hine and C. H. Howell. It is not surprising either that a specialist prison designer like Jebb was engaged to plan the Criminal Lunatic Asylum at Broadmoor (1863), in Berkshire, despite the multiple defects that ultimately marred the building.

Typically, an asylum plan was mirrored along a central axis, allowing for separation of the sexes (wholly consistent in Victorian institutions), as well as division according to age and severity of illness, or what was sometimes referred to as a patient's state of 'tranquillity'. Much, but not all, of the accommodation was set aside for single occupation. We see an early example of this model at the Derbyshire County Asylum (1844–9), by Paterson & Duesbury, where rooms are strung along extensive corridors, connected through servicing and administrative spaces, surrounded at the front and sides by enclosed 'airing courts', all set within seventy acres of grounds **[133]**. Like many schools and hospitals, asylums were usually austere inside, but, according to theories of therapeutic attractiveness, could be architecturally pretentious externally. Various styles were employed, but Italianate Classicism and Tudoresque proved popular, as seen at Middlesex Asylum (mentioned above); the North Wales Lunatic Asylum, Denbigh (1844–8), by Thomas Fulljames; or the City of London Lunatic Asylum ('Stone House'), in Stone (1862–6), Kent, by J. B. Bunning. Some were built in the Gothic style, such as the rather elaborate Essex County Lunatic Asylum, Warley (1851–3), by Kendall & Pope; the Eglinton Lunatic Asylum, Cork (1847–52), by William Atkins; or the Finlay Asylum, Quebec City (1860–2), Canada, by Stent & Laver **[132b]**.

Indeed, the logic of the Victorian asylum system meshed with colonial needs and experience. Jebb, it turns out, was advised in the planning of Broadmoor by Dr John Meyer, who had served for nine years as medical superintendent at the criminal lunatic asylum in the penal settlement at

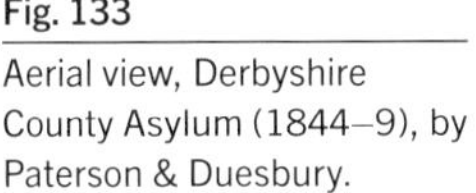

Fig. 133

Aerial view, Derbyshire County Asylum (1844–9), by Paterson & Duesbury.

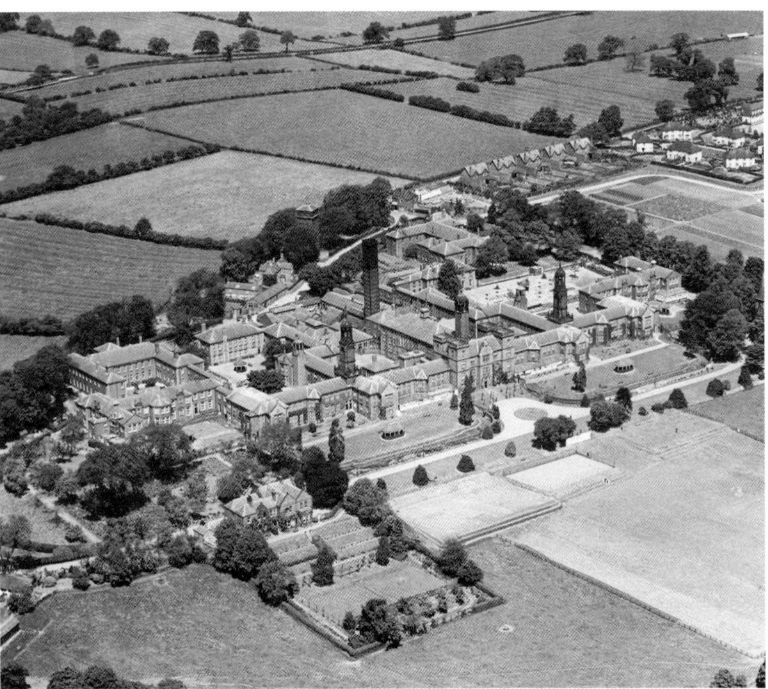

Tasmania. In other respects it departed. Specific conditions, combined with limited means, made for both a lag and a discrepancy in the effective application of metropolitan-based initiatives. As encountered in the Old Somerset (est. 1818) and Valkenberg (1867) asylums in the Cape Colony, South Africa, the initially chaotic and then carefully 'classified' relation of inmates, including mixing and later separation according to risk and race, reflected the social malaise and violence of colonialism itself.[21] In British India there was a stricter segregation not only between sex and race, but between religion and caste. Even within the nominative 'native' population, certain groups, such as the indigenous aristocracy and Parsis, were accorded additional privilege. Moreover, the British authorities were keen to extract European mental patients, establishing private 'home' asylums in London, first in Hackney (Pembroke House), and then Elm Grove House, Hanwell (Royal India Asylum), converted for the purpose by Matthew Digby Wyatt in 1870.[22]

While many asylums in colonial contexts simply followed the new moral management models coming out of Britain and the United States, with similar results, in many cases there was simply a desire to erect some (any) kind of building where those designated as insane, and therefore a danger to the public (or themselves), could be kept separate from ordinary society. In certain instances the results were disastrous, as at the Kingston Lunatic Asylum in Jamaica. Although planned by a noted asylum designer in Britain (James Harris, of Hanwell fame), the building itself, and the systems upon which it was based, were incomplete and only partially understood *in situ*. This led to neglectful and violent treatment of the patients (predominantly black) by the nurses employed for their care, including regular beatings, torture, and even rape. The Kingston episode—which precipitated an empire-wide scandal over asylum care, with direct intervention from the Colonial Office—highlighted the gap not only between metropolitan modes of practice and their effective implementation abroad, but also between views regarding the treatment and potential cure of 'inferior' races. Here architecture, and the 'asylum' in particular, had become both a tool and a cover for the actions of violent and racist colonial agency, thoroughly betraying its intended purpose of care.

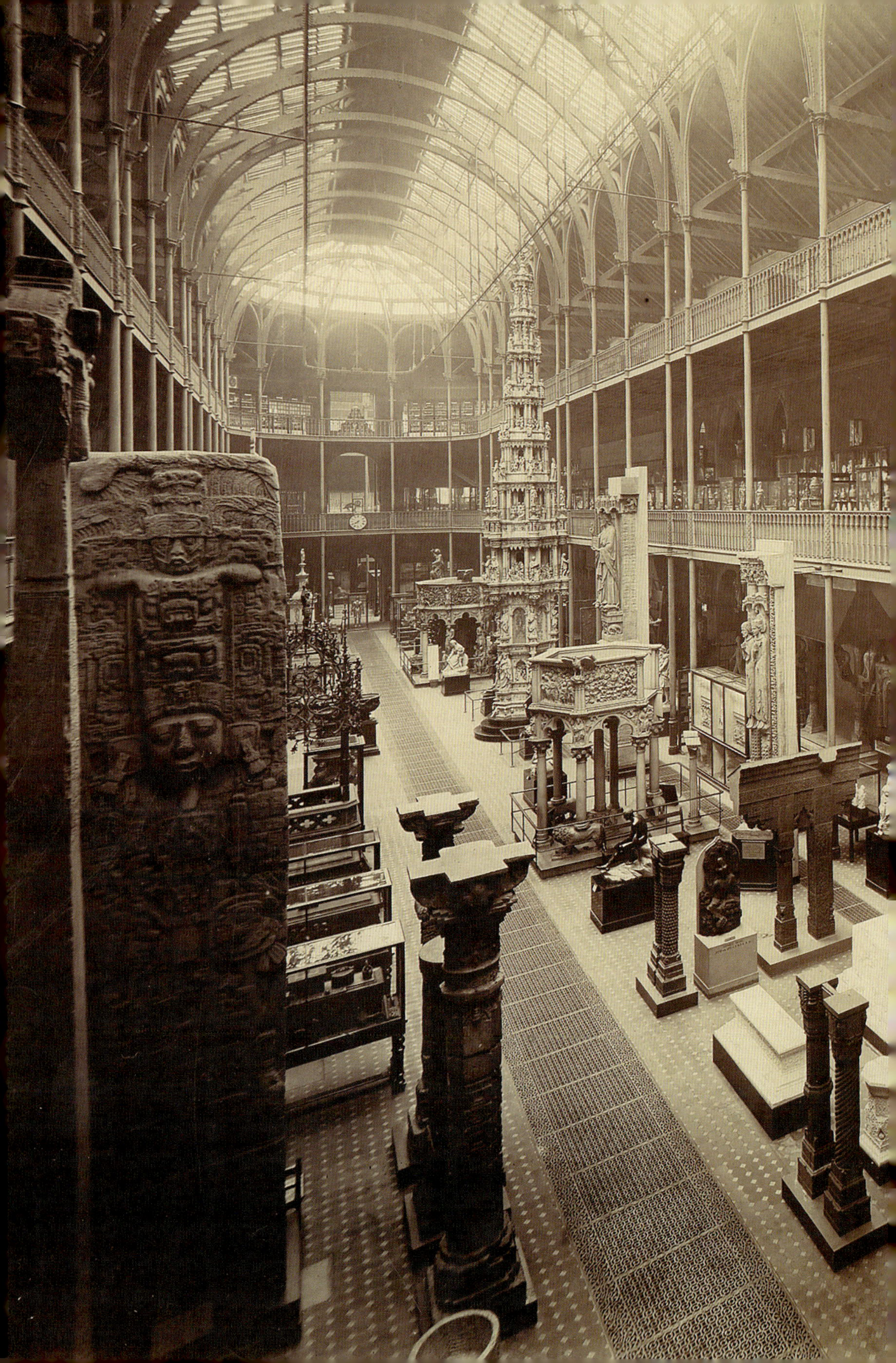

7

A World on Show: Exhibitions, Museums, and Cultures of Display

Scholars have long argued that Victorian society was both characterised and co-produced by novel ways of seeing, including innovative techniques of display. Although these modes were induced by a rapidly expanding commercial, knowledge-based economy, they were also mediated by the material conditions under which such observation took place. Everything from new types of spatial experience (museums, galleries, and exhibitions), to new and more powerful viewing apparatus (microscopes, telescopes, and cameras), to the rise of consumer culture through commodified spectacle (shopfront displays, illustrated printing, and advertising), to enhanced means of artificial illumination (gas and electric lighting) all helped transform Victorian society into a visually orientated culture like none that had come before. This is not to say that Victorians were wholly subservient to spectacle. After all, we know that among the educated elite literary culture was both pervasive and important. Rather, it is to suggest that visual means played an increasingly significant role in how Victorians related to the world and thus constructed an image of who they were.

Under these conditions, strategies for systematised viewing became a basis for constructing narrative. The way the 'viewing public' was encouraged to move through exhibitory space and engage with displays sought to imply if not impose understanding. Through the imposition of such 'regimes' of observation, the potential for fashioning a new type of citizen-subject became possible. Therefore, how, and in what relation, objects were showcased mattered. There was a social/reform dimension to this in that advocates for public museums and galleries during the Victorian period believed that such institutions provided, among other things, opportunities for autodidacticism and self-improvement, especially among the working classes. This, despite the fact that uneducated viewers often lacked the knowledge required to comprehend the logic behind such structured displays, even if they could find the time to attend. However, as Edward Forbes remarked in 1853, although museums were perhaps powerless to educate the 'ignorant' directly, they could nevertheless 'excite a desire for knowledge'.[1] The cultures of display that developed out of this movement were crucial in orchestrating new relationships with the material world, in turn fashioning unique forms of material culture. Indeed, it was for these reasons that institutions like museums and galleries were at the forefront of knowledge distillation in Victorian Britain, including the rise of disciplines such as geology, palaeontology, archaeology, anthropology, and even art history.[2]

A number of the new building types that appeared during the period were geared around technologies of display. In this, architectural practice began to absorb these new approaches by purposely directing *what* was seen and *how*. Vast, top-lit spaces, utilising iron and glass technology, became characteristic of galleries and museums, where an even and consistent mode of illumination was desired for a convenient and satisfactory viewing experience. Likewise, adequate lighting was a key consideration in the design of Victorian art schools, where certain types of light were equated with the correct 'atmospheric' conditions for creating and assessing art. Anywhere such lighting conditions were required, architecture was specifically adapted: in factories, office buildings, railway stations, postal sorting depots, public halls, even courtrooms. Top-lit spaces of course existed before the Victorian era, but their size and frequency increased manyfold during the period.

There is a plethora of building types to which an analysis of the relationship between architecture and display might be applied in Victorian society, but here I will focus on only three: exhibition buildings, museums, and galleries. These three building types, though not invented by the Victorians (although there is a case that the former indeed was), are certainly characteristic of the Victorian urban scene, often occupying prominent sites in the centre of towns and cities across Britain and the wider British world. Museums and galleries were developed and refined in their purpose to such an extent during the period, and erected in such numbers, that it would not be unreasonable to describe them as a Victorian 'invention' in their modern sense. They also supported a myriad of adjunct spaces, including staff offices, teaching rooms, storage facilities, and laboratories. Thus, these types enable us to draw out the nature and implications of the 'cultures of display' to which I refer in the chapter title. While there is some overlap in the function of museums and galleries, exhibition buildings represent a unique building typology, associated with a commercially driven, event-inspired culture that proliferated throughout the late nineteenth century, originating in the Crystal Palace and the Great Exhibition of 1851. All three tell us something about how the Victorians viewed themselves, their world, and the aesthetic utility of their contributions to the built environment.

Exhibition Buildings: Commodity Spectacle and Consumerism

The culture surrounding national and international exhibitions, on a grand scale, is something that characterised the relationship between industry, manufacturing, and commercial consumerism during the late nineteenth century, not just in Britain, but throughout much of the industrialised world. As far as Britain was concerned, the first major event associated with this culture was the Great Exhibition of 1851, staged in Hyde Park, London, between May and October that year **[40a]**. Although it took some time for officialdom to warm to the idea, eventually proposals for the exhibition gained the full backing of parliament and of royalty, in the form of the Prince Consort, Albert, who became something of a figurehead with respect to its orchestration. Other personages who featured prominently in the event's promotion and organisation included the indomitable Henry Cole, who was in many respects the prime mover behind the scheme. Cole's involvement necessarily implicated his 'circle' of associates, drawing in architects and designers such as Matthew Digby Wyatt and Owen Jones (see Chapter 3).

The building in which the exhibition was held—dubbed the 'Crystal Palace', on account of the fact that it was effectively a giant glasshouse—is significant in itself not just as a piece of engineering but as a piece of commercial technology. During its conception, the key question of how to select, categorise, and arrange (i.e., display to greatest affect) those objects chosen for exhibit remained central. Deliberations were guided by more than merely a desire to showcase items of interest to a curious public. Concern over a certain 'taxonomy of things' was ever present in the discussion. Through the lobbying of Cole and his associates, the organisers were determined to emphasise a classification system connecting capital investment, manufacturing, design, and retail **[134a]**. Moreover, in highlighting this connection, their hope was that vast improvements might be gained in demonstrating to British manufacturers how to associate mechanical industry with good, art-based design, all with a view to attaining commercial advantage. In this respect, the Great Exhibition of 1851 was, apart from its rhetorical refrain of promoting 'peace among all nations', primarily an economic event for the purpose of not only showing and comparing the supposed manufacturing prowess of the United Kingdom, but also, and perhaps more importantly, constructing (literally and figuratively) an industrialised market economy.

Fig. 134a

A great commercial fanfare. Interior, Crystal Palace, Great Exhibition of 1851, Hyde Park, London.

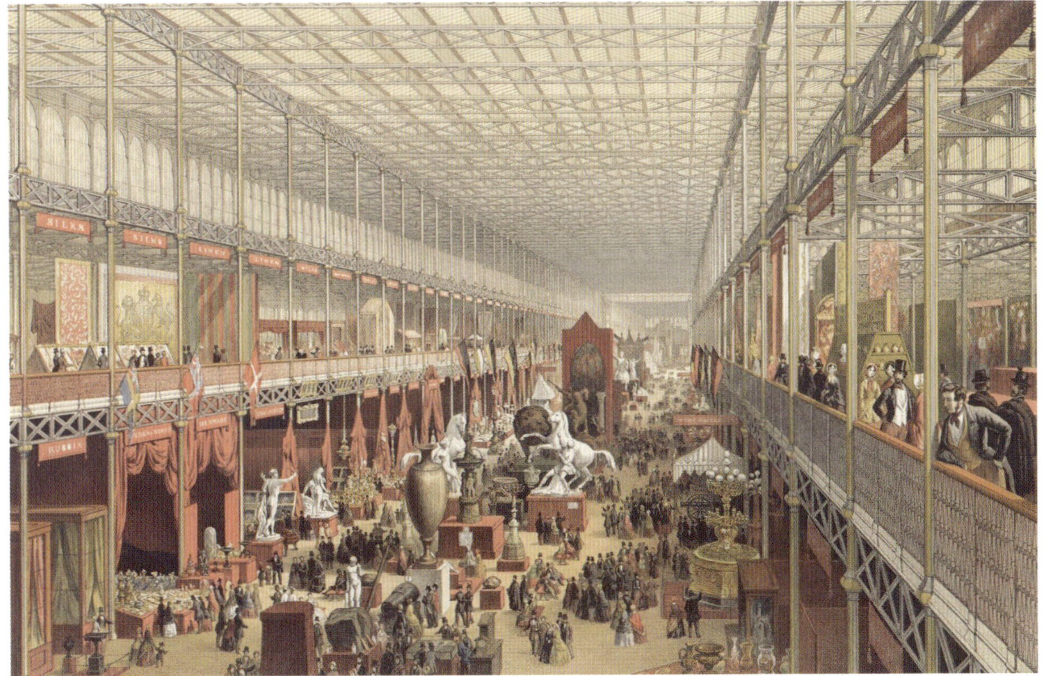

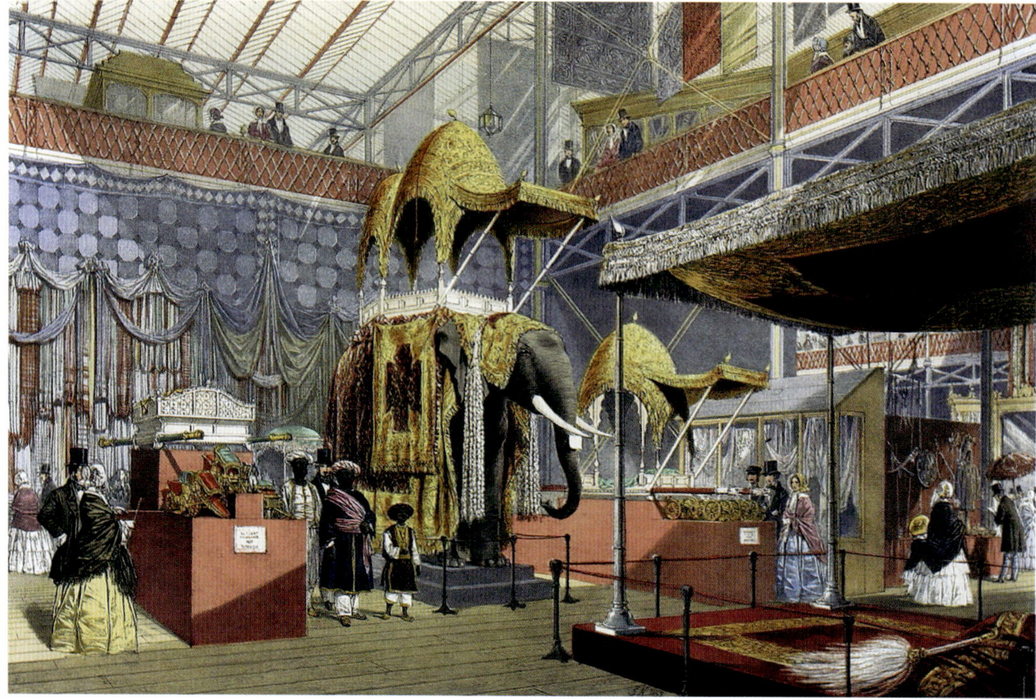

Fig. 134b
Indian Court, Great Exhibition of 1851. The famous Koh-i-Noor Diamond, presented to Queen Victoria in 1850, was on display here. The stuffed elephant was loaned from Saffron Walden Museum in Essex.

These themes were reflected in the *Official Catalogue*, with its broad distinction between raw materials, machinery, manufactures, and fine art, ranging from such things as chemicals, mineral and vegetable substances; through machines, tools, and agricultural implements; to fabrics, ceramics, sculpture, and enamels—over 100,000 exhibits in all. The building's plan attempted to map these complex relationships spatially. Although there was no direct correspondence between the catalogue and the building's organisation, the general idea was to work from the perimeter inwards, from raw products to the exterior, then machinery, to manufactured goods at the centre. This was not entirely consistent, however, leading to some befuddlement on the part of visitors and commentators. Given the structural limitations of the building, physically lighter displays were purposefully located on the upper level. Nevertheless, the end result, as one walked down the central nave, was an overwhelming spectacle of industrialised commercial output.

Floodlit through the transparency of the building itself, these tightly gathered displays showcased the splendour, colour, and richness (in effect the possibilities) of a new consumer society, pointing the way to a future of progress and prosperity. In this sense, the Great Exhibition inaugurated a way of seeing 'things' that initiated a new kind of commercial life in Victorian Britain, in turn fashioning what has been called a 'mythology of consumerism'. As one reporter noted at the time, the spectacle was essentially 'a representation to the eye'. The building itself became the place in which the spatial mechanics of this 'seeing' was realised.[3] Lauded by some as the ultimate convergence of human ingenuity and dignity, by others as a confusion and coercive middle-class delusion, the forced 'hot-house' environment of the

Crystal Palace—with its allusions to contemporary ferrovitreous constructs such as conservatories, railway stations, and covered markets—gave the impression of a type of monstrous accelerated growth, as disturbing as it was exhilarating.[4]

But this was not all. Some, such as the former slave William Wells Brown, viewed the Crystal Palace as representing a certain kind of freedom, in enabling an untrammelled intermingling of individuals, classes, and even races.[5] Indeed, as visitors walked through the building, perusing its exhibits, they could not have helped noticing this, including the extent of exotic, non-European objects on display. Although this spoke to the ambitions on the part of the organisers in bringing the peoples and manufactures of the world together into one place, it also highlighted Britain's status as a great and burgeoning imperial power. The Crystal Palace, as a structure, may not have been a monument to empire per se, but it was nevertheless a receptacle that presented Britain with an unparalleled opportunity to reveal to the world the products and manufactures associated with its industrial capacity and ever-expanding territorial interests. Paxton himself, it turns out, was a substantial investor in imperial railway ventures, enabling him to appreciate precisely the Crystal Palace's role in translating a globally unifying imaginary of people and objects into a single optical field of industrial commodification. As it happens, the comparison between British- and foreign-made crafts and manufactures was often unfavourable, leaving the organisers and the government with much to contemplate regarding the state of British design. This in turn led to further pressure for increased museum facilities and schools of art and design, such as those established in London and elsewhere following the exhibition.

The gathering of produce from Britain's colonies, and showcasing this as part of 'Britain', was highly suggestive of an unbounded British world. This 'world' was presented as an immense treasure-trove of abundance, primarily in the form of raw materials and cheap labour. This served to create a disjuncture between the symbolic meaning of the exhibition (peace and progress) and the material conditions of commodity capitalism embedded within it, resulting in the image of colonialism as a pendant to commercial growth and prosperity. The oppression, subjugation, and stripping of human and natural resources from such places was concealed beneath the spectacle of the building and the fanfare surrounding its exhibits. Nowhere was this more evident than in the Indian Court, with its visually arresting display of exotic objects, including the Koh-i-Noor Diamond and a stuffed elephant complete with howdah. Organised with the assistance of the East India Company, the display was situated strategically at the very heart of the building **[134b]**. Here 'India' was glorified and domesticated for a European audience; not on display in its own right, but as 'conquered', now the 'brightest jewel in Victoria's crown'. This was obviously calculated to leave a particular impression upon the minds of those who attended the exhibition, particularly foreigners.

The Exhibition Movement: National and Imperial Currents

The Great Exhibition proved highly successful, drawing over 6 million visitors. So popular was it that it set a precedent for a succession of similar events which took place in London and other parts of the world during the late nineteenth and early twentieth centuries. Its most immediate local successor was the London International Exhibition of 1862, established in anniversary of its illustrious progenitor. The building, also located in South Kensington, did not attempt to imitate the wondrous glass confection that was the Crystal Palace, opting instead for a far more substantial-looking structure in brick and cast iron, with two large and prominent glass domes **[135a]**. Importantly, events of this kind subsequent to 1851 became increasingly orientated towards British imperial themes and interests. At the 1862 exhibition, for instance, Britain's colonies were given much more room than they had been in 1851. One of the most prominent exhibits was the famous 'Gold Pyramid' sent from the colony of Victoria, Australia, representing the total amount of that metal extracted from the colony—some 800 tons, or £103,000,000 worth **[135b]**. The message was that Victoria, along with many of the other so-called white settler dominions, was a prosperous place and one that was ripe for systematic European colonisation.

Among the spate of exhibitions following that of 1851 may be included the Dublin Great Industrial (1853), the 'metropolitan' exhibitions at Melbourne, Sydney, and Bombay (all 1854), the Calcutta Agricultural (1864), the Sydney Metropolitan and International (1870), the Queensland Intercolonial (1876), the Jeypore Art and Industrial (1883), the Toronto Industrial (1885), the Adelaide Jubilee International (1887), the Melbourne Centennial (1888), the South African and International (1892), and the New Zealand International (1906), to name but a few. A number of such exhibitions were staged in Britain, too, including the Colonial and Indian (1886), the Empire of India (1895), Greater Britain (1899), and the Festival of Empire (1911), all in London; while others were held in Glasgow (1888 and 1901), Manchester (1887, 1894), Cardiff (1888), and Liverpool (1886). A striking feature of the

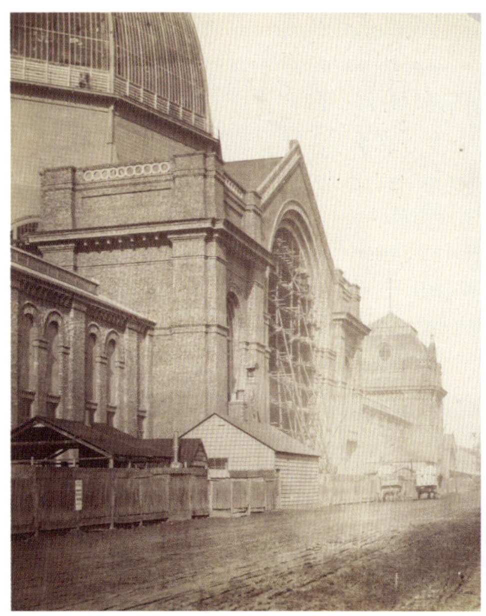

Fig. 135a
The 1862 International Exhibition building, London, in the final stages for construction.

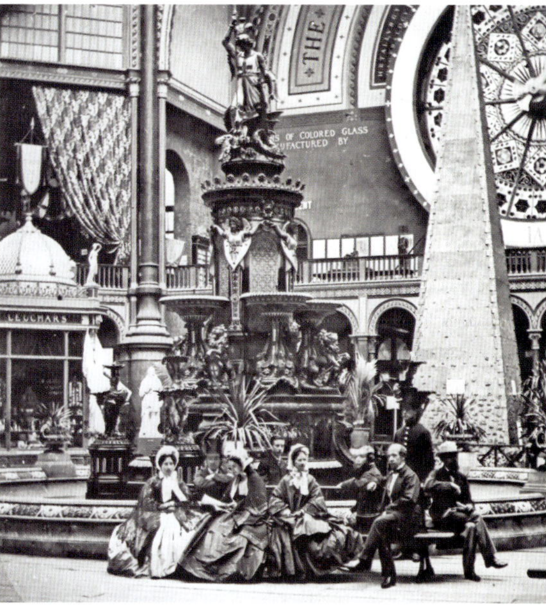

Fig. 135b
Visitors at the 1862 International Exhibition. They are sitting at the base of the great Majolica Fountain, beneath the eastern dome. In the background can be seen the 'Gold Pyramid' sent from the colony of Victoria, Australia.

Festival of Empire exhibition, staged at the Crystal Palace, was its three-quarter-size replicas of the parliament buildings of Australia (Melbourne), Canada, South Africa, New Zealand, and Newfoundland, enabling visitors to take an 'all red' stroll around the empire in the space of a few hundred metres. Indeed, so popular were exhibitions of this kind that one major event was held every year or so in Britain and its empire between 1851 and 1914, not to mention the numerous others that were held in Europe, the United States, and elsewhere. Many of these produced spectacular buildings, most of which have since disappeared, including the Crystal Palace, which, after its move to Sydenham following the Great Exhibition, burned down in 1936. One of the few still standing is that in Melbourne (1879–80), designed for the Melbourne International Exhibition of 1880 by Joseph Reed in a bold neo-Renaissance style, and used for such purposes to this day **[136]**.

The backcloth to the increasingly imperial agenda behind these exhibitions was economic depression and command over limited global resources. This realisation was given definite shape in the 'New Imperial' politics of Benjamin Disraeli during the 1870s (whose famous speech on imperialism was delivered at the Crystal Palace, no less), from which emerged a desire for closer economic and political cooperation between Britain and its colonial empire. Born of this enthusiasm was perhaps the greatest 'imperial' exhibition of the age: the Colonial and Indian Exhibition, held in the Royal Horticultural Society's garden at South Kensington in the summer of 1886. As its name suggests, this exhibition's agenda was clear. Its leitmotif was to showcase the idea and image of a united empire, a kind of 'Greater Britain' spanning the world. To emphasise this notion the building's main façade was clad with two huge hemispheric depictions of the British world, above which were located five clocks synchronising various time zones within that world (Greenwich, Ottawa, Cape Town, Calcutta, and Sydney), all sur-

Fig. 136
Melbourne International Exhibition building (1880), Melbourne, Australia, by Joseph Reed.

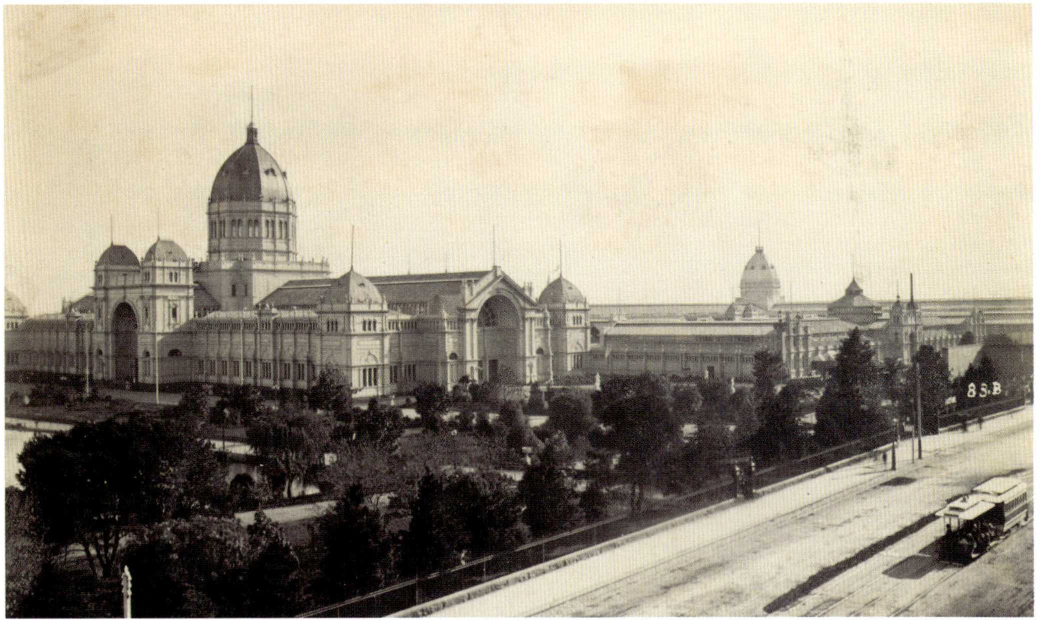

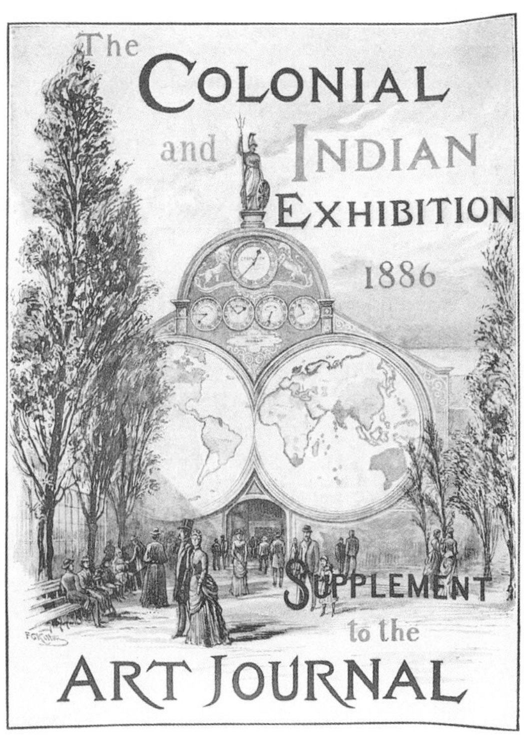

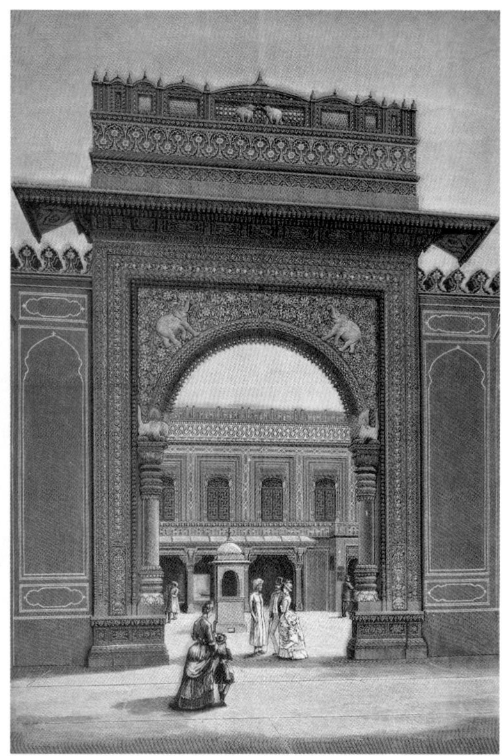

Fig. 137a

Façade to the Colonial and Indian Exhibition building, South Kensington, London, 1886.

Fig. 137b

Gwalior Gateway at the Colonial and Indian Exhibition. Designed by Maj. J. B. Keith for the Calcutta International Exhibition of 1883–84, and executed by Indian craftsmen, it was dismantled and later transported to Britain.

mounted by a large and conspicuous figure of Britannia triumphant **[137a]**. The message could not have been clearer: the measuring, marking, and celebrating of knowledge and commerce across the empire.[6] Inside, perhaps the most indicative if not spectacular exhibits were again those from India. Complete with reconstructed Durbar Hall and Palace, including the hand-carved Gwalior Gateway, these were symbolic of the imperial mission to rescue, preserve, and exhibit India's past through its rich handicraft traditions **[137b]**. The reconstructed and simulated architectural environments, with their aura of 'authenticity', including entire bazaars of imported Indian craftsmen, would certainly have transported British spectators to the Indian Subcontinent, right in the convenience and comfort of the empire's capital.

The Glasgow exhibitions of 1888 and 1901 were also spectacular events in this vein, showcasing local alongside national and international manufactures, including many that purposefully emphasised the city's imperial connections. Oriental features were conspicuously evident, while Glasgow's claim as 'second city of empire' was represented via its vast ship and locomotive manufacturing industry that had done much to extend British rule across the globe.[7] A permanent legacy of the 1901 exhibition was the Kelvingrove Art Gallery and Museum, designed by J. W. Simpson and E. J. Milner Allen in a lavish Spanish or 'imperial' baroque style. Today one of Glasgow's largest and most impressive buildings, it originally served as the 'Palace of Fine Arts' adjacent the equally spectacular but now demolished white and gold 'Eastern Palace' (Industrial Hall), by

Fig. 138a

'Eastern Palace' (Industrial Hall), Glasgow International Exhibition, 1901, by James Millar.

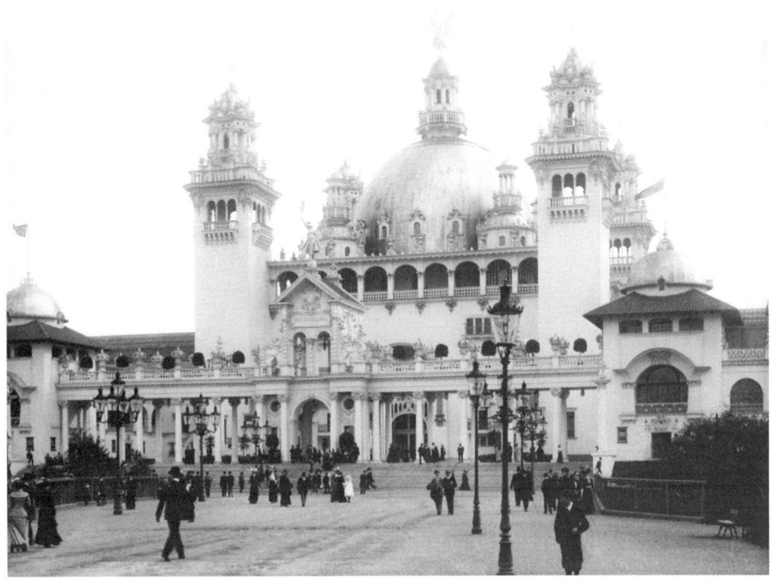

Fig. 138b

Brisbane Exhibition Building, Queensland (1889–91), Australia, by George Addison.

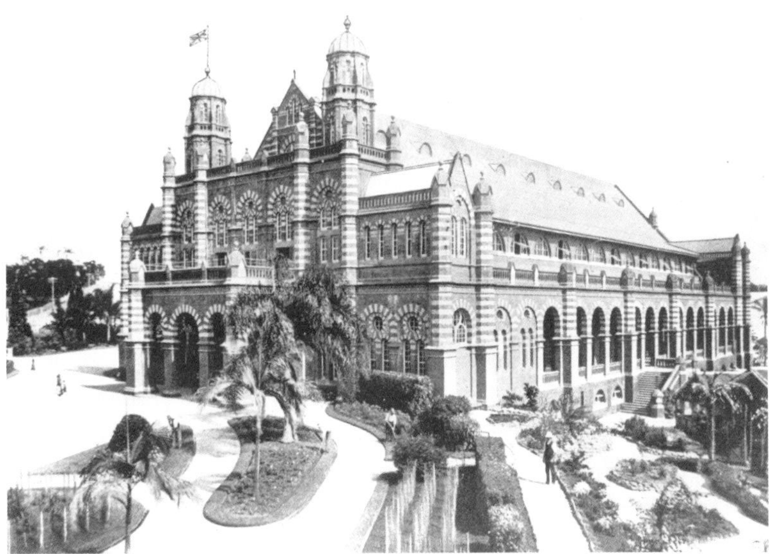

James Millar, with its conspicuous oriental flourishes **[138a]**. In some cases, as exhibition culture took hold, buildings were erected for general purposes, only later fulfilling their role as locations for international exhibitions. This was the case with the Brisbane Exhibition Building, in Queensland (1889–91), by the Welsh-born, English-trained George Addison, which became the locale for the Queensland International Exhibition of 1897 **[138b]**. Because this building was not built as a one-off exhibition structure, it survived such events, eventually becoming the Queensland Museum and Art Gallery. Moreover, from the start, it was built solidly in brick, in an elaborate, climatically adapted Byzantine-cum-Romanesque style.

Museums: Collecting, Classifying, and Comprehending

As we have seen, in the case of some of these exhibitions, the buildings used were repurposed as museums, galleries, or as facilities for further exhibition-style events, if not designed for these future purposes in the first place. Although this did not occur with the Colonial and Indian Exhibition of 1886, it was later decided that many of the items exhibited would be transferred to a new building, and put on permanent display, in celebration of Queen Victoria's golden jubilee the following year. This building, known aptly as the Imperial Institute (1887–93; demolished 1957–62), was one of the most ambitious architectural undertakings of the age **[139]**. Located in South Kensington, which was by this time London's—indeed, the nation's—museum and exhibition capital, it was designed by Thomas Collcutt, who received the commission via limited competition. As a memorial to the Queen's jubilee, as well as a monument to the perceived greatness and unity of the British empire, it was considered imperative that the edifice be 'worthy' in every respect.

Designed in an eclectic 'free classic' style, it established a link not only between Victorian architecture's propensity towards stylistic variability and notions of developmental change, but also between the need for such variability and the promulgation of British culture abroad. This idea was embed-

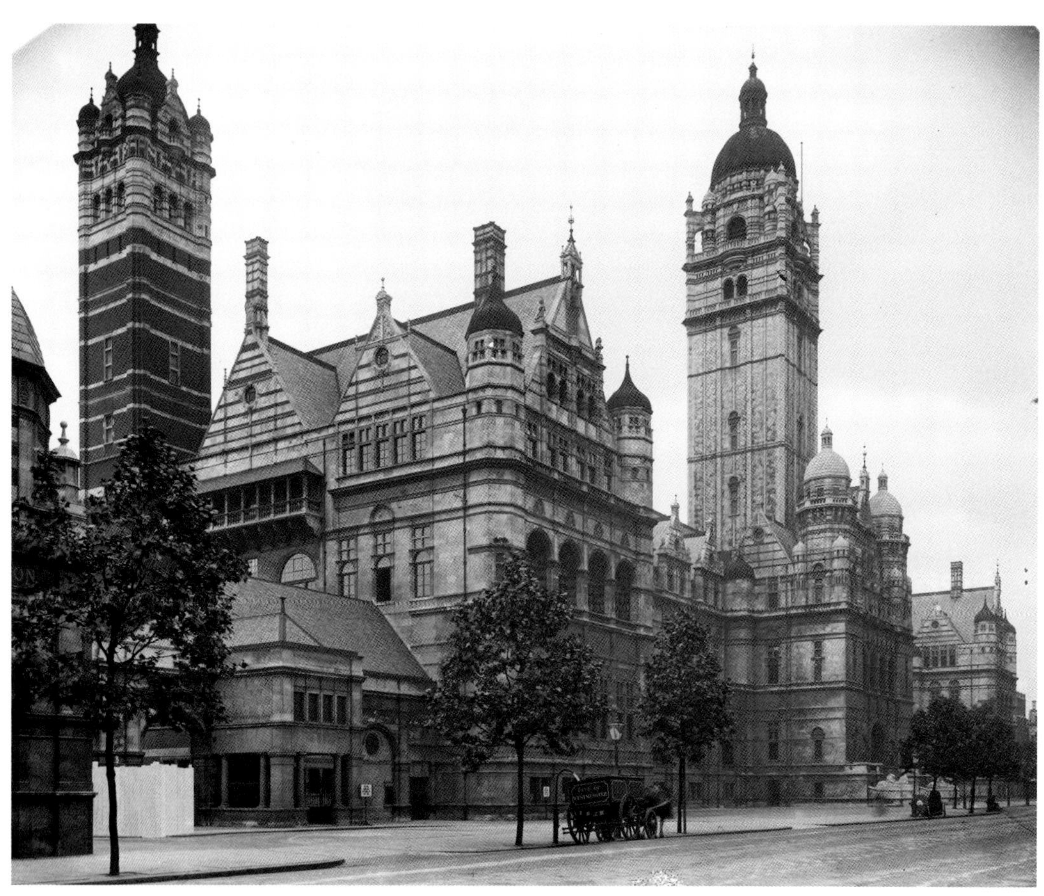

Fig. 139
Imperial Institute, South Kensington (1887–93), London, by Thomas Collcutt.

ded in the very fabric of the building, with its foundation stone of 'colonial granite' being laid upon a footing of 'British and Indian Bricks'—a gesture intended to symbolise, quite literally, the idea of common bond. Through this act, the Institute (as a building) and the concept of imperial cooperation rooted in it, were made to appear as one and the same thing. As the Prince of Wales remarked in a speech at the official stone-laying ceremony, it was his 'confident hope that this Institute may hereafter not only exhibit the material resources of the Empire, but may be an emblem of that Imperial unity of purpose and action'. The idea was extended into the building's superstructure, in which an assortment of motifs and materials from around the empire were employed.

Inside, the items were arranged in museum-like fashion, open to businessmen and the general public alike, in an effort to encourage greater knowledge and understanding of the commercial and migratory opportunities available across Britain's empire **[140]**. In this sense, the Imperial Institute may be seen to have had a propagandistic agenda. On this, *The Times* noted that it would be the 'great intelligence department of the Empire'; a place where information could be 'concentrated, organised, tabulated, and rendered accessible'. Again, the backcloth to this initiative was a desire to strengthen and further stimulate colonial development under the political banner of imperial confederation. Although never particularly successful in that capacity, the Institute nevertheless brought the wider British world 'home', acting as a centre of debate and exchange on matters imperial, as well as being the headquarters of the Royal Colonial Institute.

By this time there already existed in London a number of museums in which one could glimpse the exotic and otherworldly presence of Britain's empire. Principal among these was the India Museum at East India House. Established in 1801, this 'oriental repository' was home to all manner of fantastical objects trafficked and channelled through the exploits of the East India Company. Its architecture, too, was designed to impress, with the 1858 extension by Matthew Digby Wyatt recalling the exuberant Saracenic forms of ancient Mughal palaces **[141a]**. Such exotica could be found at the premises of Christian missionary organisations as well. Items of anthropological interest, including weapons, textiles, and votive objects from places as far afield as India, China, Polynesia, and Africa were deposited in the head offices of both the Church Missionary Society and London Missionary Society, the latter having its own dedicated museum (est. 1814) that became a feature on the London tourist circuit.[8] Further north, in Glasgow, was the enormous collection of the noted Scottish physician William Hunter, which included everything from antiquities, coins, and natural history, to anatomical specimens and works of art. This, too, included a large number of cultural artefacts from Capt. James Cook's voyages to the South Pacific, all of which eventually ended up in a purpose-built facility in G. G. Scott's new university buildings (1867–91) on Gilmorehill **[141b]**.

Given their scale and educational ambition, such structures spoke to the then prevalent tension between the 'museum' as a place primarily for display, show, and spectacle (*à la* the exhibition) and one of contemplation, learning, and serious scientific scholarship. In reality it was both. But the debate over exactly how a museum ought to present knowledge through the display

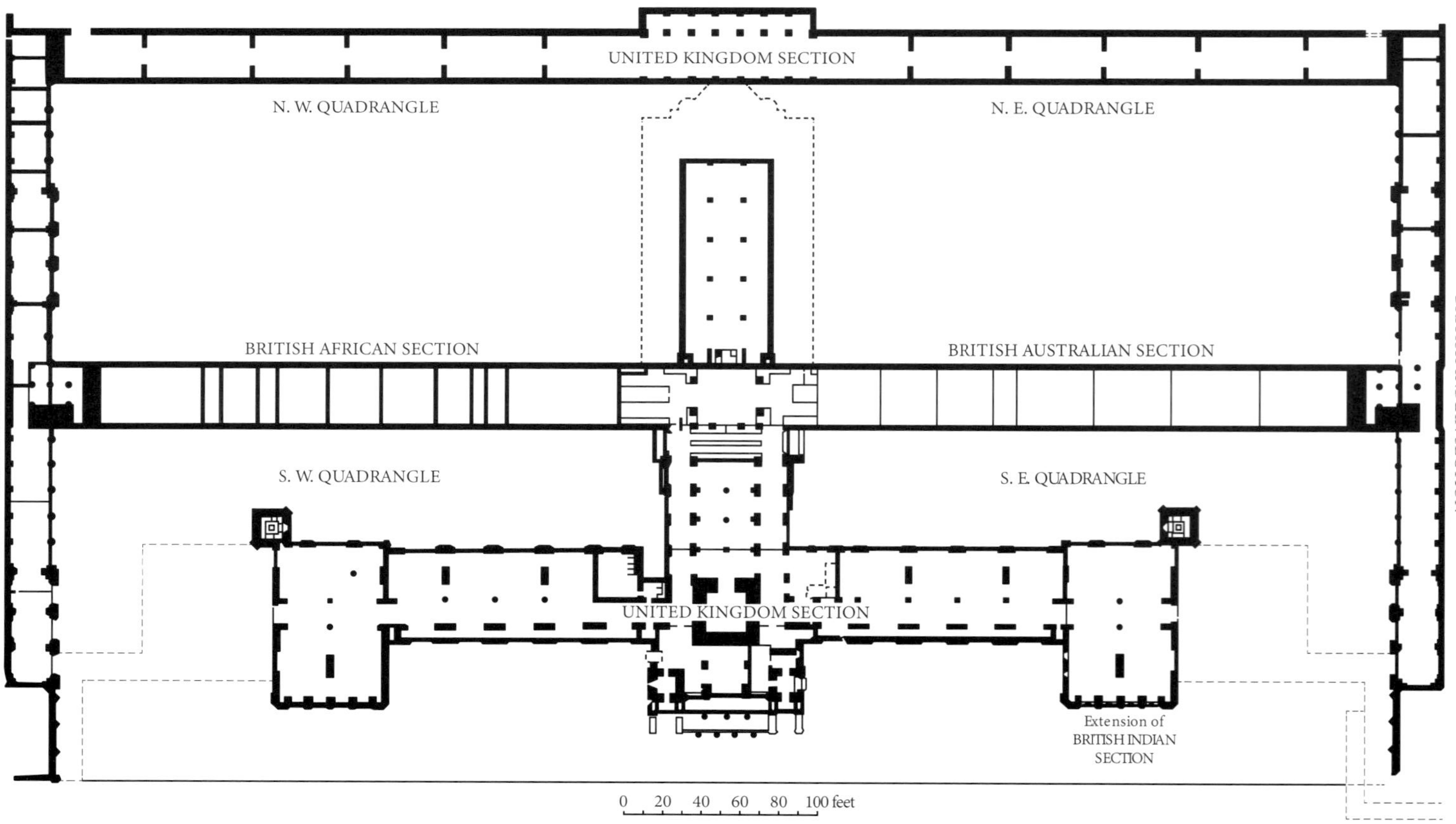
UNITED KINGDOM SECTION
N. W. QUADRANGLE
N. E. QUADRANGLE
BRITISH AMERICAN SECTION
BRITISH AFRICAN SECTION
BRITISH AUSTRALIAN SECTION
BRITISH INDIAN SECTION
S. W. QUADRANGLE
S. E. QUADRANGLE
UNITED KINGDOM SECTION
Extension of
BRITISH INDIAN
SECTION
0
20
40
60
80
100 feet

Fig. 140

Plan, Imperial Institute. It is noticeable here how the British empire is presented in a roughly accurate geographical layout. Notwithstanding the United Kingdom occupying the main entrance pavilion (being front and centre), we see an additional United Kingdom pavilion at the top (north) of the building, with Africa located to the 'south', British North America to the 'west', and India and Australasia to the 'east'. This way, visitors could take a global circuit around the empire, with the idea of Britain, as the 'metropolis', being the most important constituent element in the imperial firmament.

and study of specimens remained live as architects and trustees grappled with the limits and expectations of the typology. Size was also understood as reflecting the perceived importance of a collection, along with the growing prestige of the subject (or subjects) to which it was dedicated. Hence the scale of the new British Museum. As collections of national and regional significance grew and bifurcated, so too came calls for additional accommodation. As noted at the beginning of this chapter, the application of specific spatial requirements was fundamental in orchestrating particular patterns of circulation, enabling curators to 'construct' not only ways of seeing but also systems of knowing.

In the case of the new British Museum, the impulse was to curate an encyclopaedic-style arrangement of its vast collection **[43b]**. This was driven in part by advances in the relationship between science, knowledge, and the application of taxonomic systems of understanding that had become increasingly codified and settled upon by the mid-nineteenth century. But no sooner was the building complete and opened to the public, than certain voices were raised regarding the facility's inadequacy. The concern was that the natural history collection, in particular, was getting something of a raw deal in comparison to antiquities, with specimens crammed into spaces suited neither to their storage nor proper display. This resulted in the splitting of the antiquities and natural history collections from one another in 1860, and the proposal to erect a new, purpose-built museum. This would become the Natural History Museum in South Kensington, which, apart

Fig. 141a

Interior, extension (1858) to India Museum, London, by Matthew Digby Wyatt.

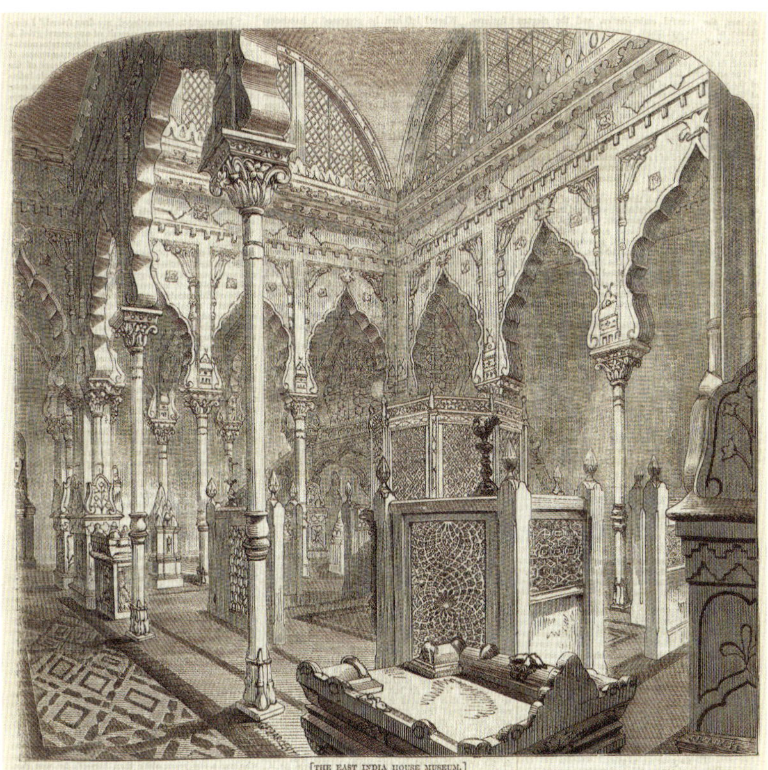

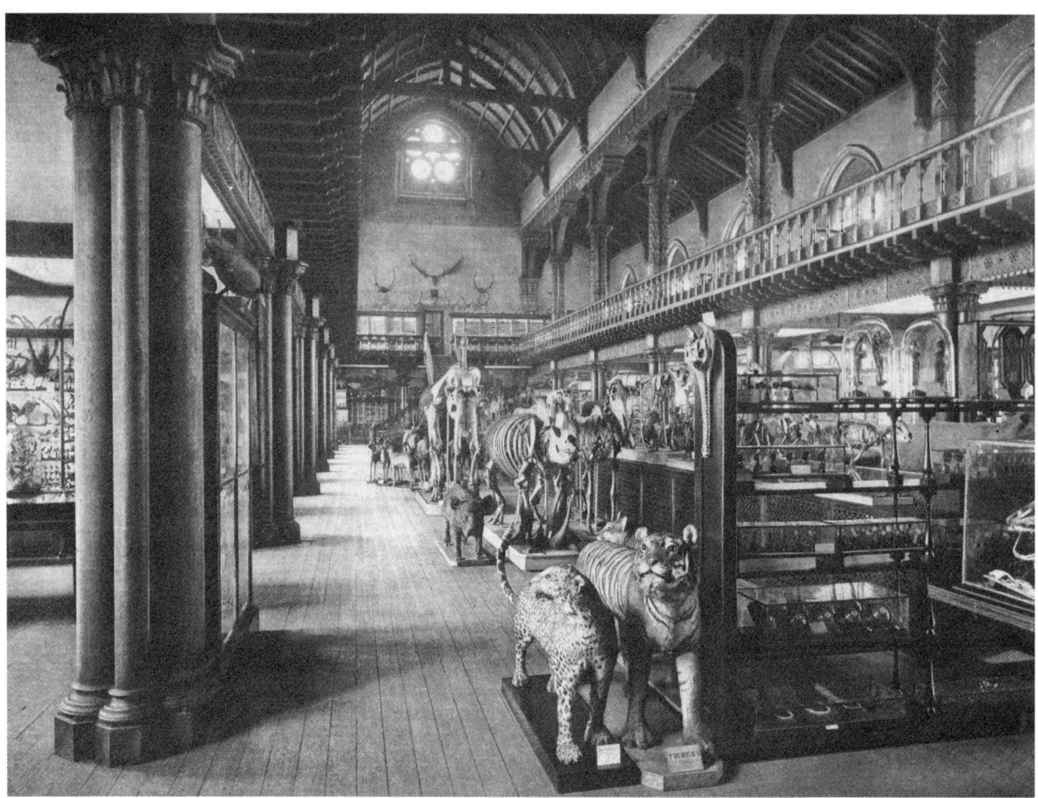

Fig. 141b
Hunterian Museum, University of Glasgow (1867–91), by George Gilbert Scott.

from its impressive architectural programming, highlighted the growing revisions and tensions within disciplinary knowledge-making and the cultural politics that accompanied it.

Developing a Type: Natural History Museums

There is a backstory to such uses of natural history in Britain. The universities of Oxford and Cambridge had been devising their own plans for the increasing knowledge of the natural world for some time. In the case of Cambridge, this stretched back to the late 1820s. With the study of the physical sciences increasingly recognised as essential to a university education, pressure mounted for the erection of facilities for the display and examination of specimens, including laboratory space for subjects such as zoology, geology, mineralogy, and botany. But the transition came too early, and C. R. Cockerell's ambitious plans for a Classically inspired library, combined with museums of science, were commuted to a library only **[142]**. But momentum was now firmly behind the idea of science as a worthy component of a young gentleman's education.

The idea only came to fruition at Oxford some 20 years later. In the meantime, a number of other museums had appeared. These were scattered among major urban centres and smaller provincial towns. Here one might point to the collections comprising the Whitby Literary and Philosophical Society (1823); the Natural History Society of Northumberland, Durham, and Newcastle upon Tyne (1829); the Saffron Walden Natural History

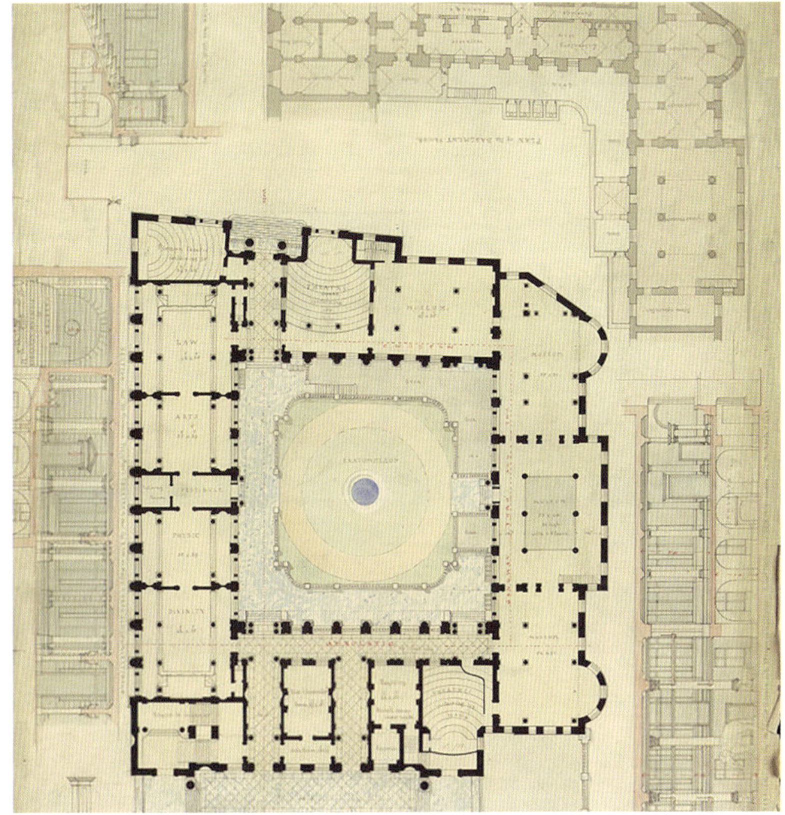

Fig. 142

C. R. Cockerell (and assistants), competition drawing for new Cambridge University Museum (1836): ground and basement plans and sections.

Society (1835); and the Derby Museum, Liverpool (1851). The museums in such settings were often combined with public libraries, linking book learning with specimen observation and analysis. In the case of Liverpool (now World Museum Liverpool), a magnificent neo-Classical edifice was raised for the purpose between 1857 and 1860, to the designs of London architect Thomas Allom **[143]**. Like town halls, the raising of such institutions was also connected to civic and regional identity and pride.

But perhaps the most significant of these early museums were the Hunterian Museum of natural history at the Royal College of Surgeons (1833–7), and the Museum of Practical Geology (1846–51), both in London **[144a&b]**. Among their key architectural innovations was the continued importance of top-lit space in conjunction with the spatial indexing of taxonomic knowledge systems. While the former reinforced the idea that good, even light was fundamental not only to seeing objects but also to understanding them, the latter allowed for a spatio-ocular comprehension of a given order of things through the methodical placement and labelling of items in space. In this sense, both the Hunterian and Practical Geology museums were library-style arrangements, encouraging their collections to be 'read' like a textbook.[9] This had to do with hierarchies of organisms in the case of the Hunterian, and the representation of geological time (lithology) and the economic development of mineral resources in the case of the Museum of Practical Geology. It is worth

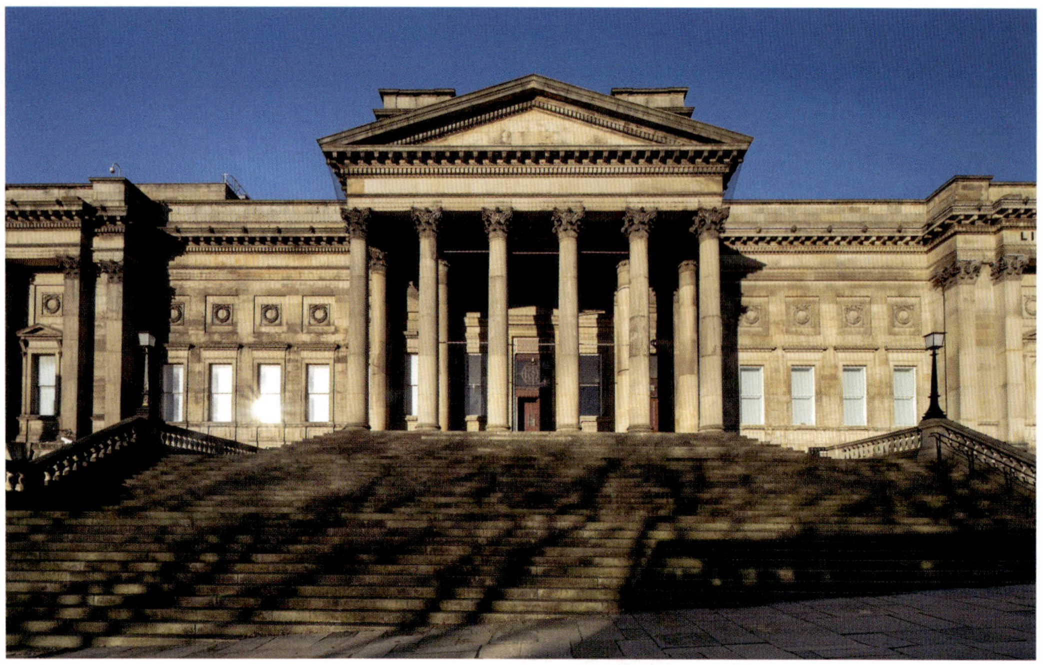

Fig. 143
Classical edifice designed for the Derby Museum (now World Museum Liverpool), Liverpool (1857–60), by Thomas Allom.

recalling that the Museum of Practical Geology in fact began life as the Museum of Economic Geology, and was a place where lectures were delivered regularly on the economic exploitation of the earth's crust, especially those relating to the curriculum of the Royal School of Mines. Indeed, the crescent-shaped lecture theatre in the basement of the new Jermyn Street building by James Pennethorne determined the form of the exhibition galleries above. Thus, visually and spatially connected, these spaces were designed to reinforce the link between knowledge, learning, and applied science.

God and Science: The Oxford Natural History Museum

In the case of Oxford, the decision to erect a dedicated museum to natural history was underpinned by the fact that the university had in 1850 reformed its curriculum by introducing an honour school in natural science. At this time the ancient universities of Oxford and Cambridge were still dominated by their affiliation with the established Church of England. This meant that, although scientific study was now recognised as a serious and worthy enterprise at university level, it would still have a close connection to official religiosity. There were those who of course took a more secular view of science, but the age of science as entirely disconnected from religion was yet to come. Despite broad evolutionary or 'developmental' concepts having gained in credence through the work of geologists such as Charles Lyell in the 1830s and 1840s, the thunderous claims of Darwin and his theory of natural selection were still a few years off (see Chapter 3). Thus, the idea for and deliberations over a new Museum of Natural History at Oxford were couched, initially at least, within the view that the physical sciences were

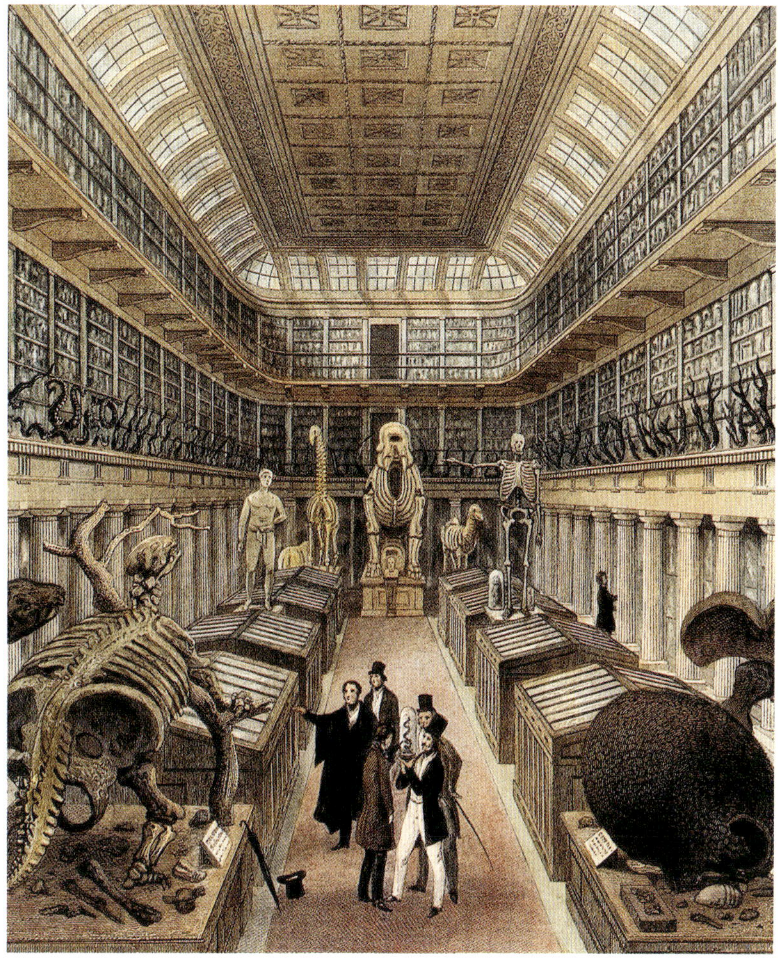

Fig. 144a

Hunterian Museum (1833–7), Royal College of Surgeons, London, by Charles Barry.

about illuminating the work of God, what was known at the time as 'natural theology'.

Having decided a museum was necessary, a competition for a facility encompassing not only museum displays, but also teaching, laboratory, and office space for academics and students was held in April 1854. By October that year, a little over thirty entries had been received. The two that caught the assessors' attention were a Classical ensemble by E. M. Barry (son of Charles), and a Gothic one by the Irish firm of Thomas Deane and Benjamin Woodward. Given the wider 'battle' over style in mid-Victorian architecture, and the fact that the museum's display was supposed to reflect not just the diversity of God's creations but also their relative hierarchy, the question of which style would best facilitate this aim was paramount. In the end it was decided that Barry's Classical proposal would not do, mainly because it would have been difficult to extend owing to its rigid symmetry. Moreover, as Henry Acland, a leading Oxford professor and one of the prime movers behind the scheme, observed, an attachment between the new sciences and the old medieval associations of the university was only fit and proper. This is crucial, for it was among the first instances where patrons, architects, and

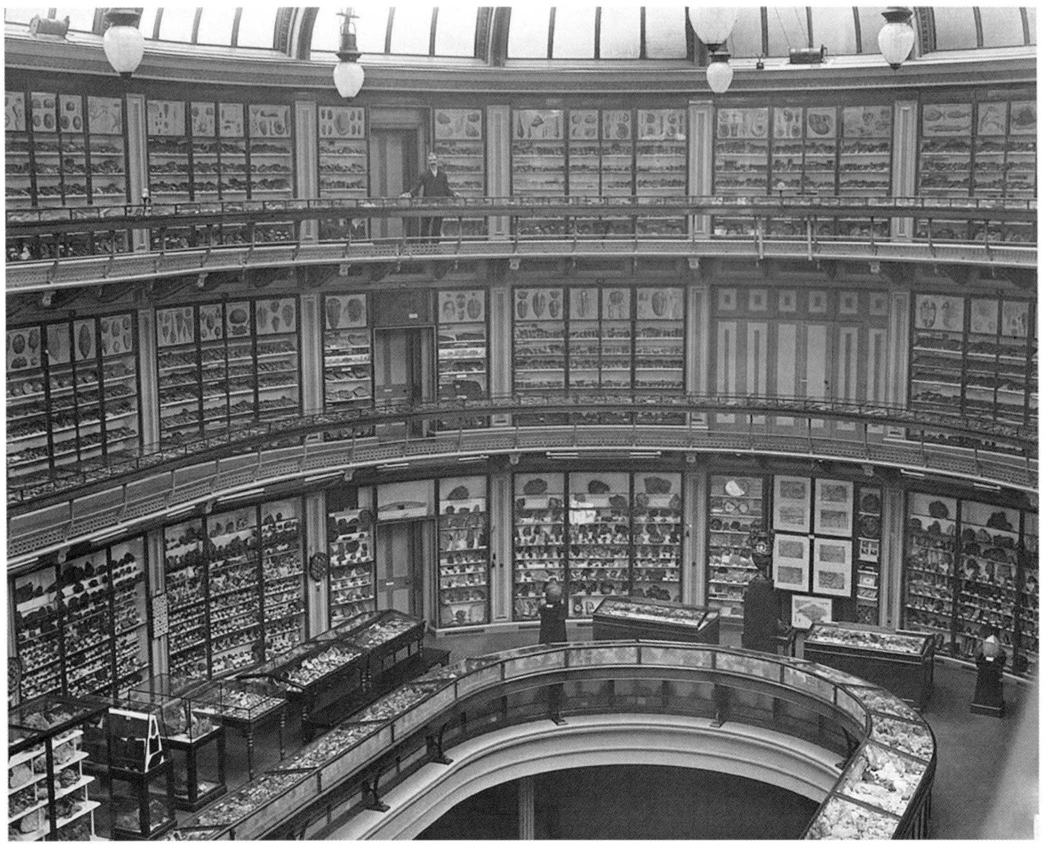

144b

Specimen display area, Museum of Practical Geology, Jermyn Street (1846–51), London, by James Pennethorne.

critics alike insisted upon a closer relationship between the idea of natural history and naturalistic design in architecture. Indeed, it was on this point that George Edmund Street argued that Gothic architecture was better suited to such a facility not only because it was more technologically advanced and therefore of greater 'scientific' merit than Classical architecture, but that Gothic forms lent themselves more easily to naturalistic detailing and the organic arrangement of space.[10]

With Deane and Woodward duly awarded the commission, construction began in 1855 **[145]**. Considering the location and ecclesiastical associations evoked, it is hardly surprising that the museum was planned around a cloistered quadrangle. This in fact became a glass-covered atrium. Around it were arrayed the laboratories, lecture rooms, and offices in an asymmetrical fashion, catering for subjects such as experimental physics, mineralogy, chemistry, geology, and zoology **[146a]**. The glazed atrium, or 'court' as it was known, was devised to enable a copious and evenly distributed amount of light to enter the building for the observation of specimens. Although the atrium did not please everyone, especially John Ruskin (who was advising on the project), it was nevertheless an ingenious and aesthetically sympathetic solution comprising a number of artistically treated, pointed-arch frames in iron **[146b]**. It was produced by Skidmore of Coventry, one of the country's leading metalworkers. Glass and iron architecture had been seen before, of course,

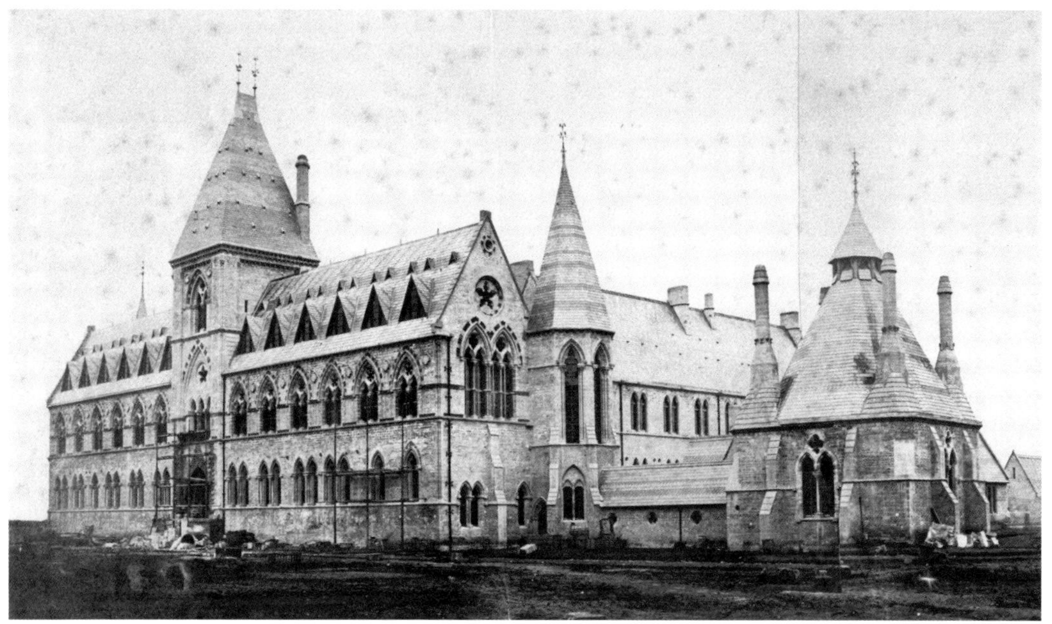

Fig. 145

Natural History Museum, University of Oxford (1855–60), Parks Road, Oxford, by T. N. Deane and Benjamin Woodward.

namely at the Crystal Palace, but the Natural History Museum at Oxford went much further in using it to enhance the general stylistic theme of the building. Here was a space, indeed building, that was historically aware yet entirely modern; knowingly anchored in the past whilst burnishing its progressive credentials. When completed in 1861, it stood as one of the first examples of modern Gothic applied to what was essentially a secular purpose: the museum.

The museum's display of specimens was laid out in a dispersed fashion, allowing freedom of movement in comprehending the taxonomic patterns evident in what Acland described as the 'unwritten Word' of the 'Supreme Master-Worker' (i.e., God). This married a particular regime of 'seeing' with certain pedagogical initiatives, whereby observation and experimentation were combined *in situ* in formulating new knowledge about the natural world. In this the architectural setting itself played an important role. For instance, as in the vestibule at the Museum of Practical Geology, granites and marbles sampled from across the British Isles were used in the construction of the arcades, in particular the columns. These were labelled explicitly as such, enabling students to discern the geological composition and diversity of those islands through engaging with the building as a type of teaching aid **[147a]**. Moreover, the structural systems of the building may be seen (and were no doubt intended) to strike appropriate analogy with those of an organic nature, such as the unavoidable synergy between the skeletal iron frame of the atrium and the outsized specimen skeletons displayed within.[11] The same may be said for the use of the oolitic Bath Stone in both the interior and exterior facing of the building, with its sedimented compaction of shells alluding to the museum's own mollusc collection; or, indeed, the layered effect of the interior brickwork echoing geological stratification.

The collaboration between scientists and artists in the decoration of the building conjured further such association. Pre-Raphaelite principles of

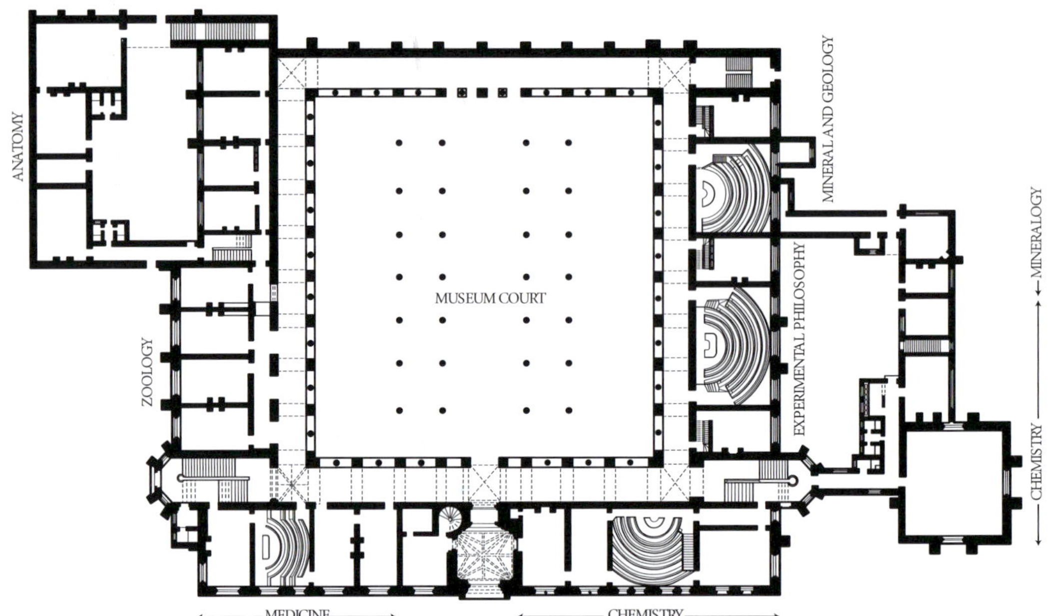

Fig. 146a

Plan, Natural History Museum, Oxford.

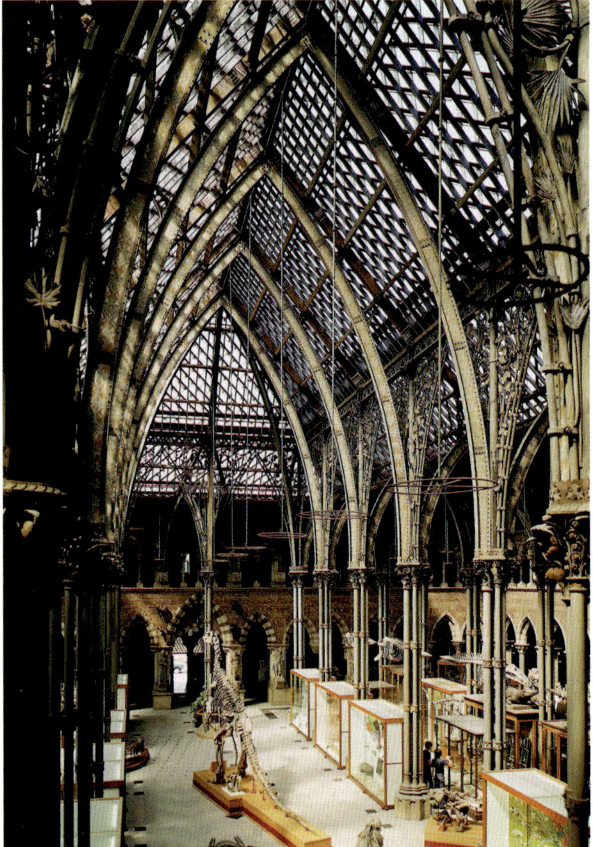

Fig. 146b

Gothic iron arches in the glazed atrium (court) of the Natural History Museum, Oxford.

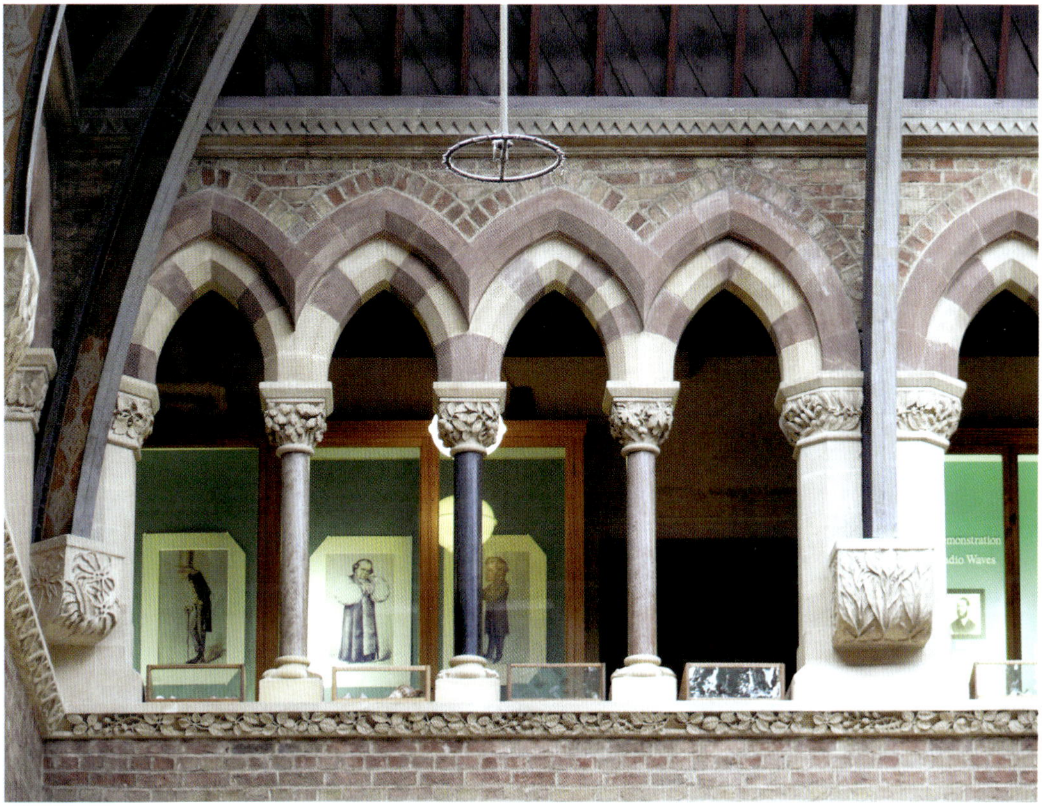

Fig. 147a

Arcade columns, upper gallery, Natural History Museum, Oxford. These represent different stones from around the British Isles.

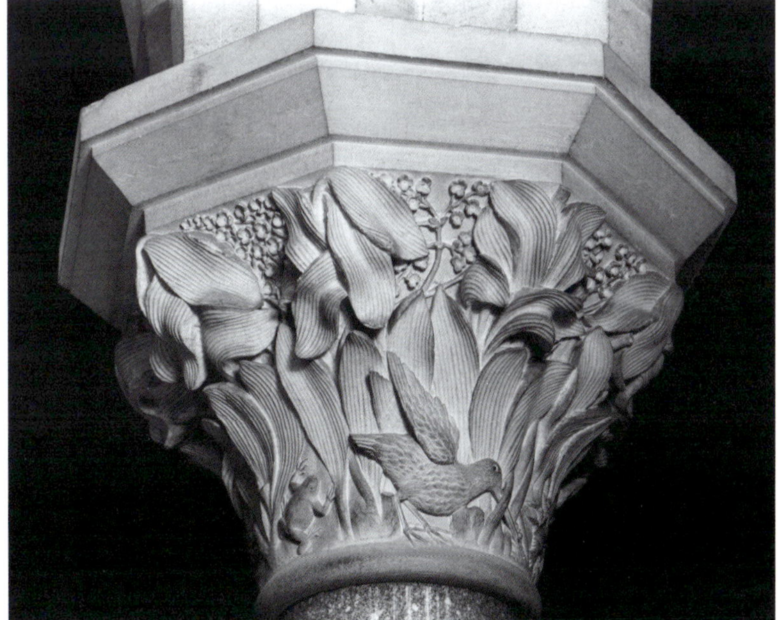

Fig. 147b

Carved capital and corbel from lower arcade, Natural History Museum, Oxford.

truth to nature were embedded in the designs for the many column capitals and corbels that embellished the court arcade, sculpted by the likes of James O'Shea and Edward Whelan. Far from random or merely illustrative, they carefully depict flora and fauna within given environmental ecologies, both local and exotic **[147b]**. This enriched the building's didactic ambition. Similar attempts at genus specificity are also evident in the wrought iron floral decoration on the capitals of the atrium frame. The 'story' of science was told through the installation of nineteen, life-sized statues around the court perimeter of prominent men of science, from Aristotle and Bacon, through Galileo, Newton, and Leibnitz, to Linnaeus and Darwin. Indeed, the all-encompassing theme of the building impressed itself upon the visitor at its very entrance, where, stretching along the pointed archway of the main portal, allegorical sculpture depicting Adam and Eve culminates in a roundel motif at its apex containing the relief of an angel. This, declared Acland, was 'the Angel of Life, bearing in one hand an open book, the emblem of intellectual and spiritual life, in the other the dividing nucleated cell, the type of all material function, growth, and decay'.

Evolving Patterns: Variations on a Theme

Similar to the Natural History Museum at Oxford was the Museum at Trinity College, Dublin (1853–7). Designed slightly earlier by the same architects, this building, inspired by Ruskin's musings on the polychromy of medieval Italian architecture, also incorporated at least eight different coloured marbles from Ireland and Cornwall in its grand vestibule and staircase, including in columns, handrails, and banisters **[148]**. Although not labelled in the same way as at Oxford, this decorative schema was nevertheless intended to illustrate and therefore provide something of a lesson in British ornamental stones. Similar but different still was the Edinburgh Museum of Science and Art (1860–89, now National Museum of Scotland), designed by the English engineer-cum-architect and Cole circle affiliate, Francis Fowke **[149a]**. Given the stronger links between industry and learning that came through the Scottish Enlightenment, including in formal educational settings, emphasis was placed on the practical and economic history and outcomes of the museum. Whereas in England there was the growing propensity to bifurcate collections along natural and anthropogenic lines, in Scotland their juxtaposition was encouraged. The principal motif here was that nature was in the service of human ingenuity, and the application of this through industry and art would foster commerce and civilisation. In this sense, natural history and human industry were seen as complementary rather than opposing categories. For the exterior of the building, Fowke, no doubt influenced by both Cole and Prince Albert's insistence on looking to German institutional models for South Kensington, adopted a rather utilitarian Renaissance-cum-German *Rundbogenstil* ('round-arched style') architecture, behind which he placed a magnificently light, cast-iron and glass 'great hall', inspired not only by the Crystal Palace, but also by his own design for the 1862 London International Exhibition building—a most appropriate allusion given the museum's commercial and civilisational imperatives **[149b]**.

Fowke appeared prominently again shortly afterwards, this time in the design of the Natural History Museum in South Kensington (first designed

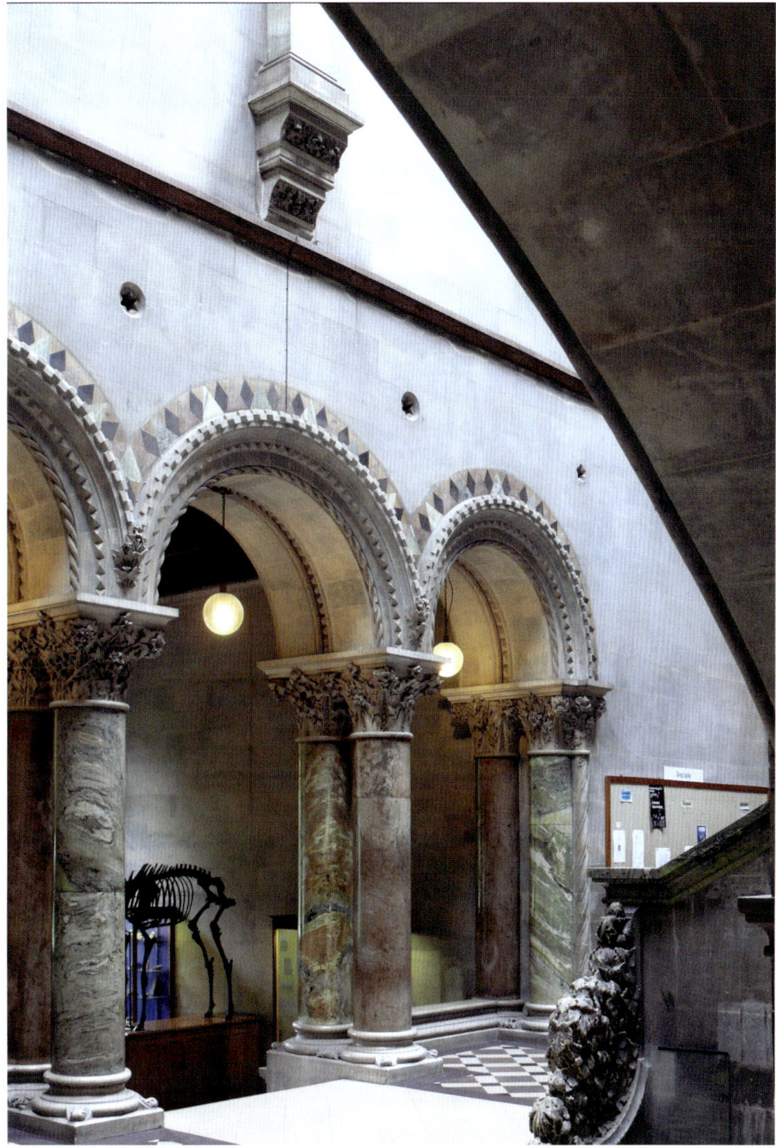

Fig. 148
Museum, Trinity College Dublin (1853–7), Ireland, by T. N. Deane and Benjamin Woodward. View from Inner Hall looking through marble colonnade to Hall (entrance).

1864; built 1873–81). As mentioned, this museum was considered necessary for housing the now hived-off natural history collections from the British Museum. Orchestrated by the noted biologist Richard Owen, under the watchful eye of parliament, its ambition was to showcase and therefore place 'natural history' on a public footing like never before. A building that would aid this agenda was obviously an important consideration, especially given the collection's widely acknowledged national (indeed, international) significance. For Owen, who became the museum's first director, such an institution was nothing less than a matter of national pride, a 'material symbol' befitting 'the greatest commercial and colonizing empire in the world'.[12] A competition for the new building was therefore held in 1864, from which Fowke initially emerged victorious. Fowke's design was in many respects

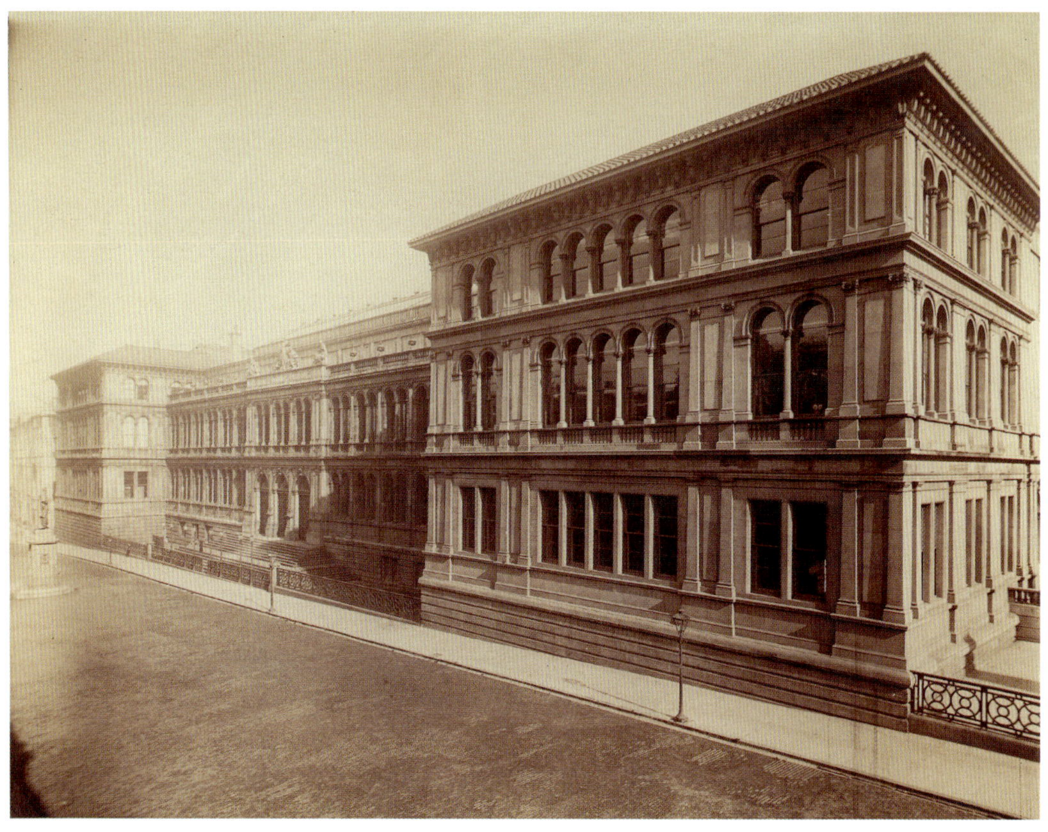

Fig. 149a

Edinburgh Museum of Science and Art (1860–89), Chambers Street, Edinburgh, now National Museum of Scotland, by Francis Fowke.

merely a much larger and slightly more elaborate version of his earlier proposal for the Edinburgh Museum of Science and Art, with the insertion of a number of domes and pavilion ends. As it happened, Fowke died unexpectedly in 1865. At this point, Alfred Waterhouse was appointed 'executive architect', seeing the project through to completion.

Among the more interesting aspects of the building was its plan. As with the planning of the other museums discussed here, there was a specific schema at work in Owen's strategies for display. Being a natural theologian, Owen believed that the collection, however it was arranged, should communicate the idea of God as the supreme creator. His initial 1859 sketch plan for the museum showed a rectangular building at the heart of which was located a large circular gallery and lecture theatre. Considering the museum's location and Owen's nationalist and imperial enthusiasms for it, this gallery was labelled 'British Collections' and other 'typical' specimens. In front was 'ethnology' (i.e., humans), and to either side—arrayed in distinct, comb-like rows perpendicular to the building's main front, and working from the perimeter inwards—were located mammals, mammalian osteology, and reptiles, on the one side, and birds, plants, zoophytes, and molluscs, on the other. Mineralogy and geology were placed towards the rear. Each row thus functioned like a drawer in a grand taxonomist's cabinet. With visitors encouraged to take a certain route through the collection, this arrangement not only reflected Owen's own nationalism, but its phylo-

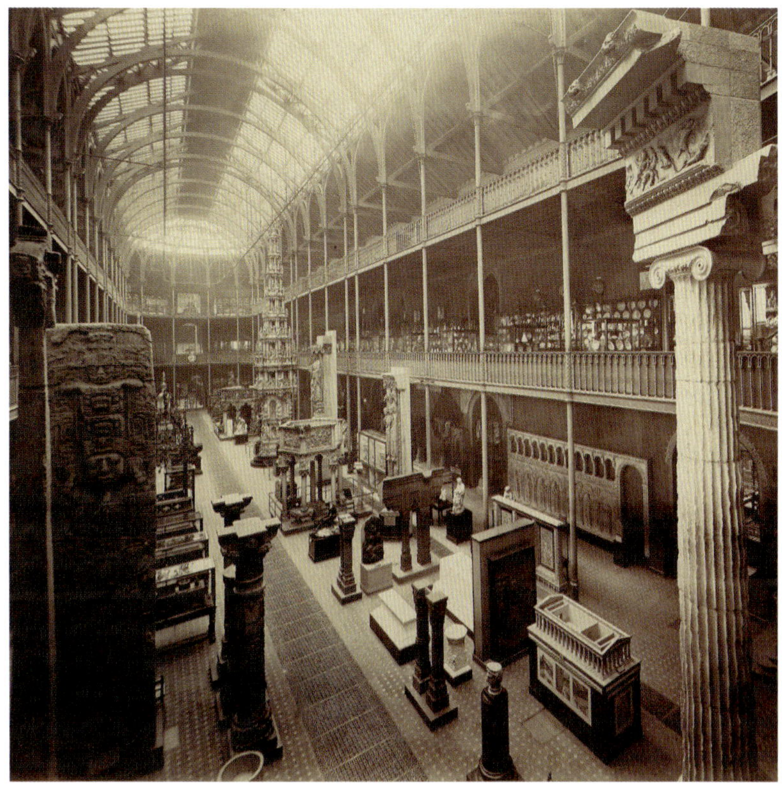

Fig. 149b

Great Hall, Edinburgh Museum of Science and Art.

genetic layout also revealed his views on divine hierarchy in the natural world. Although this schema would not survive the planning process, its essential elements remained intact. Indeed, this circuit-based approach to museum planning was later deployed at the Imperial Institute, which would rise immediately behind the Natural History Museum. Here visitors were inspired to take a geographical 'tour' around the empire, with Britain and its collections located firmly at the centre of this 'world' in microcosm. In both cases, architecture was marshalled specifically to force a particular narrative about the planet, its creatures, and idealised political constitution.

When Waterhouse took over the museum commission, rather than simply following Fowke's proposal, he redesigned it (1868–71). As mentioned, in terms of planning the comb-like array of Owen's display schema remained evident, although the central circular spaces were replaced by a large, nave-like hall, with the British collections now occupying the head (i.e., top, north) of the layout **[150]**. In terms of the architecture, however, Waterhouse proposed something entirely different, with far greater aesthetic power. Foregoing Fowke's rather bland neo-Renaissance facades, he opted instead for a bulky German Romanesque **[151]**. There were several reasons for this, not least Waterhouse being a committed medievalist. But the clear religious undertones of the style alluded to the notion that the museum, in the context of natural theology, was something of a great cathedral of science ('Temple of Nature'), reflected in its entrance pavilion and unmistakable nave-like central hall. True to Waterhouse's interest in the application of

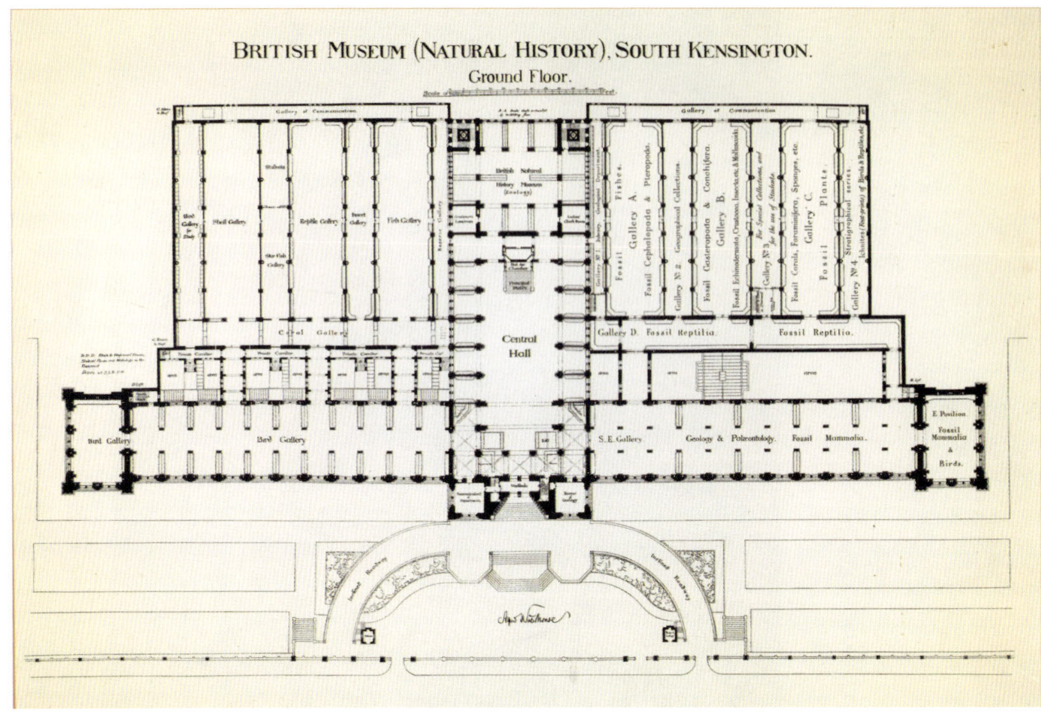

Fig. 150

Plan, Natural History Museum, London. Redesigned by Alfred Waterhouse following the death of Francis Fowke between 1868 and 1871.

technologically advanced building materials, the whole was clad in beige and grey-blue terracotta tiles.

Like the Oxford Museum before it, the building's decoration also spoke directly to the nature and purpose of the collections it kept. Here we see myriad types of flora and fauna, both extinct and living, fully formed or in relief, arrayed across the building. Some of these are repeated many times throughout the structure, such as the birds and monkeys that perch and cling around the arches that comprise the central hall **[152]**. Unlike at Oxford, however, these are patterned types, moulded and mechanically produced. This 'terracotta menagerie' reflected Owen's own view that God produced types as opposed to individuals, established forms rather than evolving populations.[13] Again, architecture serves a didactic purpose here, only in a different way. But not everyone liked or accepted this schema, especially Owen's chief professional rival, the Darwinian evolutionist T. H. Huxley. With biological science now bending towards the increasingly secular hypothesis of evolution by natural selection, Huxley and his colleagues' critique of the building for its religious connotations was not without merit. Perhaps most irksome of all was the statue of Adam standing aloft the gable to the main entrance, hands raised heavenwards, reinforcing the hierarchy of God's creation. It would take some 50 years before this statue was finally toppled, reputedly an innocent casualty of the Blitz.

Branching Out: Colonial Knowledge and the Museum

As we have seen, museums do not exist in a social or cultural vacuum. Their conception, techniques of display, and architectural setting were all

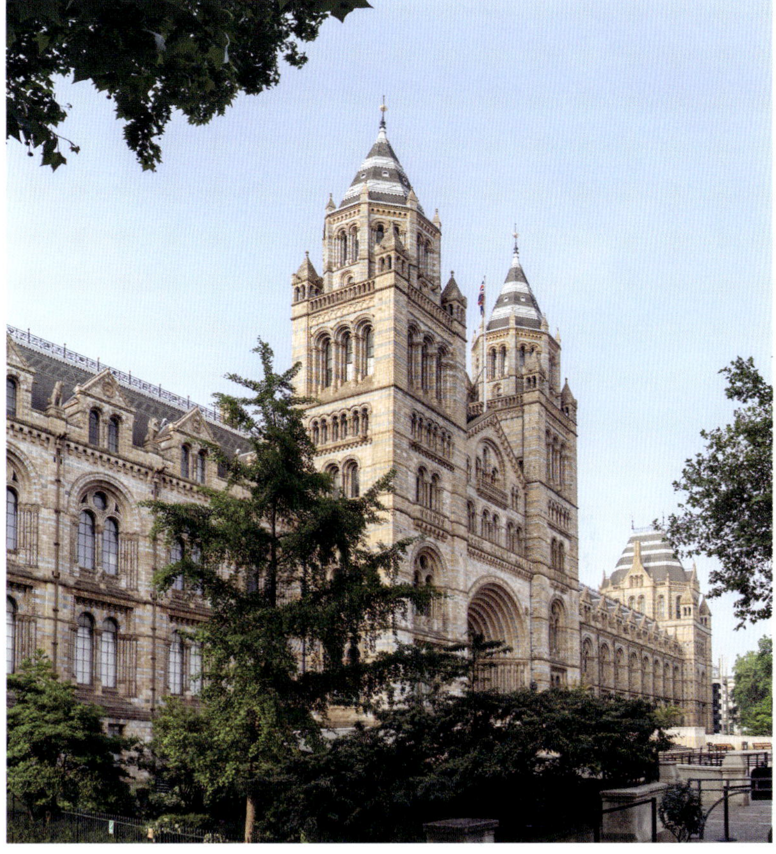

Fig. 151

Cromwell Road façade, Natural History Museum, London. The building was erected between 1873 and 1881.

contingent upon time and place. Britain during the Victorian period was at the centre of a burgeoning global empire, and this was necessarily reflected in how museum collections and spaces were organised and promoted. As the collections of missionary societies and the Imperial Institute revealed, museums in Britain relied to a considerable extent on maritime exploratory endeavours, the mission field, and colonialism to enhance and diversify their collections. Such institutions and their meaning were infused with an imaginary of Britain as a command centre of global resources, celebrated at the time as a rightful (indeed, God-given) benefit of civilisational leadership and commercial expansion. Moreover, the rise of ethnographic collections in British museums (e.g., the Pitt Rivers and Horniman museums), especially tribal items gathered and traded from places such as Africa and the Pacific, reflected contemporary anxieties concerning racial degeneration. These collections, as seen through the concomitant disciplines of ethnography and anthropology, were interpreted as indicators of robust cultural identity on the one hand, and civilisational precarity on the other, informing debates around national efficiency, eugenics, and social imperialism. In this sense, museums literally displayed Britain's relationship with the outside world, and how that relationship could be mediated and manipulated through particular narrative strategies and their related spatial configurations.

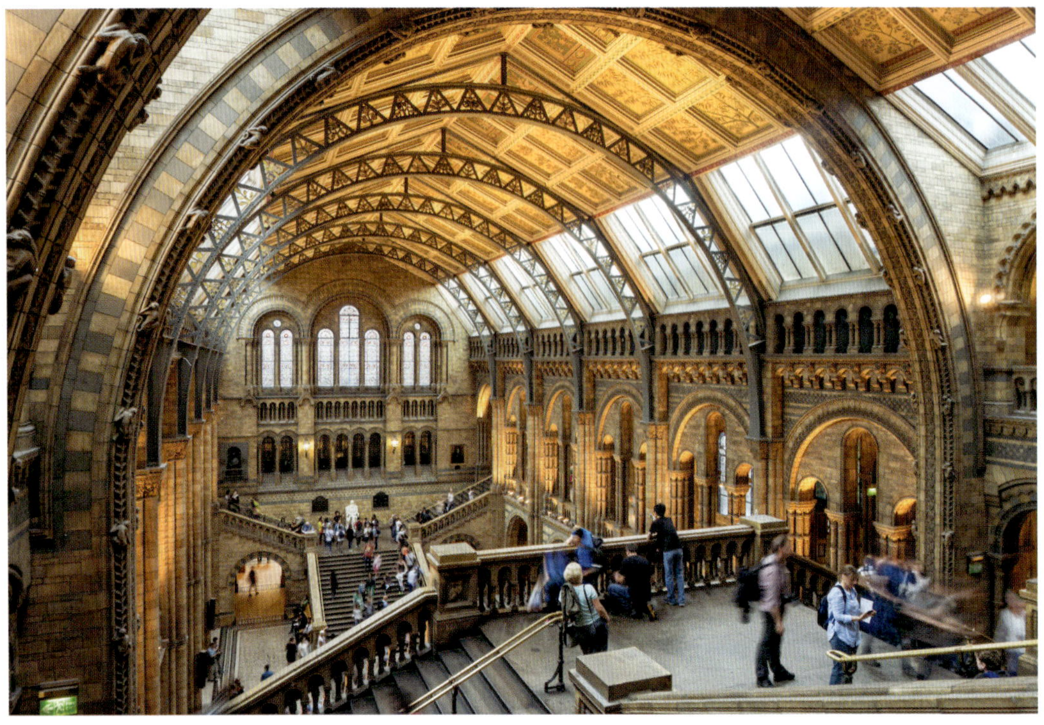

Fig. 152

Teeming with wildlife: Central Hall, Natural History Museum, London.

Modern museums of this kind had of course sprung up in other parts of the world: throughout Europe, in the United States of America, and across parts of the British Colonial world. Many expanded in the nineteenth century, adding new buildings as their collections grew; others were founded from scratch. Two of significance in the wider context of Victorian architecture are the Smithsonian Institution in Washington, D.C. (1849–55), by James Renwick Jr., and the University of Pennsylvania library and museum (1888–90), by Frank Furness. The latter of these is especially noteworthy for its powerfully articulated neo-Romanesque forms in red brick, terracotta, and stone **[153a]**. Based on similar collecting and display principles to those museums discussed above, the Smithsonian was noted for its extensive mineralogical and zoological collections obtained during westward settlement of the North American interior, with the neo-Romanesque 'castle' that housed them working to construct a reassuring and bountiful image of the American West to a nation shaken and divided by civil war.[14] Indeed, New World 'national' and colonial museums, rather than focusing on showcasing what globally sourced objects they might obtain, were better suited, and often better known, for their collections of local raw materials, artefacts, and ethnographic displays, servicing practical knowledge and commercial exploitation.

There are many other buildings of this type one could point to. Those which warrant mention here include a number of Neo-Classical examples, such as the Australian Museum, Sydney (1846–66), by Mortimer Lewis and Alexander Dawson **[153b]**; the Redpath Museum, McGill University, Montreal (1882), by A. C. Hutchinson and A. D. Steele; and the (Iziko) South African Museum, Cape Town (1892), by J. E. Vixseboxse. On the

Fig. 153a

University of Pennsylvania library and museum (1888–90), Philadelphia, United States of America, by Frank Furness.

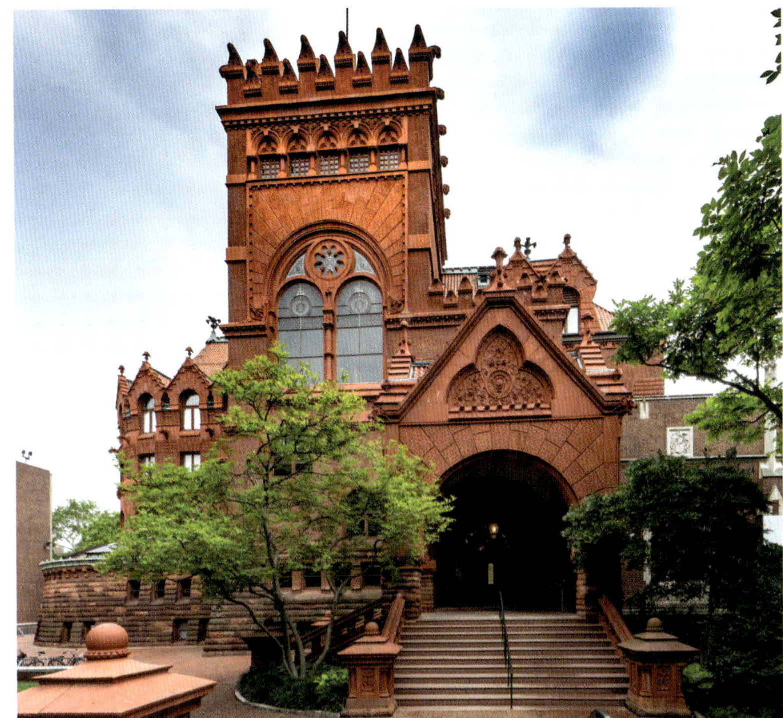

Fig. 153b

Australian Museum, Sydney (1846–66), Australia, by Mortimer Lewis and Alexander Dawson.

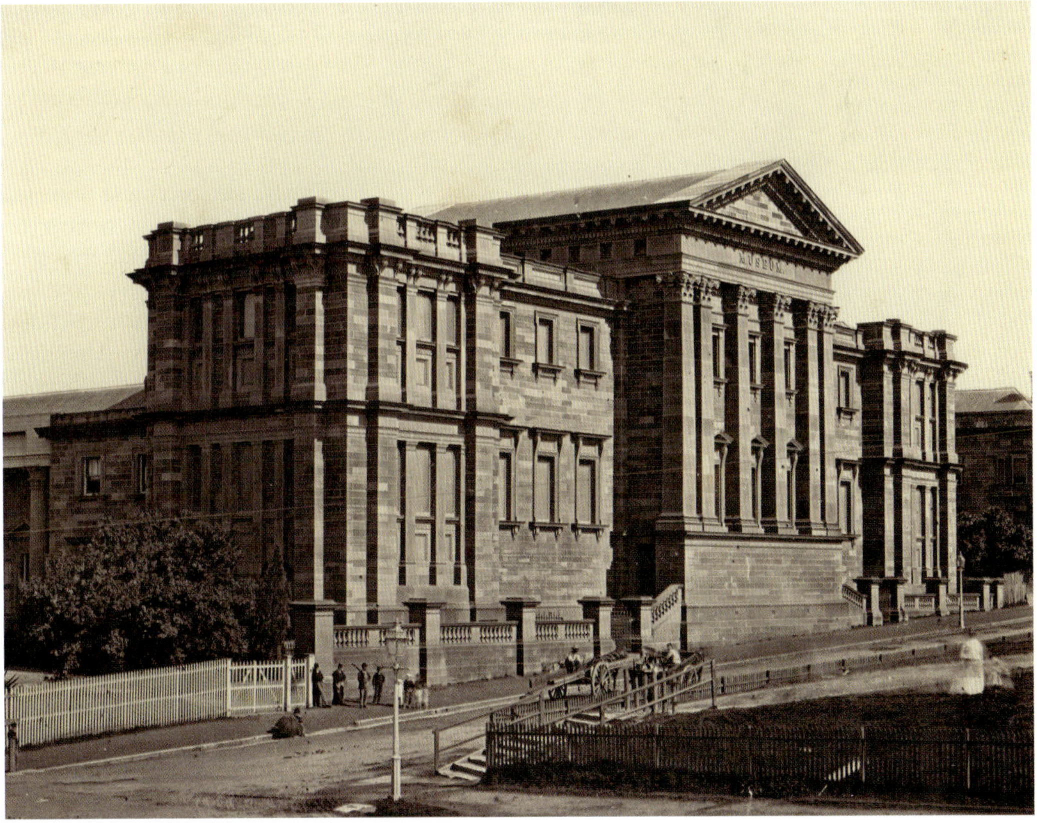

Gothic side there is the Canterbury Museum in Christchurch, New Zealand (1869–82), by Benjamin Mountfort; and the National Museum of Victoria, Melbourne (1862), by Reed & Barnes **[154a]**. In British India there were some more traditional architectural types, such as the Victoria and Albert (Dr Bhau Daji Lad) Museum, Bombay (1862–71), by William Tracey, erected with much financial support from the local Parsi elite; the extraordinary Indo-Saracenic confection that is the Albert Hall Museum (1876–87), Jaipur, by Swinton Jacob; and the Prince of Wales Museum (1905–15), Bombay, by the Scottish architect George Wittet **[154b]**.

The National Museum of Victoria is an interesting case in point. Given its serious academic pretensions, the museum was initially attached to the nascent University of Melbourne (est. 1851). It was headed by the Dublin-born scientist Frederick McCoy, who moved to Melbourne in 1854, and who had previously been an acolyte of Adam Sedgwick at Cambridge. Also an associate of Owen, McCoy was an anti-Darwinian 'typologist'. He built his collection at Melbourne through networks in Britain, Australia, and other parts of the world, either purchasing specimens outright, or via formal exchange. In this McCoy showed how operating within imperial networks enabled the expert assessment and transferal of specimens across the globe, in turn providing the colonial public with a valuable educational asset. This aspiration on the part of colonial society to replicate and extend European cultural and knowledge-based practices was evident also in the museum building. Completed in 1862 to the designs of Melbourne firm Reed & Barnes, it looked to models in Britain for inspiration, including multi-layered, top-lit exhibition spaces. Apart from the professional literature available in the Australian colonies at the time, Reed had probably experienced such spaces first hand in Britain before emigrating to Melbourne in 1853.

Considering its location within the university, the early buildings of which were based on Oxbridge collegiate archetypes, it is not surprising

Fig. 154a

National Museum of Victoria, Melbourne (1862), Australia, by Reed & Barnes (photo 1871).

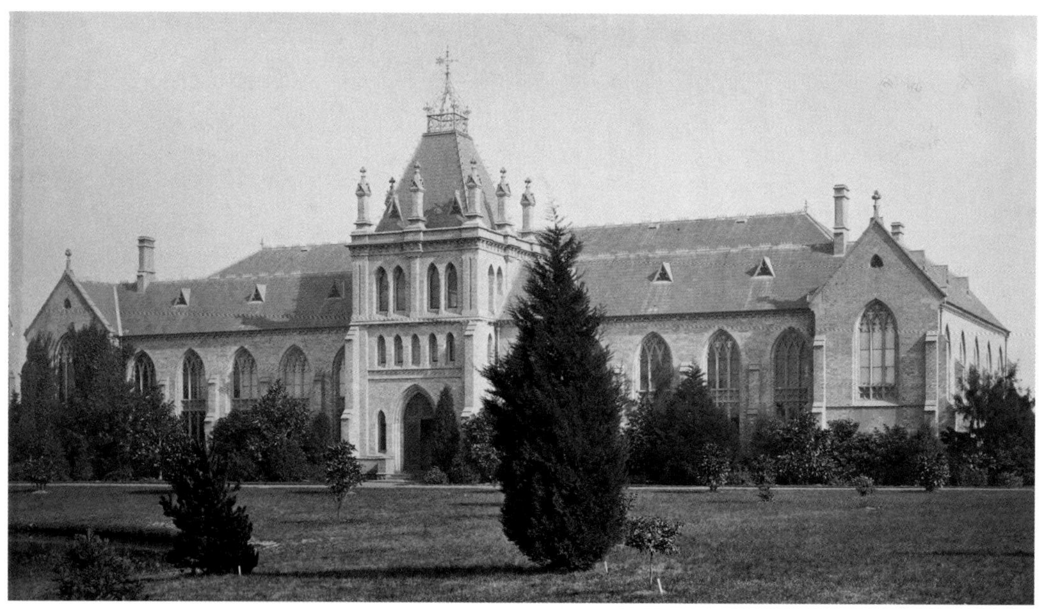

Fig. 154b

Prince of Wales Museum (1905–15), Bombay (Mumbai), India, by George Wittet.

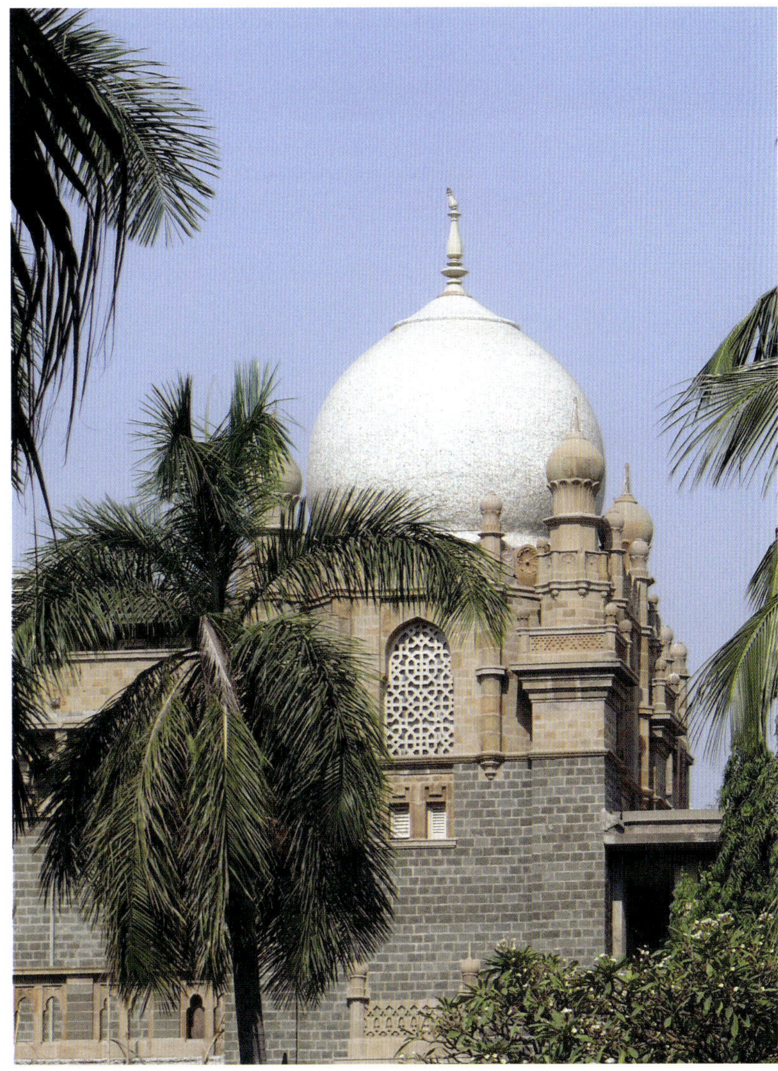

that the museum referenced its recently completed Oxford counterpart in terms of massing and choice of style, along with other possible sources, including G. E. Street's proposal for the same building (1853), or G. G. Scott's original published design for the Foreign Office (1857). These references were also evident at the Canterbury Museum. Materially, like its Oxford progenitor, the medium was to be the message. According to the civic authorities who commissioned it, the Canterbury Museum, it was hoped, would utilise 'every variety' of granite, slate, and marble available in the area, including 'crystals from our mountain ranges introduced with the best effect'. This, it was further claimed, would allow the building to 'show our appreciation of its contents, and through them of the refined pursuits, and ennobling idea of which it ought to be an exponent'.[15] In both cases, architecture played an important role not only in shaping the respective collections of these museums but also in signalling professional connection, credibility, and cultural identity. Just as museums in Britain had presented the empire in microcosm, so too museums in the wider British world worked to stimulate and reinforce the imperial circuitry that underpinned scientific expertise, planning, and architectural know-how.

Art Galleries: Framing the Nation

The Victorian period may be considered the golden age of the art gallery. Prior to the 1820s, very few galleries as such existed in Britain, and those that did were either small, private, or restricted in opening hours, or to fee-paying visitors (or both). There were the royal academies of art in London and Edinburgh, with their periodic exhibitions, but these were elitist. There was the Dulwich Picture Gallery, too, but this was difficult to access. The age of the 'national' gallery had not yet dawned. In this sense, the rise of the art gallery as a public good had much in common with the new museum, both in its architectural ambition and in its strategies for display. As noted, there was a degree of overlap in the perceived remit of these allied institutions, with some museums containing their own picture galleries. Moreover, inquiry into the nature of such institutions occurred in the same fervid atmosphere of reform that exercised the political classes in the early nineteenth century, including their industrial and wider public purposes. Coming into the early Victorian period, the momentum for this may be credited not only to parliament's newly interventionist zeal on matters concerning the public utility of cultural largesse, but also to the administrative powers, scholarly acumen, and sense of public duty of those who would go on to play a leading role in establishing and managing the new art institutions, such as Charles Eastlake, Henry Cole, and George Scharf.[16]

Much of the sentiment around the socially ameliorative capacities of art in Victorian Britain can be found in the 1835–6 and 1841 Select Committee reports on art, design, and access to public 'monuments' in Britain. To this may be added the 1841 Fine Arts Commission on the decoration of the Houses of Parliament (see Chapter 4). These inquiries fed into the establishment of the Government Schools of art and design, the Great Exhibition of 1851, and the creation of public museums and galleries of art. While there was interest in the commercial opportunities that might be realised through such initiatives, concern was also raised over what one of these reports termed 'the moral and intellectual improvement of the People', which really meant (and later clarified as) the 'minds and manners of the working classes'. In a context of poor life chances and rising social unrest among an increasingly large proportion of the population, 'rational' recreational pastimes, such as looking at art, were promoted not only as having a soothing-cum-civilising effect on the observer, but also as a means of sparking curiosity and thus an impetus to self-improvement. Anything, it was surmised, that would keep the 'lower classes' off drink and away from other popular vices, allowing them to mix with and learn from their betters, was considered beneficial. Indeed, as George Godwin put it in 1859, in bringing Britain's 'two nations' together (rich and poor), art was considered 'a social bridge of no ordinary size and strength'.[17]

As trite as some of these aspirations may seem to us today, they did find tangible expression. For instance, coming in the wake of the Great Exhibition

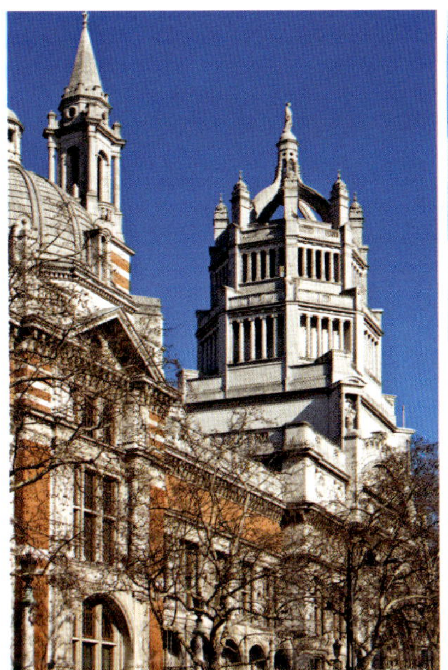

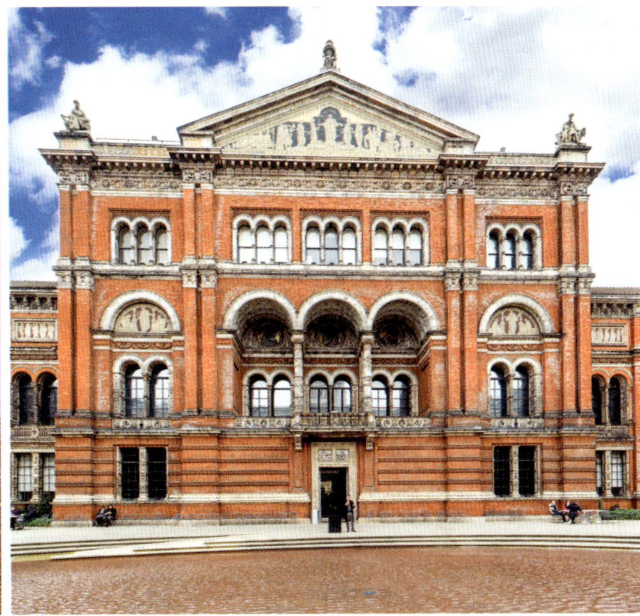

Fig. 155a

Victoria and Albert Museum, Cromwell Road front (1899–1909), South Kensington, London, by Aston Webb.

Fig. 155b

South Kensington (now Victoria and Albert) Museum, Exhibition Road, London, by Francis Fowke, with Henry Y. D. Scott and Godfrey Sykes.

of 1851 was the South Kensington Museum (est. 1854). This was an attempt to capitalise on the exhibition's success by providing dedicated spaces for further and continued public engagement. The museum was a place where specimen artefacts were collected and curated, and where these could be utilised in aid of art education and commercial development. The latter of these aims was advanced with the move of the recently established Government Schools of art and design from Somerset House, in central London, to South Kensington upon the museum's establishment. Combined, these institutions would eventually become the Victoria and Albert Museum, with its grand, neo-Baroque frontage to Cromwell Road designed by Aston Webb (1899–1909) **[155a]**. The initial buildings (1859–72), along Exhibition Road, were a more modest affair. Designed by Fowke, in conjunction with Henry Y. D. Scott and Godfrey Sykes, they were nonetheless distinctive in their terracotta-emblazoned, red-brick Italianate facades, typical of 'Cole circle' architecture of the period **[155b]**. The South Kensington Museum, as envisaged, was not only for manufacturers and students, however. With extended opening hours and the installation of gas lighting, it was very much intended as a site for the edification of the working classes, if they were willing to make the effort in getting there. In this respect, the South Kensington Museum represents the beginnings of Prince Albert's vision (under the management of Henry Cole) for transforming South Kensington into a permanent centre for the national advancement of art, design, and public education—hence the attachment of the somewhat facetious moniker 'Albertopolis'. As such, it was necessarily a site where the world met South Kensington, with all the imperial entanglements that entailed **[156]**.

One of the greatest legacies to emerge from the governmental agenda concerning public utility was the National Gallery in London. First established in 1824 through the largesse of the state for the public purchase of

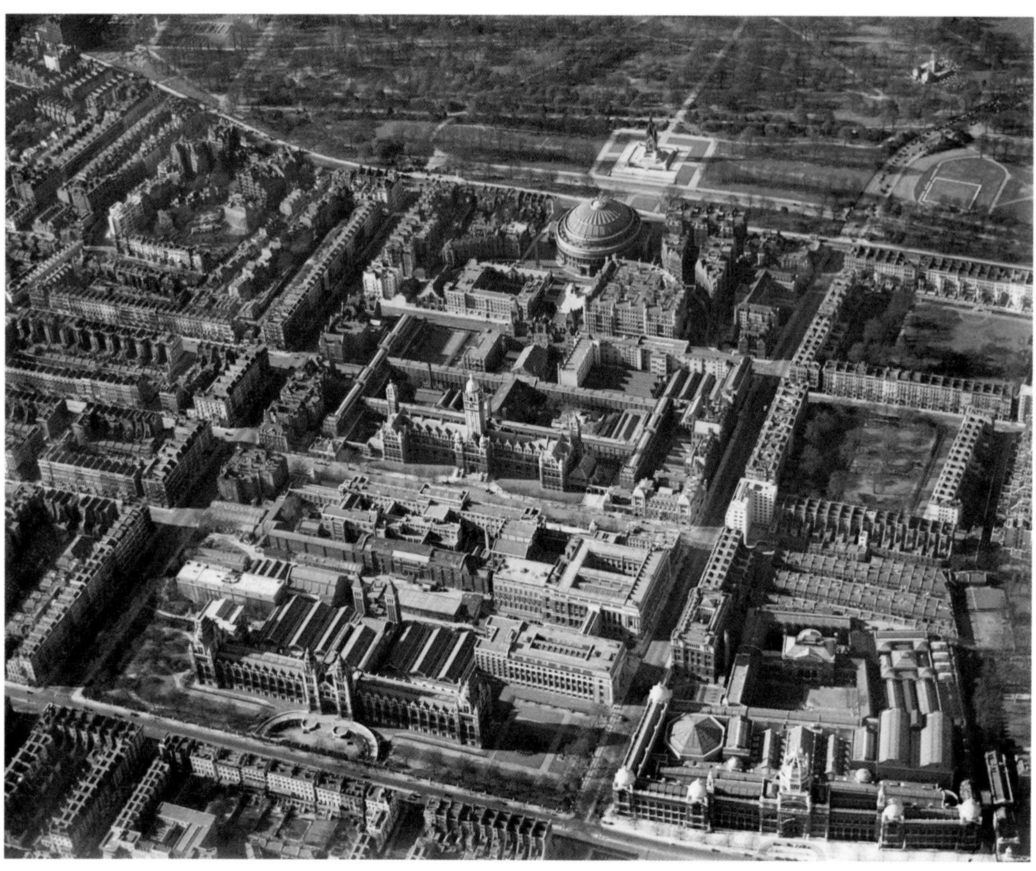

Fig. 156

March of the cultural and scientific institutions. Aerial view of 'Albertopolis', South Kensington, London. Front, middle: Natural History Museum; centre (with single tower): Imperial Institute; centre, top: Albert Hall (oval-shaped building) and Albert Memorial (directly opposite); bottom right: Victoria and Albert Museum.

paintings, it soon came to occupy the decidedly austere, Neo-Grecian pile that now characterises the northern edge of Trafalgar Square. Designed by William Wilkins under a heavy burden of official parsimony, it was built between 1833 and 1838 **[157a]**. It was not long, however, before it was considered too small. By the 1860s Charles Eastlake, the gallery's first director, had amassed a formidable collection, especially of Italian masterworks. Apart from the stated programme of ameliorating the masses via free, unrestricted access, one of Eastlake's aims in curating the collection was to present a 'visible' history of art, laying the foundations for the discipline of professional art history, of which he was an early leading exponent. Bursting at the seams, the gallery was extended from 1868 to 1876 to designs by E. M. Barry, the interiors of which were in a far richer, polychrome Italianate Classicism, including extensive gilding, deep crimson damask wallpaper, and palatial marble columns **[157]**. These effects, such as the red walls, were determined by nineteenth-century colour theory and the evolving science of sight, applied in order to enable closer and better scrutiny of the works on display. Different strategies for lighting were also experimented with, including degrees of side-lighting in addition to lighting from above.[18] Through these developments, and the seriousness that attended them, the idea of a national collection for public display was institutionalised, with the

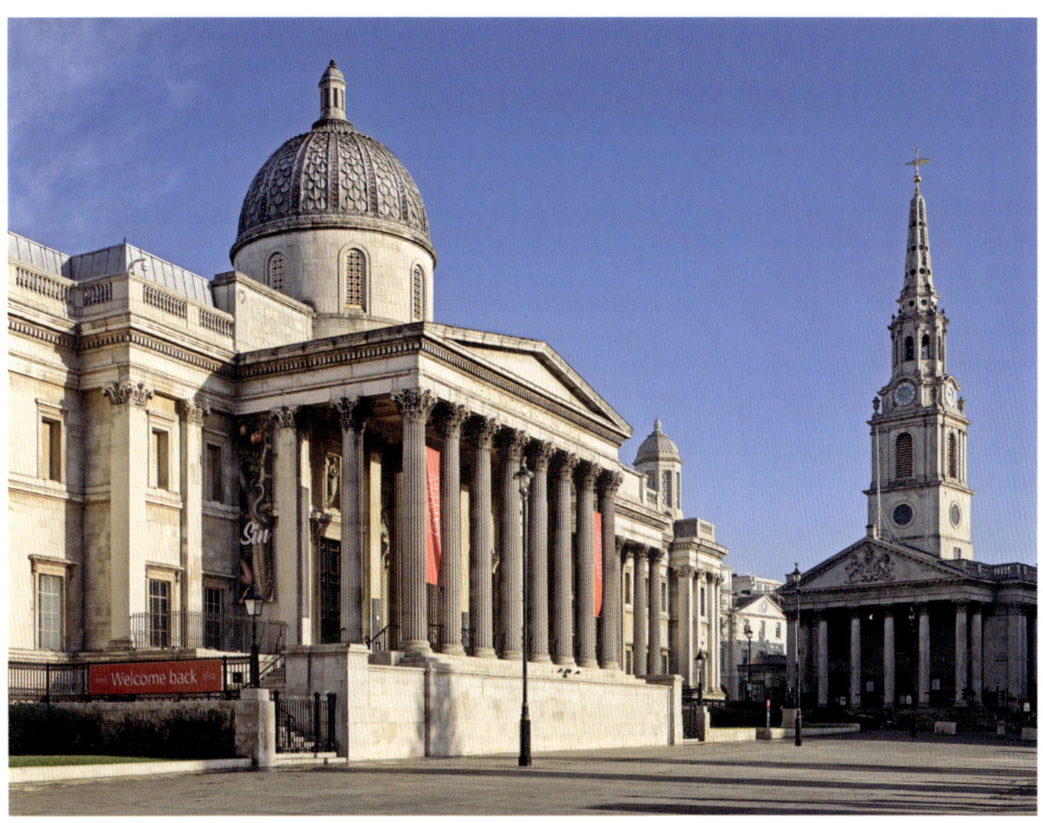

Fig. 157a

National Gallery, London (1833–8), by William Wilkins.

opulence of Barry's extension embodying this ambition, both architecturally and scientifically.

Indeed, a great nation, it was supposed, had to have great cultural institutions. A prize collection of paintings was understood in some quarters as exhibiting the more elevated attributes of a people who would pretend to be masters of the world, particularly in the context of nineteenth-century European nation building and imperial expansion. But such emoluments were not reserved for the imperial capital alone. Provincial, and even colonial, galleries sprang up. Collections of pictures were gathered in many of Britain's major industrial cities, often backed by the 'improving' patronage of manufacturing wealth. In upstart conurbations such as the Victorian goldfields town of Ballarat, some 10,000 miles away, similar sentiments prevailed. These 'municipal' museums and galleries were often seen in relation to the enlargement of societal aspiration, civic identity, and cultural connectedness; an attempt to bring morality through beauty in the creation of spaces for the display of art. Although some artists argued in defence of beauty for its own sake, other interlocutors, including the influential John Ruskin, insisted upon the link between aesthetics, ethics, and society at large in answering the ugliness of industrial capitalism. Such galleries and their art were thus perceived as an antidote not only to the chaotic forces of industrialisation and cultural isolation, but also to the dangers of empty materialism and rampant consumerism.

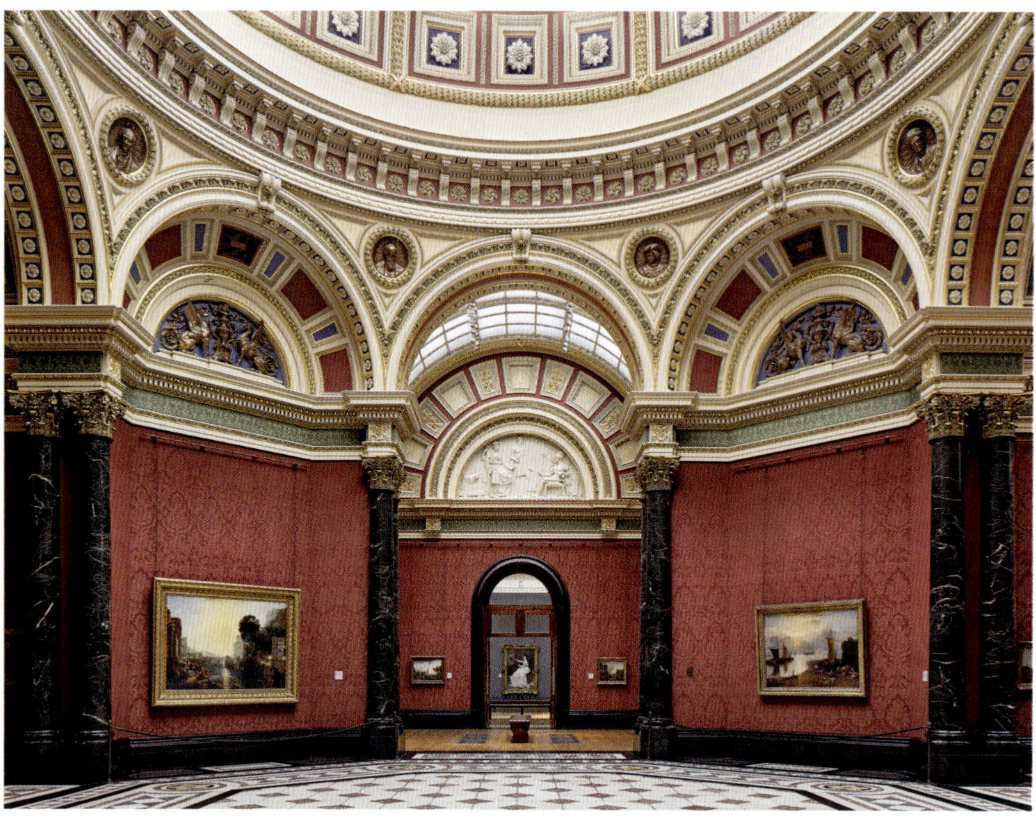

Fig. 157b

Interior of E. M. Barry's extension to National Gallery (1868–76).

Such middle-class anxieties were an imposition on the discourse of civic reformation in Victorian Britain. Real questions over who could access such spaces, and what the actual benefits would be, were never entirely settled. But evidence of their apparent efficacy is to be found in the buildings—often grand buildings—that were erected for these purposes. Much like the myriad other public institutions and spaces that appeared at this time in Britain's industrial cities (libraries, museums, town halls, parks and gardens), galleries of art were understood as monuments to a civic ideal, structures deliberately made conspicuous so that they might emanate a spirit of progressive and perpetual social transformation, while simultaneously projecting an image of civic order and stability. The cities of Liverpool, Manchester, and Birmingham, for instance, all had artistic societies that predated the Victorian period. But with the coming of government legislation in the 1840s and 1850s that allowed local authorities to raise taxes for cultural amenities, including museums, these societies became official municipal galleries. Erected adjacent to the recently completed Derby Museum in Liverpool was the Walker Art Gallery (1874–7), a stately Neo-Grecian edifice with Corinthian portico, to the designs of local architects Cornelius Sherlock and H. H. Vale **[158a]**; while in Birmingham a new museum and art gallery (1881–5) was got up through the revenues generated by the municipal gasworks. This was a rather eclectic but no less imposing building in a Free Classic style, designed by Birmingham-based architect Yeoville

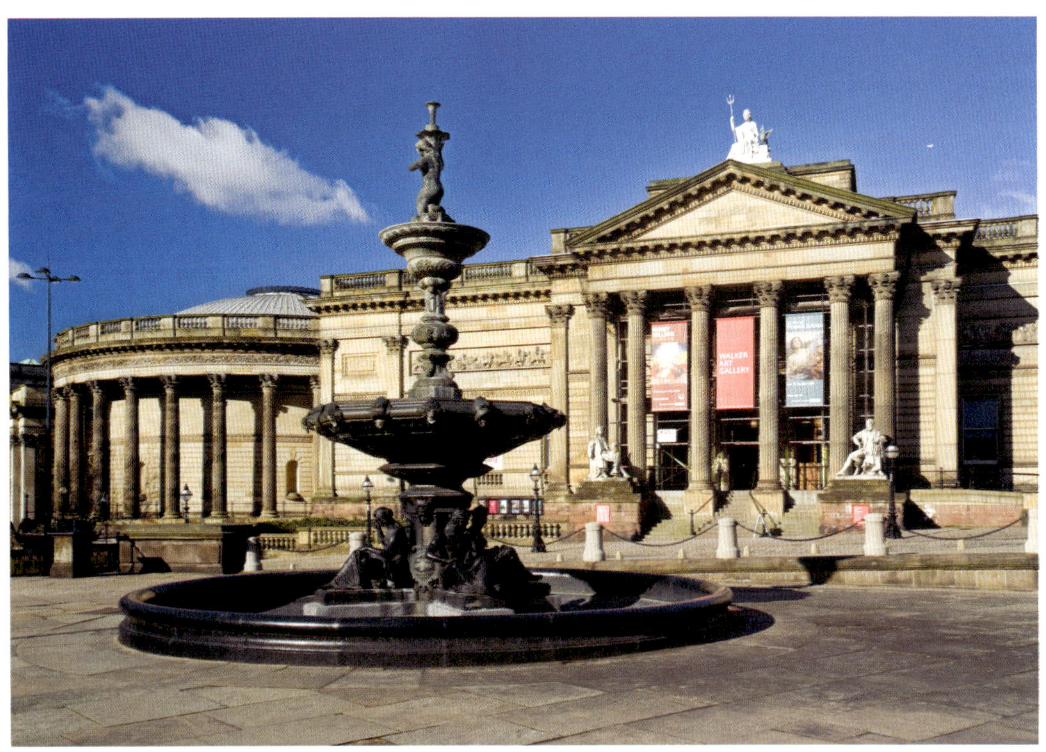

Fig. 158a

Walker Art Gallery, Liverpool (1874–7), by Cornelius Sherlock and H. H. Vale.

Thomason. Manchester City Art Gallery had existed previously as the Royal Manchester Institution (est. 1823), in a stout Neo-Greek building designed by Charles Barry in 1824 (completed 1835), becoming the official municipal gallery in 1883. Other provincial cities followed suit. In Sheffield, for instance, Weston Hall, a private residence, was brought by the municipal authorities and converted into the handsome, Neo-Greek city museum (1875), with the Mappin Art Gallery extension opening in 1887.

Through the lobbying of eminent historians such as T. B. Macaulay and Thomas Carlyle, the Victorian period also witnessed the advent of the modern portrait gallery. Realising the importance of collecting likenesses of the good and the great as a pendant to national identity formation, parliament legislated for the creation of a National Portrait Gallery, which was finally established in London in 1856. Initially under the direction of George Scharf, it had a peripatetic existence during its first 40 years, before taking up permanent residence (1885) in its current home at the side of the National Gallery in an Italianate palazzo-style building by Ewan Christian. Not surprisingly, Scotland insisted on its own portrait gallery. Established in 1882, and located in the Caledonian capital of Edinburgh, its current building on Queen Street was completed in 1890 to designs by Rowand Anderson **[158b]**. Given Anderson's earlier connection to the office of G. G. Scott, the design was in an eclectic secular Gothic 'of the latter half of the 13th century'.[19] It was erected in locally sourced Dumfriesshire sandstone, radiating a distinctive red hue, and was undoubtedly conceived as something of a challenge to William Playfair's Classically inspired National Gallery (1850–7)

Fig. 158b

Scottish National Portrait Gallery, Queen Street (1885–90), Edinburgh, by Rowand Anderson.

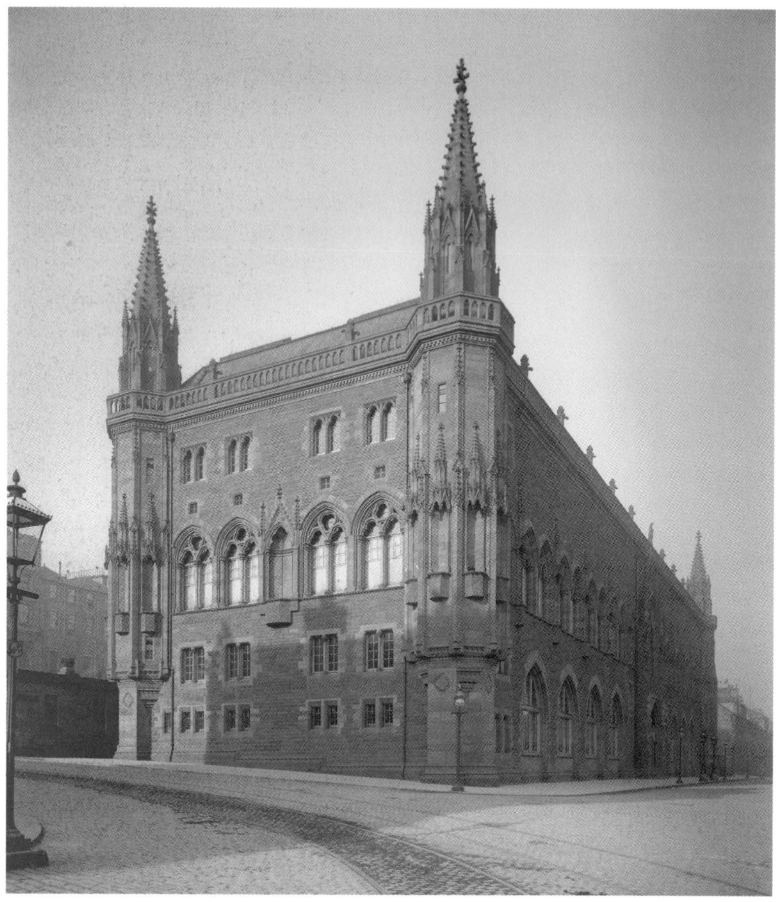

on The Mound. Both its exterior and interior are lavishly emblazoned with sculptures and murals of 'heroic' figures relating to Scottish history, including from the domains of religion, science, the arts, and monarchy. In typically Victorian fashion, the building itself thus stood—aesthetically, decoratively, and materially—as a didactic emblem of Scottish identity.

From the second half of the century art galleries of various kinds, both big and small, began popping up across the wider British world. Most of these had peripatetic beginnings, such as the National Gallery of Canada (est. 1880), Ottawa, which passed through three premises before ending up at the Victorian Memorial Museum (1905–11) on O'Connor Street, a large Tudor Gothic building by local government architect David Ewart. Other nascent collections had better luck, with dedicated accommodation being erected sooner. In the case of the Art Gallery of New South Wales, for instance, an 'annex' to the Sydney International Exhibition Building was erected in 1879 to designs by William Wardell, eight years after its initial establishment. This was in preparation for its ultimate move to a new building (1896–1909) in the Domain by government architect W. L. Vernon, a building not unlike the National Gallery of Scotland. It was a similar story in Melbourne. With much wealth from the central Victorian goldfields passing through the city in the early 1850s, one of the earliest colonial galleries was established there in 1861. The initiative was spurred by Melbourne's newly elevated sense of identity and cultural worth inspired by Victoria's separation from New South Wales as a crown colony in 1851. The collection was originally housed within the public library, moving to the purpose-built McArthur Gallery as part of the new State Library of Victoria (1854–1911), designed by Joseph Reed, in 1875.

By comparison with these larger urban developments, smaller, regional galleries also began to appear. These were often got up in the context of initiatives to provide training for local artists, in addition to such services already offered by the growing number of mechanics' institutes. The art gallery in Ballarat, central Victoria (est. 1884) has already been mentioned. This was one among a number that appeared in the regional vicinity of Melbourne at the time, including Warrnambool (1886), Bendigo (1887), and Geelong (1896). Promoted by James Oddie, a soon-to-be wealthy immigrant from Preston, Lancashire, the idea was to found a gallery along similar lines to those that had begun appearing in provincial England, and, through it, to adorn the fledgling 'city' of Ballarat with a Classical building of distinction.[20] To this end local architect William Tappin was engaged, and a modest building in an assured Italianate style was opened for the purpose on Lydiard Street in 1890. The Dunedin Public Art Gallery, the first public art gallery in New Zealand, was similarly established in 1884. Like so many embryonic collections, it began life in the local Otago Museum (1874–7), before eventually moving to Queen's Gardens in 1907. In the case of all these colonial museums, efforts were made to accumulate not only European works as emblems of taste and cultural memory, but also paintings by local artists with a view to encouraging a type of 'national' canon. Art institutions at 'home', in Britain, were specifically looked to as models of what might be achieved, especially the utilitarian museum-cum-school type established at South Kensington. Through the movement of works, artists, and teachers, art societies and galleries across the colonies became nodes in a wider imperial commercial art network. At the same time, strong egalitarian sentiment and civic pride vested such institutions with an 'ideology' of open access as a means to societal cohesion and improvement. Thus, colonial art galleries acted as incubators for self-reflection and the fomenting of colonial nationalist aspirations, ultimately helping smooth the way, somewhat ironically, to political independence.

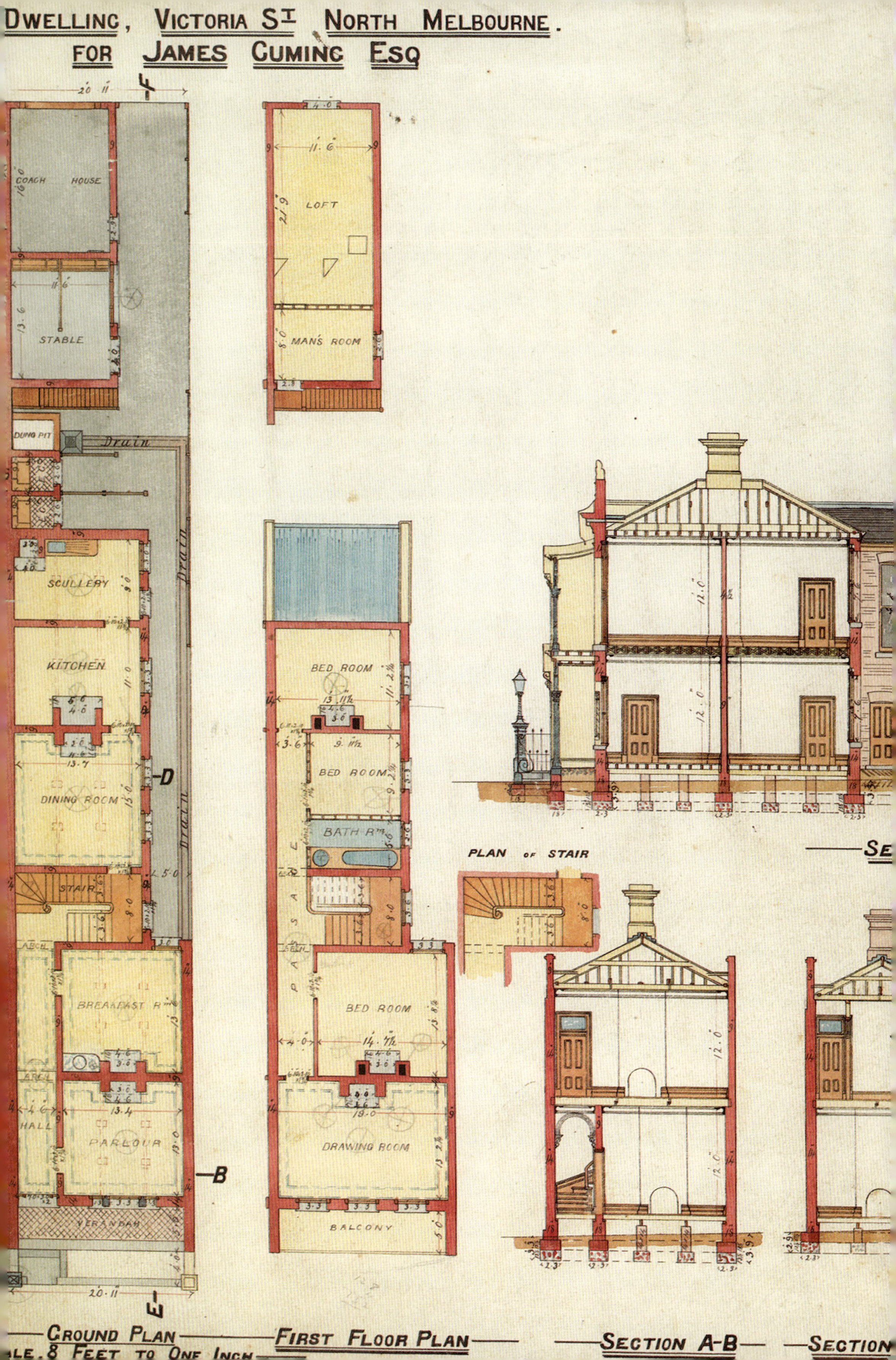
DWELLING, VICTORIA ST NORTH MELBOURNE.
FOR JAMES CUMING ESQ
COACH HOUSE
STABLE
LOFT
MAN'S ROOM
DUNG PIT
Drain
SCULLERY
KITCHEN
DINING ROOM
STAIR
BREAKFAST RM
HALL
PARLOUR
VERANDAH
BED ROOM
BED ROOM
BATH RM
PASSAGE
BED ROOM
DRAWING ROOM
BALCONY
PLAN OF STAIR
GROUND PLAN
SCALE 8 FEET TO ONE INCH
FIRST FLOOR PLAN
SECTION A-B
SECTION

8 Habits and Mores: Domesticity and the Victorian House

The one domain where we gain perhaps the greatest insight into the collective Victorian psyche, as well as the period's increasingly codified social mores, is the domestic house. In one form or another, domesticity and the domestic abode was the physical and psychological stronghold of the family. As both the practical and communal dimensions of familial life became ever-more circumscribed, in which the activities that were permitted (such as work) and the number of extended 'family' present in a household were curtailed, the ideal of family existence was sacralised as a marker of social and economic standing, especially among the middle classes and emerging industrial bourgeoisie. In this sense, the Victorian home nominally aspired to a separation between public and private, between the worlds of work and the family. Indeed, the family itself was marked by strict hierarchy and prescribed gender roles during this time, with the 'home' reflecting the influence of these separate spheres in its planning, function, and decoration. So important was this ideal considered to be that it spawned a whole genre of advice literature on how to create, manage, and maintain a comfortable and 'respectable' home. To this extent, the Victorian house was the outward expression of a profound and abiding commitment to a social economy of order, stability, and propriety.

Outside this aspirational ideal the situation was of course far more unstable, even chaotic. There was no one Victorian family type, even though discernible patterns were evident, and for the working and destitute classes, as we have seen, it was sometimes just enough to hold a family together. The concept of house and home was rather different for such people, who might find themselves in slum accommodation or, worse still, the workhouse. Nevertheless, the emotional cachet attached to the middle-class 'ideology of domesticity' had great currency during the period, and drove much of the architectural response in providing new household accommodation across Britain and the British world's burgeoning towns and cities. This necessarily resulted in a dynamic, ever-expanding, and often disruptive housing construction industry. Mostly speculative, this industry sought to keep pace not only with Britain's growing population but specifically with its mushrooming middle-class market, which was where the greatest and quickest profits were to be made. This industry catered for all types in this middling stratum, and although tremendous innovation and variety were achieved architecturally, with many excellent houses and flats erected, some of the outcomes were undoubtedly shoddy. The Victorian age witnessed the advent of the 'jerry builder'—a term denoting substandard construction that remains with us to this day.

Much of the growth in the Victorian middle-class housing market occurred in the expanding suburbs, which were beginning to spring up around major towns and cities. Some of the reasons for the advent of suburbs were discussed in Chapter 1, including the desire to escape the noise and pollution of the inner cities, but the possibility of better-appointed, more modern, and aesthetically pleasing domestic housing was also a major draw. This played into middle-class anxieties about identity and appearance, with families needing to be seen to reside in accommodation befitting their social status. It also encouraged social clustering. In these contexts we see the rise of the suburban villa type, either fully or semi-detached, as well as the ubiquitous Victorian town- and terraced houses that came to characterise many an inner-city suburb. Such anxieties were also evident in new country house design, suited to an age where immense, new-found wealth required corresponding degrees of luxury and grandeur. Indeed, the Victorian country house marked one extreme of what was deemed possible in the realm of domestic architecture during the period, even if it sometimes attracted accusations of vulgarity. In each of these scenarios architecture played a significant role as a medium of class distinction and expression, redolent of what these days we would term conspicuous consumption. This was especially so in an environment that was progressively saturated with industrially manufactured domestic product lines, increasingly accessible (and comparable) through catalogues and the rise of the department store. As we shall see, the ideal of the Victorian home was thus often hidebound by the 'tyranny' of Victorian taste.[1]

Planning and Typology: Space, Form, and Style

If the middle-class home may be understood as a kind of moral machinery in aid of propagating the separate gendered spheres of Victorian respectability, then its spatial and material dimensions were likewise divided to appeal to the norms of feminine and masculine power relations. Cultivating the protective intimacy of the home's interior was widely understood as a woman's obligation, with all the emotional effort and authority that entailed, while the idea of the 'home' as a physical object, in the world, was considered a manly preserve. In so far as a house was a piece of 'architecture', it was understood to embody a certain 'character'. Part of the building's social function as such was to convey this character, in turn communicating something of the standing and propriety of its occupants. This was the home's public face, so to speak, and naturally concerned the politics of identity that typified the Victorian class system. Thus, other similarly attuned observers could both interpret and judge the propriety of a home's occupants—their 'taste' and cultural attainment, etc.—partly through its physical structuring.[2]

In this sense, while the rather intangible, emotional qualities of day-to-day household management were down to women (organising, nurturing, caring), the 'design' and construction of houses was considered the task of men. Where intellectual effort was not required beyond expertise regarding issues of style and spatial arrangement (i.e., professional architectural knowledge), then physical effort was, in the construction process. Both these were worldly pursuits appropriate to masculine energies. To be sure, only a fraction of houses were designed by professional architects (then as now), but even where speculative builders were concerned, as in most cases, the requisite architectural knowledge was either acquired through consultation or gleaned from reputable texts and treatises on architecture, of course written by men. This is not to say that women played no role in the design of houses, for no doubt they did discretely and indirectly. Indeed, the decoration of particular rooms in a typical Victorian middle-class home, such as the drawing room, was considered to be the task of the 'lady of the house'.

Principles of the Victorian House Plan

These roles extended to an understanding of spatial planning, including a grasp of how rooms were linked and coordinated in making apparent and thus reinforcing domestic relations. In this respect the Victorian house plan reflected middle-class values *tout court*. Although rooted in much older forms of domestic arrangement, these practices were theorised during the Victorian age. One of the most reliable and popular guides on the subject, Robert Kerr's *The Gentleman's House* (1864), observed that the character of a 'gentlemanlike residence' was wholly dependent upon the 'domestic habits of refined persons', and this a concern 'chiefly of plan'. Whether a palace or a parsonage, essential divisions of space were aligned according to usage: semi-public, private, and service areas. These would include reception rooms, such as a hall/vestibule/saloon at point of entry, a drawing room (a type of sitting or lounge room), dining room, perhaps a parlour (informal dining-cum-sitting room), a study or library which could double as a morning room, and a gentleman's room, sometimes used for business. All of these can be described as semi-public. Next in line came the bedrooms, a dressing room (or two), and the bathroom(s). These were the private family rooms. Then, bringing up the rear, literally, were the kitchen, scullery, pantry, larder, and servants' rooms. These last were the service areas, usually positioned at the back of the residence.

In grander properties this basic layout might be augmented with subsidiary spaces, including a billiard room, music room, ballroom, picture gallery, boudoir, a separate serving room (adjacent to the dining room), a conservatory, as well as various butler's rooms, a servants' hall, laundry, and extensive wine cellar. At the lower end of the class income bracket, including what might be termed 'upper working' or artisan class, separate drawing and dining rooms would often be pared back to a single parlour, with adjacent kitchen and other service areas. These would usually be accessed off a small entrance lobby, or directly into the 'living room', with minimal use of corridors. Off-the-peg designs could be found in any one of the numerous guides and pattern books that had appeared on domestic architecture by the mid-nineteenth century. Many 'model' instances of the latter type mentioned here could be found in one of the most influential manuals of the period, J. C. Loudon's *Encyclopaedia of Cottage, Farm, and Villa Architecture* (1833), which captured something of an early Victorian mood in connecting architecture, 'taste', and morality **[159]**.[3]

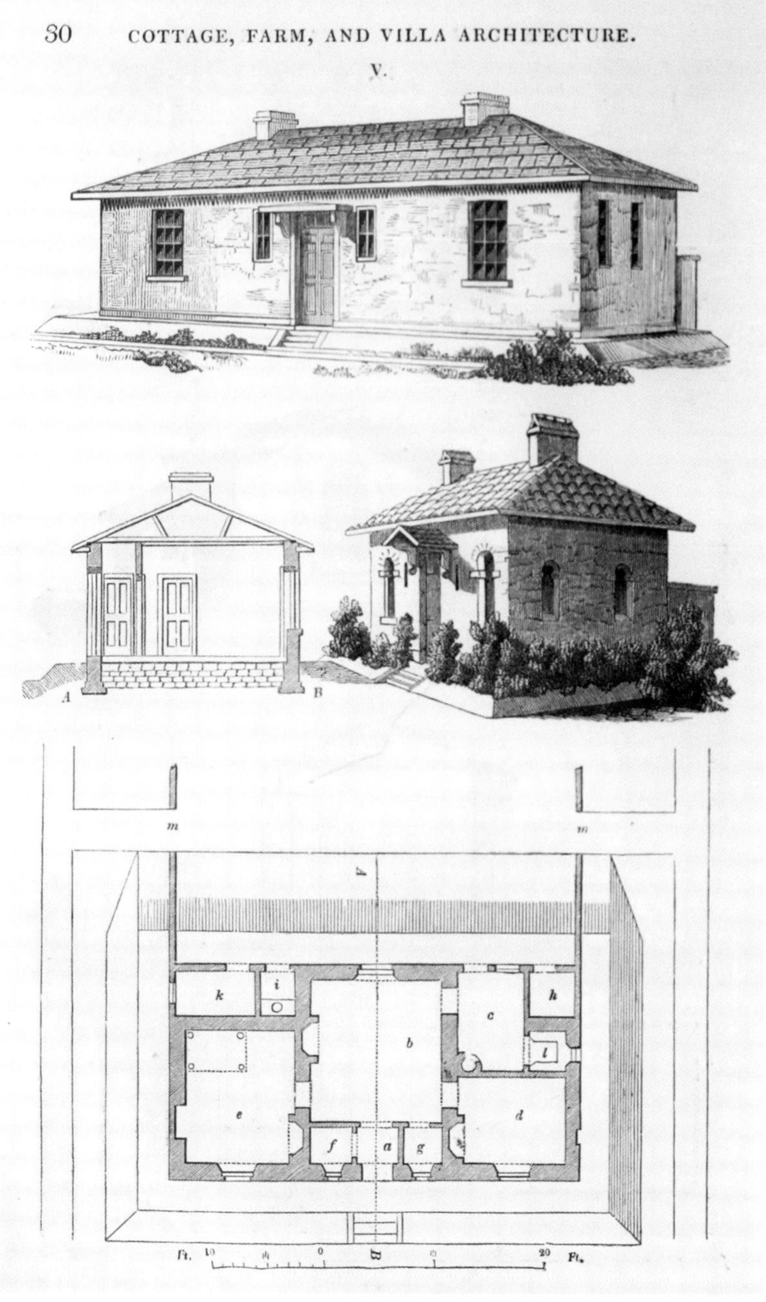

Fig. 159

'Design for a Man and his Wife and Two or more Children, with a Cow-house and Pigsty', from J. C. Loudon's *Encyclopaedia of Cottage, Farm, and Villa Architecture* (1833).

Patterns of arrangement varied according to building size and shape, but the semi-public rooms were generally arrayed towards the front, near the entrance, with the bedrooms either towards the centre, or above, in the case of multi-storey dwellings. Again, the service spaces were to the rear or in a basement, mainly to insulate the principal rooms from unwanted noise and odours. Judicious use was made of corridors and stairs in connecting—or blocking, as the case may be—the various rooms and spaces in keeping with prevailing ideas on privacy and propriety. Such devices helped occupants surveil and conceal movement within the house, as well as manage interpersonal relations. These were fundamental characteristics of the Victorian middle-class home. The number of servants varied according to household income, which for this class ranged between about £100 and £2,000 per annum. With at least one servant requisite to be designated middle class, those in the lower income bracket (£100–£300) were able to afford only one, while those at the upper end might have three or more. Very well-to-do households would certainly have had more, with country houses often requiring a small army of servants to keep them running efficiently. For instance, the household of Jane Emily Monk, one of the sisters mentioned in Chapter 5, who was an upper middle-class resident of Chelsea in London, maintained six servants by 1901 in her multi-storey townhouse at 4 Cadogan Square (designed by G. E. Street): a cook, lady's maid, house maid, kitchen maid, butler, and footman (for her and her sister's carriage).

Rather than discuss examples of noted Victorian house plans, of which there are far too many, I will instead highlight some generic specimens by way of illustration. In another of the influential manuals of the period, Kerr's *The Gentleman's House*, we see a number of planning solutions that were typical of middle-class housing requirements. Many of these were specific designs taken from professional sources such as *The Builder*, *The Building News*, and *The Civil Engineer and Architects' Journal*, and were presented by Kerr as ideal in some sense. In the example illustrated here we see floor plans of two houses: Fillongley Vicarage, Warwickshire (1859), by the Irish architect, James Murray; and Woodheyes Park, near Manchester (1859), by Horace Jones **[160]**. Both have layouts comprising the essential component spaces of respectable middle-class living identified above. Apart from this, what strikes us are the means of regulating access in order to maintain the divide between the public and private domains of the house, as well as providing a transitional zone to the outside. In this respect each plan shows a porch-type space, followed by a small hall. These are linked visually and spatially to further circulation spaces such as stairs and corridors connecting the separate parts of the house. Both also have two sets of stairs: a main stair for family use, and a back stair for the use of servants. Certain other features are also apparent, such as bay windows, which were common in this class of Victorian domestic architecture, not only for creating a more ample effect, but also for allowing greater ventilation, more light, and for taking in additional views, whether to the street or the landscape beyond.

The same pattern prevailed in better-known examples, such as A. W. N. Pugin's own house, The Grange (1843–4), in Ramsgate, Kent, and Holmwood House (1857–8), Cathcart, Renfrewshire, by Alexander 'Greek' Thomson **[161a&b]**. In other domestic typologies, too, such as semi-detached, terraced, and town houses the same ideal more or less held sway. For instance, taking just two examples from the architect E. W. Godwin—one for a semi-detached dwelling, the other for a townhouse—the requisite divisions are apparent, whether in a slightly compressed scenario, for a lower middle-class family, or amply over several levels, for an upper middle-class one **[162a&b]**. In such compact situations there was not always room for two sets of stairs. Even in the case of flats these arrangements were replicated

Fig. 160

Reproduced plans from Robert Kerr's *The Gentleman's House* (1864) of Fillongley Vicarage, Warwickshire (1859), by James Murray, and Woodheyes Park, near Manchester (1859), by Horace Jones. Sections shaded in grey indicate service areas.

Fillongley Vicarage, Warwickshire

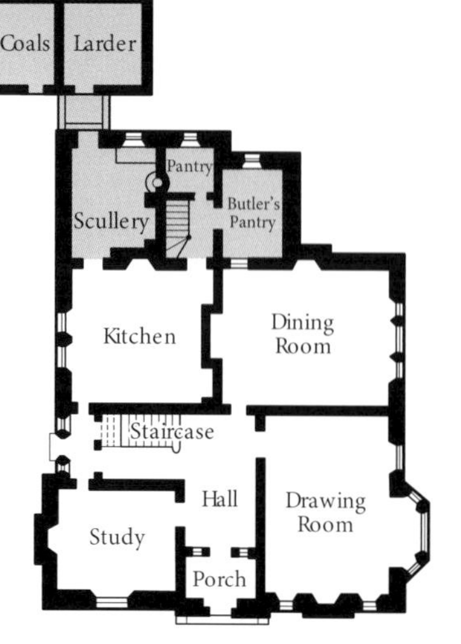

GROUND FLOOR

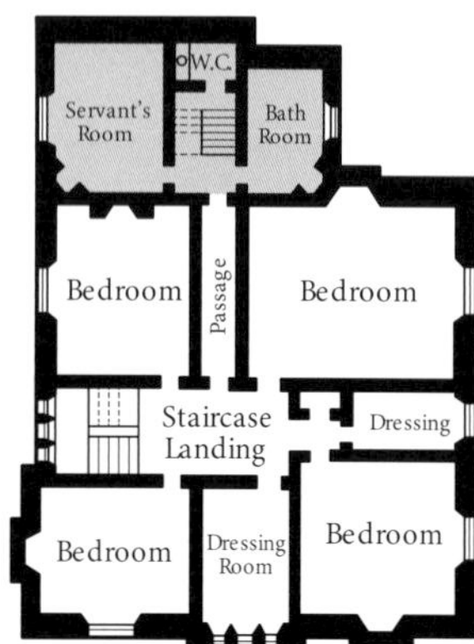

FIRST FLOOR

Woodheyes Park, near Manchester

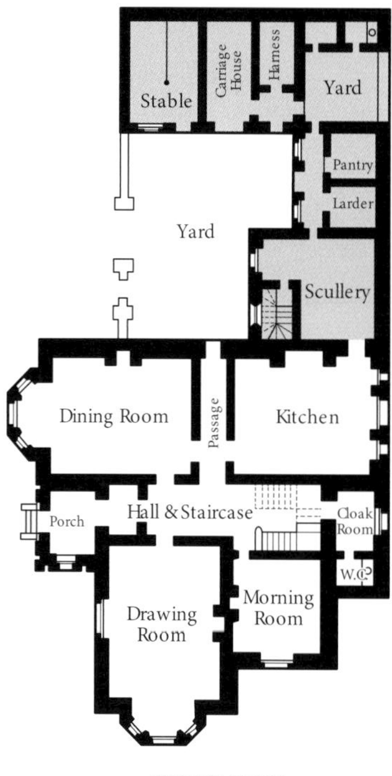

GROUND FLOOR

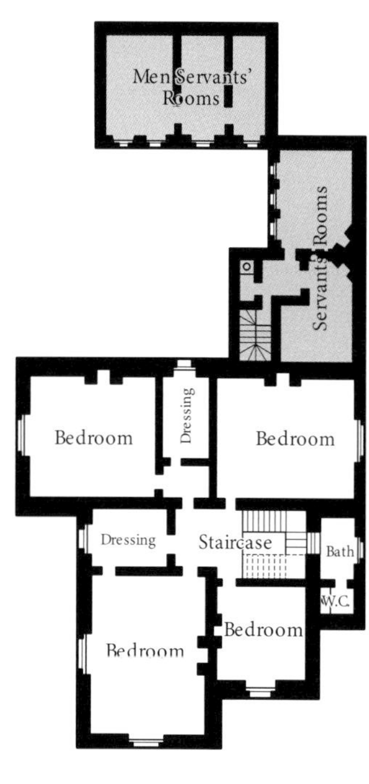

FIRST FLOOR

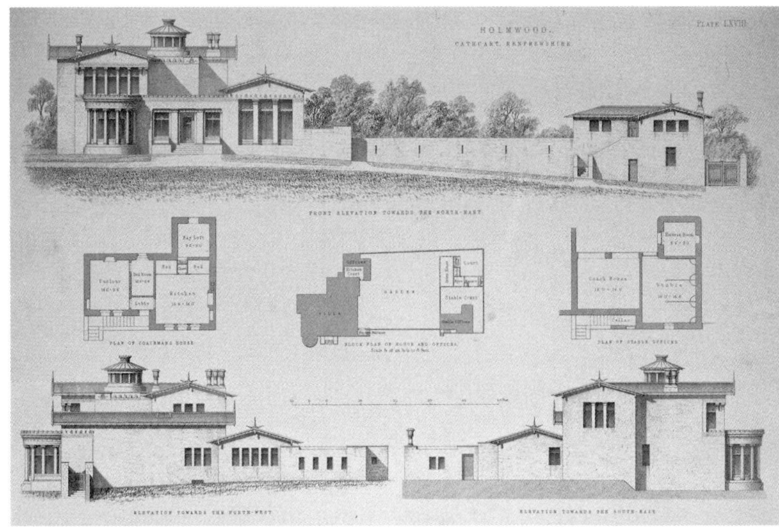

Fig. 161a

Drawings for Holmwood House (1857–8), Cathcart, Renfrewshire, by Alexander Thomson.

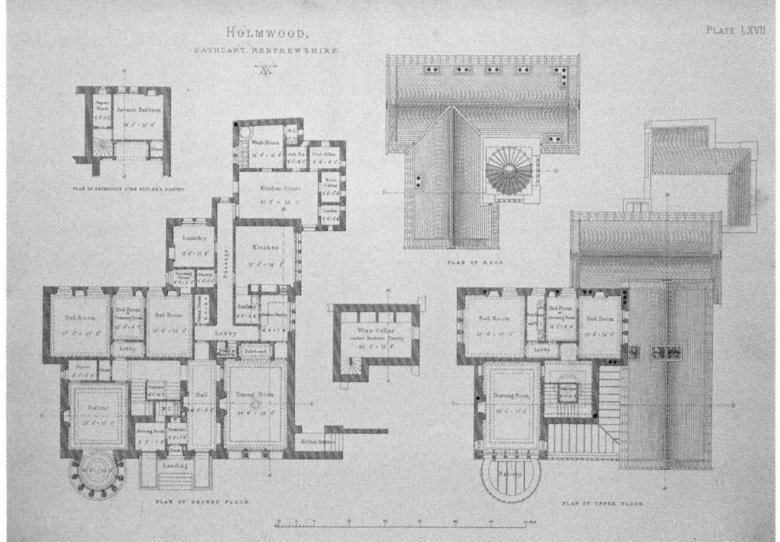

Fig. 161b

Plans of principal floors, Holmwood House.

as far as possible. In the plan for a late-nineteenth-century tenement building in Edinburgh shown here **[163]**, we see two flats (in a multi-storey development): a single-floor dwelling to the left, and a so-called 'double upper' (two-storey) one to the right. These are separated by a party wall. In the rather modest three-bedroom, single-floor flat, we still have an entrance lobby, off the main communal stair, separate drawing and dining rooms, as well as bathroom and kitchen. In the kitchen there is a small space marked 'Bed'. This was a tiny recess where the maidservant slept, the kitchen being her domain.

The demand for middle-class housing was such by the mid-nineteenth century that the leading professional magazines began to publish standard plans and pro-forma specifications, such as that illustrated here for a 'subur-

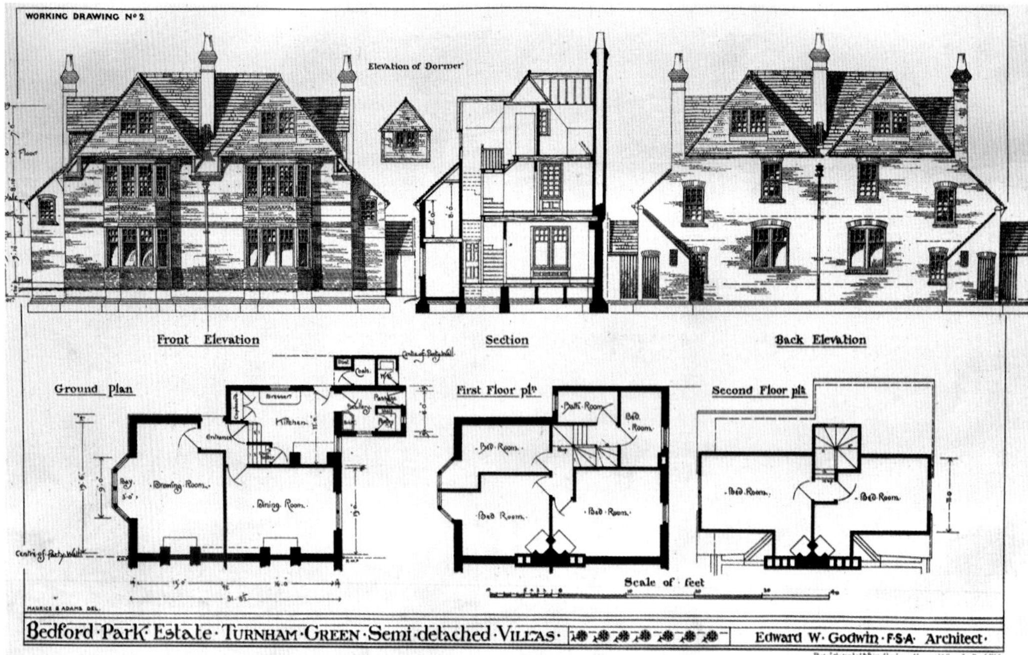

Fig. 162a

House designs by Edward William Godwin: semi-detached villas, Bedford Park (1877), Turnham Green, London.

ban villa' **[164a]**. This phenomenon was exacerbated by the explosive growth in suburbs around Britain's major cities during the late nineteenth century, as the middle classes clamoured to escape the noise, grime, and other hazards of inner-city living, aided in their exodus by the ever-expanding networks of train, tram, and omnibus transportation. As *The Building News* observed in 1859, 'such facilities of travelling as we now possess have created the innumerable villas with which every hillside round London is thickly studded'. The desire for suburban existence incentivised new forms of urban planning, as whole suburbs were built by developers purchasing extensive land leases on the outskirts of cites. This phenomenon was also connected to the nascent Garden City movement, which gained in credence as the century wore on. A classic example of this type of development was the Bedford Park Estate, Chiswick, in London. Orchestrated in the late 1870s by the cloth merchant turned developer Jonathan Carr, it was built around a limited number of pattern plans for detached and semi-detached villas, set within green and airy environs **[164b]**. It was laid out precisely to attract middle-class occupants, with compact but dignified villa designs by Godwin, R. N. Shaw, and others. It is perhaps most noted for the 'old English'-cum-Queen Anne style architecture that Godwin, and Shaw in particular, derived for the scheme.

In much larger houses the same pattern prevailed. It is worth noting that the Victorian period represented something of a golden age for country house building, in both Britain and the wider British world. In Britain alone, the period 1860 to 1875 saw large-house construction of this kind jump by nearly 60 per cent at its peak.[4] The increase was owing in large part to the entrance of 'new families' who had acquired their vast wealth off the back of industrialisation and British global expansion. Despite the diminishing value of agricul-

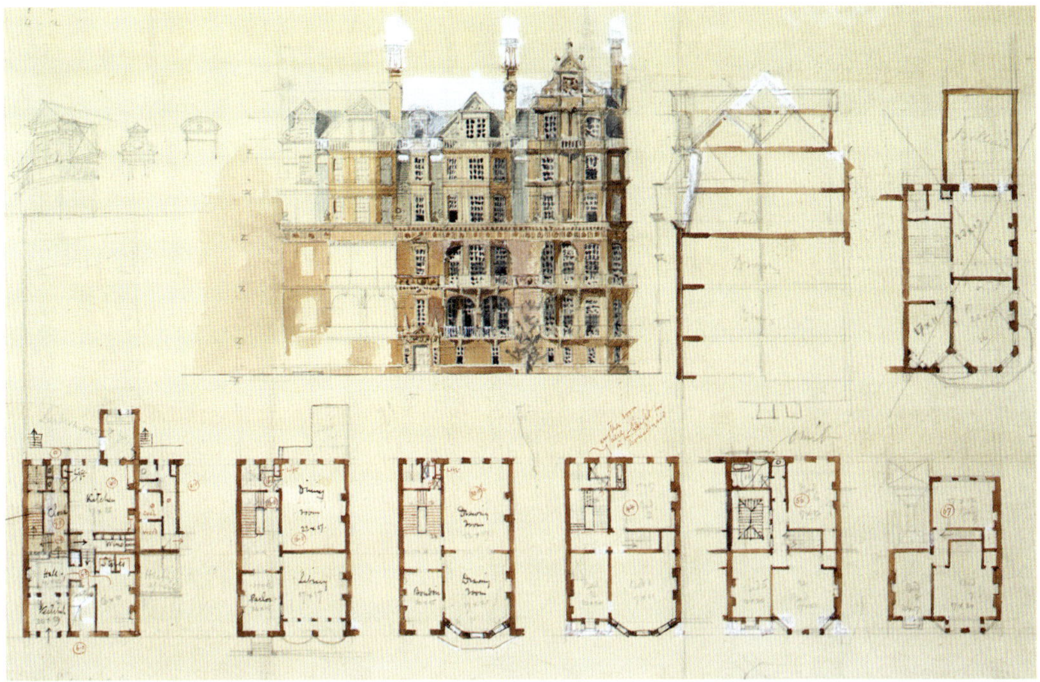

Fig. 162b

Preliminary sketch design for houses (1877), 4–6 Chelsea Embankment and corner of Tite Street, London, for Messrs Gillow and Company.

tural land itself, the social prestige associated with landed pedigree, and owning and maintaining a large house, drove the *nouveaux riches* to purchase and develop country estates. Nevertheless, the old aristocracy also continued to erect, refurbish, and modernise their family seats during this period. Many of the great architects of the day were involved, such as Charles Barry, A. W. N. Pugin, G. G. Scott, Alfred Waterhouse, William Burges, R. N. Shaw, to name but a few, with some specialising in country house design, including Anthony Salvin, William Burn, and Edward Blore. Through emigration and the making of fortunes abroad, in the colonies, the British country house model was naturally exported wherever the need for social distinction of the kind arose, making the type something of a global phenomenon. Where the captain of industry had largely led at 'home', in Britain, abroad the pastoralist and natural resource magnate was keen to follow.

In terms of planning, we may again turn to Kerr, whose book showcased the designs for a number of such houses, big and small. Among these he presents a model of his own design for illustrative purposes (all but identical to the plan he would use for Bear Wood, Berkshire [1865–74]), exemplifying what he considered to be those 'principles' indispensable to any stately home **[165]**. Apart from scale, what is immediately noticeable upon analysis of this plan is the way the ground floor is distinctly divided into the main semi-public reception rooms of the house, to the right (and front), and the service areas, to the left (and rear), including an entire, isolated service wing. In some instances there might be a separate family wing, too, but in this case Kerr has placed the private family apartments directly above the semi-public domain of the house to the front, with servants' bedrooms at the rear, and guest accommodation above. The planning of most modern country

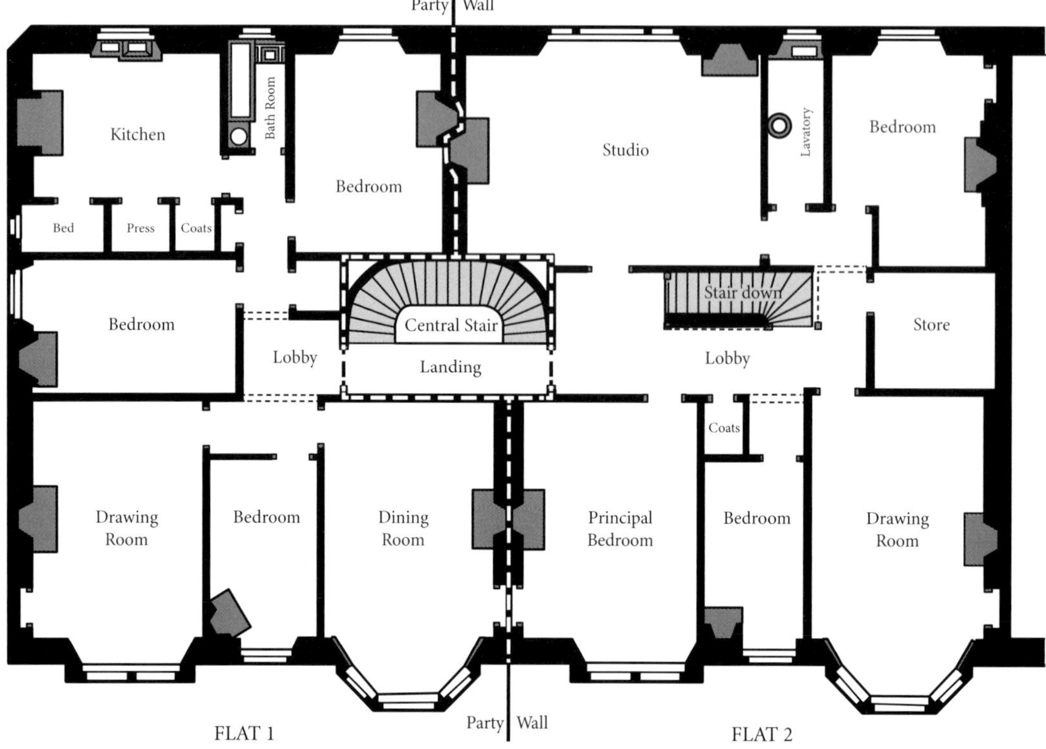

Fig. 163

Floor layout in multi-storey tenement development by Robert Paterson (1881), Warrender Park Road, Edinburgh. In the kitchen of the flat to the left-hand side of the main stair (top left) can be seen a small recess marked 'Bed'. This is where the maidservant slept.

houses was understood as a variation of this basic spatial theme. Again, these arrangements reflect the propriety expected in a 'gentleman's' abode, with a strict 'upstairs/downstairs' separation between family and service staff. In particularly large houses, with extensive grounds, the service staff could number as many as thirty or forty, or more, with the local lord or squire seeing himself as an important role model and employer for the estate community.

Questions of Form and Style

The question of what a house should look like—what form it should take, and what style it might be designed in—depended upon many factors, including the means of its occupants, the nature of the site, and the materials used for construction. In this respect, domestic housing in the United Kingdom at this time varied enormously, with the same questions over style at play that vexed the designers of major religious, public, and corporate buildings. Often this was dictated by cost and what the developer or client could afford. Obviously, at the lowest end of the spectrum, with working-class housing, production was very simple indeed. As people poured into the cities and towns seeking employment in industry, whole areas in many of Britain's industrial centres began to fill up with row after row of workers' 'cottages', usually poorly built, with only a few rooms and little sanitation. This phenomenon included what were in effect immigrant ghettos, as many poor Irish, for instance, fled their homeland for cities such as Liverpool and

Fig. 164a

'Design for a Suburban Villa' (*The Building News*, Oct. 1859).

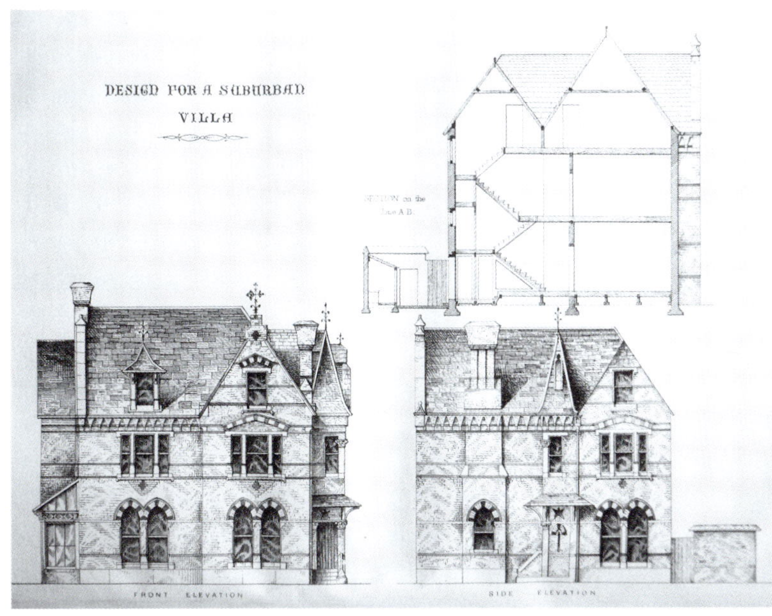

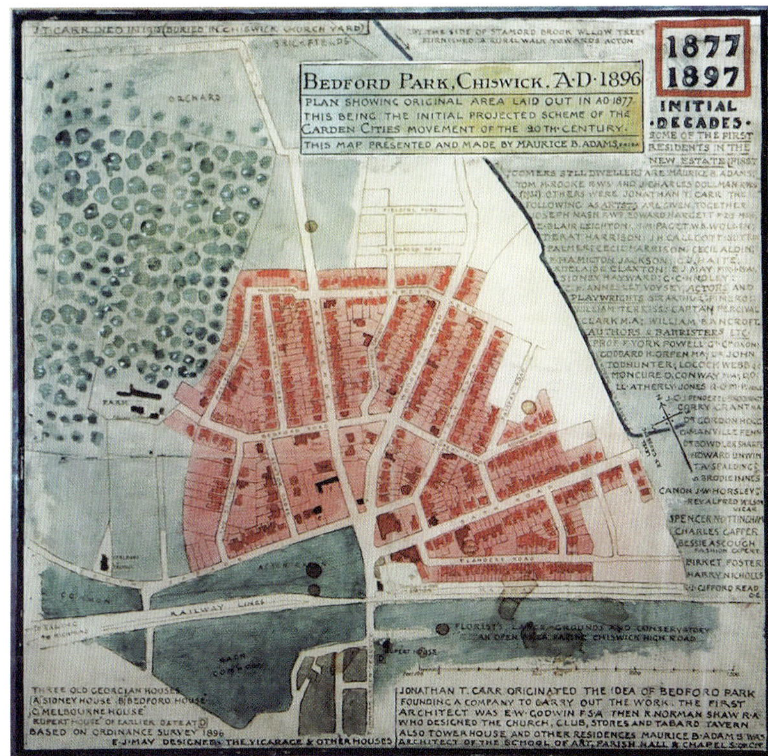

Fig. 164b

Map drawn in 1889 by Maurice B. Adams showing the original layout (1877) of housing development at Bedford Park, Chiswick, in London.

Fig. 165

Plan for 'An Elizabethan Mansion, Berkshire', from Robert Kerr, *The Gentleman's House* (second edition, 1865). Section shaded in grey indicates service areas.

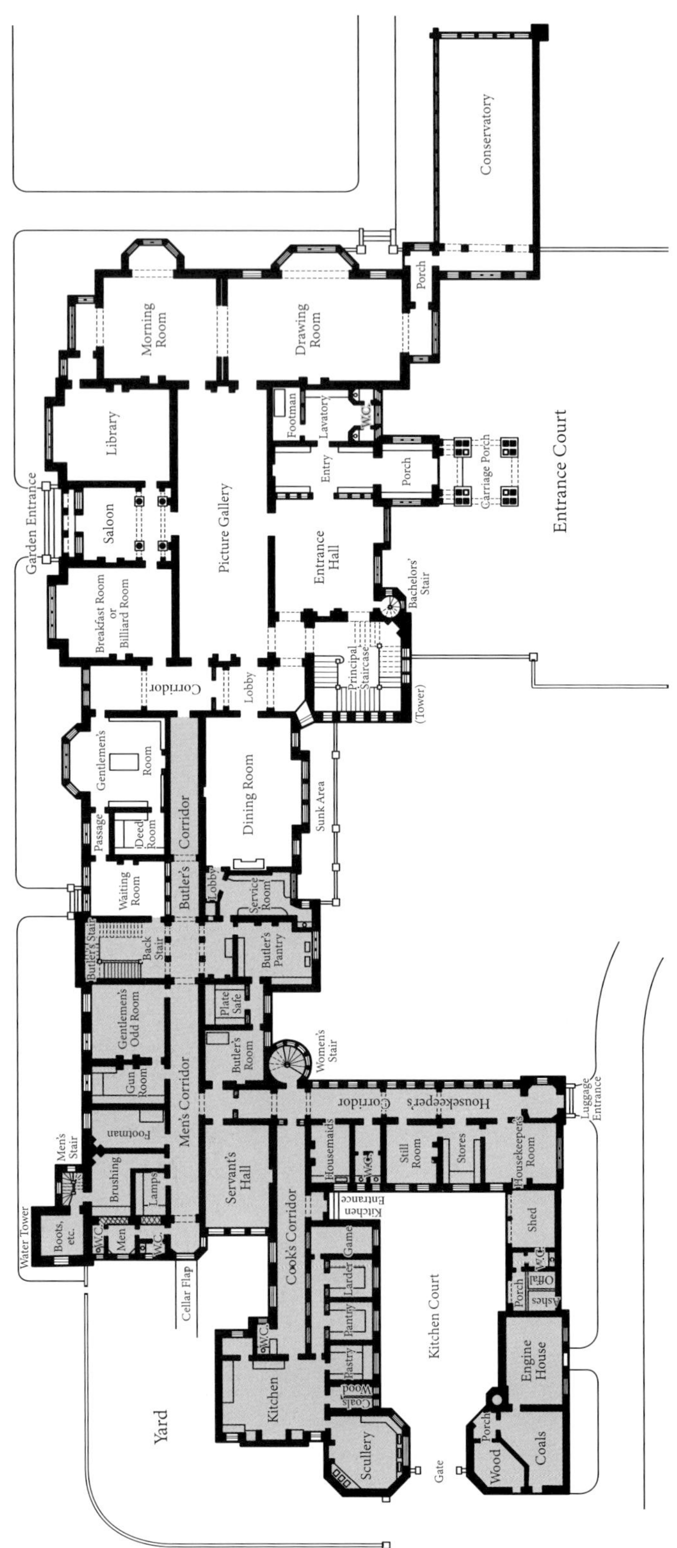

Manchester in the wake of the Potato Famine. In most cases, the houses such people occupied were nothing more than brick boxes, built in long, straight terraces. The worst kind had communal 'privies' (external toilets) backing onto an open gutter-cum-sewer. Often these led to overcrowding and slum-like conditions, rife with disease and mortality. Little decoration or aesthetic worth was attached to such housing. Even humble rural cottages, examples of which were to be found in Loudon's *Encyclopaedia*, were plain in the extreme.

The royal commission into the sanitary conditions of the working poor, led by Edwin Chadwick in the early 1840s, highlighted many of the problems. In seeking good economy, a number of far-sighted industrialists had already been thinking along these lines by building model workers' 'villages' for their employees, in the belief that a contented workforce was more productive. In addition to those mentioned in Chapter 1 (Saltaire, Port Sunlight, and Bournville), a good early example was Copley (1849–53), near Halifax, by W. H. Crossland in conjunction with G. G. Scott, with its small but neat terraced and semi-detached dwellings **[166a]**. But increased regulation brought issues of its own. Minimum standards led to the repetitive nature of many of the new working-class housing estates, as developers looked to extract maximum value from their investment. Indeed, the Public Health Act of 1875, and subsequent by-laws, determined to a great extent the formal proportions of such dwellings in the latter part of the nineteenth century, including minimum street width, room dimensions (per occupant), wall thicknesses, widow size and operability, etc.[5]

A prominent and somewhat typical example of this type of working-class accommodation was that in the Elswick area of Newcastle, alongside the Armstrong armaments factory. By 1900 the population of the area had swelled to nearly 60,000 (from around 300 in 1801), with hundreds of humble, plain brick terraced cottages running down the nearby hill to the river Tyne **[166b]**. Another example of this type is the so-called double-fronted, back-to-back terraced house found in others parts of the industrial North, in places like Leeds and Bradford. The terraced worker's cottage also found its way to the colonies, becoming ubiquitous in many new settlements, if adapted in certain ways. Such adaptations might include one storey only, with the principal rooms running off a long corridor down one party wall of the house, leading to a kitchen and scullery at the rear; or, where appropriate, the fitting of devices such as verandahs to provide shade from intense sunlight **[125b]**.

The Middle-Class Villa

Moving up from this we have artisan to middle-class accommodation. A lot of this housing was also rather plain and often substandard, as regularly complained about in the press, particularly in the earlier part of the Victorian period. As mentioned, speculative builders were out to make a few quid, and cutting corners on quality and materials was common. However, depending on the developer and prospective client base, such housing might also be embellished with quite elaborate if somewhat standardised decorative features, affording degrees of architectural pretence. Unlike the typical Georgian terraced house, for which plain, flat surfaces were favoured,

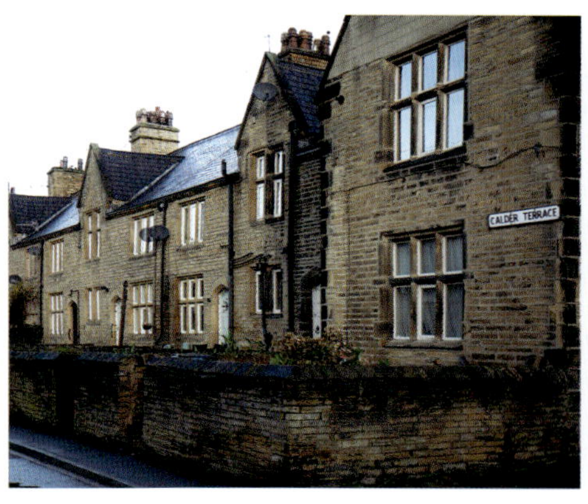

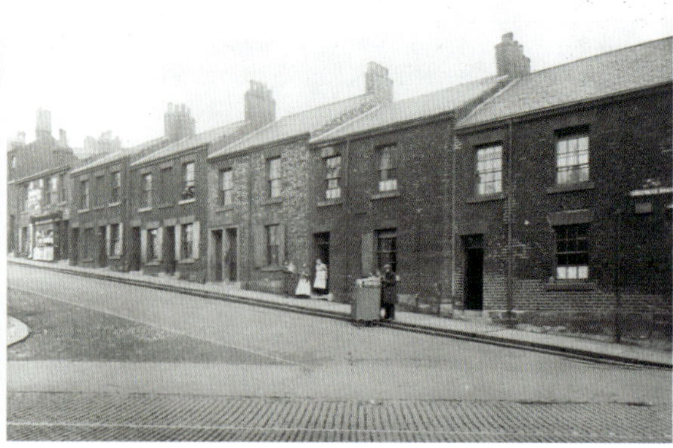

Fig. 166a

Terraced cottages at Copley (1849–53), near Halifax, to designs by W. H. Crossland and George Gilbert Scott.

Fig. 166b

Simple, working-class brick terraced houses, Edgeware Road, Elswick, Newcastle (photo c.1930).

the Victorians were keen to enliven their architecture. This was especially the case in good middle-class terraced and semi-detached housing. Here the question of style was a live one, as developers sought to increase marketability, latching onto the latest trends in an attempt to mollify more cultivated sensibilities. Indeed, although terraced rows remained largely repetitive into the late nineteenth century, variability across the façade increased. It became common to divide the façade of each house into two halves: one with the main reception room window (often bay), and the other with the entrance door. This double-fronted design initiative allowed for a break in symmetry, increasing the picturesque effect, enhanced by the addition of various elements such as gables, projecting dormers and hips, recessed or protruding porches, and prominent chimney stacks, all of which provided opportunities for ornamentation, often elaborate, including decorative ironwork **[167a]**. The creative use of brick, terracotta, moulded stucco, and carved stone and timber, in a range of often strongly contrasting colours and patterns, came to characterise the Victorian terraced house all over the British world.

Some of these features became more cost effective as taxes on such things as bricks and windows were abolished in the 1850s. Again, in the cities of Britain's principal 'white settler' colonies—in places like Adelaide, Cape Town, Melbourne, Montreal, Sydney, and Toronto—the terraced house format was commonly adapted for inner-city, middle-class living. Colonial contexts also provided opportunity for extensive use of cast-iron filigree ornamentation on verandah structures **[167b]**. Although not unheard of in Britain, especially in the South along the coast, this type of ornamentation was much more common (and often more spectacular) in sunnier climes, such as Australasia and the Caribbean, distinguishing this kind of architecture from its British relative **[175b]**. The phenomenon of the terraced house also extended to the United States in the form of town and row houses, especially in places of extensive nineteenth-century development, such as San Francisco.

It was a similar situation with the semi-detached villa, where an effort was made to articulate the façade in such a way as to make the two conjoined properties appear like a single house, thus enhancing its perceived grandeur. Again, tricks of asymmetry were subtly employed to distinguish the properties, which might include a split roofline, prominent gable to one side, and/or projecting

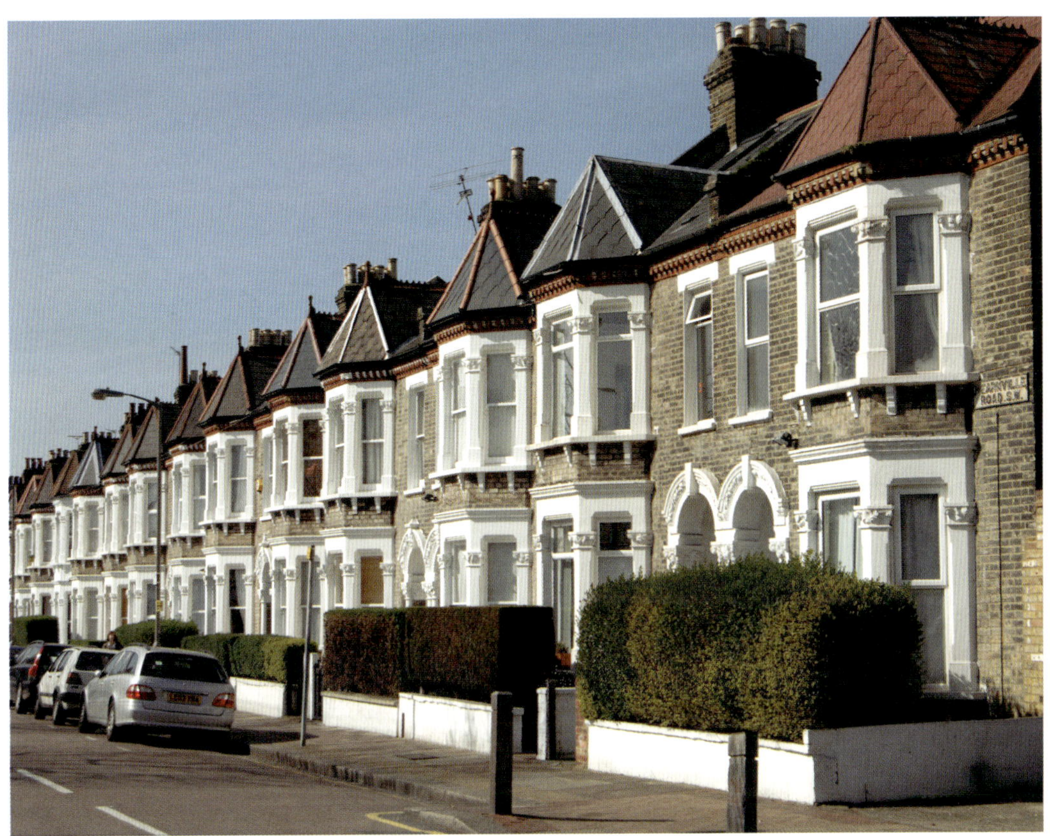

Fig. 167a

Typical brick and stucco Victorian terraced housing (c.1860s), Hearnville Road, Balham, in London.

bays and varied window arrangements. This was especially the case where the floor plans of each property were different (larger or smaller). Often, however, where the conjoined properties mirrored the same floor plan, the 'house' front was made symmetrical with projecting bays at each end, still giving the effect of a larger house **[168]**. The material quality and decorative finish of such housing was interpreted as projecting the social station of its occupants, not merely their income bracket but also their levels of 'taste' (see below), reflecting what may be termed the building's cultural capital.

As Kerr had observed, the question of style in British housing had been muddled somewhat by what he saw as too much learning, or what we might describe as information overload. 'We live in the era of Omnium-Gatherum', he mused; 'all the world's a museum, and men and women are its students'. Any 'style' might seem possible, although he conceded that there were 'chief accepted varieties', being Elizabethan, Palladian, rural and palatial Italian, French Classical, Continental Renaissance, different types of Medieval, and what he called 'the Scotch style'. The Classical and Gothic were common enough, but the latter of Kerr's named styles is interesting as a Scottish phenomenon. It will be touched upon presently; suffice to say here that it became a common style in places such as Victorian Edinburgh, in detached, semi-detached, and tenement flat homes, particularly on the south side of the city developed from the 1870s, including Marchmont, Bruntsfield, and

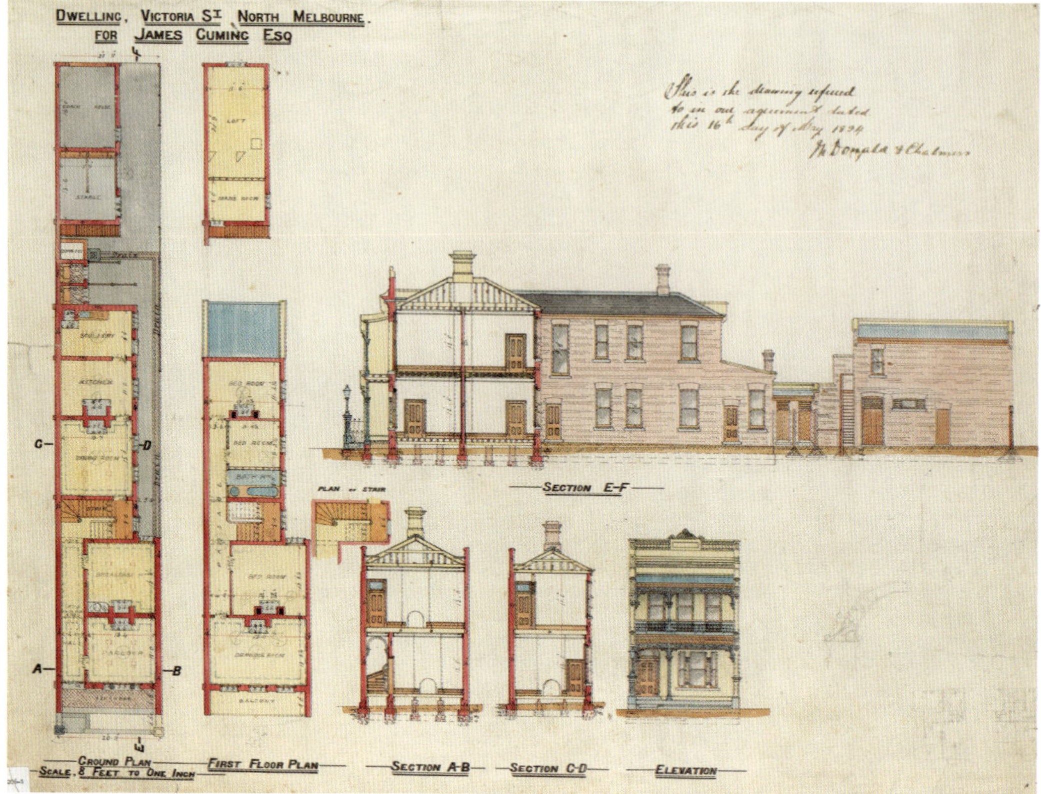

Fig. 167b

'Dwelling, Victoria St, North Melbourne, for James Cuming Esq.' (1894). Classic deep-plan, double-storey Melbourne terrace house, Australia, by Donald & Chalmers. The verandah to the front and its accompanying iron lattice-work can be seen on the elevation bottom right.

Merchiston. This played into desires over the expression of national identity in architecture.

In larger homes, both detached villas and country houses, there was much greater scope for decorative effect. This was not only because more money was available, but also because such homes were statement pieces, especially country houses, which were seen as signifying social prestige and power. The detached villa/house catered for solid middle- to upper middle-class needs (what some would term the capitalist or industrial bourgeoisie), while the country house was for the aristocracy and *nouveau riche*, on the whole. Here we see architecture being used to highlight and, in some respects, monumentalise class distinction. The advice that pundits like Kerr gave was that so long as the utilitarian nature of a good plan remained the 'first consideration', then style was effectively a matter of personal preference. But there were important factors to consider, such as suitability to scale, comparative cost, and the relationship between interior and exterior. His 'chief' styles, mentioned above, were broadly divided into 'Classical' and 'Picturesque'. On this point, he observed:

> The Classic character, the reader may be reminded, is that of stately, symmetrical, refined balance and repose, with simple elaborated elegance in the ornament: the Picturesque character is that of unsymmetrical, vigorous, sparkling piquancy, with ornament not so much refined as animated.[6]

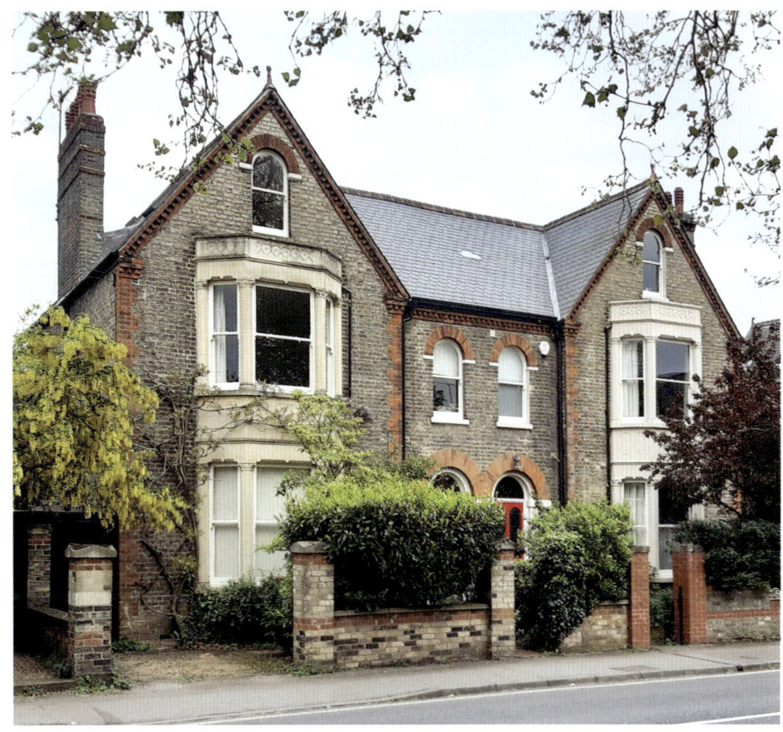

Fig. 168
Semi-detached house (*c.*1860), Tenison Road, Cambridge.

Generally, in the context of competing styles, this is what we see in larger house design in Victorian Britain and its colonies. Various forms of the Classical were a mainstay, but variants of the Italianate and medieval-cum-Gothic were popular. In the latter quarter of the nineteenth century Queen Anne and old English/Tudoresque types rose to prominence, especially in suburban villa architecture. The Arts and Crafts brought its own, 'homely' vernacularised English aesthetic to bear, which, in the domestic sphere, was grounded (and idealised) in medieval traditions of craftsmanship (see Chapter 3). Here the work of architects such as Philip Webb, C. F. A. Voysey, and Robert Lorimer stand out, with Red House (1859–60), Bexleyheath, by Webb being the most celebrated exemplar **[169a;** see also **55]**. Arts and Crafts qualities eventually filtered through into colonial contexts in the domestic work of architects such as Herbert Baker in South Africa, in his Cape Dutch aesthetic of the 1890s, and in places like Australia, where the so-called Federation-style suburban home became a common sight in the early twentieth century. In Canada, American influence was apparent, in locations such as the suburban Annex district of Toronto, where Richardsonian and 'shingle-style' impulses blended with Queen Anne elegance **[169b]**. In more tropical contexts, such as north-east Australia, detached suburban villas, known as 'Queenslanders', were built of timber and raised high on stumps with ample verandah space. Suburban housing of this kind in the colonies, the United States, and to a lesser extent in Britain, was part of the wider global conquest of the bungalow, a domestic housing type of Indian origin that, having been adapted for modern living, spread quickly throughout the anglosphere new world. Ideally situated on an

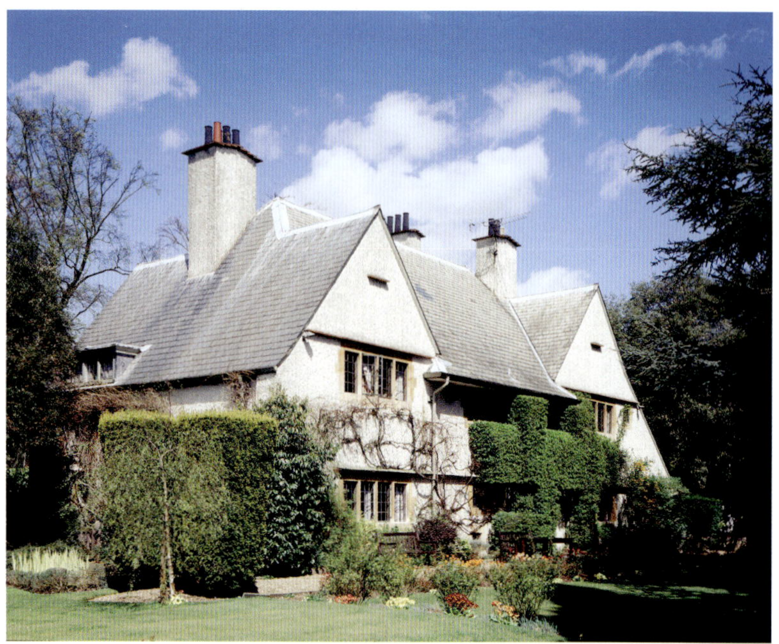

Fig. 169a

The Orchard, Shire Lane (1899), Chorleywood, Hertfordshire, by C. F. A. Voysey.

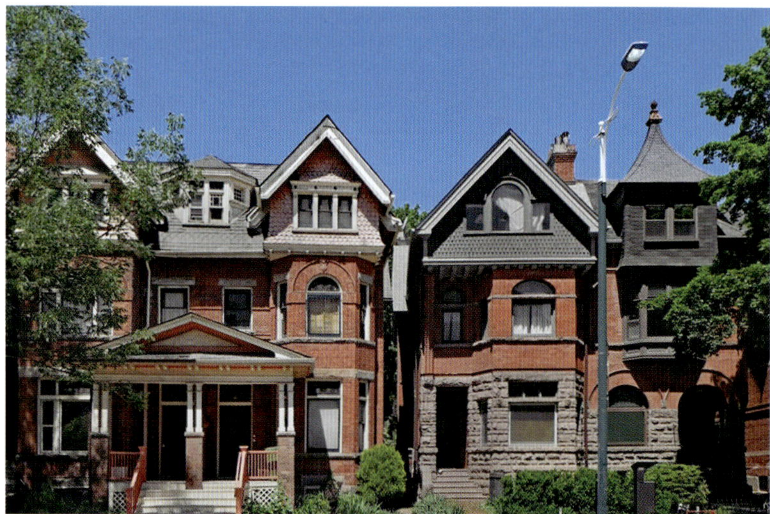

Fig. 169b

Semi-detached houses (*c.*1890), The Annex, in Toronto, Canada.

individual block of land of between one-quarter to half an acre, the ubiquitous bungalow became fatefully associated with suburban sprawl.

The Country House

But the large country house was the most conspicuous manifestation of Victorian domestic architecture. Such buildings may have drawn criticism, then as now, for their fastidiousness and apparent over-the-top grandeur, but in an age of new materials and technologies, experimentation and a certain pushing of aesthetic boundaries was to be expected. Indeed, Victorian architects dragged the country house into the modern world. Prominent early examples include Merevale Hall, Warwickshire (1838–44),

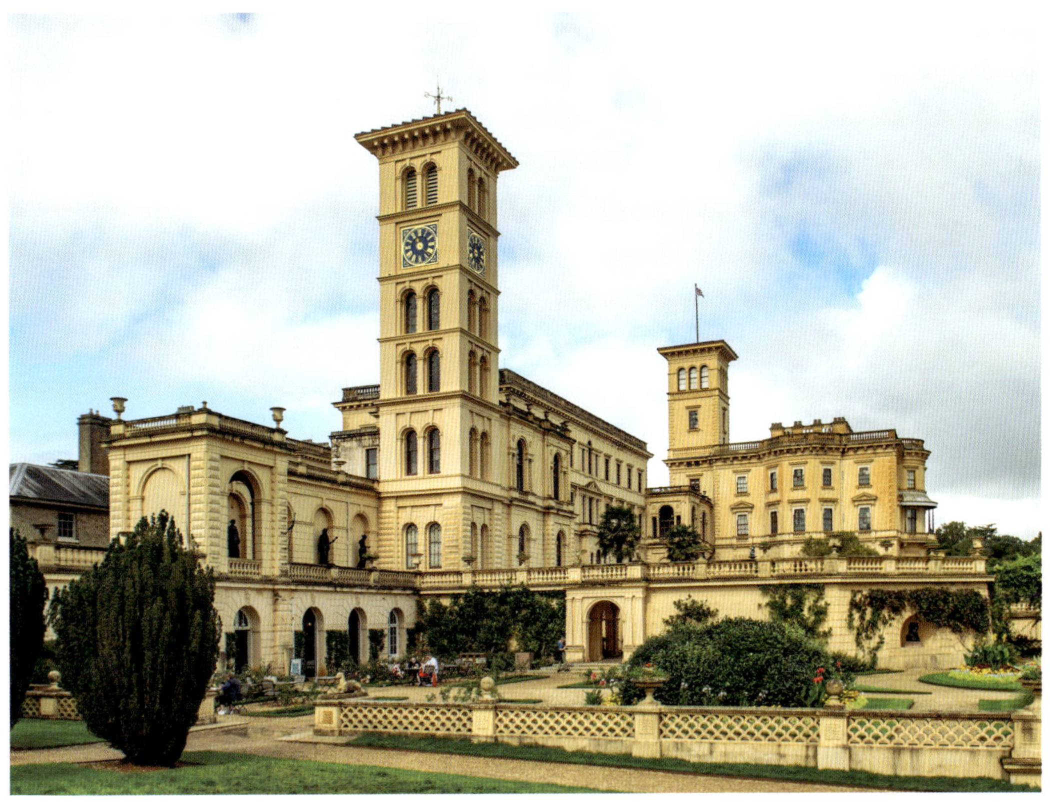

Fig. 170

One of Queen Victoria's own houses. Osborne House, Isle of Wight (1844–8), by Thomas Cubitt, with Prince Albert.

by Edward Blore, for the Tory grandee William Stratford Dugdale; and Dartrey House, Co. Monaghan, Ireland (1846), by William Burn, for Richard Dawson, 3rd Baron Cremorne. Both of these were in a Jacobethan style relatively popular in country house design at the time. In a more decidedly Gothic manner is Scarisbrick Hall, Lancashire (1837–45), by Pugin, for the prominent landowner Charles Scarisbrick. At the other end of the stylistic spectrum we have the Classical but no less picturesque Osborne House, Isle of Wight (1844–8), by Thomas Cubitt, for none other than Queen Victoria, whose husband, Albert, helped to design **[170]**. The latter is what Kerr would have designated 'Rural Italian', or what today we would call Italianate Classicism.

The High Victorians brought a distinct flavour, even vim, to country house design, showcasing the possibilities of the Gothic and broader medieval revivals. Here we can point to the small but no less impressive Milton Ernest Hall, Bedfordshire (1853–8), by William Butterfield, for his brother-in-law, the wealthy London merchant B. H. Stanley; or the more substantial and distinctly polychrome Kelham Hall, Nottinghamshire (1858–61), by G. G. Scott, for John Henry Manners-Sutton, a relative of the Duke of Rutland **[171]**. Turning up the dial were the idiosyncratic creations of S. S. Teulon at Elvetham Hall, Hampshire (1859–62), for Lord Calthorpe, and the rather muscular Bestwood Lodge, Nottinghamshire (1862–4), for the Duke of St Albans, the former of which was a visually arresting if somewhat bizarre polychrome Jacobethan-style chateau spliced with Gothic

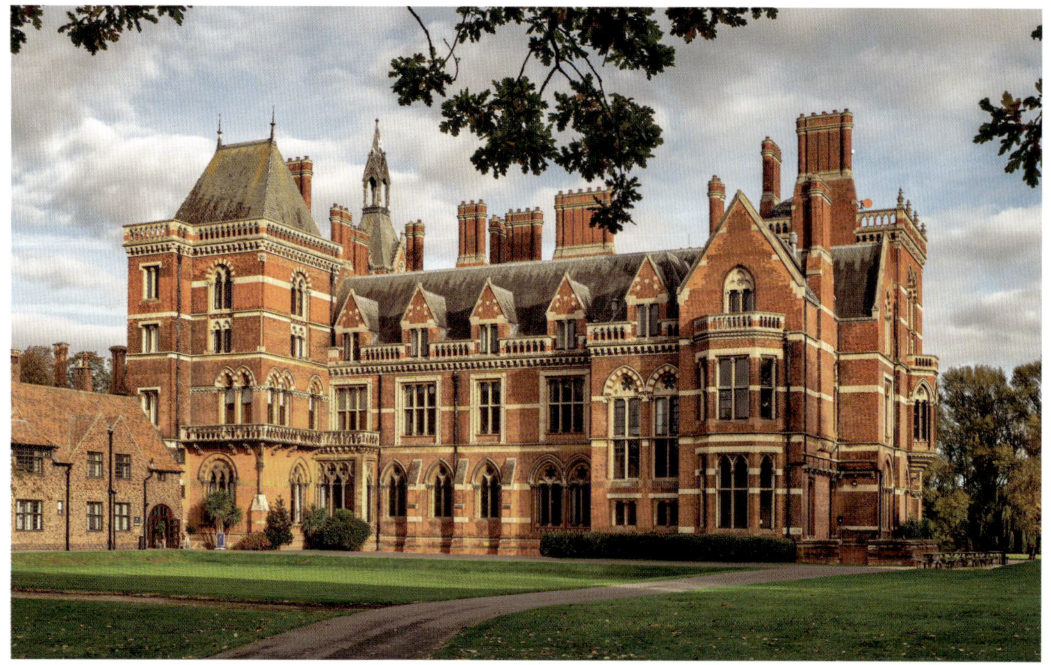

Fig. 171
Kelham Hall, Nottinghamshire (1858–61), by George Gilbert Scott.

motifs. To this group can be added the extraordinary Eaton Hall, Cheshire (1870–82), by Alfred Waterhouse, for the fabulously wealthy Duke of Westminster, with its similarly Chateau-cum-Gothic-style countenance, including its huge, free-standing chapel with clock tower **[172]**. This confection, in its entirety, cost a whopping £600,000, or around £57 million in today's money. Indeed, French influence had long affected the English elite, cropping up in country house design from time to time, both inside and out. Perhaps the grandest set-piece expression of this idiom during the Victorian era is Waddesdon Manor, Buckinghamshire (1874–89). Having set upon the idea of a French Renaissance-style chateau, the estate owner, the Jewish financier Ferdinand de Rothschild, went so far as to commission the Parisian architect Gabriel-Hippolyte Destailleur.

These examples alone reveal something of the range of stylistic possibilities (*à la* Kerr) that were open to Victorian architects when it came to large-house design. Some among the British aristocracy, harking back to their familial roots, opted for medieval castellated forms, especially where the ancestral seat remained on the site of an ancient castle. Here modern convenience met feudal romance. One accomplished practitioner in this mode was Anthony Salvin, whose efforts include the remodelling of Alnwick Castle, Northumberland (1854–66), for Algernon Percy, 4th Duke of Northumberland. Another notable example is the muscular Humewood Castle, Kiltegan, Co. Wicklow, Ireland (1866–70), by William White, for W. Wentworth Fitzwilliam Hume Dick, a rich Irish landowner. But perhaps the greatest medieval dreamer of the age was the eccentric but hugely wealthy 3rd Marquess of Bute, John Crichton-Stuart. Drawing extensive income from the leasing of mineral rights (i.e., coal) to his ancestral lands in

Fig. 172

Eaton Hall, Cheshire (1870–82), by Alfred Waterhouse.

Wales, Crichton-Stuart was able to indulge his passion for the Middle Ages, creating two of the most extraordinary country houses of the period: Cardiff Castle (1868–81), by William Burges; and Mount Stuart, Isle of Bute, Scotland (1878 onwards), by Rowand Anderson—both in a remarkably sumptuous, no-expense-spared Victorian Gothic, rich in symbolism **[173a&b]**.

Other noteworthy examples include Cragside (1870–*c.*1885), by R. N. Shaw, the lively Tudoresque forms of which rise dramatically out of its thickly wooded site in the hills just north of Rothbury, Northumberland **[174]**. Built for William Armstrong, the inventor and armaments manufacturer whose Elswick factory is mentioned above, it was one of the first houses in Britain to be lit by electricity. Towards the close of the century and into the Edwardian period fewer and fewer large country houses were built in Britain. The declining fortunes of the aristocracy, along with agricultural depression and growing expenses, made the erection (let alone maintenance) of a grand country pile increasingly impractical. Those that were built, by architects such as William Lethaby, Edward Prior, and Edwin Lutyens, tended to be smaller, 'homely' looking structures, influenced by Arts and Crafts principles. Examples include High Coxlease House, Lyndhurst (1900–1), by Lethaby, and Marsh Court, Stockbridge (1901–4), by Lutyens, both in Hampshire.

The desire to assert social distinction through large-house construction was extended to the colonies. Through agriculture and natural resource extraction, many a colonial immigrant became wealthy enough to emulate their British counterparts (after all, most such people were either British or saw themselves as British in some from or other). Among these were the Australian and New Zealand pastoralists mentioned in Chapter 1, who,

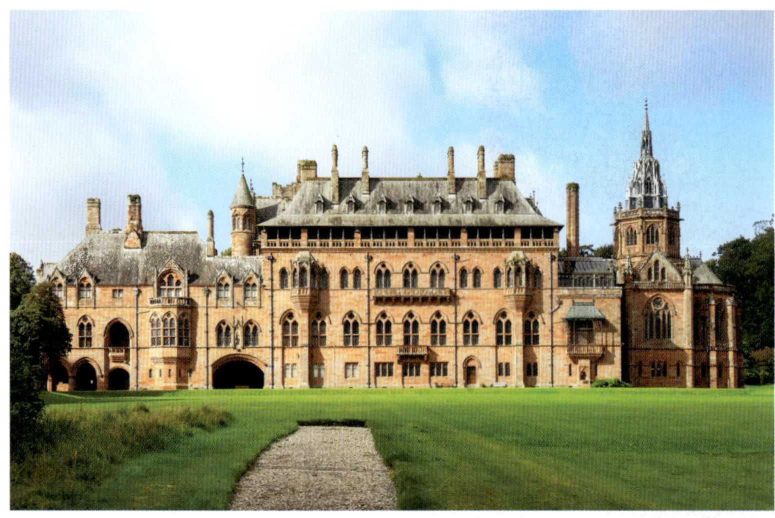

Fig. 173a

Mount Stuart, Isle of Bute, Scotland (1878 onwards), by Rowand Anderson.

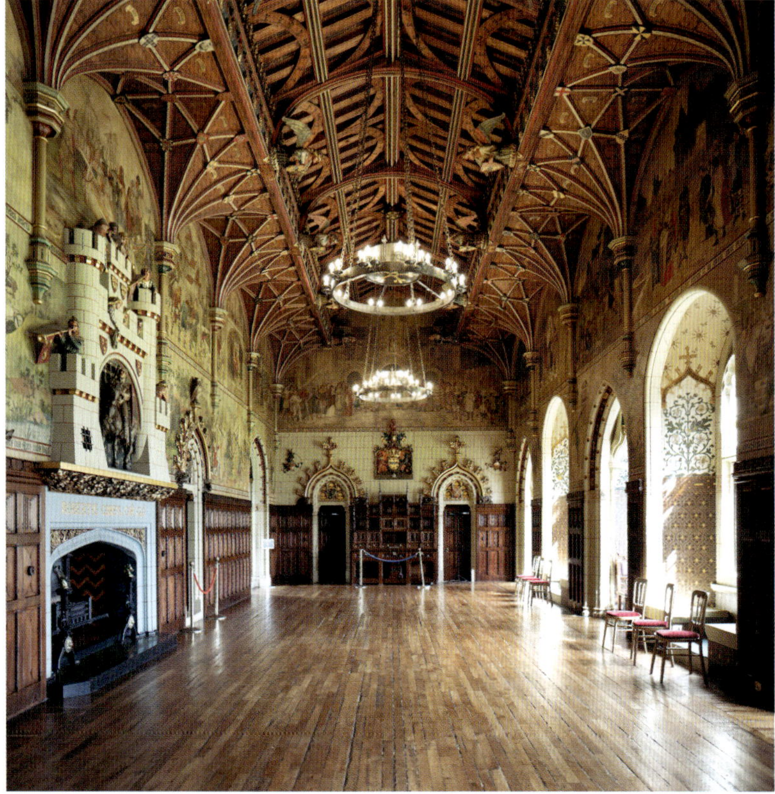

Fig. 173b

Great Hall, Cardiff Castle (1868–81), Wales, by William Burges.

running livestock on leases (or freehold land) amounting to tens of thousands of acres each, were able to erect the antipodean equivalent of country houses, colloquially referred to as homesteads. Although most of these were no more than large, well-appointed houses over one or two stories, built either of brick (rendered or plain) or local stone (often basalt or sandstone), some were quite sizable for their context, with no small amount of architectural

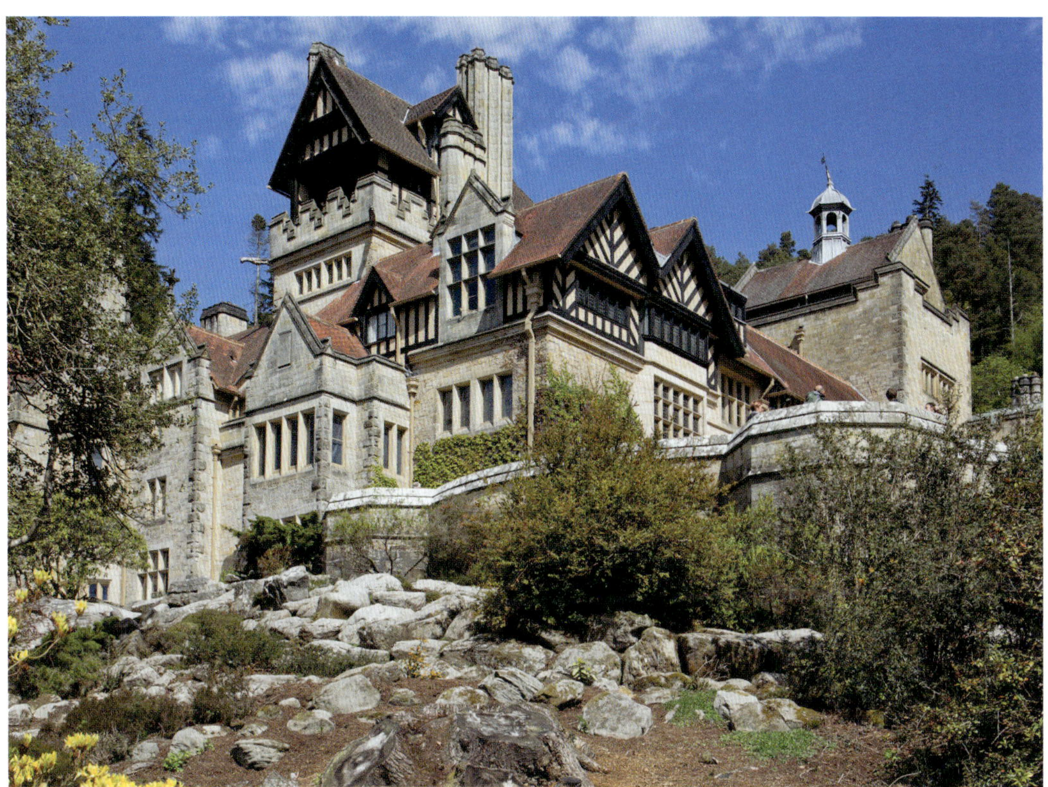

Fig. 174
Cragside (1870–*c*.1885), near Rothbury, Northumberland, by Richard Norman Shaw.

pretence. A number of such houses were built in the Western District of Victoria during the period, including Barwon Park, Winchelsea (1871), designed by the Scottish-born and -trained architect, Alexander Davidson. But two of the most prominent examples are Mona Vale, Ross (1865–7), Tasmania, by William Archer, and Werribee Park Mansion (1873–7), about 20 miles south-west of Melbourne, by J. H. Fox, both built from pastoralist fortunes **[175a]**. Others include Rupertswood, Sunbury (1874–6, extended 1881–2), near Melbourne, designed by George Brown for wealthy pastoralist W. J. Clarke; and Larnach Castle (1871–4), near Dunedin, by R. A. Lawson, for local Otago financier and businessman William Larnach **[175b]**. The first four (including Barwon Park) are variants of Italianate Classicism, the latter a form of medieval castellated. In Canada there were, among others, the spectacular Craigdarroch Castle (1887–90), Victoria, British Columbia, by Oregon architect W. H. Williams, for the Scottish-born coal magnate Robert Dunsmuir; and later the spectacular Casa Loma (1905–13), Toronto, by E. J. Lennox for the anglophile imperialist Henry Pellatt. The latter of these, the largest house in Canada, was designed in an ostentatious Scots Baronial style referencing Pellatt's Scottish heritage.

Larger colonial cities such as Melbourne, Sydney, and Toronto also witnessed a spectacular rise in the number of large suburban mansions built during the period, seen in examples such as Como (1847), Rippon Lea (1868–97), and Raheen (1870–84), in Melbourne; Carthona (1841–4), Retford Hall (1865–6), and Swifts (1876–83), in Sydney; and Oaklands (1860) and

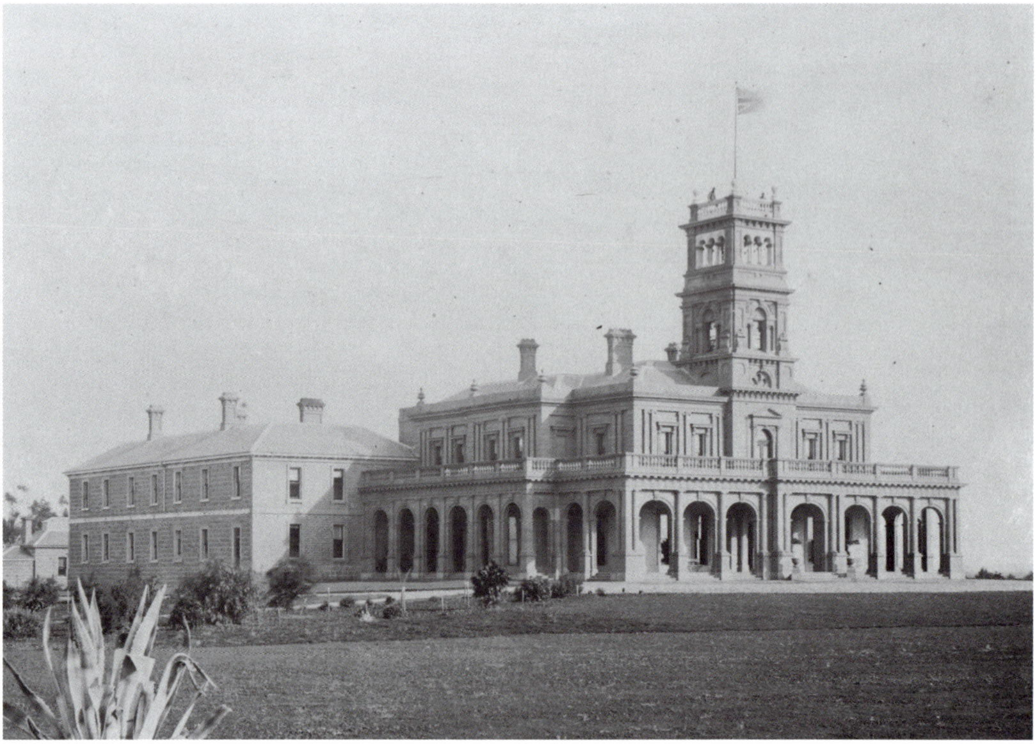

Fig. 175a

Taking the big house abroad: Werribee Park Mansion (1873–7), south-west of Melbourne, Australia, by J. H. Fox.

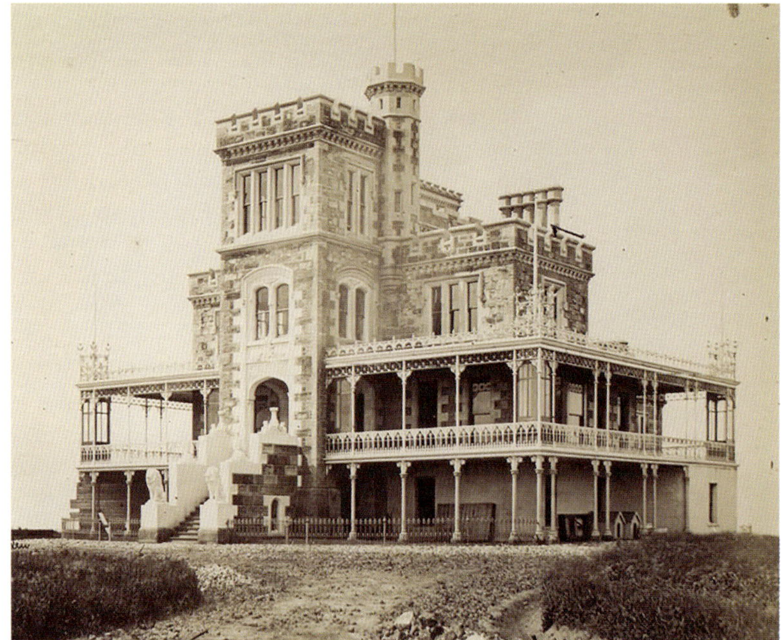

Fig. 175b

Larnach Castle (1871–4), near Dunedin, New Zealand, by R. A. Lawson.

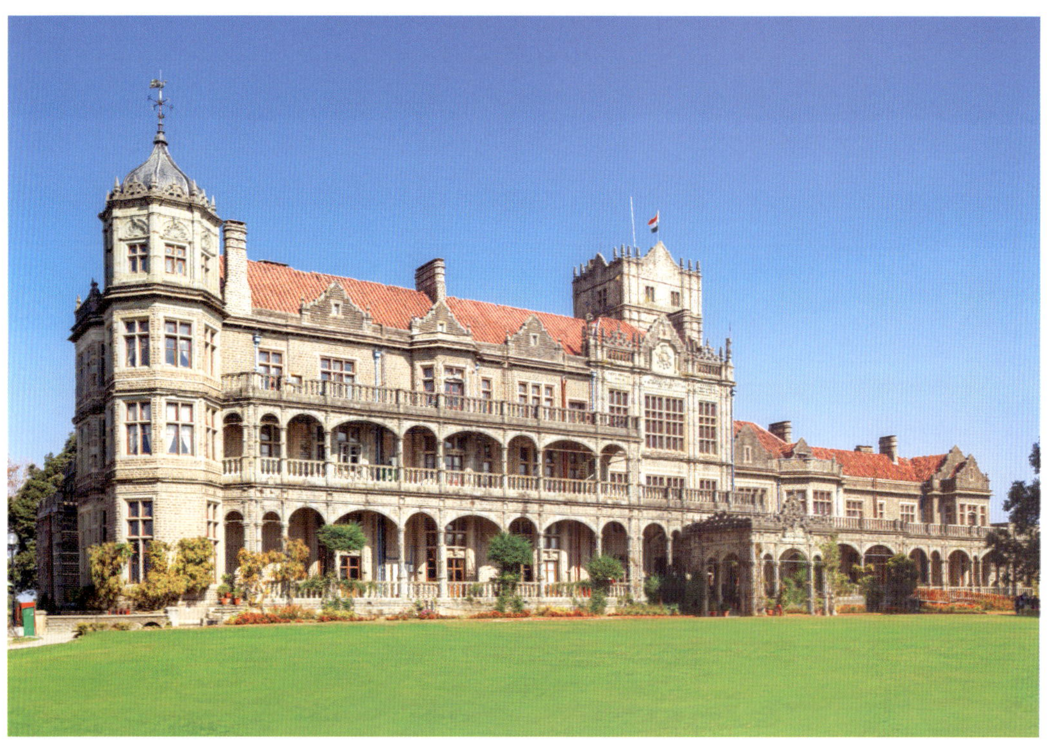

Fig. 176

Jacobean splendour. Viceregal Lodge (1880–8), Simla, north of Delhi, India, by Henry Irwin.

Gooderham House (1889–92), in Toronto. The latter of these is noteworthy for its American influence, in particular the Richardsonian Romanesque.

Some of the greatest houses in the wider British context were official government residences, such as the crenelated late Gothic mansion of Government House, Sydney (1837–47, later extended), by Edward Blore; Government House, Melbourne (1871–6), by William Wardell, in an Italianate Classicism inspired by Osborne House; or the extraordinary Jacobean-style Viceregal Lodge (1880–8), the viceroy of British India's summer residence, in the Himalayan foothills of Simla, north of Delhi, by Henry Irwin **[176]**. In the case of Government House, Hobart (1855–8), a Jacobethan-style mansion designed by James Blackburn, William Porden Kay, and others, the then governor's wife, Lady Jane Franklin, was influential in devising the plan. As discussed in relation to colonial infrastructure in Chapter 1, these kinds of houses extended not just political and economic sovereignty over British colonial territory, literally, but were also symbolic of a peculiar cultural idea of land ownership and husbandry alien to the indigenous inhabitants, who were routinely dispossessed.

Colonial wealth coming back the other way, to Britain, was often ploughed into country house construction. An example of this are houses built by the Jardine and Matheson families of the China Trade firm Jardine, Matheson & Co. The truly astounding fortunes raised from the activities of this Hong Kong-based firm, including opium smuggling, enabled the purchase of hundreds of thousands of acres of land in Scotland, the families' ancestral homelands. Evoking their ancient Scottish roots, the houses they built, including Castlemilk (1864–73), Dumfriesshire, by David Bryce, and

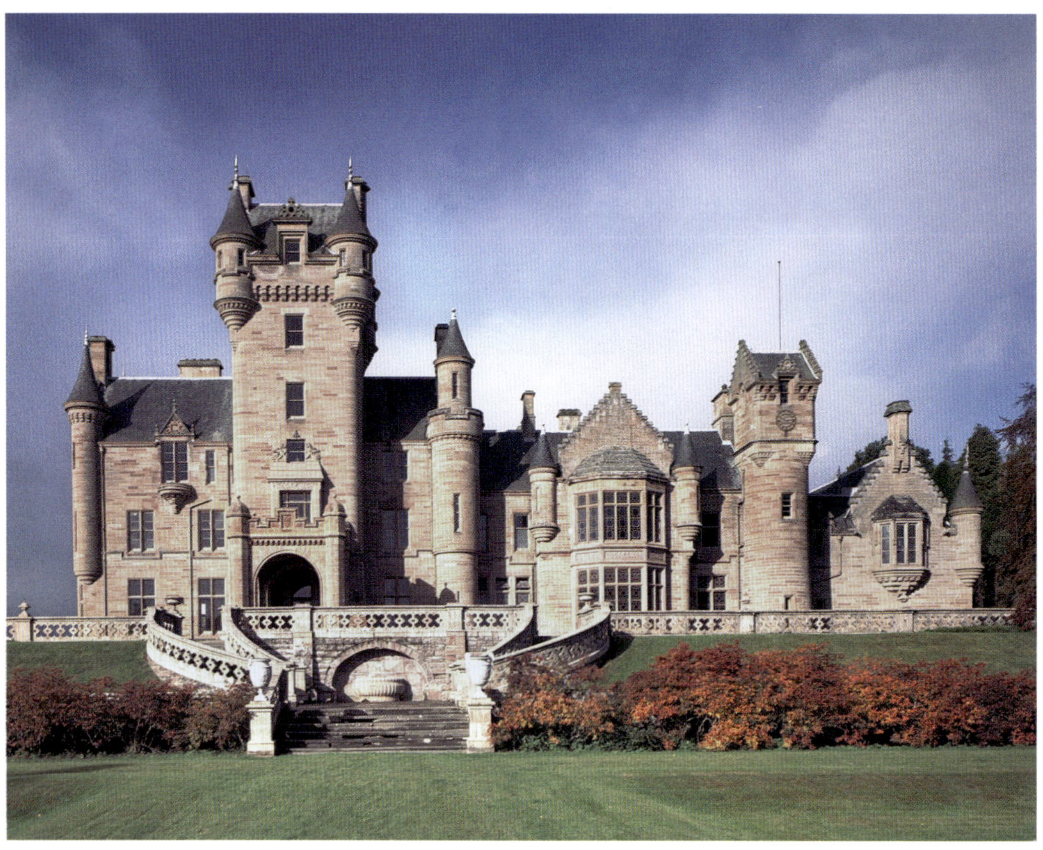

Fig. 177

Baronial aspirations. Ardross Castle (1880), near Inverness, Scotland, by Alexander Ross.

Ardross Castle (1880), near Inverness, by Alexander Ross, are fine specimens of the Scots Baronial **[177]**. Here, again, this style was used as a way of articulating national and cultural identity, in much the same way it had been at the Queen's Scottish retreat of Balmoral Castle, Aberdeenshire (1853–6), by William Smith.

Gendered Duties and Interior Transformation

Houses of these various kinds may have been 'designed' well enough, but living in them was another matter. As mentioned, patterns of Victorian domesticity and mores around familial hierarchy were heavily inscribed into the planning of such buildings. To this extent, these patterns and mores were both reinforcing and co-productive of Victorian domestic environments, manifesting a type of social hegemony. For middle-class Victorians, 'correct' management of the spaces and surfaces of the home, as well as the bodies that inhabited and moved through/over them, was viewed as a key indicator of social group self-perception.[7] Women, as wives and mothers, were considered especially suited to this role because they were understood as being morally superior to men, less corruptible, and therefore uniquely qualified to cultivate feelings of comfort and homeliness. Alongside this sat the not incompatible notion that the home was also a locale for the exercise of male power over dependeants, and a place of refuge (i.e., retreat) and discipline. This was different to the idea of 'architecture' as a manly preserve. Presiding over a well-ordered home was increasingly seen as a marker of masculine, indeed gentlemanly, esteem. Both these gendered and spiritually ordained responsibilities worked in tandem to create the Victorian home as an antidote to the grubby and calculating outside world. In this sense, it has been argued, the Victorian middle-class domestic unit and its abode represented the final stage in the process whereby the rationale for family existence shifted from being primarily economic to sentimental.[8]

So entrenched was this 'cult of the home' by the mid-nineteenth century that a large and widely consulted genre of advice literature concerning home management and decoration arose, in both book and periodical form. It was aimed primarily at women. Indeed, this literature was by and large responsible for promoting the Victorian ideology of domesticity, creating an authoritative (some might say suffocating) atmosphere around family life from which it was difficult to demur. Perhaps the most noted among such guides were Sarah Stickney Ellis's series of manuals, including *Wives of England: Their Relative Duties, Domestic Influence, and Social Obligations* (1843), Isabella Beeton's *Book of Household Management* (1861), and Jane Ellen Panton's *From Kitchen to Garret: Hints for Young Householders* (1893). Beaton's book alone sold some 2 million copies in its first seven years of publication. This was an astonishing feat given that Britain's middle-class population was estimated at around 6.6 million in 1867.[9] Magazines were also popular among the ranks of Victorian homemakers, such as *The Ladies' Treasury*, *The Englishwoman's Domestic Magazine*, and *Sylvia's Home Journal*, to name but a few. Some guides were aimed at the socially aspirant, such as Eliza Warren's *How I Managed my House on £200 a Year* (1864), while others took a decidedly highbrow tone concerning feminine conduct, such as *The Lady's Own Book: An Intellectual, Moral, and Physical Monitor* (1859). Either way, there was no shortage of advice.

As an example of the effects of this phenomenon on the material dimensions of the home, we may consider the drawing room. The Victorian 'drawing' room is what today we would refer to as a sitting, living, or lounge room. Apart from the hall or vestibule, it was the most public of the semi-public rooms in a typical Victorian house: a place for the reception and entertainment of guests, and the space to which women would 'withdraw' after dinner. This space was sometimes identified as a 'parlour'. In any case, it was considered a formal setting. Moreover, it was a feminine one. There were other rooms in the house that were considered masculine, such as the dining room, which was generally more heavily furnished with a darker palette, or those with specific functions, such as smoking or billiard rooms. But the drawing room was the domain of the 'lady' of the house. Given that middle-class women, removed from the drudgeries of the world, were expected to discover and fashion their identities within the home, the drawing room became the place where they could best express themselves and their homely ideals. Indeed, commenting on the English home from a foreign perspective in 1904, Hermann Muthesius noted that if an Englishwoman was 'the absolute mistress of the house', then the drawing room was her 'throne-room'.[10]

But the drawing room was a potentially perilous domain in terms of its decoration and arrangement; a place where a delicate balance had to be struck between individuality and 'character', personal expression and moral display. In this rarefied atmosphere of judgement, religious connotation hung heavily in the air. The incarnationalist tendencies among some to draw a line between the moral symbolism of a drawing room's contents and the spiritual constitution of the woman of the house could be brutal. In this sense, the drawing room was seen as an extension of the woman herself, where her character and discernment were objectified and exposed to scrutiny, including her choice in everything from wallpaper and carpet to furniture and decorations **[178a]**.[11]

The advice literature was full of warnings about either going too far with 'vulgar' showiness in the decoration of a drawing room, or not adequately representing one's true standing in life—both were considered social *faux pas* of the highest order. This naturally caused much anxiety among middle-class homemakers. The balancing act proved difficult, as the number and type of manufactured household furnishings, surface finishes, ornaments, and other home improvement aids and devices proliferated exponentially during the late nineteenth century. Many things that were once expensive or difficult to obtain became much cheaper and more freely available, not to mention the bewildering degree of choice **[178b]**. In order to meet growing middle-class demand, retailers of household furnishings, such as Silber & Fleming, James Shoolbred & Co., Chamberlain, King & Jones, and Oetzmann & Co. produced extensive catalogues showcasing a range of fashionable wares. In this, the middle-class woman was as much a creature of the new department stores as she was a homemaker. The result was often the Victorian drawing room seen as an environment of confusion, cluttered with objects and garishly furnished; a space that was stuffy, often pedantic, and thus uneasy in its apparent incoherency. This became a common trope in revealing a homemaker's 'bad taste'. As one home decorator observed in 1853, it was as 'morally injurious to keep company with bad things, as it is to associate with bad people'.[12]

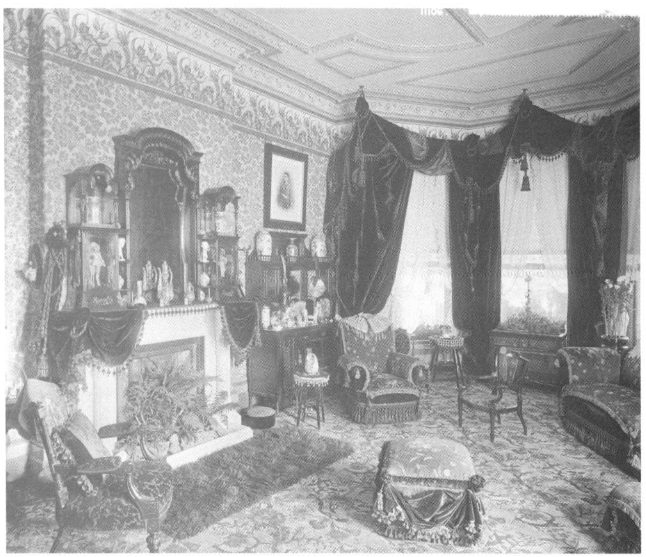

Fig. 178a

Interior design by Turner Walker & Co., for a fruit merchant's house on Aigburth Drive, Sefton Park, in Liverpool (photo 1891).

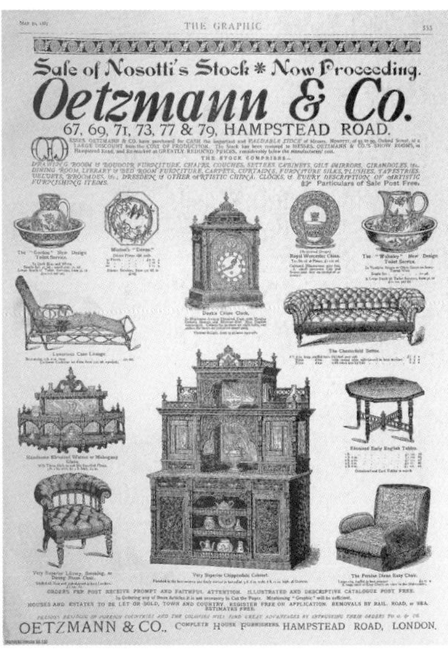

Fig. 178b

Household consumerism. Oetzmann & Co., advertisement, *The Graphic* (May 1885).

In order to combat this perceived degeneracy, Charles Eastlake produced his *Hints on Household Taste in Furniture, Upholstery and other Details* in 1868. This was aimed at 'aesthetical reform' among the general public, but women especially. For although it might offend an educated woman to suggest otherwise, he cautioned, her artistic judgement could not be assumed. In furnishing a drawing room, his first piece of advice was to avoid the recommendation of 'shopmen'. For instance, terms bandied around, such as 'handsome', had come to mean 'something which is generally showy, often ponderous'; while the word 'elegant' was 'applied to any object which is curved in form (no matter in what direction, or with what effect)'. These were fundamentally false ideas. 'The best and most picturesque furniture of all ages has been simple in general form', he counselled. It may have been 'enriched by complex details of carved-work or inlay, but its main outline was always chaste and sober in design'.[13]

The Evolving Interior: Comfort and the Arts and Crafts Ideal

This encouragement towards a kind of comfort and convenience through simplicity in home decoration was steadily presented as an essential Anglo-British trait. In their *Suggestions for House Decoration in Painting, Woodwork, and Furniture* (1876), Rhoda and Agnes Garrett advised that it was not money but 'discrimination' that was required when tastefully decorating a drawing

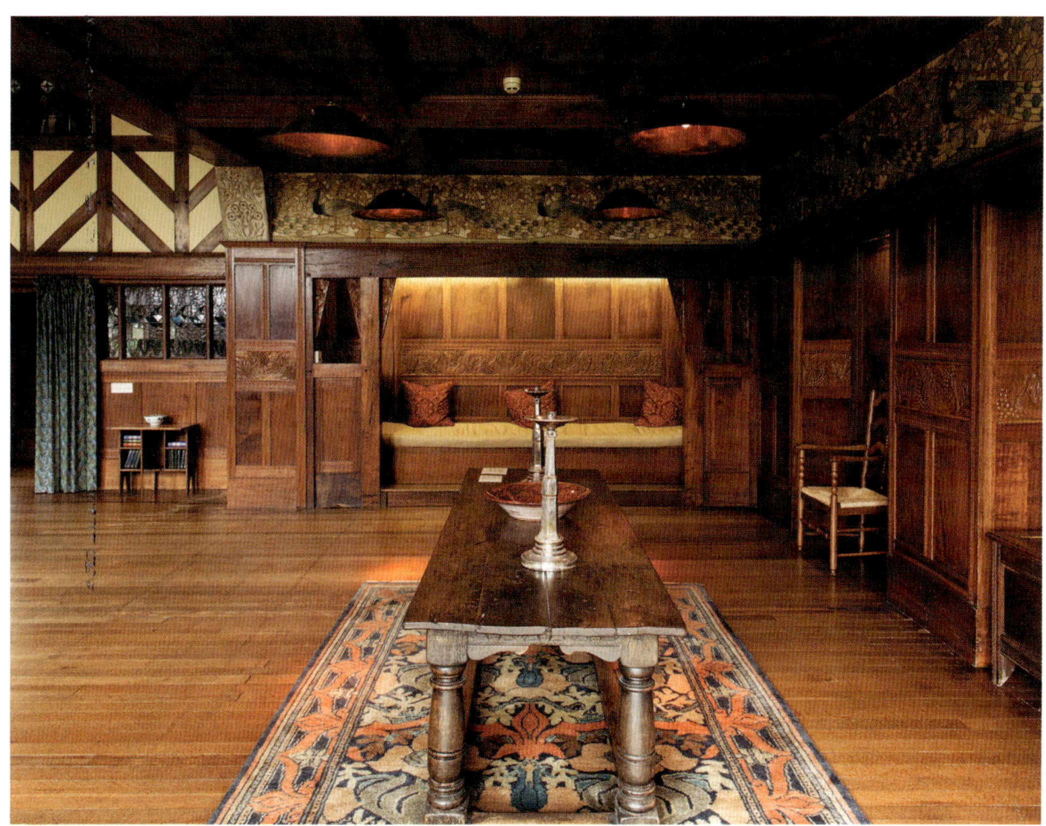

Fig. 179

Arts and Crafts comfort. Blackwell House, Bowness-on-Windermere (1898–1900), Lake District, by Mackay Hugh Baillie Scott.

room, as if arriving at such discernment ought to be innate for an Englishwoman. Professionally trained in architecture in the office of John McKean Brydon, the Garrett cousins were trailblazers as female designers in Victorian Britain, specialising in interior design, having opened their own company in London in 1874, R&A Garrett House Decoration. Much like Eastlake, in advising on furniture they noted how 'theatrical' looks were to be avoided, with a simple 'general rule': that furniture 'should be well constructed, suitable to its purpose, and thoroughly good of its kind'. Such advice reflected the growing influence of Arts and Crafts principles in interior design, of which the Garretts were noted advocates. Other companies specialising in household furnishing along these lines, such as Morris, Marshall, Faulkner & Co. and Watts & Co., rose to prominence, utilising the design skills of some of the leading artists and architects of the day, such as William Morris, Philip Webb, G. F. Bodley, William De Morgan, and Edward Burne-Jones.

Invoking straightforward notions of honesty, ease, and naturalness in design, the Arts and Crafts interior, along with its associated Queen Anne and Aesthetic Movement variants, sought to impart a well-designed, largely hand-crafted look that expressed the best in natural finishes and quality materials. As Morris himself quipped: 'Have nothing in your house which you do not know to be useful, or believe to be beautiful.' Although a self-conscious endeavour, the effects achieved through Arts and Crafts design, at its best, gave the appearance of effortless charm through coordinated,

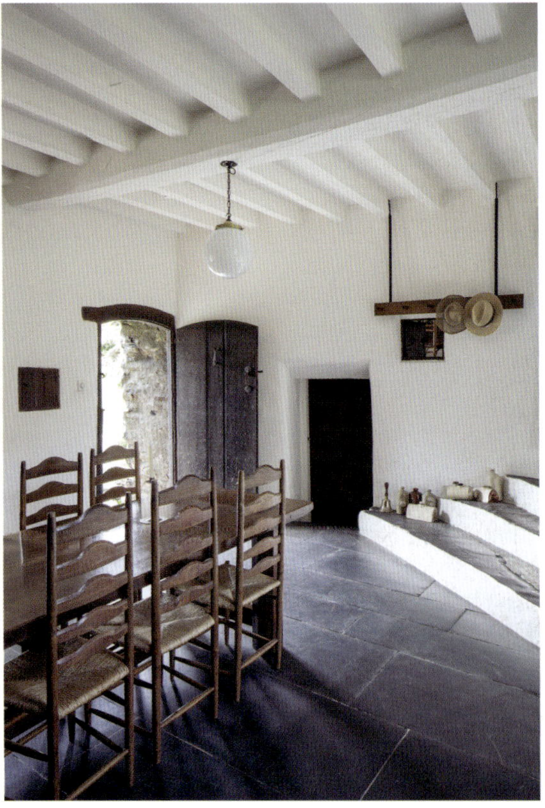

Fig. 180

Dining room, Stoneywell, Leicestershire (1897–9), by Ernest Gimson.

unfussy combinations of soft, hard, and in many cases, raw furnishings and materials, often bringing aspects of the exterior of houses into their interiors, such as exposed brick fireplaces and unrefined timber elements. This included making visible the character of natural materials, such as woodgrain, as well as showcasing general processes of craftsmanship **[179]**. Again, rooted in medieval vernacular precedent (see Chapter 3), the movement was considered quintessentially British, with variants across the British Isles. In Scotland, for instance, architects such as Robert Lorimer and Charles Rennie Mackintosh produced buildings in this manner with clear local inflections, including Ardkinglas, Argyllshire (1906–8), and Hill House, Helensburgh (1902–3), the latter noted for its Art Nouveau flourishes. Red House, in Bexleyheath near London, by Webb is obviously the classic exemplar of the 'manicured' Arts and Crafts approach to interior design, where the celebration of natural materials and surfaces, in conjunction with Morris-designed furnishings, is very much in evidence.

The beauty of this approach, however, was that it could be achieved at almost any scale, on a varied budget. We see it in palatial settings, such as Cragside, or in much more modest ones, such as Stoneywell, Leicestershire (1897–9), by Ernest Gimson **[180]**. It was popular abroad, too, throughout Britain's colonies and beyond, including in the United States. Examples include Herbert Baker's Cape Revival houses in South Africa, such as Rust en Vrede, Stellenbosch (1905); or Wombat Park, near Daylesford (1910), in

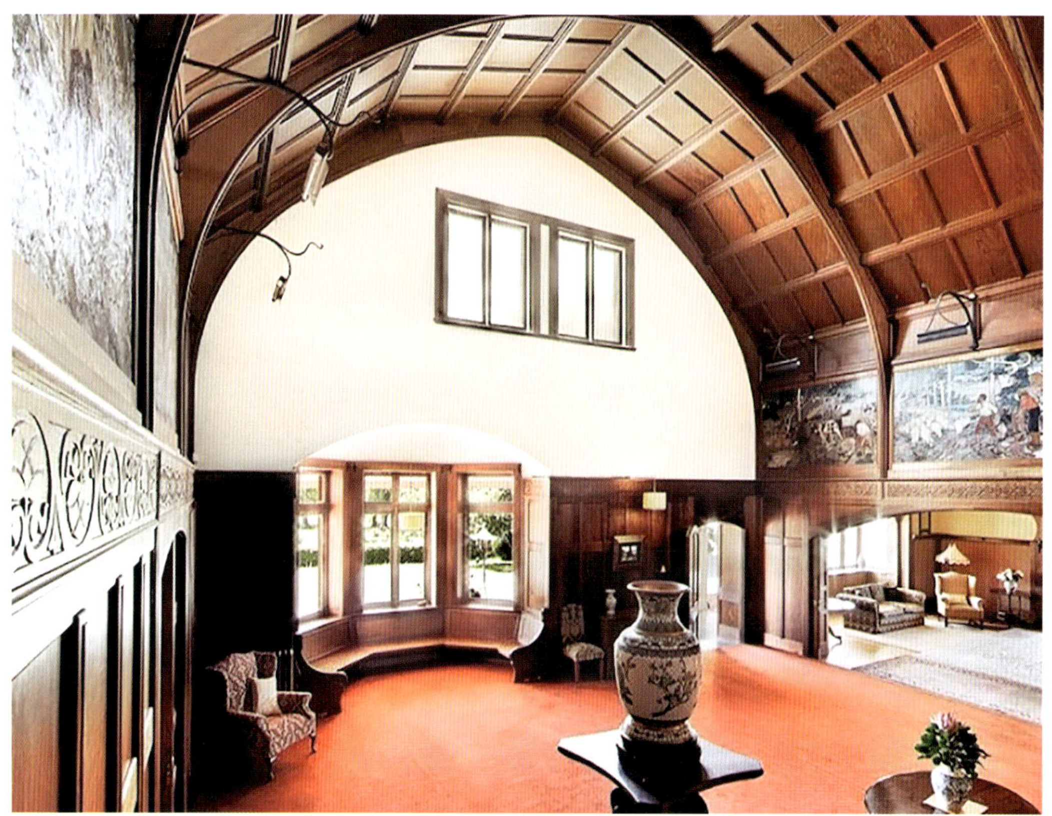

Fig. 181

Arts and Crafts down under. Purrumbete homestead (1842, extended and rebuilt 1901–2), near Camperdown, in the Western District of Victoria, Australia, by Guyon Purchas.

Victoria (Australia), by Rodney Alsop; and, of course, the exquisitely crafted houses of Greene & Greene in California, such as the Gamble House, Pasadena (1908–9), not to mention the early works of Frank Lloyd Wright, such as his own home in Oak Park, Illinois (1889). In some cases, as at Purrumbete homestead (1842, extended and rebuilt 1901–2), near Camperdown, in the Western District of Victoria, Arts and Crafts design was deployed to reinforce narratives of pioneering European settlement in what had previously been indigenous lands **[181]**. Here art and architectural motifs, including murals and handcrafted timber interiors, were devised to invoke time-honoured traditions of vernacular culture and nascent nationalist sentiment, with a view to bolstering a certain rootedness, productivity, and thus legal claim to the land.[14] In this sense, the Arts and Crafts ideal also operated as a vector of imperialism.

Labour and Dirt: Keeping the Victorian Home Clean

A certain fastidiousness around cleanliness was one of the outcomes of the modernisation of the home during Victorian times through the reforming of family life and the incorporation of new products and services, including better-connected mains water and sewage. The hallmark of the middle-class home was of course access to servants. As mentioned, the presence of such home help left its own imprint on the formal and spatial arrangements of the house, with 'back' stairs and servants' rooms appearing as recurrent features in Victorian house planning. This in turn foregrounded the degree of labour required to maintain the pretences of Victorian middle-class existence. Moreover, with industrialisation and its environmental effects came greater opportunities for the accumulation of dust and grime, especially as the number and complexity of interior decorative objects proliferated. There was a virtuous dimension to this idea of cleanliness, too, as 'dirt' was considered a form of pollutant, and thus a corrupting presence. One's home had to be 'clean' (i.e., pure), both morally and spiritually. The idea that 'cleanliness is next to Godliness' resonated widely.

This led to a surge of inventiveness, as a market response, to combat these day-to-day problems of modern existence, including the increasingly common incorporation of dedicated wet- and bath-room spaces for washing. These were specifically designed for ease of cleaning, with porcelain and enamelled metal basins and baths, as well as tile or linoleum floors, and dado walls. One noteworthy intervention was the push for cleaner-burning, more efficient fireplaces. As the domestic hearth was the locus of familial cohesion, the presence of coal dust and smoke was an irritant that potentially threatened the institution of the family. Coal's centrality to modern life and the economy was well appreciated, but its by-products were hazardous. By the 1880s sanitary activists were hosting 'smoke abatement' exhibitions at which awards were given for the cleanest, best-performing coal-fired household appliances.[15] This places the Victorian economies of domesticity within larger interpretative frameworks concerning the history of fossil fuel extraction, consumption, and its long-term health and environmental impacts.

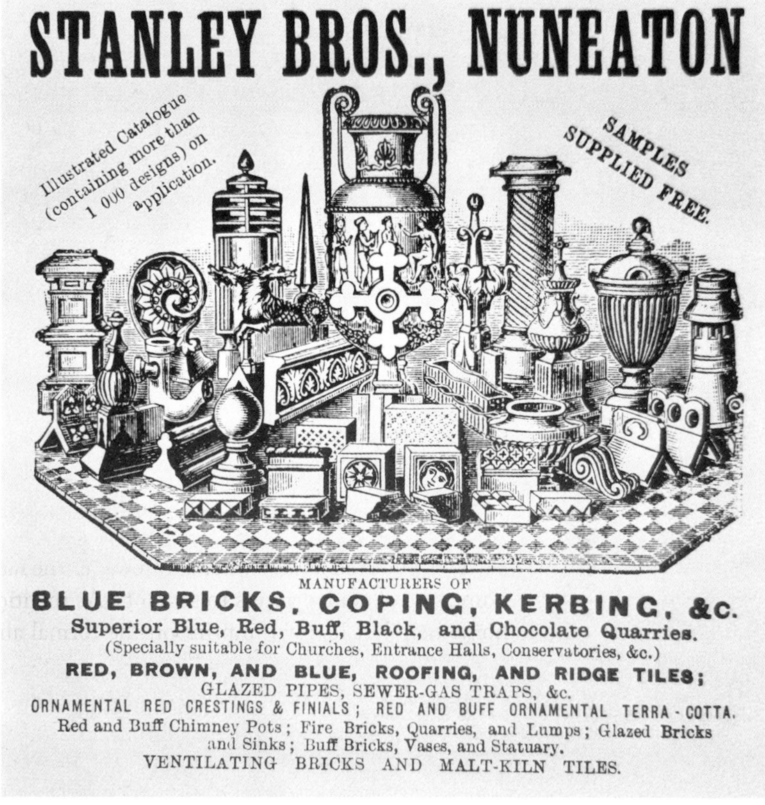

Fig. 182

Building products advertisement for Stanley Bros., Nuneaton (Warwickshire).

Materials and Construction

The range and quality of materials used in Victorian architecture was covered to some extent in Chapter 2. Many if not most of the same materials used in public and commercial architecture were also used in domestic house construction. In Britain it was most common for houses to be built in brick or natural stone, or a combination of both. This might entail a mostly brick building finished with natural stone detailing, such as door and window aedicules and other stone dressings, or solid brick construction behind a stone veneer. Brick construction was dictated primarily by fire regulations, especially in urban areas. But timber was also used, not just for framing and flooring but also for exterior elements, as seen, for instance, in Tudor Revival buildings which sought a half-timbered effect. Again, we see this at Cragside, but also on much more modest edifices, such as with some of the many workers' cottages at the Port Sunlight soap factory village (1888–1921), near Liverpool. It is also worth remembering that during the Victorian period many timber buildings, including houses, remained from the Georgian and earlier periods, making for quite a different urban complexion than we see today.

Brick was of course an extremely robust, versatile, and relatively cheap material, that by the mid-Victorian period could be obtained in a vast array of colours, shapes, and sizes. Stone was more expensive, and was usually reserved for higher-quality housing, as the procurement and finishing of stone required greater effort—although, where quarries of good building stone resided near sites of construction, it could be reasonably cost effective. In any case, stone, aesthetically speaking, spoke of a higher order of architecture. Added to these were a range of other common materials, such as slate for roofs, terracotta elements to the exterior, and plate glass for windows. It is worth reminding ourselves that during this period numerous companies appeared that specialised in the manufacture of building products, at scale and to order, offering a degree of choice that was previously unknown **[182]**. Encaustic tiles were one such product, with Mintons and Maw & Co. dominating the market. These tiles came in all shapes, sizes, and colours, and could be used outside, around porches, as well as inside. As Eastlake observed in his *Hints*, such tiling had 'not only reached great technical perfection as far as material and colour are concerned, but, aided by the designs supplied by many architects of acknowledged skill, it has gradually become a means of decoration which for beauty of effect, durability, and cheapness, has scarcely a parallel'.

As explained above, the Arts and Crafts aesthetic often required a more natural finish, which could include the deliberate sourcing of hand-made bricks for their 'imperfections', or leaving the grain and texture of timber elements exposed. Outside Britain, in the colonies, rough-and-ready, hand-made materials were often all that could be used, at least until industrial processes were systematically installed. Indeed, in places like New Zealand, Canada, and Australia timber was a very common house-building material (much more so than in Britain), not only because it was plentiful, comparatively cheap, and quick to assemble, but also because ready supplies of good building stone were not always available. As industrialised sawmilling technology increased (see Chapter 1), timber getting for building purposes became a major industry in these places. Even in Britain, the advent of steam-powered timber moulding mills, processing wood mainly from abroad, enabled an influx of decorative, off-the-shelf elements, from balusters and architraves to skirting. It was the same in the United States, where whole genres of architecture were based around timber construction, such as the so-called Stick Style, which came in a number of variations. Moreover, in seismic locations such as New Zealand, timber had its advantages in being more flexible and therefore somewhat earthquake resistant. In frontier environments timber was also the easiest material to procure, leading to basic yet recognisable forms, as pioneers built makeshift accommodation while clearing land, mining, or establishing settlements **[183a]**. In such contexts wattle and daub, mud bricks, and even bark were used, leading to the rise of colonial vernacular traditions **[183b]**. Although such structures were extremely primitive, they were not so far removed from those that could be found at the time in isolated rural areas of Scotland and Ireland. The use of stone could lead to quite distinct local effects, too, such as basalt (blue stone) employed widely in southern Australia and New Zealand. Sandstone could also range in colour from beige, through red, to brown. The distinctive and vibrant red sandstone of Dumfriesshire, in Scotland, for example, characterised many a domestic tenement block in Glasgow and Edinburgh.

In some cases entire houses were prefabricated, flat-packed, and shipped to colonial contexts, especially where industrial processes were lacking

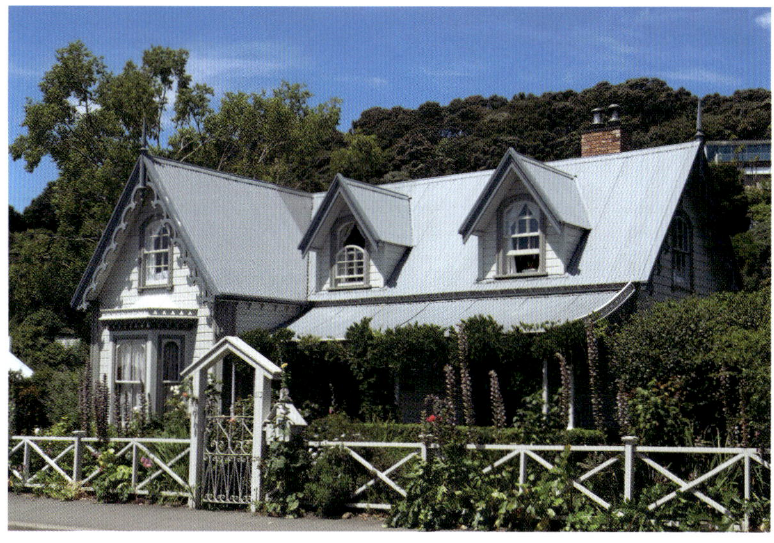

Fig. 183a

Timber Victorian cottage, Akaroa (South Island), New Zealand.

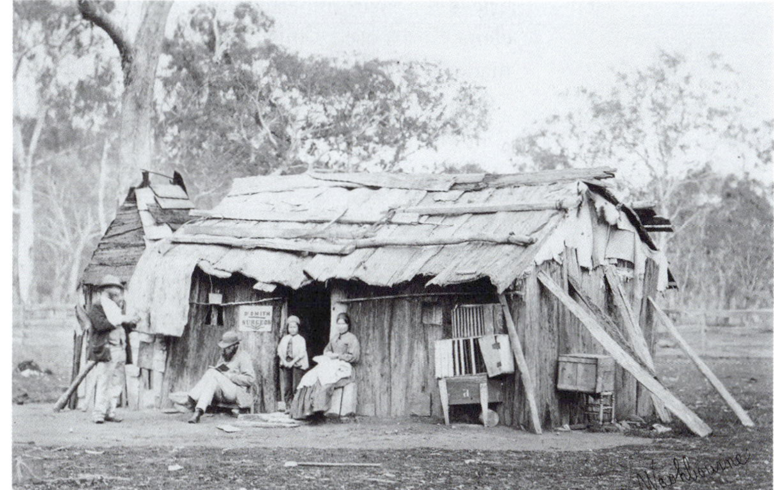

Fig. 183b

Making the best of materials to hand. Bark (slab) hut, Australia (*c.*1870).

in situ. These were often made of wood or iron, or a combination of both. One of the materials commonly used on such buildings was corrugated iron, which, owing to its repetitive curvilinear profile, was a strong, versatile, and comparatively durable material. In many colonial settings, corrugated iron became a common roofing material for domestic housing, mainly for its lightweight, durable qualities. In Australia, for instance, it gave a distinctive appearance to the roofline of many houses built during the Victorian period. Its major drawback, however, was that it conducted heat extremely well, which was not ideal in hot climates.[16]

As mentioned in previous chapters, procedures of standardisation, as well as the division of labour into specialised trades (bricklayers, carpenters, stonemasons, plumbers, roofers, etc.), was necessary to meet demand and maintain certain benchmarks in the building industry. Without this standardisation, and the networks of supply that evolved through transport infrastructure, the rate, quality, and variety of domestic house construction in Victorian Britain would have been impossible. The rise of the large, 'master builder' contracting firm, through which materials, tradesmen, and labourers were systematically coordinated around carefully planned and costed processes, also facilitated the scale and quantity of housing. In London alone fifty-seven such firms employing over fifty men each existed by 1851, of which nine employed over 200; by 1872 there were reputedly some 250.[17] Not all of these were building houses. But some, such as Watts of Catford and Edward Yates, built as many as 100 houses per year in the 1890s, rising in the case of Watts to 400 in 1899. This number was rare, however. Most firms (about 80 per cent), which were much smaller, managed only around six or so per annum, with some medium-sized outfits reaching as many as sixty.[18]

As professionalisation of the building industry increased, so too did procedural and legal complexity. Processes were formalised, such as tendering, with organisations like the RIBA issuing guidelines, while associated professions such as quantity surveying came into their own. With the number of surveyors having reached 749 in London alone by 1861, they established their own professional body (Institution of Surveyors) in 1868.[19] Practices around the leasing and development of land for domestic housing, particularly in the vicinity of large and ever-expanding cities, also diversified. Responsiveness and flexibility in the face of rapidly changing market conditions was crucial. All of this was plugged into a growing building information

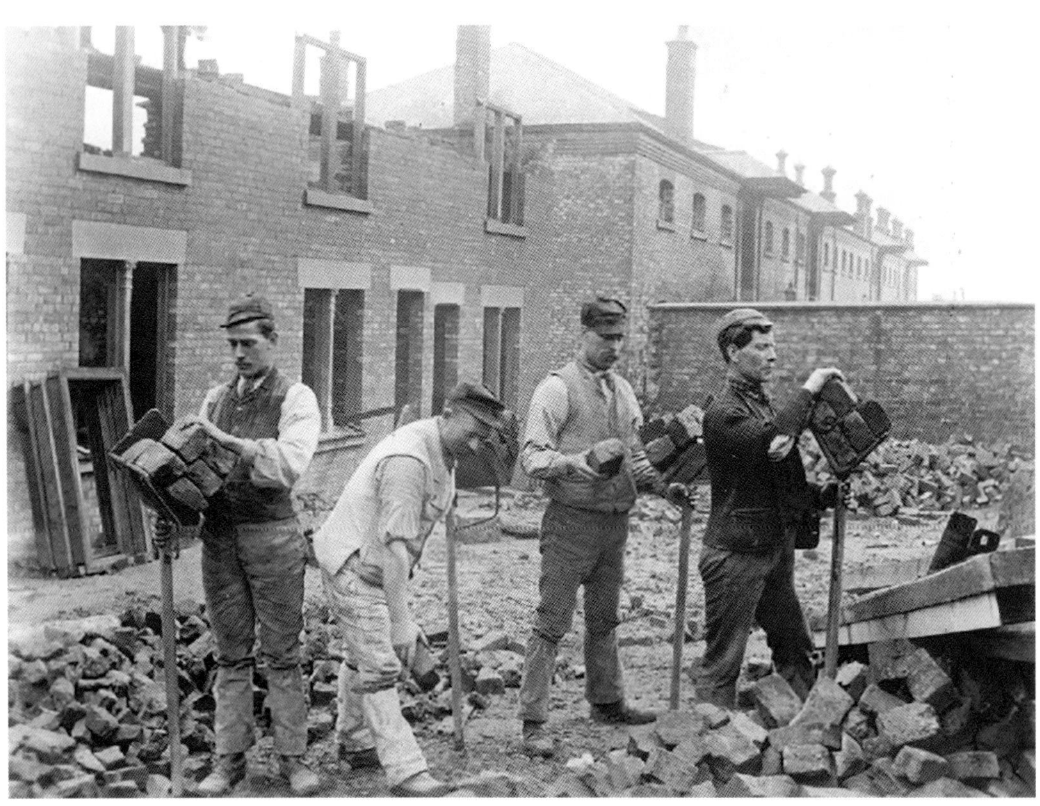

Fig. 184
Manchester bricklayers on housing development, c.1900.

economy, where manuals, trade journals, and pattern books (mentioned above) circulated with much greater frequency during the Victorian period than they had previously. In relation to speculative building may be cited *The Builder's Practical Director* (1855) and the architecture volumes in *Weale's Rudimentary Series*. These publications naturally found their way to the colonies, but in such places local, context-specific information resources also emerged.[20]

Speculative building in the housing sector had its problems, however. This was especially the case at the lower end of the market. This speculation was in effect the practice of building to sell, whereby a 'speculative builder' (and/or his investors) would shoulder the cost of construction with a view to selling for profit. This opened the door to what these days would be termed 'buy-to-let', as the buyer then looked to make a return through long-term rental **[184]**. Given that upwards of 80 per cent of homes were rented in the Victorian period, one can understand the economic pressures acting on all parties (builders, investors, tenants). This led to the rise of 'jerry building'. The pages of the building press often attracted vituperative opinions on the rise in substandard house construction owing to speculation, resulting in unfit, even dangerous, accommodation. Accusations of dishonesty and evasiveness abounded. Such problems were largely universal, occurring in both Britain and its colonies. Indeed, it was fraudulent practices that led some architects and builders to be sent to penal colonies in the first place. Once there they went on to contribute to the local built environment, in some cases significantly, such as James Blackburn mentioned above. Only with tighter building regulations, along with a more savvy customer base, did these problems slowly abate in the last quarter of the nineteenth century. As with the planning, decoration, and habitation of houses, their construction was an equally fraught moral domain.

Notes

Introduction

1. Although this was true for many architects, Murzban did travel to Britain and Europe in 1874.
2. Graham Wynn, *The Timber Colony: A Historical Geography of Early Nineteenth Century New Brunswick* (Toronto, 1981).
3. Pallavi V. Das, 'Railway Fuel and Its Impact on the Forests in Colonial India: The Case of the Punjab, 1860–1884', *Modern Asian Studies*, 47:4 (2013), 1283–1309.
4. David Ward, 'The Place of Victorian Cities in Developmental Approaches to Urbanization', in J. Patten (ed.), *The Expanding City: Essays in Honour of Professor Jean Gottmann* (London, 1983), pp. 369–377.
5. For a useful discussion of why this is so, see Martin Hewitt, 'Why the Notion of Victorian Britain Does Make Sense', *Victorian Studies*, 48:3 (2006), 395–438.
6. John Summerson, *Victorian Architecture: Four Studies in Evaluation* (New York, 1970), p. 10.
7. Hugh Casson, *An Introduction to Victorian Architecture* (London, 1948), pp. 9–11.
8. A. J. B. Beresford Hope, *The English Cathedral of the Nineteenth Century* (London, 1861), p. 250; Charles L. Eastlake, *A History of the Gothic Revival* (London, 1872), p. 279. For the idea of 'Victorian' in contemporary architecture, see Kelly J. Mays, 'How the Victorians Un-Invented Themselves: Architecture, the Battle of the Styles, and the History of the Term *Victorian*', *Journal of Victorian Culture*, 19:1 (2014), 1–23.
9. For instance, see Isobel Armstrong, *Victorian Glassworlds: Glass Culture and the Imagination 1830–1880* (Oxford, 2008), pp. 13–14; Lynda Nead, *Victorian Babylon: People, Streets and Images in Nineteenth-Century London* (New Haven and London, 2000), pp. 3–10.
10. G. G. Scott, *Remarks on Secular & Domestic Architecture, Present & Future* (London, 1857), pp. 8, 19.
11. Jerome Hamilton Buckley, *The Triumph of Time: A Study of the Victorian Concepts of Time, History, Progress, and Decadence* (Cambridge, MA, 1966).
12. Banister Fletcher and Banister F. Fletcher, *A History of Architecture for the Student, Craftsman, and Amateur, Being a Comparative View of the Historical Styles* (London, 1896), p. 293.
13. Robert Macleod, *Style and Society: Architectural Ideology in Britain 1835–1941* (London, 1971), pp. 84–105.
14. The key publications in this regard were Pugin's *Contrasts* (1836) and *True Principles of Pointed or Christian Architecture* (1841), and Ruskin's *Seven Lamps of Architecture* (1849) and *Stones of Venice* (1851–3).
15. See Thomson's lectures 'On the Unsuitableness of Gothic Architecture to Modern Circumstances' (1864) and 'An Inquiry as to the appropriateness of the Gothic style for the proposed buildings of the University of Glasgow, with some remarks upon Mr. Scott's plans' (1866), in G. Stamp (ed.), *The Light of Truth and Beauty: The Lectures of Alexander 'Greek' Thomson Architect 1817–1875* (Glasgow, 1999).
16. G. E. Street, *Brick and Marble in the Middle Ages* (London, 1855), pp. 286–287.

Chapter 1

1. Chris Otter, 'The Technosphere: A New Concept for Urban Studies', *Urban History*, 44:1 (2017), 145–154.
2. For statistics on Britain, see Dan Bogart, 'The Transport Revolution in Industrialising Britain', in R. Floud, J. Humphries, and P. Johnson (eds), *The Cambridge Economic History of Modern Britain—Volume 1: 1700–1870* (Cambridge, 2014), pp. 368–391. For India, see Tirthankar Roy, *How British Rule Changed India's Economy: The Paradox of the Raj* (London, 2019), pp. 13, 56.
3. R. C. Allen, 'Why the Industrial Revolution Was British: Commerce, Induced Invention, and the Scientific Revolution', *The Economic History Review*, 64:2 (2011), 357–84.
4. George Edmund Street, 'The True Principles of Architecture and the Possibility

of Development', *The Ecclesiologist*, 13 (August 1852), 247–262 (p. 250).
5. E. A. Wrigley, *The Path to Sustained Growth: England's Transition from an Organic Economy to an Industrial Revolution* (Cambridge, 2016), p. 146.
6. Paul Dobraszczyk, *Iron, Ornament and Architecture in Victorian Britain* (Farnham, 2014), pp. 229–273.
7. For instance, see James Belich, *Replenishing the Earth: The Settler Revolution and the Rise of the Anglo-World, 1783–1939* (Oxford, 2009).
8. E. J. T. Collins, 'Food Supplies and Food Policy', in Collins (ed.), *The Agrarian History of England and Wales*, VII, *1850–1914*, 2 vols (Cambridge, 2000), I, p. 37;
Rebecca J. H. Woods, 'Breed, Culture, and Economy: The New Zealand Frozen Meat Trade, 1880–1914', *Agricultural History Review*, 60:2 (2012), 288.
9. Jane Hutton, *Reciprocal Landscapes: Stories of Material Movements* (Abingdon, 2019).
10. A. Isenberg, *The Destruction of the Bison: An Environmental History, 1750–1920* (Cambridge, 2000).
11. Graham Wynn, *The Timber Colony: A Historical Geography of Early Nineteenth Century New Brunswick* (Toronto, 1981).
12. James Anthony Froude, *Oceana; or England and Her Colonies*, new edition (London, 1886), pp. 15, 102.
13. J. T. Critchell and J. Raymond, *A History of the Frozen Meat Trade* (London, 1912).
14. Rebecca J. H. Woods, 'Breed, Culture, and Economy: The New Zealand Frozen Meat Trade, 1880–1914', *Agricultural History Review*, 60 (2012), 288.
15. T. W. Freeman, *The Conurbations of Great Britain* (Manchester, 1959), p. 1.
16. H. J. Dyos, 'Railways and Housing in Victorian London', *Journal of Transport History*, 2:1 (1955), 11–21.
17. Quoted in Peter T. A. Jones, 'Redressing Reform Narratives: Victorian London's Street Markets and the Informal Supply Lines of Urban Modernity', *London Journal*, 41:1 (2016), 73.
18. Lynda Nead, *Victorian Babylon: People, Streets and Images in Nineteenth-Century London* (New Haven & London, 2000), pp. 13–56.
19. John Summerson, 'The Victorian Rebuilding of the City of London', *London Journal*, 3:2 (1977), 163–185.
20. Mark Crinson, *Shock City: Image and Architecture in Industrial Manchester* (London and New Haven, 2022), p. 36.
21. Ibid., p. 65. See also Tristram Hunt, *Building Jerusalem: The Rise and Fall of the Victorian City* (London, 2004), pp. 141–192.
22. C. M. Allan, 'The Genesis of British Urban Redevelopment with Special Reference to Glasgow', *Economic History Review*, new series, 18:3 (1965), pp. 598–613.
23. Peter Hall, *Cities of Tomorrow: An Intellectual History of Urban Planning and Design in the Twentieth Century*, third edn. (Oxford, 2002), pp. 14–32.
24. Felix Driver, *Geography Militant: Cultures of Exploration and Empire* (Oxford, 2001), pp. 170–198.
25. Anthony D. King, *Urbanism, Colonialism, and the World-Economy* (London, 1990), pp. 141–142.
26. Laura Harper, 'Gold Rush Urbanism: Continuing Effects of Gold Mining on the Urban Form of Victorian Towns', in A. Brennan and P. Goad (eds), *Proceedings of the Society of Architectural Historians, Australia and New Zealand: 33, Gold* (Melbourne, 2016), pp. 236–248.
27. Lindsay Weiss, 'Exceptional Space: Concentration Camps and Labor Compounds in Late Nineteenth-Century South Africa', in A. Myers and G. Moshenska (eds), *Archaeologies of Internment* (New York, 2011), pp. 21–32.

Chapter 2

1. 'The First Half of the Nineteenth Century', *Fraser's Magazine* (Jan. 1851), pp. 1–15. Britain's population doubled between 1801 and 1851, rising from 9 million to nearly 18 million.
2. Christopher Powell, *The British Building Industry Since 1800* (London, 1996), p. 42. Others put it at around 1.5 billion by 1849. For tables, see Robin Lucas, 'The Tax on Bricks and Tiles, 1784–1850: Its Application to the Country at Large and, in Particular, to the County of Norfolk', *Construction History*, vol. 13 (1997), p. 32.
3. A. J. B. Beresford Hope, *The English Cathedral of the Nineteenth Century* (London, 1861), p. 250.
4. *The Builder* (19 June 1852), p. 385.
5. Beresford Hope quoted in Paul Thompson, *William Butterfield* (Cambridge, MA, 1971), p. 163; G. E. Street, *Brick and Marble in the Middle Ages: Notes on a Tour in the North of Italy* (London, 1855), p. 284.
6. Susan Galavan, *Dublin's Bourgeois Homes: Building the Victorian Suburbs, 1850–1901* (London, 2017), pp. 134–136.
7. *The Argus* (7 Sept. 1870), p. 7.

8. Stuart Allen Smith, 'Alfred Waterhouse: Civic Grandeur', in J. Fawcett and N. Pevsner (eds), *Seven Victorian Architects* (London, 1976), pp. 118–120.
9. Margaret Henderson Floyd, 'A Terra-Cotta Cornerstone for Copley Square: Museum of Fine Arts, Boston, 1870–1876', *Journal of the Society of Architectural Historians*, 32:2 (1973), 83–103.
10. Zerah Colburn, 'The Manufacture of Encaustic Tiles and Ceramic Ornamentation by Machinery', *Journal of the Society of Arts* (19 May 1865), p. 449.
11. Lily Crowther, 'Innovation and Revivalism: Powell & Sons' Opus Sectile Mosaic', *Journal of Design History*, 36:2 (2023), 112–113.
12. W. Stanley Jevons, *The Coal Question; An Inquiry Concerning the Progress of the Nation, and the Probable Exhaustion of Our Coal Mines* (London, 1865), pp. vii–viii.
13. Andreas Malm, *Fossil Capital: The Rise of Steam Power and the Roots of Global Warming* (London, 2016).
14. E. A. Wrigley, *Energy and the English Industrial Revolution* (Cambridge, 2010), p. 37.
15. Street, *Brick and Marble*, p. vii.
16. Mari Hvattum and Anne Hultzsch (eds), *The Printed and the Built: Architecture, Print Culture, and Public Debate in the Nineteenth Century* (London, 2018), p. 3.
17. See Andrew Barry, 'Technological Zones', *European Journal of Social Theory*, 9:2 (2006), 239–253 (p. 239); Thomas Hughes, *Networks of Power: Electrification in Western Society, 1880–1930* (Baltimore, 1983).
18. George Edmund Street, *An Urgent Plea for the Revival of True Principles of Architecture in the Public Buildings of the University of Oxford* (Oxford, 1853), p. 4. He would also later remark: 'We not only know what materials we may obtain, but we have at the same time marvellous facilities for their conveyance between all parts of the country.' See Street, *Brick and Marble*, p. 284.
19. Michael Hall, 'G. F. Bodley and the Response to Ruskin in Ecclesiastical Architecture in the 1850s', in R. Daniels and G. Brandwood (eds), *Ruskin & Architecture* (Salisbury, 2003), pp. 260–261.
20. Beresford Hope, *The English Cathedral*, p. 249.
21. J. O. Taylor, 'Storm-Clouds on the Horizon: John Ruskin and the Emergence of Anthropogenic Climate Change', *19: Interdisciplinary Studies in the Long Nineteenth Century*, issue 26 (2018). doi: https://doi.org/10.16995/ntn.802.
22. R. A. Buchanan, 'The Diaspora of British Engineering', *Technology and Culture*, 27:3 (1986), 501–524.
23. Margot Gayle and Carol Gayle, *Cast-Iron Architecture in America: The Significance of James Bogardus* (New York, 1974).
24. Louis P. Nelson, 'Global Houses of the Efik', in J. Stobart (ed.), *Global Goods and the Country House Comparative Perspectives, 1650–1800* (London, 2023), pp. 285–305.
25. Naomi Yuval-Naeh, 'Cultivating the Carboniferous: Coal as a Botanical Curiosity in Victorian Culture', *Victorian Studies*, 61:3 (2019), 419–445 (esp. 423–426); 'The New Coal Exchange', *Illustrated London News* (3 November 1849), 302–303.
26. Daniel M. Abramson, *Obsolescence: An Architectural History* (Chicago, 2016), pp. 12–37.
27. Chris Otter, *The Victorian Eye: A Political History of Light and Vision in Britain, 1800–1910* (Chicago, 2008), pp. 16–19.

Chapter 3

1. P. Ayres, *Classical Culture and the Idea of Rome in Eighteenth-Century England* (Cambridge, 1997).
2. Frank M. Turner, *The Greek Heritage in Victorian Britain* (New Haven and London, 1981), p. 2.
3. Joseph Gwilt, *An Encyclopaedia of Architecture* (London, 1842), p. 224.
4. Cockerell quoted in David Watkin, *The Life and Work of C. R. Cockerell* (London, 1974), p. 105.
5. For instance, see Boyd Hilton, *The Age of Atonement: The Influence of Evangelicalism on Social and Economic Thought 1785–1865* (Oxford, 1986).
6. E.g., Simon Schaffer, 'Metrology, Metrication, and Victorian Values', in B. Lightman (ed.), *Victorian Science in Context* (Chicago, 1997), pp. 438–474.
7. William Whewell, *Architectural Notes on German Churches*, new edition (Cambridge, 1835), p. 111.
8. Ibid., pp. xi–xii. This notion of 'principle' is also very clear in the Preface to the original edition (1830).
9. Michael J. Lewis, *The Gothic Revival* (London, 2002), p. 85.
10. *The Symbolism of Churches and Church Ornaments: A Translation of the First Book of the Rationale Divinorum Officiorum* . . ., trans., with introductory essay, by J. M. Neale and B. Webb (London, 1843).
11. E. A. Freeman, *A History of Architecture* (London, 1849).

12. *Ecclesiologist*, 4 (Jan. 1847), 16.
13. *Ecclesiologist*, 4 (March 1847), 89–90.
14. A. J. B. Beresford Hope, *The English Cathedral of the Nineteenth Century* (London, 1861), pp. 30–33, 81–93.
15. Mark Crinson, *Empire Building: Orientalism & Victorian Architecture* (London, 1996), p. 5.
16. John Steegman, *Victorian Taste: A Study of the Arts and Architecture from 1830 to 1870* (London, 1970), p. x.
17. For the Victorian theory of architectural communication, see Edward N. Kaufman, 'Architectural Representation in Victorian England', *Journal of the Society of Architectural Historians*, 46:1 (1987), 30–38.
18. John Ruskin, 'The Lamp of Beauty', in *The Seven Lamps of Architecture* (London, 1849), p. 126.
19. John Ruskin, *The Ethics of Dust* in E. T. Cook and A. Wedderburn (eds), *The Complete Works of John Ruskin* (London, 1903–12), vol. 9, p. 331.
20. John Ruskin, *Modern Painters* in Cook and Wedderburn, *The Complete Works*, vol. 4, p. 163.
21. For Street and polychromy, see Neil Jackson, 'Clarity or Camouflage? The Development of Constructional Polychromy in the 1850s and Early 1860s', *Architectural History*, 47 (2004), 201–226.
22. Charles Saumarez Smith, 'The Institutionalisation of Art in Early Victorian England', *Transactions of the Royal Historical Society*, 20 (2010), 113–125.
23. *Journal of Design and Manufactures*, 1 (1849), 65.
24. Matthew Digby Wyatt, 'An Attempt to Define the Principles which Should Determine Form in the Decorative Arts', in *Lectures on the Results of the Great Exhibition of 1851*, 2nd series (London, 1852), p. 233.
25. Elena Chestnova, '"Ornamental Design Is . . . A Kind of Practical Science": Theories of Ornament at the London School of Design and Department of Science and Art', *Journal of Art Historiography*, 11 (Dec. 2014): https://arthistoriography.files.wordpress.com/2014/11/chestnova.pdf.
26. William Morris, 'The Prospects of Architecture in Civilisation', in W. Morris, *Hopes and Fears for Art: Five Lectures Delivered in Birmingham, London, and Nottingham 1878–1881* (London, 1882), pp. 169–170.
27. Ibid., p. 214.

Chapter 4

1. For this idea, see Francis Dodsworth, '*Virtus* on Whitehall: The Politics of Palladianism in William Kent's Treasury Building, 1733–6', *Journal of Historical Sociology*, 18:4 (2005), 282–317.
2. British Parliamentary Papers, 'Report from the Select Committee on Public Offices,' 14 (18 July 1856), p. 23.
3. G. G. Scott, *Remarks on Secular & Domestic Architecture, Present and Future* (London, 1857), pp. viii, 269–270.
4. G. E. Street, *An Urgent Plea for the Revival of True Principles of Architecture in the Public Buildings of the University of Oxford* (Oxford, 1853), p. 5.
5. Linda Mulcahy, 'Architectural Precedent: The Manchester Assize Courts and Monuments to Law in the Mid-Victorian Era', *King's Law Journal*, 19:3 (2008), pp. 525–549.
6. Clare Graham, *Ordering Law: The Architectural and Social History of the English Law Court to 1914* (Aldershot, 2003), p. 278.
7. Bright quoted in William E. A. Axon (ed.), *An Architectural and General Description of Manchester Town Hall* (Manchester, 1878), p. 53.
8. See 'Industrial Greatness: The Town Hall as a Gothic Machine', in Mark Crinson, *Shock City: Image and Architecture in Industrial Manchester* (London and New Haven, 2022), pp. 101–135.
9. Axon, *An Architectural and General Description*, p. 2.
10. F. E. Scott, *Shall the New Foreign Office Be Gothic or Classic? A Plea for the Former* (London, 1860).
11. Godwin quoted in Michael W. Brooks, *John Ruskin and Victorian Architecture* (London, 1987), pp. 201–203.
12. M. Casey et al. (eds), *Early Melbourne Architecture 1840–1888* (Melbourne, 1975), pp. 20–22.
13. H.-R. Hitchcock, *Architecture: Nineteenth and Twentieth Centuries*, 2nd edn (Baltimore, 1977), p. 195.
14. Preeti Chopra, *A Joint Enterprise: Indian Elites and the Making of British Bombay* (Minneapolis, 2011), pp. 73–115.
15. 'Architectural Art in India', *Journal of the Society of Arts*, 21:187 (1873), 286–287; William Emerson, 'A Description of Some Buildings Recently Erected in India, With Some Remarks on Domes and the Mingling of Styles of Architecture', *Transactions of the Royal Institute of British Architects* 34, 1st series (1883–84), pp. 149–157.
16. *The Builder* (5 June 1869), p. 449; (31 Dec. 1870), p. 1074.
17. Colin Cunningham, 'Iconography and Victorian Values', in C. Brooks (ed.), *The Albert Memorial. The Prince Consort National Memorial: Its History, Contexts, and Conservation* (New Haven and London, 2000), p. 210.

18. Edmund Gosse quoted in Benedict Read, 'The Sculpture', in Brooks, *The Albert Memorial*, p. 205.
19. John Brydon, 'The English Renaissance', *The Builder* (2 March 1889), pp. 169–170.
20. *Building News* (13 July 1900), p. 35.
21. For this idea, see Patrick Joyce, *The State of Freedom: A Social History of the British State since 1800* (Cambridge, 2013).

Chapter 5

1. Paul Thompson, *William Butterfield* (Cambridge, 1971), p. 27.
2. The architecture of these other religious traditions has been the focus of dedicated studies in recent years. See Sharman Kadish, *The Synagogues of Britain and Ireland: An Architectural and Social History* (London and New Haven, 2011); Talinn Grigor, *The Persian Revival: The Imperialism of the Copy in Iranian and Parsi Architecture* (University Park, 2021).
3. W. G. Lumley, 'The Statistics of the Roman Catholics in England and Wales', *Journal of the Statistical Society of London*, 27:3 (1864), 310.
4. David Lewis, *A. W. N. Pugin* (Liverpool, 2021), pp. 17, 26.
5. For instance, see Francis Close, *The Restoration of Churches is the Restoration of Popery* (London, 1844), and William Peace, *The Reformation and the Cross* (London, 1859).
6. M. S. Lawson (ed.), *Letters of J. M. Neale* (London, 1910), p. 17.
7. G. E. Street, 'On the Proper Characteristics of a Town Church', *The Ecclesiologist*, 11 (1850), 227–233.
8. Edward N. Kaufman, '"The Weight and Vigour of their Masses": Mid-Victorian Country Churches and "The Lamp of Power"', in J. D. Hunt and F. M. Holland (eds), *The Ruskin Polygon: Essays of the Imagination of John Ruskin* (Manchester, 1982), pp. 94–121.
9. Charles L. Eastlake, *A History of the Gothic Revival* (London, 1872), p. 317.
10. Michael Hall, 'What Do Victorian Churches Mean? Symbolism and Sacramentalism in Anglican Church Architecture, 1850–1870', *Journal of the Society of Architectural Historians*, 59:1 (2000), 78–95.
11. *The Symbolism of Churches and Church Ornaments: A Translation of the First Book of the Rationale Divinorum Officiorum*..., trans., with introductory essay, by J. M. Neale and B. Webb (London, 1843), p. xxvi.
12. Hall, 'What Do Victorian Churches Mean?', p. 83.
13. William Whyte, *Unlocking the Church: The Lost Secrets of Victorian Sacred Space* (Oxford, 2017), p. 68.
14. Thompson, *William Butterfield*, pp. 32–33.
15. Diana Orton, *Made of Gold: A Biography of Angela Burdett Coutts* (London, 1980), pp. 106–107.
16. Susan S. Lewis, 'The Artistic and Architectural Patronage of Angela Burdett Coutts' (PhD, University of London, 2012), p. 215.
17. John Shelton Reed, '"A Female Movement": The Feminization of Nineteenth-Century Anglo-Catholicism', *Anglican and Episcopal History*, 57:2 (1988), 199–238.
18. Rosemary Hill, *God's Architect: Pugin and the Building of Romantic Britain* (London, 2007), p. 230. See also Kate Jordan, 'Ordered Spaces, Separate Spheres: Women and the Building of British Convents, 1829–1939' (PhD, University of London, 2015), pp. 122–155.
19. Kathryn Ferry, *The Old Convent East Grinstead: John Mason Neale, George Edmund Street, and the Society of St Margaret* (East Grinstead, 2021), pp. 72–76.
20. Michael Hall, 'The Rise of Refinement: G. F. Bodley's All Saints, Cambridge, and the Return to English Models in Gothic Architecture of the 1860s', *Architectural History*, 36 (1993), 103–126.
21. Michael Hall, *George Frederick Bodley and the Later Gothic Revival in Britain and America* (New Haven and London, 2014), p. 108.
22. Annabel Wharton, 'Westminster Cathedral: Medieval Architectures and Religious Difference', *Journal of Medieval and Early Modern Studies*, 26:3 (1996), 530–532, 539. See also John Jenkins and Alana Harris, 'More English than the English, more Roman than Rome? Historical Signifiers and Cultural Memory at Westminster Cathedral', *Religion*, 49:1 (2019), 48–73.
23. Richard A. Sundt, *Whare Karakia: Māori Church Building, Decoration and Ritual in Aotearoa New Zealand, 1834–1863* (Auckland, 2010). See also Allan K. Davidson, 'Culture and Ecclesiology: The Church Missionary Society in New Zealand', in Kevin Ward and Brian Stanley (eds), *The Church Mission Society and World Christianity, 1799–1999* (Richmond, 2000), p. 199.
24. Jeffrey Cox, 'Were Victorian Nonconformists the Worst Imperialists of All?', *Victorian Studies*, 46:2 (2004), 243.
25. Christopher Wakeling, *Chapels of England: Buildings of Protestant Nonconformity* (Swindon, 2017), p. 104.
26. Henry-Russell Hitchcock, *Early Victorian Architecture in Britain*, 2 vols (New Haven and London, 1954), pp. I, 114.

27. F. J. Jobson, *Chapel & School Architecture, as Appropriate to the Buildings of Nonconformists*... (London, 1850), pp. vii, 4, 40.
28. James Cubitt, *Church Design for Congregations: Its Development and Possibilities* (London, 1870), pp. 40–43.
29. Stewart J. Brown, *Thomas Chalmers and the Godly Commonwealth in Scotland* (Oxford, 1983), pp. 337–349.
30. Miles Lewis, 'The Ecclesiology of Expediency in Colonial Australia', in G. A. Bremner (ed.), *Ecclesiology Abroad: The British Empire and Beyond*, themed issue of *Studies in Victorian Architecture and Design*, 4 (2012), 40–43.
31. Barry Magrill, *A Commerce of Taste: Church Architecture in Canada, 1867–1914* (Montreal and Kingston, 2012), pp. 103–105.

Chapter 6

1. Alexander Tzonis and Liane Lefaivre, 'The Mechanization of Architecture and the Birth of Functionalism', *Via*, 7 (1984), 121–144.
2. Mark Crinson, *Shock City: Image and Architecture in Industrial Manchester* (London and New Haven, 2022), pp. 101–135.
3. Edward J. Gillin, *The Victorian Palace of Science: Scientific Knowledge and the Building of the Houses of Parliament* (Cambridge, 2017).
4. *The Builder* (23 July 1859), p. 481.
5. Robin Evans, *The Fabrication of Virtue: English Prison Architecture, 1750–1840* (Cambridge, 1982), pp. 354–357.
6. Head quoted in Kathryn Morrison, *The Workhouse: A Study of Poor-Law Buildings in England* (Swindon, 1999), p. 56.
7. Felix Driver, *Power and Pauperism: The Workhouse System, 1834–1884* (Cambridge, 1993).
8. Forster quoted in Deborah E. B. Weiner, *Architecture and Social Reform in Late-Victorian London* (Manchester, 1994), p. 23.
9. Edward Robert Robson, *School Architecture* (London, 1874), p. 6.
10. Booth quoted in Weiner, *Architecture and Social Reform*, p. 54.
11. For instance, see William Whyte, *Redbrick: A Social and Architectural History of Britain's Civic Universities* (Oxford, 2015).
12. G. A. Bremner, *Imperial Gothic: Religious Architecture and High Anglican Culture in the British Empire, c.1840–1870* (London and New Haven, 2013), pp. 333–336.
13. A. King, 'Hospital Planning: Revised Thoughts on the Origin of the Pavilion Principle in England', *Medical History*, 10:4 (1966), 360–373.
14. Preface to Florence Nightingale, *Notes on Hospitals* (London, 1863), p. iii.
15. Jiat-Hwee Chang, *A Genealogy of Tropical Architecture: Colonial Networks, Nature and Technoscience* (London, 2016), pp. 94–128.
16. Annmarie Adams, *Medicine by Design: The Architect and the Modern Hospital, 1893–1943* (Minneapolis, 2008), p. 2.
17. Preeti Chopra, *A Joint Enterprise: Indian Elites and the Making of British Bombay* (Minneapolis, 2011), pp. 73–115.
18. Andrew Scull, *The Most Solitary of Afflictions: Madness and Society in Britain, 1700–1900* (New Haven and London, 1993).
19. For this argument, see Carla Yanni, *The Architecture of Madness: Insane Asylums in the United States* (Minneapolis, 2007).
20. Mark Jarzombek, 'Corridor Spaces', *Critical Enquiry*, 36:4 (2010), 728–770.
21. Sally Swartz, 'The Great Asylum Laundry: Space, Classification, and Imperialism in Cape Town', in L. Topp, J. E. Moran, and J. Andrews (eds), *Madness, Architecture and the Built Environment: Psychiatric Spaces in Historical Context* (London, 2007), pp. 131–148.
22. Waltraud Ernst, 'Madness and Colonial Spaces: British India, *c.*1800–1947', in Moran and Andrews (eds), *Madness, Architecture and the Built Environment*, pp. 215–238.

Chapter 7

1. Forbes quoted in Sophie Forgan, 'The Architecture of Display: Museums, Universities and Objects in Nineteenth-century Britain', *History of Science*, 32:2 (1994), 144–145.
2. Amy Woodson-Boulton, 'Victorian Museums and Victorian Society', *History Compass*, 6:1 (2008), 116.
3. Thomas Richards, *The Commodity Culture of Victorian England: Advertising and Spectacle, 1851–1914* (London, 1990), pp. 17–53.
4. Isobel Armstrong, *Victorian Glassworlds: Glass Culture and the Imagination 1830–1880* (Oxford, 2008), pp. 133–166, 167–202.
5. Christina Henderson Harner, 'Rebuilding the World at the Crystal Palace: Architectural Discourse at the 1851 Great Exhibition,' *Victorians: A Journal of Culture and Literature*, 136 (2019), 138–158.
6. Jonathan Sweet, 'The World of Art and Design: White Colonials', in J. M. MacKenzie (ed.), *Victorian Vision: Inventing New Britain* (London, 2001), p. 336.
7. John M. MacKenzie '"The Second City of Empire": Glasgow—Imperial Municipality', in F. Driver and D. Gilbert (eds), *Imperial Cities: Landscape, Display and Identity* (Manchester, 1999), pp. 226–228.

8. Rosemary Seton, 'Reconstructing the Museum of the London Missionary Society', *Material Religion*, 8:1 (2012), 98–102.
9. Forgan, 'The Architecture of Display', p. 148.
10. G. E. Street, *An Urgent Plea for the Revival of True Principles of Architecture in the Public Buildings of the University of Oxford* (Oxford, 1853).
11. Kelly Freeman, 'Iron and Bone: The Skeleton Architecture of the Oxford University Museum of Natural History', *Object*, 18:1 (2016), 9–44.
12. Owen quoted in Mark Girouard, *Alfred Waterhouse and the Natural History Museum* (London, 1981), p. 13.
13. John Holmes, *The Pre-Raphaelites and Science* (London and New Haven, 2018), pp. 219–221.
14. Sally Gregory Kohlstedt, 'Place and Museum Space: The Smithsonian Institution, National Identity, and the American West, 1846–1896', in D. N. Livingstone and C. W. J. Withers (eds), *Geographies of Nineteenth-Century Science* (Chicago, 2011), pp. 399–438.
15. Ian Lochhead, *A Dream of Spires: Benjamin Mountfort and the Gothic Revival* (Christchurch, 1999), pp. 262–272.
16. Charles Saumarez Smith, 'The Institutionalisation of Art in Early Victorian England', *Transactions of the Royal Historical Society*, 6th series, 20 (2010), pp. 113–125; Peter Mandler, 'Art in a Cool Climate: The Cultural Policy of the British State in a European Context, *c*.1780 to *c*.1850', in T. Blanning and H. Schulze (eds), *Unity and Diversity in European Culture c.1800* (London and Oxford, 2006), pp. 101–120.
17. Godwin quoted in Jonathan Conlin, *The Nation's Mantlepiece: A History of the National Gallery* (London, 2006), p. 68.
18. For instance, see Charlotte Klonk, 'Mounting Vision: Charles Eastlake and the National Gallery of London', *The Art Bulletin*, 82:2 (2000), 331–347.
19. Helen Smailes, *A Portrait Gallery for Scotland: The Foundation, Architecture and Mural Decoration of the Scottish National Portrait Gallery, 1882–1906* (Edinburgh, 1985), p. 26.
20. Anne Beggs-Sunter, *Not for Self But for All: A History of the Art Gallery of Ballarat Association* (Ballarat, 2018).

Chapter 8

1. 'Tyranny' was a term in fact used by Hermann Muthesius in describing the apparently immovable traditions of English domestic living. See Herman Muthesius, *The English House* (*Das englische Haus*, 1904), trans. J. Seligman and S. Spencer, 3 vols (London, 2007), pp. II, 6.
2. Andrea Kaston Tange, *Architectural Identities: Domesticity, Literature, and the Victorian Middle Classes* (Toronto, 2010), pp. 39–41.
3. Another such example was *Villa and Cottage Architecture: Select Examples of Country and Suburban Residences Recently Erected* (London, 1868).
4. Mark Girouard, *The Victorian Country House* (Oxford, 1971), pp. 5–6.
5. For a comprehensive study of Victorian working-class housing, see M. J. Daunton, *House and Home in the Victorian City: Working-Class Housing 1850–1914* (London, 1983).
6. Robert Kerr, *The Gentleman's House; or, How to Plan English Residences, from the Parsonage to the Palace, with Tables of Accommodation and Cost, and a Series of Selected Plans*, second (revised) edition (London, 1865), p. 344.
7. Kay Boardman, 'The Ideology of Domesticity: The Regulation of the Household Economy in Victorian Women's Magazines', *Victorian Periodicals Review*, 33:2 (2000), 162.
8. John Tosh, *A Man's Place: Masculinity and the Middle-Class Home in Victorian England* (New Haven and London, 1999), p. 13.
9. R. Dudley Baxter, *National Income: The United Kingdom* (London, 1868), p. 16.
10. Muthesius, *The English House*, pp. II, 36.
11. Juliet Kinchin, 'Interiors: Nineteenth-Century Essays on the "Masculine" and the "Feminine" Room', in P. Kirkham (ed.), *The Gendered Object* (Manchester, 1996), pp. 12–29.
12. Quoted in Deborah Cohen, *Household Gods: The British and Their Possessions* (New Haven and London, 2006), p. 25.
13. Charles L. Eastlake, *Hints on Household Taste in Furniture, Upholstery and other Details*, second revised edition (London: Longmans, 1869), pp. 142–143.
14. Karen Burns, 'Between the Walls: Remembering Colonial Frontier Space at Purrumbete, 1901–2', in *Interspaces: Art + Architectural Exchanges from East to West*, conference proceedings (Melbourne, 2010), pp. 1–15.
15. Colin Fanning. '"The Indispensable Agent": Coal and Its Displacement in Victorian Britain', *Journal of Design History*, 34:3 (2020), 221–222.
16. Anne Warr, 'Corrugated Iron: Forming New Perceptions in the Australian Landscape', in P. Dobraszczyk and P. Sealy (eds), *Function and Fantasy: Iron Architecture in the Long Nineteenth-Century* (Abingdon, 2016), pp. 181–198.

17. E. W. Cooney, 'The Origins of the Victorian Master Builders', *Economic History Review*, New Series, 8:2 (1955), 173.
18. Kit Wedd, *Victorian Housebuilding* (Oxford, 2012), p. 15; H. J. Dyos, 'The Speculative Builders and Developers of Victorian London', *Victorian Studies*, 11 (Supplement: Symposium on the Victorian City [2]) (1968), 660.
19. John Summerson, *The Building World of the 1860s* (London, 1973), p. 9.
20. Paul Hogben, 'The Tender Information Economy of the Colonial Building Press in Australia', *Fabrications*, 20:2 (2011), 108–127.

List of Illustrations

background can be seen the 'Gold Pyramid' sent from the colony of Victoria, Australia.
136. Melbourne International Exhibition building (1880), Melbourne, Australia, by Joseph Reed (State Library of Victoria).
137a. Façade to the Colonial and Indian Exhibition building, South Kensington, London, 1886.
137b. Gwalior Gateway at the Colonial and Indian Exhibition (RIBA Collections). Designed by Maj. J. B. Keith for the Calcutta International Exhibition of 1883–84, and executed by Indian craftsmen, it was dismantled and later transported to Britain.
138a. 'Eastern Palace' (Industrial Hall), Glasgow International Exhibition, 1901, by James Millar (Historic Environment Scotland).
138b. Brisbane Exhibition Building, Queensland (1889–91), Australia, by George Addison (State Library of Queensland).
139. Imperial Institute, South Kensington (1887–93), London, by Thomas Collcutt (Historic England).
140. Plan, Imperial Institute. It is noticeable here how the British empire is presented in a roughly accurate geographical layout. Notwithstanding the United Kingdom occupying the main entrance pavilion (being front and centre), we see an additional United Kingdom pavilion at the top (north) of the building, with Africa located to the 'south', British North America to the 'west', and India and Australasia to the 'east'. This way, visitors could take a global circuit around the empire, with the idea of Britain, as the 'metropolis', being the most important constituent element in the imperial firmament.
141a. Interior, extension (1858) to India Museum, London, by Matthew Digby Wyatt (*The London Journal*).
141b. Hunterian Museum, University of Glasgow (1867–91), by George Gilbert Scott (Chronicle / Alamy Stock Photo).
142. C. R. Cockerell (and assistants), competition drawing for new Cambridge University Museum (1836): ground and basement plans and sections (Cambridge University Library).
143. Classical edifice designed for the Derby Museum (now World Museum Liverpool), Liverpool (1857–60), by Thomas Allom (robertharding / Alamy Stock Photo).
144a. Hunterian Museum (1833–7), Royal College of Surgeons, London, by Charles Barry (Wellcome Collection).
144b. Specimen display area, Museum of Practical Geology, Jermyn Street (1846–51), London, by James Pennethorne (British Geological Survey).
145. Natural History Museum, University of Oxford (1855–60), Parks Road, Oxford, by T. N. Deane and Benjamin Woodward (RIBA Collections).
146a. Plan, Natural History Museum, Oxford.
146b. Gothic iron arches in the glazed atrium (court) of the Natural History Museum, Oxford (photo: A. F. Kersting).
147a. Arcade columns, upper gallery, Natural History Museum, Oxford (photo: G. A. Bremner). These represent different stones from around the British Isles.
147b. Carved capital and corbel from lower arcade, Natural History Museum, Oxford (RIBA Collections).
148. Museum, Trinity College Dublin (1853–7), Ireland, by T. N. Deane and Benjamin Woodward (photo: G. A. Bremner). View from Inner Hall looking through marble colonnade to Hall (entrance).
149a. Edinburgh Museum of Science and Art (1860–89), Chambers Street, Edinburgh, now National Museum of Scotland, by Francis Fowke (National Museums Scotland).
149b. Great Hall, Edinburgh Museum of Science and Art (National Museums Scotland).
150. Plan, Natural History Museum, London. Redesigned by Alfred Waterhouse following the death of Francis Fowke between 1868 and 1871 (The Natural History Museum / Alamy Stock Photo).
151. Cromwell Road façade, Natural History Museum, London (Graham Prentice / Alamy Stock Photo). The building was erected between 1873 and 1881.
152. Teeming with wildlife: Central Hall, Natural History Museum, London (eye35.pix / Alamy Stock Photo).
153a. University of Pennsylvania library and museum (1888–90), Philadelphia, United States of America, by Frank Furness (jimfeng / Getty Images).
153b. Australian Museum, Sydney (1846–66), Australia, by Mortimer Lewis and Alexander Dawson (State Library of New South Wales).
154a. National Museum of Victoria, Melbourne (1862), Australia, by Reed & Barnes (photo 1871) (State Library of Victoria).
154b. Prince of Wales Museum (1905–15), Bombay (Mumbai), India, by George Wittet (photo: G. A. Bremner).
155a. Victoria and Albert Museum, Cromwell Road front (1899–1909), South Kensington,

Bibliographic Essay

Victorian Architecture: A Changing Historiographic Scene

Scholarship on Victorian architecture up until around the turn of the last millennium was characterised by a broadly documentary and formalist approach. This is less the case for scholarship on the Victorian city, which necessarily engaged with sociology, economics, and geography, but certainly for the literature that focused primarily on buildings, architects, and their patrons. This highlights the fact that scholarship (and writing in general) on Victorian architecture was a relatively stable and contained genre up to the 1990s, and that it was directed and dominated primarily by a limited cadre of mostly male historians, conservationists, and heritage activists who had direct links to organisations such as the Victorian Society. In this it had a recognisable and consistent set of literary features, not least being its reference to Britain and the British Isles alone.

This began to change in the late 1990s. The primary reason for this was not just increasing globalisation but our heightened consciousness of it. This had the effect of enticing scholars studying architecture, especially younger researchers at the time, to consider the global dimensions of what constituted 'Victorian architecture'. The second reason concerned changes that were taking place in the wider humanities, with the impact of post-structuralist analytics, and with methodological movements addressing various 'turns' in historical scholarship more broadly (i.e., 'cultural', 'linguistic', 'spatial', 'material', 'imperial', etc.). The cultural turn, in particular, enabled (if not demanded) a new kind of interpretive framework for studying architecture, seeing it as a kind of 'artefact' and thereby form of cultural production. This reflected a broader shift from a more archaeologically orientated approach, concerned with documentary evidence and descriptive exposition, onto which could be grafted forms of connoisseurship, to an approach that was more anthropologically inflected. What came with this broader historiographic shift was a significant renewal of and transformation in the study of British imperialism, heralding the advent of 'New Imperial History'. A revitalised interest in Victorian architecture worldwide emerged which considered the built environment as part of Britain's wider imperial project. More latterly we have seen the impact of feminist and gender studies, including the history of emotions, which has begun revising our understanding of the various settings of Victorian architecture in new and interesting ways. This has also accompanied shifts in the gender balance of those who now study Victorian architecture seriously.

What this transformation in historical scholarship over the past 30 to 40 years demonstrates is not only the rise but the explicit encouragement of inter- or cross-disciplinarity. This is particularly conspicuous in the intersections between architecture and science in the Victorian age. It concerns not only the study of buildings relating directly to science, such as museums and laboratories, but also the way architecture can be understood as a science in its own right, and how it engaged with and was immersed in scientific discourses of the period. This has seen historians of architecture turn to Science and Technology Studies, as well as the history and philosophy of science, for the insights they offer on the culturally contingent and applicable nature of the Victorian scientific world-view, revealing the technologically framed and inspired conception of architecture in surprising ways.

Related to this is research into the object materiality of Victorian architecture and its relationship to energy consumption. This refers not simply to the range of materials employed by Victorian architects, but rather to the constitution of those materials: how they were procured, manufactured, and transported, and what this actually tells us about the ontology of Victorian architecture. We therefore need to take further account of the inherent nature of Victorian architecture in order to better understand what Victorian architecture actually is, and how it is unique in its own way (as a matter of substance) beyond any prima facie considerations of style or form-making. This is what the present study has attempted to do, and the following bibliography reflects many of these historiographic and methodological changes.

N.B. The following bibliography, for the most part, does not include specific, non-built-environment literature. Where appropriate, such literature has been cited in the notes to the text. The texts listed here consist primarily of general and focused works, either those on the built environment per se, or those that cover aspects of the built environment in some substantive way, including leading architects. The bibliography is broken down into broad sections that accord with the various themes running through each chapter. Where the specific buildings of individual architects are not mentioned, information on these can be found in the numerous architectural biographies listed. The aim is not to offer a comprehensive list of publications relating to the topic, but to provide a working bibliography for the student of Victorian architecture.

General Studies

The most comprehensive, general overview of Victorian architecture to date is **Roger Dixon and Stefan Muthesius**, *Victorian Architecture* (London, 1978). Although a more formalist account of Victorian architecture, it is a very useful source book, with a unique catalogue of architects and their major works listed at the back. Beyond this, there is **Henry-Russel Hitchcock**'s magisterial two-volume *Early Victorian Architecture in Britain* (New Haven, 1954), which covers part of the period in detail, and the less enthusiastic *Victorian Architecture* (London, 1966), by **Robert Furneaux Jordan**, with its rather strange and equivocal analysis of the period. Alongside these sits **H. S. Goodhart-Rendel**'s *English Architecture Since the Regency* (London, 1953), which, originating in the Slade lectures at Oxford, is amusing and insightful, if highly subjective. In addition we have a small number of introductory texts and essay collections under the general heading 'Victorian Architecture', including **Hugh Casson**'s *An Introduction to Victorian Architecture* (London, 1948), which is a brief essay on some of the major themes and principles observable in the genre, and **Peter Ferriday**'s *Victorian Architecture* (London, 1963), being a multi-authored series of essays, mostly covering the lives and careers of major architects of the period. Also, originating in a series of lectures given at Columbia University in 1968, is **John Summerson**'s *Victorian Architecture: Four Studies in Evaluation* (New York, 1969). Apart from a brief introduction, this text is largely a comparative study of paired buildings (churches and stations), concluded by an analysis of the Royal Courts of Justice by G. E. Street on the Strand in London. Later, he produced the more specific *The Architecture of Victorian London* (Charlottesville, 1972), again from a series of lectures, delivered at the University of Virginia. More recently there is **James Stevens Curl**'s *Victorian Architecture: Diversity and Invention* (Reading, 2007), which is a solid, informative, and superbly illustrated account, covering nearly all aspects of the architecture of the period, although only within the British Isles, and largely on architecture proper. It sits next to Dixon and Muthesius's account in terms of comprehensiveness. On the Edwardian side of things, we must also point to **Alistair Service**'s *Edwardian Architecture: A Handbook to Building Design in Britain, 1890–1914* (London, 1977), which is a good overview of the period, covering domestic, religious, and secular architecture. There are also other studies that deal significantly with Victorian-era architecture, such as **J. Mordaunt Crook**, *The Dilemma of Style: Architectural Ideas from the Picturesque to the Post-Modern* (London, 1987), and **Barry Bergdoll**, *European Architecture 1750–1890* (Oxford, 2000). In this category it is also worth highlighting **John Steegman**'s *Victorian Taste: A Study of the Arts and Architecture from 1830 to 1870* (London, 1970 [originally published in 1950 as *Consort of Taste 1830–1870*]), which contains numerous insights on architectural thought and practice in the first half of the Victorian period.

All these studies are modern interpretations looking back at the period, separated by at least 50 years or more, and, for the most part, conducted in the methods of modern art-historical scholarship. But there was also a body of writing on 'Victorian architecture' that rose up during the period itself. There was of course much written on the built environment at the time, in pamphlets and journals, but there were a few texts that presented themselves as 'histories' that dealt specifically with the recent past. By far the most important of these is **Charles Locke Eastlake**'s *The History of the Gothic Revival* (London, 1872), which remains an excellent source for those studying Victorian architecture, brimming as it is with anecdotes and insights that capture the mentality of architectural design and practice during the period. Alongside this there were a number of books that sought to promote a particular agenda, more or less, couched in quasi-historical terms. These include **A. J. B. Beresford Hope**'s *The English Cathedral of the Nineteenth Century* (1861), where the term 'Victorian' architecture is adopted, and **T. G. Jackson**'s *Modern Gothic Architecture* (1873). In addition to these books there was a spate of publications that presented themselves as actual histories of architecture, including **Edward A. Freeman**'s *A History of Architecture* (1849) or **James Fergusson**'s *History of the Modern Styles of Architecture* (1862), along with **Robert Kerr**'s additions to the latter, which nearly always took their accounts up to the present. Architects' memoirs can also be included here for their commentary on the profession over a given period, the most notable example being **George Gilbert Scott**'s *Personal and Professional Recollections* (1879), as well as biographies, including **Alfred Barry**'s *The Life and Works of Sir Charles Barry* (London, 1867). Later in the century, even those books concerned with discrete periods or particular architects, such as **W. J. Loftie**'s *Inigo Jones and Wren* (1893), could not resist having a swipe at the architectures of the recent past; while the first iteration of **Banister Fletcher**'s *A History of Architecture Upon the Comparative Method* (1896) included ten pages on late-nineteenth-century architecture in Britain. These contemporary histories of architecture, as it were, helped establish not only the historical lineaments of Victorian architecture as we understand it today, but also the discipline of architectural history itself.

Although I could break this list down further into sub-topics, such as the Gothic Revival, the Arts and Crafts, Classicism, Queen Anne, or even the Edwardian Baroque, I shall cover the scholarship on these, where appropriate, in the chapter-by-chapter listings below.

Individual Architects

Since about 1970 there has been a near-continuous stream of masterful and comprehensive monographs on Victorian architects and architectural practices. The most prominent of these include, in chronological order of publication: **Paul Thompson**, *William Butterfield* (London, 1971); **David Watkin**, *The Life and Work of C.R. Cockerell* (London, 1974); **Andrew Saint**, *Richard Norman Shaw* (New Haven and London, 1976); **Anthony Quiney**, *John Loughborough Pearson* (New Haven and London, 1979); **Ronald McFadzean**, *The Life and Work of Alexander Thomson* (London, 1979); **David Cole**, *The Work of Sir Gilbert Scott* (London, 1980); **J. Mordaunt Crook**, *William Burges and the High Victorian Dream* (London, 1981); **Anthony J. Pass**, *Thomas Worthington: Victorian Architecture and Social Purpose* (Manchester, 1988); **Roger Dixon** (ed.), *Sir Gilbert Scott and the Scott Dynasty* (London, 1980); **Eve Blau**, *Ruskinian Gothic: The Architecture of Deane and Woodward 1845–1861* (Princeton, 1982); **Michael Darby**, *John Pollard Seddon* (London, 1983); **Jill Allibone**, *Anthony Salvin: Pioneer of Gothic Revival Architecture* (London, 1988); **Colin Cunningham** and **Prudence Waterhouse**, *Alfred Waterhouse, 1830–1905: Biography of a Practice* (Oxford, 1992); **Geoffrey Tyack**, *Sir James Pennethorne and the Making of Victorian London* (Cambridge, 1992); **Stuart Durant**, *C. F. A. Voysey* (London, 1992); **Wendy Hitchmough**, *C. F. A. Voysey* (London, 1995); **Frederick O'Dwyer**, *The Architecture of Deane and Woodward* (Cork, 1997); **Gavin Stamp**, *Alexander 'Greek' Thomson* (London, 1999); **Susan Webber Soros** (ed.), *E. W. Godwin: Aesthetic Movement Architect and Designer* (London, 1999); **Gavin Stamp** and **Sam McKinstry** (eds), *'Greek' Thomson* (Edinburgh, 1999); **Sheila Kirk**, *Philip Webb: Pioneer of Arts & Crafts Architecture* (London, 2002); **Carol A. Hrvol Flores**, *Owen Jones: Design, Ornament, Architecture, and Theory in an Age of Transition* (New York, 2006); **Gill Hunter**, *William White: Pioneering Victorian Architect* (Reading, 2010); **Michael Hall**, *George Frederick Bodley and the Later Gothic Revival in Britain and America* (New Haven and London, 2014); **Paul Barnwell**, **Geoffrey Tyack**, and **William Whyte** (eds), *Sir George Gilbert Scott 1811–1878* (Oxford, 2014); **Gavin Stamp**, *Gothic for the Steam Age: An Illustrated Biography of George Gilbert* Scott (London, 2015); **Peter Howell** and **Andrew Saint** (eds), *Butterfield Revisited* (London, 2017); **Geoff Brandwood**, *The Architecture of Temple Moore* (Donington, 2019), and (with P. Howell and P. C. W. Taylor) *George Edmund Street* (Swindon, 2024); **Timothy Brittain-Catlin**, *Edwin Rickards* (Swindon, 2023); and **Robert Thorne**, *Matthew Digby Wyatt* (Swindon, 2025).

There are a number of books on A. W. N. Pugin, including **Phoebe Stanton**, *Pugin* (London, 1971); **Alexandra Wedgwood**, *A.W.N. Pugin and the Pugin Family* (London, 1985); **Paul Atterbury** and **Clive Wainwright** (eds), *Pugin, A Gothic passion* (New Haven and London, 1994); **Paul Atterbury** (ed.), *A. W. N. Pugin: Master of Gothic Revival* (New Haven and London, 1995); **Rosemary Hill**, *God's Architect: Pugin and the Building of Romantic Britain* (London, 2007); **David Frazer Lewis**, *A. W. N. Pugin* (Swindon, 2021).

There is also an assortment of studies that discuss or cover only part of a noted architect's career. These include: **Jane Fawcett** (ed.), *Seven Victorian Architects* (London, 1976); **David Brownlee**, *The Law Courts: The Architecture of George Edmund Street* (Cambridge, MA, 1984); **Fiona Sinclair**, *Alexander Greek Thomson: The Glasgow Buildings* (Glasgow, 1990); **John Elliott** and **John Pritchard** (eds), *George Edmund Street: A Victorian Architect in Berkshire* (Reading, 1998); and **William Whyte**, *Oxford Jackson: Architecture, Education, Status, and Style 1835–1924* (Oxford, 2006).

To these may be added studies of noted British colonial architects or those that cover the work of British architects in the Colonies: **Doreen E. Greig**, *Herbert Baker in South Africa* (Cape Town, 1970); **J. M. Freeland**, *Architect Extraordinary: The Life and Work of John Horbury Hunt, 1838–1904* (Melbourne, 1970); **Ursula De Jong**, *William Wilkinson Wardell, 1823–1899: His Life and Work* (Melbourne, 1983); **Margaret Archibald**, *By Federal Design: The Chief Architect's Branch of the Department of Public Works, 1881–1914* (Ottawa, 1983); **Joan Kerr**, *Our Great Victorian Architect: Edmund Thomas Blacket (1817–1883)* (Sydney, 1983); **Ian Lochhead**, *A Dream of Spires: Benjamin Mountfort and the Gothic Revival* (Christchurch, 1999); **Brian Andrews**, *Creating a Gothic Paradise: Pugin at the Antipodes* (Hobart, 2002); **Philip Goad** (ed.), *Bates Smart: 150 Years of Australian Architecture* (Fishermans Bend, 2004); **Margaret Alington**, *An Excellent Recruit: Frederick Thatcher—Architect, Priest and Private Secretary in Early New Zealand* (Auckland, 2007); **Norman Ledgerwood**, *R. A. Lawson: Victorian Architect of Dunedin* (Dunedin, 2013); and **Dorothy Mindenhall**, *Thomas Fuller: Architect for a Nation* (Victoria, 2015). The movement of architects around the British empire is also germane to understanding Victorian architecture in the wider British world, discussed, for instance, in **Julie Willis**, 'Architectural Movements: Journeys of an Inter-Colonial Profession', *Fabrications*, 26:2 (2016), 158–179.

Chapter 1. Steam and Speed: Industry, Infrastructure, and the City

Railways, Infrastructure, and Industrial Processes

Simon Bradley, *St. Pancras Station* (London, 2007); **G. A. Bremner**, 'Tides that Bind: Waterborne Trade and the Infrastructure Networks of Jardine, Matheson & Co.', *Perspecta*, 52 (2019), 31–47; **Steven Brindle**, *Paddington Station: Its History and Architecture* (London, 2006); **Paul Dobraszczyk**, *Iron, Ornament and Architecture in Victorian Britain* (Farnham, 2014); **Francis T. Evans**, 'Roads, Railways, and Canals: Technical Choices in 19th-Century Britain', *Technology and Culture*, 22:1 (1981), 1–34; **Peter Freeman**, *The Woolshed: A Riverina Anthology* (Melbourne, 1980); **Susan Galavan**, 'Transoceanic Networks of Exchange: New Brunswick Lumber, Merchant Trade, and the Building of Victorian Britain', *Acadiensis*, 48:2 (2019), 90–116; **Carroll L. Meeks**, *The Railway Station: An Architectural History* (New Haven and London, 1957); **John Minnis** with **Simon Hickman**, *The Railway Goods Shed and Warehouse in England* (Swindon, 2016); **Lynne Pearson**, *Victorian and Edwardian British Industrial Architecture* (Marlborough, 2016); **Tom F. Peters**, *Building the Nineteenth Century* (Cambridge, MA, 1996); **A. Pugsley**, *The Works of Isambard Kingdom Brunel: An Engineering Appreciation* (New York, 1976); **Andrew Saint**, *Architect and Engineer: A Study in Sibling Rivalry* (New Haven and London, 2007); **Jack Simmons**, *The Victorian Railway* (London, 1995); **Gavin Stamp**, 'Rail, Steam and Speed', in R. Hill and M. Hall (eds), *Studies in Victorian Architecture and Design: The 1840s*, vol. 1 (2008), pp. 43–59; **Patricia Vervoort**, '"Towers of Silence": The Rise and Fall of the Grain Elevator as a Canadian Symbol', *Histoire Sociale/Social History*, 39:77 (2006), 181–204.

The City and Urbanism in Britain

C. M. Allan, 'The Genesis of British Urban Redevelopment with Special Reference to Glasgow', *Economic History Review*, new series, 18:3 (1965), 598–613; **William Ashworth**, *The Genesis of Modern British Town Planning* (London, 1954); **Asa Briggs**, *Victorian Cities* (Harmondsworth, 1968); **David Cannadine**, 'Victorian Cities: How Different?', *Social History*, 2:4 (1977), 457–482; **Gordon E. Cherry**, 'The Town Planning Movement and the Late Victorian City', *Transactions of the Institute of British Geographers*, 4:2 (1979), 306–319; **Mark Crinson**, *Shock City: Image and Architecture in Industrial Manchester* (London and New Haven, 2022); **Felix Driver**, *Geography Militant: Cultures of Exploration and Empire* (Oxford, 2001); **H. J. Dyos**, 'Railways and Housing in Victorian London', *Journal of Transport History*, 2:1 (1955), 11–21; **H. J. Dyos** and **Michael Wolf** (eds), *The Victorian City: Images and Realities*, 2 vols (London, 1973–8); **T. W. Freeman**, *The Conurbations of Great Britain* (Manchester, 1959); **Mark Girouard**, *Cities & People: A Social and Architectural History* (New Haven and London, 1985);

Simon Gunn, 'Urbanization', in C. Williams (ed.), *A Companion to Nineteenth-Century Britain* (Oxford, 2004), pp. 238–252; **Peter Hall**, *Cities of Tomorrow: An Intellectual History of Urban Planning and Design in the Twentieth Century*, third ed. (Oxford, 2002); **Tristram Hunt**, *Building Jerusalem: The Rise and Fall of the Victorian City* (London, 2004); **Peter T. A. Jones**, 'Redressing Reform Narratives: Victorian London's Street Markets and the Informal Supply Lines of Urban Modernity', *London Journal*, 41:1 (2016), 60–81; **John R. Kellett**, *The Impact of Railways on Victorian Cities* (London, 1969); **Eric de Maré**, *Victorian London Revealed: Gustave Doré's Metropolis* (London, 1973); **R. J. Morris** and **Richard Rodger**, *The Victorian City: A Reader in British Urban History 1820–1914* (London, 1993); **Lynda Nead**, *Victorian Babylon: People, Streets and Images in Nineteenth-Century London* (New Haven & London, 2000); **D. J. Olsen**, 'Victorian London: Specialization, Segregation and Privacy', *Victorian Studies*, 17:3 (1974), 265–278; **Andrew Saint**, *London: 1870–1914—A City at Its Zenith* (London, 2021); **C. J. Stewart**, *The Housing Question in London* (London, 1900); **John Summerson**, 'The Victorian Rebuilding of the City of London', *London Journal*, 3:2 (1977), 163–185; **Nathaniel Robert Walker**, *Victorian Visions of Suburban Utopia: Abandoning Babylon* (Oxford, 2020).

The Colonial City

Nezar AlSayyad (ed.), *Forms of Dominance: On the Architecture and Urbanism of the Colonial Enterprise* (Aldershot, 1992); **G. A. Bremner** and **D. P. Y. Lung**, 'Spaces of Exclusion: The Significance of Cultural Identity in the Formation of European Residential Districts in British Hong Kong, 1877–1904', *Environment and Planning D: Society and Space*, 21:2 (2003), 223–252; **Preeti Chopra**, *A Joint Enterprise: Indian Elites and the Making of British Bombay* (Minneapolis, 2011); **Laura Harper**, 'Gold Rush Urbanism: Continuing Effects of Gold Mining on the Urban Form of Victorian Towns', in A. Brennan and P. Goad (eds), *Proceedings of the Society of Architectural Historians, Australia and New Zealand: 33, Gold* (Melbourne, 2016), pp. 236–248; **Robert Home**, *Of Planting and Planning: The Making of British Colonial Cities*, 2nd edition (London, 2013); **Anthony D. King**, *Urbanism, Colonialism, and the World-Economy* (London, 1990); **Anthony D. King**, *Colonial Urban Development: Culture, Social Power and Environment* (London, 1976); **Miles Lewis**, *Melbourne: The City's History and Development* (Melbourne, 1995); **Brenda Yeoh**, *Contesting Space: Power Relations and Urban Built Environment in Colonial Singapore* (Oxford, 1996).

Chapter 2. Material Abundance: Energy and the New Building Ecology

Primary Sources

'The Manufacture of Bricks by Machinery', ***The Builder*** (16 Aug. 1856), pp. 442–444; 'Foreign Marbles', ***The Building News*** (13 July 1866), p. 457; 'The First Half of the Nineteenth Century', ***Fraser's Magazine*** (Jan. 1851), pp. 1–15; **Zerah Colburn**, 'The Manufacture of Encaustic Tiles and Ceramic Ornamentation by Machinery', *Journal of the Society of Arts* (19 May 1865), pp. 445–450; **George Edmund Street**, 'On Colour as Applied to Architecture', in *Reports and Papers Read at the Meetings of the Architectural Societies* (London, 1855); **Matthew Digby Wyatt**, *On the Influence Exercised on Ceramic Manufactures by the Late Mr. Herbert Minton* (London, 1858).

Building and Materials, Systems and Processes

Julian Barnard, *Victorian Ceramic Tiles* (London, 1972); **R. W. Brunskill**, *Brick and Clay Building in Britain* (New Haven and London, 1990); **Lily Crowther**, 'Innovation and Revivalism: Powell & Sons' Opus Sectile Mosaic', *Journal of Design History*, 36:2 (2023), 109–124; **T. Donnelly**, 'Structural and Technical Change in the Aberdeen Granite Quarrying Industry 1830–1880', *Industrial Archaeology Review*, 3.3 (1979), 228–238; **Pamela R. Healey** and **E. M. Rawstron**, 'The Brickworks of the Oxford Clay Vale', *The East Midland Geographer*, 4 (1955), 42–48; **Henti Louw**, 'The Mechanisation of Architectural Woodwork in Britain from the Late-Eighteenth to the Early-Twentieth Century, and its Practical, Social and Aesthetic implications' (Parts I & II), *Construction History*, 8 (1992), 21–54, and vol. 9 (1993), 27–50; **Robin Lucas**, 'The Tax on Bricks and Tiles, 1784–1850: Its Application to the Country at Large and, in Particular, to the County of Norfolk', *Construction History*, 13 (1997), 29–55; **Lynn Pearson**, 'In the Latest London Style: Decorative Tile and Terracotta Exports by British Manufacturers, 1840–1940', in Malcolm Dunkfield et al. (eds), *Proceedings of the Second International Congress on Construction History*, vol. 3 (Exeter, 2006), pp. 2433–2450; **Christopher Powell**, *The British Building Industry Since 1800* (London, 1996); **Michael Stratton**, 'The Terracotta Industry: Its Distribution, Manufacturing Processes and Products',

Industrial Archaeology Review, 8:2 (1986), 194–214; **Michael Stratton**, 'Science and Art Closely Combined: The Organisation of Training in the Terracotta Industry, 1850–1939', *Construction History*, 4 (1988), 35–51; **Michael Stratton**, *The Terracotta Revival: Building Innovation and the Image of the Industrial City in Britain and North America* (London, 1993); **Kathleen Ann Watt**, 'Nineteenth Century Brickmaking Innovations in Britain: Building and Technological Change' (PhD, University of York, 1990).

Architecture, Infrastructure, and Energy Systems

Aleksandr Bierig, 'Building on Ghost Acres: The London Coal Exchange, circa 1849', in K. Förster (ed.), *Environmental Histories of Architecture* (Montreal, 2022), pp. 1–27; **Barnabas Calder**, *Architecture: From Prehistory to Climate Emergency* (London, 2021); **Barnabas Calder** and **G. A. Bremner**, 'Buildings and Energy: Architectural History in the Climate Emergency', *Journal of Architecture*, 26:2 (2021), 79–115; Esther **da Costa Meyer**, 'Architectural History in the Anthropocene: Towards Methodology', *The Journal of Architecture*, 21:8 (2016), 1203–1225; **Colin Fanning**, '"The Indispensable Agent": Coal and Its Displacements in Victorian Britain', *Journal of Design History*, 34:3 (2021), 212–226; **Bruce G. Trigger**, 'Monumental Architecture: A Thermodynamic Explanation of Symbolic Behaviour', *World Archaeology*, 22:2 (1990), 119–132.

Technology and Production in Relation to Architecture

G. A. Bremner, '"In Bright Tints…Nature's Own Formation": The Uses and Meaning of Marble in Victorian Building Culture', in J. Nicholas Napoli and William Tronzo (eds) *Radical Marble: Architectural Innovation from Antiquity to the Present* (New York, 2018), pp. 78–84; **R. A. Buchanan**, 'The Diaspora of British Engineering', *Technology and Culture*, 27:3 (1986), 501–524; **Paul Dobraszczyk** and **Peter Sealy** (eds), *Function and Fantasy: Iron Architecture in the Long Nineteenth-Century* (Abingdon, 2016); **Ronald Firman** and others, 'Brick, Stone and Iron: Building Materials at St Pancras', *British Brick Society Information*, 96 (April 2005), 5–20; **Susan Galavan**, *Dublin's Bourgeois Homes: Building the Victorian Suburbs, 1850–1901* (London, 2017); **Thea Goldring**, 'Recovered or Perfected: The Discourse of Chemistry in the Nineteenth-Century Revival of Stained Glass in Britain and France', *19: Interdisciplinary Studies in the Long Nineteenth Century* 2020 (30). doi: https://doi.org/10.16995/ntn.2893; **Dean Hawkes**, *Architecture and Climate: An Environmental History of British Architecture 1600–2000* (London, 2012); **Henry-Russell Hitchcock**, 'London Coal Exchange', *Architectural Review* (1 May 1947), pp. 185–187; **Mari Hvattum** and **Anne Hultzsch** (eds), *The Printed and the Built: Architecture, Print Culture, and Public Debate in the Nineteenth Century* (London, 2018); **Lucia Juarez**, 'Documenting Scottish Architectural Cast Iron in Argentina', *ABE Journal*, 5 (2014): doi.org/10.4000/abe.821; **Michael Kerney**, 'Polished Granite in Victorian Architecture', *Victorian Society Annual* (1987–8), 20–32; **Stuart King**, 'The Architecture of Van Diemen's Land Timber', *Fabrications*, 29:3 (2019), 338–358; **Stefan Muthesius**, '"The Iron Problem" in the 1850s', *Architectural History*, 13 (1970), 58–63; **Louis P. Nelson**, 'Global Houses of the Efik', in J. Stobart (ed.), *Global Goods and the Country House Comparative Perspectives, 1650–1800* (London, 2023), pp. 285–305; **Henrik Schoenefeldt**, *Rebuilding the Houses of Parliament: David Boswell Reid and Disruptive Environmentalism* (Abingdon, 2021); **Robert Thorne**, 'Inventing a New Design Technology: Building and Engineering', in J. M. MacKenzie (ed.), *The Victorian Vision: Inventing New Britain* (London, 2001), pp. 173–185.

Chapter 3. The Quest for Modernity: Theory and Style

Primary Sources

'Mr. Hope's Essay on the Present State of Ecclesiological Science in England', *The Ecclesiologist*, 7 (1847), 85–91; **A. J. B. Beresford Hope**, *The Condition and Prospect of Architectural Art* (London, 1863); **Christopher Dresser**, *The Art of Decorative Design* (London, 1862); **James Fergusson**, *An Historical Inquiry into the True Principles of Beauty in Art, More Especially with Reference to Architecture* (London, 1849); **E. A. Freeman**, *A History of Architecture* (London, 1849); **E. A. Freeman**, 'Development of Roman and Gothick Architecture, and their Moral and Symbolical Teaching', *Rules and Proceedings of the Oxford Architectural Society* (November 1845), pp. 23–51; **Owen Jones**, *The Grammar of Ornament* (London, 1856); **William Morris**, 'The Prospects of Architecture in Civilisation', in W. Morris, *Hopes and Fears for Art: Five Lectures Delivered in Birmingham, London, and Nottingham 1878–1881* (London, 1882), pp. 169–217; **William Morris**, *Gothic Architecture: A Lecture for the Arts and Crafts Exhibition Society* (Hammersmith, 1893); **A. W. N. Pugin**, *Contrasts: or, A Parallel Between the Noble Edifices of the Middle Ages, and Corresponding Buildings of the Present Day;*

Shewing the Present Decay of Taste (London,1836); **A. W. N. Pugin**, *The True Principles of Pointed or Christian Architecture* (London, 1841); **Thomas Rickman**, *An Attempt to Discriminate the Styles of English Architecture* (London, 1817); **John Ruskin**, *The Seven Lamps of Architecture* (London, 1849); **John Ruskin**, *The Stones of Venice*, 3 vols (London, 1851–3); **John Ruskin**, *On the Nature of Gothic Architecture: And Herein of the True Functions of the Workman on Art* (London, 1854); **G. E. Street**, *Brick and Marble in the Middle Ages: Notes on Tours in the North of Italy* (London, 1855); **G. E. Street**, 'The True Principles of Architecture, and the Possibility of Development', *The Ecclesiologist*, 10 (Aug. 1852), pp. 247–262; **Alexander Thomson**, 'The Unsuitableness of Gothic Architecture to Modern Requirements', *North British Daily Mail* (20 April 1864); **William Whewell**, *Architectural Notes on German Churches* (Cambridge, 1835); **Matthew Digby Wyatt**, *The Industrial Arts of the Nineteenth Century* (London, 1851). See also Alexander Thomson's writings in **Gavin Stamp** (ed.), *The Light of Truth and Beauty: The Lectures of Alexander 'Greek' Thomson, Architect 1817–1875* (Glasgow, 1999).

General Secondary Sources

Anna Antonowicz, 'Pioneers of Modern Design: From the Cole Circle to Walter Gropius', in A.-F. Gillard-Estrada and A. Besnault-Levita (eds), *Beyond the Victorian/Modernist Divide: Remapping the Turn-of-the-Century Break in Literature, Culture and the Visual Arts* (New York, 2018), pp. 142–160; **G. A. Bremner**, 'An Aryan Descent: Race, Religion, and Universal Civilization in E. A. Freeman's *A History of Architecture* (1849)', in P. Brouwer, M. Bressani, and C. Drew Armstrong (eds), *Narrating the Globe: The Emergence of World Histories of Architecture* (Cambridge MA, 2023), pp. 277–293; 'Part Three' (pp. 145–179), in **Chris Brooks**, *Signs for the Times: Symbolic Realism in the Mid-Victorian World* (London, 1984); **David B. Brownlee**, 'The First High Victorians: British Architectural Theory in the 1840s', *Architectura*, 15 (1985), pp. 33–46; **Mark Crinson**, *Empire Building: Orientalism & Victorian Architecture* (London, 1996); **Colin Cunningham**, 'James Fergusson's History of Indian Architecture', in C. King (ed.), *Views of Difference: Different Views of Art* (New Haven and London, 1999), pp. 43–66; **Michael Hall**, '"Our Own": Thomas Hope, A. J. B. Beresford Hope and the Creation of the High Victorian Style', in R. Hill and M. Hall (eds), *The 1840s, Studies in Victorian Architecture and Design*, vol. 1 (London, 2008), pp. 61–75; **G. L. Hersey**, *High Victorian Gothic: A Study in Associationism* (Baltimore, 1972); **Olivia Horsfall Turner**, *Owen Jones and the V&A: Ornament for a Modern Age* (London, 2023); **Deborah Howard**, 'Ruskin and the East', *Architectural Heritage*, 10:1 (1999), 37–53; **Neil Jackson**, 'Clarity or Camouflage? The Development of Constructional Polychromy in the 1850s and Early 1860s', *Architectural History*, 47 (2004), 201–226; **Edward N. Kaufman**, 'Architectural Representation in Victorian England', *Journal of the Society of Architectural Historians*, 46:1 (1987), 30–38; **Robert Macleod**, *Style and Society: Architectural Ideology in Britain 1835–1914* (London, 1971); **J. Mordaunt Crook**, *The Architect's Secret: Victorian Critics and the Image of Gravity* (London, 2003); **Stefan Muthesius**, *The High Victorian Movement in Architecture 1850–1870* (London, 1972); **Nikolaus Pevsner**, *Some Architectural Writers of the Nineteenth Century* (Oxford, 1972); **Charlotte Ribeyrol**, *William Burges's Great Bookcase & The Victorian Colour Revolution* (New Haven and London, 2023).

Classicism

Peter Kohane, 'Charles Robert Cockerell's Formation of Architectural Principles', in P. Hogben and J. O'Callaghan (eds), *Proceedings of the Society of Architectural Historians, Australia and New Zealand*, 32 (2015), 310–318; **John Lowrey**, 'From Caesarea to Athens: Greek Revival Edinburgh and the Question of Scottish Identity within the Unionist State', *Journal of the Society of Architectural Historians*, 60:2 (2001), 136–157; **J. Mordaunt Crook**, *The Greek Revival: Neo-Classical Attitudes in British Architecture 1760–1870* (London, 1972); **J. Mordaunt Crook**, 'From Neo-Classicism to Imperial Baroque', in J. Mordaunt Crook, *The Dilemma of Style: Architectural Ideas from the Picturesque to the Post-Modern* (London, 1987), pp. 193–224; **Frank Salmon**, 'British Architects, Italian Fine Arts Academies and the Foundation of the RIBA, 1816–43', *Architectural History*, 39 (1996), 77–113; **Frank Salmon**, *Building on Ruins: The Rediscovery of Rome and English Architecture* (Aldershot, 2000), pp. 73–99; **Frank Salmon**, 'The Ideal and the Real in British Hellenomania, 1751–1851', in K. Harloe, N. Momigliano, and A. Farnoux (eds), *Hellenomania* (London, 2018), pp. 73–99; **David Watkin**, 'Stuart and Revett: The Myth of Greece and its Afterlife', in S. Weber Soros (ed.), *James 'Athenian' Stuart 1713–1788: The Rediscovery of Antiquity* (New Haven and London, 2007), pp. 19–57; **Katherine Wheeler**, *Victorian Perceptions of Renaissance Architecture* (Abingdon, 2016).

Medievalism, the Gothic Revival, and John Ruskin

Megan Aldrich, *Gothic Revival* (London, 1994); **Cornelis J. Baljon**, 'Interpreting Ruskin: The Argument in the Seven Lamps of Architecture and the Stones of Venice', *Journal of Aesthetics and Art Criticism*, 55:4 (1997), 401–414; **Simon Bradley**, 'The Englishness of Gothic: Theories and Interpretations from William Gilpin to J. H. Parker', *Architectural History*, 45 (2002), pp. 325–346; **Michael W. Brook**, *John Ruskin and Victorian Architecture* (London, 1987); **Chris Brooks**, *The Gothic Revival* (London, 1999); **Anuradha Chatterjee**, 'Tectonic into Textile: John Ruskin and His Obsession with the Architectural Surface', *Textile*, 7:1 (2009), 68–97; **Kenneth Clark**, *The Gothic Revival: An Essay in the History of Taste* (London, 1928); **J. M. Frew**, 'Gothic Is English: John Carter and the Revival of the Gothic as England's National Style', *Art Bulletin*, 64 (1982), 315–319; **Kristine Ottesen Garrigan**, *Ruskin on Architecture: His Thought and Influence* (Madison, WI, 1973); **Michael Hall**, 'Modern Gothic', in M. Hall, *George Frederick Bodley and the Later Gothic Revival in Britain and America* (London and New Haven, 2015), pp. 51–65; **H.-R. Hitchcock**, 'High Victorian Gothic', *Victorian Studies*, 1:1 (1957), 47–71; **Stephen Kite**, *Building Ruskin's Italy: Watching Architecture* (Farnham, 2012); **Michael J. Lewis**, *The Gothic Revival* (London, 2002); **Chris Miele**, 'Freeman and the Culture of Gothic Revival', in G. A. Bremner and J. Conlin (eds), *Making History: Edward Augustus Freeman and Victorian Cultural Politics* (London and Oxford, 2015), pp. 139–156; **J. Mordaunt Crook**, 'Modern Gothic', in J. Mordaunt Crook, *The Dilemma of Style: Architectural Ideas from the Picturesque to the Post-Modern* (London, 1987), pp. 133–160; **Nicholas Penny**, 'Ruskin's Ideas on Growth in Architecture and Ornament', *British Journal of Aesthetics*, 13:3 (1973), 276–286; **Geoffrey Tyack**, 'Architecture', in F. O'Gorman (ed.), *The Cambridge Companion to John Ruskin* (Cambridge, 2015), pp. 100–115; **James F. White**, *The Cambridge Movement: The Ecclesiologists and the Gothic Revival* (Cambridge, 1962). See also essays in **Rebecca Daniels** and **Geoff Brandwood** (eds), *Ruskin and Architecture* (Reading, 2003).

The Arts and Crafts and William Morris

Stephen Coote, *William Morris: His Life and Work* (Oxford, 1995); **Alan Crawford** and **Collin Cunningham** (eds), *William Morris and Architecture* (London, 1996); **Peter Davey**, *Arts and Crafts Architecture* (London, 1980); **W. R. Lethaby**, *Philip Webb and His Work* (Oxford, 1935); **Chris Miele** (ed.), *William Morris on Architecture* (Sheffield, 1996); **Chris Miele**, 'Morris and Architecture', in F. S. Boos (ed.), *The Routledge Companion to William Morris* (New York, 2021), pp. 169–187; **Mark Swenarton**, 'The Architectural Theory of William Morris', in M. Swenarton, *Artisans and Architects: The Ruskinian Tradition in Architectural Thought* (London, 1989), pp. 62–95; **Paul Thompson**, *The Work of William Morris* (Oxford, 1991); **Grzegorz Zinkiewicz**, *William Morris' Position between Art and Politics* (Newcastle upon Tyne, 2017).

Architecture and Science

Barry Bergdoll, 'Of Crystals, Cells, and Strata: Natural History and Debates on the Form of a New Architecture in the Nineteenth Century', *Architectural History*, 50 (2007), 1–29; **Alexandrina Buchanan**, *Robert Willis and the Foundation of Architectural History* (Woodbridge, 2013); **Sophie Forgan**, 'Bricks and Bones: Architecture and Science in Victorian Britain', in P. Galison and E. Thompson (eds), *The Architecture of Science* (Cambridge, MA, 1999), pp. 181–208; **Graeme Gooday**, 'Architectural Acoustics: Thomas Roger Smith and the Science of Hearing Buildings in Nineteenth-Century Britain', in Edward Gillin and H. Horatio Joyce (eds), *Experiencing Architecture in the Nineteenth Century* (London, 2019), pp. 101–114; **John Holmes**, *The Pre-Raphaelites and Science* (London and New Haven, 2018); **Matthew Mullane**, 'The Architectural Fossil: James Fergusson, Geology, and World History', *Architectural Theory Review*, 20:1 (2015), 46–66; **Henrik Schoenefeldt**, 'Powers of Politics, Scientific Measurement and Perception: Evaluating the Performance of the House of Commons' First Environmental System, 1852–4', in Edward Gillin and H. Horatio Joyce (eds), *Experiencing Architecture in the Nineteenth Century* (London, 2019), pp. 115–129; **Carla Yanni**, 'On Nature and Nomenclature: William Whewell and the Production of Architectural Knowledge in Early Victorian Britain', *Architectural History*, 40 (1997), 204–221; **Carla Yanni**, 'Development and Display: Progressive Evolution in British Victorian Architecture and Architectural Theory', in B. V. Lightman and B. Zon (eds), *Evolution* *and Victorian Culture* (Cambridge, 2014), pp. 229–237.

Chapter 4. Building the State: Architectures of Power and Pride

Primary Sources

'Architecture in Madras', *The Builder* (5 June 1869), p. 449; *The National Memorial to His Royal Highness The Prince Consort* (London, 1873); *Remarks on a National Style in Reference to the Proposed Foreign Office* (London, 1860); (**A. Alison**), 'The British School of Architecture', *Blackwood's Edinburgh Magazine*, 40 (1836), 227–238; **William E. A. Axon** (ed.), *An Architectural and General Description of Manchester Town Hall* (Manchester, 1878); **A. J. B. Beresford Hope**, *Public Offices and Metropolitan Improvements* (London, 1857); **William Emerson**, 'A Description of Some Buildings Recently Erected in India, With Some Remarks on Domes and the Mingling of Styles of Architecture', *Transactions of the Royal Institute of British Architects*, vol. 34, 1st series (1883–84), pp. 149–157; (**E. A. Freeman**) 'The Foreign Office: Classic or Gothic', National Review (Jan. 1860), pp. 24–53; **F. E. Scott**, *Shall the New Foreign Office Be Gothic or Classic? A Plea for the Former* (London, 1860); **G. G. Scott**, *Remarks on Secular & Domestic Architecture, Present and Future* (London, 1857).

General Secondary Sources

G. A. Bremner, *Building Greater Britain: Architecture, Imperialism, and the Edwardian Baroque Revival, c.1885–1920* (London and New Haven, 2022); **Richard Butler**, *Building the Irish Courthouse and Prison: A Political History, 1750–1850* (Cork, 2020); **Mark Crinson**, 'Industrial Greatness: The Town Hall as a Gothic Machine', in M. Crinson, *Shock City: Image and Architecture in Industrial Manchester* (London and New Haven, 2022), pp. 101–135; **Colin Cunningham**, *Victorian and Edwardian Town Halls* (London, 1981); **Philip Davies**, *Splendours of the Raj: British Architecture in India 1660–1947* (Harmondsworth, 1987); **Harold Kalman**, *A History of Canadian Architecture*, 2 vols (Toronto, 1994); **Paul Larmour**, *Belfast City Hall: An Architectural History* (Belfast, 2010); **M. H. Port**, Imperial London: Civil Government Building in London, 1851–1915 (New Haven and London, 1995); **William Whyte**, 'Building the Nation in the Town: Architecture and Identity in Britain', in W. Whyte and O. Zimmer (eds), *Nationalism and the Reshaping of Urban Communities in Europe, 1848–1914* (London, 2011), pp. 204–233.

Houses of Parliament and New Government Offices

T. S. R. Boase, 'The Decoration of the New Palace of Westminster, 1841–1863', *Journal of the Warburg and Courtauld Institutes*, vol. 17 (1954), pp. 319–358; **G. A. Bremner**, 'Nation and Empire in the Government Architecture of Mid-Victorian London: The Foreign and India Office Reconsidered', *Historical Journal*, 48:3 (2005), 703–742; **David Brownlee**, 'That "Regular Mongrel Affair": G. G. Scott's Design for the Government Offices', *Architectural History*, 28 (1985), 159–197; **Andrea Fredericksen**, 'Parliament's Genius Loci: The Politics of Place After the 1834 Fire', in C. and J. Riding (eds), *The Houses of Parliament: History Art Architecture* (London, 2000), pp. 99–111; **Edward J. Gillin**, *The Victorian Palace of Science: Scientific Knowledge and the Building of the Houses of Parliament* (Cambridge, 2017); **E. K. Morris**, 'Symbols of Empire: Architectural Style and the Government Offices Competition', *Journal of Architectural Education*, 32 (1978), 8–13; **M. H. Port**, 'Government and the Metropolitan Image Ministers, Capital City, 1840–1915', in D. Arnold (ed.), *The Metropolis and Its Image: Constructing Identities for London, c. 1750–1950* (Oxford, 1999), pp. 101–126; **M. H. Port** (ed.), *The Houses of Parliament* (New Haven and London, 1976); **W. J. Rorabaugh**, 'Politics and the Architectural Competition for the Houses of Parliament, 1834–1837', *Victorian Studies*, 18 (1973), 155–175; **Gavin Stamp**, 'The Nation's Drawing-Room: Restoring the Foreign Office', *Apollo* (July 1992), pp. 23–29; **Ian Toplis**, *The Foreign Office: An Architectural History* (London, 1987), pp. 95–135.

The Albert Memorial

Stephen Bayley, *The Albert Memorial: The Monument in Its Social and Architectural Context* (London, 1981); **G. A. Bremner**, 'Between Civilisation and Barbarity: Conflicting Perceptions of the Non-European World in William Theed's *Africa*, 1864–69', *Sculpture Journal*, 15 (2007), 94–102; **G. A. Bremner**, 'The "Great Obelisk" and Other Schemes: The Origins and Limits of Nationalist Sentiment in the Making of the Albert Memorial 1861–63', *Nineteenth-Century Contexts*, 31:3 (2009), 225–249; **Chris Brooks** (ed.), *The Albert Memorial. The Prince Consort National Memorial: Its History, Contexts, and Conservation* (New Haven and London, 2000); **Colin Cunningham**, 'The Albert Memorial', in G. Perry and C. Cunningham (eds), *Academies, Museums and Canons of Art* (New

Haven and London, 1999), pp. 190–206. For the Wallace Monument in Stirling, see **Helen E. Smailes**, 'A Pride of Lions: Noel Paton and the National Wallace Monument', *Architectural Heritage*, 25 (2014), 85–106.

Government Architecture in the Colonies

G. A. Bremner (ed.), *Architecture and Urbanism in the British Empire* (Oxford, 2016); **Julius Bryant**. 'Kipling and Architecture', in J. Bryant and S. Weber (eds), *John Lockwood Kipling: Arts & Crafts in the Punjab and London* (New York and New Haven, 2017), pp. 107–121; **Preeti Chopra**, *A Joint Enterprise: Indian Elites and the Making of British Bombay* (Minneapolis, 2011); **Robert G. Irving**, 'Architecture for Empire's Sake: Lutyens's Palace for Delhi', *Perspecta*, 18 (1982), 7–23; **Christopher London**, *Bombay Gothic* (Mumbai, 2003); **Sarah Longair**, 'Scottish Architects, Imperial Identities and India's Built Environment in the Early Twentieth Century: The Careers of John Begg and George Wittet', *ABE Journal*, 14–15 (2019), doi.org/10.4000/abe.5767; **John M. MacKenzie**, *The British Empire Through Buildings: Structure, Function and Meaning* (Manchester, 2020); **Thomas Metcalf**, *An Imperial Vision: Indian Architecture and Britain's Raj* (London, 1989); **Sten Nilsson**, *European Architecture in India 1750–1850* (London, 1968); **Peter Scriver**, 'Empire-Building and Thinking in the Public Works Department of British India', in P. Scriver and V. Prakash (eds), *Colonial Modernities: Building, Dwelling and Architecture in British India and Ceylon* (London, 2007), pp. 69–92; **Gavin Stamp**, 'British Architecture in India, 1857–1947', *Journal of the Royal Society of Arts*, 129:5298 (1981), 357–379; **George Tibbits**, 'Parliament House, Melbourne', in *Historic Public Buildings of Australia*, vol. 2 (North Melbourne, 1971), pp. 152–163; **Andreas Volwahsen**, *Splendours of Imperial India: British Architecture in the 18th and 19th Centuries* (Munich, 2004); **Carolyn Young**, *The Glory of Ottawa Canada's First Parliament Buildings* (Montreal and Kingston, 1995).

Chapter 5. New Jerusalems: Fabricating Faith in the Victorian World

Primary Sources

The Symbolism of Churches and Church Ornaments: A Translation of the First Book of the Rationale Divinorum Officiorum…, trans., with introductory essay, by **J. M. Neale** and **Benjamin Webb** (London, 1843); **A. J. B. Beresford Hope**, *The English Cathedral of the Nineteenth Century* (London, 1861); **Cambridge Camden Society**, *A Few Words to Church Builders* (Cambridge, 1841); **Francis Close**, *The Restoration of Churches is the Restoration of Popery* (1844); **James Cubitt**, *Church Design for Congregations: Its Development and Possibilities* (London, 1870); **Charles L. Eastlake**, *A History of the Gothic Revival* (London, 1872); ***The Ecclesiologist*** (1841–68); **Ecclesiological Society**, *Instrumenta Ecclesiastica, or, A Series of Working Designs for the Furniture, Fittings, and Decorations of Churches and Their Precincts* 1 (1847), 2 (1856); **F. J. Jobson**, *Chapel & School Architecture, as Appropriate to the Buildings of Nonconformists* …(London, 1850); **William Peace**, *The Reformation and the Cross* (1859); **G. G. Scott**, *A Plea for the Faithful Restoration of Our Ancient Churches* (Oxford, 1850); **G. E. Street**, 'On the Proper Characteristics of a Town Church', *The Ecclesiologist*, 11 (1850), 227–233; **George Truefitt**, *Designs for Country Churches* (London, 1850); **Benjamin Webb**, 'On the Adaptation of Pointed Architecture to Tropical Climates', *Transactions of the Cambridge Camden Society, 1843–45* (1845), 199–218.

General Secondary Sources

Brian Andrews, *Australian Gothic: The Gothic Revival in Australian Architecture from the 1840s to the 1950s* (Melbourne, 2001); **G. A. Bremner**, *Imperial Gothic: Religious Architecture and High Anglican Culture in the British Empire, c.1840–1870* (Newhaven and London, 2013); **G. A. Bremner** (ed.), *Ecclesiology Abroad: The British Empire and Beyond*, themed issue of *Studies in Victorian Architecture and Design*, 4 (2012); **Timothy Brittian-Catlin**, **Jan De Maeyer**, and **Martin Bressani** (eds), *Gothic Revival Worldwide: A. W. N. Pugin's Global Influence* (Leuven, 2016); **Chris Brooks** and **Andrew Saint** (eds), *The Victorian Church: Architecture and Society* (Manchester 1995); **Jim Cheshire**, 'Space and the Victorian Ecclesiastical Interior', in Sandra Alfoldy and Janice Helland (eds), *Craft, Space and Interior Design, 1855–2005* (Aldershot, 2008), pp. 27–44; **Basil F. Clarke**, *Anglican Cathedrals Outside the British Isles* (London, 1958); **Basil F. Clarke**, *Church Builders of the Nineteenth Century: A Study of the Gothic Revival in England*, revised (London, 1969); **James Stevens Curl**, *Piety Proclaimed: An Introduction to Places of Worship in Victorian England* (London, 2002); **Edmund Harris**, *The Rogue Goths: R. L. Roumieu, Joseph Peacock and Bassett Keeling* (Swindon and Liverpool, 2004); **Peter Howell** and **Ian Sutton**, *The Faber Guide to Victorian Churches* (London, 1989); **C. M. Smart, Jr.**, *Muscular Churches: Ecclesiastical Architecture* *of the High Victorian Period* (Fayetteville, 1989); **Phoebe B. Stanton**, *The Gothic Revival & American Church Architecture: An Episode in Taste, 1840–1856* (Baltimore, 1968); **Christopher Webster**, *'Temples worthy of His presence': The Early Publications of the Cambridge Camden Society* (Reading, 2003); **Christopher Webster** and **John Elliott** (eds), *'A Church as it should be': The Cambridge Camden Society and Its Influence* (Stamford, 2000); **William Whyte**, *Unlocking the Church: The Lost Secrets of Victorian Sacred Space* (Oxford, 2017); **Nigel Yates**, *Buildings, Faith, and Worship: The Liturgical Arrangement of Anglican Churches, 1600–1900* (Oxford, 1991).

Specific Buildings and Themes in Ecclesiastical Architecture

G. A. Bremner, 'A Tale of Two Churches: "Protestant" Architecture and the Politics of Religion in Late Nineteenth-Century Rome', *Papers of the British School at Rome*, 88 (2020), 259–296; **G. A. Bremner**, 'Colonial Themes in Stained Glass, Home and Abroad: A Visual Survey', *19: Interdisciplinary Studies in the Long Nineteenth Century*, 30 (2020): doi.org/10.16995/ntn.2900; **Michael Hall**, 'The Rise of Refinement: G. F. Bodley's All Saints, Cambridge, and the Return to English Models in Gothic Architecture of the 1860s', *Architectural History*, 36 (1993), 103–126; **Michael Hall**, 'What Do Victorian Churches Mean? Symbolism and Sacramentalism in Anglican Church Architecture, 1850–1870', *Journal of the Society of Architectural Historians*, 59:1 (2000), 78–95; **Erin A. Hammond**, 'Sight Unseen: Mediating Vision and Emotion in Gothic Revival Churches c.1830–50', *Emotions: History, Culture, Society*, 6:1 (2022), 117–134; **Peter Howell**, 'Newman's Church at Littlemore', *Oxford Art Journal*, 6:1 (1983), 51–56; **Neil Jackson**, 'Christ Church, Streatham, and the Rise of Constructional Polychromy', *Architectural History*, 43 (2000), 241–246; **Edward N. Kaufman**, '"The weight and vigour of their masses": Mid-Victorian Country Churches and "The Lamp of Power"', in J. D. Hunt and F. M. Holland (eds), *The Ruskin Polygon: Essays of the Imagination of John Ruskin* (Manchester, 1982), pp. 94–121; **David Lawrence** and **Ann Wilson**, *The Cathedral of St Fin Barre at Cork: William Burges in Ireland* (Dublin, 2006); **J. Mordaunt Crook**, 'Early French Gothic', in S. Macready and F. H. Thompson (eds), *Influences in Victorian Art and Architecture* (London, 1985), pp. 49–58; **David Prout**, '"The Oxford Society for Promoting the Study of Gothic Architecture" and the "Oxford Architectural Society", 1839–1860', *Oxoniensia*, 54 (1989), 379–391; **Gavin Stamp**, 'High Victorian Gothic and the Architecture of Normandy', *Journal of the Society of Architectural Historians*, 62:2 (2003), 194–211; **Paul Thompson**, 'All Saints' Church, Margaret Street, Reconsidered', *Architectural History*, 8 (1965), 73–94; **Annabel Wharton**, 'Westminster Cathedral: Medieval Architectures and Religious Difference', *Journal of Medieval and Early Modern Studies*, 26:3 (1996), 523–555; **William Whyte**, 'Sacred Space as Sacred Text: Church and Chapel Architecture in Victorian Britain', in J. Sterrett and P. Thomas (eds), *Sacred Text—Sacred Space: Architectural, Spiritual, and Literary Convergences in England and Wales* (Leiden, 2011), pp. 247–267.

Women and Victorian Religious Architecture

'Women in Architecture', *The Victorian* (Nov. 2020); **Kathryn Ferry**, *The Old Convent East Grinstead: John Mason Neale, George Edmund Street, and the Society of St Margaret* (East Grinstead, 2021); **Michael Hall**, 'Emily Meynell Ingram and Holy Angels, Hoar Cross, Staffordshire: A Study in Patronage', *Architectural History*, 47 (2004), 283–328; **Kate Jordan**, 'Ordered Spaces, Separate Spheres: Women and the Building of British Convents, 1829–1939' (PhD University of London, 2015); **R. R. Langham-Carter**, 'South Africa's First Woman Architect', *Architect and Builder* (March 1967), pp. 14–18; **Susan S. Lewis**, 'The Artistic and Architectural Patronage of Angela Burdett Coutts', (PhD University of London, 2012); **Desmond Martin**, *The Bishop's Churches: The Churches of Anglican Bishop Robert Gray* (Cape Town, 2005).

Nonconformist and Dissenting Architecture

Nonconformist Chapels and Meeting-Houses (London, 1986); **Bridget Cherry** (ed.), *Dissent and the Gothic Revival* (London, 2007), pp. 5–18; **Ruth Mason**, 'The Design of Nineteenth-Century Wesleyan Space Re-reading F. J. Jobson's Chapel and School Architecture', *Wesley and Methodist Studies*, 7:1 (2015), 78–99; **Christopher Wakeling**, *Chapels of England: Buildings of Protestant Nonconformity* (Swindon, 2017).

Colonial Church Architecture

G. A. Bremner, 'Narthex Reclaimed: Reinventing Disciplinary Space in the Anglican Mission Field, 1847–1903', *Journal of Historical Geography*, 51 (2016), 1–17; **G. A. Bremner**, 'The Architecture of the Universities' Mission to Central Africa: Developing a Vernacular Tradition in the Anglican Mission Field, 1861–1909', *Journal of the Society of Architectural*

Historians, 68:4 (2009), 514–539; **Peter Coffman**, *Newfoundland Gothic* (Quebec, 2008); **Paola Colleoni**, 'The Extraordinary Partnership Between Goold and Wardell', in J. Anderson, M. Vodola, and S. Carmody (eds), *The Architecture of Devotion: James Goold and His Legacies in Colonial Melbourne* (Melbourne, 2021), pp. 63–79; **Mark Crinson**, *Empire Building: Orientalism and Victorian Architecture* (London, 1996); **Harold Kalman** and **J. de Visser**, *Pioneer Churches* (Toronto, 1976); **Ursula de Jong** (ed.), *W. W. Wardell: The Architect and His Era* (Geelong, 2000); **Ayla Lepine**, 'Gothic Portability: The Crimean Memorial Church, Istanbul and the Threshold of Empire', in M. Gharipour (ed.), *Sacred Precincts: The Religious Architecture of Non-Muslim Communities Across the Islamic World* (Leiden, 2015), pp. 203–218; **Miles Lewis**, *Victorian Churches: Their Origins, Their Story, and Their Architecture* (Melbourne, 1991); **Ian Lochhead**, 'Antipodean Gothic: Gilbert Scott, Benjamin Mountfort and the Medieval Vision in New Zealand', *L'art et les révolutions: Actes [du] XXVIIe Congrès International d'Histoire de l'Art* (Strasbourg, 1992), pp. 215–230; **Barry Magrill**, *A Commerce of Taste: Church Architecture in Canada, 1867–1914* (Montreal and Kingston, 2012); **Barry Magrill**, '"Development" and Ecclesiology in the Outpost of the British Empire: William Hay's Gothic Solutions for Church Building in Tropical Climates (1840–1890)', *Journal of the Society for the Study of Architecture in Canada*, 29:1–2 (2004), 15–26; **Jonathan N. Mané**, 'Gilbert Scott's Colonial Churches', in M. Belcher and H. Debenham (eds), *Australasian Victorian Studies Association: Conference Papers 1987* (Christchurch, 1987), 31–42; **Shane O'Dea** and **Peter Coffman**, 'William Grey: "Missionary" of Gothic in Newfoundland', *Journal of the Society for the Study of Architecture in Canada*, 32:1 (2007), 39–48; **Douglas S. Richardson**, 'Hyperborean Gothic, or Wilderness Ecclesiology and the Wood Churches of Edward Medley', *Architectura*, 1 (1972), 48–74; **Reyhan Sabri** and **Oluseyi A. Olagoke**, 'The Genesis and Evolution of Anglican Ecclesiastical Architecture in British Yorubaland: Postcolonial Reflections', *Journal of Architecture*, 26:8 (2021), 1271–1293; **Richard A. Sundt**, *Whare Karakia: Māori Church Building, Decoration and Ritual in Aotearoa New Zealand, 1834–1863* (Auckland, 2010); **Malcolm Thurlby**, 'Two Churches by Frank Wills: St. Peter's, Barton, and St. Paul's, Glanford, and the Ecclesiological Gothic Revival in Ontario', *Journal of the Society for the Study of Architecture in Canada*, 32:1 (2007), 49–60; **Emily Turner**, 'The Church Missionary Society and Architecture in the Mission Field: Evangelical Anglican Perspectives on Church Building Abroad, c.1850–1900', *Architectural History*, 58 (2015), 197–228.

Chapter 6. Correction, Reform, Discipline: Shaping Institutional Architectures

Primary Sources

First Annual Report of the Poor Law Commissioners for England and Wales (London, 1835); 'French Opinions and French Art', *The Builder* (23 July 1859), pp. 481–483 (481); **John Conolly**, *The Construction and Government of Lunatic Asylums* (London, 1847); **M. M. Murzban**, *Leaves from the Life of Khan Bahadur Muncherji Cowasji Murzban* (Bombay, 1915); **Florence Nightingale**, *Notes on Hospitals* (London, 1863); **Edward Robert Robson**, *School Architecture* (London, 1874).

General Secondary Sources

Annmarie Adams, *Medicine by Design: The Architect and the Modern Hospital, 1893–1943* (Minneapolis, 2008); **Samantha F. Barnes**, *Manchester Board Schools 1870–1902* (London, 2009); **G. A. Bremner** and **Louis P. Nelson**, 'Propagating Ideas and Institutions: Religious and Educational Architecture', in G. A. Bremner (ed.), *Architecture and Urbanism in the British Empire* (Oxford, 2016), pp. 188–195; **Allan Brodie, Jane Croom**, and **James O. Davies**, *English Prisons: An Architectural History* (Liverpool, 2002); **Lawrence Burchell**, *Victorian Schools: A Study in Colonial Government Architecture 1837–1900* (Melbourne, 1980); **Richard Butler**, 'George Gilbert Scott and the University of Bombay', *The Victorian*, 37 (2011), 10–13; **Robyne Calvert**, *The Mack: Charles Rennie Mackintosh and the Glasgow School of Art* (New Haven and London, 2024); **Felix Driver**, *Power and Pauperism: The Workhouse System, 1834–1884* (Cambridge, 1993); **Robin Evans**, *The Fabrication of Virtue: English Prison Architecture, 1750–1840* (Cambridge, 1982); **Christienna D. Fryar**, 'Imperfect Models: The Kingston Lunatic Asylum Scandal and the Problem of Postemancipation Imperialism', *Journal of British Studies*, 55:4 (2016), 709–727; **Elain Harwood**, *England's Schools: History, Architecture and Adaption* (Swindon, 2010); **A. King**, 'Hospital Planning: Revised Thoughts on the Origin of the Pavilion Principle in England', *Medical History*, 10:4 (1966), 360–373; **Ranald Lawrence**, 'Halls, Lobbies, and Porches: Transition Spaces in

Victorian Architecture', *The Journal of Architecture* 25:4 (2020), 419–443; **Kathryn Morrison**, *The Workhouse: A Study of Poor-Law Buildings in England* (Swindon, 1999); **Amona Pieris**, *Hidden Hands and Divided Landscapes: A Penal History of Singapore's Plural Society* (Honolulu, 2009); **Sarah Rutherford**, 'Landscapers for the Mind: English Asylum Designers, 1845–1914', *Garden History*, 33:1 (2005), 61–86; **Sarah Rutherford**, *The Victorian Asylum* (Oxford, 2008); **Jeremy Taylor**, *The Architect and the Pavilion Hospital* (London, 1997); **Leslie Topp**, **James E. Moran**, and **Jonathan Andrews** (eds), *Madness, Architecture and the Built Environment: Psychiatric Spaces in Historical Context* (London, 2007); **Geoffrey Tyack**, 'The Architecture of Art Education: Provincial Art Schools in Britain, 1850–1914', in Edward Gillin and H. Horatio Joyce (eds), *Experiencing Architecture in the Nineteenth Century* (London, 2019), pp. 61–74; **Geoffrey Tyack** and **Marjory Szurko**, *William Butterfield and Keble College* (Oxford, 2002); **Deborah E. B. Weiner**, *Architecture and Social Reform in Late-Victorian London* (Manchester, 1994); **William Whyte**, 'Building a Public School Community 1860–1910', *History of Education*, 32:6 (2003), 601–626; **William Whyte**, *Redbrick: A Social and Architectural History of Britain's Civic Universities* (Oxford, 2015); **Julie Willis**, 'The Four Pillars: The Architecture of the Government School in Australia 1835–1885', *Oxford Review of Education*, 47:5 (2021), 556–575; **Carla Yanni**, *The Architecture of Madness: Insane Asylums in the United States* (Minneapolis, 2007).

Architecture as Machine

Robert Brucemann and **Donald Prowler**, '19th Century Mechanical System Designs', *JAE*, 30:3 (1977), 11–15; **Moritz Gleich**, *Inhabited Machines: Genealogy of an Architectural Concept* (Basel, 2023); **Henrik Schoenefeldt**, 'The Temporary Houses of Parliament and David Boswell Reid's Architecture of Experimentation', *Architectural History*, 57 (2014), 175–215; **Herbert Sussman**, *Victorian Technology: Invention, Innovation, and the Rise of the Machine* (New York, 2009); **Alexander Tzonis** and **Liane Lefaivre**, 'The Mechanization of Architecture and the Birth of Functionalism', *Via*, 7 (1984), 121–144;

Chapter 7. A World on Show: Exhibitions, Museums, and Cultures of Display

Primary Sources

Reports from the Select Committees on Arts and Manufactures (London, 1835 and 1836); **Henry W. Acland** and **John Ruskin**, *The Oxford Museum* (London, 1859); **Peter Berlyn** and **Charles Fowler**, *The Crystal Palace: Its Architectural History and Constructing Marvels* (London, 1851); **George Edmund Street**, *An Urgent Plea for the Revival of True Principles of Architecture in the Public Buildings of the University of Oxford* (Oxford, 1853).

General Secondary Sources

Jonathan Conlin, *The Nation's Mantlepiece: A History of the National Gallery* (London, 2006); **Sophie Forgan**, 'The Architecture of Display: Museums, Universities and Objects in Nineteenth-century Britain', *History of Science*, 32:2 (1994), 139–162; **Ranald Lawrence**, *The Victorian Art School: Architecture, History, Environment* (London, 2020); **J. Mordaunt Crook**, *The British Museum: A Case-Study in Architectural Politics* (Harmondsworth, 1973); **Christopher Whitehead**, *The Public Art Museum in Nineteenth Century Britain: The Development of the National Gallery* (Aldershot, 2005); **Marjorie Caygill** and **Christopher Date**, *Building the British Museum* (London 1999); **Peter H. Hoffenberg**, *An Empire on Display: English, Indian, and American Exhibitions from the Crystal Palace to the Great War* (Berkeley, 2001); **Amy Woodson-Boulton**, *Transformative Beauty: Art Museums in Industrial Britain* (Stanford, 2012); **Carla Yanni**, *Nature's Museums: Victorian Science and the Architecture of Display* (New York, 2005 [first published 1999]).

Great Exhibition of 1851, the Crystal Palace, Colonial Exhibitions

Jeffrey A. Auerbach, *The Great Exhibition of 1851: A Nation on Display* (New Haven and London, 1999); **Jeffrey A. Auerbach** and **Peter H. Hoffenberg** (eds), *Britain, the Empire, and the World at the Great Exhibition of 1851* (Aldershot, 2008); **Patrick Beaver**, *The Crystal Palace, 1851–1936: A Portrait of Victorian Enterprise* (London, 1970); **Kathryn Ferry**, 'Owen Jones and the Alhambra Court at the Crystal Palace', in G. Anderson and M. Rosser-Owen (eds), *Revisiting al-Andalus: Perspectives on the Material Culture of Islamic Iberia and Beyond* (Leiden, 2007), pp. 225–245; **Paul Greenhalgh**, *Ephemeral Vistas: The* Expositions Universelles, *Great Exhibitions and World's Fairs, 1851–1939* (Manchester, 1988); **Christina Henderson Harner**, 'Rebuilding the World at the Crystal Palace: Architectural Discourse at the 1851 Great Exhibition', *Victorians: A Journal of Culture and Literature*, 136 (2019), 138–158; **Lara Kriegel**, 'Narrating the Subcontinent in 1851: India at the Crystal Palace', in L. Purbrick (ed.), *The Great Exhibition of 1851: New Interdisciplinary Essays* (Manchester, 2001), pp. 147–178; **John McKean**, *Crystal Palace: Joseph Paxton and Charles Fox* (London, 1994); **Henrik Schoenefeldt**, 'The Crystal Palace, Environmentally Considered', *Architectural Research Quarterly*, 12:3–4 (2008), 283–294; **Deborah Swallow**, 'Colonial Architecture, International Exhibitions, and Official Patronage of the Indian Artisan: The Case of a Gateway from Gwalior in the Victorian and Albert Museum', in T. Barringer and T. Flynn (eds), *Colonialism and the Object: Empire, Material Culture and the Museum* (London, 1998), pp. 52–67.

Museums and Galleries

Tim Barringer, 'The South Kensington Museum and the Colonial Project', in T. Barringer and T. Flynn (eds), *Colonialism and the Object: Empire, Material Culture and the Museum* (London, 1998), pp. 11–27; **Anne Beggs-Sunter**, *Not for Self But for All: A History of the Art Gallery of Ballarat Association* (Ballarat, 2018); **G. A. Bremner**, '"Some Imperial Institute": Architecture, Symbolism, and the Ideal of Empire in Late Victorian Britain, 1887–93', *Journal of the Society of Architectural Historians*, 62:1 (2003), 50–73; **J. B. Bullen**, 'Alfred Waterhouse's Romanesque "Temple of Nature": The Natural History Museum, London', *Architectural History*, 49 (2006), 257–285; **Annie Coombes**, 'Museums and the Formation of National and Cultural Identities', *Oxford Art Journal*, 11:2 (1988), 57–68; **Mark Crinson**, 'Imperial Story-lands: Architecture and Display at the Imperial and Commonwealth Institutes', *Art History*, 22:1 (1999), 99–123; **Ray Desmond**, *The India Museum 1801–1879* (London, 1982); **Sophie Forgan** and **Graeme Gooday**, 'Constructing South Kensington: The Buildings and Politics of T. H. Huxley's Working Environments', *British Journal for the History of Science*, 29:4 (1996), 435–468; **Kelly Freeman**, 'Iron and Bone: The Skeleton Architecture of the Oxford University Museum of Natural History', *Object*, 18:1 (2016), 9–44; **Trevor Garnham**, *Oxford Museum: Deane and Woodward* (London, 1992); **Mark Girouard**, *Alfred Waterhouse and the Natural History Museum* (London, 1981); **Caroline Jordan**, 'The South Kensington Empire and the Idea of the Regional Art Gallery in Nineteenth-Century Victoria', *Fabrications*, 20:2 (2011), 34–59; **Gareth Knapman**, 'Curiosities or Science in the National Museum of Victoria: Procurement Networks and the Purpose of a Museum', in S. Longair and J. McAleer (eds), *Curating Empire: Museums and the British Imperial Experience* (Manchester, 2012), pp. 82–103; **Ranald Lawrence**, 'The Evolution of the Victorian Art School', *Journal of Architecture*, 19:1 (2014), 81–107; **John Peponis** and **Jenny Hedin**, 'The Layout of Theories in the Natural History Museum', *9H* 3 (1982), 21–25; **Rosemary Seton**, 'Reconstructing the Museum of the London Missionary Society', *Material Religion*, 8:1 (2012), 98–102; **Helen Smailes**, *A Portrait Gallery for Scotland: The Foundation, Architecture and Mural Decoration of the Scottish National Portrait Gallery, 1882–1906* (Edinburgh, 1985); **Paul Walker** and **Stuart King**, 'Style and Climate in Addison's Brisbane Exhibition Building', *Fabrications*, 17:2 (2007).

Chapter 8. Habits and Mores: Domesticity and the Victorian House

Primary Sources

Isabella Beeton, *Book of Household Management* (London, 1861); **Charles L. Eastlake**, *Hints on Household Taste in Furniture, Upholstery and other Details*, second revised edition (London: Longmans, 1869); **Robert Kerr**, *The Gentleman's House; or, How to Plan English Residences, from the Parsonage to the Palace, with Tables of Accommodation and Cost, and a Series of Selected Plans*, second (revised) edition (London, 1865); **J. C. Loudon**, *Encyclopaedia of Cottage, Farm, and Villa Architecture* (London, 1833); **Herman Muthesius**, *The English House* (*Das englische Haus*, 1904), trans. J. Seligman and S. Spencer, 3 vols (London, 2007).

General Secondary Sources

M. J. Daunton, *House and Home in the Victorian City: Working-Class Housing 1850–1914* (London, 1983); **Kathryn Ferry**, *The Victorian Home* (Oxford, 2012); **Judith Flanders**, *The Victorian Home: Domestic Life from Childbirth to Deathbed* (London, 2003); **Mark Girouard**, *The Victorian Country House* (Oxford, 1971); **Mark Girouard**, *Sweetness and Light: The Queen Anne Movement, 1860–1900* (Oxford, 1977); **Michael Hall**, *The Victorian Country House: From the Archives of Country Life* (London, 2009); **Neil Jackson**, *Built to Sell: Attitudes Towards Speculative House Building in Nineteenth Century London* (London, 1981); **Anthony D. King**, *The Bungalow: The Production of a Global Culture* (London, 1984); **Stefan Muthesius**, *The*

English Terraced House (New Haven and London, 1982); **John Summerson**, *The Building World of the 1860s* (London, 1973); **Kit Wedd**, *Victorian Housebuilding* (Oxford, 2012).

Themes in Victorian Domestic Architecture

John Belchem, '"Housing the poorest poor": The Irish Other in Nineteenth-Century Liverpool', in G. A. Bremner and D. Maudlin (eds), *Inner Empire: Architecture and Imperialism in the British Isles, 1550–1950* (Manchester, 2024), pp. 78–99; **Kay Boardman**, 'The Ideology of Domesticity: The Regulation of the Household Economy in Victorian Women's Magazines', *Victorian Periodicals Review*, 33:2 (2000), 150–164; **G. A. Bremner**, 'Foreign Mud, Home Comforts: Taipans, Opium, and the Remitted Wealth of Jardine, Matheson & Co. in Scotland', in G. A. Bremner and D. Maudlin (eds), *Inner Empire: Architecture and Imperialism in the British Isles, 1550–1950* (Manchester, 2024), pp. 193–217; **Deborah Cohen**, *Household Gods: The British and Their Possessions* (New Haven and London, 2006); **E. W. Cooney**, 'The Origins of the Victorian Master Builders', *Economic History Review*, New Series, 8:2 (1955), 167–176; **Lisa Daniels**, '"Houses as they might be": Rediscovering Rhoda and Agnes Garrett and their Influence on the Victorian Middle-Class Home', *Journal of the Decorative Arts Society, 1850–The Present*, 35 (2011), 82–101; **H. J. Dyos**, 'The Speculative Builders and Developers of Victorian London', *Victorian Studies*, 11 (Supplement: Symposium on the Victorian City [2]) (1968), 641–90; **Miranda Garrett**, 'Interior Decoration and Domesticity in the Women's Penny Paper/ Woman's Herald', *Victorian Periodicals Review*, 51:2 (2018), 289–306; **Joanne Harrison**, 'The Origin, Development and Decline of Back-to-Back Houses in Leeds, 1787–1937', *Industrial Archaeology Review*, 39:2 (2017), 101–116; **Catherine Karusseit**, 'Victorian Respectability and Gendered Domestic Space', *Image & Text: A Journal for Design*, 13 (2007), 39–53; **Juliet Kinchin**, 'Interiors: Nineteenth-Century Essays on the "Masculine" and the "Feminine" Room', in P. Kirkham (ed.), *The Gendered Object* (Manchester, 1996), pp. 12–29; **Thad Logan**, *The Victorian Parlour: A Cultural Study* (Cambridge, 2001); **Andrea Kaston Tange**, *Architectural Identities: Domesticity, Literature, and the Victorian Middle Classes* (Toronto, 2010); **John Tosh**, *A Man's Place: Masculinity and the Middle-Class Home in Victorian England* (New Haven and London, 1999).

Arts and Crafts Domesticity

Sylvia Backemeyer and **Theresa Gronberg** (eds), *W. R. Lethaby 1857–1931: Architecture, Design and Education* (London, 1984); **Annette Carruthers**, *The Arts and Crafts Movement in Scotland: A History* (New Haven and London, 2013); **Harriet Edquist**, *Pioneers of Modernism: The Arts and Crafts Movement in Australia* (Carlton, 2008); **James Macaulay**, *Hill House: Charles Rennie Mackintosh* (London, 1994); **Fiona MacCarthy**, *Anarchy & Beauty: William Morris and His Legacy 1860–1960* (London, 2014); **Jan Marsh**, *William Morris & Red House: A Collaboration Between Architect and Owner* (Swindon, 2005); **Margaret Richardson**, *Architects of the Arts and Crafts Movement* (London, 1983); **Peter Savage**, *Lorimer and the Edinburgh Craft Designers* (Edinburgh, 1980); **Pamela Todd**, William Morris and the Arts & Crafts Home (London, 2012).

Domestic Architecture in the Colonies

James Broadbent, *The Australian Colonial House: Architecture and Society in New South Wales, 1788–1842* (Sydney, 1997); **Karen Burns**, 'Between the Walls: Remembering Colonial Frontier Space at Purrumbete, 1901–2', in *Interspaces: Art + Architectural Exchanges from East to West*, conference proceedings (Melbourne, 2010), pp. 1–15; **Tom Cruickshank** and **John de Visser**, *Old Toronto Houses* (Toronto, 2003); **J. M. Freeland**, *Architecture in Australia: A History* (Harmondsworth, 1968); **Davina Jackson**, *Australian Architecture: A History* (Sydney, 2022); **Ursula de Jong** and **Jacqueline Healy** (eds), *Barwon Park: People and Place* (East Melbourne, 2023); **Miles Lewis**, *Victorian Primitive* (Carlton, 1977); **John Macarthur**, 'Colonies at Home: Loudon's Encyclopaedia, and the Architecture of Forming the Self', *Architectural Research Quarterly*, 3:3 (1999), 245–258; **Matthew M. Reeve** and **Michael Windover** (eds), *Casa Loma: Millionaires, Medievalism, and Modernity in Toronto's Gilded Age* (Montreal and Kingston, 2023); **James Robertson**, 'Jamaica's Victorian Architectures, 1834–1907', in T. Barringer and W. Modes (eds), *Victorian Jamaica* (New York, 2018), pp. 439–473; **Jeremy Salmond**, *Old New Zealand Houses 1800–1940* (Auckland, 1986); **P. B. Simons** (and Alain Proust), *Cape Dutch Houses* (Vlaeberg, 2000); **John Stacpoole**, *Colonial Architecture in New Zealand* (Wellington, 1975).

Index

Note: Figures are indicated by an italic "*f*", following the page number.

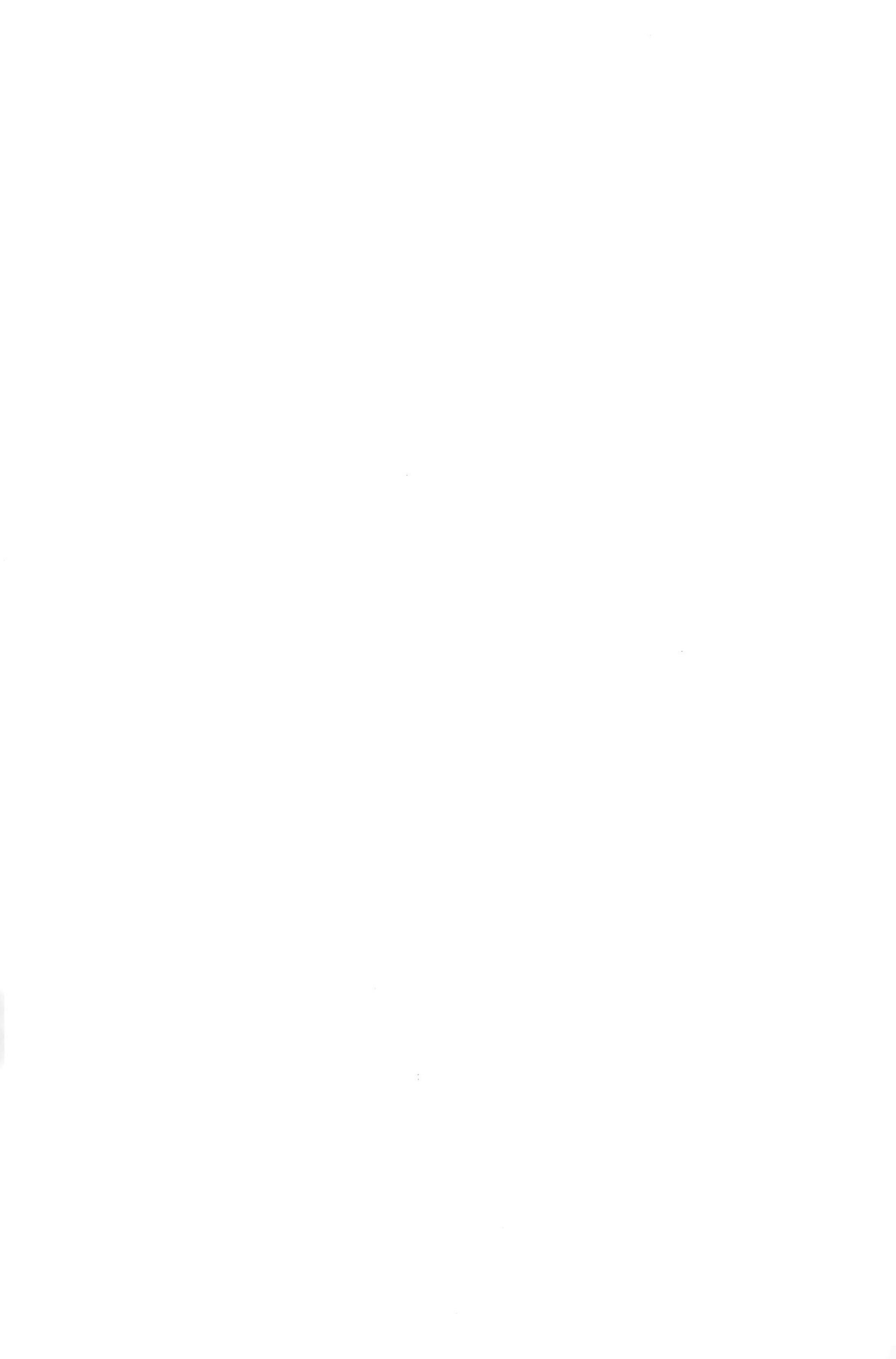

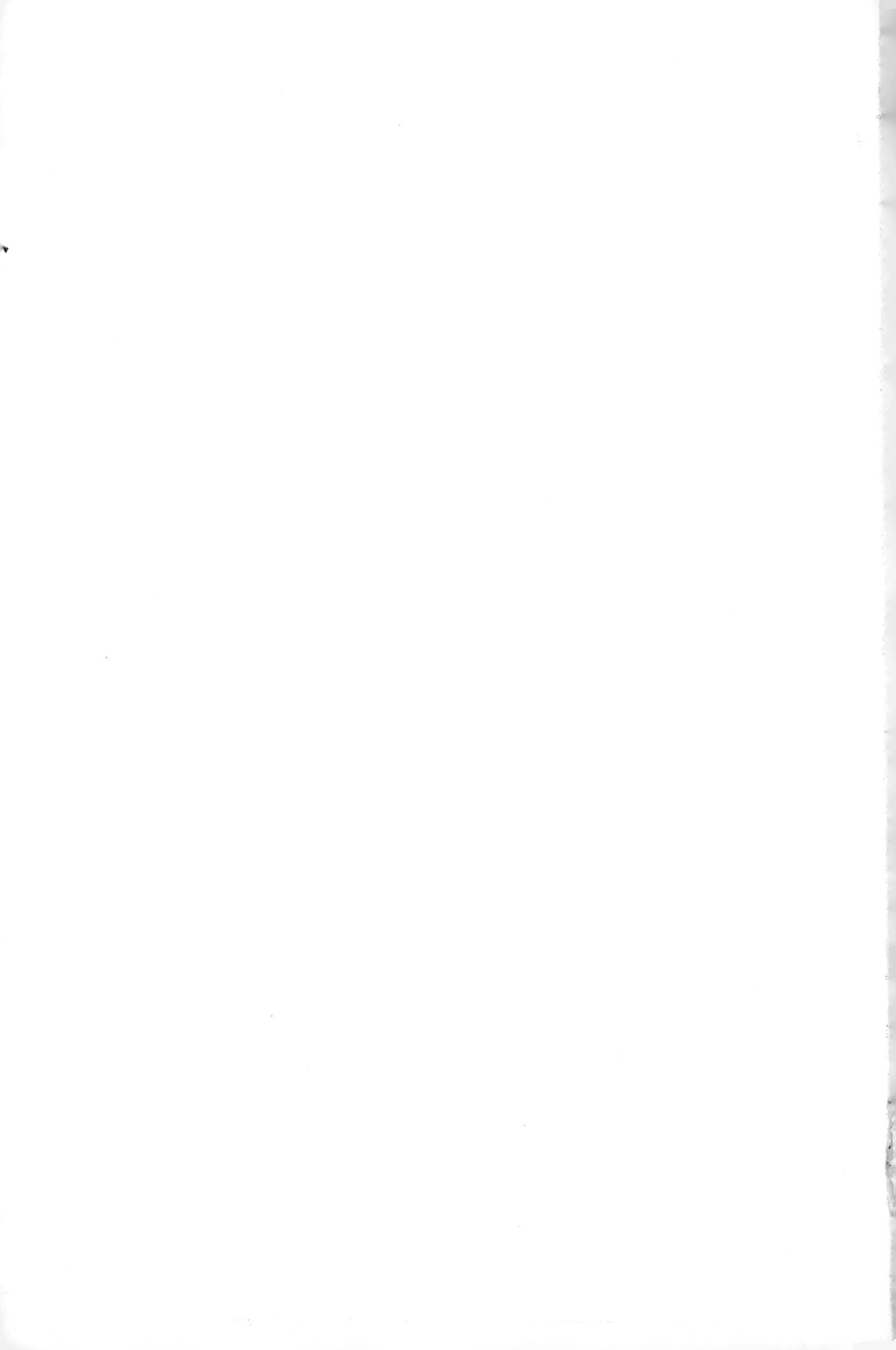